S0-BSE-045

CHANGES IN THE ROMAN EMPIRE

CHANGES IN THE ROMAN EMPIRE

ESSAYS IN THE ORDINARY

Ramsay MacMullen

PRINCETON UNIVERSITY PRESS

PRINCETON, NEW JERSEY

COPYRIGHT © 1990 BY PRINCETON UNIVERSITY PRESS
PUBLISHED BY PRINCETON UNIVERSITY PRESS, 41 WILLIAM STREET,
PRINCETON, NEW JERSEY 08540
IN THE UNITED KINGDOM: PRINCETON UNIVERSITY PRESS, OXFORD
ALL RIGHTS RESERVED

LIBRARY OF CONGRESS CATALOGING-IN-PUBLICATION DATA

MacMULLEN, RAMSAY, 1928–

CHANGES IN THE ROMAN EMPIRE : ESSAYS IN THE
ORDINARY / RAMSAY MacMULLEN.

P.   CM.

INCLUDES BIBLIOGRAPHICAL REFERENCES.

ISBN 0-691-03601-2 (ALK. PAPER)

1. ROME—CIVILIZATION. I. TITLE.

DG77.M28   1990   945'.63201—dc20   90–35552 CIP

THIS BOOK HAS BEEN COMPOSED IN LINOTRON TIMES ROMAN

PRINCETON UNIVERSITY PRESS BOOKS ARE PRINTED
ON ACID-FREE PAPER, AND MEET THE GUIDELINES FOR
PERMANENCE AND DURABILITY OF THE COMMITTEE ON
PRODUCTION GUIDELINES FOR BOOK LONGEVITY
OF THE COUNCIL ON LIBRARY RESOURCES

PRINTED IN THE UNITED STATES OF AMERICA BY
PRINCETON UNIVERSITY PRESS, PRINCETON, NEW JERSEY

1   3   5   7   9   10   8   6   4   2

CONTENTS

24

ILLUSTRATIONS

PREFACE

IN THE PAGES that follow, I have gathered about a third of my essays published previously,* and added another fifth of the volume, to make a whole, all of a single character. It is defined by its focus on a certain historical period (say, A.D. 50 to 450) and on sociocultural phenomena—meaning, common beliefs and forms of behavior among broad groups of people. Such phenomena happen to be well reported for the period in question, and happen also to be of increasing interest to historians in recent decades, regardless of their field of specialty. Perhaps that explains why there has been such a marked shift of interest from the earlier, more evocatively "classical" epochs, to the Roman empire. I would like to contribute something to that interest, in an accessible form.

Then, too, as Plato with pleasant irony declares at midpoint in his last great dialogue (*Laws* 811 D), "there is a feeling of decided pleasure, and perhaps not a surprising one, that comes over me when I survey all these words of mine as one single work."

* One essay, published in Italian ("Distrust of the Mind in the Fourth Century"), has been a great deal expanded beyond its English original; to the rest I have made no changes at all, or only a few little ones indicated in square brackets.

ACKNOWLEDGMENTS

I WOULD like to thank the following for granting permission to reprint articles under their copyright:

"Roman Elite Motivation." World Copyright: The Past and Present Society, 175 Banbury Rd., Oxford, England. This article is reprinted with the permission of the Society from *Past and Present: A Journal of Historical Studies*, no. 88 (August 1980), pp. 3–16.

"Provincial Languages in the Roman Empire" and "Personal Power in the Roman Empire." These articles are reprinted with the permission of the *American Journal of Philology*, Johns Hopkins University Press, 701 West 40th St., Suite 275, Baltimore, MD 21211.

"The Celtic Renaissance," "What Difference Did Christianity Make?" "Women in Public in the Roman Empire," "Roman Attitudes to Greek Love," "The Legion as a Society," and "Late Roman Slavery." These articles are reprinted with the permission of *Historia: Revue d'Histoire Ancienne*, Rutimeyerstr. 52, CH-4054, Basel, Switzerland.

"Barbarian Enclaves in the Northern Roman Empire." This article is reprinted with the permission of *L'Antiquité Classique*, c/o Inst. d'archéologie, Collège Erasme, Place Blaise Pascal 31.

"Notes on Romanization." This article is reprinted with the permission of the *Bulletin of the American Society of Papyrologists*, Loyola University of Chicago, 6525 North Sheridan Rd., Chicago, IL 60626.

"Roman Bureaucratese." This article is reprinted with the permission of *Traditio*, Fordham University Press, Bronx, NY 10458.

"Some Pictures of Ammianus Marcellinus." This article is reprinted with the permission of *The Art Bulletin* (1964, vol. 46), College Art Association of America, 275 Seventh Ave., New York, NY 10001.

"Constantine and the Miraculous." This article is reprinted with the permission of *Greek, Roman, and Byzantine Studies*, P.O. Box 4715 Duke Station, Durham, NC 27706.

"Distrust of the Mind in the Fourth Century." This article expands on an article printed in the *Rivista Storica Italiana*, Via Po 17, 10124 Torino, Italy, with permission of the review.

"Two Types of Conversion to Early Christianity." This article is reprinted with the permission of *Vigilae Christianae*, published by E. J. Brill, Postbus 9000, 2300 PA Leiden, The Netherlands.

"Women's Power in the Principate." This article is reprinted with the permission of *Klio*, Akademie-Verlag, DDR-1086 Berlin, Leipziger Strasse 3-4, Postfach-Nr. 1233.

"How to Revolt in the Roman Empire." This article is reprinted with the permission of *Rivista Storica dell'Antichità*, Via Zamboni 38, Bologna, Italy.

"Judicial Savagery in the Roman Empire." This article is reprinted with the permission of *Chiron*, Kommission für Alte Geschichte und Epigraphik des Deutschen Archäologischen Instituts, Amalienstrasse 73b, D-8000 München 40, West Germany.

"Social History in Astrology." This article is reprinted with the permission of *Ancient Society*, Katholieke Universiteit Leuven, Afdeling Oude Geschiedenis Erasmushuis, Blijde Inkomststraat 21, B-300 Leuven.

CHANGES IN THE ROMAN EMPIRE

1

INTRODUCTION: AN ABUNDANCE OF DATA IN

ANCIENT HISTORY

W EAK MINDS, like mine, unable to sustain a focus very long, slip sideways into irrelevancies not meant for their attention by the speaker addressing them half-heard, or by the assiduous historian whose text drops into his readers' laps unfinished. Rather than the focus, it is some little detail that claims at least their idle notice: the fact that Caesar, as Dio and Suetonius describe for us his last seconds of life and dying words, spoke Greek, or the fact that Apuleius' unprincipled accuser in that most Roman of African towns, Oea, could show around the forum a private letter written by a prominent citizen to her son, which any chance stroller there could read, likewise in Greek.[1] When and how did the upper classes, Roman or provincial, become at least partly Hellenophone, in the Latin west? The question has never aroused much interest. It lacks the drama that Suetonius or Apuleius, historian or courtroom orator, chose instinctively as their focus: focus, for instance, on the weaving of a plot against a great dictator, or against some innocent young traveler abroad. Changes in details of setting, changes without apparent meaning and barely detectable, will catch the interest only of the inattentive.

To the extent that historiography is story-telling, its emphasis must of course fall on the actors, not the stage. The stage is a given, serving only to support and complete the action that readers are meant to follow with their mind's eye. The faster the action, the less attention to the stage—and, it may be added, the more "historic" that action, in the sense of producing noticeable change. So the historical setting is easily dismissed as something strictly insignificant. If interest should perhaps be directed to points around and behind the figures in the foreground—figures in rapid motion, assassinating each other, plotting, or engaged in similar exciting acts—it will still seek change across time. What is changeless is background at best, to be included in the story only for necessary verisimilitude.

Yet background may control change. Whatever happened, it is recognized, could only have happened in the way it did because of certain features in its setting. Therefore those features must be examined in their own right. The Roman Republic was a democracy, even under a dictator, where friends and associates could cluster close around him—and so riddle him with wounds. Nothing of the sort could have happened to a Caesar of the Dominate. Therefore conventional historiography, at least of the modern sort, might certainly concern itself with such things as "Die Ausgestaltung des monarchischen Ze-remoniells."[2] The author of a monograph on that subject, possessed of a wonderful eye for the drama of the past, sensed change, meaning history, even here in a matter of mere posturing. He could trace the elaborating of monarchic ceremony across time. It had made a difference. But change was very slow, spread across whole centuries. His was not a book for Everyman.

In the 1930s, indeed, when it was written, change in the Roman empire had not been investigated at many points or to any great depth, if comparison is made with the decades that were to follow. There were exceptions. What was then still called "the dismal science," economics, was in fashion. Scattered totals of taxes from some individual province, totals of value of eastern imports in a given year, or similar rare figures caught almost at random in surviving works of ancient literature, like flies in amber, allowed at least some description of the economy based on numbers, not compounded of adjectives and anecdotes. To these could be added archeological data. Regarding pottery, they accumulated especially early and in especial bulk, beginning with the researches of an American physician resident in France from the 1870s on. Perhaps not sufficiently interested in the serious business of medicine, his attention wandered to an ancient kiln for the production of terra sigillata discovered in his very garden, and by 1885 he had assembled from chance finds and excavations in his vicinity the names of some three thousand potters of Roman times, and one cluster of kilns for which a wholesale store served as outlet. On the foundations he laid, a truly remarkable mountain of evidence today allows from its heights a view over much of the western Mediterranean. What articles were chiefly traded within its shores, in what bulk, and from what point of production to what point of consumption? Partial answers to such questions were available well before the 1930s.[3] They become steadily less lacunose, so that specialists are in a position to offer substantiated statements about significant change, at least in the economy of the west.

Modern experience directs attention to technology as the chief cause of economic change. But the ancient world was different. A new way of blowing glass that developed in Syria and spread rapidly under the emperor Augustus, as likewise innovations in patterns of textile-weaving that were developed in the same region in the third century, only show that technical improvements in production were few and insignificant. Although the screwpress for wine and olive oil represented an advance over the levered variety, it was little used outside of Italy, and not even widely taken up inside the peninsula. The water wheel was fairly well known though not prevalent in Asia Minor by Augustus' reign; but it was not adopted elsewhere save in Gaul, late. There and then, too, the quite remarkable mechanical reaper is attested both by written report and in relief representation; but it never became common. All of which illustrates the relative changelessness of the ancient economy, at least in its industrial parts. What advances can be noticed were due rather to the minute sub-division of production, with correspondingly high levels of skills.[4] It would be easier to show that agriculture, accounting for a vastly greater portion of the gross national product, underwent significant, continual development, at any rate in the west. New strains of fruits, grains, and domestic animals were introduced. They enriched as well as diversified the rural economy.

Besides economics, religion received attention very early. In that aspect of the historical setting, a change of overwhelming interest took place: the population became progressively converted. Christianity, announcing a new ethic, could not fail to make a new world. In the more obvious ways, indeed just that appeared. Bishops joined bureaucrats as the nouveaux arrivés of the later empire. On a scale matching that of their cities, large or small, they financed public building, attracted clients and dependents, exerted influence, lodged in luxury, and made a space for themselves among the older aristocracy, all, ex officio. Yet of course they were also drawn from that older aristocracy, municipal-senatorial or better. What might be attributed to their new ethic can better be found in their inheritance of class: for example, the moderating of servitude at certain points, as had been the tendency, however, in legal thought untouched by the Church; the norms laid down for marriage, yet anticipated by independent developments in Roman morals; or disgust at gladiatorial combat—that, too, a tendency developing in non-Christian thought independently.[5]

Dynamic aspects of the historical setting were then discoverable, if one cared to look for them, though they might turn out to be different from one's first expectations. In the later nineteenth and earlier twentieth centuries, the search was predictably directed according to major interests of that period, modified by subsequent study. In time, beyond changes in the empire's economy and religion, a third locus began to receive closer attention: the aristocracy, as it was reflected in useful numbers of inscriptions. Analytical inventories of some completeness were already being made in the 1930s. More recently, a total of nearly a hundred new men joining the senate from an eastern origin can be distributed over the reigns of the Julio-Claudii (eight), Flavians through Trajan (twenty-three), and later Antonines (fifty-nine), to suggest the opening up of noble rank to Greek-speakers. Of course the process was grudging: not one lucky candidate came from Cappadocia or Thrace until near the end of the period of study.[6] But the figures are a little misleading: the total of all surviving inscriptions of any sort rises as times goes on, and so floats upward those tabulated senators of later decades. Until the epigraphic pool as a whole is analyzed chronologically, which has not yet been attempted, all that can be inferred from the figures is that it was easier to join the empire's most exclusive club from the east in the second century than in the first. The finding does not represent any great advance in knowledge.

However, within the far larger total of 3,362 individuals native to three areas of the west, and known to us overwhelmingly from inscriptions, it is possible to distinguish much more significant and more reliably demonstrated trends (Figure 1).[7] As percentages, not absolute numbers, they need not be discounted; for example, men of Italian origin constitute 97 percent of known senators in the empire before the reign of Claudius, and that is true regardless of the fact that the total of all senators known in this period from inscriptions is smaller than in the succeeding one. What is easily seen in the data is the steady loosening of the hold of Italy on the inner circles of power and influence. The phenomenon could be illustrated in other ways, though less graphically: even emperors spring from provincial families, as time goes on. So do the leading lights of literature; so too, at a quite different level, the enlisted men in the legions. The shift in their patterns of origin can be quantified, though the surviving samples are not very large. History's stage on which the Hellenomane Nero and the Spain-born Seneca play out their parts, to which Trajan introduces his Spanish friends and Septimius Severus, his, from Africa, is continually changing shape; and the fact deserves the emphasis ordinarily given to it because of its effect upon the more dramatic actors and actions of the time. If weak minds should weary of the plots and pretenders, the assassinations and uprisings that brought to an end this provincializing of the empire, in the third century, they might turn instead to the less dramatic but less dreadful consequences of the process: the bestowal of universal citizenship in 212, the tolerance of contracts in Celtic or Punic in Ulpian's court, and the building of a most elegant temple to a Syrian ba'al by the emperor himself,

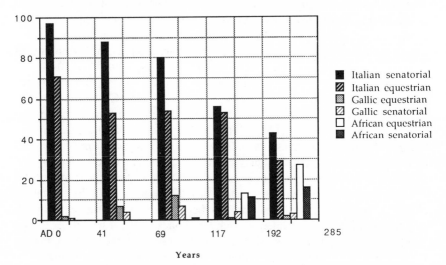

1. Percentage of senators and equestrians from western provinces in the Principate

on hand for its inauguration in the largely east Mediterranean slums of Tras-
tevere. Its remains have been excavated—testimony to imperially endowed
ecumenism.

My object so far has been to draw attention to the aspects of the empire's
history which lack the speed and interest of the political narrative, but which
still have their importance, and which were indeed receiving some scholarly
treatment a half-century or even a century ago. Economics, religion, and prosopography (or capitalism, Christianity, and the upper classes, defining the
world of the observers) have supplied the best illustrations. From the study of
such topics, the gain has long been acknowledged. It is by no means mere
errant attention that picks them out of the historical record for special focus,
where more classical traditions of historiography ignored them. The classical
(and on through Guicciardini and Clarendon and Montesquieu and Gibbon
. . .) were wrong because too narrowly devoted to the narration of doings
among persons prominent in public life, without looking aside at details of
context, or, as one might say, not looking deeply enough into the layers of
causation. Underlying motives they treated as personal or of the times—
hence, a page on the moral character of Scipio or Savanarola, a Melian dialogue, reflections on the singing friars of Rome. Details, however, that regard
national wealth and the capacity to field an army year after year, or regarding
the reinforcement of national resolve through belief in divine approval, or,
again, such as reveal the numbers of the leadership and their acceptance
among the masses of their countrymen—all these help very much in the understanding of why one side won a war and the other lost it. Surely that is a
kind of question acceptable even to classical historians; therefore, the vision
that seeks out details illuminating such matters is well directed and readily
approved.

But it may range much more widely still. To illustrate the possibilities,
nothing serves so well as the school of the *Annales*; and, as anyone interested
in history well knows today, nothing has been more of a force within the discipline over the past several decades. Its initiates have made great use of lateral vision, the sideways glance and more than a glance at details of nautical
maps, mortality statistics, age at marriage, preferred basic grains, and a thousand other matters of the sort. A thousand, or a million. It is characteristic of
this school to investigate and give weight to phenomena which are of interest
only because they are a part of so many lives, and within each, important,
whether or not those individual lives are also important; and the massing of
great quantities of data, and the presenting of very broad statements about
behavior with adequate substantiation, also belongs to the *Annales*; so that an
account of the school intended to show its influence and nature may be, with
wit but truth, presented in the form of graphs comparing continuity of editorial
leadership among leading historical journals, bulkiness of their volumes, and
the influence of their style among courses of instruction in the national center

of higher education.[8] For historians of recent decades, as everyone knows, style (or, if one deplores it, mere fashion) has meant something close to sociology *cum* anthropology *cum* economics *cum* political science—in short, alliance with the social sciences.

Within the world of classical antiquity, however, lateral vision and the social sciences have had very little to look at. Even in periods for which the ancient historians survive, much more is needed and does not exist in adequate amount, in order to say much about Solon's Athens or Sulla's Rome. It is in fact only the first four centuries of the common era (and later times only after the interruption of several more centuries) that offer more than a very occasional opportunity for study à la mode, the reason being the survival of so very much more material within that period. In both bulk and variety, it surpasses anything in other periods before A.D. 1000 quite enormously. *Enormously.* Let the reader in imagination stand before the body of ancient law, from A.D. 150 back to Hammurabi, as compared with what survives from 150 to 450. The latter is bulkier by a factor of fifty (at a guess). Or compare the art favored by Demosthenes, ennobled in Latin by Cicero, and central to the culture of classical antiquity: in the period from Quintilian to Chromatius and from one Chrysostom to another, oratory is transmitted to us in works fifty times more abundant than before. By a similar factor, urban architecture, villas known at least in ground plan, mosaics from both types of site, carved or painted portraits, coinage in all metals, personal letters, astrological and magical literature, both Latin and Greek inscriptions (especially Latin), all, increase in bulk over the empire, compared with the total of everything in these categories across all earlier time. Add, further, pottery, with all that it can reveal through modern scientific techniques. That was mentioned, above; and medical writings will appear for mention, below. The data base underlying the study of the empire has an absolutely distinctive character of its own.

Therefore it lends itself to *Annalysis.* One is not obliged, as in other periods, to describe the past in terms methodologically unacceptable to the present, through eleven potsherds, a few snippets of ancient comedy, some single excavated house, and suchlike pitiful little collections of fact, without statistical significance. All kinds of things that constituted the fabric of the empire's everyday life are open to a more satisfactory study because they have left signs of themselves in such numbers. They allow the substantiation of general statements about routines; in those routines, changes may be detected across time; and changes are the stuff of history. In proof of the possibilities is graphic representation, peculiar to the pages of modern historiography. And an example: in the early 1960s (though not published till some years later) I presented to a meeting of specialists a graph of material arranged by decades to show the quantity of surviving papyri classifiable as private (contracts, letters, wills, personal accounts) as opposed to public. The latter, though very largely tax receipts, included all sorts of documents about obligations toward the state. Patterns of behavior were revealed which seemed to require some rede-fining of the so-called Dominate. The question asked was whether a govern-ment characterized among modern historians as particularly oppressive and intrusive actually touched people's lives much more after A.D. 284 than ear-lier. The answer at least for Egypt was no. Such a question could not be ad-dressed through a bar graph for any earlier periods, with any degree of credi-bility, since no adequate data base could be developed. Where, on the other hand, it did exist, it could be compressed within this medium of description without becoming unintelligible; and the striking quality of visual argument has invited me to use graphs in many other contexts, to describe modes of tax payment, wealth distribution within the empire's society, religious prefer-ences, resort to epigraphy for memorial purposes, and so forth.

Bar- or linear-graphic presentation has gradually become less unusual in scholarly argument, as others have explored its suitability.[9] For the most part, it draws on epigraphic evidence for presentation, and topics in demography and economics. However, material in the *Digest* may be compared with mod-ern statistics to study life expectancy (a favorite subject for statistical repre-sentation, with a history reaching back to the last century);[10] or again, the same, from papyri;[11] or such other subjects as names in Egypt showing reli-gious affiliation, or eras of flourishing of different manufacturers of oil am-phorae in Spain.[12] The point being made, of course, is not that drawing is better than writing, even if that be true; rather, that it is increasingly resorted to as a vivid and economical way of presenting a large number of similar pieces of information such as the period of the empire affords, and no other. And indeed the numbers *are* large, however they are displayed: for purposes of discussion, nearly ten thousand inscriptions studied by Harkness in 1896, over twenty thousand by Macdonell in 1913, over forty thousand by Szilagyi in 1961; and, of papyri, nearly a thousand by Hooper in 1956. How could one possibly lay out so much information before one's readers in mere words?

Past economics, past religion and demography, curiosity about life in the empire has moved on to other aspects. Of all phenomena the hardest to write about, the affective have come under inspection, not only as they can be stud-ied through scattered anecdotes or among the highest aristocracy of a single city (Rome), but among the lower classes. Since these latter are never heard in literary sources doing any of our generalizing for us, once again, a lot of little scattered semi-tangential bits of evidence have to be collected to provide an adequate base for any statement. They can be combed out of inscriptions, and serve then to correct various expectations, anachronisms, and stereotypes regarding, for example, ties of affection within conjugal units (the phrase needed to cover slave "marriages").[13] As an object of study, the family nat-urally belongs among the social sciences and received little attention until it was drawn into the ancient historian's dialogue through the school of the *An-*

between the age of Cicero and the century of the Antonines: a metamorphosis in sexual and conjugal relations''; there, too, appeared a study of female sexuality in the Roman empire, drawing on medical writings of the period of the empire; and the surviving corpus of those works, though of course not requiring a statistical approach, was enormous enough to invite at least tabular presentation; for, among the score or so of writers preserved from the period, accounting for many thousands of pages (!) of discussion, it was possible to find answers to questions about general health care, not merely the practices of chance individuals.[14] Nothing similar could be done for periods before the common era, or for much of the medieval period, either.

In people's feelings toward each other and toward each other's general behavior lie the most difficult questions for exploration. But they underlie the conduct of the political narrative as gravity beneath our feet defines our motions on the surface of the earth. Human values, to the ancients an explanation for so much that is nowadays explained in far more complicated socioeconomic terms, turn out to be worth looking at after all, to discover whether the criminal was deemed responsible for his acts, what was thought to be the proper conduct of men toward women or children toward parents, what was the good perceived in gratitude or aggressiveness, and so forth. Such questions would have been dismissed by historians of a generation past as too ''soft,'' unimportant, and in any case incapable of anything but the most impressionistic answers. Now they reappear, quite respectable, at the front door of the historical discipline: they concern ''mentalités.'' And they are not unimportant.

As to ''mentalités'': imagine someone born in A.D. 50 but still magically traveling around the empire in A.D. 350. What would he see about him that would strike him as quite strange?—that being a way of asking, what big obvious changes had taken place? While a very great deal had happened that brought the peripheral areas closer to the civilization of the center, in the form of sedentary farming, urbanization, consumption of wine and olive oil, use of Latin, and similar things, in the central areas life would no doubt have seemed in most ways still quite recognizable across the lapse of time. The rural scene would be just about the same, so far as might be observable. In the urban, forms of architecture would present some differences—much more use of brick, more curvy lines—but nothing overwhelming, in physical terms. What would most startle and alarm the time-traveler would be the manifestations of official violence toward citizens (himself the next?): at the heart of the town, ''the jail crowded with people awaiting torture and death,'' the judge in the forum conducting interrogation by torture, the local senator being conducted by cart along the main streets to exhibit his back torn by a recent flogging.[15] Ideas of permissible brutality had all too obviously changed.

Then, too, monks. Views of the body and its demands had undergone an extraordinary redirection. Ascetic behavior was not only to be seen, but seen to be valued, as never before, transforming parts of Egypt and already drawing the curious to that province and Palestine by A.D. 350 from all over the empire. A new ideal of life that was till recently described by historians only through its visible signs and its theology can also be tracked in its origins through all those medical writers mentioned previously.[16] But the exaltation of abstinence, reshaping ancient society, would also have been manifest to casual observation through public beheadings for adultery. Changes long under way behind the screens of decency and taboo had prepared an altogether unpredictable reception for the ideas of St. Anthony.

What those changes were in turn must raise the largest and most difficult questions of all. Most students of the empire would probably look for answers in the direction of religion. There, it would be agreed, the Decline was not like the Principate, by any means. "Compared with the age of Cicero and Caesar, for instance, the fourth century was an age when religion was in the forefront of men's minds, when they were obsessed by their relations with the divine."[17] But "obsession"—that needs a very profound examination. In an age looking to the social sciences for help in historical analysis, there could be no one better suited to the job than a past president of the London Society for Psychical Research, E. R. Dodds—also, a most learned classicist. The title of his book, *Pagan and Christian in an Age of Anxiety*, presents him rather in the first of his two capacities. In his listening to the Geist of the Zeit recumbent on the confessional couch, in fact he discovers "the conflict of love and hate in the unconscious mind," "the sense of guilt," "unconscious guilt," "introjection of hostile feelings" leading to "physical acts of self-punishment . . . self-mutilation or suicide," and, in sum, "a period when earthly life was increasingly devalued and guilt feelings were widely prevalent."[18] In proof that affective history, the story of how people feel at different times, may be easier to write than to read, this book may serve as well as any; for it is greatly admired. It undertakes to define the first half of the first century all the way to the second half of the fifth as one period, and then to open up the psyche of a population of sixty millions over that length of four hundred years through a sampling of a dozen or so of its inhabitants, all quite extraordinarily interested in philosophy and theology, and highly educated. Well, really, who can take all this seriously? Let us divide the witnesses as we divide the period studied, and take a quarter of each; and then let us offer an opinion of the Geist of our own Zeit, call it a round century, on the basis of three professors or seminarians. That is the attempt.

What it makes all too clear is the importance of numbers, of mass of evidence, of substantiation proportionate to one's statements. This must be understood before the unique potential of the first four centuries of the era can be appreciated as a period for study. Here, one can indeed find the materials for *Annalysis*.

It is of interest to Dodds to demonstrate "the insecurity of the times," so as to explain certain other phenomena. "This is illustrated by a papyrus," he says—and adduces only the one piece of evidence. Alas, it turns out to belong to a largely irrelevant genre of text; but even the great Braudel occasionally misused his evidence.[19] Who doesn't? Against the kind of slip which anyone may make, however careful he is trying to be, there is safety only in numbers: *many* facts, of which one may be wrong without destroying the argument.

A last word: the quality as well as the quantity of documentation needs to be weighed, in arriving at conclusions about those broad, slow-moving aspects of history on which inquiry increasingly focuses. Some facts imply many facts and so, though singly, allow generalization. In illustration, a scene carved on a tombstone. It shows the deceased, man and wife, holding hands. "We think it unlikely," say the commentators, "that this couple would have advertised qualities that were not held as ideals by others around them."[20] The comment is surely justified, taking account, as it obviously does, of the ancient audience to whom an act or an opinion is openly presented. Man is a social animal, does not gratuitously issue a challenge to the values of the surrounding human community, and especially avoids challenge in what are meant as formal statements, verbal or symbolic. So the bas relief on the tombstone may be gingerly used to speak about much more than the preference of the one person who commissioned it. As it turns out, the great bulk of communications surviving from the past were offered to a public, not to an individual or private audience. They are epitaphs by the hundreds of thousands; other types of stony statement; works of art; works of literature, even apparently private correspondence consciously prepared for publication, unless written on papyri (rarely, on other surfaces). All that needs to be avoided is the too-tidy clearing aside of uncongenial exceptions to what one wants to say. Nothing is true that leaves out untidiness; for there may in fact be more than one audience for a document, more than one human community addressed, each holding to patterns of behavior and values quite at odds with some other in the same city—to say nothing of the whole empire.[21] They cohabit quite conubially; a member of one may even pass into another on the same given day without awkwardness, though with discretion. The historian must listen to both, or all, before he ventures on any general description of their society; he must expect such variety of life as is always to be found, but is not always adequately reported; therefore he must *know* both or all audiences or communities. In this respect, once more, it is the first four or five centuries A.D. that present a record sufficiently detailed to satisfy the needs of believable generalization, satisfying reasonable doubt that some relevant group may not have been left out of account entirely, because of the perishing of evidence. The Roman empire offers that detailed record, uniquely, and the pages that follow are offered in celebration of the fact.

2

ROMAN ELITE MOTIVATION: THREE QUESTIONS

E VEN A HISTORIAN impatient of debate about method, who would rather do history than discuss how it is done, may find himself drawn into such a discussion; he may even do more than tolerate it, if it can be shown to bear nearly and effectively on the actual practice of his art. But that is the case, as may be illustrated by following out a certain train of thought.

It begins with a well-known passage from Polybius,[1] in which he reports a conversation he had with Scipio. Scipio was then in his twentieth year. He speaks of people's general opinion that he is likely to turn out a weak spokesman for his family, not a stirring and active man but a stranger to Roman ways and beliefs. He is keenly sensitive to what those of his circle are saying about him, their estimation of him causes him great distress, and he is especially aware of the standard set for him by his descent. The conversation reveals the strain felt by the young men (and no doubt, in different ways, by women) of the ruling class through their need to live up to expectation.

To this anecdote we may add a group of four more having a common focus: Lucius Junius Pullus lost his fleet in the First Punic War and "anticipated his conviction by a voluntary death"; one of Cato's aides, caught by his commander in the purchase of boy captives (for homosexual purposes, that is) killed himself; so did Decimus Junius Silanus, praetor in Macedonia, after he had been found guilty of extortion by a family hearing and banished by his own father; and Marcus Aemilius Scaurus was found guilty of cowardice in the face of the enemy, likewise by his father, and killed himself.[2] These examples from the later third and second centuries B.C. reinforce the impression we receive from Scipio's confession of suffering, the impression that what one's circle expected of one might produce strains literally insupportable. For suicide is, after all, a most extreme act, quite against nature. It draws attention to motive with unique emphasis, especially where (as with these cases) the loss of one's cause, or of all one's material possessions, or of life itself at the hands of an executioner, was not in question. No, it was the terrible eye of the community that men could not bear. And our examples are not presented in our sources as anything utterly strange, rather as representative of a tragedy well known if not common among Romans.

But this is the people who, beyond such institutions of public praise and reward as all societies possess—an Honors List annually, or whatever form it may take—every five years staged before the entire citizen body the ceremonious humiliation of their fellows who were most in the public eye anyway, that is, senators and members of the upper class who had been detected in some fault beyond the reach of law and who could be made to suffer the most sharply from exposure. It would be hard to name a match, in any century or country, for the *censoria nota*, whose *ignominia virtutem acuit*, the censors' annotation, that spurs on virtue by ignominy.[3] The Romans set great value on it. Scipio for instance enjoyed recalling stories and recommending the example of particularly strict censors.[4] Institutionalized dishonoring belonged to *mos maiorum*. It belonged to the Roman army as well, in which misconduct was not only punished on the spot but, beyond that, insured that offenders would be taunted and banished from their home circle when they came back from the wars.[5]

And names: in this period, unlike later days that had fallen more under alien fashions and paraded men as The Great or The Fortunate (Felix, very close to "Epaphroditus"), or Achilles (a certain Occius), Romans somehow acquired the names Gurges, Porcina, Caudex, Asina, Balbus, Catulus, Cicero, Flaccus, Strabo, Spendthrift, Piglet, Puppy, Cross-Eyes, Flabby: a striking contrast with the Greeks, all wonderful in their very cradles, all Famed-Everywhere, Foremost-in-the-Assembly, and so forth.

Cicero sees the value of customs that inflict disgrace on the citizens of a state who "are not so much deterred by fear and punishment that laws lay down as by the sense of shame that nature has afforded to man in the form of a certain fear of reproach." He goes on to expand on the point.[6] It cannot have needed much emphasis for an audience whose experience had regularly exposed them to the stigmatizing of faults by nicknames and *nota*, by state or family judgment, to a degree and with a force not found in other western societies.

But if the depths of disgrace were so pronounced, so too were the heights of fame. Polybius describes how Lucius Anicius hired a whole lot of the best Greek instrumentalists and ballet-dancers and (what was unknown to their art, and boorish absurdity to Polybius) got them to perform like two armies on the stage, to illustrate his victorious campaigns in Thrace.[7] Lucius Hostilius Mancinus, back from the wars, campaigned for the consulate in front of immense posters he had had painted and set up in the Forum, before which he gave illustrated lectures on his own heroic actions. Scipio resented being upstaged.[8] But Scipio's grandfather at his own celebrations in 201 B.C. had prefigured both practices by adding to the triumphal parade illustrative posters and pictures, and interpretive dancers, some in massed formation, one miming victory over enemies.[9]

The praetor Marcus Sergius about the same time and after service in the same war delivered and handed down to posterity in written form a speech on his own exploits: "in his second campaign, lost his right hand; in two campaigns was wounded twenty-three times; yet, disabled, served in numerous subsequent campaigns; twice taken prisoner by Hannibal, twice escaped; fought four times with only his left hand, having two horses stabbed under him,'' and so on and so forth.[10] To this hero we can compare that other who displayed *his* scars to the crowd in the Forum, until he displayed a bit too much, and was laughed at for his remembered and present pains—*not* (which is the point here) laughed at for what we would call extravagant boastfulness.[11]

And still in the same decade or so, Cato, on whose continual self-praise even a Greek biographer remarked:[12] *his* addresses to his fellow citizens, which he carefully transmitted also to later generations, are regularly punctuated by the emphatic use of the first person singular, as a glance at the surviving quotations can tell us: for example, "And I myself have long realized . . . ," "notice how differently I myself would have done it . . . ," or in his speech "On His Own Virtues," where he declares how "I myself from the very beginning, in reduced expenses and straitened life . . . ," or in his speech "On the Blessedness of His Term as Censor."[13] These self-gratulatory exercises happen only to be preserved somewhat more fully than, for example, those of Scipio's father,[14] or, from about Scipio's own lifetime, those of the inscription: "and as praetor in Sicily I tracked down runaway slaves of Italian owners and gave back 917 to their masters. Furthermore, I was the first to force shepherds to make room on state land for farmers," and so on.[15] We may compare Cicero's two epic poems "On My Times" and "On My Consulate." Had any of these compositions seemed preposterous to their audience, so too would their authors. Their careers would have ended. But advertisement of one's own virtues and achievements was expected. It picked out the summits of pride.

Epic (or more or less epic) versification of one's deed could also be insured by those who were not up to it themselves, and (unlike Cicero) would accept the fact. They attached a poet to their campaign retinue, as did Scipio's great-uncle, and Marcus Fulvius Nobilior, and various other prominent men in later times.[16] Heroizing poetry was in general circulation, and esteem. Cicero expects an open-air audience—that is, not a specially literate one in the Forum—to know by heart certain edifying lines of Accius, and to agree that such lines "spur us on to efforts and fame."[17] It was common knowledge in Polybius' day that older Romans had had some sort of ballad tradition to keep green the memory of patriotic deeds, and Valerius Maximus expects from them very much the same effect as Cicero: "they make youth the more eager to emulate outstanding deeds."[18] Polybius offers to his Greek readers the full tale of Horatius at the bridge, Horatius whose statue stood in the most frequented corner of the Forum and whose heroism, no one can doubt it, every Roman lad knew by heart. "Some impulse and thirst for honor like this, directed at splendor of achievement, is thus engendered," as Polybius says;[19] or as Macaulay says, sitting at his desk in Ootacamund in India in 1834, and from that strange vantage point reconstructing the *carmina* that Cato recalled:

And how can man die better / Than facing fearful odds,
For the ashes of his fathers / And the temples of his Gods . . .
Never, I ween, did swimmer / In such an evil case
Struggle thro' such a raging flood, / Safe to the landing place;
But his limbs were borne up bravely / By the brave heart within,
And our good father Tiber / Bore bravely up his chin . . .
And they made a molten image / And set it up on high,
And there it stands unto this day / To witness if I lie.
It stands in the Comitium, / Plain for all folk to see . . .
And underneath is written / In letters all of gold,
How valiantly he kept the bridge / In the brave days of old.[20]

Polybius set about his recording of Roman history because of the turn it had taken recently: it had overspread the world—at least *his* world. He would like to explain that interesting fact. He approached his task like a sociologist as much as a historian, giving close attention to institutions and national character. The connection between what a people *is* and what, over a stretch of a generation, that people *does*, he obviously sensed, perhaps even so far as to grant that the various very familiar practices we have surveyed with his help, taken all together, open a view on the chief determinant of Roman imperialism. They made such a striving people, under such striving leadership, as could not fail to expand. With this view Macaulay, for one, would surely have agreed. If we could ask him how he would account for the spread of Roman dominion over the Mediterranean, surely he would look for the answer, or an important part of the answer, in the story of Horatius—just as his readers were prepared to believe that the battle of Waterloo was won on the playing-fields of Eton. The myths that infuse the boyhood of the officer class can be seen as shaping the men of a nation, later.

One assumption should be made explicit here: that the behavior of a group of leaders acting in their public capacity will not differ in quality from their behavior as private individuals. By way of illustration: Polybius remarks on "how much making money by good-faith means is held in honor"; and in a funeral oration delivered at the death of Lucius Metellus in 221 B.C. his son lists among the ten things that all wise men strive for, "the obtaining of great wealth in an honorable way." It is obvious from many passages in Cato's book on farming that the author endorsed this pursuit, though in it one should, he repeats, behave "like an honest landowner."[21] He means, one may increase honor even beyond what wealth bestows, through not extorting every penny of advantage out of one's position; just so, when Scipio acted generously in a family matter, witnesses "were tremendously impressed by his goodness and largeness of mind . . . something quite remarkable in Rome, where absolutely no one ever gives away anything to anyone . . . such being the sharpness about money among everyone, along with the love of gain."[22] The two characteristic impulses are seen at work on a large scale, and at cross purposes, it so happens, in 172 B.C. The king of Macedonia was about to declare war on Rome, for which his preparations were complete. A consul deceived him into delay, greatly to Rome's advantage, "and boasted of nothing more than of this."[23] Most senators also saw it as a very shrewd bit of business, though some considered it un-Roman. Polybius examines a similar occurrence of some years later, noting that "Romans prided themselves on conducting their wars in a straightforward, honorable fashion," with perhaps not too much of that showing recently toward Carthage.[24]

These anecdotes and comments serve as a reminder, if any were needed, that traits valued in a confined setting one should expect to find valued and at work in a wide setting. Historians therefore should be able to treat the conduct of a state and of an individual in similar terms, noting as Polybius does that Roman government was "extremely ambitious of honor in every endeavor."[25] For "Roman government" we may read "Scipio," and "every endeavor" may include the settling of a family affair as naturally as it does the state's dealings with an overseas power.

Such terms of historical analysis sound sadly dated and simple when contrasted with the current style. But if we asked one of the latter's most able practitioners, Keith Hopkins, the same question we put to Macaulay, he might invite us to:

> take a closer look at the Roman war effort. One obvious measure is the size of the army. . . . Right down to the end of the Republic, Rome is best seen as a warrior state. The empire was won only through the massive involvement of the lower classes in war, an involvement which mirrored the militarism of the elite. We can see this clearly enough if we consider the average length of military service . . . the conclusions seem staggering. An army which accounted for thirteen per cent of all citizens (the median of the last two centuries) could be raised by enlisting eighty-four per cent of seventeen-year-olds for five years, or c. sixty per cent for seven years, or forty-four per cent for ten years, or twenty-eight per cent for sixteen years. (The cohort of seventeen-year-olds (at $e_0 = 25$) equalled about three per cent of the adult male population . . .).[26]

Unfortunately, however, we know neither the length of service nor, within pretty large limits, the available number of possible conscripts.[27] The range of possibilities dangled before us, being further enlarged to account for freely acknowledged uncertainties in the data base itself, therefore reduces to the statement that the Romans exerted themselves in war very greatly. They made a big effort.

"They made a big effort" says all that the more refined calculations say, working from age cohorts and so forth; but it does not appear to say anywhere nearly so much. On the other hand, Polybius' perception of "the impulse and thirst for honor like this" (of Horatius) among Romans, or Macaulay's "brave days of old,'' while they appear to give us only a naive, old-fashioned romantic bit of Romanophilism, in reality direct us to a point of inquiry quite essential: national motive. The former statement, the quantified one, is mere description and on the surface; the latter is explanatory and interpretive and aims at the heart of what happened (namely, how did the Romans come to conquer everybody?). Quantification may belong to science and the 1970s, but explanation is better reached by way of Ootacamund and 1834.

We need not, perhaps, go quite so far back for a good model of historiography. Early in our own century, Max Weber attacked a question somewhat like ours and Polybius'—that is, what ''lashed 'capitalist man' into his frantic race?''[28] He sought the answer through the study of ideal types, the bourgeois businessman, the entrepreneur or putter-out, Benjamin Franklin and his like. In certain parts of his argument he had no difficulty. Imagining (for example) two groups of people, one of which was a little more inclined to save than the other, be it by only a few percent, then in a couple of decades he could show it to have grown twice as rich. That was mathematically unexceptionable; for a *settled* tendency at work continuously over any length of time need not be a *marked* tendency, in order to produce differences of significant historical magnitude. Though we might be surprised at the size of the results, we readily grant their validity. At the heart of Weber's argument, however, lies the necessity to demonstrate the heightened degree of the required tendencies in the ascendant group. He does not claim them as unique to his ideal type,[29] any more than one might claim competitive striving and acquisitive impulses to be unique among Romans. No, the ideal type that he describes is a human being like any other, differing only in susceptibility to this or that particular (but not peculiar) motive or motives. Only the amount of the difference remains to be established. But just here lies the rub. The necessary numbers cannot be developed from available sources to prove a striving quality x percent greater among Romans or a saving quality y percent greater among the Protestant bourgeoisie than among other contemporary groups. We must be content with the observed phenomena (whether or not, results): the troops under arms or the capital accumulated.

Before surrendering to this logic, and in order to be sure that the problem of historical method is correctly addressed, let us look at a second Roman question: not ''What drove the Roman elite to conquer the world of Polybius' time?'' but ''What drove the city elite of the empire to lavish its money on its fellow citizens?''

If our understanding of Roman history were best advanced through purely numerical description, then no scholar today could help us more than R. Duncan-Jones, who has gathered into one volume a dense and meticulously arranged display of data on costs, population, private fortunes, productivity, and so forth from one relatively well-documented sector of the empire. For illustration: he gives us from the central Italian town of Aquilonia two inscriptions recording how local priests of the imperial cult paid for the paving of 800 and 880 feet of road:

> The amounts appear close enough together to suggest the fulfilment of a fixed charge translated into differing construction costs. If the figures are read as lengths of road of standard width, the implied outlay would be considerable, of the order of HS [sesterces] 16,000 in each case. This seems implausible as the amount of a fixed charge. . . . Aquilonia was an extremely obscure town which can scarcely have had high charges for office. An alternative would be to see the totals as a square measure; on this basis, the longitudinal road distance notionally represented would be . . . lengths . . . quite compatible with the familiar charge for the Augustalitas of HS 2,000. The construction costs that would be implied are HS 22.4 and HS 20.4 per longitudinal foot; both figures are very close to the attested examples ranging from HS 20.7 to HS 24.2.[30]

The evidence here is laid out so scrupulously that every detail of the calculation can be tested. But unfortunately the paving costs then appear to change before our eyes, depending on whether we take a certain abbreviation in one sense or another or accept or reject the idea of a "familiar charge."[31] In looking closely at such minutiae, of course, our object is merely to illustrate how exiguous are the statistical data from antiquity, how hard they are pressed to yield up any useful sense at all, and (as might be shown easily enough from other pages, or from less careful scholars) how far exactness of calculation exceeds the inherent firmness of the results. Indeed, many favorite subjects such as the size of Rome's population, or of the population of less important cities, or the average life expectancy, the proportion of slaves to free men, the profitability of large versus small farms, the size of the imperial army, or mortality under the great plagues, can be described only in the roughest approximations, which it is time wasted to carry to the second decimal place. And this is a criticism which may be made even without raising the further challenge: whether the results offered, if they were exact, would really advance our knowledge. Suppose we did discover that in Aquilonia, or for that matter in some place not "extremely obscure," two of the richest citizens made a present to their fellows of a certain sum for road-paving, at a date not precisely known, would that carry us very far along the path to the truth? Statistical data can be put to use only when they appear in a close texture. Widely scattered, they avail nothing. So far at least as the favorite subjects are concerned, it has long been evident that the requisite texture is lacking.

But in fact these two inscriptions from Aquilonia are part of another dossier as well, one that describes not the costs of building in stone but rather the dimensions of civic generosity. The data from one region, so far as they can be quantified, are collected by Duncan-Jones. They include such projects as those just seen in Italy, and cash handouts, and entrance contributions by municipal senators or magistrates elect, feasts for the citizenry, endowments of all sorts—in sum, the great bulk of everything that later ages or the Romans themselves pronounce admirable in their civilization, derived from free gifts of private individuals. From the more illuminating items in the dossier we can find out, not how many sesterces it cost per foot of paving around Aquilonia, but why the town's residents gave to this end out of their own pockets, untaxed and unconstrained. We can, that is, discover motivation.

One writer of the era that concerns us says in a speech:

> I need not tell you that my father was a good man, for you [that is, his compatriots] are always saluting him approvingly, in your gatherings or singly, whenever you recall him, as a most estimable citizen. . . . Nor could anyone say of my grandfather, too, that he disgraced his city, or that he spent nothing on it out of his own means; for he lavished the entire property he inherited from his father and grandfather on civic generosity [*philotimia*] till he had nothing left at all.[32]

So there, almost by inadvertence, we have the words we would expect to explain the whole phenomenon: ''salute,'' ''gatherings,'' ''disgrace,'' ''citizens.'' A generation later we can find another writer saying: ''We [the urban aristocracy] have run into debt not for our bread and wine . . . but through spendthrift staging of games and shows for our cities. We lavish our generosity in barren and ungrateful competition''[33] — from which we gain a sense of the emptiness felt by civic benefactors, not only because they had literally bankrupted themselves—had committed a kind of economic suicide reminiscent of the real deaths touched on in an earlier page—in their pursuit of honor, but because their sacrifice had not brought its proper reward. It was a sacrifice taken by their fellow citizens, and taken for granted. Yet social constraints, peer expectation, the sense of father, grandfather, and the whole weight of place and pride continued to compel the gifts that made Roman cities what they were. To the very end, an observer like John Chrysostom saw how at Antioch:

> the theater fills, and the whole citizenry is seated up there, presenting the most brilliant spectacle made up of so many faces, that the very topmost gallery and its covering is blocked out by men's bodies. . . . Upon the entrance of that benefactor who brought them together, they leap to their feet, uttering a salute as from a single mouth, with one voice calling him guardian and leader of their common city. They stretch forth their arms; then at intervals they compare him to the greatest of all rivers; they liken the grandeur and flow of his civic generosity, in its abundance, to the waters of the Nile, and they call him a very Nile of gifts, himself; and some who flatter still more, declaring the comparison with the Nile too mean, set aside rivers and seas and bring in Ocean, and say that is what he is, as Ocean among waters, so he in his gifts. They omit no possible term of praise. . . . He himself bows to them, and by this pays his repects, and so he seats himself amid the blessing of all, who, every one, pray to be such as he—and then to

die. . . . And while he revels in his heart's desire like a person drunk with vain-
glory, to the point that he would spend his very self, he can take in no least sensation of his losses. But when he is at home, . . . then at that moment he understands they were no dream but a reality in hard cash.[34]

To sum up so far: in Roman history the salient fact in the earlier half appears
to be the assembling of an empire, and in the latter half the decorating of it.
To explain these two great facts, corresponding to the two questions I have
discussed, we have no knowledge that seems to me more helpful than our
knowledge about the characteristic inclinations of the elite. Those inclinations
produce the results universally familiar, which may almost be said to constitute Roman history itself as it is conventionally written. But the underlying
inclinations themselves are relatively little studied. Why (my third question),
why is this so?

The answer must be sought somewhere among the processes by which the
raw facts about the past, recent or remote, come before our judgment, and are
arranged in series, and so offered to an audience. But here I would like to refer
to matters of quite ordinary experience. Let me at the start divide the historian's facts or data into two kinds, for convenience termed "irrational" and
"sensible." By the first, I mean whatever data lie inside the mind, apart from
reasoning itself: therefore passion, emotion, prejudice, mood, personality,
ideals. By the sensible, I mean whatever data lie outside the mind. They are
taken in through the senses; they show us the coins that we see being paid for
some item (Duncan-Jones's paving costs), the lads that we see enlisting (Hopkins's recruits), any field of action, a battle, a debate and vote in the senate, a
whole sequence of scenes. Part of the historian's job lies simply in putting this
sort of data down on paper. For my purposes, however, it is important to note
that one can if one wants to describe all this numerically: the distance tra-
versed, the exact time or date, the size of the meeting, the majority enjoyed
by one party or army over another, the very wounds in Caesar's body, everything can be counted; and furthermore, that numbers have a unique capacity
to clarify the outline of data. It follows that anyone wanting to make his report
of an action particularly persuasive will express its salient parts numerically,
as Hopkins does with Rome's degree of militarism or as the Romans themselves did with their own exploits: "in two campaigns was wounded twenty-
three times," "gave back 917 runaway slaves to their masters." The full quotations are given above, carrying a special conviction. "That is the good of
counting," said Dr. Samuel Johnson, "It brings everything to a certainty
which before floated in the mind indefinitely."

The characteristic weight and ease of handling that we discover in sensible
data carry over into those debates by which historians, using such material,
determine the truths they can agree on. Of course the material may be totally

lacking, or reports of it erroneous; hence controversy and uncertainty; but to the extent that it is available, conflicting interpretation can always be resolved.

So much for sensible data, by definition outside the mind. In trying to explain, however, not *what* happened but *why*, historians must somehow penetrate to the inside. In that realm they would like to continue working with equally tractable evidence and arguments. Such can be found: motivation reaching out to tangible benefits—at its simplest, the instinct for self-preservation in every form, all appetites and bodily needs, or greed, and all the reaching out also to intermediate objectives that will help one to attain the more fundamental—such motivation deals with or is stimulated by sensible data, at least on the conscious level. So does the scholarly examination of it. As in the minds of their subjects, so in the minds of historians themselves, and yet a third time in the minds of their readers, survey may be made of lands to be conquered, trade improved, wages raised, Sabines raped. All, quantifiable. Not only the process of survey and material of calculation, but the original force of motive may be reproduced. The mere listing of the desirable things to be gained, in however inartistic a style, addresses basic and universal wants, arouses those wants vicariously, and so produces undiminished the feeling of being convinced and moved. The sensation really experienced by a given person at a given moment in the past is experienced again by someone else, the student. It being the historians' aim to present explanatory pictures of the past that carry conviction, at least this part of their task they thus find quite satisfactory. Indeed, to sum it up in quite different words, materialistic motivation is easy to treat. That fact, by the way, may have something to do with the popularity of the socioeconomic approach dominant in historiography for so long—more recently than 1834, shall we say?

By contrast there remains a most refractory kind of motivation that historians must deal with. The evidence is "irrational." No one entirely denies its existence; indeed everyone concedes that in every event in the past there were various emotions at work. Were they strong, however, and their role important? *Very* strong? Or perhaps very, *very* strong? The questions are childish only because we are asked to quantify what cannot be measured. If historians disagree about such motivation, however, by what other means than measurement can disagreement possibly be resolved?

What are we to do with motivation that reaches toward a satisfaction wholly or largely internal? What are we to do with resentment, compassion, outrage, the need for excitement, the sheer spirit of adventure, the need for love or for relief of anxiety? What are we to do with Alexander's vision of the unity of mankind, Hannibal's boyhood oath of revenge on Rome, whatever induced the jeopardy of material interest or of life itself by Horatius Cocles, Marcus Sergius, Spurius Ligustinus, Lucius Junius Pullus, and, in a later age, all those bankrupted magnates? How easy to brush aside the naivety that would accept all these figures just as they appear in our sources; how far more sober to interpret their actions in fashionably modern terms of expected advantage and profit, how difficult on the other hand to give persuasive force to explanations of conduct that rest on nothing but people's alleged feelings!

Consider, for example, Paul Veyne's discussion of civic generosity, in which he confronts first the quantitative benefits gained by Roman noblemen through their public benefactions, and next, the question whether:

> they may not have sought popularity for its own sake, even among the poor who could be of no use to them, but could only look up to them. It is not pleasant, when one knows oneself to be one of the powerful, to be jeered at in the street by a whistling crowd, even if the crowd's contempt is powerless and, to a realist, of no effect. In other words, benefactions by public figures looked toward a satisfaction that was, one might say, irrational or in any case basic.[35]

What Veyne is trying to do, and in the field of ancient history today no one does it better, is to invite our serious attention to the irrational. But he must do it through tricks not usually employed by historians, offering for instance a purely imaginary street scene with its hooting mob, and merely asserting what is pleasant or unpleasant, unsupported by the usual scholarly citations.

But these and similar tricks are needed because, in the effort to make clear why people in the past behaved as they did, plain prose suffices to replicate sensible motives in the reader's mind, but not the irrational ones. The latter must rather be stimulated through the novelist's, playwright's, or poet's skill. They must be evoked through a street scene, by Veyne, or through a scene in a theater, by John Chrysostom. Language must be used that touches, stirs, or makes the spine tingle. Only then will the written account yield those moments of marvelous illumination in which at last the reader realizes: *"That's* how it was! *Now* I can see!"

If advances in our understanding of the sensible evidence from the past appear to be so hard-won nowadays and so seldom on a satisfactory scale, our concentration rather on the irrational would involve a radical change in the nature of serious historiography. Let us return to a problem already touched on: historians' disagreements. Would one reconstruction, one richly worded evocation, have to be pitted against another? And judges of "what really happened" (in Ranke's famous phrase) would somehow have to compare them, and somehow empathetically determine which one felt more likely to be true? And would not scholars have to adopt approaches very hard to contemplate: the consulting of their own emotions as they study the past; the reading of fiction, even of anthropology; the use of adjectives and other touches of color in their argument? They might find themselves exploring aspects of national character, or at least the character of elites, or writing about peer pressure or feuds in the later Republic, the sense of clan in the same period, the acceptability of laughter and tears in public, or humanitarianism in the Antonine empire, inter-rank relations in the army, or gender differences in the acculturation of new citizens. None of these subjects might appear very rewarding were it not for the possibility, at least the theoretical possibility, that Weber's thesis and others similar, although beyond demonstration in conventional terms, might be right—and the terms wrong. That does make one think.

3

HISTORY IN CLASSICS

SUPPOSING THAT classical philology draws people to its study because it fits the focus of their own natural curiosity and their intellectual capacities, and supposing that they are drawn, too, not only by the subject matter itself but by the particular kinds of questions asked by its specialists—then it makes best sense to develop their capacities under the direction of others like themselves but more advanced in that study: in short, under the direction of classical philologists. In this same manner, *mutatis mutandis*, anthropologists and biologists and economists are also trained. Their training is entrusted to people well suited by demonstration: they have shown their mastery to each other, the best jury, by means of their masterful essays and public lectures. Manifestly they know the discipline. They are therefore the best suited to impart it to others. At the same time, they themselves continue to develop, professionally, as their discipline does; for it undergoes continual inspection, is tested by its yield, and is corrected, revised, improved, and kept up to date with the whole wide front of other related, vital disciplines.

Self-evident, all this, and true—except for the study, students, teachers, and discipline of Greek and Roman history. Alexander the Great and Tiberius Gracchus, unlike Napoleon and Lord Grey of the Reform Bill, are not thought to be the proper care of historians but of philologists. It has been for philologists to explain to us the wars, economies, legal systems, religions, mass cultures, and every other aspect of past life, not of the Renaissance, not of the twentieth-century United States, but only in the period of classical antiquity.

Has this most peculiar anomaly been a good thing? On the face of it, one would imagine not, since it opposes the wisdom accepted in every other field of special study. No one would think to produce a good practitioner or even a very good undergraduate understanding of anthropology through a course of instruction from economists, or of physics, from political scientists. Why ever, then, were the rules of common wisdom set aside for classical antiquity? The answer is obvious, and applies incidentally to one or two other odd corners of history: the languages that the student needs are difficult to acquire and in their difficulty stand as an obstacle against entrance to the field by all but those who gained the languages for their own sake, first, and only by related curiosity came to read and enjoy Herodotus or Plutarch. Then perhaps they said, with these writers as their models, "I like it. I'll try my own hand at it."

In trying, they may perhaps discover a good fit with "the focus of their own natural curiosity and their intellectual capacities" (as the matter was expressed, a moment ago). That is, they reach over from philology to history; for there are indeed lucky individuals who have and demonstrate some gift for two quite separate disciplines. Yet they are, in the past century or so, surprisingly hard to think of, whether the doubling of disciplines has involved philology and history, or economics and physics, or any other pair. Conventional wisdom is thus confirmed. Cobblers, to be any good at all, had better stick to their last.

Still, there is an awful lot of historiography carried on by classical philologists—a very great majority of all that has been written, comparing the authors' academic origins with the titles of their books and articles and the journals they appear in. Who is to say it is all bad, and they should stick to literary criticism and history, exegesis of texts, linguistic change, and so forth? No attempt at so broad a condemnation could rise much above name-calling, and very invidious and unconvincing it would be: "Smith's book is folly, Jones' book is worse"—and so on, dismissively, through whole libraries, a little like the unpleasant Mommsen's dictum delivered to his son-in-law in a letter of May 18, 1878: "Scholarly writing is almost as corrupting a trade as playacting. The great majority of one's colleagues are vulgar and petty and devoted to the business of bringing these characteristics to ever fuller bloom. Anyone who enters it with any idealistic notions will have a hard time controlling his disgust and hatred." And he continues to excoriate "the ignorance among far the majority of colleagues . . . , archeologists, comparative linguists, and whatever else they call themselves" (ed. E. Schwartz, *Mommsen und Wilamowitz. Briefwechsel*, 1935, 42).

There is quite another approach possible to the question, "Has it been a good thing to leave the history of classical antiquity largely to classical philologists?" We can look at the models they encounter in the natural course of their studying, and we can measure these against the historical discipline as it has developed over the last half-century (still more clearly in the last quarter-century). Have they kept up? Consider only biography. From the Greek and Roman world we have a generous amount of literature devoted to the lives of the most eminent figures, either whole as it is encountered in Plutarch and Suetonius or in bits and pieces as it is provided by the anecdotal parts of Polybius and Tacitus. Such material can be compared with the pages devoted by modern historians to their not-ancient subjects, the great figures of the fourteenth century, the fifteenth, or later. Depth of documentation for these latter sometimes allows very searching analysis, and searching it must be to reach the truth—though, even without such modern models, nobody past adolescence needs to be told that human motivation can be infinitely complicated, above all in complicated or important junctures of a person's life. Those are the very moments on which our focus must rest, in our efforts to understand the past. We may learn as much from Page Smith's *John Adams* (1962), Richard Shannon's *Gladstone* (vol. 1, 1982), or any ongoing study of the living such as Stephen Gillon's *Walter Mondale*. Considering the absolutely monumental evidentiary base, including great diaries, that underlies these latter works and the uncertainties that still obscure their authors' findings, who then can turn with satisfaction to the exiguous record for (let us say) Tiberius Gracchus? Who can take it seriously? By reading Plutarch in the light of Appian, and Appian in the light of snippets of Cicero, and so on, it once proved possible to advance a few inches beyond the understanding of any single ancient account, and so to arrive at a scholarly consensus about the very broadest outlines of Gracchus' tribunate. But that was long ago. Surely the ancient record will not allow so much as a millimeter of further progress, in which new findings may be worth arguing against all prior contrary opinion. The closest argument cannot satisfy because modern biography has shown us what we require, and what we will never have, to resolve any more detailed disagreements.

Much study of the Greek and Roman past nevertheless continues to strain at the narrative of political careers. It might be expected to turn instead to other aspects of the past that would prove more rewarding; but scholars find little encouragement to that in their historiographical models. The latter teach only that it is leaders who change the world; or, as it was asserted a half-century ago, "Roman history, Republican or Imperial, is the history of the governing class" (R. Syme, often quoted since). In this belief, and entirely in accord with classical models, students of classical antiquity struggled to learn more and more about a very few of the most prominent figures. That is, they pursued prosopography. Exactly what it was in aid of—exactly what new ground it would eventually open up—needed no debate, because, after all, it was contributing to knowledge of the leadership stratum.

But, for the understanding of periods other than the Greek and Roman, the truth has long been recognized that leaders must have followers, and that the connections between the two, and followers in their own right, are as important as the people at the top. Indeed, there have been interesting moments in the past when "leaders" have commanded but no one obeyed, when ringing orations were delivered but no one listened. There is Napoleon before Moscow: the submissive boyards must attend him at the gate and learn of his generosity. But they didn't care to. No followers! Tolstoy exposes the moment in *War and Peace* (part 11 chap. 14, "le ridicule"). In classical antiquity there is the fatuous prince Germanicus described by Tacitus (*Annals* 1.35—teaching how necessary it is that leaders must know *how to* posture); and there are the officers at Thapsus and Placentia whose troops grew tired of pursuing other men's—gentlemen's—quarrels even if it might be called "making history" ("Caesar," *African War* 85, and Appian, *Civil Wars* 2.47). The leaders in these scenes had briefly blundered: they had forgotten the limits to relationships within which they could ordinarily count on compliance from others.

Such limits and such posturing, the structure and the style of a society, have always counted heavily among the determinants of events. Were they at any time different, "history" would be different. They evidently deserve study. So does technology, obviously; so does transportation, commerce, finance, demography, mobility, sense of place, and class structure—a hundred things of that sort. But the general conditions of life in the classical models of historiography are either taken for granted as the weather is taken for granted or the seasons of safe sailing, or they are ignored as unimportant, or they are not understood; for both writers and readers, belonging to the elite, were to some extent simply ignorant of how their more humble contemporaries lived and thought. The three reasons taken together explain why Plutarch and Appian seldom afford the material which is today the most common focus of historical study in all fields but ancient.

Holistic explanation is what most obviously characterizes modern historiography: it takes into account not only all regions of a country and all types of person but their perceptions of each other, how they are accustomed to react to each other, what values they hold to, how they gain and spend money, their relations with the law, sense of participation in the state, and so forth. Most important by far is the recognition of all these phenomena *as mutual influences*, not as disconnected parts of the historical setting. In interaction, they produce change, but change at different rates too slow to catch the interest of the unreflecting observer. Indeed, it is rather that most rapid change involved in surface events—the battles of Bedriacum, let us instance—which is most easily dismissed as uninteresting. Their study, no matter how detailed, explains too little.

Not long ago, at long last, someone referred in a scholarly review to a truth that scholars have conspired to ignore: a learned book may be "dull" (*Journal of Roman Studies* 1978, p. 185). At least by their never using the term, or any like it, they had encouraged the impression that anything alleged as fact or argument (and very little of scholarly publication cannot qualify as one or the other) everyone must find interesting. How absurd! Professor Hopkins confronted the pretense and exposed it; and, right or wrong in his judgment of the particular book under his inspection at the moment, he deserved a medal for his courage. He then went on to consider just what it might be that makes a piece of historical literature not dull—interesting. He offered, as the chief part of his answer, the power to draw a reader in imagination to the center of the scene described. It should "evoke a lost world and make it live in the reader's mind." One could perhaps go even further, and demand the reader's emotional involvement as an instrument of scientific analysis (see the discussion in chapter 2). In so doing, one could admit, too, the merits of a good deal of historical literature that survives from classical antiquity, full of dramatic power, while thankfully consigning much larger amounts of what modern professionals write, and even read, to eternal darkness. Classical philology could certainly claim a role in assessing and explaining this aspect of interest.

But Hopkins recognized also the intellectual reward to be had from any good treatment of the past. Surely, this can only be gained where the material is presented in adequate depth to reveal the operation of mutual influences among many factors in change. By this depth, the mind is directed to successive levels of understanding, at each one encountering different forces at work at different rates of speed. Classical historians are incurious about these levels; hence they are generally dull, in the intellectual sense, no matter how much they sometimes appeal to the reader's imagination. Moreover, as they are bad models in respect to their method, so also they do not offer very much to supply the demands of a better, a more modern style of historiography. Their poverty, resulting from the operation of three reasons, was described a little earlier. At least by intent, and with exception made of certain pages in Thucydides and very rarely in other authors, they do not provide the material for any very penetrating understanding of the past. Inquiry must turn instead to other sources of information and, in the search, must reach beyond the ordinary range of classical philology.

Where to turn, for a supplement or alternative to the likes of Xenophon or Livy, was made plain at least by the 1920s through the independent vision and energy of Michael Rostovtzeff—Braudel *avant la lettre*. He actually went down into the basements of museums to see what he could find; he took clay lamps seriously as informants about life in classical antiquity; he took lead seals seriously, and the crudest grave reliefs, not to mention coins and papyri and inscriptions and the ground plans of structures other than temples and fora—wonder of wonders! He really believed that *everybody* had helped to make history and must be included in its accounts. Naturally he was not popular among classical philologists, however much historians admired him. On the Hellenistic world his work was (is) little used by them: his plain mistakes of interpretation about the third century, in his work on the Roman empire, became a favorite target for gratuitous refutation; so the challenge to the traditional style of historiography was turned back quite easily. For a time.

His coeval Marc Bloch with others in France and other countries in good time produced the vindication of Rostovtzeff's genius. Undeniably, it has taken strange forms, at least in contrast to the familiar library of classical authors. There is, for example, a huge quantity of Roman law (and the four illustrations of method that follow all focus on the Roman empire, since that is where they are most naturally to be found); besides questions of the intellectual processes involved, the corpus can be made to yield a picture of who used the law, and how much. Liselot Huchthausen (in *Klio* 1974 and elsewhere) combed out the names, civic status, and problem at law of some fifteen hundred persons referred to in the Justinianic Code to whom the emperors responded on appeal. The discovery of slaves among these appellants most students of the period must find very surprising; similarly, the fact that women suing in their own name accounted for better than an eighth of the total at the outset of the reigns of Hadrian up to Diocletian, rising to a fifth and then to a quarter and more; and that an unexpected number of women can be seen not merely protecting their dowry or inheritance but actively engaged in profitable businesses of various sorts. There are other instructive points that emerge, too; but no doubt the two matters of most interest concern the accessibility of government and the active role in affairs played by women.

Second, there exists an enormous brambly mass of numismatic evidence needing to be opened up to non-specialists: the coinage of hundreds of urban mints in the Greek-speaking half of the Roman empire. At last, from a comprehensive description of its history by Kenneth Harl (*Civic Coins and Civic Politics*, 1987), there now emerges a far clearer because more broadly illuminated picture of the eastern cities in their relations with the dominant power. The Romanizing of the municipal elite (and their parade of the face on the local small change which received the most active circulation) is one impression now gained from this study. Another is the extreme sensitivity of that elite to its duties vis-à-vis the emperor, whose military accomplishments are advertised with increasing particularity in the second century and whose fact and titles are brought up to date with instant patriotism. Joint portraits, showing two emperors, are even recalled by the mints for censorship, at the instant that one of the two (Geta, for example) suffers official condemnation. His face is chiseled or stamped out.

Third, the scores of thousands of inscriptions from the capital even before their recent indexing invite study of the classes never thought worthy of mention in literature. They had lived—yet nobody cared. Marleen Flory (in the *Classical Journal* 1984 and elsewhere) was remarkably successful in reconstructing their interrelationships not only in terms of status but of sentiments as well. From nomenclature and position in inscribed texts, she could demonstrate the sense of place in large households of slaves, its principal determinants, the survival devices of those in servitude, and much else that governed their efforts in life. Since slaves and freed constituted so enormous a part of the population not only in Rome but in Italy over-all, they obviously cannot be excluded from Rome of the history books.

And last, there is no doubt that the more familiar parts of classical civilization rested on a broad base of productive relations, nowhere of more historical interest than at the interface between developed and undeveloped regional economies; but explanation of that interface cannot go far without drawing on information from regions or periods quite remote from classical antiquity. Brent Shaw (*Antiquités africaines* 1981) has brought to bear not only Apuleius, Tertullian, Cyprian, and Augustine for the subject as it can be studied in north Africa, but Optatus' discussion of Donatism; not only Optatus but inscriptions from the hinterlands; and not only inscriptions but, as the chief part of his discussion, comparative material on periodic markets in many other regions and periods of Africa, up to the very present: for example, among the

Nuer, in Evans-Pritchard's well-known work. Comparative anthropology may be only heuristic, not probative; but it adds detail, concreteness, and authority to otherwise almost unusably incomplete material.

These four pieces of historical research share two important characteristics. None of them had anything to do with classical philology, either in regard to the questions asked (the chosen focus of inquiry) or the types of information made use of: law codes, coins, inscriptions, and the yield of sister disciplines. All four have, as their focus, levels of causation which classical historians are embarrassed to acknowledge, among provincial municipal senators at the best and slaves and semi-nomads at the worst; and all four borrow from quite discrete disciplines just as modern historiography does, in order to reconstruct in the reader's imagination the whole of the past—not just of "the governing class." It is the challenge of such reconstructions that provides intellectual interest to the pursuit of history extra-philological; it is their success that makes older approaches appear dull; and it is their reasonable abundance, among the last generation or so of students of the ancient world, that seems to show the integration of their specialty with the larger discipline of modern history.

4

PROVINCIAL LANGUAGES IN THE ROMAN EMPIRE

SEVERAL LANGUAGES in the Roman empire proved their ability to sustain themselves in spoken and even in written form against the competition of Greek and Latin. The latter two define a civilization without filling it; for "Greco-Latin" indicates a mixed culture in which, to the very end, a majority of the population must have spoken neither Latin nor Greek in their homes, whatever they spoke of necessity in the courts and market-places. Bilingualism, even trilingualism, was common, then as now, in cities like Beirut, Alexandria, or Marseilles. In the back country, local dialects persisted for a long time, some destined to emerge into the full light only in the Middle Ages (Welsh, Berber, and Basque, for example), others destined to recede slowly before the pressure of classical languages: Celtic in Spain, Galatia, or northern Italy, or Thracian, Dacian, or Lydian—though, before they disappeared, these too laid their distinctive marks on their successors. So the descendants of Latin differ from each other, Roumanian from Spanish. Technical aspects may be left to the experts in linguistics, whose surveys of the minor tongues show the obscurity of the subject:[1] the vitality, the distribution according to social classes or to any but the most general geographical areas, the extent of literacy of the speakers or their bilingualism, are matters for mere guess-work, in almost every case. But there are four languages about which a little more can be learned: Syriac, Coptic, Punic, and Celtic. The present paper sketches their history.

An entrance to the subject is offered, surprisingly, by two opinions of a lawyer, Ulpian, writing in roughly A.D. 215: "*Fideicommissa*," he says, "may be devised in any tongue, not only Latin or Greek, but Punic or Gallic [= Celtic] or any other."[2] In *fideicommissa*, to be sure, a greater freedom of formulation may have existed from the start, but the reference to Punic or Celtic is a new departure. Again, Ulpian says (*Dig.* 45.1.1.6),

> It makes no difference if the answer [to a *stipulatio*] is given in some other language. So if someone asks in Latin, the answer may be in Greek. . . . But whether this is extended to Greek only or to other languages as well, Punic or Assyrian [= Syriac][3] or some other, may be questioned. . . . Yet according to what Sabinus has written [ca. mid-first century] and in fact as is clear enough, any kind of speech contains the obligation of its words, provided that each party understands the other's language himself or through accurate interpreters.

A narrower opinion meets us in Gaius, *Inst.* 3.93, written in the time of Marcus Aurelius. Among verbal contracts, while some are valid only between Roman citizens,

> others [*obligationes*] belong to *ius gentium*, and so are valid between all men whether Romans or non-Romans. And even if they are expressed in Greek, as in this form, *Doseis? Doso. Omologeis? Omologo*, etc., these too are binding on Romans so long as they know Greek. *Per contra*, though they are expressed in Latin, they are valid between non-citizens if they know Latin. But the formula, "Are you a sponsor?" "I am a sponsor," is so peculiar to Roman citizens that it cannot be properly put into Greek even by interpretation.

These passages are relevant, or at least one of them has been brought in by several inquirers, as proving the revival of Celtic in Ulpian's day. Sherwin-White dismisses the whole argument along with the text. "This proves too much," says he[4]—as much for Punic as for Celtic; but the wider result which he brushes aside is exactly what this paper aims at. The other texts which have been cited show at first, in the earlier Empire, some tolerance of Greek, but tolerance of more exotic languages only in Ulpian's day. The problem had apparently not much exercised his predecessors, but did elicit several comments from him. Moreover, though his concessions to foreign languages are indeed very limited and grudging, they are granted in the face of a long-established prejudice against anything but Latin in the courts. Legal substance was strictly tied to legal terminology, was really untranslatable, as Gaius says. So the Romans generally insisted on the use of Latin for suits and contracts, making exceptions only for procedures under *ius gentium*, for honored individuals, or for persons like veterans who stood in special need of favor.[5] The connection between Latin and Roman law accounts for the presence of interpreters, private or public, who appear in the sources generally as in Ulpian on *stipulationes*;[6] the same connection is the most important single factor in the intrusion of Latin loan-words into Greek, and in its predominance in the eastern provinces to an astonishingly late date.[7] This is the background against which we must understand those concessions, limited as they are, in Ulpian's opinions. They are the first sign of a new position for provincial languages.

One of Ulpian's contemporaries leads us further into the subject. It is Bardesanes (154–222) in his *Book of the Laws of Countries*, written against the Romans who "abolish the laws of the countries they conquer"—whereas the very variety of those laws, in Britain, Gaul, or Syria, on marriage, theft, libel, or homicide, expresses man's freedom in moral definition. It is a work of protest, asserting the distinctness of cultures, and curiously enough, written by a man credited with the chief role in the creation of a national literature. For Bardesanes, despite a knowledge of Greek, despite even a willingness to send his son to school in Athens, wrote in Syriac. He focused upon ideas and an audience that combined elements of Greco-Roman civilization with others purely local. If some of his thought drew on the common currency of Hellenistic philosophy, other elements like his fondness for writing in verse or his doubts about Chaldaean astrology would appeal principally to the un-Hellenized common folk.[8] Their knowledge of Greek was limited. For, in the Near East from Syria into Mesopotamia, what prevailed in the streets was one or another of the closely related members of the Aramaic family, notably Syriac. The speech habits attested in the New Testament still meet us at a much later date. Evidence for Syriac is especially good in the area around Antioch and among Christians—monks and church dignitaries as well as the ordinary members of congregations.[9] What is at once clear and surprising is the high proportion of the people, concentrated in the more backward districts, who spoke only their native dialect, after centuries of domination by another civilization, compared with the much smaller number of people who knew only Greek. Bilingualism was of course common. In inscriptions, names show a thorough mixture of roots and races. Almost all, however, are written in Greek, joined by a few in Syriac only in the fifth century. They demonstrate the complete supremacy of Greek as the language of the educated.

Syriac produced little literature of its own until the second half of the second century. It then began to spread from the church in Edessa. Edessene Syriac came to prevail in all Oriental Christianity. A beginning was made in the second century with translations of short parts of the Bible, and especially with a popular and quickly diffused gospel harmony, Tatian's *Diatesseron*,[10] but it was Bardesanes who was responsible for a sudden advance in literature. He wrote, besides homilies and treatises, 150 hymns of enormous influence and doubtful doctrine. They were added to by his son Harmonius, and corrected by Ephraim (Afrem) in the later fourth century in counter-hymns of more careful orthodoxy. In Bardesanes' own lifetime other genres of Christian literature, including dialogues, apocryphal Acts, and treatises, appeared in Syriac, along with a few pagan works, a gathering number of further Christian ones, and Monophysite and Nestorian writings from the fifth century on. For a while, this literature was much under the spell of Greek. It did not entirely free itself until the fourth century. From its beginnings, however, in its richness of symbolism and its emphasis on verse forms, it had characteristics peculiarly its own, and left traces in the style and thought of men like Eusebius, Basil, and Theodoret who wrote in Greek. Many works, for example, of the famous Ephraim, were translated from Syriac into Greek, and spread into other areas.[11]

A Gnostic element in one or two early pieces of Syriac, and in Bardesanes himself, must show the penalty paid for being out of the mainstream of language as of theology. Another example is to be found in Manichaeism. Its founder (d. ca. 276) wrote seven works we know of, one in Persian, six in Syriac, prophetic of the fate of his beliefs, since, when the Manichaeans were driven out of Persia by King Bahram and his successors, some went east and their doctrines took root in Iranian and Chinese, while others speaking Syriac spread in the opposite direction, and had established their mission in Egypt by 300, further west in Africa by the mid-fourth century. St. Augustine was their best-known convert. One of the earliest Syriac Manichaean writings, dated to the late third century, is Thomas' *Psalm-Book*, which "seems to have been inspired by the example of [Bardesanes] and his son Harmonius."[12] Egyptian Manichaeans presented a problem to the Christian Church by the end of the third century, and to the Roman government also, since they seem to have played a part in the revolt of Achilleus (296–297).[13] Their teachings, except for a few extant fragments in Syriac, were spread through translation into Greek at first, and shortly afterward through Coptic, by which they were able to reach the less-Hellenized population of Upper Egypt. A large find of Coptic Manichaean texts in Egypt, including Thomas' *Psalm-Book*, was made in 1930, another more recently, and still to be published.

Coptic was the Egyptian language rendered in written form by the use (mostly) of the Greek alphabet. Previous efforts to find a more convenient system than hieroglyphic had begun, long before Alexander conquered the land, with Demotic, but while the everyday speech went on evolving, Demotic set into a scribal form, and was at any rate never a very satisfactory vehicle for reaching the common people. A second experiment of little success, sometimes called Old Coptic, used Greek characters, and texts mostly magical have survived, dating from about A.D. 100 on.[14] Coptic proper, however, gradually displaced both this and Demotic, because it made a more intelligent use of Greek letters and because it was the chosen medium of Christianity. It was first employed for the translation of Scripture out of Greek in the second century—the persecutions of 189 show that the Church was by then established, perhaps even conspicuous, in Egypt—and the earliest figure in the progress of translation became a bishop of Alexandria in that year, Demetrius (189–231). A Coptic Bible was complete by 300, and at about that time the first known original works in Coptic were written, by Pachomius; a century more and the language in its written form was approaching maturity, its literature (much of it translated from Greek) large and vital. The competition among the dialects, especially Bohairic and Sahidic, had been settled, at least for a long time, in favor of the latter representing Upper Egypt. Herein lies the obvious explanation for the invention of written Coptic. For Greek was the language only of a minority of the population, though a very prominent and respected minority, concentrated in Lower Egypt (i.e., the Delta) and the Church in that area was less cut off by its original adherence to Greek. With the appointment of bishops of Upper Egypt in the episcopacy of Demetrius, a mission to the less Hellenized part of the country was announced, necessitating hymns and gospels which would be accessible directly to the fellahin, or indirectly through the interpreters attested in each church.[15] Sahidic actually included a larger number of loan-words, mostly Greek; yet because it was a more essential invention in Upper Egypt, it considerably antedated Bohairic of the Delta. It was more used, more filled with a literature of its own, and made more perfect through practice, than any other dialect.

The connection that existed between Syriac and monasticism in Asia Minor, because monks were so often from the poorer, less Hellenized classes, helps to explain the close ties between Syrian and Egyptian monks. Whereas the former knew the rules of St. Pachomius and translated for their own use the Lives of St. Anthony and his successors, the latter welcomed both Syriac works and Syrian monks even to the more remote parts of Upper Egypt.[16] Egyptian and Syrian shared, beyond their religion, the same social outlook. And as Syrian monks generally used their mother tongue, not Greek,[17] so Egyptian monks used Coptic. People of the upper classes made up a minority in the monasteries, occasionally an isolated Greek-speaking enclave, while on the other hand St. Anthony, the real founder of monasticism, and Pachomius its legislator, spoke only Coptic.[18] Coptic tales of heroes like these two were written in and for ascetic communities, and drew upon traditions of old Egyptian folk-tales for the development of the genre. It has been noticed, too, that many martyrs and monks bore names of a native, not Hellenized, type, like the famous Paphnutius = Pa-p-noute, "God's man," who from monk became bishop and was sent to Nicaea in 325.

But names offer a valuable sign of linguistic allegiance. The displacing of Syrian Hierapolis by the older native name Bambyce finds a parallel in Hermopolis-become-(Coptic) Shmun, and in similar revivals of their ancient titles for other Egyptian cities.[19] Personal names trace a similar history. The Greeks in Egypt called their children by straight Greek names like Apollonius, or Timagenes—much less often Dionysius (Greek translation of Petosiris through the equivalence of Dionysus and Osiris), hardly ever Ammon (pure Egyptian). The natives, on the other hand, sought to rise into the dominant class by the Hellenizing of their names either in an arbitrary fashion or through some likeness of origin or sound. Often, despite considerable legal difficulties, they took a double name: "Dionysius also known as Petosiris," "Theon who is Thionis," or the like. These double names have been several times analyzed, for different times and districts.[20] In the great majority of cases, the Greek half of the names comes first, and the Egyptian half may be dropped, indicating the social ambition of the bearer. They belong to the big cities, to the educated and official strata (as opposed to Egyptian names usually among the poor, the rural, and the priesthoods). They increase enormously in popularity in the second century A.D., drop off in the third, and become rare in the fourth century. Examples of single-name sons of double-name fathers are few, and not early, and the compositions of names with the Egyptian feminine prefix "ta–" (Taapollos, "daughter of Apollon," a mixed example) increase toward the third century.[21] What all this points to is a decline in the prestige of Greek, perceptible in the first half of the third century, pronounced over the next century, and accompanied by some revival of native nomenclature among the literate classes. The carelessness of Greek spelling, grammar, and syntax in papyri and ostraca—especially ostraca, which better reflect the linguistic habits of the lower classes; the decreasing popularity of Greek literature in Egypt; and the history of Coptic just described—all these fit neatly together.[22]

The story of personal names in Egypt involves one particular difficulty. Are people who seem to stand for some kind of separatism also the bearers of native names? The question can be answered, if at all, only through a study of the major heresies of the late third and fourth centuries, principally Meletianism; but leaders of the Church, whether or not orthodox, arose mostly from the better-educated classes, where the conservatism in nomenclature found among Egyptian families perpetuated the same names, generation after generation, regardless of changes in religious or political allegiance. Thus the chief men in the Church for the most part bore Greek names in the fourth and fifth centuries,[23] with the possible exception of the Meletian bishops of the list of A.D. 327. It is perhaps more than a coincidence that these Meletians were backed by a strong monastic element, that their partisans were concentrated in the less-Hellenized Upper Egypt, and that their center was Lycopolis in the Thebaid, center also of a Coptic dialect (Achmimic). Meletianism, in short, may have expressed a long-standing dissatisfaction with a foreign and intrusive civilization, and its adherents may unconsciously represent what was Egyptian, rural, indigenous. Yet the patterns of thought and movement do not emerge very clearly. One scholar tries to show that Coptic was the language of dissent, Gnostic, Manichaean, or other. So he naturally emphasizes that Meletius supported Arianism versus Athanasius. Yet Athanasius propagandized in Coptic, evidently with hopes of an audience among the non-Hellenized, and did have the friendship of two Coptic speakers, and those the most influential, Anthony and Pachomius. Meletius' bishopric was one that changed its name, I do not know when (Lycopolis-Siut), and in its neighborhood the abbot Shenoute, who certainly stood up for the poor, wrote Coptic, and presided over a famous monastery made up of Coptic speakers; yet the population was half-pagan, tinged with Gnosticism.[24] This jumble of facts is offered only to illustrate the uncertainties involved in the subject. It seems impossible to sort out all the various hints of one loyalty or another.

E. R. Hardy nevertheless suggests the grouping of these phenomena—language, heresy, monasticism—under the heading of nationalism. "There is," he says, "a real parallel with the Donatists of Africa. In each case a schismatic movement that made a special appeal to a national group arose out of disputes about church order, and took disciplinary rigor as its distinctive principle."[25] The parallel is an interesting one, and has received powerful support in the past generation. There is no need to go into it at length, if only because it seems to yield no firm conclusions; but beyond that, the evidence, little and confused as it is, seems rather to tell against the parallel. Briefly, north Africa was a land of three languages, Berber (Libyan), Punic, and Latin, in order of their age in the country. It is argued that Donatism found its chief support in the rural parts, where the real natives, speaking Berber, rallied against an aristocracy doubly alien: both Punic and Roman, urban and orthodox. While there are strong reasons for saying that the movement had a social character and that its distribution on the map of the African provinces conformed roughly to differences in class and occupation,[26] the specific matter of its language cannot be bent to the same shape. The inscriptions in Berber, it has most recently been argued, are not Berber at all, but debased Punic in Latin characters, while, if this be wrong, it is at least generally admitted that Berber was deeply penetrated by Punic, and touched also by Latin.[27] Besides these purely linguistic points, the "Berber" inscriptions, though notoriously hard to date, are much rarer in the days of Donatism than in the second and earlier third century, even though the relative prosperity of Africa in the fourth century might be expected to have stimulated an increase in writing among the peasant population. And Donatism did not produce any Berber literature, either. The explanation may lie in the competition of other languages for written purposes, for when the sources refer to the trilingualism of the country, they mean Latin, Punic, and *Greek*.[28] For literary ends, Berber obviously offered no challenge to Punic; Punic, in which parts of the Bible were probably translated, may have enjoyed a kind of resurgence against the language of Rome, in the fourth century; but beyond all this, it is not even clear that Donatist congregations understood spoken Berber more naturally and easily than Punic.[29] Both languages were widely used, the native tongue among the poor (to survive to the present day with some loan-words from Punic surprisingly embedded in it). What is known of their relations with each other, however, and of their comparative vitality, is best interpreted by assuming a very wide prevalence of bilingualism, Punic and Berber, with Latin strong in the elite of the north African provinces.

If we stopped here, our evidence might seem to rest upon a uniform base, and to fit together remarkably well. The language of the conquerors (first Macedonian, then Roman, and the latter alone in the west) advanced steadily over the Mediterranean world, within the areas marked out by need—for naturally no one abandoned his native speech without some special necessity. Thus trade and tribute, commerce and administration, made the first converts, and thereafter ambition, to rise into the ruling classes. In the lower classes and remoter countryside, however, where these needs were not felt, Greek and Latin yielded place to a score of local languages. Here could be seen the phenomenon on which this paper concentrates: a positive counter-attack by two or three minority languages toward the close of the second century, demonstrating the height of its strength by the end of the fourth. The population least Hellenized or Romanized discovered something of their own that needed saying, something quite unconnected with the way of life of their rulers, or even hostile to it, and desperately important: namely, a new faith.[30] On the Tigris or Nile, the conversion of some backward peasant could be accomplished only in his own language; and it was conversion to a religion based on sacred texts. Meter aids memory, among illiterate people. Concession could be made to them—hence the immense popularity of Bardesanes' hymns, incorporating his lessons in a form easy to remember and to repeat. If he was tinged with Gnosticism, the orthodox Ephraim had to meet him on his own ground, correcting Bardesanes in other hymns of different teaching, as Arius, to reach a like audience, "composed songs to be sung by sailors, millers, and travelers, and others of the same kind, which he adapted to certain tunes . . . and thus seduced the unlearned by the attractiveness of his songs to his own impiety."[31] But at the foundation lay the prose of scripture, joined in due course by biographies of heroes of the Church, by collections of divine sayings, theological treatises, and sermons. If they were produced in the larger Christian centers where orthodoxy was hammered out, they bore that mark; if in isolated villages, then they might well combine oddities of both language and belief, even angry rejection of an orthodoxy tainted at its source: for cities, in the minds of rustic farmers, were the abode of tax-collectors and recruiting-sergeants as well as of bishops.

Religion thus seems to be the key to the appearance of written Coptic, Syriac, Phrygian, and perhaps Punic. But before leaving it at that, let us go on to Celtic, the last of the three languages (along with Punic and Syriac) in the Ulpian passages cited earlier. We may begin with the statement of Irenaeus (*Contra haeres.*,1. 3 = *P.L.* 7 p. 444) that, in the 170s, he had to speak Celtic to his congregation. Ausonius (*Epicedion in patrem* 9) describes his father's imperfect knowledge of Latin and Greek—i.e., neither was his natural speech—and this in a rank of society by no means the lowest. His father's lifespan must have lain in the later third and earlier fourth centuries. Between the dates of these passages, Celtic comes more often to the notice of our sources than in the first century (Aulus Gellius, *N.A.* 11. 7. 4; several passages in the *Scriptores Historiae Augustae*; and so on); and in some parts of France and Switzerland, Celtic habits of nomenclature definitely reasserted themselves. Place-names revert to a pre-Roman form, Lutetia becoming Parisii, Julia Equestris becoming Noviodunum[32]—just as happened in Egypt and Syria. And a further parallel: Celtic prevails among the rural population. Working with the epigraphic evidence around Trèves, L. Weisgerber shows that personal names of a Celtic root make up 0–15 percent of the total in or near the city, 40–50 percent in outlying districts. Further into the countryside he cannot go, because the number of inscriptions sharply decreases. Presumably Celtic increases.[33] The lack of evidence for written Celtic in places where it was undoubtedly the vehicle of ordinary speech is striking, and perhaps requires a special explanation; for in fact the Gauls seem to have made no effort to develop an alphabet of their own, hardly any to perpetuate their tongue in Latin letters. Only a very few texts survive (mostly dedications), along with the words of medical incantations in the early fifth century. These latter, like Coptic experiments in Demotic, and Phrygian curse-inscriptions, were preserved by magic, because magic would have lost its force in translation.[34] Native beliefs, more broadly, however, contributed nothing to keep Celtic alive. It was a characteristic of the ancient priests of Gaul not to reveal their lore in writing; and to them was traditionally entrusted also the education of the aristocracy. Druids and nobles thus turned their backs on literacy, and when it came, consequently, it came through the less conservative of their subjects and through the Latin alphabet.[35]

In Gaul, then, the rising prominence of Celtic has no connection with religion. It is a phenomenon complete to itself. Yet it does share with the emerging literature of Coptic and Syriac Christianity one obvious characteristic. It represents a rural resurgence of some sort, a slight but detectable shifting of vitality and creativity from cities to countryside, and from classical culture to more truly indigenous elements. As to the date at which this phenomenon appeared, the evidence strikes no discordant note. In the general history of the empire, one can see the tide of Romanization running strong in the first century, clearly receding in the fifth. The point of slack tide is best put at the turn of the second to third, when, quite appropriately, the successor to the Antonines was chosen in a civil war that rambled from Asia Minor to Gaul, and placed a trilingual African on the throne. After him came his sons and great-nephew, half-Syrian. The men who helped them to run the government, the great jurists as well as the senatorial class, reflected the same very mixed background.[36] These facts of the period are too familiar, and besides too small a part of a large and complicated picture, to receive proper treatment here. Yet they serve to show how easily Ulpian might extend consideration to ''Punic or Gallic or any other'' language in the early third century, in recognition not only of the status of their speakers but of the very languages themselves.

There is, of course, no evidence that Greek and Latin, in terms of mere numbers of speakers, receded as time went on—quite the reverse. They continued their steady advance. But there *is* the evidence here offered that the strata of provincial society in which classical culture would once have been accepted without question realized after a time that they had a culture of their own, with its own vitality—that they had inherited a language in which to express it—and that they had, finally, learned from their conquerors the habits and techniques of saying it in writing.

5

THE CELTIC RENAISSANCE

EXPERTS in most fields fall easily into the habit of talking to themselves, and an outsider may be excused for trying to open their conversations to a wider audience. A generation has now passed since the very phrase "Celtic renaissance" came into use, and it recurs in several of the more recent works I refer to in the notes. It indicates the revival, in the later second and third centuries, of certain traditions of art common before the Romans came, and uncommon during a long period of Roman cultural ascendancy. There exists no general sketch of the subject and no treatment of its historical importance.

Among the materials that can survive a burial of many centuries (i.e., not wood and fabrics, about which we know nothing), the Celts liked best to work in metal, and least well to work in stone. When they tried the latter, they applied techniques better adapted to other media, and beyond that, were naturally more susceptible to foreign influence than in, say, the sculpting of silver. Their stone temples, even to their own gods, were not of their own design, but generally Greek.[1] In jewelry, however, and in armor and ornaments, in pottery, and less often in stone sculpture, the Celts, despite heavy borrowings from Scythian and Greek models, developed an art of their own. Its works survive in great profusion. During the last four centuries before Christ, in the La Tène period, it displays in its maturity a fondness for abstraction, sometimes "geometrizing," as for instance in the reduction of faces to triangular forms or in the rendering of hair by straight lines drawn back from the forehead, or in the reduction of the joints of an animal's legs to mere circles; sometimes abstraction of a more fluid type, in powerful swinging curves or wild whorls and volutes. The dolphins and horses, or the hair and beard of heads, shown on their coins, trace a remarkable transformation from their Greek models, along just these lines.[2] Their ultimate design may be purely abstract, verging toward the motifs already mentioned as favorites—S-shapes, arabesques, chevrons, and many others. The human face and figure are rarely shown in works of any material. Animal forms are more popular. But even hunting dogs and stags, horses and birds, are used to fill a space, not to tell a story. The artist turns from the realistic to the ornamental. It is not surprising to find him, then, reducing three dimensions to two, in a final characteristic of his tradition: a tendency to flatness, to decorative line rather than to form.[3]

In the course of the first century B.C. and the first century and a half A.D., men and manufactures from the Greco-Roman world flooded into the west.

Cultural backwaters, poor mountainous districts, and areas remote from natural lines of travel retained more of their old way of life: in Gaul, the areas north of the Loire, much of Aquitania, north of the Seine, in the Vosges and Pyrenees; in Switzerland, the eastern part especially.[4] The new ways prevailed most obviously and completely in the cities and among the rich. Of course the convert to Roman ways, still more the Roman himself, from Italy, was in the minority, but the style of his art nevertheless penetrated far and wide, by a combination of technical superiority, prestige derived from conquest, and adaptability to the demands of mass production. For all this, pottery provides the best evidence.

Coarse ware favoring certain shapes—wide mouth; little or no base ring or neck or spout—continued to be turned out everywhere. In pottery of a more pretentious quality, terra sigillata had established its ascendancy by the mid-first century, often produced in the same centers from which the older Celtic pots had issued (Lezoux is the best-known case), and so popular that it drove its competitors out of the market. Native potters made sporadic efforts to resist the popularity of terra sigillata through (for example) the improvement of the older black or dark gray ware;[5] they asserted themselves in certain techniques of manufacture and, more than was realized until recently, in the handling of decoration. The unity of composition proper to the Arretine tradition was sometimes dissolved into isolated decorative elements, borrowed at random from an alien repertoire; shapes verged toward the local traditions, the decoration was divided into fields by bands of geometric motifs.[6] But the sum of all this was not very significant.

Romanization in the north of Gaul, making great strides in the early Empire due to the stimulus of the armies of occupation, was outstripped by the Romanization of the south.[7] The northern market for Arretine ware remained large, but reached for a better product beyond the local potters, who continued to produce their best-known ware, the so-called Belgic, right through the first century. It was very widely bought, most of all in the southern part of Belgica.[8] Imitating terra sigillata, it soon diverged from its traditional motifs until it disappeared in the early second century. What drove it out, however, was not only its unsuccessful compromises, or the competition of the classicizing pots of the south, but a new kind of pottery produced in the region of the Argonne forest. Some of its centers were Trier and Rheinzabern. By the mid-second century, Argonne pottery had entered the export market, even to the upper Danube. Pots of this type were decorated in relief, by roulette. They showed sometimes in their shapes, and in the arrangement of reliefs in bands and panels, and in the choice of motifs—often geometric, or symbolic (stars and crosses), or chevrons or leaves in running spirals—the continued popularity of an indigenous style. Even the technique of wheel-molding was pre-Roman. After a major disruption in the third quarter of the third century caused by the invasions, Argonne pottery took on a second lease on life, displacing

terra sigillata throughout northern Gaul, Germany, and Rhaetia, and display-
ing an increasingly close affinity to terra nigra and the whole range of older
native pottery.[9] To explain this return to La Tène, there is evidence of a third-
century revival of Celtic forms in pottery produced across the Rhine,[10] from
which the inspiration might have been transmitted through invasion and commerce; and in the second place, there is the clearer fact that Gallo-Roman
pottery deteriorated from the later second century, encouraging, by the corruption and carelessness of its manufacture, the competition of other styles;
but only the second of these factors can explain why, not only in the Rhine
region but throughout Gaul, and in Rhaetia and Spain as well, the late Empire
witnessed a ubiquitous assertion of the oldest traditions in pottery. The evidence is abundant.[11] One must first assume that, for the service of the kitchen
and for the needs of poorer people, local artisans had gone on working in their
accustomed way untouched by foreign influences,[12] but their sporadic activity
under the last Antonines, and their more obvious resurgence in the late third
century and after, fit neatly with the downward trends of the empire's economy. To train potters in the art of Arretine, and to buy their products, required
a wealthy world. Before saying more about this, however, it would be best to
go on to the other arts.

Celtic sculpture differed from classical sculpture in its tendency to find
dominant curves, circles, and triangles in its subjects; to emphasize line and
decoration against the claims of roundness and chiaroscuro; to present itself
stiff and full face; and to pursue abstraction and symbolism at the expense of
realism. Foreign influences, not only Roman but eastern and Hellenistic too,
prevailed in Gaul in the first century and a half of the Empire. The old ways
lingered only in the poorer workshops. In isolated regions, however, in the
second half of the second century, and over all of the west a hundred years
later, Celtic styles reasserted themselves, not of course with complete thoroughness, but very strongly. Aquitania seems to have led the way.[13] For illustration we may turn first to the rendering of hair, in portraiture, which the La
Tène artist almost drew upon stone, by combing straight lines back from the
forehead, in a fashion found occasionally in the earlier Empire and very commonly in the later Empire;[14] or we may turn to the use of opposed facing
animal heads, in heraldic position, which also was traditionally Celtic, and
which regained popularity after a century or so of classicizing.[15] To these few
details dozens more could be added, and indeed the revival of the native spirit
in sculpture has a full and complicated history. Yet stated most simply, it
shows itself first in certain regional deviations from classical standards,[16] and
in the third century penetrates more and more thoroughly into all areas and
types of work. It combines the Celtic characteristics already mentioned, in that
flat, linear, frontal art once dismissed as merely "crude."

Metal-work was the favorite outlet for the Celts' genius. They adorned
themselves with torques, bracelets, rings, and brooches (fibulae); their horses

they adorned with elaborate plates, buckles, and disks (phalerae); their weapons, with repoussé work in gold and silver and bronze. Their own coinage, first modeled upon Greek examples, they changed in the direction of pure design, and Roman coins they incorporated into jewelry—so much did the spirit of decoration dominate among this people. But although the styles in metal embodied the principles appropriate also to the other arts—low relief, frontality, abstraction; geometric, animal, and plant motifs—and while even some of the techniques were borrowed, from woodworking or ceramics, yet the Celts added two devices adapted especially to metal: the use of a chisel to achieve a decoration of wedge-shaped marks arranged in bands or panels, and the use of fretwork. In the late second century a famous center in Baden advertised its trade name in the cut-out letters of bronze strips, AQVIS HELVETICIS, GEMELLIANVS F(ECIT), distributed very widely in the West,[17] and the same technique can be seen turned to a more appropriate use in some pieces of harness decoration with a fretted pattern of leaves and vines. They "represent a rebirth of the Celtic spirit."[18] As for wedge-shaped decoration, this revives strongly from the second century and goes on into Merovingian times.[19] Fibulae show features reminiscent of La Tène practices, spread over Gaul, Switzerland, and Germany, and imported to the North.[20]

Bronze phalerae dating from the fifth century B.C. to the third century of the Empire, found scattered from Italy to Denmark and from south Russia to Germany, exhibit a frieze of heads running around the rim. On these heads, the hair is combed straight back, the mouth turned down, the eyebrows formed in a single arch in characteristically Celtic fashion. Moreover, the whole motif springs from the gruesome custom of decapitating an enemy, showing "the reminiscence of the old warrior rites of the Gauls. It is one example among many of the survival of Celtic civilization in the midst of the Gallo-Roman period."[21] An especially useful example: it illustrates one obvious means by which a pre-Roman style might survive for centuries, by being attached to a religious belief. By this connection, it is easier to understand the stubborn appearance of lunettes, rosettes, and stars, even in otherwise classicizing pottery. The symbols had a meaning.[22] Religious conservatism influenced also the portrayal of native deities.[23]

But here other questions suggest themselves. To discover the meaning of the "Celtic renaissance" in the ceramic and other arts, we should ask also, how the whole culture of the Celts fared in the late Empire, and whether a renaissance penetrated elsewhere into their life as well. Their worships offer an obvious starting point for the enquiry and, without entering on any detail, it is nevertheless clear that a revival of its pre-Roman forms took place, beginning in the second half of the second century.[24] The imported pantheon, having for long enjoyed a preeminence among resident Romans and among the richer Gauls alike, began to give way before resurgent native gods and goddesses (for instance, Epona), whose temples flourished once more, whose symbols and attributes appeared more often in the plastic arts, and whose altars attracted new devotees. The priestly class of Druids, having been driven into hiding by the decrees of the early emperors, had sustained themselves and some shadow of their influence in obscure places, and emerged less tentatively in the third and fourth centuries.[25] The Celtic language also survived, and literary references to it belong to the later second century or after, though whether one can speak of a spread of its use, or any improvement in its status, is doubtful.[26] It had receded demonstrably before Latin, in the graffiti of Gallic potters, before the mid-first century, and the mottoes written on drinking cups produced for the everyday buyer were in Latin. On the other hand, it certainly remained the first language of the poorer classes in the less Romanized districts, who are hardly likely to have left their records upon stone. The small number of inscriptions in Celtic thus proves nothing. Yet epigraphical evidence may be considered with a different end in view, to determine whether the names recorded succumbed wholly to Roman forms and the adoption of the *tria nomina*, or whether the Gauls stuck to their old habits of a single name of Celtic root. At the larger ceramic centers of the south, the workers rather early adopted Latin names; less so in the north.[27] While, in general, Gallic inscriptions show something of a decline in Celtic nomenclature, due perhaps to the movement of the richer, "inscribing" Gauls into cities in the second and third centuries, in the same period the proportion of native names doubles in Lyon, Reims, Metz, and Langres and quadruples in Autun, while in Aquitania and Switzerland as a whole native names became far more common in the late Empire.[28] Place-names often revert to an older, pre-Roman form, Lutetia becoming Parisii and Forum Claudii becoming Octodurus.[29]

If the histories of the different aspects of Celtic culture are compared, pottery with religion, language with sculpture, the results are certainly very striking. What can be seen, most clearly in the plastic arts, least clearly in language, is a re-awakening of the Celtic genius, which produced, for example, a cult statue marked by a wholly un-Roman rendering of hair, mouth, and the line of the brows, and which showed to the devotee not only a flat, frontal, linear appearance, but the face of a Celtic god as well, rather than of some Mars or Jupiter. To this deity, in Marcus Aurelius' reign, libations might be offered from a cup shaped like those that Claudius had seen in his passage through Gaul, and which had thereafter vanished from the market—a cup decorated with the same incised patterns and strings of chevrons typical of the La Tène period. These various Celtic practices had been submerged by the high tide of Romanization. If they later revived, then they must always have existed hidden beneath the surface of imported culture; for no one supposes that some antiquarian impulse, leaping a gap of six or eight generations, inspired the Gauls of a later period. Instead, those Gauls must have found all the materials for a renaissance still surviving somewhere inconspicuously. It is agreed that the countryside as opposed to the city, and the northwest as opposed to the southeast (but regional differences do not easily lend themselves to a general summary) retained the ancient customs.

It is not agreed where the renaissance originated. So far as the arts alone are concerned, a change to frontality and to the other peculiarities of the so-called "late antique style" has been detected very widely throughout the empire,[30] but since the evidence for this change is based partly on findings in the western provinces, it would be circular to invoke it here as explanation. A different view attributes the Celtic renaissance to renewed contacts with the peoples across the Rhine, whether by commerce or by their invasions of Gaul. To be sure, certain things like Kerbschnitt technique could have been borrowed from the areas both east and north of Gaul; and from the second century on along the Rhine and even well to the south, in isolated pockets, archeological evidence reveals a rapprochement between Roman provincial and "barbarian."[31] Alföldi has a particularly interesting explanation for this rapprochement. "To understand the Celtic renaissance," he writes, "one must keep in mind that in the last century B.C. the Celtic branches of Great Britain, France, Spain, and the Danube lands, and on the other hand the Illyro-Thracian races of the Danube and Baltic lands, formed a single cultural unit. This was split by the Roman conquest."[32] Much of this culture survived, he goes on, but could not successfully challenge Romanization until the renewal of commercial links between East and West "revived the general atmosphere of the La Tène period." The encouragement of mutual tastes and the exchange of manufactures in the second century initiated a movement which continued even after the links were later broken.

These arguments that an older culture in Gaul was aroused by kindred races, whether from beyond the Rhine or from the Danube, and whether through the contacts of trade or war, may well contain some truth. They are, however, not easy to substantiate, nor is it easy to apply them to those areas of Gaul like Aquitania which, when still untouched by Germanic or Danube peoples, felt a stirring of pre-Roman memories. Other arguments based on economic and social considerations must be brought in. Briefly: Romanization depended on cities and wealth. The peace on which trade, and the trade on which cities, depended was shaken by heavy if isolated raids in the 160s and 170s[33] and again more or less continuously over the last two thirds of the third century. Markets were cut off from each other, producers from buyers, artists from patrons. The urban population, suffering from these troubles, and oppressed by heavier and heavier obligations to the state, increasingly took refuge in rural estates. Such circumstances favored local production on the countryside, either in lonely little clusters of bronze-, glass-, stone-, or ceramic-workers, or in villas adapted to the production of wool, pottery, metal, or wine.[34] Since it was the rural artisan who held to his ancestral styles, he simply went on doing as he always had done, yet to a widening market and against competition of declining vigor—the competition, that is, of men working in the classicizing styles. Gallic civilization in all its aspects gradually re-assumed the face it had worn before the Romans came.

Political history at first sight seems to confirm this picture: the rural classes assume a new importance in the later Empire, beginning with the peasant marauders of late Antonine times and developing into the wider scourge of the Bagaudae. Apparently the Bagaudae intended to split themselves off from the empire.[35] It is an obvious assumption that they represented the least Romanized parts of the population, and they thus present that mingling of political and cultural assertions which we call nationalism. While we know almost nothing about the Bagaudae, we do have the histories, in more detail, of the Gallic pretenders of the third and fourth centuries, to whom the same word "nationalistic" has been applied. Can the evidence of these figures be used to explain the Celtic renaissance?

Coinage offers the best clues to the intentions of the pretenders. It has been often discussed. We need concentrate only on whatever cultural overtones it may have. While the old Gallic *minimi* revived; while the coin types were distorted by the local artist from standard Roman ones into others reminiscent of the Armorican staters, and the legends from AEQVITAS AVG into HEQVIS HIIS or some other illiterate jumble; while Postumus might celebrate Hercules or two Gallic cities, HERC DEVSONIENSI and MAGVSANO, or appear, with Carausius, as the first rulers to be shown nearly full face instead of in profile, under the influence of the Celtic taste for frontality[36]—while these signs point to some consciousness of Celtic nationality, others point in exactly the opposite direction. Carausius' coins alone of all Roman issues contain a tag of Vergil;[37] Postumus makes no effort to conceal his *nomen* Latinius, nor his devotion to ROMA AETERNA, and is unique in his century in his preference for the Roman *milia passuum* on his milestones rather than the Celtic word *leuga*.[38] The picture, then, is very confused. Most scholars are inclined to delete the word nationalism entirely from any description of the third- and fourth-century Gallic pretenders.[39] It seems fairer to say, of this collection of contradictions, that while the people who supported the pretenders represented impulses both cultural and political, the latter impulse alone was explicit and conscious, and the former showed itself only accidentally, because it had become so powerful in all aspects of Gallic life.

For the Celtic renaissance there are thus three explanations: that of stimulation by contact with kindred, less Romanized races; that of economic decline; and that of nationalism. In fact, the three should not be separated, because of obvious overlapping, but it is convenient to weight them one by one. The last is the weakest. Tetricus' beard is reduced to the chevron design dear to the La Tène sculptor, and Postumus is represented full face, on their coinage, only because the artists in their mints were now trained in a native, not a Roman tradition. No pretender appealed to his countrymen to rise in defense of their ancient way of life. As to the first explanation, whatever strength it may have for a later period (the fourth century, say) or for the northern parts of Gaul, the truth is that pottery or jewelry had begun to revert to La Tène styles in the second century. Even the second explanation, the economic, must be here modified. It cannot be tied too closely to the inflation or the invasions of the late Antonine reigns, since, even before then, in the use of the *leuga* as a unit of length, or in the various arts as they were practiced in Aquitania, the Celtic had begun to thrust up through the Roman layer. This is the really extraordinary lesson of the Celtic renaissance: that it showed itself so early, in the very century so generally thought to have confirmed and established the victory of Greco-Roman civilization. The work of the conquerors, remarkable as it certainly was, suffered from a kind of fragility and superficiality which should not be forgotten.

6

BARBARIAN ENCLAVES IN THE NORTHERN ROMAN

EMPIRE

THERE WERE always barbarians within the Roman empire, left to themselves in remote mountains and deserts, or recently incorporated by conquest. When Trajan died, however, the great days of expansion were over, and his successor's Wall in Britain, with similar lines along other frontiers later, indicated a wish to separate Roman from non-Roman by a permanent barrier, symbolic and controlled by more than symbolic regulations, troops, forts, and check-points. Along the Rhine and Danube, soldiers put up market buildings, sometimes very large ones, in which trade with barbarians could be carried on under military supervision. We have, for instance, the fortlet in Pannonia advertising its purpose in its name, *cui nomen Commercium*; the *signiferi leg. III Aug. agentes curam macelli* in Africa; and a *macellum* itself at Vindonissa, roughly 150 yards square.[1] Trade was restricted not only to certain places but to certain days as well—the *nundinenses* known in inscriptions—or was banned entirely;[2] barbarians who were allowed entrance for a longer visit as seasonal laborers promised their good behavior on oath before the officer of the frontier (Augustine, *Ep.* 46), and intermarriage with barbarians was forbidden, at least in 368 (*Cod. Theod.* 3.14.1). These and a great many similar measures, attested all along the frontiers of the western empire and throughout the second, third, and fourth centuries, aimed at the fulfillment and defense of the civilization within the frontier, by marking it off clearly from the peoples beyond.

In the same period, however, with increasing frequency, barbarians appeared in the provinces. Their dispersion from Britain to the Black Sea, from the northern *limes* to Africa, has been traced in studies of nomenclature by Pflaum, Mocsy, and many others, using the evidence of inscriptions; and since they were most often found in irregular troop units, they have been traced, too, by scholars of Roman military history. We thus know in surprising detail the whole process that brought the members of friendly, or newly conquered, tribes into the service of Rome's armies and, after that service, into the inner citadels of Roman citizenship, the imperial civil administration, or peaceful retirement far from the frontier.

Among these intruders a special category was formed by the entire tribes or the very large parts of tribes admitted to the empire as settlers. They were intended to fill the gaps created in the army and on the countryside by a manpower shortage of undoubted gravity.[3] Five texts give specific numbers: "50,000 Getae from beyond the Danube" received into Moesia under Augustus;[4] "40,000 Germans settled on the Rhine and in Gaul" by Tiberius (Eutropius 7.9); "more than 100,000 Transdanubians" received into Moesia under Nero;[5] "3,000 Naristae who deserted" to Roman land under Marcus Aurelius (Dio 72.21); "100,000 Bastarnae settled on Roman soil" by Probus (SHA *Probus* 18.1); and "more than 300,000" Sarmatians received into Thrace, Scythia, Italy, and Macedonia under Constantine (Anon. Vales. 32). The fact that one of these figures was written on stone should not inspire special confidence. "In lapidary inscription a man is not upon oath," as Dr. Johnson observes; and all of these round numbers were probably meant to express only what is less precisely described in other texts as *plurimi, tot, copiosissima multitudo*, or even *omnes barbari*. Against this caution, it is fair to set the very large number of mentions of such controlled folk-wanderings. Over the centuries they included most tribes bordering on the empire, in a total certainly mounting to the millions.[6] Where the custom of transplantations had so full a history, one should not expect consistency. While the bulk of barbarians were settled on deserted land and in border provinces, others joined the army; some were enslaved; if most lived on in large concentrations, some were assigned to individual plots or masters, as far within the empire as Italy; and while some were planted forcibly in the most desolate districts, others clustered around cities. Most paid tribute. All seem to have been subjected to some degree of control, rarely private or municipal, regularly military. What we find in the majority of cases is a large group established in a *regio*[7] under a *praepositus* or *praefectus*[8] with a fort nearby to remind them of their obligations to Rome.[9] The terms of their settlement would have been agreed on in the original treaty drawn up between their leaders and the representatives of Rome.

So they poured in, a heavy tide. Under Constantine, it is a fair guess that the inhabitants of the northern provinces saw in every twentieth man the example or descendant of these migrations. We even have a picture of such a migration, stamped on the lower and upper fields of a lead medallion: above, two emperors with bodyguards receiving suppliants, women and children; below, men, women, and children crossing a bridge across the FL(UMEN) RENVS, from one towered town CASTEL to another, MOGONTIACVM.[10]

The medallion offers a visible reminder of an exceedingly important fact: that barbarians admitted to the empire brought with them their wives and children, and their domestic animals, and their baggage, and that they settled, for the most part, as families in reservations. Everything was thus propitious to the preserving of their way of life, even in the midst of Romans. From such alien enclaves must certainly have radiated cultural forces long undiminished; into such enclaves Roman manners could penetrate only with difficulty. Surely some traces of them must remain for the archeologist.

A) Treveri? G. Behrens, "Neue Funde von der Westgrenze der Wangionen," *Mainzer Zeitschrift* 29 (1934) 441., using the criteria of cremation, Germanic coins, fibulae types, pottery (Belgic ware, almost no terra sigillata), glass, and burial with arms, traces the movement of Treveri into the empire and its army, the latter attested in inscriptions of a number of Treveran soldiers around Worms and Mainz. The date of the movement, which Behrens ascribes to conscious Roman policy, falls in the early Empire. To satisfy their taste for their favorite Belgic ware, the immigrants built their own kilns for its production.

B) Vangiones? An enclosed cemetery about twenty miles south of Mainz, with twenty-five graves running from the first to the third centuries. The contents were generally sparse and poor (no coins), reflecting strong but not complete Romanization (un-Roman construction of the graves, some non-Roman pottery). The graveyard perhaps belongs to a settlement of Vangiones, by Caesar's arrangements, from which the men enlisted in the *coh. Vangionum* (J. Curschmann, "Ein Römische Friedhof und römische Villen bei Dautenheim, Kreis Alzey," *Mainzer Zeitschrift* 37–38 [1942–1943] 69f.; idem, "Die germanische Siedlung von Dautenheim," ibid. 41–43 [1946–1948] 129f.).

C) Brittones. On the Upper German *limes* (Mainz, Obernburg, etc.) in the mid-second century, techniques of stonecutting in construction, and inscriptions with characteristic lettering set in elaborately ornamented *tabulae ansatae*, both also found in Britain, and a kind of pottery favored by the Brittones, produced in family kilns and reflecting an increasing Romanization, identify a settlement of this tribe moved to the area by Antoninus Pius (F. Drexel, "Bauten und Denkmäler der Brittonen am Limes," *Germania* 6 [1922] 31f.; W. Schleiermacher, "Der obergermanische Limes und spätrömische Wehranlagen am Rhein," *BRGK* 33 [1943–1950] 143f.; and E. Birley, "Eine neue Inschrift von Corstopitum," *Germania* 20 [1936] 23f.)

D) Chatti? In the *canabae* around two camps in the Taunus region a kind of pottery is plentiful, hand-made, crude, and with parallels among the free Germans. Its occurrence covers the period from Antoninus Pius to Alexander Severus. It is attributed to a long-term settlement of Germans, probably Chatti. See R. von Uslar on "Die germanische Keramik in den Kastellen Zugmantel und Saalburg," *Saalburg Jahrbuch* 8 (1934) 63f., esp. 84–96, and in *Klio* 8 (1935) 294f.

E) Alammani? A cemetery belonging to the soldiers of a fort at Augusta Raurica, containing thirty graves of the fourth century, most of the first half of that century. The contents (fibulae, glass, pottery) and orientation of the burials are closely similar to those of sixth- and seventh-century Alamannic graves. See R. Laur-Belart, "Spätrömische Gräber aus Kaiseraugst," *Beiträge zur Kulturgeschichte. Festschrift Reinhold Bosch* (1947) 137–49.

F) Germani. K. Böhner, "Archäologische Beiträge zur Erforschung der Frankenzeit am Niederrhein," *Rheinische Vierteljahrsblätter* 15–16 (1950–1951) 22f., discusses a number of burials presumably belonging to soldiers, on the left bank of the lower Rhine (e.g., around Cologne). The graves date from ca. 300 without change of custom or contents into the seventh century. Their orientation, their pottery and glass, the weapons left with the dead, all are German, but details of decoration and place of manufacture of the richer articles show a union of Germanic and Roman provincial influences. A similar rapprochement of styles shows in a number of objects in use along the northern borders, e.g., fibulae produced in army camps, characterized by purely linear decoration and gross simplification from prevalent types, "the result of slow penetration of Germans into the empire" (R. Lantier, "Un cimetière du IVᵉ siècle au Mont Augé," *Antiquité classique* 17 [1948] 395f.). Some of the fourth-century graves in which such fibulae were found also contained weapons (ibid. 401). Further south, in central France about one hundred miles east of Bordeaux and north of Toulouse, a third-century cemetery of thirteen burials shows remarkable affinities with contemporary customs of the Germans of the lower Rhine just mentioned. The small size of the cemetery, the poverty of the burials, the pottery types, and the lack of cinerary urns establish the resemblance, and suggest a local German settlement (M. Labrousse, "Un cimetière romain du IIIᵉ siècle de Brive," *Gallia* 6 [1948] 363f.).

G) Laeti. These were troops of many tribes and peoples drafted into the western defenses under Diocletian and later emperors. A few were recaptured Romans, the great majority barbarians (Franks, Suevi, Alamanni, Batavi, Nervii, Teutones, and Lingones). They were organized in ethnic units kept at full strength by recruitment from lands assigned to them and their families near cities or scattered in villages. *Praefecti* and *praepositi* supervised them (Zos. 1.54.1; *Not.* Dig. *Occ.* 42.34f.; *Cod. Theod.* 7.20.10; 13.11.10; Ammian. Marcel. 20.8.13; *Paneg. vet.* 4.21.1; and discussion of these references by Jullian, *Hist. de la Gaule* 7.53f. and 8.81f.; Mommsen, *Ges. Schriften* 6 [1910] 166f. and 256f.; R. Grosse, *Röm. Militärgesch.* [1920] 207f.; and A. Grenier, *Manuel d'arch. gallo-romaine* 1 [1931] 398f.) The origin of the word *laetus* has been sought in Ger. *leto, litu, laet,* etc., denoting a sort of serf, and on the derivation O. Seeck, *Untergang,* I, Anhang, p. 589, builds a theory of the history and civil status of the *laeti* within the empire. The theory, right or wrong (and generally not accepted), is not relevant here. Another connection, however, must be rejected more firmly: that between *laeti* and the *lai* or *Laoi* of the lower Danube (see V. Parvan, *Dacia* 2 [1925] 242; S. Lambrino in *Mélanges de philol. . . . offerts à J. Marouzeau* [1948] 334f.).

Mentions of *laeti* in literary sources have provided a natural explanation for certain fourth-century burials of a non-Roman character in the western empire. The explanation cannot be proved but it is plausible and widely accepted, and the burials are themselves numerous and interesting enough to excite curiosity. Typically, they are not associated with villas or cities; the cemeteries, usually small, exhibit a wide spectrum of wealth, from a few very rich burials of the nobility down to the poorest; the richer ones, of both men and women, contain many articles of personal adornment; graves in most but not all cemeteries are oriented north-south (earlier) or east-west (later); many offer examples of pottery typical of the free Germans, some even produced in family kilns by the settlers; and many contain weapons: axes, long swords, lances, arrows, daggers. To the study of these graves J. Werner has devoted two articles, in *Archaeologica geographica* 1 (1950) 23f. and *Bonner Jahrbücher* 158 (1958) 372f., of which the first received a long and very damaging treatment from S. J. De Laet, J. Dhondt, and J. Nenquin, in *Études d'hist. et d'arch. Namuroises dédiées à Ferdinand Courtoy* (1952) 149f. Other examples are reported in *Gallia* 1 (1943) 203, in the Marne region; ibid. 14 (1956) 131f., by R. Lantier; and in H. Schönberger's study of "Provinzialrömische Gräber mit Waffenbeigaben," *Saalburg Jahrbuch* 12 (1953) 53f.

There are two important features in these graves. In the first place, they show the closest relations between the cultures within and without the empire. While *spathae*, conic fibulae, etc., are Germanic, the treatment of detail is Roman, the place of production is Gaul. The exportation of Roman manufactures to the most distant points, in Scandinavia or Poland, is well known. In the *laeti* burials, however, we have an importation of such Germanic customs as burial fully clothed, not only into the lower Rhine area and northeastern Gaul, though they are indeed especially concentrated there, but as far south as Auvergne (*Gallia* 7 [1949] 307). The approximation of Roman and barbarian, through the exchange of production and practice, has suggested to Werner the origin of Merovingian civilization. Whether this be correct or not, it is certain that there existed a remarkable degree of uniformity in culture in what is now northern France, Belgium, the Netherlands, and Germany.

In the second place, a considerable number of these graves contained weapons. Burial with weapons was a practice common before Caesar, but begins to die out first in the west, then in the Danube lands, from the first century on. Its revival in the third century Schönberger (op. cit. 56) explains only by reference to "the changed relations between soldier and civilian," but Lantier (*Gallia* 14 [1956] 131) more satisfactorily points to the widespread presence of *laeti* and *gentiles*. In their cemeteries it is clear, too, that wealth and weapons went together: the nobility were warriors, enriched by their services to Rome. And it was through this aristocracy that the embers of Roman civilization warmed the barbarian north.

H) Quadi? The contents of scattered graves in Pannonia reflects a civilization from beyond the Danube, settled within the empire in the first century, and confirmed, perhaps, by habits of local nomenclature (A. Mocsy, *Die Bevölkerung von Pannonien* [1959] 33–34). One such grave not far southeast of Vienna held a shield boss, possibly belonging to a follower of king Vannius when he crossed the river (Tac., *Ann.* 12.30; L. Franz, *BRGK* 18 [1928] 138).

I) Gepidae. From their home in the region of Prussia, they moved to the middle Danube, and entered Dacia before the middle of the third century. The presence there of certain characteristic fibulae supports what is found in literary sources. See C. C. Diculescu, *Die Gepiden* (1923) 1.24f. and 32.

J) Sarmatians. In the later third century two Sarmatian graveyards were in use in the neighborhood of Brigetio (L. Barkoczy, *Acta antiqua acad. sci. Hung.* 7 [1959] 444). An inscription refers to another settlement of the same people in Britain, who left, however, no further trace of their own civilization (I. A. Richmond, *JRS* 35 [1945] 19f.). In France, dozens of modern place-names like Sermaize and Salmaise remember Sarmatian settlements (Grenier, *Manuel* 1.402; J. Soyer, *Mém. de la Soc. arch. et hist. de l'Orléanais* 37 [1936] 200f.). The wide diffusion of this evidence is explained by the use of the Sarmatians as irregular troops, often linked with *laeti* and *gentiles* in the *Notitia Dignitatum*, throughout the empire.

While this catalogue could doubtless be expanded, and while it should be supplemented by a general study of the rising or falling popularity of native names, as against Roman, over the last three centuries of the Empire, it still suggests some interesting conclusions. It suggests, to begin with, one powerful means by which the ascendancy of Roman culture was broken down. Not only were representatives of alien cultures admitted in hundreds of thousands, but they brought with them, in their wives and children, the whole of their life. Their homes were entered by no drill sergeant, no notary, or young equestrian, such as were encountered in auxiliary camps.

Machinery sufficient to Romanize a *man* could not touch his family. So the later settlements en masse possessed a very different character from the systematic recruitment of individual soldiers among friendly tribes, in the earlier Empire. An indication of the difference is supplied by the little private kilns for the production of kitchen ware, on barbarian models (above, A, C, D, F) or the homemade fibulae (above, F); by the showy bracelets, brooches, and necklaces of the women; or by the placing of passage money in the mouth of the dead, to help them into the Beyond.

Moreover, a cultural superiority sufficient to Romanize whole provinces in Caesar's day clearly declined in the third and fourth centuries. True, the immigrations were much larger, later; but a comparison of the survival power of

Sarmatian settlements in Britain, of the Vangiones or Brittones near Mainz, or the Quadi and Marcomanni on the lower Danube, with the *laeti* of the fourth century, shows a significant change. The aliens of the first and second centuries could be absorbed. They left little trace of their individuality, or succumbed, from the start, to an admixture of Roman ways. The *laeti*, on the other hand, resembled their hosts within the empire only, or at least largely, because these hosts had already come to resemble the barbarians—had gradually adopted, by trade, or by the revival of far earlier native customs, or by other influences, a good part of non-Roman civilization. From Gallienus on, "the power of Romanization diminished, and groups within the population began to form in border provinces which, in manners, speech, and ethnic background, remained united with their parent race beyond the frontier. These enclosed settlements, however, were continually and silently spreading outward in a fashion never historically understood, and only occasionally known through some chance find such as a grave-stone."[11]

7

NOTES ON ROMANIZATION

THE SUBJECT here is very broad and often explored; and if there are a few points which seem still to invite more discussion, it is because discussion keeps opening up the old to question and challenge. A few generations ago it would have been hard to convince readers of the very limited powers exercised by ancient conquerors over the daily lives and *mores* of their subjects. The high claims of Europeans in vast scattered empires south and east over the globe would have been too much to the fore in people's minds; they would have credited merely technological or military superiority with the ability to accomplish absolutely everything; and, moreover, the dominant view of the Roman world was that of a historian who had been a lawyer, Theodore Mommsen.

Everywhere Mommsen looked he found, and scholars for long after him also found, legal structures giving shape to life. His view seemed reasonable: if men who could build military camps and roads declared that things must be done in such-and-such a manner, surely they were obeyed. If they declared a census and a rate of tribute to be exacted, surely "all went to be taxed, every one into his own city"; and if it was laid down in Italy that registration in municipalities, colonies, and prefectures should list their citizens by nomen, praenomen, father or patron, tribe, cognomen, and age,[1] then surely it followed throughout the provinces that registrants would adopt Roman names and thus identify themselves in their epitaphs. From warfare to political organization and to a person's very name, the civilizing process seemed to move forward as straight as any Roman road.

It very much fostered this impression that the historical record most readily at hand was the literary, looking out (not very far) from the centers of the Greco-Roman world, occupied with commanders and conquests, addressed by and to the ruling classes, and serenely ignorant of nonconformity beneath them. If scholarly investigation were to be pressed beyond these historical accounts to the less obvious sources, one might encounter the corpus of *agrimensores* or the Elder Pliny's remarks on provincial life, showing lands and peoples carved up, distributed, named, and duly recorded on government rolls. And if epigraphy were to be called in additionally, the best known text was what Mommsen christened the "Queen of Inscriptions," the *Res Gestae* of Augustus, well suited to illustrate the mastery of the center over all the rest. What the coming of Rome meant to those unhappily come upon was thus reported in rather official terms, that is, in terms of what the conquerors and their collaborators gave orders for, as if those orders were really and fully obeyed.

Was that really what resulted from the formation of the Roman empire? "Not everyone," as Professor Gilliam observed, "will be satisfied with an answer based on legal status";[2] not everyone will agree that lawful citizenship represented a triumph, or even an important ingredient in the making of One World (Roman); and other merely formal and mandated changes in civic relations and structure will not be treated by everyone these days as the aspect or level of Romanization that, in the long run, made the most difference in history.

It is, instead, increasingly recognized in recent decades that even the best of ancient governments in its most strenuous age was obliged to act within quite narrow limits.[3] The more closely we consider the Roman emperors' power, indeed, the narrower those limits appear.

A moment in history very likely to be recalled in any discussion of the Romans' power to make the conquered into their own image is described by Tacitus (*Agricola* 21). He presents a governor of Britain who "encouraged people in private and supported them officially to build temples, fora, houses." He had sons of leading men taught Latin. "Hence even honor for our costume, togas common." A nice case of acculturation. It is sometimes used to suggest a settled Roman policy. But if such really existed, why is it that, for every sestertius spent by the Roman government on such projects in the west and north, we can find a hundred spent in the eastern provinces? The east needed no Romanizing, nor accepted it; yet its cities could tap the imperial treasure almost at will. That broad fact we must set against our little glimpse of Agricola smiling upon his barbaric subjects. It pleased his benevolence to assist their struggles upward. But there was no policy behind him, not even a tendency.

Could he have *forced* compliance, not bought it? With that question, I turn to the first of three headings I wish to consider: compulsion, capacity, choice. Romans did transplant whole tribes, Cisalpine or Spanish, thereby obliging them to find new modes of food production, for example. That in turn would involve a long train of further adaptations. Similarly, tribes were everywhere forbidden warfare. As anthropologists would say, their value systems and sex roles would be affected. And self-help—that is, the settling of disputes and wrongs without resort to law—the Romans discouraged also, not very thoroughly. Beyond these several measures, however, all of which aimed at the conqueror's monopolizing of the force of arms, it is hard to think of any area of life on which actual compulsion was brought to bear by any ancient government. Areas of life beyond reach were correspondingly broad.

My second heading, *capacity* for cultural change, directs attention to mechanical, technical, tangible resources. So long as these were lacking, the non-Roman population remained physically unable to adopt the master civilization even had it wished to do so. For example, the art of the fresco painter required a long apprenticeship and only a certain kind of wall surface in a certain style of house. In turn, that required among the painters' customers the support of a concentration of wealth. Stable peace must first permit such wealth to accumulate; a road system must permit the expansion of markets by which it might be increased; urban centers that might buy the surplus of the countryside must develop, in their turn needing supplies of water, streets, a rational town plan; and it would help greatly if there were a trusted currency so that commerce might advance beyond mere barter. All these preliminaries to fresco painting were needed if the art were to flourish. And all were in the gift of the conquerors.

Almost at the very moment of conquest they became available, through the presence of Roman troops. Legionaries as bearers of far more than arms are among the most familiar figures in modern accounts of the civilizing process.[4] Beyond the better-known and grander marks they left on the ancient landscape, such as the aqueduct that fed Caesarea in Palestine, they contributed to small structures of all sorts: so much we may guess from their skill in building, providing models to the untutored natives; more still we may be sure of, through finding the stamp of military units on bricks in construction. The bricks are discovered in non-military structures in Pannonia, Germany, Raetia, Moesia, and elsewhere, along with characteristic forms of Roman architecture. It is a sure sign of acculturation wherever "la tuile romaine fait une timide apparition."[5]

But in the remotest corner of the empire, in northwestern Spain, Lucius Terentius, *figlinarius* of the Fourth Macedonian Legion, manufactured not only bricks but amphorae.[6] An article of daily use like this, or still more strikingly the molded red dishes whose manufacture the army oversaw in other western provinces through its own kilns, brought the Roman way of life into the natives' very homes. It both brought in and at first satisfied a demand, until initiative passed into civilian hands. And potsherds attesting to this process may stand for a broad range of articles not so likely to survive for excavation. Small wonder that Strabo, speaking of Cantabria, should have concluded, "Tiberius, establishing in this area a force of three legions he had received from Augustus, succeeded in rendering parts of it fit not only for peace but even for city life."[7]

The shape of vessels for the table may show us further how new items first were introduced into the native diet. Those, too, could be learned from the forces of occupation. Thereafter they became established and lasted even when the troops had moved away. Favored crops and methods could be picked up from the agricultural territory set aside for army use—for example, from the *prata* of the Fourth Macedonian Legion just mentioned. They spread over much of the Celtiberian region.[8] The outline of that military land is known through the termini that have been discovered. Paradoxically, the demands of resident troops for agricultural products of all sorts might actually enlarge and nourish the local economy, through requiring more land to be farmed and surpluses to be produced—surpluses which thereafter were spent on the local market.[9]

Our survey of the indigenous capacity to accept an alien culture thus arrives at the most fundamental matter of all, wealth; for what natives could not afford could never become a part of their lives. But it has long been recognized that the presence of the forces of conquest and occupation attracted traders (for example, around Caesar's camps in Gaul) because the troops had money to spend; and when the quantity of that money is estimated even approximately, and measured against what was likely to be in circulation before conquest, it becomes clear that conquest brought with it enormous stimulation.[10] An illustration may be found in the army camp at Orléansville in Algiers a century or more ago, to which was drawn a civilian population serving army needs, especially in wine shops, and merchants supplying small manufactures (bangles or rugs) and horses at the weekly market. Four or five thousand Arabs attended every Sunday.[11] Altogether similar crowds and economic forces came together at ancient army camps as well. "It is significant," writes Lucian Musset, "that many terms relating to trade, transport and measurements have been borrowed from the Latin of the garrisons" and so brought in to German and even Danish and Old English.[12]

So much for the capacity to be Romanized. Before passing on, however, to the third and last category of reasons why people came to adopt other ways of life—I mean the category of *choice* or free preference—it would be well to consider what degree of homogeneity was actually achieved in the empire.

We may conveniently begin, as historians generally do begin their accounts, with the externals of life. In the surviving record, political and administrative organizations of course leave many traces. They particularly attract the notice of students in the tradition of Mommsen; nor is there any possibility of their being ignored by the ancient authorities. Throughout the eastern provinces, nevertheless, the preexisting forms of local government remained quite undisturbed by the Romans, whereas among more backward, vulnerable populations in the west the units of self-government seem generally to have persisted in the countryside and in scattered urban centers as well; so we find a variety of native terms in government in Thrace, Gaul, Africa, or Spain.[13] Cities retained the right to issue their own currency, though only of base metal, in eastern cities throughout the Principate, and in areas of the west for some decades after conquest.[14] Evidently the imperial authorities took no active interest in the matter.

I referred to the charter of Caesar's time discovered at Heraclea, in which is prescribed the proper way to list a citizen's name. To return to that now: it is often assumed that the rulers pressed their own habits of nomenclature on their subjects through its connection with citizenship. In a sense this is certainly true. On the other hand, the advantages bestowed by citizenship are not likely to have been much on the mind of the ordinary man in the provinces. He therefore cannot have felt much need to change his name in order to improve his civic status. The right of appeal that St. Paul availed himself of is rarely referred to in our sources, and the other significant benefit derived from citizenship, bestowing the right to inherit from other *cives Romani*, would be of interest principally to the rich. They had other reasons for desiring entry into the ruling classes.[15] It is instructive to note the absolute indifference of the masses to the gift of citizenship in A.D. 212, an indifference eloquent in the silence that greeted the gift.[16]

The point is worth dwelling on because the phenomena I aim to understand are, if not of the masses, at least to be measured across broad samples of the population; and the adoption or refusal of the Roman three-name custom is one of the very few indices which our evidence allows us to examine in some bulk. If everyone in the provinces bore the *tria nomina*, then Rome had indeed triumphed; if no one, then acculturation still had a long way to go.

Nomenclature known through inscriptions presents many, many peculiarities. The one thing not discovered in all the evidence, however, is a clean break from indigenous to a correctly Roman style. Instead, as we move from records on stone to records on cheaper materials,[17] or as we move from urban to rural settings,[18] we descend through various degrees of correctness to quite strange local practices. At points in the descent, it is impossible to tell whether we have yet left the truly Romanized strata. Individual bearers of the name Fortunatus, for example, in Africa had nothing clearly un-Roman about them; yet when all Fortunati around the empire are surveyed together, we find that this cognomen in particular is likely to identify a native—so fond were the Africans of auspicious names like this, and of the suffix *-atus* as well.[19] Even in appearing to conform to Roman practices, indigenous preferences thus made themselves felt, and differentially, too: more in some times, strata, and regions than in others.

And a further difficulty: in a very high percentage of cases within our most important category of evidence—among individuals in inscriptions—we cannot determine whether we are dealing with Italians or true indigenes. The word "native" only hides the problem, since it applies to both; yet the two are vastly different. Suppose we had before us Gaius Iulius Rufus from Gaul: son of a freedman, Greek by descent but Roman in citizenship and way of life? Or rather a Gallic chieftain? From what he called himself, we could not tell. In a recent catalogue of over a thousand persons prominent in Roman Spain in local or provincial government, in the imperial cult, or the like position, perhaps no more than five percent are demonstrably ethnic Spaniards—that is, the degree of Romanization among the classes most likely to have been Romanized at all cannot be *proved* to rise above that proportion. No doubt, of course, it was in fact much greater.[20] In inscriptions from Gaul (excluding Provence), the figure may approach a third.[21] In both areas, however, we would like to assess the impact of the conquering civilization through its conversions among the true indigenes; and these conversions we cannot generally distinguish from immigrants who simply brought their own customs to Gaul and Spain.

If we cast around for a parallel that might make more concrete the possibilities of the situation, the modern African nation of Liberia suggests itself. Here neither race nor religion (in any very powerful sense) marked off the nineteenth-century settlers from the indigenes.[22] The former, however, generally kept themselves apart from the latter: "What shall we, what *can* we do with such an appalling amount of heathenism, superstition, and barbarity all at once?" asked one of them, regarding the influx of natives into the urban preserves of the settlers. Settlers for their part did penetrate into the hinterlands, not in large numbers. There they took women, though not often in marriage, and adopted native ways of life and native ways of working the land. There remained, as there still remain, however, "two distinct and unequal societies."

When we turn back to our subject proper, and there discover semi-Romanized persons in provincial hinterlands, may they not be descendants of Italians who had indeed descended, representing a loss of their own culture, rather than indigenes risen half-way to Roman manners? At least the Liberian analogy suggests the possibility. Or when we discover great estates in Spain bearing names derived from Porcius or Marius, may these not indicate, not rising natives, but exploiting immigrants whose own ancestors were once drawn as slaves from the east?[23] Questions of this sort are as urgent as they are hard to answer. They are urgent because, after all, it is self-evident that in every province there was some interchange of culture; only by determining *how much* can we claim to have refined that knowledge; yet quantification requires tools of analysis that we seem still to lack.

Besides nomenclature, there exist a few other well-reported aspects of civilization which invite generalization. These include, in an odd little list, gods, pots, and Latin. Occasionally several aspects may appear in a cluster—for example, in a dedication to the local deity Erudinus (and at a surprisingly late date, A.D. 399) set up in a rural corner of Spain. The dedication is offered by someone who betrays non-Roman habits of nomenclature, bad Latin, and membership in a local tribe.[24] For another cluster of signs, we may look at a single province, Noricum, where the women did the hard work in the fields, not the men, and wore jewelry, turbans, and smocks peculiar to the land; where their names were Patevilla, Resatira, Aveta; where modes of worship and funerary cult were maintained against all outside influences; and where relief sculpture that renders all this in pictures for us exhibits a characteristic Celtic, linear style and geometric "feel," straight through to the mid-fourth century, blending at that point with other dominant traits of late antique art.[25] Of that art, one of the finest examples is the gold portrait of Julian discovered less than half a century ago in Aventicum. It serves to remind us that indigenism, in its effects if not in its motives, was more than a primitive or purely negative phenomenon.

Its manifestations can be arranged in patterns so as to bring out its principal characteristics. Most obvious and familiar is one tendency of non-Roman, that is, non-Italian elements of Roman imperial civilization to assert themselves among the poor and the rustic. In contrast, Roman fashions established themselves most easily among the urban wealthy. Much the same can be said of Greek expansion into Sicily and south Italy centuries earlier: the results appear to be a sort of decapitation of the conquered culture. The leading representatives adapt themselves; their homes, their dinner tables, their very graves exhibit a range of imported wares and ways. Everyday objects, on the other hand, and the homes of the poor are little influenced.

That the latter predominated numerically, everybody knows. We know the world was not made up of the likes of Annaeus Seneca, Cornelius Fronto, Cornelius Balbus—provincial millionaires who had risen into our natural field of vision and who were of course as Roman as Cicero. Yet nothing adequately prepares us for the discovery that native languages prevailed in parts of eastern Spain still in the sixth century or that, at the other end of the Mediterranean, Coptic had by then taken on written form and overspread Egypt.[26] How, we are bound to ask ourselves, how could such broad-based and at times even dynamic cultures entirely escape our view over the preceding three or four centuries? An unsettling fancy takes us: that a whole second world may have existed beneath the one familiar to us, containing an actual majority of the population, of a wholly un-classical civilization, hidden from us by some deficiency in our sources.

A fancy, nothing more: the sprawling supremacy of imperial Rome cannot be so easily confined to an upper stratum. Nevertheless it might be seriously argued that in the western half of the empire in the fifth century there was as much that derived from the forgotten countryside of the earlier Empire as from the civilization of the Caesars. The range and strength of practices emerging from the dark into the light of history in the later empire is really most striking.[27]

Moreover, we are indeed reminded that our sources have failed us. Not only, of course, do they speak in the language of the conquerors, but they speak very rarely of life outside their own circle. Outside are mere "barbarians," meaning often no more than peasants;[28] and natives rising into the circle, by the point in their acculturation at which they have mastered the language, have shed most of their earlier way of life. They are known to us through more durable building materials, no longer thatch, wattle, and clay; they dispose their dead no longer under mere heaps of stones, doubtfully identifiable, but under shaped monuments that gradually come to be inscribed.[29] Only then, but too late, do we learn their names or sense their religious beliefs.

The Noricans Patevilla, Resatira, and Avita mentioned earlier remind us of another kind of person whose beliefs and practices are largely hidden from us, namely, women. Yet among indigenous groups on the road to Romanization, we find them traveling at a different pace from their men—generally more slowly.[30] They are slower to adopt an alien costume, their names longer retain a native sound, their speech likewise. As Cicero says (De orat. 3.45), "it is easier for women to preserve old ways unchanged, for they know little of the varieties of speech and cling forever to what they first learned."

It is very likely that ancient life was divided into men's and women's spheres, according to bargains differing in different Mediterranean regions, and that women administered their sphere more conservatively not only in the respects we can occasionally detect but in many others as well that are unknown to us. Surely they traveled less, were seen less in city streets, and compared ideas less often with strangers. So their cultural loyalties would be the less disturbed.

To summarize the broader findings that emerge within my second category of reasons for change, namely, capacity: there was plenty of movement and flowering in the upper branches of provincial society, but little detectable in the broad roots. Or, in terms less poetic: persons in the lower socioeconomic strata and living closer to the soil enjoyed the least capacity for change, while those who stirred about in the cities were constantly exposed to alternatives, and, if they were rich as well, could afford to buy a new dress, a new style of wine cup, a new design of headstone for their last resting place.

But why should they want to? Up to this point we have considered only symptoms—indeed, there seems to have been no scholarly attention paid to anything but the symptoms—of a broad urge to become Romanized.[31] Turning to my third and final category of explanation, choice, I should at least briefly examine on what grounds it might be made. Motive is after all the essence and center of historical explanation. Moreover, where our first category, sheer compulsion, appears to have had so limited a scope, the scope remaining to free preference is too large to be passed over. We must therefore consider why any indigene possessed of the capacity to change would want to do so.

We cannot say, for example, that a Roman name was intrinsically more attractive to the human ear. Indeed, excluding hot baths, central heating, softer beds, and the pleasures of wine as opposed to beer, Roman civilization was not obviously more to be desired than the indigenous. It was preferred for indirect reasons. Just what sort, we are rarely told, but can perhaps advance a little through conjecture.

First, I would suppose one adopts someone else's practice if one admires him generally, not if one holds him in contempt or finds him wholly incomprehensible. Students of acculturation must therefore look first among the people who are about to change, in order to discover what their inherited values are—values which approve an alien custom over a traditional one. Unfortunately most indigenous groups in the Roman empire are not adequately known to us for this sort of inspection; but Caesar, Strabo, and less often other writers offer help. Exactly as we would expect, they portray non-Romans chiefly as enemies: the Bracari in the second century B.C. "are the most warlike of people, they are armed along with their womenfolk who fight, too, and they offer their lives eagerly, not one of them turning his back" (App., *Hisp.* 72); the Helvetii in the next century are *homines bellandi cupidi* (Caes., *B. G.* 1.2); throughout Gaul (ibid. 6.21f.) male chastity is valued greatly because it preserves strength for fighting, and farming is valued lightly because it lessens the *studium belli gerendi*. "Men are warriors rather than farmers" (Strabo 4.1.2); "the whole people now called Gallic or Galatic is war-mad, passionate and quick to war" (ibid. 4.4.2). If their senates of leaders will not vote them a war, then—Gallic tribes or Celtiberi (Caes., *B. G.* 3.17; App., *Hisp.* 100)— they will destroy them with fire and sword. And other testimonies, some archeological, confirm this broad picture.[32] We cannot doubt that power in arms beyond everything else conferred prestige, just as we are specifically told that the objects of trade from what we would call higher civilizations were scorned and excluded by various tribes as likely to diminish that power.[33]

The Romans possessed it, of course, in greater measure than the peoples they defeated. For the latter to assume the toga worn by the master warriors of their world, to assume the language of challenge and command, to take the very name of their conqueror, can only have seemed a natural step up even in terms of their own familiar values. Alien ways were recommended by prestige won in exactly the ways already most widely accepted among the conquered.

There was also advantage to be gained. The masters had their own values: for example, scorn of *bracati*, trousered men such as were the Celts.[34] They scorned and kept down those who did not know their tongue, who babbled barbarously. Natives could learn better: so, in a passage already quoted, Britons are seen taking up Latin and the toga. Why? *Honoris aemulatio* is Tacitus' explanation (*Agr.* 21.1): "ambition for promotion." Exactly as we would expect. In A.D. 21 one could find at Autun (Tac., *Ann.* 3.43) the young Gallic noblemen getting their (thoroughly) Romanized education. And again in Spain, Sertorius could induce young aristocratic warriors to go to school in the language of the conquerors "with the assurance that when they became men he would give them a share in administration and authority. So the fathers were wonderfully pleased to see their sons in purple-bordered togas" (Plut., *Sert.* 14.2f.). Fortified with such little tags of Greek and Latin as can alone give courage to the classical historian, perhaps we may now trust our common sense: *of course* indigenous ways were put aside, not because the Roman ways were, or were thought, inherently superior, but through desire for status, money, influence, ease, and self-esteem that accrued by a sort of magic to the members of the master civilization. So it was then, so it has been at a thousand junctures in the history of conquest.

A last tag, drawn from a setting long past the moment of conquest: in a city on the edge of Rome's eastern empire the main population in their own fashion all wore beards. Only one man decided to shave. "And it was said this was his practice not without a purpose but in flattery of the Romans and so as to demonstrate his friendliness to them."[35] With this scene we have passed the generation when warlike tribes are beginning to settle into the *pax Romana*; we have passed all those half-Romanized Iulii making their way in the western provinces through service in the army; and we have entered a peaceful world of subtler calculations. Flattery procures favor; favor is in the gift of the master class; and "imitation is the sincerest form of flattery," as the saying declares. So imitation continues from the first to the last generation, until adaptation is complete.

Complete, however, only for those who attempted it. We have perhaps seen into the process when it worked. We have not seen why it did *not* work—why some people evidently did not seek prestige within their own community or favor from the ruling class, by adopting Roman ways of speech, dress, and so forth. But I think the answer lies most likely in the oppressive sense of one's place that may be felt in the empire's society: this sense entirely discouraged attempts by the bulk of the population to improve their lot.

I find it useful to think through such matters with the aid of the mind's eye. Let us imagine, then, a one-room dwelling such as is attested in many parts of the ancient Mediterranean countryside. Across the room, to divide it in two, are hung rush mats and the tatters of blankets. On each side is a small chest to hold clothes and a larger chest or chiffonnier with mats on it serving both for bed and storage. There is one table. The owners, man and wife, farm a few acres and pay tribute or rent to someone else. On this house a Roman soldier is billeted for the winter. It is the owners' first close view of Roman civilization. They do not much like it, since their guest shows a good appetite and all too healthy an interest in their daughter. They feel no faintest attraction in the soldier's language, costume, or equipment, no part of which can be of the least use to them in their life; and when at length they look upward for the means to control his burdensome behavior, it is to a man of their own people that they turn, the man to whom they pay their tithe. The soldier's officer they would never dare approach, nor of course will they ever learn Latin. His world and theirs are and will always remain too far apart for that.[36]

Adjust the picture as I may to what little I know of rural life in ancient Numidia or Northumbria, or to a house in a hamlet or to one more isolated still, I cannot find much place in it for the natural learning of new ways of life. I must therefore conclude that "resistance" to Romanization among most of the population need not have been a positive force of any strength. It may in fact have been only negative. It was not (or was not likely to be) anything we could call nationalism, it was no passionate attachment to ancestral traditions or heroic refusal of the foreign; rather, among people whose whole experience taught them that they could not live through an experiment that failed, reluctance in the face of Romanization was a mode of survival.

Before we leave it at that, we have yet to explain those apparently dynamic phrases, those times when indigenous customs came to the fore. How are they to be reconciled with the passivity and deprivation discovered in the picture I have presented? Yet the fortune of the unhomogenized, the excluded, and the deprived may always turn: the son of a shepherdess may become an emperor—Maximinus or Galerius—and so bring forward to the sunlight a whole new range of tastes and traits. It is by such somersaults that history turns corners.

8

ROMAN BUREAUCRATESE

T HE THEORY and fact of the Roman emperor's position were strikingly at variance in the fourth century. *Quod principi placuit legis habuit vigorem* may have been the established doctrine, but when he spoke to his proconsuls, the emperor said rather, "You must order the proceedings [of civil suits] to be concluded on the third day, or at the latest on the fourth day, or at any rate on the fifth"; or, to the civil service, "Let the greedy hands of the officials now forbear, let them forbear, I say."[1] The stutter and shrillness do not fit an autocrat, nor the repetitions; but repetitions are characteristic of the Codes. An entire decree might have to be re-enacted, in almost identical form, eight or ten times, evidently because no one had paid any attention to it.[2] Against this merely ornamental legislation, against "the ruler who lays down a law and is reckoned unable to enforce it," Libanius might protest, yet, three times imperatively summoned to the capital, he simply remained in Antioch.[3] A contemporary, Valerianus *v. c.*, flouted one decree after another, one judicial decision after another, and flouted, too, the authority of the praetorian prefect, the proconsul, the urban prefect, and the imperial secret police, one of whom he allegedly killed with his own hands.[4] Between the emperor and his subjects, and between his theoretical omnipotence and his actual powers, the essential link was the bureaucracy. Plainly, it was not doing its job. It is the argument of this paper that part of the difficulty lay in the failure of all ranks of government to get through to each other.

This bureaucracy was made up largely of guilds of clerks. Within each, new members might buy or inherit a position, *cum suis commodis*; paid an additional fee to their superiors; and entered thus on the course of extortion necessary to recoup the cost of entrance. Higher positions went at a price more than twenty-five times the official salary (which was clearly a mere token). By the middle of the fourth century this extraordinary, immoral, and workable system was established openly in the Codes, and the payments involved—so much by a plaintiff to have his *libellus* registered, so much due to a governor's usher to admit a petitioner, so much added to the ordinary tax as perquisite of the collector—were all reduced to an official schedule.[5] The guild as a whole had a juridic personality, its own private interests, its slaves and places of meeting.[6] It had a joint treasury from which it paid to its members, in portions jointly decided, some periodic dividend, and, on the analogy of troop units, it may have made a joint yearly payment to the magistrate whom it served.[7] Its corporate strength was opposed to its superiors by imperial legislation, if they attempted anything illegal.[8]

Having obligations, dues, bylaws, officers, treasury, and traditions, and often filled by sons of members from generation to generation, the guilds within civil *officia* presented a highly professional appearance. This did not include professional education. We hear of judges *humanitatis litterarum rudes*, of clerks rising to the first ranks of the Roman *decuriae* who still stumbled in their grammar and spelling—all part of the general decline of letters everywhere.[9] Yet the very ignorance of these men, tightly knit, semi-educated, helped in the development of a particular language of the trade. We know better what happened to Latin among soldiers, to Greek among medical practitioners. A jargon of the lower secretaries of the fourth century is attested only by the faintest traces. It is significant, however, that, in "an age in which symbolical and abstract values predominated," the names of staff positions should shift somewhat from those like *scriba, tabularius, librarius*, denoting a specific kind of job, to others like *melloproximus, proximus, sexagenarius, ducenarius, trecenarius, scholasticus, princeps, maior*, denoting only a certain place or rank of employment. It is more significant that so rich a vocabulary of corruption should have developed. Promises sold, which one had no intention of keeping, were *fumus*, "smoke."[10] The *suffragium*, "vote," of big men needed by little men for promition, was so regularly bought that it came to mean "money given or promised for the sake of securing some honor."[11] As we have "tip," "douceur," "largesse," and (in the days of Fox) "gratification," to mean what is really a bribe, so Latin spawned "overflow" or "drippings," *stillatura*; "pickles," *salgamum*; "little baskets," *sportulae*; "little favor," *munusculum* (in Greek, "guest-present," *xenia*).[12] Since the only justification for such payments was the one much respected in the period, namely, that they had always been exacted, they came to be called simply "the usual";[13] and in the course of time their recipients claimed them "honestly," *recte, sophronos*.[14]

The fourth century was the great age of tax-collectors. Under titles increasingly polysyllabic and obscure, new exactions were laid by the government upon its subjects—*aurum coronarium, collatio glebalis, superindictiones*. A number originated in the Greek East and the names were taken over by Latin with little change: *anabolicae species, aerica*, or by Greek from Latin, with or without change: *indiktion* (*indictio*) or *arouration* (*iugatio*). Government servants with a good ear for the music of these words were detected in the invention of wholly illegal taxes: "contributions" (*syneisphora*), "wheel-wear and services" (*rotarum tritura ac ministeria*), and "superstatutory food-money" (*cenatica superstatuta*), the word *cenatica* clearly formed on Greek principles.[15]

But most of the peculiarities of government language, then as now, filtered down to the ranks of mere scribblers from higher levels—from bureau chiefs and ministers of state. Among these, the most valued accomplishment was a command of literature. It was to Constantius "the greatest of all virtues," to Julian, "the second ornament of peace"— second only to service in some government uniform.[16] Emperors pursued it, and after their death historians judged them as good or bad on this one basis. For civil positions they often chose men only for their ability with words: a linguist, with Hebrew, Greek, and Latin letters, was made head of an imperial dye factory; and from that level up, we find *literati* drawn on to supply ambassadors, a vicar of Rome, many provincial governors, several *comites* and diocesan vicars, seven praetorian prefects, a *comes sacrarum largitionum* (advanced to *magister officiorum*), a *comes rerum privatarum*, a *praepositus sacri cubiculi*, and an urban prefect. All of these were men famous, some even active professionally, as grammarians, philosophers, poets, playwrights, historians, and (most of all) rhetoricians. Most of them belong to the second half of the fourth century.[17] Their power we do not have to account for here, but it must be accepted as a prominent feature of late Roman government.

It is easier to understand why civil servants connected with law should be valued for their eloquence; why rhetoric and law should be taught together, by professors skilled equally in both subjects; why the graduates of Bordeaux or Beirut should look on the post of *advocatus fisci* as a natural reward of their training, even as a way station to a higher charge; and why the emperor should choose his legal advisers from men of this background. Best illustration is the *quaestor sacri palatii*, whose duty originally to read the emperor's messages to the senate developed into the actual making of law, as those messages became more and more autocratic, so that, by the fourth century, legislation was nothing less than an address from on high, delivered by the empire's foremost orator. The inevitable influence of rhetoric on law has been much studied.

From what has been said, a picture emerges of the fourth-century bureaucracy lacking, in its lower ranks, sufficient sense of language to control the excesses of the higher ranks; among whom the love of belles-lettres, of philosophy and science and grammar and especially of rhetoric grew more passionate as one moved up the hierarchy to the top; so, if a man of administrative skills and another of literary skills were both in a position to shape some document, it was the latter, without doubt, who asserted his claims and stamped the character of his accomplishments on bureaucratic style.

Typical of this style was a love of synonyms, seen already in the half dozen words for bribe. Rhetorical schools were to blame, from which issued men half-trained in law, "an ill-educated type, broken away too soon from the elementary classes," who tried to drown judges under a flood of "disarranged circumlocutions."[18] That, at least, is what Ammianus says. But when his own writings are tested, scholars interested in military history are exasperated by his use of twenty-eight synonyms for "die," twenty-four for "kill," thirty-five for "at dawn," and by his use of *numerus, cohors,* and *turma* simply for variety, applied indifferently to all sorts of troop unit.[19] Libanius and the Latin panegyrists show the same fault, as well as official documents and the Codes, which, "to avoid clumsy repetitions, made a free use of synonyms, thereby often blurring the precise meaning of technical terms."[20] What such habits of profusion must have done to confuse government can be easily imagined.

Confusion, however, has its uses. It may be said of late Roman times as it has been said of our own, that "political speech and writing are largely the defence of the indefensible . . . political language has to consist largely of euphemism, question-begging and sheer cloudy vagueness."[21] Thus, in the proliferation of synonyms, words could be deliberately misused so regularly as to acquire a new sense. The grain tax wrung from the peasants of Egypt was "the happy shipment" (*aisia embole*), remissions of which were *indulgentiae*; where *praestatio* once meant "aid," it came to mean an assessment or obligatory payment; *devotio* (later, "tax-payment") and *functiones publicae* ("fiscal charges") show the same twist; while payments to government servants are *donativa* and *largitiones*.[22] The object was to present the actions of the state in the best possible light by a device familiar to the propaganda of today; better still, the high purpose of the state, and the wickedness of its enemies, might be set forth more openly, in some long, contorted, rambling, even shambling preamble, such as the introduction to Diocletian's price edict. "Who, therefore, does not know that insolence, covertly attacking the public welfare . . . comes to the mind of the profiteer to extort prices for merchandise, not fourfold or eightfold, but such that human speech is incapable of describing either the price or the act."[23] For the establishing of this sort of grotesque long-windedness Diocletian is largely to blame, but an address to Septimius Severus by the authorities of Mylasa provides one of a great many prototypes: "In very truth, the security of the city is shaken by the malice and villainy of a few people, who assail it and rob the community. Through them speculation has entered our market-place and prevents the city from securing supplies."[24]

The history of the ample style that ultimately prevailed in official documents must take account of several divisions in the bureaucracy. Early in the Empire, the secretariats were fewer, and all dispensed a Latin more or less unaffected, intelligible, succinct—especially legal Latin, which persisted, though decreasingly in favor, until the days of its revival under Justinian.[25] It was written by men trained in law; rhetoric attracted other men; and the two kinds of training remained generally distinct until Hadrian's reign. It was then that rhetoric and law were commonly joined in the same person, that a more elaborate style came into favor for official documents, and that the competence of jurists in government was diminished by the creation of new bureaus. Only the office of the *a libellis*, entrusted with matters of civil law, continued, so to speak, pure, until it too, in Diocletian's day, passed under the shadow of the rhetorizing *a memoria* and *ab epistulis*. In Constantine's day we have the culmination of the process.[26] Its dominant feature is obscurity.[27] That it prefers two words where one will do, or a long one where a short one would be clearer; that it avoids, wherever possible, the *mot juste*, or envelops its meaning in synonyms, baroque fancies, archaisms, superlatives, and analogies; that it introduces perfectly unnecessary *loci communes*, or moralizes, or rants—all this is too obvious in the sources to need much illustration. One text may serve as typical. Its intention is simply to proclaim an Easter amnesty to all but forgers.

> The day of Easter joy permits not even those persons that have committed crimes to be afraid. The terrible prison shall at that time be open to the unaccustomed light. We decree, however, that any person shall be excluded from this grant of pardon who . . . by copying the sacred imperial features and thus assailing the divine countenance, has sacrilegiously coined their venerable images.[28]

Another decree wishes to denounce (since the emperor evidently cannot check) the desecration of tombs. "Criminal audacity extends to the ashes of the dead and their consecrated mounds, although our ancestors always considered it the next thing to sacrilege even to move a stone from such places or to disturb the earth or tear up the sod." As if this were not enough inflated, the original text, three times as long as the law of which this is the beginning, itself began, "It was my duty, after considering with myself, to restore the ancient custom [about funerals]. . . . For when they considered the matter, the men of old, who made wise laws, believed that there was the greatest possible difference between life and death." This last bit of ancient lore, rescued by a rhetorician, and the assurance that "the sun is the cause of day and night . . . by his departure and arrival," is embroidered with a tag from Homer, with a syllogism, and with other elegances, to a length of several pages.[29] Its author, the emperor Julian, may well accuse himself of being too lengthy (*lalisteros*: *Ep.* 30).

To prolixity were added tricks of eloquence, each with a technical term attached, each taught in the schools, and all, of course, figuring in the writings of an *advocatus fisci* or *magister memoriae* deliberately.[30] A letter of investiture to the consulate, sent by Gratian to Ausonius (*Grat. actio* 4), contains some particularly obvious examples—for example, *solvere te dicis quod debeas et adhuc debere quod solveris.*

Affectations and contortions, appearing first in the emperor's edicts, were carried down to a lower level. They were copied for the sake of their author. Provincial bureaucratese, from the very beginning of the third century, and especially in Greek, grows almost unintelligibly obsequious. The agent of a procurator, speaking for his superior, says, "it is pleasing to His Greatness . . ."; a petition to an Egyptian *strategos* begins, "unlawful conduct, my Lord Prefect, is suppressed by none other than Your Worthiness"; and a governor is thanked, who, "by his mere passing-by, by the mere efficacity of his high dignity, recalled our city . . . to splendor."[31] The third century gives birth to the optative protasis of courtesy (delightful term): "if it should meet with the approval of thy most gracious name," "if it should please your goodness" (*sou tei aretei*), "if it should suggest itself" (*ei parastaie*);[32] and to these examples from papyri, others could be added employing rhetorical, even poetical, mannerisms. In one, we have "a thoroughly rhetorical style: antithesis used twice . . . with parallelism carried through, the second time picking up the concluding word of the first phrase in the initial word of the second phrase . . . far-fetched and affected . . . the expression of poetry and exalted prose."[33] Another really poetical circumlocution meaning only that the writer resides in Oxyrhynchus reads, *to ephestion echon en tei lamprai kai lamprotatei Oxyryngchiton polei*, an instance of a practice regular in legal documents, by which residence was indicated not as "NN of New York" but by phrases like *hormomenos apo, oikon en*.[34] A preference can be seen here for the circumvention of the verb: not "I feel" but "it is my feeling;" not "I live" but "my habitation is," and so forth; in Greek, *oikesin echon, phrontis hymin esto*, even *ktenaphairesin hemon epoiesen*, "accomplished the cattle-removal." With this preference went, necessarily, the greater use, or new invention, of abstract nouns coupled to verbs like *didonai, echein, poiein, tithenai, tyngchanein, chresthai*.[35] While this type of expression can be seen in the early Empire, its full development belongs only to the period after Diocletian. It is found as often in Latin as in Greek,[36] and characterizes documents not only issuing from the central government, but those submitted to it by private persons, imagining that such was the only language understood by so incalculable an eminence as the *magister memoriae* or the pretorian prefect. Ordinary little town magistrates wrote this way. Small civil suits were initiated in this style, and its influence can be seen also in private letters.[37]

One use of abstract nouns was especially typical of the late Empire: that applied to officialdom. *Exceptio* = the office of the secretary, *exceptor*; *obsequium* = court or retinue; *officium* (= *taxis*) = official staff members; *proteion* = head official; *potestas* (*exousia*) = holder of authority; and, better known, titles like *claritas* (*lamprotes*), "Your Gravity," "Your Illustrious Authority," "Your Admirable Prudence," "Your Exalted Eminence."[38] The emperor claimed specially for himself a large vocabulary of virtues, used more or less at random in his writings.

But then the emperor was God's agent on earth. "His wishes have the force of law."[39] And to so high a pinnacle of power a form of address particularly reverent, and from such a pinnacle, a form particularly dignified and impressive, seemed only fitting.

Here we enter on a different aspect of the problem of government language: the intercourse between rulers and their subjects. For the good side—that is, showing an effective contact between ruler and subject—there are two kinds of evidence, the first consisting of references, in constitutions and imperial letters, to *petitiones, suggestiones, preces, desideria*, and the like, in answer to which relieving laws were passed. These petitions are not very numerous, though there is no special reason why they should always be mentioned in the legislation which they called forth.[40] The second kind of evidence concerns a handful of orators whose works have survived, and between whose embassies to the capital or published speeches, and subsequent changes in government policy, there is some evident relation. Libanius, to take the outstanding example, enjoyed a close friendship with Julian, which he used to influence the course of government. Symmachus, Synesius, and Themistius had their friends in high places; and all wielded the tremendous prestige of their literary accomplishment (see above, at n. 16). Themistius' oration (Sozomen, *Hist. eccl.* 6.36) "had some effect in mitigating the resentment of the emperor [against non-Arians], and the persecution became in consequence less cruel." There is the difficult question, how often such published speeches were actually delivered to the throne, how often merely circulated to concentrate public opinion; but, leaving doubtful cases aside, enough remains to justify the conclusion that "Libanius and the orators of his time personified, in many occasions, the public conscience," and made it known directly to the throne.[41]

But, against this happy picture of confidence and advice shared between emperor and orators, the latter themselves often testified. Beyond this emphasis laid on the necessity of free access to the throne for all plaintiffs—an emphasis which makes one a little suspicious whether such access really existed[42]—complaints are frequent pointing out the isolation of the throne.

> May you [Arcadius] be able to bear with intercourse of this sort [open and easy], and may your ears not be utterly corrupted by the praises which you are wont to hear. . . . Accordingly, this majesty and the fear of being brought to the level of men by becoming an accustomed sight, causes you to be cloistered and besieged by your very self, seeing very little, hearing very little of those things by which the wisdom of action is accumulated. . . . You have taken to keeping your lairs like lizards, scarcely peeping out at all to enjoy the sun's warmth, lest being men you should be detected as such by men. (Synesius, *De regno* 1 and 10–11)

> Now the emperor, who is shut up in his palace, cannot know the truth. He is forced to know only what these men [his corrupt agents] tell him. (SHA *Aurel.* 43.4)

> [An investigation of corrupt practices in government was frustrated] in the way in which supreme powers are usually deceived among the distractions to which the powerful are liable. (Amm. 28.6.9)

Those who had something to say to the emperor speak with discouragement of the obstacles in their way. They would be sidetracked like the plaintiffs against Count Romanus, with the excuse "that amid the more important and pressing business of the emperor such trivial and superfluous communications could not be read until opportunity offered" (Amm. 29.5.2). Approach to the throne of course lay only through great personages; so Synesius (*Catastasis* 1) says, "since they who wield the scepter of the Romans ought, themselves also, to know this, do you write to whomsoever you may of those empowered to bring a statement before the council of the emperor." But Symmachus, foreseeing trouble from a certain quarter, felt helpless to avert it: "Providence, I hope, may cut off the sad paths of misfortunes by instructing the emperor's sacred ears" (*Ep.* 4.54.2–3). Even so influential a man as Symmachus had to leave the sacred ears to Providence.

What of men and messages, filtered through the faction and chicanery of government, that did eventually reach the emperor? Among set speeches some at least were not only bombast but utter hypocrisy. Julian and Symmachus delivered panegyrics of men they hated, while an envoy redoubling the praises of a praetorian prefect before Valentinian was only by chance discovered as a chief, frightened witness against that prefect's crimes.[43] Speeches not suspect in this way, though still panegyrics, naturally distorted, omitted, and colored the truth very freely, and one tradition should be specially mentioned, by which rhetors, who had already suppressed reference to imperial blunders and defeats, hid also the name of enemies vanquished, under a variety of circumlocutions: "that monster," "the savage beast," "that wicked brigand."[44] Avoiding ill omen or offense, avoiding the subject of the emperor's setbacks, avoiding an easily understood, straightforward explanation of their mission, rhetors hid the truth under a haze of words. It might be thought that, in a less formal occasion than the presentation of an address to the throne, men spoke to the emperor differently; but in fourth-century court life there were no less formal occasions. Surrounded by his closest advisers, within his very council chamber, the emperor remained apart. The sessions were named first the *consistorium* because all must stand in his presence, later the *silentium* (*silention*), because, theoretically at least, his presence imposed a ritual silence.[45]

Besides petitions, speeches, and council meetings addressed to the emperor, there was a final avenue of approach, by pamphlet. Two examples are known, Vegetius' *De re militari* and the *De rebus bellicis* of an unknown author. Phrases from their dedicatory portions are interesting. Vegetius undertakes to speak of arms etc.,

> not, Invincible Emperor, because these matters are unfamiliar to you but that you may know that the measures you yourself take for the security of the realm the founders of the Roman empire formerly observed . . . not so much for your instruction as for your review . . . What could be more presumptuous than to suggest, to the master of the human race, and to the conqueror of all the barbarian races, anything to do with military practice and discipline? (Prefaces to bks. 1 and 2)

The second author writes:

> It will be fitting for the Head of the State to learn of desirable reforms from a private person, as useful measures sometimes escape his inquiries. . . . True, these [suggestions] are not unknown to those closest to Your Clemencies, men harassed by many other cares to which I am a stranger. But preoccupied as they are, many points escape them.[46]

The contortions of the style display some embarrassment, the explanation for which is, of course, the constitutional theory, fostered by flattery, that the emperor is omniscient (yet ignorant), omnipotent (yet his rule must be strengthened). How can one instruct the *divina mens* that foresees the future, how direct the *caelestis nutus* by which the universe is run? How dare to advise? "For the reverence that surrounds [the emperors] rejects observation, even in the vestibule [of the palace], and any who approach that countenance closer are deprived of their sight, its rays cut off, as with eyes which challenge the sun."[47]

The key word, in the preceding pages, is certainly "rhetoric." Lifeless and mechanical drill in the ornaments of speech increasingly dictated how a man should arrange his thought, or create the illusion of a thought, when he sat down to a lease or will, a notice of appointment, a response to a petition, or the drafting of some new law. Among higher civil officials, rhetoric probably flavored private conversation, and certainly flavored what was said in an official capacity, to a colleague in government or to the emperor. The style shows as its chief trait a fondness for upholstered verbiage, in which the meaning is hidden, like a penny in a sofa. Synonyms, especially adjectives, occur in profusion, along with much extraneous material: moralizing, literary allusion, hyperbole, circumlocution. Words are arranged for their rhythmic or poetic effect. Archaisms are popular; new words are coined, especially long ones, and abstract nouns, for example, in *-sis* or *-tio* (Gr. *-sis* or *tes*). The very handwriting of the chancery is of the same quality: florid, archaizing, affected.[48]

In all this, the very object of language—to be understood—was forgotten. One kind of proof is the great difficulty experienced by modern scholars in making out just what an ancient writer was trying to say. It would be easy to give a score of examples of this happening, in comments to Constantine's alleged letters, or to Symmachus or Cassiodorus; or to papyrus texts or imperial edicts. Particularly confusing is the lack of a technical terminology. A half-dozen words may (or then again, may not) mean the same tax, bureau, official, troop unit, or type of document. In the course of use, if one word within such a choice of circumlocutions prevails, it is not necessarily the most obvious or appropriate; and the exchange of words between Latin and Greek (*dephenteusis* [= *defensio*], for example, or *anabolicae species*), though contributing to some technical vocabulary, contributed also to the confusion—witness the errors of translation in Diocletian's edict of prices.[49] People in the fourth century must often have labored through contracts, laws, and so forth, not quite certain that they understood what they were reading or writing; and the fog grew thicker as one moved upward to the more important levels of government. To a provincial governor, the most roundabout courtesies were due. By the time one reached the emperor, it was insulting to be explicit.

The point need not be labored. The machinery of the state was clogged not only by corruption, and red tape, and triplicate copies, but by the nature of governmental language. There is, however, another matter already touched on, the positive value of inflated language. "Rioters shot," becoming "restless elements of the population brought under control," softens the cruelties of dictatorship. Constant assurance that taxes were "happy," paid by mere loyalty (*devotio*) to "the ever-victorious soldiers" of "Our Invincible Emperor," that government payments were "mercies" from "the largesse" of "Our Clemency"—this and similar humbug may actually have made for a more contented realm.

Finally, the effect of bureaucracy, as such, on language. Why do large governments, modern or Roman, favor the same style? The question has, I think, never been studied,[50] yet it is beyond coincidence that so many features of late Latin and late Greek should be familiar today. The answer for Rome must lie in the enormous powers claimed by the government, and in the kind of men and life found within the resulting bureaucracy.[51] The average civil servant, after a kind of trade-school education, found himself the representative of the representative of God. His position called for words like *intributiones* and *primiskrinios*. These strengthened his profession, on the Tacitean principle, *omne ignotum pro magnifico est*; strengthened the sense of belonging, in guild or caste, by being nearly unintelligible to outsiders; strengthened the bureaucracy against its own errors by blurring the edges of responsibility. Abstractions like "Your Magnificence" or "the diligence of the judicial capacity" meant, but did not seem to mean, simply "the prefect" or "the governor." Bureaucratic forms, and the long words and repetitions they called for, could be shrugged from one office to another. And phrases like "if it should appear good," "if it should suggest itself," took away from the urgency of the business.[52] Moreover, most civil servants, as was described, bought their posts and looked on their life in government not as a career but as an investment. Strictly by seniority they inched upward to the more profitable ranks, which, nevertheless, they were allowed to enjoy only for a short time, in order "to keep the procession moving."[53] Unlike a single ruler or politician who, under attack, takes the offensive—"Look at my opponent," or "Look at all the good things I've done"—the posture of bureaucrats was typically passive, since they had more to lose by being outstandingly wrong than to gain by being outstandingly right. The place in the queue, the corporate life, and a defensive mentality all went together, and with it, a final feature of government language: the avoidance of strong verbs, the preference for participles, and (most characteristic) the transfer of the sense of action to an abstract noun: ''Our thinking is,'' ''my habitation is.''

9

SOME PICTURES IN AMMIANUS MARCELLINUS

READERS OF Ammianus are struck by the pattern which certain scenes of greeting follow (21.10.1, etc.), in an author who tries so hard to avoid pattern and repetition: a personage approaches a city; the populace streams out to receive him with torches and flowers; troops and senators cluster around; there are shouts hailing his presence and virtues; and thus accompanied he enters the city gates. From other sources, however, we know that such occasions, through a very long history, had accumulated features which were indeed patterned, which included also details passed over by Ammianus such as chants and incense, and which were advertised to a larger audience in imperial coinage or in inscriptions set up by the local magistrates.[1] It would be interesting to find out how deeply into the society of Ammianus' time the impression of such events penetrated, and whether they were imposed by the rulers of the Dominate from above or whether they satisfied more widespread tastes. They are prominent enough in art, notably in relief sculpture; but most surviving art presents us with emperors, consuls, saints, great patrons. It is natural to attribute to the high position of men like these the qualities so often detected in the works they commissioned: grandiloquence, pose, theatricality, and dramatic richness. The present paper, however, pursues these qualities beyond painting and sculpture, into other forms and customs, and into lower levels of society. Its object is to add the support of some social history to the history of art; its conclusion is that, far from being isolated in the upper classes, fourth-century art reflected with fair accuracy the enthusiasms and tastes of a popular audience.

Architecture, Language, Costume

The first question to ask is whether there was much communication or movement of ideas of any sort up and down through the various layers of society. Ancient authors concentrate on the doings only of the higher classes. They rarely dip below a senatorial level. To this point, indeed, evidence is plentiful. Ammianus fixes a sour stare (14.6. 9–17; 28.4. 8–19) upon those senators who can afford armies of servants mustered in brigades under their officers; upon their carriages, out-riders, and uniforms for the day; upon their rigid receptions and the degrees of condescension offered to the different members of their circle. But in much of this, emperor and noble copied each other. The hem of the senator's mantle that swept the marble floors of Constantine's palace as that senator kissed the imperial purple had lately been kissed by some much humbler client, and if the senator had been ranged among the privileged of the emperor's First Admission, that rank derived from the formalities of Republican levées to which even one's meaner acquaintance were admitted. The aristocracy, at least, could enjoy an elaborate ceremony of which they were themselves the direct heirs, without feeling wholly dependent on some still higher model. They brought it somewhat closer to the common man. From the emperor down at least to a town councillor's petitioners, the same customs were in use.

But of course society, however one divides it for analysis, is not really made up of grades and distinctions, nor are its customs really kept in compartments. Was ceremonious behavior, for example, generally accommodated in an appropriate arrangement of rooms? By way of answer, we find a series unbroken from the emperors' reception halls of Spalato, Piazza Armerina, or Constantinople down through the mansions of rich provincials, and so to the houses of the middle class: all indulge in a showier use of marble; the opening out of public rooms at the expense of bed-chambers and servants' quarters; apsidal recesses to give focus to a room; monumental entrances.[2] The point cannot be pursued here, so far as architecture is concerned, but it can be supported in various other ways. Take the recently discovered panegyric directed apparently by Constantius to one of his praetorian prefects:

> Innate virtue holds this extraordinary advantage for tested and faithful men, that when such a man is constantly on the alert to promote the interests of his emperor and the republic, the glory of the thing weighs as much as the disadvantages of the life itself and besides he is considered to have sought for himself in respect to fame this recognition, that by merit in the service of his emperor he has prospered as a result of industry and hard work. If anyone among all these men remains fixed in our sight and mind—and the felicity of our age has drawn from fortune a great supply of them—Philip would be the outstanding man whom I rightly proclaim our parent and friend.[3]

The self-consciousness, sense of role, and importance which inflate the emperor can be found again and again throughout the period, more fully in the speeches of trained rhetoricians (a good example, keeping to the reign of Constantius, is Julian's *Oration* I.50C–D), less lengthily in the letters of Symmachus, and so to an unknown and ill-educated Egyptian monk, writing in the 330s:

> To the most genuine and most enlightened, most blessed, beloved and in God's keeping and filled with the Holy Ghost and most valued in the sight of the Lord God, Apa Paieou, greeting in our master Jesus Christ. Before all things I pray for prosperity for you with the Lord God. This our letter I wrote on this papyrus that

you might read it with joy and with most secure peace from the Holy Ghost and with cheerfulness in God's keeping and with entertainment of long-suffering filled with the Holy Ghost. To you, then, I write, most genuine and most secure in the sight of the Lord God, Apa Paieou.[4]

To these two lines of illustration, architecture and language, a third may be added: costume. We are fortunate enough to have an early fourth-century procession fresco, showing soldiers, "magistrates, and high functionaries" parading with the emperors, and a mosaic street scene of the next century with people walking about or sitting at tables (Plate 1).[5] Here, too, the styles that one can see in use among the great men of the realm prevailed at a lower level, so far as lesser riches, leisure, and sophistication allowed—many-colored clothing, and the embroidered patches and ribbons to be discussed later—giving to Ammianus' world a homogeneity of which he was himself hardly aware.

But the three features of fourth-century society collected here are chosen not only because they can be traced at several levels, but also because of a characteristic that they share. They may all be said to contain a kind of theatricality. Halls and courts in imperial palaces are deliberately adapted to dramatic appearances—appearances generally of the emperor, from behind a curtain, after the observers have been lined up formally like an audience; or, less often, appearances of consuls or high officers of state, surrounded like their ruler by a bodyguard. The fronts of private villas and the internal arrangements of the better town residences betray a similar purpose, to impress, even at some expense of comfort. A particularly significant liking for that most spectacular achievement, the marble stage-backdrop or *scaenae frons*, grows upon the empire as time goes on, in the first century in frankly ornamental fountains, *nymphaea*, in private homes, or shown in frescoes and mosaics; then as palace facades, by Septimius Severus' reign, and so to the palace architecture

1. Mosaic border from Yakto near Antioch. Antioch Museum

of late antiquity.[6] The advantages of color and drama in curtained doorways are much more fully exploited in the same late period than earlier, especially for churches and the emperor's residence (Plates 2–4).[7] As for the hyperbole of panegyrists, it was of course completely conscious, and completely artificial. This we might suspect from common sense. No man can have deserved the praise that Julian offers to Constantius. Our suspicions might be aroused, too, by the very emphasis so regularly placed on protestations of sincerity. Beyond that, we have Julian himself admitting that "this kind of praise is gravely suspected because of those who misuse it, and is considered base flattery rather than trustworthy testimony of noble deeds."[8] But this being so, we are hard put to imagine the scene of a panegyric. All stood except the target of praise. The rhetor spoke slowly, in a singsong manner, to bring out the rhythm, and with carefully rehearsed gestures, "Uttering platitudes / In stained-glass attitudes." Possibly Julian's mind wandered while Mamertinus addressed to him a text that now spreads over forty pages. And all to what purpose? We can only suppose that the participants in the occasion, quite aware of its falsity, valued themselves for their patience, saw themselves the custodians of an ancient literature, perhaps even savored the skill of the rhetor—but above all, felt themselves part of a *tableau vivant*. We have many monuments to show this, tombstones and mosaics featuring the deceased among the Muses or in the company of Plato and Aristotle.[9] There was a pride in such poses of cultivation.

Another form of address was also popular: acclamation. The custom shades off into its opposite, malediction, into magic spells common in this and earlier periods, into the army's shouts that hailed a man emperor, savior, bringer of prosperity, and the rest. What is common to these is the repetition of a set of words. The origin of the practice can be traced to Hellenistic audiences cheering their favorite actors or jockeys rhythmically;[10] the custom penetrated in the earliest Empire into the meetings of the Roman senate[11] and turns up once more in a session of the town council of Oxyrhynchus.[12] A famous example is the shouts of senators hailing the Theodosian Code: "Augustuses of Augustuses, the greatest of Augustuses [repeated eight times], God gave You to us, God gave You to us [twenty-seven times]. As Roman emperors, pious and felicitous, may You rule for many years [twenty-two times]," etc., etc. We have at a still higher level the words dictated to an emperor by an angel, so he said, and distributed in copies like an actor's script to his soldiers, who obediently called to the Deity, "Greatest God, we beseech you, Holy God, we beseech you, To you we commit all care of justice, To you we commit our salvation, Through you we conquer," etc. [three times repeated].[13]

But the mob shouted like this too, in Rome, Egypt, or Africa: "May the gods keep you!"[14] "Rejoice! May you prosper!" they wrote on their drinking vessels, for their toasts,[15] and "May we conquer" was the cry of the slaves as they entered the master's house in the evening.[16] Pieces of jewelry had accla-

2. Gallus Caesar as consul, copied from a Carolingian manuscript in turn a faithful copy of a fourth-century original (Rome, Bibl. Apost. Vat., MS Barb. Lat. 2154)

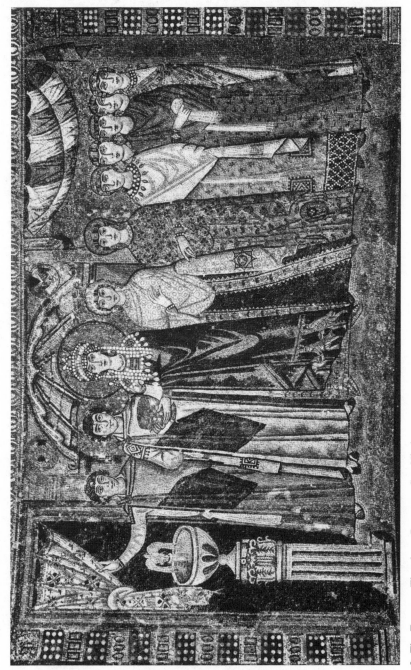

3. The Empress Theodora. Ravenna, San Vitale

4. Tapestry panel, Boston, Museum of Fine Arts

mations inscribed on them: "God save the wearer!"[17] All this testifies to the very wide diffusion of a social practice, in every class and activity. The emphatic cheers, short phrase by short phrase, that greeted a triumphator upon his entrance into Rome greeted the eyes of more ordinary folk as they looked above the lintels of their homes. Language itself had become static and stagy.

The Power of Pomp and Glitter

Yet "static and stagy" fits nothing so well as the imperial entrance, into whatever city. No ceremony was more carefully managed, more contrived and impressive, than the *adventus*. Ammianus' frequent references to *adventus* have been mentioned already, but there is one instance (16.10.2–10) quite well known and worth quoting fully. Constantius approached Rome from Ocriculum

> accompanied by a formidable armed retinue, led in battle formation, . . . in order to show an inordinately long parade, banners stiff with gold, and the splendor of his retainers. [He entered] with the standards preceding him on both sides, he himself seated alone upon a golden car shining with the beauty of precious stones of various kinds, which seemed to hold a light of mingled luster. And behind those that preceded him, many other dragons surrounded him, inwoven with purple, fastened to the gold and jeweled spear tips, with their wide mouths open to the breeze and as if hissing thus aroused with rage, trailing their twisted tails in the wind. And on both sides marched a double line of armed men with shields and crests, shining with a shifting light, clad in gleaming scale mail, and here and there the cavalry in full mail whom they call *clibanarii*, masked, breast-plated, girt with iron belts, whom you might take not for men but for statues polished by the hand of Praxiteles. . . . [As for Constantius himself] he showed himself immobile . . . keeping his gaze straight ahead, nor turned his face to left or right, and like a statue of a man was never seen either nodding when the wheel jolted, nor spitting, nor wiping or rubbing his face or nose, nor moving his hands.

This long passage contains a number of points that deserve discussion. We may begin at the end, with the immobility of the emperors, which they assumed to make more perfect their resemblance to a god, and which was upon need completed by painting their eyes or by adding a wig lest their hair blow.[18] Makeup went back to Oriental monarchy, the motionlessness of the emperor to the rules of the stage: "not to sit down if weary, not to wipe away the sweat save with the robe [the performer] wore, to allow no discharge from nose or mouth to be seen" (Tac., *Ann.* 16.4). Such traditions ended in a curious rapprochement: at the same time that imperial statues were coming to resemble their subjects by being borne about in processions, carried in chariots,

wreathed and hailed and addressed as witnesses to oaths, the emperors themselves copied their own statues. They were increasingly forced into an ideal
impersonal mold, encompassing the whole list of virtues necessary in a ruler,
expressed outwardly in strength of body, in the splendor of their eyes, in their
gait and voice, in the serenity of their behavior. Individual differences tended
to recede in official representations. Once the commissioned artists had caught
the proper character, it was repeated again and again: "The flattened head,
low forehead, the enormous muscles of the jaw, great eyes glassy and placed
somewhat too far apart, the bull neck, short snub nose, beard with stiff short
hair like bristles," recur from one portrait to another, and emperors with a
change only of the title re-used the portraits of their predecessors, even of
pretenders against them, in coins and busts.[19] In all of these, however, nothing
is so striking as their rigidity. Metal or stone seems only to delineate a man
made of the same substance, whose expression is fixed in a show of imper-
turbable omnipotence, and who is addressed as Your Serenity. He could be
complimented on "the gravity of his visage, the tranquillity of his eyes and
countenance."[20] And if he responded to the artistic and philosophic impulses
of his time, he transformed himself into a sort of icon, for display and adoration. He did not even scratch his nose in public.

It is hardly necessary to mention here the quality of frontality, which is
spread so broadly across the arts of late antiquity. Theodora and her party
(Plate 3) typify it. They stand in repose, their gaze set on nothing, their motions frozen, their faces full toward the viewer. So also Stilicho, in Ammianus'
day (Plate 5). What the description in Ammianus allows us to imagine, however, is that men who wished to emphasize their own importance did so
through gestures and poses exactly resembling those of art.

In this period, the fourth century, a more heavily armed kind of elite cavalry
troops was coming to the fore. They wore scale mail, less often chain mail,
covering both man and mount. In parades they frequently added masks,
gilded, silvered, or bronze. These are what Ammianus calls, in the description
just given, *clibanarii*. The word comes from Persia[21] as did this particular
style of armor.[22]

Clibanarii received much attention in the sources, being something really
fantastic and terrifying. Ammianus returns to them in another passage
(25.1.12); a Latin panegyrist (*Pan. vet.*, ed. Galletier, 10[4].22.4), like Claudian (*In Rufin.* 2.357f.), dwells on them; Julian (*Or.*1.37C–D; 2.57C) twice
describes them at length, each time, like Ammianus, emphasizing their simi-
larity to statues. They contributed to parades and martial ceremonies exactly
the quality desired in the emperor himself: dramatic immobility.

Beside *clibanarii* moved troops with resplendent equipment, shields, crests,
mail (Amm. 16.10.8). These too entered Rome with Constantius. While soldiers like the praetorian guards in the earlier Empire might well have matched

5. Stilicho in an ivory diptych. Monza, Cathedral Treasure

the pageantry of these fourth-century ones, the latter attracted a growing attention by their greater number, their exotic splendor, and the contrast they offered to the very shabby soldiers of the regular army. They are prominent in the mind's eye of contemporaries. The commander's helmet, arms, his shield, even his horse, are decorated with gold and precious stones, his bodyguards are agleam "with the splendor of gold and colors,"[23] and wear an increasing weight of jewelry: torques, pendant medallions, rings, bracelets, engraved or stamped with the emperor's image, inscribed "Luck to the bearer," or a gift from the throne.[24] Such ornament answered an obviously barbarian demand for a wealth more intelligible than coins, especially during the third century when the increasing use of troops recruited from beyond the Empire was matched by the increasing adulteration of the coinage to pay them. In the fourth century, sculptured representations of soldiers with elaborate decoration are more often barbarians, and men (not only women) in excavated graves are buried with increasingly rich, and wholly un-Roman, jewelry. The habit of showy costume spread rapidly throughout society, along with Germanic motifs such as the opposed swans' heads on a belt buckle from Rome (Plate 6 and n. 37 below). Even a private citizen's lowest servants wore torques, fancy fibulae, and embroidered tunics.[25] Court fashions were higher. Theodora's attendant wears a big brooch on his left shoulder (Plate 3), of a type that can be studied more closely in a mid-fourth-century fresco from Bulgaria (Plate 7 and n. 25 above), and on Stilicho (Plate 5). Its exact counterparts are recovered by the archeologist in Africa, Switzerland, or elsewhere round the empire.[26] Laws that restricted the use of jeweled fibulae to the emperor suggest some similar implications of rank in slightly less sumptuous examples. At least they were found only on soldiers and officials entitled to wear the heavy cloak (*chlamys*), and *chlamydati* certainly did not include the majority of the emperor's servants.

People who commissioned their portraits naturally wanted their importance to be made evident, just as Rembrandt's sitters wanted the lace to show. Thus fourth-century reliefs, paintings, and mosaics emphasize details of costume and equipment at the expense of form, a fact often noted by critics and sometimes attributed to a contemporary theory that the reality of detail should prevail over the demands of perspective and proportion.[27] But the true explanation is probably more social and psychological than aesthetic.

So a passion for pure display took hold throughout the empire. But there is a curious interpretation laid upon this display, wholly typical of the period and echoed in a Latin rhetor (*Pan. vet.* 10[4].14.3), the Scriptores Historiae Augustae, Julian, and Ammianus. The first writer, describing an army, mentions how "their shields flashed forth something terrifying, and the awful splendor of their heavenly arms gleamed." This is slightly expanded (SHA *Sev. Alex.* 50.3) by the statement that in an army well equipped at all points, well

6. Terminal plate to a belt. Rome, Castellani Coll.

mounted, and so on, an enemy "might recognize the Roman state itself." Julian says more explicitly (*Or.* 1.23C), "the enemy were discountenanced [*ekplettomenoi*] by the close order, splendor, and calm" of the Roman troops. When we come to Ammianus, however, we find no less than seven passages ascribing the alarm of the enemy solely to the brilliant *appearance* of the Roman army.[28] Vegetius adds his support in the view that "the radiance of arms carries the greatest terror to the foe."[29] This is to attribute to something purely external a force that it cannot have possessed. The belief is puzzling. One must interpret it, I think, in terms of the psychology implied in what has already been discussed—in terms of the value placed upon the almost supernatural power supposed to lie behind a pose, a costume, an expression, a set of words. What arms and armor only represent or imply is thought to reach out against the enemy in some effectual fashion. The point I am making will be supported further in the subsequent section on symbolism in uniforms.

7. Tomb fresco, Silistra, Bulgaria

Animal Decoration and Metaphor

Roman soldiers throughout the Empire put their names on their shields, writing them, or punching the letters on some metal part. By this means, according

to Dio, they identified themselves and their exploits in the very midst of battle.[30] If that was indeed their purpose, it was better served by a custom that
developed, at least by the later Empire, of painting shields in some heraldic
way—*diversa signa in scutis pingebant, ut ipsi nominant, digmata*—and perhaps these devices can be detected even in the second century as well as later,
some in thunderbolts looking like a fleur-de-lis, some harder to describe.[31] It
seems probable, however, that most of these designs were adopted for their
own sake, for they are hard to fit into a pattern of actual legionary organization
even as early as the Trajanic and Antonine columns, and are afterward exploited for purely ornamental ends. The taste for such bright decoration was
not Roman, though whether imported from western auxiliary regiments or
from the East is not clear.[32] Shields of the third and fourth centuries unfold
scenes of the sack of Troy or of battles with Amazons (no heraldry here, at
least) or are colored a vivid red, rose, or green, or blue-green with patterns in
yellow and red, or borders of alternating red, white, and orange, or black and
gold.[33] Some are shown in the mosaic from Piazza Armerina (Plate 8). They
contribute richly to that splendor of armament thought to terrify the enemy.

On some shields were painted opposed goats' heads, giving their name to
the soldiers of these units, *Cornuti*. They were especially favored by the em-

8. Mosaic hunt scene, Piazza Armerina

perors from Constantine on, prominent and envied. Another unit which appears first in the fourth century bore the name, "The Lions," *clipeoque . . . teste Leones.*[34] The two together declare the popularity of animal symbolism among the western barbarian troops, both being called after their shield device. A. von Domaszewski pointed out that animal insignia in the earlier imperial army are almost all derived from the signs of the zodiac, chosen through horoscopy to represent important dates in the legions' history.[35] Favorite types are the Bull, Ram, Capricorn, and Lion; the ram and the griffin (sacred to Apollo, hence *leg. XV Apollinaris*?) appear on helmets in the Antonine column. The griffin is the more easily explained by the eastern home of the legion, and so also, in the third century, is the raising of units' animal signs from a lower place on the legionary standard to the very tip, a development "reflecting the spread of forms of worship from the Orient, in which animal cults had their true home."[36] Later, however, apotropaic animal symbolism comes in through Celtic and Germanic influences.[37]

In writers from Homer on, animals are used in comparisons, for the sake of vividness. Warriors are likened to lions, for instance; mythology affords a fairly complete bestiary from which further comparisons can be drawn. In the largely derivative literature of Ammianus' time, such classical comparisons are fairly frequent and fairly easy to detect, along with vaguer references to men who are "beasts" or "monsters"—*beluae, theria,* or the like.[38] Beyond these, late writers draw in a variety not found earlier, and use them with increasing freshness and effectiveness. In Claudian we find, beside the ordinary classicizing metaphors, others that involve an assortment of monkeys, boars, ostriches, and dogs.[39] Ammianus has a still larger collection: bulls, vultures, kites, lions, dogs, which he uses sometimes in extended similes, always with vigor.[40] If we look for the source of the images that come to his mind, we may assume a certain amount of borrowing, from the elder Pliny or the *Georgics*; a certain amount of ordinary observation of country life; but beyond these, a third source as well, belonging especially to the Roman world, that is, the amphitheater. Often he compares men to "wild beasts with tusks, in their cages" under the stage (19.6.4), to "the beasts of the amphitheater" (15.5.23; 28.1.10; 29.1.27; 31.8.9), "like a beast in a hunting show" (*venatio*, 30.1.15)—very much as Claudian (*In Rufin.* 2.394f.) refers to an enemy, in about the same period, "as a beast who has lately left his native mountains and, torn from the high forests, is doomed to the shows of the arena." Scholars are sometimes so scholarly that they forget the obvious, the things that came instantly to the common mind when in search of a phrase to convey excitement, ferocity, color, or danger. The Romans not only spent more public money on their amphitheaters than on anything else—it is usual to find a provincial city putting one up even before its public baths, and sometimes before it could really afford either—but when they could not actually attend a performance, they gawked at the placards in the street advertising the next day's show[41] or solaced themselves in their own homes with scenes of *venationes* and combats between animals, extremely common in frescoes and mosaics. They had a robust taste for blood. Valentinian kept two pet bears in cages by his bedroom, which he playfully called Goldflake and Innocence (Amm. 29.3.9), and a private citizen specified his favorites, Cruel and Mankiller, written over portraits of bears.[42] These theatrical scenes and gaudy paintings certainly must have made a profound impression on Ammianus and his contemporaries, and help especially to account for comparisons of people with rare animals like monkeys and ostriches.

The largest number of Ammianus' animal metaphors concern snakes, serpents, and dragons: an enemy is "like an underground serpent lurking below the hidden entrance of its hole," or "like a viper swelling with its store of poison."[43] It is tempting to find the inspiration for this in, or somehow connected with, the dragon standards which we have already seen accompanying Constantius on his tour of Rome. A closely similar passage, to which we will return a second time below, is Themistius' *Oration* 1.1–2:

> Most admirers see [not the emperor's soul but see] rather, and sing in their discourses, things such as the expanse of the realm, the number of subjects, the invincible regiments of infantry and the troops of cavalry and the great wealth of their equipment and the insuperable screens of weapons and the dragons on the delicate banners, raised high on gilded shafts, filled and shaken by the breeze. The more elegant of those speakers come a little nearer to yourself and lay hold of your crown and your gleaming robe, your strong girdle and tunic.

Here we meet again the same parade device that struck Ammianus, the dragon banner. By his day it was a familiar sight in the army. Introduced originally from the east,[44] it appears in many eastern writers: Theodoret, Claudian, Eusebius, and others (but in the Spaniard Prudentius as well).[45] Eusebius in a rather well-known passage describes how Constantine

> caused to be painted on a lofty tablet and set up in the front of the portico of his palace, so as to be visible to all eyes, a representation of the salutary sign [the cross] placed in the painting above his head, and below it [Licinius] . . . under the form of a dragon falling headlong into the abyss. For the sacred oracles in the books of God's prophets have described him as a dragon and a crooked serpent, and for this reason the emperor thus publicly displayed a painting of the dragon, stricken through with a dart, beneath his own and his children's feet.[46]

The image recalls one closely similar but far more ancient and widely diffused, that in which some hero on horseback spears a wild beast. In such a posture Claudian imagines Stilicho's son (*De cons. Stilichonis* 2.350f.) portrayed in gold in a panel of an embroidered cloak (cf. the *togae pictae*, below, p. 99). Scenes of exactly this kind survive in Coptic textiles, as in ivory reliefs, frescoes, and mosaics. The Coptic examples lead us to the suggestion that there was a symbolic aspect to the hunter's triumph, clear not only in the Babylonian and Assyrian kings' trampling upon their enemies, but, more abstractly, in the victory of Good over Evil. Strzygowski brings forward a work of Egyptian art, Horus depicted on his horse spearing a crocodile.[47] An Egyptian already quoted more than once, Claudian (*In Rufin.* pr.15f.), compares the murdered Rufinus to a poisonous, coiling serpent. "Now that second Python has been killed by the weapons of our master . . . who preserved the world unshaken for the brother emperors [Arcadius and Honorius] and held sway in peace with justice, in war with energy." But Good victorious over Evil, the one mounted, the other wriggling below, meets us in crudely carved magical amulets from Asia Minor, from Syria, and from Egypt, demonstrating the prevalence of the image in the common mind.[48] So do other animals, not only dragons but lions, boars, stags, representing vices or enemies, these being interpreted by both pagan and Christian in an abstract way, in an age devoted to symbolism. Their appeal especially to a popular audience has been emphasized.[49] Finally, the serpent in particular as the embodiment of Evil enters the literature of the fourth century through a source uniquely influential, the Bible, which offers a host of texts and images that fill the authors of east and west, not only with such hunt motifs as have been mentioned, but with other situations and metaphors also.[50] Constantine (to return to his "lofty tablet") was thus indulging in no recondite imagery. He as well as rulers after him continued to triumph over some dragon—Paganism, Pretender, or whatever—in their coins and official art, with the confidence that they would be understood.[51] The painting that offered Licinius in the guise of "a crooked serpent . . . stricken through with a dart" spoke to everyone in the most universal and intelligible language.

Perhaps Ammianus remembered this conspicuous allegory when he searched for terms of special force to describe a creature of evil. Perhaps the army dragons came to his mind, billowing sinuously in silk. Perhaps instead a man who had spent some years with the military carried over into his writing other animal emblems in use among the troops, filled out by pictures of the beasts in the amphitheater. In all these possibilities, however, are found new, non-classical sources of vividness, whether appearing in bronze standards, paintings, literary metaphors, or dragon banners.

Banners were borne by late Roman guilds as they marched in parades.[52] An orator of Autun tells us how the townsfolk went to meet the emperor: "We bore forth the *signa* of all the guilds, the statues of all our gods, with some very few instruments of brilliant sounds, reappearing on [Constantine's] path several times by the use of shortcuts."[53] The use of brass bands to lend a pleasing emphasis to the emperor's *adventus* was borrowed by his servants, among whom the more important took a trumpeter with them on their official rounds of the provinces, as Ammianus tells us.[54] There are in addition several proofs of musicians attached to the army for entertainment as well as for the usual issuing of orders to attack or retreat;[55] and trumpet-players and organists were popular in theater shows;[56] so we are once more uncertain whether Ammianus drew his horn metaphors from his army years, from the amphitheater, or from *adventus* parades. It is nevertheless striking how often he employs musical instruments in a metaphorical sense: "Those people who were powerful in the court thus blew the horns of civil discord," "the trumpets of internal slaughter sounded," etc.[57]

Symbolism in Uniforms

Themistius' and Ammianus' descriptions as well as texts quoted in the notes (nn. 23 and 52) stress the glitter of the *adventus*, the silk, the gold and silver and steel, the jewels. To glitter was joined color. Of this, one source has been mentioned, soldiers' shields. Their uniforms also became, as time went on, brighter and brighter, more and more variegated—*auro colorumque micantia claritudine* as Ammianus says (31.10.14), in a passage reinforced by the long lists of "part-silk garments with Girba purple, one undervest with Moorish purple," handed out to soldiers upon promotion (SHA *Claudius* 14.8). Such lists abound in the Augustan Histories. When we turn to surviving representations of soldiers, we find those of the first century generally clad in grey or white uniforms, whereas later ones are much gayer. But a Dura painting of the second half of the first century presents a divine figure wearing a red cloak bordered in gold with a black design on it, fastened at the right shoulder by a gold fibula, with a shield and corselet (evidently a soldier). His tunic is red.[58] Scenes on shields from the same city a century later show Trojan warriors in obviously unhistorical dress, wearing blue cloaks, brown tunics, and trousers.[59] *Segmenta*, that is, patches with embroidered pictures or designs on them, sewn to cloaks, also appear early, in Antioch,[60] and again in the early fourth century on soldiers with red tunics and the regulation red belt fastened with a dangling ribbon at the right hip.[61] These scraps of evidence, scanty but consistent with what will be said later about civilian clothes, seem to point to the eastern provinces as the home of the more cheerful costumes which ultimately spread over the empire, in a growing variety of special corps.[62]

Three points are worth making about soldiers' uniforms of the later Empire. In the first place, they reflected a barbarization, or more accurately, an un-Romanization, of the army. The general process is too familiar to need discussion. It affected the size of troop units, formations of attack, war cries, armor with corps of specialists in one type of weapon or another; it affected army slang, army worships, even the rites by which armies chose their emperors. So far as costume is concerned, soldiers' jewelry and animal emblems have already been mentioned in passing, and we may add other items: for example, trousers. These were worn both in the east and west, and in auxiliary regiments of Gauls, Sarmatians, or Osrhoenians. By the late fourth century they were so prevalent that Romans had to be recalled to their traditional toga by a law.[63] But by the same route—through native recruits—cylindrical little hats of Illyrian origin (Plate 8), a longer, sleeved tunic called the Dalmatic from its provenience (Plates 4, 5, and 7), and a kind of short German cloak, all entered into frequent use.[64] These innovations and others besides caused people in the more Romanized provinces at first to stare, later to imitate. "I myself," says Eusebius (*Vita Const.* 4.7), "have sometimes stood near the entrance to the imperial palace and observed a noticeable array of barbarians drawn up, differing from each other in costume and decorations. . . . All these in turn, like some painted pageant, presented to the emperor those gifts which their own nation valued, some offering crowns of gold, others diadems set with precious stones, some bringing fair-haired boys, others barbaric vestments embroidered with gold and flowers."

This brings us to the second point: the love of display through dress. Here too, little need be said where so much has been said before, especially by Alföldi. The Romans started with a purple cloak for a triumphator. In Marcus Aurelius' day it was still possible for the emperor himself, if he chose, "to live in a palace without wanting either guards or embroidered costumes, or torches and statues, and suchlike show" (*Meditations* 1.17). By Ammianus' day, what with red shirts, blue mantles, red leggings and belts, and even colored caps, white itself was sought out for distinction, and embroidered *segmenta* were superadded in all hues.[65] Showy garments were so much valued that they became almost a kind of currency, given out as pay to soldiers; offered by envoys to the emperor, as in the above quotation from Eusebius; more often offered by the emperor to envoys.[66]

But this value (for our third point) derived from the connotation of rank and power that belonged to rich clothing. Some items such as gems sewn to shoes had been long reserved to rulers, according to Hellenistic practice. Fourth-century rulers aimed the charge of treason against anyone who usurped an article of dress from a lengthening list of imperial prerogatives. Purple was the most famous. Diocletian officially equated the Birthday of the Purple, *natalis purpurae*, with the anniversary of his accession, thereby proving the abstracting tendencies of the times as well as the position of the imperial color;[67] but to the influence of such examples radiating from the throne, a second powerful influence was added by the army, in which ranks were indicated by different types or shades of dress[68] and on which the civilian bureaucracy modeled itself.[69] All this indeed fitted the innate sense of caste of which the Romans are often accused. The striped tunics of their senators and equestrians had been envied, and the sash (*limus*) of their public slaves had been despised, as far back as the era of the Republic. Though stripes were later very widely usurped, they seem to have raised the wearer at least above the laboring classes, and their significance, and that of the long Dalmatic robe, the embroidered mantle, and other parts of dress, established ranks in the Church also (as the next paragraphs will show). Among soldiers and civilians, laymen and clerics, importance thus expressed itself in a man's outward appearance.

This was quite openly acknowledged by contemporaries. One could tell the ruler by his "declaring the august title of supreme authority in the notable form of his vesture"—a statement which may stand for a number of similar ones spread over the period of the Empire, and which finds much earlier echoes in Hellenistic practices.[70] The ceremonial surrounding kingship was, in fact, precocious. It was complete, or nearly complete, even before the Romans had an emperor. Not till the fourth century do we find the inner spirit applied more widely. We have already discussed Ammianus' view that soldiers *ought* to wear a brilliant uniform because it somehow realized their will to conquer. The same sense of the fitness of a costume explains Salvian's saying (*Governance of God* 4.7), "When a man changes his garments he immediately changes his rank." Fourth-century legislation is filled with words and phrases which show how the insignia of a position, notably the *cingulum* but also the consular *toga picta* (Plate 2) and the chlamys, were unconsciously equated with the position itself (e.g., *Cod. Theod.* 6.10.3) and the Code goes on to forbid the usurpation of the *cingulum* etc., without letters patent, even to enjoin the wearing of certain clothes by certain people: togas by senators and lawyers, for instance.[71] The next step was to substitute the uniform for its wearer's rank, in common speech. This was done in the laws and in Ammianus: *togati* = lawyers, *palliati* = philosophers.[72] But that last word, which came to mean "pope" from the pope's *pallium*, reminds us how the Church adopted secular customs and expressed them in its own way. Salvian may be quoted a second time, here speaking to clerics: "Although you pretend religion by your clothes, although you proclaim faith by your cincture, although you feign holiness by your cloak, you do not believe at all" (*Adv. avarit.* 4.5). A longer text from Sozomenus is more remarkable:

> It is said that the other vestments of these [third-century] Egyptian monks referred to some secret of their philosophy, and did not differ from those of others by chance only. They wore tunics without sleeves, in order to teach that the hands should not be ready for any presumptuous act. They wore a covering on their heads called a cowl, to show that they ought to live with the same purity and innocence as infants who are nourished with milk. . . . Their girdle and a kind of scarf, the one around the loins, the other around the shoulders and arms, admonish them that they ought to be always ready in the service and work of God.[73]

It is not easy to understand a way of looking at things so alien to our own day. The difficulty may excuse the rather full citing of the passages in which Ammianus' contemporaries set down their thoughts most explicitly. What is apparent is their conviction that for one's role, one should dress the part. An emperor should look like an emperor and should be identifiable by his shoes alone or by the hem of his mantle; a soldier should distinguish himself visibly from his officers, and they from their commander-in-chief; chamberlains should not dress like lawyers, nor lawyers like consuls, nor consuls like monks or bishops. From each person might be expected, instead, a declaration of what he did in the world.

For these points support may be found in a great body of works of late antique portraiture. They pay less attention to plasticity and individuality in order to focus on the insignia of a role, with laborious exactitude (Plates 2 and 3). In so doing, they demonstrate a dominating harmony of tastes that could be demonstrated as well in twenty other ways: in the glitter of advent parades (for one example) corresponding to the gold leaf and precious stones that, in this period, begin to flash in the background or frames of portraits. Artists and emperors, and the emperors' subjects of all ranks and callings, join in the enjoyment of the same fashions.

A peculiar and puzzling outgrowth of these fashions is the wearing of badges. Apparently the earliest known among the Romans were sewn to the robes of Salian priests.[74] In eastern provinces over the first three centuries they display mythological scenes or warriors or *venationes*.[75] These early figured embroideries are, so far as I can discover, very rare, and it is not until the fourth century that their use spreads. We then see, in surviving pieces of clothing from Syria and Egypt or from Egypt by way of Switzerland (!), such designs as birds in blue and green; human and animal figures in red and yellow; floating putti in violet on yellow; a hunter in black and white; hunt scenes; crowned Erotes; and a white-on-black warrior standing over a lion and hare.[76] In the same period, continuing with even greater popularity into Byzantine times, appear embroidered portraits of the emperor or empress, of private individuals, and above all, of Biblical figures: Mary and John, Christ with nimbus, the Annunciation, the meeting of Mary and Elizabeth, sometimes identified with titles: IOSEPH, MAXARIOY.[77] Christian or pagan symbols are also common,[78] and others indicate degrees of rank.[79] Among various examples should be mentioned the Magi on the hem of Theodora's dress, in the Ravenna mosaic (Plate 3), the eight figures to be counted on the toga of Gallus as consul (Plate 2),[80] and, less often noticed, the reliefs even upon the terminal plates of belts (Plate 6).[81] Ammianus (14.6.9) mentions tunics "figured in different threads with the shapes of animals of many types," and other writers confirm our knowledge of sewn patches showing men and women.[82] One reference in the Augustan Histories may give a clue to the meaning of some of these badges. We read of the family of Macrinus that they carried their admiration of Alexander the Great so far as to have his portrait woven into their clothing, *ut tunicae et limbi et paenulae matronales in familia eius hodieque sint quae Alexandri effigiem de liciis variantibus monstrent*.[83] Alexander had become, when this was written—*hodie*, "even today"—a figure of pagan polemic, and those who wore his face on their clothing were perhaps asserting their loyalties. This is certainly true of the parading of the emperor's face, and of a variety of Christian scenes and symbols. The patches, then, identified the wearer more completely and explicitly than the cut and color of what he wore.

Under the term badges I have included the round, oval, or square bits of cloth fastened on tunics and mantles (*segmenta*) and the vertical strips on tunics running from shoulder to mid-chest, to waist, or to hem (*clavi*). Not all had figures on them; far more usual, in fact, were those showing some abstract design.[84] Similar designs appeared also on the collars, sleeves, cuffs, and hems of tunics. Since these were worked in a riot of color, they can indicate nothing more complicated than that love of display already described as typical of the late Empire. Decorative *segmenta* and *clavi* (not the red stripes of Roman knights) turn up sporadically in the east, in Hellenistic times,[85] rise to a wide popularity in the late third century, and are often attested even in the west in the fourth.[86] They belong to a still more general development which quite transformed styles of dress from a narrow preference for local garments, dyed in a low key or left the natural color of the wool or linen, into an eclectic enjoyment of many imported garments colored in the highest key and with the greatest possible variety. One might guess as much from the price edict of 301 alone. The sections dealing with dyes, garments, and textiles specify the products of six tribes (Treveri, Atrebates, etc.), thirteen cities (Poetovio, Mutina, Tarentum, the rest eastern), and seventeen provinces, from Britain to Arabia. At Cologne, Soissons, Halicarnassus, Rome, and Thabarca (Tunisia) one could see in mosaics the same range of choice in clothing, with the same favorite items, that prevailed in Syria or Egypt.[87]

Plates 1–4 and 7–9 illustrate what people wore. Most of these speak for themselves. A few details may be noted: that on servants we can indeed see *segmenta*, yet smaller than those on their masters (see the chlamys held up, Plate 7, and the spectator in rich dress in the Piazza Armerina mosaic, Plate 8, whether he be a great senator or Maximian himself)—rank determines decoration; or that gladiators were got up as splendidly as emperors (Plate 9). There is a useful hint here. Some fashions may have begun, or at least reached the west, in the amphitheater—perhaps *braccae*, even in Septimius Severus' reign "common at Rome, particularly for charioteers and heralds";[88] perhaps costly clothing in general, which Cyprian and Tertullian attest for the theater.[89] A procession of heralds in a Severan mosaic from Rome already shows the *clavi* on their tunics and sets them before a background that is, or resembles, a *scaenae frons*;[90] still another Severan mosaic shows a herald in yellow cloak with black fibula and decorated cuffs on his tunic, plus two swastika *segmenta* at mid-thigh. A second figure sports a costume, and a shield, equally colorful. The green and yellow curtains above them, and the architectural background, suggest a theatrical setting.[91]

Since late Roman costume is so obscure a subject, and since so much of the material is relatively recent, it has seemed worthwhile to gather a good deal

9. Mosaic from Torre Nuova (detail). Rome, Borghese Gallery

of the evidence in the plates and footnotes to this section. It should be emphasized to begin with that the developments of the later Empire were very striking. Had Cicero, had so late a figure as Marcus Aurelius, stepped into Ammianus' world, what certainly would have made him stare the most would
have been people's clothing: children in red tunics, riders on horses decorated
with silver plates and fancy harness in black and red, magistrates in long jeweled chlamydes, some wearing the red leather belt of imperial service—all
these as mosaics portray them with wonderful detail, in the new realism of the
period. The outer garment most often seen is a mantle pulled over both shoulders or held by a fibula at one shoulder. *Segmenta* often mark the shoulders as
well as the two lower corners in the front, sometimes together with embroidered edges down the front. Underneath, perhaps with no mantle at all, is a
tunic. Its short sleeves—common in the early Empire—are, except for the
costume of children or for heavy exercise, gradually replaced by long sleeves
from Severan times on, and are cut fuller in the fourth century. Its hem drops
lower, from knee finally down to ankle; and *segmenta* get bigger, up to five
inches across in surviving fourth- and fifth-century examples, three times that
size on the "magistrates and high functionaries" of the Luxor frescoes (above,
n. 5). They also become more common: earlier only two near the hem, at
about mid-thigh (later lower down, with the longer style of tunic) framed in a
deep ornamental border along the lower hem, and joined by bands of brocade
at the wrist and even down the arm. Another band runs round the collar, set

off at each corner (the shoulders) by a second pair of *segmenta*. *Clavi* become fashionable. Above all, color is accented in both mantles and tunics. It covers a spectrum of red, violet, crimson, pink, orange, yellow, ocher, brown, tan, blue, green, white, black, and gray, up to six in one piece of clothing: yellow, purple, blue, green, tan, white; and many other assertive contrasts are sought out, especially in *clavi*. A modern scholar, Forrer, speaks of the *Farbenpracht* and *Farbenliebe* of the times, attributable to the eastern shift of the empire's center; more vivid, we have an anonymous Egyptian's order to his tailors, "let them be large-handed in the coloring" (P. Oxy.1069). On top of all this, we must remember the wholly un-Roman garments such as trousers, high leggings, little capes or big cloaks with hoods, which ultimately relegated the toga to a purely symbolic use as a kind of gigantic scarf; and the greater luxury of textiles and embroidery, extracting an understatement from Ammianus: "The lavish use of silks and the arts of weaving had increased" (22.4.5).

Ammianus (14.6.9 and elsewhere) is scornful of excessive finery; a churchman ridicules the sumptuous dress of another bishop (Euseb., *H. E.* 7.30); but further attacks on mere show concentrate on that obvious target, the emperor. Several grounds of criticism can be detected. First and most common is the feeling that an elaborate costume came from the east and somehow brought with it a hated softness of spirit in the subject, a hated despotism in the ruler.[92] This line of thought, incidentally illustrating once more the tendency of the times to attribute reality to symbols, was countered by an appeal to that same tendency: a less extravagant ceremony around the emperor would diminish the awe which the monarchy aroused among the masses.[93] Somewhat similar is the view implied in Ammianus' ridicule of the pretender Procopius, who, amid other embarrassments in getting his revolt started, had to appear before the troops in some obviously makeshift regalia, "so you might think him a splendidly decorated figure [*simulacrum*] or comic puppet suddenly popped up through the curtain on the theatrical stage" (Amm. 26.6.15). What Ammianus is making fun of is not so much the regalia as its wearer. A better man, like Julian, could put a soldier's torque on his head and make it look like a crown. A more profound uneasiness meets us in a passage of Themistius quoted above (p. 93). He seems to be saying, a little obliquely, that all the pomp around the emperor is just that—pomp—and what counts is the man's inner qualities. An old, standard view, this, embodied in a Stoic emperor. There are further echoes in a set piece spoken by Eusebius. The good emperor "when he beholds the military service of his subjects, the vast numbers of his armies, the multitude of horse and foot . . . feels no pride at the possession of such mighty power, but turns his thoughts inward on himself and recognizes there the nature common to everyone. He smiles at his vesture gold-embroidered with flowers of many colors, at the imperial purple and the diadem, when he sees the multitude stare trembling, looking at the apparition like children at a spook."[94] It is not easy to imagine Constantine smiling at anything about himself; not easy, indeed, to imagine Eusebius giving up his episcopal finery for a monk's cowl. His statement, and those of Themistius, Ammianus, Symmachus, and Socrates, are chiefly valuable in showing that contemporaries had given conscious thought to the meaning of the ceremonies that filled their world.

Dramatic Exaggeration

One final scene from Eusebius (*Vita Const.* 3.10). Constantine enters the sessions of Nicaea "like some heavenly messenger of God, clothed in raiment which glittered as it were with rays of light, reflecting the glowing radiance of a purple robe, and adorned with the brilliant splendor of gold and precious stones. Such was the external appearance of his person; and with regard to his soul, it was evident that he was distinguished by his piety and godly fear. This was indicated by his downcast eyes, the blush of his countenance, and his gait. For the rest of his form, he surpassed all present in height of stature," etc., etc. Certainly Constantine may have been and seemed all these things—but I doubt it. Set against the formality of acclamations of *adventus*, of the throne's *allocutiones* to the troops, this Nicene picture is suspiciously perfect. The vaulted chamber is too high, the bishops rise in too close a unison upon the emperor's entrance, and he arranges his jeweled person too humbly upon a little stool. He is in fact playing the part of a modest moderator to his audience. It is an act from a play.

And against the behavior of Constantine, whose mildness is so much paraded, we must set his shout (*Cod. Theod.* 1.16.7), "The greedy hands of the civil secretaries shall immediately forbear, they shall forbear, I say; for if after due warning they do not cease, they shall be cut off by the sword." Or a second law of his (*Cod. Theod.* 9.24.1) that for parents accessory to the seduction of their daughter "the penalty shall be that the mouth and throat of those who offered inducement to evil shall be closed by pouring in molten lead." There is a didactic symbolism, a kind of dramatic appropriateness, in these barbaric explosions, found again in other incidents: the groom's hand that fails the emperor as he tries to mount his horse is to be hewn away; if a bureaucrat's fingers have signed false documents, their tendons are to be cut, lying tongues shall be torn out; the seller of "smoke" (*fumum* = false promises) shall be suffocated over a slow fire.[95] Theatrical edification is expected as much from the Deity as from earthly powers. "By the just judgment of God Himself, Valens was burned alive by the very men who, through his action, will burn hereafter for their heresy."[96] And a tyrant or a heresiarch, Elagabalus or Arius, dies fittingly in a latrine off the Constantinopolitan forum, others by the most incredible diseases, hardly fit to be described.[97] We may turn in bewilderment from these thoughts and scenes and laws, from heterodox enemies smitten by horrible effluxions, by worms, by insanity, back to our earlier pictures of the emperor. What has become of his *Clementia*, the most common of all his titles in the Codes? Or of his Gentleness?[98] Is the immobile Constantius of the Roman *adventus* the same who, "beyond a usual degree of indignation, blazed up, regarding them [the envoys] with sidelong glances till they feared for their lives . . . burning with anger" (Amm. 20.9.2–3)? What of similar outbursts of insane ferocity, with the emperor falling dead from apoplexy, or rendered speechless, or banging his head against the walls?[99] Is it the embodiment of *Tranquillitas* who bursts into tears at the pitiful pleas of his subjects (*Paneg. vet.* 8[5].9.5–6; cf. 7[6].8.3)? The answers to these questions must surely lie in the general customs of the fourth century. *All* emotions appropriate to a scene must be fully expressed, violently, assertively, publicly. Exaggerated grief, exaggerated calm, the flush of modesty or of rage, should be equally evident. This is the age of Theodosius' open penance at Milan, of Galerius' humiliation, running a mile on foot at the side of his senior colleague's chariot.

It would be interesting to know how the *gravitas* of the old Roman came to be so utterly changed. There is no easy answer. One influence may well have come from barbarians in the army, often rising to high positions, even to the throne. Their anger at least was freely vented, in brawling, by war cries, by raging or grinding their teeth or by banging their shields. All this is referred to in the sources, but its range is limited.

Another line of explanation is suggested by the comparisons frequently drawn in late antiquity between real events and events on the stage. Some illustrations in the writings of Ammianus (above, p. 101) and Eusebius (above, p. 96) have been given in passing. These and a number of others demonstrate how quickly the stage came to a writer's mind when he sought to make his story vivid. So a battle unfolded itself "like some theatrical show, the curtains revealing many wonders" (Amm. 16.12.57). The intrigues and investigations of courtiers are dramas (*fabulae*) seen when the curtains are drawn apart (28.6.29); people disappear from history "at the drop of the curtain" (16.6.3). Orosius (*Hist. libri sept.* 7.26) and Eusebius (*Treatise on Philostratus' Life of Apollonius* 42) also turn to the stage for metaphors, while Constantius and Athanasius attack each other with the same image, the emperor in a letter (Athanas., *Apol. ad Const.* 633B) accusing his unruly subject of drumming up sympathy "the way people in dramas recite their woes to the first comer," Athanasius (*Hist. Arian.* 52) asserting that a council "exactly resembles what one might see on the stage, being shown as a comedy by them [the Arians], the bishops like actors, Constantius like their servant." [Julian (*Or.* 8.244; 7.217 and 221) likes similar metaphors.] When we find Procopius the pretender popping up from behind a curtain, in Ammianus 26.6.15, and actual emperors or their more important agents in their offices appearing to a crowd by the same fashion,[100] we seem to have a direct link between a real theatricality and a borrowed one, which may very well have extended itself to ranting and raging, to violent open grief, or to the other instances of dramatic conduct collected above.

Though the link is not easy to establish, several further hints may help. We know the Romans' fondness for pantomime, broad gesture, and caricatured masks. Their audiences must have grown accustomed thus to the exaggerated expressions that later lent themselves to symbolic use. We know, too, that acclamations copied rhythmic applause first practiced by theater claques; that some fashions of rich dress are likely to have originated among players, heralds, and gladiators. We know the keen interest in spectacles throughout the Empire, growing to frenzy in Constantinople of the Byzantine era. The theater, then, did touch many late antique images, motifs, and manners.

Still a third comparison lies between dramatic poses and a fondness for paintings with a message, for occasional paintings reminding people of anything from a circus to a consul's accession. While these were not likely to survive, while their style must often be deduced from their mosaic imitations, there are references to prove that imperial portraits were widely distributed,[101] that emperors commissioned works to show their exploits in battle,[102] and that political and religious loyalties were allegorized. Examples have been mentioned already. If an emperor was attacked, the vile pretender was pilloried in a painting under the guise of a dragon. Pagans flaunted a badge of Alexander the Great, and the heroes of the Church stood forward in one or the other of the two forms which most appealed to popular taste, as "soldiers of Christ," with a rapidly developing language of symbolism, or as "athletes of Christ." The latter personification was certainly surprising. Christians were supposed to have nothing to do with the arena, and the Fathers scowled upon attendance at it. St. Augustine's strictures are the best known. When it came to decorating a shrine, however, the artist was expected to show the eponymous martyr in the most appropriate dress, perhaps a philosopher's cloak, present in the ring with, but really against, his captors and judge, while above sat the figure of Christ as "umpire."[103] A sort of billboard brightness thus served the uses of propaganda, Christian, pagan, or imperial. Such paintings revealed the power of popular art. It is not rare to find these clearly before an author who is describing some important moment: an acclamation hailing a man as emperor, fit subject for "a painting worthy of the ages, a scene worthy of our times" (Symm., *Or.* 3.5), or a gathering of foreign envoys before the palace "like some painted pageant" (Euseb., *Vita Const.* 4.7).

Conclusion

Here then are Ammianus or his contemporaries comparing real scenes to works of art, in color or (above, p. 86) in stone and bronze—the more naturally since the artist of the same period so often draws his inspiration (or at least his commission) from particular events: from the magistrate's appointment, from the rich citizen's gift of a hundred stags to a *venatio*, or from the emperor's victories over his enemies. Occasional art, of course, tends to be didactic. It aims not at pleasing so much as at inculcating an idea, generally political or religious (above, pp. 93–94 and 97–98). Often the idea is very simply that the principal figure is doing something wonderful, stands for something important, in which case his importance will be suitably set off. An arch or a drawn curtain will frame him, soldiers or listeners surround him, and some other person will be shown suppliant or vanquished. His own figure will be larger and more impressively costumed. Hence the care taken in even so really crude a work as the porphyry Tetrarchs of St. Mark's, to show their belts of office inlaid with jewels, the rich fibulae holding their mantles, the eagles' heads on their sword pommels, and the decorated scabbards. Details of this kind are indeed only symbols; but symbols—cross, star, human or animal heads—appear also on real costumes. Even splendor quite by itself is symbolic. Is this why it is emphasized in the Ravenna mosaics (Plate 3); or do they reveal only the same straining for color found in Syrian or Sicilian mosaics (Plate 8) and again in surviving fragments of mantles and tunics of the period?

Questions of art and social history become inextricably mixed. The unity of culture is in fact all I am trying to illustrate, as has been done many times for other periods. The flat poses of an ivory diptych (Plate 5) surmounted perhaps by some phrase of good wishes, differ hardly at all from the positions taken up by the actors in living pageants of acclamation or the like, shouting or even chanting in unison, "Long life to you," "May you conquer." The disposition of people in the late Empire to arrange themselves in *tableaux vivants* is most striking, and finds closest parallels in the fifteenth century. Whether people welcome a personage with torches and flowers, or greet him as he emerges upon a balcony; whether they play Socrates to a philosophic circle and commemorate the pose on a grave relief, or equip themselves with a brass band and guild banners for parades, the joy of an occasion is evident. They declare their roles in the most aggressive hues, augmented by jewelry and by varieties of garments; in statuesque immobility, the limbs, hands, and features arranged just so; or in public outbursts of emotion.

These cultural developments, much as they connect and mingle with each other, have nothing to do with "classical" culture. They represent the upthrust of non-Greek and non-Roman elements through an upper surface worn thin. The point is familiar, and too large to discuss here, but it can be conveniently illustrated by returning to the subject of metaphors in Ammianus. Among these, as has been said, we find statues, paintings, theater scenes, animals, and the bray of trumpets. They are not new, but the emphasis on them is his own, and non-classical. His commentators notice also that his vocabulary and metaphors agree together in giving a glimpse into the common mind, so far as it could break loose from the tyranny of classical example, and confirmation lies in the habits of other authors. Where they have any colloquial sources to draw on—that is, Christian sources—they choose such similes as occur also in Ammianus. So one can follow dragons from Revelations to Eusebius (and Ammianus), into imperial placards, and into the banners of the army; but when one turns from Eusebius to Mamertinus, from Lactantius to Symmachus or Julian, one finds the old commonplaces: the ruler a pilot, the warrior a lion. Literature of the late Empire joins with the other arts in revealing a partial vulgarization, a partial turning from stale imitations, laboriously mastered, to a richer source of images in popular culture. A movement like this cannot be hidden. Rodenwaldt saw it; more recently, and with more delicate definition, Bianchi Bandinelli, who attributes it particularly to the insurgent creativity of Christians, and to the lifetime of Constantine.[104] Surely this is a view too limited, in its basis as in its conclusions. The whole of this paper has been meant to prove the wider prevalence of a change of taste, in which an eclectic enjoyment of whatever might make men stare, from whatever province derived, took hold of the empire. In this change, the east, the army, and the theater were the principal contributors, the whole population the sharers. We can return to the first question of this paper equipped with a fuller answer. What struck the imagination of the man in the street was the ancient equivalent of today's royal marriage or bull-fight, and his delight in such vivid moments worked its way up even into the sophisticated circles of Ammianus.

10

CONSTANTINE AND THE MIRACULOUS

ONE DAY saw Constantine a pagan, the next a Christian, all thanks to the vision of a refulgent cross burning above him. So runs the familiar story. But told in this manner, apparently lacking precedent or preparation or context, it challenges belief. Readers of Lactantius or Eusebius, more alert than those historians themselves to the course of events they trace, now point to many gradual steps by which the emperor actually changed his public adherence from old gods to new, bringing his empire with him. They point, moreover, to bridges of thought touching both paganism and Christianity by which men like Constantine could pass from one to the other without need violently to repudiate their earlier worships and without need of any miraculous or magical act from on high. In fact, acts of the latter sort themselves constituted a part of the bridge, and it is on them that the following pages will focus, with citation of as many authors of Constantine's whole lifetime as are pertinent. It is the spread and prevalence of ideas as much as their content that will concern us.

Constantine's cross, a model for several similar appearances later, evidently served the credulity of his times. Such a sign was to meet the Caesar Gallus at Antioch as he entered that city, "a cruciform pillar in the sky" visible to other spectators as well, and Constantius, about to engage Magnentius in battle, was not only favored with the same miracle but the citizens of Jerusalem attested its simultaneous appearance in the East stretching from the Mount of Calvary as far as the Mount of Olives. To the pious emperor it brought victory, to Magnentius' troops terror, "because they worshipped demons."[1]

Constantius' reign witnessed divine intervention on another front. Persians beleaguered Nisibis where, among the Roman defenders, the holy bishop James of Antioch sent up his entreaties for aid. In response a kingly figure ablaze with crown and purple robe stood out upon the battlements, in whom the Persians recognized the Christian God; and James, himself mounting next, cursed the enemy with hordes of gnats that attacked their horses and elephants, putting them all to flight.[2] Plagues of stinging insects first fell at Moses' command on Egypt; more recent ones were known, attributed to divine anger;[3] and the efficacy of prayer in battle was to recur also, as that which Theodosius uttered against Eugenius in 393, raising a mighty wind to blow the rebels' missiles back in their faces.[4] In so many ways did the incidents at Nisibis build on themes which were the common property of Christians in that period, just as the story of Theodosius and Eugenius likewise could be counted on to remind its audience of a storm they all had heard about, the famous storm that saved the "Thundering Legion" under Marcus Aurelius when Germans and Sarmatians beset his army. For this miracle, in an altogether typical contention over events certainly historical (confirmed by Marcus Aurelius' sculptured Column as well as by his coin issues), Christians credited their fellows, pagans turned for explanation to a wonder-worker of the time, one Julianus, or to an Egyptian magician, Arnouphis, who "had summoned by enchantment certain demons, above all, Hermes the aerial, and through them had brought on the rainstorm."[5]

But the figure of God himself threatening Persians from the walls of Nisibis was more spectacular than these deluges and winds. Parallels are thus correspondingly rare. An early glimpse into the popular mind is offered by the *Acta Andreae* of the last quarter of the second century. It relates how the saint and his companions, "proceeding through Thrace, met a troop of armed men who made as if to fall on them. Andrew made the sign of the cross against them and prayed that they might be made powerless. A bright angel touched their swords and they all fell down."[6] Eusebius later (*Vita Const.* 2.6) tells of detachments of Constantine's forces—where none really were, hence miraculous troops—marching through eastern cities on the eve of the battle with Licinius, sent "by a divine and superior power." Two other examples are found in Socrates' *Ecclesiastical History* (6.6, 7.18): "multitudes of angels . . . like armored soldiers of great stature" who vanquished Gainas; "the angels from God [who] appeared to people in Bithynia . . . [and] said they were sent as arbiters over the war." Better yet is the "demonic apparition" drawn by Eusebius from Josephus (*H. E.* 3.8.5; Joseph. *B. J.* 290f.): "before sunset in the air throughout the country chariots and regiments [were seen] flying through the clouds and encircling the cities." Among pagan writers, on the other hand, such miraculous beings play a smaller part. A woman of gigantic form turns up in Dio Cassius' pages almost as a genre figure. Dio asserts his personal belief in her, whether in the scene of Drusus crossing the Elbe or upon the crisis of Macrinus' reign in 217.[7] Herodian (8.3.8) goes further. The occasion as he describes it is the closing in of Maximinus' legions on Aquileia in 238. To the townspeople "certain oracles were given that the deity of the region would grant them victory. They call him Belis, worship him mightily, and identify him with Apollo. His image, some of Maximinus' troops reported, often appeared in the skies fighting in defense of the city"—which returns us to Constantine.

For that susceptible emperor had *two* visions, not only of a cross but (somewhat less well known if hardly less debated by scholars) an earlier one of Apollo. It came to him on his way north to the Rhine after defeating Maximian in Marseilles. He turned aside en route to a temple of Apollo, "whom you saw, I believe, O Constantine—your Apollo accompanied by Victory holding out laureled crowns to you each of which brought the presage of thirty years [of rule]. . . . And yet why do I say, 'I believe'? You saw and you recognized yourself in the form to which . . . the reigns of all the world were destined'' (*Paneg. vet.* 7[6].21.3–5). "You saw," presumably as others by the score had seen some deity invoked by magic or freely offering himself to them, and as, in later embroidered versions, Constantine's second vision was explained to him personally by Christ.[8] Superhuman beings, then, who revealed themselves to their worshippers before armed conflict or whose agents or powers were exerted for the battalions of the pious were a feature of pagan as of Christian mythology in the third and fourth centuries; and no better illustration of this common ground can be found than the spiritual career of Constantine between 310 and 312.

His panegyrists noted elements throughout his rise and reign beyond mere mortal reach. Sometimes such notice was blurred and vague, for example, in the emphasis of Nazarius on Constantine's "celestial favor," the victims "divinely granted to your arms," "the divinity accustomed to forward your undertakings," and so forth—expressions shading off into ambiguities common among both pagan and Christian writers.[9] So victory comes to Valentinian *magni numinis adiumento*, Julian's armies feel confident *caelestis dei favore . . . freti*, spurred on by *salutaris quidam genius praesens*.[10] More often the notices of Constantine's protector are explicit, as in the paragraphs devoted by Eusebius (*H. E.* 10.8.6–9) to proving his hero God's representative on earth.

With Constantine, indeed, the sense that men, especially leaders of state, acted as servants of some supernal purpose and thus played their roles under its direction, took firm hold on the minds of contemporaries, as was bound to come about from the ascendance of so historically oriented a religion as Christianity. The view, destined long to prevail, was new to the Roman world. It left faint traces in the Augustan History, where a favorite of pagan polemic, the emperor Marcus Aurelius, was imagined Stoically receiving news of a pretender's revolt in the certainty that *di me tuentur, dis pietas mea . . . cordi est*. "We have not so worshipped the gods nor so lived that he should overcome us."[11] On the other hand, the acts of Christian emperors were frequently hailed as approved, inspired, intended, or made possible by God. God (says a writer addressing Constantine's sons) has bestowed the *imperium*, the *vexillum fidei; vobis hoc divinitas reservavit. Favore eminentis dei victores estis omnium hostium vestrorum. . . . Strati sunt adversantium cunei, et rebellantia ante conspectum vestrum semper arma ceciderunt. . . . Haec vobis deus summus . . . pro fide vestra reddidit praemia.* And if this be a view no doubt deeply colored by the established supremacy of Christian rulers in whom the devout would wish to see the workings of Providence, we may yet match it with the statement of an Alexandrian bishop a century earlier, for whom God "entrusted the monarchy to the most pious Valerian and Gallienus," whose reign he prays him to uphold.[12] So late as the fourth century, moreover, vestiges survived of a belief in guardian angels set over each people, giving to them their worships, languages, and separate characters and, beyond that, controlling their destiny through their own high or low position in God's favor. Angels might sometimes exert their power on the battlefield.[13]

Upon his conversion, Constantine entered into this whole heritage of beliefs—the belief that a pious people would receive divine protection, that their ruler ruled according to divine plan, and that God directly or through his angels could be expected to intercede in their behalf at crucial moments. Thus, to Maxentius' fateful collision with Constantine at the Milvian Bridge, "God Himself as with chains dragged the tyrant far away from the [safety of Rome's] gates."[14]

The question how pagans looked on the position of the Roman emperors vis-à-vis the gods has been surprisingly little studied, despite a mass of material.[15] It is fortunately tangential to our purpose. Two points only need be made. In the first place, the idea of national guardian angels, though familiar to writers like Celsus, Porphyry, Iamblichus, and Julian,[16] did not lead to a concept of supernatural intervention in terrestrial happenings; nor (in the second place) did the concept of the ruler favored or even chosen by the gods develop further into the expectation that they would miraculously succor him in the hour of national crisis. Not until challenged by Christianity did pagans give any sharpness to their claims that their own piety could secure the safety of the state or the victorious outcome of a campaign.[17] In Constantine's lifetime, a change can be seen. In the transition to an era of far more intense and vaunting religious propaganda, the battle of the Milvian Bridge was critical. Thereafter, through the conflicts involving Licinius and Maximin and so to the historic conversion of Clovis in the following century, battle was determined, so men said, by divine judgment.

But to return to Constantine: newly converted, he advanced into Italy in 312. His decision to make war, his march, his feelings and motives, all receive a characteristic treatment at the hands of spokesmen for the Church. But they make the meaning of the march clearer by their description of his opponent, who, we are told, huddles in Rome gripped by terror, vice, and superstition, dupe to countless religious charlatans, petitioner to countless vain spirits, convert to such revolting measures as the tearing of unborn babes from the womb for use in prognostic sacrifices. Though the picture of his *superstitiosa maleficia* is a compendium of commonplaces,[18] it sets the stage for the dramatic collision of the two religious worlds. This is the significance felt by historians of the battle of the Milvian Bridge. The old world failed, whatever devices were desperately attempted; the new conquered, in the first campaign of a century's religious strife.

This strife was carried on not merely by men but by supernatural forces too. If the Sibylline books, demons, priests, and the rest deceived Maxentius, it is at any rate they who fought as well as he; and their enemy was not the western emperor but the Savior's sign. The sign may then have been the *chrisma* and only in later battles the cross—more likely, at the Milvian Bridge as through-out the rest of Constantine's career, the cross.[19] Its cherished use in war, its invariable efficacy whether on armor or on the *labarum* and whether to protect emperor or humble standard-bearer, set it above all other forces;[20] yet the re-lation between the *labarum* and the traditional Roman *vexillum* is obvious,[21] while the painting of a declaratory or magical device on the shields of one's troops had earlier close parallels.[22] Even the tales of the defensive properties of the cross in combat are matched by the inscriptions found on pieces of military equipment from the centuries just before Constantine, reading "Luck to the bearer" or "Best and Greatest, save the corps of all our soldiers"; Mars or Victory might be depicted on armor.[23] Such evidence shows us the well-worn paths that Constantine trod when, according to the ancient arts of apotro-paic magic though with a different device, he put the insignia of Christianity in the hands of his followers.

On the history of those insignia there is no need for much discussion. Their potency to tear demons from their lairs in statues, to uproot them from un-happy maniacs, to drive them forever from shrines and temples to the accom-paniment of their anguished howls and supplications—all this is attested in dozens of accounts of Christ's cross or name in the service of the faithful.[24] So mighty was the weapon that Constantine aimed at Maxentius' weaker gods. But Constantine extended its use. His mother Helena sent him a piece of the true cross. "When he received it, confident that the city in which it was kept would be preserved forever, he hid it in a statue of himself standing in the so-called Forum of Constantine in Constantinople, on a large porphyry col-umn"—thereby producing the Christian equivalent of those images of the pa-gan gods that, both earlier and later, deflected enemies' attacks. They guarded Nero against conspiracies, Ephesus against plagues, Athens against earth-quakes, Rome against sedition.[25]

Constantine's actions fitted the times. Apotropaic magic to ward off disease was on the increase. Lucky stones with mystic signs and spells on them grew more popular in the third and fourth centuries than ever before, evidently among both Christians and pagans, since the synods of Ancyra (under Con-stantine) and of Laodicea (between 341 and 381) spoke out against "those who foretell the future and follow the customs of the heathen, or introduce persons into their houses to find out magical remedies or to perform purifica-tions," or against priests who "shall not be magicians or enchanters or astrol-ogers or make so-called phylacteries [amulets] . . . and those who wear them we order to be expelled from the Church."[26]

Eusebius tells the tale of Caesarea in Palestine where once lived the woman whom Christ cured of an issue of blood. At the gates of her house stood two statues which he himself had seen, one of a woman praying, the other of a man resembling Jesus. At the base of the latter grew a curious herb able to "cure diseases of all kinds." To this wonder we must add the power of the true cross that Helena discovered to heal the sick: thus, two illustrations of the workings of *Christus medicus*, in opposition especially to the authority enjoyed by Asclepius.[27] But it was, after all, essential for the Church to present its founder as a God of deeds equal to the performances of pagan deities, since, particularly for a mass audience, proof through miracles offered an infinitely more persuasive appeal than the type of argument carried on in written form. Simple people wanted simple proof of the superior ability of Christianity to do for them what older worships had always promised: that is, to defend them from the ills of this earth. The dreams granted at Asclepieia taught suppliants how to be healed. Could Christ or his holy men do as much? And if the answer was yes, in scores of wonders wrought especially by monks, there remained the more general affliction of epidemic disease. Throughout antiquity men attributed plagues to divine anger. A persistent conviction blamed their onset on the progress of Christianity and the resulting neglect of pagan cults.[28] It was a heavy charge variously answered; but one response as it was ultimately framed in pious myth said that even in averting disease Christians had access to a more greatly beneficent power than pagan wonder-workers.

With a few exceptions—Eusebius was one—Christians, like pagans, acknowledged the supernatural origin of plagues, as they did of other bodily ills which they could not understand. Ailments afflicting (in grotesquely disgusting descriptions) especially the intestines and genitals marked the victim as the target of a god's, or of God's, wrath; the genre is well known and meets us most often in the heated religious atmosphere of the fourth century.[29] Manic fits likewise called more for the exorcist than the doctor, and Christians claimed to possess the requisite skills more than their opponents. Palladius and Sozomen supply an abundance of case histories. It was the same with other mysterious catastrophes: sterility of the fields, insect pests, hail, drought, earthquakes, storms. Great winds, said Maximin Daia, were controlled by the gods,[30] and could be turned on or off by their favor or displeasure. Jealous courtiers of Constantine accused the influential wise man Sopater of having "chained the winds" that were to bring the grain fleet to the capital; whereupon the emperor, evidently convinced that the man was actually capable of the necessary enchantments, executed him.[31]

Believing that natural phenomena, from earthquakes to the wasting of the flesh, were in fact all supernatural, people of the later Empire saw in their afflictions a working out of divine conflicts on a terrestrial plane or stage. Pagans accused Christians of causing these conflicts and their resultant sufferings. In the Apologists the echoes of such accusations—*popularia verba*, said Arnobius—are plainly heard; individual instances of persecution breaking out in the train and, because of the typical interpretation, of droughts and earthquakes are fairly often recorded. It was thought that droughts and the like might be deliberately inflicted in response to invocation or upon people hateful to the gods, though it was still more usually argued that the protectors of cities and nations had been neglected, and had for this reason departed.[32] The sum total of the later Empire's ill-fortunes could thus, to Zosimus, appear to follow from the abandonment of ancestral cults and rites. He singles out for his criticism the decision of Constantine not to hold the *ludi saeculares*, in order that he may strike a blow at that hero of the Church.[33]

Here, then, is another part of the background to the battle of the Milvian Bridge: terrestrial events of a striking, public character were thought to result from supernatural intercession whether spontaneous or invoked. It was neither improper nor uncommon for Christians to give credence to happenings of this order, and it was frowned on only if it degenerated to the private practice of magic. Pagans of course enjoyed a wider latitude in superstition, without, however, any fundamentally different views.

To understand a further aspect of the collision between Maxentius and Constantine, some discussion of demons is needed. The term, in Greek or by adoption in Latin, had the broadest meaning. Pagan philosophers used it to designate, between the crass material of mankind and the etherial realm of pure intellect, the denizens of an intermediate world who served as agents and emissaries from the higher to the lower and (conducting the souls of the dead and the prayers of the living) from the lower to the higher. These denizens had ranks according to their insubstantiality and intellectuality, the purer ones sometimes called angels but often not differentiated under a separate category. They linked men to gods. Foreign as was most of this hierarchy of intermediaries to classical Greek thought, it can be seen developing in the second century and went virtually unquestioned in the later Empire. Its roots lay partly in a substratum of popular superstition, partly in Oriental religions.[34] To mention only points of interest to our present purpose: it was demons who occasioned earthquakes, pests, and so forth; they again who brought oracles from the gods and cured the sick; sometimes, too, harmed men when called on with the proper enchantments. Outstanding minds of late antiquity, Porphyry and Libanius, were quite sure that magic could be enlisted in the cause of personal vendettas—though the pure in spirit were beyond the reach of demons.[35] The more evil among demons longed to gorge themselves on sacrifices, to experience sexual intercourse vicariously through the bodies of the possessed, and to deceive with false revelations.[36] Sometimes demons dwelt in cult images; they would not appear in impure places and shunned a hostile presence.[37] To different ones among them different temples, even different zones or, more specifically, nations and peoples, had been assigned for oversight,[38] and they occasionally took visible human shape to meddle directly in the course of events.[39] According to a particularly common conviction, the Devil—*ho misokalos*—or his agents continually worked against the progress or unity of the Church by spreading false doctrines, libels, suspicions against Christians, and the like. Infected with these diabolical errors, heretics and persecutors became mere instruments of a wickedness from beyond.[40]

Strange views, perhaps. But as a darkness of irrationality thickened over the declining centuries of the Roman empire, superstition blacked out the clearer lights of religion, wizards masqueraded as philosophers, and the fears of the masses took hold on those who passed for educated and enlightened.[41] From the same world, reflecting of necessity the same ideas because surrounded by them in all social classes, rose the leaders of the Church. Thus all of the opinions about demons (by that specific term, *daemon* or *daimon*) just now reviewed as representing the consensus of pagan thought also reigned as orthodoxy among Christians like Origen, Lactantius, Eusebius, Basil, Gregory, and many others,[42] though with this major difference, that the intermediaries between mortal and divine were conceived of as good and bad angels, the latter being equated (under the name "demons") with the pagan gods. It hardly occurred to Christians to deny the whole infinite list of the older deities; only as many as possible were traced back to men as heroes, according to the traditional teachings of Euhemerism, while those that could not be talked out of existence in this fashion were left to deceive men with false visions, false cures, false oracles, and insidious intrusions of shameful lust. This last trial especially will be recalled by readers of Athanasius' *Vita S. Antoni.* Anthony declared himself the target of temptation by beautiful succubi some of whom, it is permissible to imagine, were simply pious peasant girls coming to venerate the saint. The mistake, at any rate, is once attested of a bishop of Constantius' time, spending the night at an inn. A woman entered in the dark, the bishop asked, "Who's there?" and hearing her voice concluded she was a demon in female form. "Straightway he called on Christ the Savior to help him."[43] The instinctive assumption that unearthly forces were at work tells us much about the spirit of the age.

Priests forbidden by the Council of Laodicea to engage in magical practices are joined by the clients of charlatans in Basil's congregation; together they and their like form the audience for one of the charges most frequently (surely, because most credibly) launched by Christians at their fellows, heretics or schismatics or simply personal foes, namely, the charges of attempted sorcery. It is irrelevant that these were no doubt often untrue; the fact remains that they were believed.[44] They could be launched, moreover, at more ambitious targets, and used in polemics of a yet graver importance. When enemies of the Church competitively inflated the reputation of that renowned wonderworker of the first century, Apollonius of Tyana, Christians could dismiss him, too, as a mere "magician"; in reply, the term was turned against Christ, lowering him to the rank of *magus*.[45] Could pagan miracles truly equal those wrought by Christ? A didactic tract pointed to his raising of the dead to life, whereas heathen wizards could only boast that *magicis carminibus non mortuorum sed daemonum spiritus evocari.*

The atmosphere of contentious comparison, the tendency to prove the superiority of one's faith by matching its miraculous powers with another's, emerged suddenly from books to the stage of real events in Constantine's life-time. The conditions making this possible were all present. What was required was a conviction that powers accessible to men through invocation, and will-ing to intervene in tangible forms and happenings—moreover, powers poten-tially hostile to each other—filled the universe. It was necessary, too, that such a conviction should be held by the great mass of people, as was indeed the case. Our sketch so far, relying more on anecdotes than analysis, has been intended to reveal society shot through at all levels with the colors of a grosser superstition, with cruder expectations of the supernatural than one could find in the Empire at its height.

The consequences appeared first in the origins of the Great Persecution, of which Constantine, incidentally, was a witness. As Diocletian was assisting in the ceremony of *extispicium*, Christians in his retinue crossed themselves, "by which act the demons were put to flight and the ritual disturbed." The chief priest explained why the entrails refused to yield their prophetic mes-sage, whereupon the emperor flew into a rage at those guilty of the distur-bance. The incident is well known; but not so often emphasized is the concep-tion of demonic conflict that lay behind Lactantius' account: one superhuman power could drive away another, magic worked only in the absence of inimical forces. Evidence for those views has been gathered above.[46] After Lactantius, Church historians multiplied imitations of the story, sometimes by retrojec-tion: for example, "The teacher and arch-priest of Egyptian magicians per-suaded him [Valerian] to get rid of them [Christians], bidding him kill and drive away the pure and holy men as being enemies and preventers of his foul and disgusting spells (for they are and were able, by being present and by watching and by simply breathing on them and speaking, to scatter the plots of baneful demons)."[47] Until the end of Eusebius' century and even beyond, though with diminishing report, the noise of battle was to sound as it were contrapuntally between Christians and pagans on earth, and between their gods invisible in shrines, in the heavens, in the nether regions, and in men's minds—a battle, however, in which the combatants struggled with identical weapons of attack and on the same field of ideas.

Men who controlled gods, great wonder-workers, launched their superhu-man agents or allies against their rivals, in duels more fit for a Greek novella; yet they were recounted in sober prose. Witness the vision of a certain perse-cutor of pagan wise men, one Festus, in which he saw a former victim "throw-ing a noose around his [Festus'] neck and dragging him down to Hades. . . . As he came out [of the temple in which the vision came to him], his feet slipped under him and he fell on his back and lay speechless there. He was borne away immediately and died, and this seemed to be an outstanding work of Providence (*pronoia*)."[48] We need change only the proportions of the story, from two individuals to two causes and armies, to have the prelude to the battle of the Milvian Bridge. On the one side is Constantine with his vision, his prayers, his divine support, his miraculous symbol borne before his troops; on the other is Maxentius busied with "certain unspeakable invocations to demons and deterrents of war,"[49] vain, as it turns out, and powerless against the mightier arsenal of Christianity.

How much in the scene can be credited? Were our whole basis of understanding the pages of Eusebius alone, we might, like Burckhardt a hundred years ago, replace the supernatural elements with others more easily acceptable to a modern mind. Anachronistic rationalism, however, only misleads; the interpretation suggested by more recent scholars, notably Alföldi, is surely right. In the light of the beliefs surveyed in the foregoing pages, we must suppose that Constantine's contemporaries (why not himself, then?) did in truth fear antagonistic wizardry, did put their faith in supernatural aid to be exerted visibly on the very field of battle, accepted without skepticism the powers claimed both for Maxentius' sacrifices and for the symbol of the cross, and looked on the whole struggle of old against new religion as being greater than, but no different in kind from, the operation of magicians' spells and counter-spells.

DISTRUST OF THE MIND IN THE FOURTH CENTURY

INTELLECTUAL DECLINE in the later empire is ordinarily demonstrated by a negative: there is no competent handbook on surveying or architecture, no encyclopedia of natural history, no Hyginus, Vitruvius, or elder Pliny; Galen in the second and Plotinus in the third century find no match in the fourth; no geographer competes with Strabo, no traveling antiquarian with Pausanias, no legist with Paul or Ulpian. The comparative survey returns a bleak report from almost any province of thought to which it is directed. But something more can be attempted. It is the aim of the present paper, reaching beyond the *argumentum e silentio*, to discover a positive hostility toward the life of the mind.

The search has something contradictory about it; for never in Roman history was a higher value set on men of intellectual attainments. Society, from diminishing resources, still lavished its gifts on them: endowed professorships, just as in the earlier Empire, or immunity from every civic obligation. The foremost among them became true celebrities, rising into consular circles, welcomed into some rich country house, honored with thanks in a provincial city's senate chamber, portrayed in bronze in its forum, applauded in its theater. Fame at court, even political power, rewarded tutors to princes: Exsuperius, Lactantius, Themistius, Ausonius, of whom the last-named found government positions in turn for his in-laws, uncles, nephews, and cousins under Gratian. Others like them, for the same reason—for the glory accorded to a career of letters—rose to great heights in other reigns. Many of the authors whose works survive from the period attained a consulship, a governorship, or the administration of some central bureau: Symmachus, Paulinus of Nola, St. Ambrose, Aurelius Victor, Macrobius, Pacatus, Festus, Eutropius, Himerius, Claudius Mamertinus, Rutilius Namatianus.[1] It is an imposing list. And the Church, while emphasizing somewhat different qualities, nevertheless demanded the same cultural eminence. Lactantius, Arnobius, Synesius, St. Basil, Gregory of Nyssa, and St. Augustine all began their rise as rhetoricians; others again—Arius, for example—studied with the foremost teachers.

Meanwhile, from the schools, issued a steady stream of young men lacking perhaps the ability to make so distinguished a place for themselves as the names just reviewed, but marked by their still rare and valuable training for posts in administrative bureaus, *litterarum gratia et magisterii*, "thanks to their knowledge of literature, and as teachers."[2] Around the inner core of the learned, and of learning pursued as a profession, gathered admirers whose devotion was none the less sincere for being shared with other occupations, who embraced cultivation as an inheritance from generations of ancestors, or as a vocation.[3]

Emperors themselves felt an obligation to encourage learning. A few were famous for energetic generosity and discrimination in this regard, most notably Julian;[4] but others also from whom we would expect little or nothing: Constantine, by no means an intellectual yet patron even to pagans, if they enjoyed sufficient renown in the academic world.[5] Among his successors, Constantius received praise for his "literary taste to the point of elegance";[6] Valentinian won a mixed assessment; Theodosius, approval for his interest if not for his taste in cultivated studies.[7] Even Valens befriended an author— Festus (*Brev.* 1 and 15).

Our sources, deriving from the intellectual elite, place a predictable emphasis on any emperor's attainments in their own field of endeavor; he is, to an absurd degree, judged as good or bad on exactly this basis; so, too, his court, officials, generals and commanders.[8] The long-established distinction between a civilian career and that of a *vir militaris* had, by the fourth century, deepened to a gulf. As we would expect, army chiefs lacked the refinements of civilians. But even in the army, men like Ammianus could be found,[9] and, as he tells us (18.6.18), when there was need for secret messages in time of war, an unmistakably bookish code was devised which substituted the names "Greek" for "Roman," "Hadrian" for "Antoninus," and "Granicus" and "Rhyndacus" for "Tigris" and "Anzaba." To be sure, this could only be deciphered "with great difficulty" by the officers for whom it was intended.

The picture so far sketched is of course perfectly familiar to students of the fourth century. It is a picture of a Mandarin society, as it has been called—by no means a new growth, rather a heightened form of tendencies already manifest in the earlier empire. One would assume, if no further shading remained to be added, that the fourth century must have been a time of cultural renascence. That, it was not, as everyone knows. A darker side remains to be filled in.

Higher studies of all kinds languished; fewer schools existed; audiences for recitations and displays of learning shrank; technical disciplines lost their apprentices; less was known, less was written and read, less was thought out afresh. Realizing the decline, the authorities multiplied remedial measures, offering subventions to students, founding institutions of learning, and extending a well-advertised patronage to talented individuals. Such efforts nevertheless proved sometimes vain, sometimes transitory. Professors were denied the friendship of officials; "crowds of young men formerly around them," as Libanius says about rhetoricians, "seeing this, flee literary studies as ineffective, to seek some other skill." Even under Julian, provincial governors knew no more than how to read and write, if that, and government clerks could not spell.[10] Illiteracy prevailed among municipal senators.[11] The legal profession sheltered the semi-educated, a fact not only noted by contemporaries but reflected throughout official documents in the contorted bombast that inflates them.[12]

For this sorry state of affairs, people could find only the emperor to blame, whichever one was thought to have set an example of boorish ignorance or actively to have sought a lowering of the empire's civilization. Inadequate as the explanation must seem, there is no denying that, at the very beginning of the fourth century and with increasing frequency as time went on, the throne was first occupied and then quickly surrounded by persons of little culture—by Diocletian and the colleagues whom he promoted, or by Valentinian and a fresh infusion of Pannonians. They brought with them the attitudes and limitations characteristic of less-developed towns, provinces, and ways of life—in brief (as one writer puts it), "of the camp and the country"; and the court so early as Constantine's reign, and more and more obviously as time went on, also contained honored and prominent men of barbarian extraction, ordinarily as high army officers, to whom the tradition of cultivated generals like Caesar was utterly alien.[13] Few processes in the later empire are more important than its militarization and "rustification." Those who suffered under the change noted the relative backwardness of the army type (above, n. 7); they continued (as throughout antiquity) to use the word "rustic" to indicate clumsiness and lack of refinement and education.[14] Still, to the camp and the country more and more frequently could be traced the origins of a new aristocracy, of a patron class that shaped the aspirations of society.

Two tendencies of the fourth century are not only detectable but, I think, attributable to these nouveaux arrivés: a distrust of what they thought was impractical, and what they thought was downright dangerous, in traditional higher learning.

First, a word about impracticality. Romans, though they put themselves to school with the Greeks, did so with typical selectivity. From Republican times onward, the full range of Hellenic and Hellenistic interests was narrowed in transmission to a curriculum in appearance broad but in actuality centered on letters, as (in successive stages, for successively older students) grammar, poetry, and rhetoric, to which other subjects served as mere tributaries.[15] Philosophy alone retained some standing—of which we will have more to say. The decline in scientific and technical studies is of course evident in itself, partly through their rarity, partly through the dependence of later writers upon their predecessors. Late antiquity was an age of handbooks and epitomes, of derivation from authorities long, long since departed—almost forgotten in the Latin west, dimly understood in the Greek east. Occasionally contemporaries made explicit their sense of decline. In Ammianus' description of Alexandria and of the great scholars of its past, such as Aristarchus and Herodian in grammar, Ammonius Saccas, and so forth, a note of despair sounds in a single *nunc quidem*: "The various disciplines," he says, "are not silent in that city *even now*."[16] Though he goes on (22.16.18) to instance the medical researches flourishing there, yet in the same period enlightened persons, we know, were willing to adopt the cures suggested by superstition, alleging that "the vulgar sometimes know more than the learned"; and the use of amulets and assorted hocus pocus against disease was taken for granted in all circles.[17]

The cult of letters alone retained great vitality. It does not at first sight seem to meet the requirement of practicality. No one can browse through the literature of the fourth century without being struck by its extreme preciosity, its exquisite or merely tedious uselessness. Surely the epistolary style of Symmachus, or the subjects of concern to Macrobius, are as far from real life as one could get; and what could less deserve the attention of a busy emperor than the versified cross-word puzzles of Optatianus Porphyrius? Yet the enthusiasms of such writers were very widely shared. Suitably diluted for younger minds, they filled the schools, while, at a higher level, university training perpetuated the idiocies of long ago—demanding of students a speech on the topic, "Epictetus is accused of impiety for denying providence," or offering for their imitation such conceits as "The contamination of adultery was dared with artful ruse, and the wretched lad evilly induced, by inebriation through the cursed cup, against his mother, while his father's hand was armed by depraved guile to the murder of his loved one."[18]

In education so conducted, substance made surrender to style. Authors happily repeated themselves, as if words and phrases had only the same decorative purpose as the ivy leaves that punctuate Latin inscriptions; or, on the contrary, to avoid repetition, they ranged through an inexhaustible list of inexact circumlocutions.[19] Even in so intelligent a writer as Ammianus, the influence of formal schooling can be seen in the *mirabilia* with which he embroiders his account. His many excursuses are successfully bizarre and colorful; they catch the attention; they leaven the body of fact he wishes to present. His fund of knowledge, used as a legal advocate might use it to make a tedious narrative palatable, is "essentially rhetorical."[20] In this major respect, his work fairly represents the culture from which it sprang, though it is of course for the least representative aspect, the description of events themselves, that Ammianus' *History* is read today.

Throughout education, the dominance of literature and, in that latter, the dominance of the ornamental, answered to a taste for style over substance. Occasions calling for command of the rhetorician's arts were many in both private and public life. A letter of recommendation, acknowledgment of some dedication or honor, an address to an official body, or the correspondence and memoranda that circulated among the bureaus of government, all demanded *elegantia* and *eruditio*, the masters of which thus did indeed possess an accomplishment of the greatest practical value.

The way-stations to a higher style, beyond mere literacy, also promised their rewards. A revealing conspectus of the opportunities which opened to those born under the constellation of cleverness is given by the astrologer Firmicus Maternus: Mercury "will make secretaries to governors, to authorities, to the senate, or persons who, associated with emperors, will have some power of instruction. . . . Sometimes they will be secretaries or registrars or agents for great men"; if more fortunate still, "by their divine gifts, [Mercury] will make orators or teachers of oratorical arts, or schoolmasters . . . or masters of studies or of tax-records."[21] The emperors kept track of recent graduates in order to draw on their talents; for, while there may have been only one or two hundred vacancies a year in the civil administration—the number, though quite unknown, must have been small—yet there were still fewer applicants boasting full credentials.[22] Although in the second half of the century the importance of legal training began to compete with rhetorical,[23] the latter nevertheless continued to enjoy immense prestige and to offer access to wonderful riches, power, and fame.

The insistence referred to earlier, that learning should be good for something, was thus quite satisfied by rhetoric. For all its artificiality, emptiness, conservatism, and pedantry, its repute gave to the fourth century a decided Mandarin quality.

Some criticism there was of rhetoric, along predictable lines. Its enemies alleged that its powers of persuasion could be enlisted in the defense of error— true, of course, and particularly emphasized in the writings of Christians early in the century. They had still to rebut the charge that Scripture was written in too-plain language, whereas later in the century Christianity found adherents enough among the educated. Thus it is Lactantius and Arnobius, under Diocletian and Constantine, who supply examples of distrust of rhetoric. Better, they say, that truth should be written "by the unlearned and crude" than "stained with lies"; deceivers "can easily snare unwary spirits by smooth talk and verse; but I wished to join wisdom with piety, so that empty doctrine might bring no hurt to the studious, and that the art of letters might be of maximum use."[24] Christian apologists, however, are not the only ones to voice such doubts about the rhetorical culture of the times. Constantius' court seems to have turned away from it, "as a pursuit involving much labor and little profit,"[25] and Licinius "was a foe of letters, which in his boundless ignorance he declared a poison and public plague, especially courtroom diligence."[26] What the emperor had in mind seems to have been too-clever lawyers.

Yet under the Tetrarchs, *humanitate parum imbuti*, we are told further that "literature was numbered among the evil arts, and those versed in it were oppressed and execrated as if they were foes and enemies."[27] The statement, though surely exaggerated, introduces the second tendency to be discussed. Not only was education oriented toward rhetoric and poetry, in which taste prevailed over content; but their very emptiness, their very unreality and emphasis on decoration, may well have protected them against profound suspicions of more substantial learning which already prevailed from the outset of the century.

Just how violent those suspicions might be appears in the well-known "Theodorus plot" of 371–372. An attempt by a small number of aristocrats and officials to find out who would next be emperor was uncovered, and further investigations of hideous cruelty were undertaken to root out all their associates. Charges of treason and black magic, both of which had long been intertwined in repressive legislation, widened still further into an attack on learning *per se*. The attack was urged forward by Valens with a thoroughness indicating genuine fear of "all those far-famed in philosophy or otherwise bred up in learning . . . [men] who had reached the heights of culture."[28] Many of its victims—Maximus, for one—are indeed identifiable as "philosophers."[29] One witness of these persecutions describes how "numberless books in piles, and heaps of tomes, were burned under the eyes of the judges, torn from various houses . . . though most were handbooks on the several liberal studies and on law . . . ; throughout the eastern provinces people burned up all their libraries."[30] A deep hostility toward the intellectual, such as he was in those times, underlies this remarkable nexus of events—not a mere isolated flash of anger; for that same Maximus had aroused a hatred even earlier that found expression in the clamor of the mob,[31] and, under Constantius as well, learned men had had to complain of "philosophy . . . suspect, and not only stripped of honors but accused and found guilty."[32]

That last passage continues with words going far to explain the phenomenon we are considering; for we must suppose that "philosophy" and "philosopher" bore some special meaning. "Now," under Julian, we are told, "one may look up to the heavens and survey the stars with untroubled eyes, though a little before, like prone and four-footed beasts, we fixed our trembling gaze on the ground. For who dared to watch the rise or setting of a star?" So the secret is out: philosophy really means astrology, according to a widening or blurring of ideas having a long history but attaining in the fourth century a form fixed for a thousand years.[33] Knowledge, *sophia* or *sapientia*, indicates quite a different domain from that which Aristotle or Plato had once ruled. Its masters, by beliefs unchanged hereafter down to the days of Friar Bacon or Doctor Faustus, are thought of as pursuers of the occult. The suspicion had a history reaching back to the days of Clement of Alexandria, reporting that "the masses are in terror of Hellenic philosophy, as children of goblins, fearing it may delude them";[34] and the suspicion was often justified. As time went on, an increasing share of publication (if that is the right term) was given over to the supernatural, ranging from the copious works of heresiarchs to the encyclopedias of practicing wizards. They were all to be burnt in the public square if the police could get their hands on them.[35] Sciences verged on pseudo-sciences: medicine on witch-doctoring, mathematics on numerology—"damnable art," in Diocletian's words—and astronomy on astrology.[36]

In its radical sense, philosophy still meant "love of wisdom"; but men asked darkly, "What kind of wisdom?" Too much of it, in whatever way displayed, incited rioting and abuse, or rumors of communion with demons and command over spells, attributed by detractors to all sorts of deeply read men: to Constantius, to Athanasius, or to Priscillian—charges vague or unsubstantiated, for the most part. Priscillian, for example, "was believed to have practiced magic arts from youth."[37]

A different cause of the distrust of philosophy is revealed in other writers of the later empire: not that it is wicked and baneful, but a waste of time. People are advised to "leave to students of ethics the more laborious questions—for instance, what is ethical and rational virtue—and what is said about *mores* and passions, to those who pursue analysis by hypotheses but who do not concern themselves with the attainment of individual virtues, and rather heap up more abstract pronouncements at random." Eristics are deplored, and loose speculations, and idle subtleties. A second author declares, "You have given credence to your wise men and those learned in every kind of study—those, forsooth, who know nothing and proclaim no one doctrine, who join battle over their views with their adversaries and forever fight it out with obstinate hostility, who overthrow, tear down, and raze each other's positions, make all doubtful, and demonstrate from their disputes that nothing can be known."[38] From the mid-second century, a growing distaste for disciplined, consecutive, analytic thought can be traced through Lucian and Hippolytus, contested by Origen,[39] and culminating in a sort of despairing repudiation of ancient philosophy. After so many centuries, it had gotten nowhere![40] Argument upon argument, the exhaustion of so many subtle minds; still, no certainty! And in a baffled and impatient spirit, men reached beyond reason to revelation. The story—of theurgy, of neoplatonism—has been often told, and need not be rehearsed again.

But rejection of another kind might be defended upon the ground that ignorance had something about it positively good. "Investigation of natural phenomena," one bishop tells us, "is superfluous and beyond the human mind, and the learning and study of these matters are impious and false," while another declares, "A certain heresy holds that earthquakes come not from God's command but from the very nature of the elements, since it does not know what Scripture says, '*Qui conspicis* (as it reads) *terram et commoves terra motu.*' . . . Not heeding the power of God, they dare to attribute the motion of force to the nature of the elements, like certain foolish philosophers who, ascribing this to nature, know not the power of God."[41] Repudiation of learned inquiry is thus express. But it comes as no great surprise. The fourth century, after all, witnessed the triumph of a religion first announced to humble folk and disseminated through *indocti* and *rudes*, in whom, nevertheless, resided truths that had eluded the wise. A view quite opposed to the Greek could now come forward: wisdom of this world counted as folly; philosophy rose above thought, becoming rather a way of life. To be "simple" earned a new respect,[42] and men who, in a secular sense, knew nothing could yet be portrayed as victorious in debate with "philosophers."[43]

Change in the image of the wise man was reflected in the very word "philosophy" in Greek and its derivatives "philosophize" and "philosopher" in both Greek and Latin. Its meaning veered off in a surprising direction. At the root for centuries had lain both the familiar sense of pursuing knowledge through ratiocination, and the special character that invested the pursuers. They might wear a sort of uniform of short cloak and beard; their conduct must be more restrained, moral, and high-minded than that of ordinary people. Fat philosphers were a contradiction in terms. By the second half of the second century, however, this ascetic aspect of the word's meaning had begun to take on an independent existence: "philosophy" could mean a regimen of self-denial without any special requirement for reasoned thought, even though persons under its rules could attain to great truths. By the fourth century the word had come to bear that ascetic meaning quite as a matter of course.[44] Eusebius in his *Praeparatio evangelica* (12.29.1) offers an illustrative text, describing the old Jewish prophets "living in deserts, mountains, or caves in order to reach the summit of philosophy."

Exactly how such a regimen could lead to enlightenment can best be seen through two passages, one written around A.D. 220, the other in 357. The first concerns the holy man Apollonius of Tyana, subject of countless stories and of more than one rather sensationally written biography. At the height of his fame, that fame had brought him under suspicion of being a *goes*, a wizard and black magician and maleficent charlatan; for it was, after all, commonly reported that he could see through time and space. He had, for example, foreseen the coming of plague to Ephesus. Envious detractors challenged him in the presence of the emperor to show that this feat had not been accomplished through some act of wicked magic. In answer "he said, 'I used, O my sovereign, a lighter diet than others, and I was thus the first to be sensible of the danger. . . . This diet, O King, guards my senses in a kind of indescribable ether or clear air, forbids them to contract any foul or turbid matter, and allows me to discern, as in the sheen of a looking-glass, everything that is happening or is to be. . . . [Only] the gods perceive what lies in the future, and men, what is going on before them, but *wise* men, what is approaching.' "[45]

The description of Apollonius may be compared with a second text, in which a bishop describes St. Anthony's instant knowledge of the death of his fellow ascetic, Amoun, far off in a different part of Egypt. The saint actually saw Amoun's soul mounting to heaven. He told his companion monks of the vision, and later they compared it with the date of the event as they learned it through normal sources. "They and others as well marveled at the purity of Anthony's soul, that what had happened at a distance of thirteen days' journey he had learned instantly, and had actually seen the soul taken up on high." In fact, he had given the explanation of his powers himself, much earlier, saying: "If we should ever be concerned to discern the events of the future, let us make ourselves pure in intellect. For I myself believe that when the soul is completely pure and in accord with its own nature, it is able through its powers of penetrating sight to see more and greater things than the *daimones*," the oracle gods like Apollo; "for it has in it the Lord that can reveal things."[46]

Search for great truths thus had no need of any academic training at all; the accomplished teachers of them might be of a radically different character from such other culture heroes as Libanius. Like Anthony, they might instead be anchorites, representing the heroization of *simplicitas* and (it is worth adding) at the same time the most historically significant and original creation of the later empire. From the gathering of disciples around Anthony in Diocletian's reign, to the dissemination of his biography in the west toward the end of the fourth century, monasticism under his inspiration grew prodigiously. In its later manifestations, to Rutilius Namatianus, as in its origins, this novel development in religious ideals set at odds the learned and unlearned.[47] Consider the founder's discountenancing of "Greek philosophers" who, the story goes, "came to him thinking to make fun of him because he was illiterate; but Anthony said to them, 'What do you say, now—which comes first, mind or letters? and which underlies the other, mind or letters?' When they answered that mind came first and was the discoverer of letters, Anthony said, 'Whoever has a sound mind has no need of letters.' By this he astonished them and the bystanders, and they left in wonderment."[48] Or consider his disciple Macarius, encountering "a certain heretic . . . of great eloquence" who "baffled his simple words with cunning arguments," but in the end suffered defeat.[49] Or again, Arsenius, being asked by his companions, "How is it that we have gained nothing from so much education and wisdom, while these rustics (*hoi agroikoi*, the monks) and Egyptians have won such virtue? . . . Why, abbot Arsenius, when you have so much Greek and Latin cultivation, *paideia*, do you question this rustic about your ideas?" But Arsenius of course upheld the greater wisdom of the illiterate peasant.[50] Knowing not even the languages of classical civilization, sharply contrasted with those who did know them, speaking generally in short and artless phrases, the monk still rose to heights beyond the reach of rational powers. It was those heights to which Arsenius paid tribute. The foremost figure of monastic mysticism, Evagrius, even declares, "Blessed is he who has attained infinite ignorance."[51]

The respect accorded to such views and persons, so dramatically in contradiction to the classical heritage, no doubt had a complicated origin. Of course—for nothing in history of much significance happens without a conjuncture of causes. So great is the blessed variety and contrariness among all the human beings required to join in the making of changes that count. Among the population of the Roman empire, no contrariety is more marked than that which distinguished the masses (especially rural) from the elite (essentially urban); and it is therefore natural to begin the search here, for the historical explanation needed. In the Principate indeed that great gulf is to be found separating the Pliny's both Elder and Younger, Plutarch, Lucian, Apuleius, and others of their class, from *hoi polloi, rusticani* and *vulgi*, in religion as in other aspects of culture.[52] With exceptions—for example, the rhetor Aelius Aristides, owing his life to Asclepius' repeated warnings, or the consular convert to the god Glycon that Lucian so angrily and amusingly describes—they acknowledged a zone of indirection separating divine powers from mortal life. Gods didn't meddle visibly and in detail with what happened down here. They wished mortals well, they should be addressed in prayer, but they were not likely to exert their benevolent effects immediately and before one's eyes. Therefore, they could not be thought the cause of earthquakes, and, if one occurred, it was best to resort to the palace for help, not to the temple. Entirely different, the view of Eusebius and others of the class that formed opinion in the fourth and fifth centuries.[53] To look for a natural cause was in their view not merely wrong but wicked. Victory in battle was determined in 312 for Constantine, in 394 for Theodosius, by God's will, which operated also at less dramatic junctures to decide disputes between individuals: those who were wrong died horribly, like Arius or the various notable apostates under Julian. It was not so that historians of earlier centuries had explained why things happened as they did.

To modern readers, this is mere superstition; and they may recall Augustine in the twenty-second book of his *City of God* ardently advocating the advertisement of miracles which they simply cannot credit, or Ambrose practising exorcism from the pulpit and conversing with the demons he has called forth from his distracted congregation members, or the veneration of relics, the ascetic's walling himself up in some tiny stone cubicle or swathing his limbs in a hundredweight of chains—all, so many demonstrations of irrationality. Where did they come from? The answer most often given in the past has been much like A.-J. Festugière's: "What Gilbert Murray called 'The failure of nerve,' speaking of the taste for the irrational in the Late Empire, must be regarded not so much as a decay of cultivated minds (those, for example, of Plotinus, Ambrose, Augustine, Boethius, Cassiodorus) as the appearance in literature . . . of the beliefs and feelings of the vulgar."[54] *Hoi polloi* had taken over elite thought, somehow; for "within the empire there is no significant distinction between the beliefs of the upper classes and those of the lower classes. . . . The christian abolition of the internal frontiers between the learned and the vulgar had clear implications. For cultured persons it meant the reception and acceptance of many uncritical, unsophisticated beliefs in miracles, relics, and apparitions." So, Arnaldo Momigliano.[55]

With this familiar line of interpretation, more recently, Peter Brown appears at one point to agree, quoting Momigliano's words and noting for approval his "characteristic wisdom and firmness." But in the course of full and repeated discussion, it becomes clear that in fact he quite rejects these views.[56] He begins from Hume, moves on to Gibbon, next to Cardinal Newman, and thereafter to more recent historians, among whom he finds and rejects a "two-tier model" of elite and popular religion in the fourth century (to be found also somewhat earlier, and somewhat later, too): there had once been rational religion and there had been superstition, the two coexisting; but, through the rise of Christianity, the latter, characteristic of the lower classes, had overwhelmed the former. Hence, magic, veneration of saints and relics, miracles. At any rate, that would be how conventional interpretation would have it.

But Brown accepts none of this. What emerges from his many pages of analysis (unless it be the view that the elite exploited "superstition" for the purpose of advancing their influence within their communities—and that must entail a class-wide, concerted deceit) is not at all clear, at least to myself;[57] nor does his treatment really address the cause of changes so characteristic of the thought of the time: veneration of saints, veneration of ascetics, working of miracles. He seems rather to

> explain a thing till all men doubt it,
> And write about it, Goddess, and about it.

Which is not to deny that these phenomena seem very puzzling at first sight.

Perhaps the difficulties in arriving at an explanation are occasioned by too judgmental a stance. In our own civilization, reason is good and its contradiction bad; therefore those terms "irrational," "simple-minded," and the like which Hume or some other modern might apply to the beliefs of "the uneducated," "the vulgar," and the like in antiquity, amount to so many indictments delivered against church leaders and common church practices. They should be spared any such insult. But they would certainly not thank us for our consideration. No, mere reason measured against authority and revelation would seem to them a very inferior thing. Their convictions need only be taken on their own terms, then, and without judgmental vocabulary, for their existence to be acknowledged without hesitation or complication; and they are in fact perfectly well attested, later, in socioeconomic strata where, earlier, they would have been quite foreign. The contrast has been drawn especially at notes 52f., above. It is particularly striking within the religious thought of the upper classes.

The question how these late Roman views came to appear there, Momigliano answers almost by inadvertence. Speaking of the court of Theodosius II, he says in passing that its dominant figures, who happened to be mostly women, had equally close ties to "the devotion of the masses" and to "monks who came from peasant stock."[58] His explanation of the religious ideas characterizing the court seems therefore to fall in line with that of Festugière and many other interpreters. I agree with their view, that is, with the "two-tier model," since it is not easy for me to imagine people who have received however little training in logic, abstract thought, analytic observation, and a written tradition of technical and scientific manuals, being *argued* out of their habits—being *reasoned* out of their respect for rationality. Far easier to imagine them being *ordered* out of it, or in their youth deterred from it, by the voice of authority issuing from the mass of the people and announcing views naturally at home among the masses.

So far as religious authority is concerned, the Church for a time found room for a generous mix of all classes within the ranks of its leadership: most revealingly, a freedman at its head well into the third century, that is, a bishop in the imperial capital, and occasional illiterate bishops even in the later empire.[59] To suppose them and their like receptive to views common among their class, if sincere and harmonious with inherited church teachings, is not unreasonable. What could they have found improbable, after all, in a woman's being healed through the touching of Ambrose's gown, the death of a persecutor through being eaten of worms, demons being so often exorcized, or the interpretation of an earthquake as a divine judgment? While these and a thousand similar episodes and beliefs are reported in surviving literature of the fourth century, they are also amply attested in writing by the most authoritative source of all, the scriptural.

When we look at secular authority, however, we discover a much wider setting for anti-intellectualism. No person better illustrates this than Constantine, toward the beginning of the period of interest here. Hear him on theology, declaring its controversies "perfectly inconsequential and quite unworthy of such contentious debate . . . extremely minor and highly inconsequential . . . suggested by unprofitable leisure . . . minor and trifling . . . few and idle disputes about words," and so forth.[60] Hear him again dismissing "Socrates, elated by his debating powers, making the weaker reasoning appear the stronger, and playing about with mutually contradictory arguments . . . , and Pythagoras as well, while pretending to practice self-control in a special degree and silence, too, was caught in imposture . . . , and finally Plato, up to a point, was wise, but in other matters he is found to have erred from the truth."[61] And when Constantine turns to the writings of the great jurists, his one desire is to "eradicate the interminable controversies of the jurisconsults. We order the destruction of the notes of Ulpian and Paul on Papinian; for, while they were eagerly pursuing praise for their genius, they preferred not so much to correct him as to distort him." "We have ruled out the quibbles of senseless verbiage."[62] That final boast, aimed at practicing lawyers, recalls a statement of the contemporary Licinius quoted on an earlier page.

Rather hidden from our view in the latter half of the third century, a great deal of upward social movement took place throughout the empire, raising to positions of more money and prestige the beneficiaries of the expansion of government and of the peace of the Church. By the same two avenues, movement accelerated in the earlier fourth century, especially under Constantine but continuing over the next several generations, too. It swept upward the members also of a barbarian aristocracy (if the phrase is intelligible) from among the armed forces. From their new eminences, it is easy to imagine all these nouveaux arrivés, like Constantine though on a smaller scale, speaking very much in the same voice: the voice of the plain man who knew what he liked, enjoyed prestige and confidence, and had no need to appeal to the school-bred for his opinions. Rather the reverse: *absint docti*, away with fancy lucubration! What counted was not what was said but the authority behind it—including the divine.

So old ideas were proclaimed from loftier platforms.

12

TWO TYPES OF CONVERSION TO

EARLY CHRISTIANITY

WHAT PAGANS saw *in* Christianity (in the sense of being drawn to it) depended greatly on what they saw *of* it. Self-evidently, their first allegiance could be inspired only by those parts and aspects of the faith that were openly displayed. So there is one topic to explore: exactly what *was* displayed, undeniably and demonstrably?

And displayed at the moment of conversion, so as to account for it—not when the process was well begun. I therefore exclude consideration of the converts made in Judaea or in or around Jewish communities in Greek cities.

But further: conversion depended greatly on the fit between Christianity and prevailing expectations regarding the world above us. No challenge on all fronts, nor a faith centered in some practice perfectly unacceptable (such as human sacrific, let us say, or ritual prostitution), could have prevailed. There is a second topic to explore—relatively accessible, at least if we limit our exploration to our surviving texts, their writers, and their readers.

They immediately confine us within a circle constituting less than a tenth of the population. A cultural elite: even St. Paul almost a member, or on the fringes, since he like the pagan Celsus or the convert Justin had added years of further study to a training in mere literacy. The basic elements of their education are well known. In one part of the Greek-speaking world, Egypt, they are known through the whole accumulation of literary papyrus fragments, in which the Iliad emerges as favorite, the Odyssey a good second; Demosthenes a poor third; Euripides next; then Callimachus, Hesiod, and Plato (and students who were aiming for law explain the popularity of the orator; but Plato's works, like the tenets of Stoicism and other chief doctrines, would circulate mostly in excerpts and condensations, and these would be commonly memorized if not discussed in advanced schools). The whole list makes specific the pair of words, "poets and philosophers," continually used by the Christian Apologists to define the written basis of their opponents' beliefs. Tertullian (*Apol.* 14) in his attack on them looks at the Trojans and Achaeans, at Venus and Mars; moves on to Euripides; next to one of the lyric poets; and so to Plato—Tertullian, a *Latin* Apologist, exactly duplicating the list from Egypt. It was very much one world, that cultural elite we are considering.

Its theology (for pagans who ventured on such speculation) supposed a world above Olympus; at the top, some version, relation, or descendant of

Plato's Supreme Being. Pagans could therefore be said, like Christians, to believe in one god, maker of heaven and earth.[1] Visions so abstract, like Immanuel Kant's "categorical imperative" or Sartre's existentialism today, were more often mentioned, and nodded to in passing, than really understood. Yet the philosophers' notion of one god, perfection complete, above all things, needing nothing, not to be touched by Achilles' spear, Eros' arrows, or the worshipper's prayers, provided a theoretical base for very widespread ideas about the nature of divinity. It precluded whatever was capricious or trivial, deceitful, harmful, or vengeful, foul, wicked, or cruel. No divine being could be anything but beneficent.

The divine *dramatis personae* of literature and myth, however—where did they fit? They stood in sharp opposition to the ideas just outlined. Christian Apologists exploited the opposition between "poets and philosophers" to the full. The philosophers, as Tertullian says (*Apol.* 46.4) "openly destroy your gods and attack your superstitions with their treatises, while you cheer them on, forsooth!" He was quite right. There was Seneca in the Latin West, in a work *Against Superstition* (now largely lost); in the Greek East, there was Heraclitus, not the famous philosopher but a figure belonging to the generation or two before Seneca, writing on myths from a very rationalistic point of view; and both of these writers only summed up and gave greater circulation to convictions long common among the educated, convictions quite incompatible with a literal belief in the stories about the gods; and should not Christians join in the debate? As one of their tormentors sourly remarks, "This is the Christians' custom, to invent many foul calumnies against our gods."[2]

In trying to determine, however, what expectations or presuppositions about religion might await evangelists of Christianity, we should not assume that people's general ideas of godhead had made no broad advances since the days of Homer and Hesiod. Not at all: in the days of Seneca or Tertullian, we do not find them expressing the belief that Apollo takes sides with one mortal against another, or that Zeus might defenestrate some second Hephaestus. The gods had grown up, in company with more advanced moral and intellectual standards than prevailed in the eighth century B.C. Attacks by Christian polemicists indeed made more public but they did not create the gulf that had long opened between literature and philosophy. They only struck at a bookish vulnerability, not at a living faith.

That living faith, if it had little room for a Supreme Being in its daily concerns, did commonly acknowledge some sort of supremacy of a more familiar, less remote figure, whether Zeus (or Jupiter) as king of all gods, directing them, or presiding over them in looser fashion in the way that Agamemnon had presided among the Achaean chiefs. Either view permitted the very widespread interpretation of local gods as no more than reflections, under various names, of some single one: Zeus was Sarapis was Jupiter was Helios,[3] and similarly Selene was Astarte was Artemis was Diana.

To repeat: none of these beings was harmful, all were kindly to each other—if they were thought to have any interrelationship at all—and kindly toward their worshippers. Prayers went up to them seeking benefits only, not to avert their wrath. We do not find in the non-Christian (and non-Jewish) world much evidence even of punishment by the gods for wicked behavior. It is attested, as we will see below, but not very commonly.

Which raises the question not easily solved by anyone, Christian or not: *pothen to kakon?*—for if divinity is beneficent, where can afflictions and evil deeds originate? If there is any broadly shared view in the Roman world about this matter, it is that the gods, like ourselves though not in the same degree, inhabit a universe they cannot control. They can modify but not entirely direct events like death, disaster at sea, or drought. Sometimes only Chance, Tyche, Fortuna is to blame, sometimes the picture is a little sharper: we find a plague caused by a particular evil power.[4] It can be driven away, then. It is not a god but some lowlier being.

For underneath the gods lie *daimones*. It is best to leave the word in its Greek and, by adoption, its Latin form so as not to confuse it with our word "demons." No one asked a *daimon* for a favor (and if that is what is meant by prayer, then no one prayed to one), nor did any *daimon* have his temple or priest. From having been, in Homer and certain later writers, a word applied to the familiar Olympians, *daimon* had sunk down below Olympus to an intermediate though still superhuman and supernatural realm, denoting powers that fill the heavens, fill the air. They are beings without name or dignity but not without capacities that set them above us. Some are beneficent, some the reverse. It is the latter that are invoked or coerced by spells for purposes alien to divinity.[5]

Such, in loose outline, are the views that Christianity must fit or challenge. But in trying to understand in what light it might appear to the holders of those views, two difficulties arise. First, the new faith could only be judged by its visible, audible parts. Yet, as Tertullian says, "no one turns to our literature who is not already Christian"[6]—meaning that, in his opinion, the New Testament and apparently the Apologists like Tertullian himself, Justin, Origen, Minucius Felix, and the rest should not be counted as either visible or audible to a pagan audience. Perhaps we should not take Tertullian's remark quite literally. The pagan Celsus in the later second century had read the Bible, if only to refute it. On the other hand, he himself was so instantly forgotten that one of the best-read men of a somewhat later day, Origen, could find no trace of him. Celsus appears to have been a quite minor oddity, then. A few generations later, a governor of Egypt, a man evidently unusually interested in religion, nevertheless shows that he knows almost nothing about Christianity—the judge of the martyr Phileas.[7] Other bits of evidence could be cited to the same effect. So when we speak of people observing and becoming acquainted with Christianity, we should be careful not to draw into our discussion too

much detail regarding doctrine or practice. As a parallel, the widespread ignorance about Judaism is instructive.

And if we exclude from our discussion St. Paul's letters, the *Didache*,
Clement's letter from Rome, in sum, the bulk of pre-Nicene Christian writings
because they are not likely to have been read outside the Church, then as our
second difficulty we confront a very puzzling poverty of sources. Just how *can*
we discover what that outer face was, that the new religion showed to the
unconverted?

The sources that can be used, I think, include three sorts. There are those
parts of the Acts of the Apostles in which, at some moment around A.D. 90,
the writer described how an earlier evangelist might have been expected to
speak (we do not know, of course, what the evangelist really did say). We also
have some early apocryphal acts.[8] Second, from about the same period as
these last—that is, from the last half of the second century—we have the bulk
of the Apologists, to the extent that they really reached non-converts. Third,
we have exchanges between the martyrs and their tormentors. As strictly as
possible we should try to limit ourselves to things that were specifically and
expressly said to non-believers. We should not use what was written for eastern pagans by Lucian or Galen or what was spoken to an audience in Rome by
Fronto and Crescens: they are looking at Christians (at behavior, that is), not
at Christianity (that is, at belief).[9]

In the canonical Acts, it may be recalled, there are from the very start some
tell-tale mis-perceptions of Christianity, revealing both what people expected
in the way of religion and what they were being actually shown. They supposed Peter, Barnabas, and Paul at various junctures to be gods come down to
earth,[10] just as they thought Simon Magus the literal embodiment of divine
force.[11] They would have better understood the reaction of Peter when he saw
Moses and Elijah before him: Should he, he wondered, set up a tabernacle for
each of the two on the spot?[12] Pagans also expected the apostles to offer their
supernatural gifts for a price, because cures, exorcism, and prophecies by itin-
erant wonder-workers evidently were for sale here and there from time to
time.[13] These incidents take us over a great span of the Greek-speaking world,
incidentally, from Samaria to the coast, up into Anatolia, and beyond to northeastern Greece. It is in these same lands that we can best become acquainted
with non-Christian circles and sources, too, to confirm in other ways the truth
of the glimpses given us by the Acts.

In Phillippi, the apostles are by error taken for servants of the All-High
God, as a woman of the crowd terms him.[14] Some dominant male deity generally stands out in the worships of both Semitic and Asianic Greek-speaking
lands. At Lystra they are taken for gods again. On this occasion, Zeus is
thought to have his younger, lesser agent with him, Hermes,[15] just as would
be expected—and just as God had Jesus, it might be said: for ditheistic con-

fusion occasionally invades the relation between Father and Son, and would have to be cleared away.[16]

Ordinarily, however, pagans are presented by Christians with a God new but one they can understand: Creator, Lord, Ruler over all things.[17] They betray no uneasiness about the implied picture of a divine monarchy. To be sure, it does not resemble the picture of paganism that is seen from a distance, embracing many worshippers, cities, and regions. Rather, it resembles what could be discovered in the mind of most single individuals. The distinction is important. In the daily practice of religion, they acknowledged some local deity as supreme without bothering about other people's preferences in the next county. It is this as much as the shadow of Plato's Supreme Being in their minds that allows Tertullian to say, "Do you not grant, from general acceptance, that there is some being higher and more powerful, like an emperor of the world, of infinite power and majesty?—for that is how most men settle divinity: with the enjoyment of the top command in the hands of one, subordinate tasks distributed among many."[18] So non-Christians in the world of St. Paul, Justin, or Origen were in reality both polytheist and monotheist.[19]

But those terms are in fact only a source of extraneous confusion when they are applied to the centuries and developments we are looking at. They did not exist in the ancient lexicon of debate.[20] What modern interpretation conceals and what ancient sources abundantly reveal is a struggle over the meaning of the word "god," *theos, deus*.

Christians and non-Christians alike supposed there was a multitude of supernatural beings above them. Non-Christians acknowledged Supreme Gods, each one illogically *hypsistos* or *kratistos* or *invictus*; next, gods of the familiar order (Venus or Hermes) with *daimones* and lesser spirits beneath them. As to Christians, they proclaimed their own particular Supreme God; His ministers, angels; what non-believers probably saw as divinized heroes, Moses and Elijah; with hordes of *daimones* or more often little *daimonia* under *their* Supreme God the Devil, *megas daimon* as Origen calls him (*C. Cels.* 1.31) or Prince (*archegetes*, 1 *Apol.* 28) in Justin's term. A pagan governor need find nothing disturbing, then, in the picture a martyr explains to him, of " 'Adonai the All-High seated above cherubs and seraphs.' Marcianus says, 'What are cherubs and seraphs?' Acacius answers, 'The agent of the All-High God and attendant on His lofty seat.' "[21]

There was thus no basis for conflict between the two structures of belief so long as the nature of "god" remained undefined. But of course Christians could not tolerate *that*. In the first place, they must re-define other people's "gods." They called them mere objects, that is, idols. Very offensive, no doubt, but more for the manner of the accusation than its matter.[22] Pagan writers in the educated circles they moved in had been making the same accusation for centuries. There remained the deeds wrought through forces which pagans called by the name Apollo or Poseidon or Zeus—miracles beyond denial by

Christians, wrought even in their own day, but which they attributed to mere *daimones*;[23] for *theoi* were no more than gods so-called and in quotation-marks.[24] Tertullian asserts and makes use of the terminological argument: "If angels and *daemones* perform the very same feats as your gods, where then lies the superiority of their godhead? . . . Is it not better to think, when they do what makes us believe in the gods, that they have *made themselves* gods, rather than that gods should be on a level with angels and *daemones*?"[25] Clearly the word *deus* was to be reserved for a being or beings of commanding power, truly sovereign, independent, superior. As Simon Magus proclaims to a crowd in Rome, " 'He that has a master is not a god.' And when he said this, many said, 'You put it well.' "[26]

But how can superiority which thus defines the word be demonstrated save by measurement against every alternative? How can Christian "monotheism," in the peculiar meaning of the term we have discovered, be asserted save through proving the inferiority of everyone else's "god"? Here, too, and in a second respect, Christians presented a new definition of divinity—but of their own God, not the pagan ones. Unlike the latter which had for centuries been hymned, acclaimed, portrayed in sculpture, or praised in oratorical performances without ever a hint of hostility among them—in this respect as in others entirely departing from Homeric tradition—the focus of worship for Christians was a being perpetually in arms, a jealous God always to be feared.

It is in this light that we ought to understand the exceptional prominence accorded by Christians to their success in overcoming demons through Jesus' name. It could only be seen as a test of strength. The winner was the "true" god; for truth in that regard must be established precisely through the demonstration of commands given by one and obedience yielded by another. Stories of Jesus' casting out of devils no doubt were among those parts of the faith first to be shown and talked about before unbelievers; exorcism was enjoined by Jesus upon his disciples when he sent them out to the Gentiles,[27] and was performed often by the apostles in their travels, too. Beyond all tales of such confrontations and triumphs, or others like them, found in the apocryphal second-century Acts of John and Peter, there were the boasts of the Apologists. One of them, Tertullian, makes clear what is at stake: through Christian exorcism "that spirit will own himself in truth a *daemon* just as he will elsewhere call himself a 'god,' falsely."[28] Exorcism and mastery of spirits—not unknown among pagans but much more practiced and proclaimed before them by Christians—exorcism thus was a demonstration of a theological position and thereby a missionary instrument. It made converts.[29]

Truly divine power also displayed itself in acts of dramatic punishment. That was common knowledge. But the Christian perception was far more dreadful than the pagan, so far at least as we can generalize about the latter. There was certainly no pagan match for the declaration with which Paul introduced his God to a pagan crowd: "The living God, the God of vengeance, the jealous god who has need of nothing . . .'' had sent him, Paul, to preach repentance from sin.[30] Non-Christians of course knew what they might expect if they defied a deity head-on, by breaking an oath taken in his name or by violating some taboo right in his sacred precinct.[31] They could have found the match for their own stories within the Christian community: the story of Ananias and his wife, for example, who were struck dead for cheating the poor box. But there was a great deal more to it than that. What Christianity put forward was the fearful novelty of a God who would burn them alive in perpetuity for their very manner of life, spying out their transgressions wherever committed, as he would correspondingly reward the virtuous. Beginning with John the Baptist's and Jesus' preaching, on through Paul's acknowledgment of "the wrath to come," the flames of hell illuminated the lessons of Christianity quite as much as the light of Grace.[32] Actual scenes of speeches delivered to non-believing crowds show that the message was made plain, for example, by Paul at Iconium very much as Jesus had told His disciples to do;[33] and we know that it got through, at least to Celsus. He remarks that Christians "believe in eternal punishments" and "threaten others with these punishments."[34] Clearest of all is the scene in the amphitheater at Carthage where the martyrs, referring to their coming torment, tell the crowd by sign language, "You, us; but God, you"; but Pionius had elaborated on similar comparisons and warnings of condemnation and suffering, in the city square of Smyrna.[35] It is likely that this particular article of faith was as widely known as any outside the Church. Despite the Apologists' attempts, however, to make eternal hell-fire credible by reference to Tartarus or to Stoic predictions of universal conflagration, non-believers found it novel and hard to accept. That much we can tell from the way the Apologists handle the subject.

No source indicates that the unconverted saw a necessary connection between eternal torture and an eventual existence after death *in the flesh*. Perhaps the connection was seen, but forgotten in the surprise and controversy roused by the latter proposition itself. "This very flesh will rise?" asks the judge of Phileas martyr, "astonished."[36] His astonishment reminds us once more of the gap that had opened between the poets and philosophers over the course of centuries: an after-life peopled with forms that were recognizably what they had been before death was indeed to be found in primitive Greek religion— for that matter, in Etruscan and therefore early Roman religion. But outside of literature, in the real Roman empire, and among real convictions throughout our period of study, there is hardly a trace of Tartarus, the Elysian Fields, or any such world beyond death. Even a belief in the immortality of the soul alone is hard to find—a fact reflected in the second-century Lucian's saying about Christians: "The poor devils have utterly persuaded themselves that they will be immortal and live forever."[37]

Christian certainty of a heavenly reward for the virtuous was known to pagans, though that knowledge is just barely attested.[38] It made a pair with eternal punishment, and was to be attained, so a non-believer might have heard, through acts of denial of the flesh.[39] This was a teaching often discussed by the Apologists, and the call to repentance had been earlier raised by St. Paul before crowds in Iconium and Athens.[40] Celsus declares all this to be familiar: pagans likewise, so he says, believed in divine retribution for wicked acts, because they were so taught by their initiators into certain cultic mysteries. He himself seems to espouse the view,[41] but it cannot be found anywhere else nor can we be sure what mysteries he is talking about.

Of course what we call paganism was an immensely rich, variform, criss-crossed, and, above all, randomly reported world of beliefs, in which no doubt you could find almost anything somewhere. But when allowance has been made for the danger in any attempt at generalizing, there still remain some conclusions to be summed up at this point.

To begin with, we *can* determine what things most educated pagans thought they knew about their own gods, and what other things they were likely to know about the God of the Christians; and we can compare the two credos and find the novelty of the latter to lie in *the dramatic polarities it presented*. This is perceived by a pagan, charging that the Christian "impiously divides the kingdom of god and makes two opposing forces, as if there was one party on one side and another one at variance with it." He means, naturally Satan and *daimones* that are falsely called "gods," versus the real deity and his angels.[42] And a Christian for his part points to "a certain rational agency, rival in its operations"[43]—again meaning the Satanic kingdom. Apologists echo such words very often. The dualism, the resulting warfare in supernatural realms, and the implied necessity that you should choose up sides and hate the one and love the other just as you were in turn loved or hated by the divine powers, was absolutely new and strange outside the Judaeo-Christian community; and it was perceived as such.

Moreover, the polarity expressed itself in the most savage terms, terms almost if not entirely novel: in an eternity of torture for the soldiers in the wrong camp, with corresponding bliss for those in the right. Right and wrong took on the starkest outlines. There was no escaping the choice between them, for neutrality counted against you; and this novelty, by which religious preference was for the first time demanded, then itself demanded a corresponding way of life. That, too—the moral implication in religious preference—was all but unheard-of among pagans. Cult and philosophy had been kept quite separate: prayer for benefits was one thing, a Stoic chaplain in one's house was another. But now the two came together. As Apollonius martyr said to his tormentor, it was through belief in "judgment after death, a reward for virtue in the resurrection, with God as judge . . . through this above all we have learned how to live a fair life, in the expectation of the hope to come."[44]

Two warring camps above and all around us, life resumed after death in eternal bliss or agony; and a choice in conduct here on earth that was at every moment scrutinized and borne in mind against the day of judgment—these remarkable images in the harshest black and white were all entirely strange. They were presented to an audience that was conservative, perhaps no more than any other people in history, yet deeply and expressly conservative in matters of religious allegiance. That we know from countless proofs and testimonies of pagans addressing other pagans; we know it also from pagans addressing Christians, and from various Christian passages in reply.[45] By what possible means, then, could such aggressively novel novelties win any adherents?

The specific moments and details of conversion seem not to have been much studied. Perhaps it is assumed that the job of winning adherents would have been a rather easy one, given the intrinsic attractions of the new faith—if only it had been fully and fairly understood. However, persecutions intervened and thus the spread of Christianity was impeded unnaturally. The horrific crucifixions of A.D. 64 were only the first in a series. From then on, even if thinly spread out in time and space, renewed attacks drove the evangelists off the streets of most cities.[46] All the more difficult to understand how the faith they preached could be communicated and diffused!

In addressing the difficulty, no doubt the first step must be to assemble some body of evidence. We may begin by excluding consideration of any rewards that awaited new recruits—rewards spiritual, social, emotional, and financial[47]—which came only *after* conversion; for it seems fair to define our topic, conversion, as that experience by which non-believers first became convinced that the Christian God was almighty, and that they must please him.

The evidence includes a very limited number of persons who speak to us as Christians but were not always such.[48] "I came," says one, "to my faith [in the Scriptures] through the unpretentious style, the artlessness of the speakers, the clear explaining of Creation, the foreknowledge of what was to happen, the excellence of the precepts, and the single ruler over the whole universe. And my soul being taught of God, I have learned that [Greek] writings lead to our being judged and condemned, but that these others put an end to our slavery." Herein, the level of internal dialogue is obviously high, high enough to place the speaker in that uppermost tenth of the population or less that we have so far been dealing with. It is an eastern immigrant to Rome, Tatian, who is quoted. His remarks, except in their length and explicitness, may stand for the group as a whole. What *they* saw in Christianity that led them to adopt it is about what we might have predicted. Its style of thought we can easily understand.

We are also familiar with the view that martyrs made converts; but with this, we take leave of the elite and enter among the masses, who supply our second type of convert.

"The blood of the martyrs is the seed of the Church"—famous epigram, long afterward endorsed by the policy of the apostate emperor Julian. The fourth-century biography of the Egyptian monk Pachomius declares, "after Diocletian's and Maximian's persecutions, conversion of pagans increased greatly for the Church."[49] Why did this happen? Just how did pagan witnesses reason, when they saw martyrdoms and became converts? There are several plausible explanations but only one bit of evidence that I know of. In Carthage in A.D. 203, Christians were incarcerated, they behaved with splendid cheer and spirit, and the jailer "began to make much of us, realizing that there was a great power in us," a great *virtus*. Shortly afterward he appears a convert.[50] His reasoning can only have been: their conduct is beyond nature, a real god must be at work—in short, they constitute a miracle.

To revert to the monk Pachomius: he himself was won over through a bargain he struck when he was held in close custody against draft-dodging. "If you set me free from this affliction," he prayed to God, "I will serve your will all the days of my life."[51] On a vastly more important scale, such was the basis for Constantine's conversion, a sort of *do ut des*, or perhaps *credo quia vinces*; and so on into the first of those early medieval conversions of entire nations for the same cause, that they might engage in war with better prospects of victory. The Burgundians in A.D. 430 decided that the God of the Romans must be a very superior one. They applied to a convenient bishop, fasted, were instructed, and within a week were all baptized.[52]

With these reports from the empire's jails, barracks, and frontiers, we have entered on calculations quite different from those of the schools, quite different from Tatian's that were quoted a little earlier. Tatian puts fear of damnation at the end of his list of considerations. By contrast, we know of a woman, also of Rome but a little earlier (the 140s) and of a lower class, who put it first: for, "coming to know the lessons of Christ" and thus being won over herself, subsequently she "recalled the teachings of Christ and warned [her husband] of punishment in the eternal flames for those who do not live modestly and according to right reason."[53] We do not know, and it is inconsequential, just who she was; but she does provide one of our very rare glimpses into someone's thought processes. We have seen that pagans were informed of Gehenna and damnation; here we see those horrors used as the chief, perhaps the only, argument for conversion.

We also have a few scenes where the thoughts of persons not among the elite are anticipated by speakers trying to bring over whole crowds to belief. The fullest are naturally the speeches given by Paul and Stephen to Jews in Jerusalem. The setting is not comparable to those involving a pagan audience, but it is worth noting the emphasis in one of the speeches that is laid on the miracle on the road to Damascus. Since Paul often refers to it in his letters as something instantly familiar to his readers, it seems likely to have been a prominent feature also in his preaching generally.[54] He had seen God with his own eyes, and his being blinded was the proof. Very similarly, when Peter preaches in Rome, he recounts how he too thought he had been blinded by the revelation granted of God, for a moment, visible in his true form.[55]

But there is another scene of Paul addressing non-believers. He is in Ephesus. He tells his listeners how, in that same period when he had been in the Damascus area, he encountered and spoke with a lion, and won it over, and baptized it in a river. After that, the lion departed in peace, thereafter even eschewing lady lions. It had become an ascetic. "And as Paul told this," our source declares, "a great crowd was added to the faith."[56] They were converted—why? Surely because the story, which audiences of the time could be credibly portrayed as believing, demonstrated *virtus* working through the man who was at that very moment addressing them.

If this scene may be taken as really written before A.D. 200 and really circulated among various churches in an interested and reverential fashion, as seems clear, then it matters not whether it transmits words actually spoken or behavior actually observed; for our concern is with the mentality of the audience—how they thought, how contemporaries who wanted to be believed would depict that thought, in short, what generally seemed familiar and credible. There is confirmation in just the same period from Tertullian's saying, "When were even droughts not ended by our going down on our knees, and fasting? At those times, too, the populace, hailing 'The God of Gods, who alone prevails!' have been witnesses to our God."[57] He is reminding his own living audience of moments of mass conversions upon the working of wonders by prayer, even if the conversions are along quite unreconstructedly pagan, "Great-is-God" lines. And there is confirmation, too, in the account Eusebius gives of the successors to the Apostles, evidently toward the turn of the first century in the Aegean area: addressing audiences who "had heard nothing at all of the word of faith, they moved about with God's favor and help, since in that time, too, many wonderful miracles of the divine spirit were wrought by them, with the result that whole crowds, every man of them upon the first hearing, eagerly espoused piety toward the Maker of all things" (*H. E.* 3.37.3).

The most precious scenes prior to the triumph of the Church under Constantine are to be found in the *Life of St. Gregory Thaumaturgus*, strangely enough, never translated into a modern tongue and therefore relatively little known. Its author Gregory of Nyssa makes clear that he had been in the region of Gregory's mission and had heard, passed down orally over the span of some hundred and thirty years, a wealth of stories which he transmits to us.[58] Through them all runs the theme of supernatural force displayed and, for no other reason and without need of any further word, conversions wrought.[59] The Wonder-worker puts an end to an outbreak of plague, for example, and the pagans thereupon turn to his God, "whom they acclaimed the One True God and ruler of all things." We can almost hear them shouting, like those around Carthage in Tertullian's day at the end of a drought, "The God of

Gods!'' or in Rome, beholding Peter's miracles, ''One is the God, One God of Peter!''[60] The *Acta Petri* develops the same theme repeatedly and at length: a miracle is wrought and thereby the onlookers are made Christians on the spot.[61]

That this is how it really happened, and the Church really grew in historically significant numbers through demonstrations, or the report of demonstrations, that seemed beyond all but divine *virtus*, I do not doubt. In evaluating the evidence, we must of course bear in mind all that has been said about the religious habits and expectations of the world evangelized. For other explanation of that great growth, there is no evidence—no mass meetings, no great sermons, no speaking in tongues or dramatic inner spiritual crisis. But our view can be confirmed from two further sorts of information: first, information about conversions to belief in pagan deities, in just the same ways that availed to make Christians, in the same period and regions—that is, through proofs of power;[62] and second, information about conversions to Christianity post-Constantine. There is a small corpus of sketches giving us the specific moment and reason that belief was inspired.[63] What they reveal is just what is found also in earlier parallels, that is, religious allegiance following upon displays of divine efficacy.

Words and logic unassisted by wonderful deeds did sometimes have the same effect among ordinary folk as we have seen them having among the elite, and they are so reported;[64] but the surviving evidence does not show them to be any considerable factor, whatever rationalists might prefer. Celsus, representing that latter view, tries to discountenance the Church by his ridicule of the supernatural element in Christian expansion; but Origen defends it head-on as operating and absolutely essential in the time of Jesus, of the Apostles, and down into his own day near the mid-third century.[65] Both he and his opponent are at one in assuming that it is an element at work only among simple folk. Both writers, like the Apologists generally, distinguish between what should be shown to the educated and the uneducated.[66]

What is shown naturally determines what is seen, and seen to be good. So we return to our subject and starting-point. The devotees of other gods saw in Christianity what could be accommodated on their level of perception. Among them, among the most highly articulate and intellectual, we ourselves feel not too ill at ease. They both produce and tend to occupy the pages of our sources. We can see how they think, we can generally understand them, and we are inclined instinctively to explain the rise of the Church in terms of these elite figures. But if we are rather to estimate Christianity as a historical force, that drew in scores of thousands, we must take account (even if we cannot quite enter the thoughts) of Everyman as well.

13

"WHAT DIFFERENCE DID CHRISTIANITY MAKE?"

THE QUESTION put by E. A. Judge to A.H.M. Jones has about it a kind of devastating simplicity: "What difference did it make to Rome to have been converted?"[1] Self-evident changes like basilica-building or people's attendance at churches instead of temples are surely not what the question is getting at. The point (or at any rate *my* point) is rather to discover how broad patterns of secular life changed as a result of the population being now believers. Inquiry promises interesting results because Christianity is known to us as a religion, along with Judaism and certain others, that offers powerful prescriptions for living this secular life. There is a Christian morality, in short; and the introduction of the new faith should thus have had historical impact.

The extent of this impact I test in five areas. The first two have to do with domestic relations: sexual norms and slavery. The latter three have to do with matters in which public authorities were more involved: gladiatorial shows, judicial penalties, and corruption.

The hundred years after Constantine's vision of 312 seem to constitute the best period on which to focus the question I address, because then the new religion can be seen still operating on the old; whereas, thereafter, when nonbelievers were too few to exert influence around them, whatever changes occurred in society must have been due to factors other than conversion.

There are a few problems of method to look at first. They arise from the nature of our sources, which distort the truth through offering too much of an upper-class view, and one that is excessively bookish. They may be illustrated out of a work from an earlier age, around A.D. 200: the *Paedagogus* of Clement of Alexandria. Here more than anywhere else we find extended discussion of how Christians ought to live: they should avoid wine, dancing, the theater, loose badinage, cosmetics, primping, jewelry, finery. Some hundreds of pages are devoted to characterizing all these things in the darkest colors, principally because they lead up to or are somehow tainted with illicit sex.[2] To the extent Clement may have been heeded, then, in all these areas of life, conversion made a difference. When we notice further in his work, however, the easiness of life he assumes and evidently finds among his audience, who toil not neither do they spin—who eat and drink too richly, have too much jewelry, and expect on their saunters around the city to be pushed up the hilly parts by their servants (3.73.5)—we must suppose Clement's Christians to be only some tiny part of the population. As they seem all to own slaves, and in numbers, too, they may cluster within only the top five percent.[3]

Beyond that, the *Paedagogus* lies wholly within the realm of books. Much of its preaching is expressly or in fact drawn from previous works of literature, for the most part pagan.[4] Clement thus introduced little that was unfamiliar to his particular audience, all, persons of the leisured classes. The *Paedagogus* "made no difference," in the phrasing of our original question. Further: we have no way of telling whether, even among its own tiny numbers of readers, it produced persuasion to the point of action, any more than similar works by Seneca had done, or homilies by Dio Chrysostom. Of course, reading books and being interested in them is in itself an important activity for some of the elite, therefore of historical significance—a little, anyway. But if we cannot demonstrate *doing* as a consequence of reading, we have reduced the whole of moral literature to the compass of a pastime. Such a reduction indeed needs to be considered seriously, if we may trust a parallel; for anyone familiar with modern study of Stoicism and Cynicism knows with what care and controversy the effect of these philosophies has been sought in the law courts or streets of the Roman empire. The two schools seem to have left little mark within their different strata of society; they were somehow encapsulated.[5] Was Christian preaching similarly encapsulated within some five percent of the already-converted?

To answer that question and in turn, therefore, to answer our question originally posed—"What difference did Christianity make?"—we require a special test. That test must show Christians not just talking but doing; and it must show them in some opposition to evidently accepted standards. Without that opposition they cannot have produced any difference.

Of course the standards must be of that time, not of some other. Anachronism must be avoided. Consider the matter of slavery. It is condemned in recent centuries as abhorrent to Christian principles. It need not have been so in the past. Morality is no fixed thing. In fact the early church took slavery entirely for granted. "In contrast to Jesus' teaching, there was no command . . . to strive to abolish slavery."[6] When, in the later Roman empire, circumstances changed as a result of toleration and Christian emperors began now to legislate on slavery, plainly they never intended its abolition—not even its mitigation, beyond the measures that flowed naturally from prior models.[7] The penalties they applied to peccant slaves grew even crueler than they had been,[8] a matter which I come back to later. If we ask, in summary, whether life was on the whole easier for slaves in Christian times than in pagan, the answer is probably no. The new religion introduced no radical innovation, only development along lines laid down earlier: in some ways a bit more humane, in some ways less so. The Church itself, corporately, and its priests individually, and its models and heroes as well as at least the richer members of congregations whom church leaders normally addressed, continued to own, buy, and sell men, women, and children.[9] In the fourth century as a result of the social advancement of its upper crust, church members while increasing their ownership of slaves lost their fellow-feeling for them too, and thereby no doubt were all the easier in their minds about administering harsh laws and treatment.[10]

In contrast to the relatively little attention bestowed by the Church on slavery, attention to sex continued quite at the high level discovered in Clement's *Paedagogus*. Suggestive social settings were identified and barred to women; suggestive sights on the stage as well; singing and erotic verse, or even poetry in general, for its presumed effects.[11] Sex itself was a prohibited subject among both pagans and Christians in Clement's world, to be censured only through its secondary or tertiary connections: that is, through a person's dress or walk, the tint or expression of the face, and so forth, as indications of sexual tendencies. Unacceptable tendencies could be easily distinguished. Respectable pagan women didn't drink wine, nor men either till they reached their mid-thirties—but these were the practices among Romans specifically.[12] Women went veiled in public[13]—or at least they did so in early days in Rome and later, too, in some but not most north African cities, and among most of the eastern populations. The veil covered the head, not the face as well. We see there were regional differences among both Christian and pagan communities, before Constantine; and Christians did not differ from their neighbors.

But there were other differences in style to which Clement draws attention (*Paedagogus* 2.114.4.): for instance, the use of purple veils that rather drew than deflected the gaze of strangers. Purple was a very rare and expensive tint. A decent woman among the Romans could be told by her dress and attendants, says Ulpian, and a stranger should only address her within the bounds of respect: a jest was permitted but nothing *contra bonos mores*.[14] Ulpian's reference to her attendants, like Clement's to purple veils, tells us he is thinking of the wealthy. But in this regard, too, there might be regional variations. In some Hellenized cities but not others, says Menander Rhetor, "it is not thought proper for a young male to be seen before the agora fills up or after late evening, nor should women engage in buying and selling or anything else that belongs in the agora."[15] He is plainly speaking of the upper classes. A man like Menander, a professional speaker who traveled around, would be observant of local practices and norms.

We can pursue the subject of variations in moral codes according to degrees of wealth. In the small towns and villages of third-century Syria,[16] we catch a glimpse of wagging tongues and almost obsessive concern for the isolation of women from men, save in marriage—this, among pagans. The standard is reminiscent not of our own world but of modern Iran, perhaps. What a difference between this and a group of young Lycian women of leisure! They are a little surprised that their friend and hostess is *not* wearing cosmetics.[17] But they are Christians! Or consider Apuleius' rather countrified accusers in the small town of Oea in north Africa, quite scandalized by the erotic poetry he wrote; but he can cheerfully defend it before the judge, a man of the world and an aristocrat: " 'desirous of her thighs and honeyed mouth,' " he quotes from another poet. "Now what is there so naughty in all my verses compared with this one line?" (*Apol.* 9.9f.). He could even better have quoted a great deal of Catullus, too, or Propertius. High life had its own code. Consider the account of a community leader anxious to secure the liberation of some members unhappily arrested; so he sought out a woman who could help through her connections at court. He is Pope Victor and, in the words of Hippolytus, she is "the God-loving concubine of Commodus, Marcia, who wished to do good deeds."[18] What an extraordinary phrase, "God-loving concubine"! But it was used of a woman almost a queen; so that was all right—just as it was all right for Christians to put off their first husbands and take another, if they were of the elite. Valentinian could do so, and Jerome defended another such case.[19]

But that case drew a storm of criticism. I instance it, with the other scenes I have sketched, not to suggest that, between Christians and pagans, there were really no differences at all in sexual norms—obviously the rules regarding remarriage were markedly different. I intend rather to underline the complexities of my subject. In trying to discover what consequences followed from the conversion of the empire's population, it is not enough to say there was a pagan code and there was a Christian code, and the latter won out. In fact, to sum up my discussion thus far, it seems to me likely that there was broad agreement between the two codes regarding slavery, and very considerable overlap regarding sexual *mores*, without either code on this matter speaking at all consistently to every region and socioeconomic stratum.

Now to continue, we must just glance at sexual proprieties as seen from the top. I instance Cicero. He was raised in the belief that every woman, like Lucretia, defended her virginity literally with her life. On the other hand, he has no difficulty in excusing gang rape. How so? His client's victim did not belong to the respectable classes.[20] Special rules protected *matronae*, "decent married women," and maidens; and there were other rules for the lower classes as seen by the upper.[21] Still in the Christian empire, legislation acknowledged the distinction.[22]

Attitudes toward homosexual relations prevailing in non-Christian society reflected similar biases and differences both of class and region.[23] With the arrogance of supremacy the noblemen of Rome did very much as they pleased. Some of them separated themselves from the majority of even their own class, in practicing homosexual relations quite out in the open, and drew around them poets and prostitutes and new fashions. Evidence for such openness in the west, fairly abundant by the mid-first century A.D., cannot be found after the reign of Hadrian, save for occasional signs of opposition.[24] The east had its own ways. Dio Chrysostom's speech to the people of Tarsus[25] is fairly representative of the culture of that broad region. In it we see male homosexuality quite out in the open; discussion of it might be likewise fairly free. For though his criticism is offered in a manner at once humorous and gingerly, nevertheless Dio does criticize. So does one of the parties to the debate in Plutarch's essay on love, very passionately. If, then, we look to see where among these various moral values the Christian might fit, perhaps the best setting would be among the everday sort of Romans, not the aristocracy, or among the more severe circles of eastern cities. Yet it must be noted that, in attacking "unnaturalness," pagans did not attribute any divine personality or intent to Nature. So in that respect they lacked the logical force in support of their disapproval that Christian doctrine certainly possessed.

A friend of Pliny (*Ep.* 9.17.1) "complains of his disgust at clowns, ballet-boys, and mimes" on display at a recent party. Pliny shares his feelings. There is, he says, "nothing attractive in the ballet-boys or enjoyable in impudent buffoons and stupid clowns." He instances (7.24.4f.) a noblewoman of his acquaintance, too, who had her own private troupe of *pantomimi* and "showed favor to them more effusively than fitted a leading personage." That is, Pliny disapproved. But she did so herself as well, and therefore always excused her son from her company when she called them in to perform. Away at Vienne in Narbonese Gaul, far from Rome, Pliny also tells us "it was decided the games should be abolished because of the ill effect they have on citizens' *mores*—just as our own have," he adds, "but more universally" (*Ep.* 4.22.7). From Alexandria, Dio Chrysostom chimes in: mimes and dancers and horse racing "bring a common ruin to whole cities"; and he goes on to spread his disapproval over the conduct of spectators generally at such spectacles, characterized by utter lack of dignity and decency.[26] When, then, we return to Clement in the *Paedagogus* (2.40.2) castigating dance music and choruses in that same city, we do not sense any gulf between his views and those of pagans—some pagans, as I must emphasize, not all or even most, for the entertainments that Pliny, Dio Chrysostom, and the Apologists speak about so harshly were of course immensely popular among non-Christians.

Among these items so far discussed we have, incidentally, focused on opinions that are openly advocated and put in practice, often among substantial minorities or even whole communities. It is obviously important in presenting the history of morals to bring forward the decisions of an entire city, like Vienne, and the express reason for its decisions; failing that, to instance views which are offered, not defensively, to a sizable audience, as if that audience would approve or at least not be shocked. In Cicero's or Dio's or Menander's speeches, or in laws, or in literary works published within some not too narrow circle, especially if they explicitly speak of a custom or opinion as widespread, we have the kind of information we can rely on, if we use it cautiously. And on the subject of entertainment it prepares us for what we find in the fourth century.

Gregory of Nazianzus describes "empty-headed people who set great value on strange leaping about [that is, dancing], the slaughter of men and killing of wild animals, which they provide to their fellow citizens in order to excel others in honor,'' just as Basil refers to "the man in the theater who offers his wealth, for the sake of some slight honor, to pancratiasts, mimes, and men pitted against wild beasts—whom one looks on with disgust—amid the shouts and clapping of the crowd.''[27] Clearly the views of the second-century Apologists on these shows had not yet prevailed. Critics remained as they had been before, a censorious minority within the Christian population, as Pliny and Dio Chrysostom had been within the pagan population. Still in A.D. 384 the emperors Theodosius and Arcadius graciously supply "theater players by every carriage and boat'' for the up-coming festivals in Rome. The urban prefect thanks them cordially. Christianity in this respect had thus made no difference.[28]

The same prefect Symmachus also writes to the emperors (*Rel.* 8.3) to endorse rules drawn up by the senate limiting, or equitably distributing, the expense of both theatrical spectacles and gladiatorial ones. He had not heard that decree, often referred to by modern scholars, in which Constantine "put an end'' to gladiatorial combat (*CT* 15.12.1, a. 325). In fact the termination of such combat began not in 325 but much earlier: in Gaul, Germany, and Britain in the course of the 200s. The reason is not quite clear but is probably compounded of economic difficulties and displacement of tastes to other enthusiasms. I stress the economic factor because most gladiators, like prize fighters today, chose the role and received extensive training; therefore they cost a lot. After training, their life expectancy was to survive only ten contests, on average. The expense of maintaining troupes of fighters was borne by the imperial treasury in Rome or in other cities by millionaire office-seekers and the very rich as a form of self-advertisement and grandiose benefaction. Such displays of all sorts were limited in the capital to certain months, chiefly December, and elsewhere limited still more sharply because of their high cost. The role of Christianity in the abandoning of most western gladiatorial combat was nil.[29]

In the wake of the law of 325 posted in Beirut, gladiatorial contests are nevertheless attested in Antioch in 328; thereafter, approved and facilitated by Constantine himself, for Italian towns; accepted without comment by his son Constantius, in legislation; and, as we have seen, supplied by Theodosius. In Augustine's and (rather rarely attested) in eastern cities also, Christians financed and in throngs attended these spectacles, which continued into the fifth century and were only banned for the last time, apparently, in the 430s.[30] In the light of the course of change in the northwestern provinces, it is difficult to show that Christianity and not some other force was at work in this final disuse of gladiatorial combat.

We need clear indications of motive—of how people felt about these spectacles. Yet evidence is very scant. We know that Constantine was not the first emperor to indicate dislike of them. Marcus Aurelius had done so, and barred duels to the death.[31] Prior to 325, Christian authorities are found condemning the institution and even attendance at its shows;[32] but so are pagan "authorities," that is, Stoic moralists. The longest and most emphatic statement on the subject issues from Seneca, and in some ways the most watered-down, from Tertullian and Novatian, who almost lose what we ourselves would call the main point in a miscellany of objections. Among the several angles of attack or causes of revulsion that we discover, however, there seems to be no clear pagan-Christian difference. The combats are seen to involve the violation of cult rules and hence contamination;[33] or watching makes us insensitive to human suffering, or it makes us accomplices to murder, even murder of the innocent.[34]

In the fourth century we have, from the first Christian emperor, a reason given for the ending of gladiatorial combats; such "bloody specatcles are displeasing in times of civil serenity and domestic peace." He does not condemn them absolutely.[35] Later we have the reactions of one non-Christian as reported to another, discovering in himself, to his utter horror, the full degree of savageness that watching murder could arouse. The account is even more telling than Seneca's anguished pages, but in the same line.[36] We look in vain, however, for any expression of pity for the combatants, in this reporter as in various contemporary Christian authors also: Gregory of Nazianzus, Cyril of Jerusalem, and others.[37]

Before concluding, however, that the conversion of the empire in this regard introduced no moral novelties, generated no special forces of disapprobation or discontinuation—in short, "made no difference"—I think one must face up to a contradiction. The level of judicial savagery rose in the fourth century but condemnations specifically to the arena seem to have diminished very sharply. Though somehow the gladiatorial troupes continued in operation, we hear almost nothing of criminals sentenced to the games. What we would call "the better view" of Eusebius but also of Seneca thus prevailed in the long run not, evidently, through any general tenderness toward one's fellow beings but out of unwillingness to feed the amphitheater through the law courts. Exactly why the courts should not be used for that purpose, we have no hint or information.[38]

Judicial savagery in the later empire is a marked and historically significant phenomenon. It both represented and produced widespread changes in the way people shaped their careers and generally comported themselves in situations that brought them into contact with government. I now turn to that topic as the fourth of my five, though only for cursory treatment.[39]

I begin with a law often noticed. It issues from Constantine (*CT* 9.24.1, a. 315) against the guardians of a girl persuaded to yield to some lover: "the penalty shall be that the mouth and throat of those who offered incitement to evil shall be closed by pouring in molten lead." But compare his decree a little later (*CT* 1.16.7, a. 331) aimed at venal bureaucrats: those "greedy hands shall immediately forbear, they shall forbear, I say; for if, after due warning, they do not cease, they shall be cut off by the sword." He specifies (*CT* 9.18.1, a. 315) that the kidnapper shall not only be condemned to the amphitheater but, "before he does anything whereby he shall be able to defend himself, he shall be destroyed by the sword." And he revives (*CT* 9.15.1, a. 318) the almost-disused penalty of tying a person into a leather sack with snakes and then drowning him. As for any rude treatment of tax-delinquents who are women, death is not enough; the perpetrator "shall be punished by a capital penalty or rather" (Constantine corrects himself) "he shall be done to death with exquisite tortures." The emperor's language, whether or not metaphorical, matches the measures he prescribes, for example against informers, "the one greatest evil to human life," whose activities "shall be strangled in the very throat, and the tongue of envy cut off from its roots and plucked out."[40]

But with that threat Constantine was not yet finished with informers. As we have seen, those who were slaves and had the "atrocious audacity" to turn in their masters for alleged treason should be "affixed to the cross"—a decree which has caused great difficulty to commentators. Once a man was converted, as they reason, he could never impose such a sentence, in violation both of the respect due to the Lord's suffering and of the Christian rules of charity: for crucifixion caused a lingering death of the utmost agony.[41] Fortunately my train of argument can pass by these perplexities; for my interest lies in large developments, not particulars; and it is uncontested that crucifixion, which had been occasionally imposed as a penalty throughout imperial history up to this point, thereafter disappeared from the record. So likewise did condemnation to death from wild beasts (though see above, n. 38). Christianity in these respects therefore did make a difference.

At the same time, however, cruelty in other forms continued on the rise, and in open, systematic, and publicly tolerated forms. Of this, Constantine's other laws just instanced are fairly representative. True, they do not initiate the rise, of which there are abundant signs both in the legislation of his immediate predecessors and in our accounts of the Great Persecution; but they extend it. They extend it over a lengthening list of new capital crimes, as the century goes on; and, if most of these speak of the times in general, especially of administrative difficulties, a number are of concern specifically to church teachings. As we might predict, some of them focus on sexual crimes; others, on religious belief, whether pagan, Jewish, or Christian.[42] The form of the death penalty they prescribe is decapitation, less often burning at the stake. We can occasionally see these laws being applied in individual cases,[43] indicating they were not a dead letter; and they are, of course, all promulgated, if not personally initiated, by Christian monarchs for execution by an increasingly Christian officialdom.

We can naturally discover in the record some officials crueler than others.

No contemporary observer of whatever religious allegiance attributes their varying degrees of mildness or cruelty to their religion;[44] nor should we. Which is not to say that there was no conscious discussion of judicial savagery among Christians as such; but only that it fell on both sides of prevailing standards.

Those standards were, to repeat, a great deal harsher in my period of study, A.D. 312 to 412, than in the preceding hundred years. Considering the whole span there covering two full centuries, is it possible to see anything in the nature or development of Christianity that might have helped produce the change toward harshness? The only evidence of that sort known to me, which is also the only sadistic literature I am aware of in the ancient world, is the developing Christian vision of Purgatory,[45] surviving principally in apocryphal apocalypses and parts of the Sibylline Oracles. In the details abundantly provided in this literature depicting the torments of the wicked—hung up by their tongues, buried to their mouths in human excrement, their eyes put out with a red hot iron, and so forth—a connection is drawn between the elaborate infliction of pain and the will of God. Such a connection may have been found and felt likewise by the persecutors, earlier. In Diocletian's edict against the Manichaeans we sense it. He concludes several strident paragraphs with the statement, "We have established pains and penalties well deserved and suited to those people . . . [who], together with their abominable scripture, are to be subject to a rather rigorous punishment: to be burned up in the fiery flames; and those who are of their allegiance, truly, and especially the more fanatical, we order to be beheaded."[46] Observing both Christianity and an aroused paganism in operation, it appears to me likely that religious beliefs may have made judicial punishment specially aggressive, harsh, and ruthless. In both, the characteristics of action were similar, producing cruelty in the service of zeal. But there was also a major difference: pagan beliefs left daily morals to philosophy. For pagans, only correct cult mattered. Christian zeal in contrast was directed over all of daily life. Hence, threats and torture, the stake and the block, spread over many new categories of offense.

Christians also display a moral defiance toward law which pagans do not offer; and they do this not only during the persecutions but after 312, as well. Ambrose confronting Theodosius comes first to mind, perhaps, not over the slaughter of the innocents at Thessalonica but over the commission of theft and arson in Callinicum. What was done there in the name of religion, he says, rises above law. It is justified violence.[47] We see him later, too, contesting the surrender of property lawfully claimed and lawfully assigned by the courts.[48] Apparently it could also be claimed by a brother bishop. And Basil in Caesarea sharply defies the judge and the law in defense of a person seeking refuge in his church.[49] Such direct confrontations with civil authority cannot be found in the pagan world of either the third or fourth century, and attest to a strength of conviction that might easily reform legislation to its own ends.

A generation of controversy has grown up around the presence or absence of Christianity in Roman law—a generation beginning with the three fat volumes of Biondo Biondi's *Diritto romano cristiano*. Near the conclusion of his work Biondi notes how "the scope of penal law greatly expands and the penalties themselves . . . take on a harshness that can be called cruel and excessive."[50] Harshness, however, he attributes to the moral seriousness of the church, focusing especially on sexual conduct, religious belief, and "administrative disorder and the corruption of public functionaries."[51] If one were to seek the roots of that moral seriousness, they would surely be found in the Christian sense of acting out God's will; and the discussion thus returns to the operation of religious zeal such as I point to in the vision of Purgatory.

Controversy over the nature of postclassical law, however, seems to me in some degree needless. I can illustrate what I mean through the third area of special severity that Biondi correctly identifies: governmental routines. Here we can see plain moral deterioration. Is Christianity somehow to blame? If it is assumed that the world after 312 was "officially" Christian, as the controversy and historians generally take it to be, then there is a sort of responsibility for everthing that rests on the Church. But surely it is mistaken to see conversion of the empire in such simple terms. Throughout the century post-312, though in diminishing degree, the empire's religion was a mixed thing.[52] On many practices and elements of life the church therefore could have no influence; and in many elements and practices there was a momentum, too, as a great ship has way on it, that no opposing force could easily re-direct. Accordingly we cannot expect a Christian world in the moral sense where there happened merely to be a Christian emperor and widely prominent churches.

"Administrative disorder and the corruption of public functionaries," in Biondi's phraseology, traced a line entirely independent of ecclesiastical history and had developed by A.D. 312 into a luxuriant jungle of shakedowns, bribes, intimidation, perquisites, and privileges. It involved the taking of money for services you should perform gratis, or money not to perform what you were instructed to do. Throughout the preceding several centuries there had prevailed a moral standard universally familiar which forbade any of this. However, there were many corners of life, very much as we have tipping in restaurants today, where a different standard prevailed. Over the course of time, it spread around and became a serious and historically significant factor in the third and later centuries. It drew the most attention and had the most effect within government and in the areas where government and private citizens had to deal with each other. In a typical scene, you would have soldiers billeted in some city, intimidating shopkeepers and practicing extortion through the fear of violence they aroused. Or you would have a court clerk holding out his hand; and you could be sure if you didn't give him money your legal papers would never reach the judge's desk. Emperors like Constantine and Julian, both Christian and pagan, all had to acknowledge the prevalence of such practices by setting legal limits to them: so much rake-off but no more. At the same time they legislated again and again and again to prevent the further growth of corruption.[53] In sum and in short, corruption represented an enormous example of what sociologists call value dissonance.

Now for some illustrations. I choose them not at large, from a society usually called Christian; for I have indicated that society was in fact very far from completely converted. Instead, I pick out from the mixture people who are manifestly believers. I begin with a civilian charged to recruit for the army in Egypt. He reports to the local commandant, "I am fighting for you, and not for any 'take' " which might arise through excusing otherwise likely recruits. "I want all your doings to go well, but we want you too to take a little, for that is good for everybody and good for God, too."[54] And similarly to the same recipient, another person writes out a contract to hand over the agreed-upon amount for bribes needed for the promotion of his son in the local camp, and he swears to the agreement "before God." So the deity was seen to smile on these nefarious little doings.

But of course there are Christians and Christians. Even the openness of these protestations (the second instance being intended to be shown in court if need arose) might prove only the bad faith of some insignificant single individuals. We may turn then to a great leader in monasticism, Saint Pachomius. One of his monks was sent out in time of famine to find grain for the monastery; and he got it in unhoped-for bulk by buying it at a cut rate illegally from the public tax stores of a nearby village. His benefactor who allowed this was "the thoroughly devout and God-fearing" village custodian of the stores, and Pachomius' only reaction was to scold the brother for buying more than was strictly needed.[55]

Perhaps that only shows moral standards in Egypt. Let us look at the bishop of Laodicea, using church funds to bribe high courtiers in the cause of his beliefs; but they were heterodox.[56] Or the bishop of Caesarea, Basil, in correspondence with the bishop of Iconium, agreeing to buy the exemption of an important congregation-member from certain civic duties, while hoping perhaps to get it free. The two bishops had to settle "on what post" of exemption "we must bring to bear our efforts, so that we may set about the asking of this favor from all our friends in power, either as a free gift or for some moderate price, however God may help us forward."[57] Again, in Italy, we glimpse the mighty Petronius Probus continually in and out of the highest offices so as to provide the more bountifully for his numerous greedy kinsmen by lowlier but useful appointments. "A good son of the Church and patron of one of its most successful bishops," Ambrose, he "was a spectacular profiteer of the empire."[58]

Last, Augustine. While making his living in Rome as a teacher of oratory he campaigned for advancement. He devoted his leisure hours, he tells us, to the cultivation of "a good supply of powerful friends," *amicorum maiorum copia*, to win their promises of support; "and, if we have nothing else," he says, "and can't wait, at least a governorship may be provided, and a wife can be taken with some money so she won't increase our expenses." The train of thought rather suggests that expenses would be incurred in gaining a word of recommendation in the right quarters.[59] Is that possible? It would be entirely according to normal practices; and after his return to Christianity and elevation to a bishopric, we hear Augustine saying to his congregation, "You would like to be a governor, and lack the qualifications of merit; so then, by purchase. For perhaps you wish to be of use to society, and buy [that governorship] that you may be of use."[60] The line of thought is clear: the end justifies the means. It appears in a much longer and more studied form in a letter he writes later to the great *vicarius* of Africa, Macedonius. Augustine speaks of the bribes taken, and taken for granted, in the courts[61]—all illegal, of course. But, while drawing the line at buying the judge and the witnesses, he defends the clerks who take bribes. Let them just keep their demands within the bounds of custom. Then, if they grow rich, they may "lavish their goods on the poor"!

While, then, heralds in the public square of every city were bellowing out the angry threats of capital punishment—fire and sword, no less—offered by Christian emperors in thirty separate laws aimed in thirty separate directions, but all at various forms of money-making from one's administrative authority—while this din of rage resounded through the empire, servants of government continued quietly about their business as usual, the Christians exactly like the non-Christians. If we ask again our central question, whether conversion had made any difference, the answer is an easy no—except in the justification offered for what was going to be done anyway. There, Christians had their own reasons.

But we can observe how corruption spread even within the Church itself. Partisan accusations of that tendency in the course of sectarian strife[62] perhaps should not be dismissed out of hand, since we have bishops reproaching their own priests for extortion in various forms.[63] The bishop of Antioch, "being of a great city, and having the governors under his influence, put it all up for sale"—that is, he involved other bishops in the routine purchase of church office. We notice incidentally that appointment lay in part with secular officials, here as also in Egypt.[64] Our source for this, Palladius in his biography of St. John Chrysostom, goes on to report on still more widespread and ineradicable purchase of episcopal thrones in the province of Asia, centered in Ephesus and protected from Constantinople. John himself determined that the buyers whom he discoverd in the province should remain in office. They alleged the hardship they had undergone in assembling the money in the first place: "some of us," they told him, "put up the property of our wives."[65] So they were to be forgiven.

Not that John generally approved of what they were doing. Simony was condemned. In condemnation of it, Basil quotes the text from Acts that gives us the very word. Bishop after bishop quotes Luke 3.14, where John the Baptist bids soldiers abstain from extortion.[66] Augustine praises honesty on the bench,[67] Ambrose groans at the corruption he sees around him, ''most of all among those persons set in office. . . . Everything is for sale.''[68] The morality these leaders subscribe to is exactly the same preached to society at large by imperial legislation. Nevertheless, just as emperors themselves occasionally put up offices for sale when they needed the cash (and is not that extraordinary?),[69] so the same persons in the Church who condemn corruption also engage in it, as we have seen, or condone it. They offer justification drawn from their own morality, above the law. And we have seen that before, too (above, p. 150).

At the end, now, I should attempt some summary of my findings, or at least pick out their chief features. I begin by pointing out the need to take the times on their own terms without importing into them our modern sympathies. Ancient unbelievers do not require our reproach, nor Christians, our apology.[70] That said, it remains true that different points for ethical emphasis were favored by Christians in the century I survey than were favored either earlier or later—as, taken on their own terms, of course, all different times display their own moral preferences. There were evidently changes also in non-Christian moral standards, at least so far as they can be sensed in the west. I have in mind developing second- and third-century views about male homosexuality and gladiatorial combat; also, everywhere, more frequent resort to torture and executions in the name of justice. Attitudes toward venality in public office became more and more tolerant as time went on, in both east and west. In these respects as in respect to the institution of slavery, where I can really detect no change in attitudes across time, non-Christian moral history runs parallel to Christian. Or the two are one. In both we can discover some variation in moral values up and down the social spectrum. In both we can detect the views of individuals especially interested and sensitive about morals, who rise above everyday norms of actual behavior. We know them from their words, which inspire. If we look to deeds, however, and try to see patterns of action in the population at large that clearly reflect Christian preaching, we are hard put to find anything very significant. Of that most aspiring virtue, charity to the point of loving one's enemies—hardly a sign.[71]

The identification of areas where Christianity made a difference can perhaps best focus on sexual conduct. In this regard Christian ideas induced a change of law to legitimize slave marriages (but not to free the offspring thereof) and changes also to sharpen penalities against sexual deviance or misbehavior. Misbehavior was defined much more broadly. Pederasty, rape, any roughness toward respectable women, adultery, and seduction were all newly attacked by death penalties;[72] and a letter of Jerome (above, n. 43) shows us the enforcement of such laws, or similar ones, in the courts. There were demonstrable changes in literature, too. Nothing similar to Heliodorus', Apuleius', or Petronius' novels could be published, nor poetry like Catullus' or Ovid's. There was a difference! Above all, the entire abnegation of sexual intercourse was actually espoused and practiced in scattered odd places in the west[73] and Asia Minor in the east,[74] quite apart from orthodox monasticism there. Monasticism had its deepest roots in Egyptian Christianity,[75] spread rapidly to other provinces in the period I deal with, and produced toward the end literally scores of thousands of adherents. Here we see an absolutely remarkable impact on manners and morals that was to shape the whole millennium to come.

14

ORDINARY CHRISTIANS IN THE

LATER PERSECUTIONS

IN THE EARLIER persecutions [before Julian's], what was confounded
and distracted was a small thing, for our teachings had not yet spread to
many; but truth was established still among only a few.'' So, Gregory of
Nazianzus, looking back from the position of political dominance and numerical parity enjoyed by the Christian population within the eastern empire of his
own day.[1] Like many such statements in ancient Christian writers offering
some sense of numbers, their context and their purpose must be borne in mind,
whether to minimize or maximize. It is really impossible to put much faith in
them; so modern attempts at estimating the size of the church throughout the
empire at the time of the Decian or Great persecutions do not and should not
venture beyond round numbers. We might hazard the figure of five millions of
Christians in A.D. 300.[2] Given the statements by Eusebius and others, that the
preceding generation or so had been so fortunate for the faithful, those five
millions would have to be diminished by a fifth, perhaps, to approximate the
total in A.D. 250. Attempts at estimating the numbers of martyrs must be similarly tentative. Henri Grégoire, master of persecutions history in general,
gave this matter his special attention, and arrived at a figure of two to three
thousand as a maximum, under the Great Persecution, to be added to W.H.C.
Frend's ''hundreds rather than thousands'' in the 250s.[3] The difficulties of the
question are of no importance here. It is enough to draw out, by subtraction,
the obvious conclusion: roughly one one-hundredth of one percent of Christians by their dying for their faith constitute the focus on which historical interest, then and now, ordinarily rests.

Whether or not rightly, from consideration merely of their total, needs no
arguing. Historical importance is not to be estimated by the mechanical counting of heads. But, on the other hand, what happened to the remaining 99.99
percent is also of interest, surely; and, as the material has been repeatedly
sifted, chance comments in ancient sources have been noticed, and assembled,
and in fact provide some picture of the ordinary truth.

It must be understood in terms both of the persecutors' purpose—to assure
divine favor through displays of universal piety—and of their administrative
capacities. What they could do was quite limited. In gathering their subjects
together to express submissive loyalty toward the gods, they were often to be
seen making some unhappy Christian go through the motions of compliance,

struggling all the while. Then he would be released. Appearances were enough.[4] If they were determined on more substantial compliance, then they must go beyond public proclamation, to compulsion under the direction of local agents. The latter, appointed by municipal senates, came in various shapes and sizes—untitled civic leaders, unspecified "magistrates," duovirs and *strategoi*, cult administrators, scribes, heralds, and accountants.[5] All available machinery such as could have been seen in raising taxes, relieving famine, or handling any sort of emergency was put in motion. Occasionally, as we can see in Eusebius' *Martyrs of Palestine* (4.8), it was reinforced by soldiers; but normally there was no physical force that could be called on until victims had been brought into the custody of a governor's staff. His office would include both body-guards and torturers, but no men to spare. As G.E.M. de Ste. Croix has pointed out,[6] recalcitrants would have had little to fear from pursuit. Yet there were occasional exceptions: Gregory Thaumaturgus and Dionysius were hunted actively if briefly beyond their cities' walls; and there always remained the most common and important means of law enforcement, namely, the citizenry's active cooperation. Informers, including the most deadly, Christians themselves, not only can be seen in effective operation from time to time but were in people's minds as they considered what response they should make to the government's demands.[7] In Egypt, doubtless compliance with Decius' registration of the pious through sacrifice-receipts, *libelli*, was as broad as it can be seen to have been, because of Egyptians' habituation to tax receipts: it was not that they were especially zealous to prove their good faith before the emperors; rather, that they were used to providing themselves with some protection against later charges of delinquency. A neighbor's malice or greed was always to be feared; for he could expect to be rewarded with a part of the property of anyone convicted with his help. Even without the need for *libelli*, later, betrayals are recorded. Money is reported as the motive. Similarly, in the collection and registration of confiscated Bibles and other Christian writings in north Africa in the Great Persecution: the town officers scrupulously recorded through their scribes just what they did, when and where, and kept those records for decades, because, as it actually turned out, they might need them for their own defense later in court.

From the statement that "thousands of certificates [of forgiveness for having offered pagan sacrifice] were being issued every day" in Carthage in the summer of 250 by the few persons who had stood up to the persecutors, some idea is given of the numbers of Christians in need of such documents, confirming the looser wording of Cyprian in particular (the Decian persecution a *vastatio*, and similar testimonies).[8] The same impression is conveyed of the Great Persecution by an official's remarking, "The whole of Africa has sacrificed," as by Eusebius' account of Antioch, where one "saw a great number of men, women, and children in crowds coming to the idols and sacrificing," and the more specific description of Optatus: "In the demons' temples the devil reigned victorious, the altars smoked with the foul fumes, those who could not attend the rites were made everywhere to offer incense, so that every temple was made a temple for the crime, and old men on their deathbeds were defiled, mindless infants were polluted, little children were brought to the wicked deed by their mothers." The crowds included "a great number of clergy, . . . deacons, . . . priests, . . . and some bishops."[9] It is plain from such unhappy witnesses that some very large proportion of the victim population succumbed to their dread of the consequences of disobedience or were swept along in the flood of compliance, itself constituting a demonstration of piety that must have been very impressive; for there are instances of permanent apostasy.[10]

But there were also ways of circumventing persecution short of surrender. Various dodges are described for us: feigning madness, hiring an obliging pagan or Christian to offer sacrifice in one's own name, or buying a certificate of having sacrificed from an official. Such measures because of their expense counted in the Alexandrian church as an acceptable substitute for resisting the emperors' demands head-on.[11] Simple acceptance of compulsion might also be tolerated, as, for example, by "Plutarchus bishop of Sbeht [in Egypt]; this man for the excellence of his wisdom is worthy of all respect. He was prudent and reverenced the emperor's gods, and offered up sacrifice to them; and look at him now! He is alive, with everyone who sacrificed with him, and is bishop over them."[12] At the other extreme lay the inviting of death by provocative behavior, even thrusting oneself on official notice. This was generally condemned by the Church,[13] though the teaching was not heard by numbers of martyrs especially in Numidia and Palestine. The persecutions presented novel challenges more quickly than the Church as a whole could agree on the best response; and, notoriously, the variety of responses was a cause of the deepest imaginable divisions; but Plutarchus and his congregation, like the purchasers of *libelli* of sacrifice, of course thought of themselves as Christians and transmitted the faith to their children no less than their more heroic comrades.

The scattered fragments of evidence regarding the later persecutions have so far yielded a picture only of various forms of accommodation, and generally within an urban setting. True, rural settings occasionally were disturbed by the persecutions—in Theadelphia in Egypt, quite a tiny place yet the point of issue of a number of sacrifice-certificates, fitting Eusebius' mention of pagan violence reaching into cities and villages alike. Edicts calling for persecution in the eastern provinces prior to A.D. 311 had been directed to *logistai* (= *curatores*), *strategoi*, and "the people in the countryside"; and, when Eusebius reports on Palestine, he speaks of "the leaders of the native churches" being haled before the authorities in the city, seeming to mean churches in the city's surrounding territory.[14] Otherwise, however, the fact that Christianity was an urban religion appears clearly enough in the history of the persecutions as in its other trials and triumphs.

What underlines that fact are the many stories of refuge sought and found in the rural parts around cities, or still further, into craggy or barren regions. Christianity was not much expected or much pursued there. From Decius' decrees, people in north Africa took to "flight among the lonely mountains," as others did in Palestine, there initiating a monastic movement, and still others in Egypt likewise, to mountains and deserts, from which at least a few of the fugitives never returned.[15] Retreat to barely habitable parts brought one into dangerous proximity with lawless, fierce people living on the edge of civilized society. But nothing so extreme was generally necessary. Instead, one sought a hiding place and protection in country dwellings proposed by one's friends (Cyprian's, for example)[16] or, if the danger of the moment was limited in its reach, in another, safe province entirely.[17] Merely changing residence from one city to another evidently could provide the same security as flight into the rural areas,[18] presumably because the neighboring population wouldn't know you or have any grudge against you. In any case, who could say who lived in the rabbit warrens of metropoleis like Alexandria or Antioch, with all their twisting back streets and high-walled houses?

Indications of the scale of the different responses to persecution show quite clearly that the preponderant one was flight. That was true in Alexandria in 203 as in Cappadocia in 234 and again in Alexandria in 248/249; in Pontus in 250 as in north Africa at the same time; and in the east generally in the early fourth-century troubles, when, under Licinius, "once more the pious took their flights, and once again the barren or wooded parts, once again the mountains, took in the servants of Christ."[19] Eusebius' emphasis is on the *pattern* of response, for a last time repeated. It cannot have been universal, of course, given the great variety of administrative institutions in the empire's cities and little towns, and given the freedom of governors to interpret the law as they chose.

Those who fled were not only separated from their homes and belongings but lost them to the state forever. Confiscation of property was likewise the punishment for any sort of head-on non-compliance.[20] The loss of all one owned, on which rested so much of one's place in society, too, was a heavy blow. Many feared its effects, and were no doubt influenced by it in deciding what to do. In particular, Eusebius shows in his church history (6.41.11) how "many of the more prominent [Christians], fearful of the threats or induced through their public responsibilities," complied with the edicts of the mid-third century. The phrasing recalls similar passages in other authors showing how riches and magistracies together not only involved people ex officio in ceremonies repulsive to a Christian, but made evasion of the edicts well-nigh impossible.[21]

There were exceptions. We would like to know, for example, how it was possible for the bishop of Emesa as an elderly and then very aged man to remain on his throne for forty years through the difficulties reported in Aurelian's reign, and those under Diocletian, Galerius, and Maximin, until he at last came forward for identification as a Christian in 311, and was martyred.[22] Most bishops of both larger and smaller towns were simply too well known to escape detection for any length of time. Therefore, of course, a special weight fell on them, even without their being picked out as particular official targets in both the 250s and early 300s. Some not very large number complied with the edicts (above, nn. 9 and 12), at one extreme, or, at the other, suffered martyrdom; others for a term endured terrible conditions in jails and quarries; but most—Clement, Peter, and Dionysius in Egypt, Gregory Thaumaturgus and Meletius in Pontus,[23] Cyprian in north Africa under Decius—fled into hiding. Cyprian (*Ep.* 58.4.1) writes to the people of one town under his general oversight that they can expect their bishop to disappear. That was simply what happened. And he alone of his rank suffered in the persecutions under Valerian in north Africa, as, in Palestine and Syria under the Great Persecution, only the bishops of Antioch and Jerusalem.[24] These three stand out among several hundreds holding episcopal office in the provinces concerned. Of the lower clergy, the persecutions were likely also to make very nearly a clean sweep.[25]

In their own terms, Christians of the period here under examination looked on those of their number in the persecutions who preferred to die rather than deny their religious beliefs as wonderful models for their imitation; and their descendants thereafter to the present day have seen them as the heroes they were. Indeed, they have not seen much else within the history of the later persecutions. If that history is examined from a distance, however, and from what might be described as a Darwinian point of view, the martyrs diminish in significance. They were objects of enormous pride to their local communities and eventually to the united Church as a whole, from the later fourth century on; but before that, their cult did not claim any large part of religious life. It is not easily interpreted as a result of the part they played. Around them more promptly developed rigorist schisms under the names Donatism, Valentinianism, Meletianism; but martyrs were certainly not the cause of division, however much they were appealed to for partisan purposes. As to the force of their example, it is not clear that they aroused more imitation in the Great Persecution, proportionate to the numbers of Christians then and the duration of their trials, than in 177 in Gaul, or in 203/204, or 234, or at any subsequent date. The fact is important. To die for a belief not in the course of war, not bearing arms, not in the grip of him-or-me, required extraordinary resolve; and as in other historical settings—some religious, some secular, some of this very day when tanks are sent against civilians—only the tiniest proportion of adherents possessed the qualities needed for that death.

Regardless of period, whether of Decius or Diocletian, the edicts aimed at the churches had indeed reduced them to ruins. At least, so it appeared. Their congregations like their leaders had either complied or fled, with very few exceptions. Their meeting places and personal property had been seized. Persecution, however administratively primitive it might appear to a modern view, had attained its near goals, the empire once more deserved the favor of the gods, there was not an atheist in sight. Then and only then did emperors and governors relax from their savagery.

But if, in the accounts of these times and trials, historical significance is sought rather than "melodrama"—"sensational incident and violent appeals to the emotions, but with a happy ending," as my dictionary defines the word—that significance is indeed to be found, of overwhelming mass: it is to be found in the enormous fact that the Church as a whole survived, not that some tiny handful of its members did not. It survived despite having been leveled. And it did so because of ordinary Christians, in their quite ordinary responses to adversity, not martyrs: ordinarily fleeing, complying, buying their way out, dodging, lying, hiding in cellars or haylofts, communicating with each other only in secret, but (with few exceptions, perhaps no more numerous than the martyrs) remaining Christians. They won by a sort of guerrilla. Therefore, the search for an understanding of the persecutions should properly focus on the Church's endurance in flight and apparent surrender, and on the patterns of behavior, ties, and values established among ordinary Christians that gave to their union an indestructible elasticity without loss of corporate character. It was as so often the ordinary, the un-melodramatic, who shaped the future.

15

WOMEN IN PUBLIC IN THE ROMAN EMPIRE

IN THE COURSE of research begun nearly a decade ago, I noticed that the study of women in the Roman empire had not reached to inscriptions and therefore had not reached beyond Pompeii. That remains very nearly the case still today.[1] There was, however, in the nineteenth century in more laborious times, something written in Latin on the subject of my title, which carried into the Greek-speaking world. Until it is brought up to date properly and competently, a few notes in its margins may be useful.[2]

By way of background, however, a passage from Valerius Maximus (6.3.10) might first be cited, in which he describes "the frightful marital severity of Sulpicius Gallus, who dismissed his wife because, as he learned, she had gone about in public unveiled." He adds, and a little reading in other authors easily supplies, still more examples of Roman wives and daughters punished for conversing or being seen out of the house with any but their own immediate family. So the more muscular half of the human race imposed its sense of sexual territoriality upon the other half "once upon a time" (*olim*, 6.3.12, to use our source's word).

The period in which this incident lay was back in the second quarter of the second century B.C., far removed from the days of Valerius Maximus himself.[3] Roman women were not in his time hidden from men's sight. But Plutarch reports "it is more often the custom for women to be veiled," evidently in the Greek half of the Mediterranean world, and evidence confirms this for Pamphylia, Cilicia, Palmyra, and Palestine on the coast.[4] Did this difference really exist, and did it indicate broadly different mores, Greek compared with Roman?

The well-known evidence in Pompeii strikes even the least-informed tourist right away. On the forum, one of the largest and most notable buildings is that given by Eumachia to a workman's association, and her name and office, *sacerdos publica*, are there advertised.[5] Of the two deities served by women, Venus and Ceres, it was the former who held the higher rank, being patroness of the colony itself, invoked on occasion even in favor of political candidates (*CIL* 4.26). To be chosen priestess brought one before the public eye very sharply. For Eumachia as for others we know of, election was connected with great wealth, wide business associations, a husband an office-holder, and forebears the same. We can only guess that certain personal qualities were needed as well. After a lifetime of prominence, for one's burial the local senate might vote a funeral and assign a plot at public expense, as to the distinguished Arellia Tertulla or Septumia or Mamia.

Declarations of political support are painted up on the street-side walls of all sorts of buildings in the town, typically in the form "So-and-So asks you to make So-and-So aedile." Quite a few of the supporters who speak are women and can be identified in some further way, as wife of a café-owner, workers at a mill-cum-bakery, waitresses at soup kitchens, apparently all of them slaves or ex-slaves or in any case of a lowly condition.[6] While the form *Hilario cum sua rogat* is readily understood, in which the husband and his wife (not even named) ask the passer-by to vote for their candidate, it is also common to have a woman's name written ahead of a man's, *Caprasia cum Nymphio* or *Recepta nec sine Thalamo*,[7] an inversion of status explained by neither of the parties having any sense of status between them at all, or by the woman being free or freed, the man freed or slave.

At both the top and the bottom of society, women thus appear to take an active part in the common business of the city, at the former level because among them could be found, at the least, a lot of money and the ability to bestow it in one form or another on those who sought it through their offers of flattery, respect, and support; at the latter level, because women obviously wanted to take a part and no one told them it was useless or ridiculous. The fact carries its own implications.

One of the painted announcements on a wall in Pompeii offers for rent all or portions of a block of buildings *in praedis Iuliae Spurii filiae Felicis* (*CIL* 4.1136); another on an interior wall in a sort of gambling house shows a certain Faustilla as a pawnbroker making short-term loans on articles of small value.[8] She did business widely. Between the two extremes in scale of operation, we also have Pompeiian records showing women selling properties of middling size or less. The sellers appear to be mostly ex-slaves and the sources of their wealth, such as it is, may have included the manufacture of condiments (*garum*) and textiles.[9] Women might have effective management of estates of a wide range, and could do with them pretty much what they wanted, in the process drawing the attention of their community; for transfers normally took place very much in public, often through auctions.[10] The Justinian Code contains hundreds of imperial responses to women litigants, many of course concerning civil status, obligations of freed condition, marriage, divorce, support, dowry, minority status, and child custody—essentially private matters, though also among those most often of concern to men, too. It is worth noting, however, that financial affairs bulk very large in this collection, and they may involve substantial transactions. From just a single year we can pick out mention of "the income from estates [note the plural] given as a dowry"; "the gift of slaves and other things given by wife to husband"; "assessed estates given as dowry"; "fully equipped estates by bequest," one farm of which yields oil and wine for the market at the disposal of the *mater familias*; finally, a certain

Marcia suing her debtors and getting hope of satisfaction even though she has lost the IOUs.[11] Over a period that begins with Hadrian and runs to Diocletian, women *sui iuris* and over the age of twenty-five make up a fifth of all rescript addressees, a quite surprising percentage on the rise as time goes on.[12]

With this kind of evidence we move beyond Pompeii to Italy more broadly. But some of the features visible in Pompeii reappear in other Italian cities. Naples buried at public expense an honored citizen Tettia Casta, the senate voted a statue to her to be erected, and offered its sympathies to the next of kin. She had been priestess of a women's cult association.[13] At Tarentum, Reate, and Milan young women belonged to an imperial cult association, the *invenes*.[14] In a population so universally given to incorporation into social and religious groups, it is possible to find exclusively women's groups, very rarely;[15] and a host of women not of the highest class are requested to serve as patrons under one or another title, most often *mater*, to one or another men's *collegium*, sometimes centered in a cult, sometimes in a shared profession.[16] Throughout the west, Italy plus the provinces, perhaps a tenth of the protectors and donors that *collegia* sought were women.[17] Honors paid to a patroness *ob merita*, or some similar hint, indicate how the game was played: the members of a college inflated themselves with titles for their officers and with rules for their self-government that most closely approximated to institutions (like whole cities, for instance) enjoying substantial dignity; and in that important condition, they passed a motion empowering their representatives to confer with the esteemed object of their interest, extending a respectful invitation to become their benefactress. The minuet can be observed best in a decree not of a college but of a city, Corfinium, whose senate and populace paid court to a (now ludicrously nameless) local worthy, with suitably worded praise; offered the usual engraved plates, *tabulae patrocinales*, of compliment and honorific enrollment; and had no long wait for reward from the honorand, "who accepted the honor and instantly gladdened the hearts of the most distinguished Senate, offspring and wives, plus the populace, by feasting them all with great rejoicing" (*CIL* 9.3160).

The foregoing shows quite clearly how women in a town could come to the notice of large groups of fellow citizens, in ways bound to make observers look up to them, or at least not to look down on them; and those who were observed constituted a good sampling of society, with some over-representations of wealth. But it might be doubted whether the latter category was not sought out solely to be drawn on for money, in encounters away in the privacy of large homes. Or did donors actually attend big gatherings in their honor, and stir about in the crowds? On these questions (not easily answered for male honorands) perhaps the only facts that can be brought to bear are, first, that set assemblages in the Roman world for cult purposes or joint action or mere conviviality more often than not involved eating and drinking; and, second, that women could be naturally included in these activities, as is commonly recorded. As a general rule, then, women as benefactors should be imagined playing their part personally and visibly, out in the open.

The evidence regarding the presence of women at public banquets in Italy is widely scattered through inscriptions.[18] People attended and received a meal, wine, pastries, oil, cash, in categories by rank: "town senators (*decuriones*), the male populace, women," "town senators . . . , Augustales . . . and citizens (*municipes*) of both sexes, as is our custom," "citizens and residents and married women," "town senators, Augustales, women of magistrates' families and the populace."[19] Not only were women, more often than not, excluded altogether from these occasions, however, and from apparently all-inclusive phrases like "all citizens" or "the entire people";[20] beyond that, if they were indeed invited, they were generally put at the bottom of the pecking order, as the sequence of mention indicates, and as is sometimes made mathematically clear in differential distributions: largesses might be given out in the ratio 30:20:3 to town senators, Augustales and women (*AE* 1971, 85; [cf. 1976, no. 176]). The proportions fit not badly with those so far discovered in imperial rescripts or electoral signs, that is, showing the female sex, as such, entirely excluded from no role or aspiration at all, in the public affairs of their community, nor required to demonstrate merits much different from men's in claiming respect and participation, but yet included only in far, far smaller numbers.

Turning at last to the Greek-speaking provinces, we can make use of still another kind of evidence, the bronze coins minted by hundreds of cities. Sometimes they bear on them the names of their incumbent magistrates. From his prosopographical files on those coins, K. W. Harl very generously answers two questions for me: what sort of posts did women hold, and in what proportion to men? He produces 17 women in 13 cities, where 214 men are also named on coins.[21] The larger the city (Pergamon, Tralles, Laodicea, Smyrna), the fewer the women relative to the men. But generally, the implications of the ratio are no doubt the same for this region as for Italy. As to the positions held, they are of the highest that municipal politics afforded: stephanephoros at Attuda, for instance, Ulpia Carminia Claudiana, whose father was a magistrate and high-priest (that is, of the imperial cult) before her and whose mother Flavia Apphia was "high-priestess of Asia, mother and sister and grandmother of senators, local patriot, daughter of the city and of Flavius Athenagoras procurator of the emperor, father and grandfather and great-grandfather of senators," as an inscription tells us.[22] Other notables: Secunda, prytaneus of Cymae; Pedia Secunda, epimeletes of Eucarpia; Flavia Asclepia, strategos of Germe; Cosconia of Smyrna, stephanephoros and daughter of the populace; Marcia Aurelia Glaucia, grammateus of Tralles; and so forth. It should be pointed out that, despite local variations in title, these are all eponymous magistracies, giving a date to each year, representing the city to the world, and so constituting the very top of the whole pyramid of offices.

This numismatic material strikingly confirms the picture presented in the nineteenth-century work already referred to, by Pierre Paris. It contains names on coins of high-priestesses, for example, Julia Severa at Acmoneia, her husband thrice high-priest, or Pedia Secunda, already mentioned, a priestess of Artemis like Apphia of the same town in Phrygia—just as Paris finds in the inscriptions more about women in sacred offices than in secular ones;[23] but the post most publicized is naturally that of the person presiding over the worship of the imperial house within an entire province. It is generally agreed that incumbents held the title high-priestess not in their own right but as wives of those high-priests who happened to be married.[24] It goes without saying, too, that they can often be identified as, and always assumed to be, members of the provincial aristocracy, therefore naturally marrying at their own social level. So it follows that one or another of them will be chosen for other prominent positions as well: "high-priestess of Asia of the temple in Ephorus, prytanis and stephanephoros," "prytanis and gymnasiarch, the high-priestess Favonia Flacilla," "the most distinguished high-priestess Mamia Belleia Alexandria . . . , Mother of the Gerousia" of Thasos.[25] Pierre Paris draws special attention to a certain Menodora from a city in Pamphylia, whose father and great-grandfather had been gymnasiarch, demiourgos, decaprotos, and high-priest before her, her son and daughter gymnasiarchs after her, and she herself holder of most of these plus certain other offices. She was person of great wealth, able to pay for the building of a temple with porticoes, and so forth—also to pay for largesses distributed publicly to town senators (88 *denarii* and a bushel of wheat), gerousiasts (81*d*. and a bushel), Assembly voters (78*d*. and a bushel) and their wives (3*d*.).[26]

These figures invite comparison with the largesses offered by the locally wealthy to various civic categories in Italy. The sequence of ranks and the proportions are similar. It is harder, however, to compare the ratio of women to men in high office, since apparently in the eastern provinces women sometimes received titles solely through being the wives of office-holders. That practice extends beyond the high-priesthoods to the presidency of provincial federations (Asiarchs, Pontarchs, and so forth),[27] and occasionally to the presidency of the local gymnasium.[28] In Macedonia, apparently the wife of the Macedoniarch became high-priestess, or she was Macedonarchissa, her husband high-priest.[29]

Pierre Paris spends many pages discussing whether women in public positions actually *did* very much. If that is a real question, it is not easily answered for male magistrates and liturgists, either. They used private and municipally owned slaves as their agents, and they had elected or appointed assistants.[30] But surely the heart of the matter and what most concerned contemporaries had nothing to do with the personal arranging of this or that detail of civic administration or ceremony. Rather, it was the deference secured forever from one's fellow citizens through one's being, for only a day, or for only a few days in a year, at the head of the parade, or in front of crowds, and thereafter known by a new title and memorialized in stone in the forum. Rewards of this sort were had quite as easily in religious offices as in civil, quite as much through titular elevation as through the direct responsibility for executive decisions, and quite as fully (though nowhere near so often) by women as by men.

Certainly the town senate as willingly voted its honorific decrees to those in charge of ceremonial and sacred duties as to the administrative.[31] Moreover, priestesses are seen aloft on a throne in the theater, there to preside over the shows, or are crowned by the city or by the women and men of some cult group, or even thrice honorably received by the emperor himself;[32] the deity they serve, they serve on an equal footing with priests;[33] or they alone must preside over certain religious associations.[34] In any case, women are by no means restricted to priestly honors. As we have seen, they appear with those joined to other, secular titles, in combined careers that include being head, for example, of the gymnasium or gerousia.[35]

It is correctly noticed, nevertheless, that women are rarely found in roles like that of grammateus which would require their speaking in public. They are to be seen, then, but not heard. They may, as Pierre Paris points out, be accompanied by a spokesman, husband or son; and in addition to the long list of terms of praise applied indifferently to them or to their male counterparts, there are some that suit their sex alone: *sophrosyne*, for instance, "modesty."[36] What insures some place for them unconstrained by prevailing ideas about propriety is, first, the very easily understood and amply documented importance of money in the pursuit of fame and high standing, evident in that phrase that meets us so often in inscriptions, "out of her own resources," *ek ton idion*, or sometimes a little more specifically, "assigning all her fields to her largesses" (*IGR* 3.584); second, the never-enough-revealed means and relations by which women, as well as men, exerted political influence.

At the center of the Roman world, as any reader of Tacitus knows, women had a great deal to say about the decisions that determined the lives and fortunes of the most important people (and "politics" rarely rose above that courtier level, to the level of what we would call "policy"). Claudius' reign offers the best illustration, pictured as wholly under the control of his latest wife. He even received embassies "with the matrons present";[37] and no one can doubt, though no evidence allows us to demonstrate, that, in such groups of the wives of the great in the capital, the stronger personalities stood out, and altered others' opinions, and those opinions were in turn carried home, there to influence at least some husbands, sons and fathers. In essentially the same way at a much smaller center of power, and yet a large city, Corinth, which served as a provincial capital, a certain Junia Theodora opened her house to merchants, envoys, and travelers from all over Lycia, and received their thanks later in the form of senatorial decrees for having "rendered sympathetic to the province most of the authorities, helping to promote a friendly disposition toward us among all the leading people," "contributing to all the affairs that mattered most to all Lycians."[38] But she never accomplished all this with money alone, she never *bought* "the leaders," nor did she content herself with formal appearances on balconies or the like. No, what she was able somehow to bring to bear, from (of course) a naturally favored social position, can have been nothing but a network of connections woven and made to work for the objects of her interest, in the way politicians of both sexes and every period in history have done since time began.

Less in the public eye than the court at Rome, less the stage on which events were made than a provincial capital like Corinth, we have the little town of Cragae on the road from Side to Antioch. It lies in a plain only a couple of miles across, overlooked by a Zeus temple on the hills. There also was built a watch-tower. Some miles off into steeper country there rises another tower, thirty-odd feet high and strongly constructed, marking the center of a fortified farm such as can be found all over the empire at this time, the mid-Principate. This structure, along with its match at the town and the temple and the cult statue, inscriptions declare all to be the work of one or another member of the house of Hermogenes. The local founder of the house came from the large center in the region, Selge, thirty-five miles away. He and his descendants maintained their relations and high standing there. When the populace of Cragae voted a decree of honor to a certain Cassia for having been "priestess of Zeus and, in her short life, of service to her city in many matters,"[39] it is hardly surprising to find her at the heart of the house of Hermogenes by descent and marriage alike, and (with the plain half-owned, we may suppose, and daily scanned from their eyries by the heads of the family) it is quite inevitable that she should have been indeed a force in the community. She it would be who must be asked to intervene with Zeus, or with the hardly less remote authorities of Selge (who recorded their respects to her in stone), or finally, with all her cousins, determining whatever ambitions or needs of Cragae would be met.

And yet, to return to our starting-point, we have the many testimonies to women in the eastern provinces going about veiled, and the implication therein, that they were to avoid notice by all means possible. What is to be done with this picture? Against it must be set others in mosaics, without exception showing women with their faces and generally with their heads, too, quite uncovered—perhaps the better to display the modish arrangement of their hair.[40] Here may be the clue that resolves the conflict in evidence: women who imitated the changes in style that went on at the imperial court, changes depicted in the provinces by portraits of the ladies of the imperial house, were the richer ones, the more open to the new ways, and the more likely to belong to families on the rise. Women of humbler class went veiled, but these others behaved exactly like their counterparts observed in Italy, fully visible, indeed making their existence felt very fully in public.

16

WOMEN'S POWER IN THE PRINCIPATE

THERE IS no novelty in saying that the women of the empire were listened to on important business; but demonstration of the fact is likely to be drawn from the Palatine, where they were Tiberius' mother, Claudius' wife, Nero's old servant, Vespasian's mistress, Domitian's niece, Elagabalus' grandmother—in short, where they had access to the emperor himself and belonged therefore to a peculiar category.[1] They are recorded as his other and better self in the handling of ordinary government business; if not better, then at least highly effective and not much concerned to hide the fact. They took care of their own in a way specially Roman: that is, for payment in cash or credit, they could supply praetorian prefectures, consulships, governorships, procuratorships, lesser offices, favors, pardons, and judicial decisions sometimes tantamount to murder on behalf of their adherents. That is power.

An example or two: In A.D. 240 the chief Vestal, Campia Severina, received public thanks from one dependent "for the favor of equestrian rank and a second term of service conferred on him, Aemilius Pardalas, honored with the tribunate of the First Aquitanian Cohort through her request," and from a second dependent "made procurator of the emperor's Library Funds through her favorable intervention," *suffragium*.[2] She was a potent friend. Consider, next, a certain Calvia Crispinilla. Of high rank, nevertheless she assumed a sort of chamberlain's job under Nero, custodian also of a boy treated by him as mistress. Presumably through her young charge she had the emperor's ear. In any case she practiced methodical, wide-reaching extortion and grew vastly rich. A little after Nero's death she set off for Africa, there to rouse the legionary commander to revolt. His movement failed. She managed in spite of that to keep her head safely on her shoulders right through the twists and turns of the years 68, 69, and 70, under Galba, Otho, and Vitellius, one of whom (probably Otho) even defended her against loud clamor for her punishment. She had perhaps by then remarried (her first husband had been executed for a single night in the empress' bed). The second was an ex-consul; and they had no children. So, "potent through her money and absence of heirs," "she extended her influence throughout the capital."[3]

And we are reminded that women enjoyed power even in the provinces as companions to their husbands posted abroad. A very unfortunate business that was, too: debated in the senate, where note was taken of their ordering people about, including high military officers; of their engaging in intrigues, no doubt mostly in regard to promotions; and of their practicing extortion.[4] The most remarked-on female presence in a province may have been Munatia Plancina, married to a consul of 7 B.C. Her conduct (matched by her husband's, to be sure) amounted to high treason: rudeness toward Prince Germanicus during his eastern sojourn; poison and hexing aimed against him; and meddling with the troops' loyalty. Returned to Rome and formally charged, her friendship with the queen mother protected her for the nonce, even when her husband was driven to take his own life. Tiberius publicly acknowledged the weight of his mother's prayers; and Tacitus, besides telling us of Plancina's high birth and riches, attributes even greater influence to her than her husband once possessed. "Thus it was unclear what freedom of action toward her the emperor enjoyed."[5]

We hear of no governors' wives her equal—indeed, very little about any of them at all, after Tacitus' time. Perhaps just a matter of our sources? At about the same point, epigraphic evidence approaches the height of its amplitude and detail. Women then step forward into our ken who are certainly very well known and deferred to in Italian and western provincial cities: the wife of a consul, daughter-in-law to a praetorian prefect, to whom the patron of the town publicly records his gratitude "for her most singular, preeminent, and bountiful good will displayed toward himself and his children"; a second, Ummidia Quadratilla, benefactress of Casinum, providing the town with a temple and amphitheater even though the family had long since made its chief residence in the capital; and a third, Vitrasia Faustina, of a family likewise long famous in their home (Cales) despite still greater fame in Rome, who now pays the bill for some expensive project in her native place—before the emperor killed her.[6] All three were of senatorial rank, and addressed as such. The title advertised prestige and wealth as matters of course; but those advantages were enjoyed actively. Their possessors were visible, stirred about, even achieved (one of them) a position felt to be some threat to the throne; for Vitrasia's name in our literary sources occurs in the context of Commodus' paroxysms against the dangerous and disloyal.

At lower levels of standing and social rank, and in more confined settings, quite similar persons appear in the epigraphic record, too unimportant to be noticed in literary productions: for example, a woman of Nemausus accorded a public funeral by the town council, without mention of her status or claims (no need for that among her fellow townspeople), or a priestess of the imperial cult in a Spanish province honored by council decree in her native place.[7] Is there, however, some qualitative difference as well as a quantitative one between these provincial examples and the women whose scene or source of influence is the capital? In any case, what exactly is meant by the term "power"? Power to do what? When the structure of authority across the whole empire is taken in at a single glance, no doubt the center predominates over the periphery, the official over the unofficial, and the imperial over the provin-

cial. To the center belonged control of arms, of plain brute force, and of whatever respect the law commanded. Women had no part in this directly. They
could not hold office. And whatever influence some of them might enjoy indirectly over appointments and agents in government, they could not all live
in Rome. No matter: Rome was not the world. Most of the time, most people
were rather concerned about material ease and the respect accorded to their
wishes and opinions in their own city—at most, in their own province. Ease
and respect could be gained apart from office; they could, as we will see, then
lead to office, if it were local and provincial. So power need not be defined
only in the terms that describe Munatia Plancina or Ummidia Quadratilla.

Perhaps, nevertheless, Roman power was different from every other, and
Roman women were given a greater part of it, than in the Hellenistic world.
Why else should "matrona stolata" be taken over as a loan phrase in Roman
Egypt?[8] It defines a special, imported, desirable degree of privilege before the
courts. There is no need to emphasize that the legal right or reality of handling
one's wealth as one pleased gained one a very great deal of control over others,
at least in the private sphere. It gave access to the public sphere as well, since
official ranks and positions of any sort in cities throughout the empire were
tied to donations, subscriptions, minima of total worth, or all three of these in
combination, even for a village headman. Yet, without special grants on any
Roman model, women in the eastern provinces are nevertheless seen bestowing their money where they wish, in loans or purchases or gifts.

Such gifts are sometimes enormous and amply recorded by their beneficiaries—temples, for example, or the donor's city at large.[9] The free handling
of money may then be combined with high birth and wielded by someone
"descended of a father and remoter ancestors belonging to the first people, the
establishers of the city" of Aphrodisias; also (and the cause for the inscription)
high-priestess.[10] As priestess, did "power" extend to any significant action?
Would she be more than a face and a lineage, or bank account, so as actually
to make a difference in her world and earn a place at least in the footnotes of
its history? Yes is the answer, qualified of course to allow for some merely
ceremonious elite. Women holding the post of city secretary (*grammateus*) or
president of the city's youth- and sports-parks (*gymnasiarch*) or of the Elders'
Association (*gerousiarch*) not only had, as we can tell, certain inescapable
public duties but acted in offices much more often occupied and keenly sought
out by men. Their real position is indicated by someone boasting in a public
notice that he is "husband to a Lyciarch," that is, the presiding officer of the
Lycian provincial congress. His deference is highly instructive.[11] Such as she
are recorded as helping to shape community opinion in Pisidian Antioch—
"women of distinction and the leading men of the city," Acts 13.5—or in
Thessalonica ("many of the leading women," *ton proton*, Acts 17.4 and
above, n. 10).

Notice a second sign seeming to show that Roman power was special and different: a second loan-word, "patroness," taken over into Greek from Latin. The elements from which Romans as individuals or collectively as a state assembled their power are all familiar: *beneficia*, *officia*, *gratia*, *clientelae*, *clientes*, *patroni*. Several of these are transliterated for use in the eastern provinces; but *patronissa* is, for our purposes, most apposite. "Patronesses" in Roman form are recognized in a small eastern city, being honored both by individual citizens and by "the council and people," by individuals alone, the person honored being the wife of a consul; even by an entire city, a great one (Ephesus or Thessalonica).[12] As a thoroughly Greek name like Thoas (in Figure 2) in time gives way to "Thoantianus," and as Greek law yields slowly to Roman, so it seems likely that relations of dependency à la Grecque, such as can be seen in these instances, gradually grew closer to some form of patronage that Cicero would have understood. But the details of the development have escaped record.

In Termessus the artisans advertised their gratitude to a benefactress for distribution of free "grain to all the masses" of the city.[13] Granted, the same sort of client-patron relation is more easily found in Italy or the west. For Sossia Polla dedicating honorific statues in Apamea, there is a match in Sosia Falconilla (I draw both illustrations from the stemma, Figure 2). Falconilla in the lordly way of her place and time picked up the cost of no less than five portraits of her father voted by the town council in Cirta while also having her own statue set up at public expense in Minturnae (perhaps the family's point of origin).[14] She too represents a type more readily found in the west. Yet the ratio of surviving epigraphic texts, western and eastern, Latin and Greek, is ten to one or worse; and, for the control of wealth and access to civic prominence, our evidence is largely found in inscriptions. The imbalance between west and east therefore loses significance.

This essentially similar control of power by women of the local aristocracy in both halves of the empire can be discovered in another of the usual arenas of the day: in the law courts. I instance, first, a pair of contests in Italy. Rutilia Polla, otherwise unknown to us, at some point in the first half of the first century bought up Lake Bracciano in southern Etruria, along with a ten-foot strip of shoreline.[15] The lake now and presumably then measures some forty kilometers round. But it was not enough. In the spring run-off it might get bigger. Then she claimed the same ten-foot strip, but further into the land; and she went to court to assert the claim. At least in her own district she was a figure to be reckoned with.

Then, second, a case emerging in the private correspondence of Marcus Aurelius' day, though in a letter sadly chewed up by the centuries. We discover a certain Baburiana's failed petition to the emperor. It had concerned public construction in which she was interested as a backer, perhaps, or more likely as donor to her city. Also it concerned sums of money out at interest.

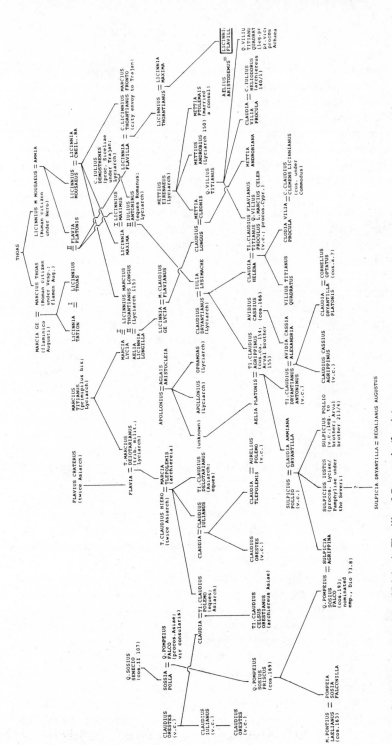

2. The better-known kin of Licinnia Flavilla of Oenoanda (Lycia)

Being refused once, she resumed pressure to get her way, acting through Fronto. He was of course one of the persons closest to Marcus Aurelius.[16] Not to take no from the emperor indeed showed a formidable tenacity.

Third, however, is an eastern litigant, Furia Prima. She is entangled with the enterprising and rather alarming Archippus in Prusa. He had once been sentenced to the mines for forgery; somehow balked justice; waved aloft his testimonials from the emperor himself, not to mention recognition decreed him by the city; and has the cunning to tie up another opponent (no less a celebrity than Dio Chrysostom) in a most sinister charge of lèse majesté. None of which deters Furia Prima from attack.[17] I am not concerned here, obviously, with details or technicalities of legal position; rather, with the effective ability of women to engage in serious struggles, and win. Without confidence in that ability, they would not be found so often in the courts, accounting as they do for close to a third of the docket.[18]

In estimating their strength, the importance of money and of the independent handling of it has been emphasized more than once (and it must be said again, too, that the sources allow discussion only of the local or imperial aristocracy, all relatively rich). Women can be seen doing a great deal more with their estates than spend the rents. At Pompeii or Ostia their speculative ventures in real estate turn up; also, in manufacture.[19] The port city itself was largely built of bricks brought down in barges from brick yards up the Tiber valley and further north. Of those that we can identify from trade marks on their product, nearly one in five is owned by a woman. Indeed a sizable number of the actual producers leasing the yards, putting up the cash, and operating as the moving force in the works, were also women.[20] Such evidently direct engagement in various kinds of business affairs naturally engaged them also in litigation, where we have just seen what role they played.

The consequence of money, business, litigation, patronage, municipal office, influence, and, of course, the individual determination to apply any or all of these things in action, appears in casual phraseology. For example, Tacitus describing a confrontation between Otho and the praetorian guardsmen. They burst in on him when he is banqueting "the leading women and men."[21] If the women do not enjoy quite the precedence implied in the word order, at least they have a separate importance. It is not an assembly of "the leading men and their wives." In the next century another scene and phrase: in the theater (of Marcellus?) and around the statue of an empress, special seating is reserved for "the women foremost in power."[22] Last, a phrase taken from Epictetus, as he imagines a venal Roman official. The man contemplates using his posting to Greece as an opportunity for theft and extortion. He says to himself, "if it's done neatly and guardedly, we'll never be detected; and besides, we have powerful friends in Rome, men and women, and the Greeks are a flaccid people. No one will dare to come up to the capital on this account."[23] So there we have some little glimpses into the minds of three persons

across two centuries, reflecting what seem to be everyday, unconscious ap-
praisals of the power structure. Both sexes have to be reckoned with, in the
capital as in Antioch or Thessalonica (above, p. 171).

Between those cities, however, and Rome, the difference in weight was
obvious. As a final illustration of the fact, and of the weight of women as
against men in their localities, we have one further type of evidence, in the
form of a genealogy. It is displayed on the tomb of Licinnia Flavilla of Oenoanda in Lycia: some hundreds of lines of fine Greek script, a regular fifth
chapter of Genesis (Figure 2).[24] It shows a dozen generations: among them,
many Lyciarchs, a procurator of Trajan's, an army officer or two, a couple of
consuls, a line of several generations of Roman senators, and a highly distinguished pancratiast (!). This family, one of the most completely known
throughout all antiquity, branches out into kin that the lady of the tomb specifically passes over. However, they are likewise to be traced in the epigraphy
of the corner of the world and in connections drawn to similar elites of other
substantial centers—Patara, Cadyanda, Cibyra—and still larger rural districts;
for of course the income that supported claims to local office drew upon very
extensive landed possessions. One member of her family was Opramoas. His
belongs among the really great private fortunes that we can reckon up in the
whole empire's history. He gave way enough money to make a good handful
of Roman senators.[25] Another relative, Avidius Cassius, came measurably
close to gaining the emperorship in Marcus Aurelius' place, a third (but post-
dating Licinnia) was offered the throne after Commodus' death, though he
declined it (Pompeius Falco), while a fourth was married to the briefly successful pretender Regalian.

As to Licinnia Flavilla, now: it is simply not to be imagined that she could
ever have been injured unavenged, or that, if she persisted, she could not have
brought to bear the leverage of wealth and kin, dependent villages, and Roman
senatorial aunts and uncles (for both men and women were accorded rank-
titles like ''senatorial'' or ''consular''), against any human target she might
choose.

Yet at the same time the epigraphy of her region, expanded beyond that of
her tomb itself, yields only a tiny handful of women among many men achiev-
ing public notice. Claudia Vilia Procula paid for a part of the theater at Patara
in 147 (it was apparently an ancestress of the same name who dedicated some
imperial statues in the 120s in the same town). Marcia Ge and several others
served as priestess in the imperial cult, either in their home town or representing the entire province; and Sosia Polla set up an honorific statue to such a
priest in Phrygian Apamea. So much the inscriptions tell us. But among
eighty-odd persons named in that web of kin, as among half as many again
that I have chosen not to show at all in the stemma, there is no further hint of
prominence. A survey of other Greek-speaking regions as they can be known
through the record on stone, whether Syria or Asia, confirms the impression;

so do various non-epigraphic written sources like Apuleius' or Heliodorus' novels, Philostratus' biographies of the sophists, the latters' works (Menander or Aelius Aristides), interpreters' handbooks on dreams and horoscopes, Plutarch's *Moralia*, or the straight histories of the time. Religion generally required female ministrants for female deities, and piety of another sort moved the survivors in a family to memorialize the dead, often very richly; hence, two roles in which women left their mark in the record. These excepted, however, opportunities to make history in any conventional sense were offered to them far, far more rarely than to men. That is the first broad conclusion that can be based on everything that has been said so far; and it is entirely unsurprising.

A second conclusion suggests itself very clearly in Licinnia's stemma: as one moves through the names from east to west (and right to left), the weightier ones begin to appear—those that actually count in the historical record. They are not only male but generally Rome-based, just as we would expect. It was said before, however, and may be said again: Rome was not the world, nor can its ways fairly be taken as those of all the empire round it. Elsewhere than in the capital, local lives could be lived on local terms.

That was so because the disruptions that might intrude in times of rapid political change, such as had characterized the late Republic—sudden conscriptions or new taxes, alarms and movements of troops—became markedly less frequent. Let us set the moment at 15 B.C., not quite arbitrarily; perhaps a decade or two later. In many regions thereafter, generation after generation passed in unbroken peace; or, if peace was broken, it was on distant frontiers: Scotland, the Atlas Mountains, or Armenia yet again at issue. High magistracies and army commands from which women were excluded had correspondingly less significance. What rather mattered in Oenoanda as in Cirta, Nemausus, Casinum, Tarraco, Thessalonica, or the other cities of scattered regions that have by chance been mentioned, were local decisions about property, prominence in the community, advancement of careers, occasional serious rivalries, and similar everyday concerns. At this level and among these concerns, women who wished it could indeed attain power. We have seen them exercising it—as a minority but no doubt more effectually during the pax Romana than ever before.

ROMAN ATTITUDES TO GREEK LOVE

THE EASIER PARTS of the story of Rome's Hellenization over the period from Plautus on have been often told: literary genres and philosophy were taken over and a mythology developed. Various arts were copied. Other parts are seldom surveyed. Some day, someone, writing the right book, will crack open the great eggshell still called "Roman civilization" and show us in full the Greco-Roman creature that we all know lies within; and we can then properly study the nature and origins of its hyphenation.

To illustrate the process of Hellenization, we have the younger Scipio's remarks on the novelties he had observed and reports on in 129 B.C. Speaking of the young in the city, he says:

> They learn shameful arts. Along with ballet-boys (*cinaedi*), and carrying their violins and saxophones (*sambuca psalterioque*), they attend the entertainers' schools; they learn singing—all these things that our ancestors wanted to be judged disgraceful, for freeborn persons. They attend, I repeat, the very dancing schools—unwed girls and freeborn lads among the ballet-boys. Though someone might have reported these doings to me, I could not have taken in the notion of noblemen instructing their own offspring in these things. Yet, when I was conducted to a dancing school, by Jove, there I saw more than fifty lads and maids in the school, one of them a boy (and this caused me the sharpest pain, on our state's behalf), a boy marked out as noble (*bullatum*), son of a candidate for public office, under twelve years of age, dancing to castanets such a dance as some shameless slave could not decently have performed.[1]

Some years earlier Scipio had also described P. Sulpicius Gallus, *homo delicatus*: "For one who daily perfumes himself and dresses before a mirror, whose eyebrows are trimmed, who walks abroad with beard plucked out and thighs made smooth, who at banquets, though a young man, has reclined in a long-sleeved tunic ["called 'chirodotae,' " explains our source] on the inner side of the couch with a lover, who is fond not only of wine but of men—does anyone doubt that he does what ballet-boys commonly do?"[2]

Emphatic passages; reminders, however, that the state contained not only Scipio and those fellow citizens he thought he was addressing, but a prominent and opposed group living a life in certain respects provocatively at odds with his own. It would be a great mistake, then, to say that "Romans" had been gradually picking up the new ways. Some Romans had; some, angrily and bitterly, had not. In Scipio's day as in any other, society was divided into more or less encapsulated groups and strata, by no means approving of each other's behavior.

Some of the questions that exercised him were still being debated two centuries later. Persius describes himself at a leisure moment, giving himself to some serious sun-bathing, when a total stranger attacks him. "And these are your habits indeed!" begins the man; and goes on (in a passage rarely translated, because so uncompromisingly anatomical) to castigate the poet for being so depilated: all the pubic shrubbery has been trimmed back, each hair on the buttocks has been grubbed out with tweezers. The vocabulary belongs entirely to farming. Evidently the critic of Persius' cosmetic practices is from the country, not up to date with all the fashions of the capital. He expresses his disapproval with ferocity (*inspuare* is the word used).[3]

There existed, then, two views on the matter; and since they can be discovered not only in these scenes but in many another as well, there is no reason to doubt that they were really championed by real people. That much could not be denied even by scholars who see in some of the discussions or portrayals the presence of literary convention. It follows that no one should speak of *the* Roman attitude toward male homosexuality, in the singular, nor should anyone try to describe perceptions of that subject in the Roman world from a small range of texts.[4] The true picture must show all sorts of exceptions, contradictions, and tensions.

The origin of those tensions, if we should try to treat them historically, is not easily discerned. From analogies that it would be useless pedantry to cite, I simply assume that the early Roman population contained some minority of males that preferred sexual relations with other males, and a minority that enjoyed (or, given unchecked opportunity, would have enjoyed) relations with both sexes equally. I do not see any reason to think these proportions changed later, or differed from those among the Greeks themselves. What can it mean, then, to say these preferences were Greek? Yet that is just what Ennius, Cicero, and later sources do say, or imply. Polybius, for one, speaking of Scipio's coevals, says "some gave themselves up to love affairs with youths . . . having quickly adopted Greek laxity in this regard, during the war with Perseus."[5]

But further, there seems to be some confirmation of these statements suggested in three kinds of circumstantial evidence.

First, the vocabulary of homosexuality contains many Greek terms like *paedico*, *pathicus*, *catamitus*, and *cinaedus*, of which some had to be explained to contemporary readers as novelties.[6] By analogy with familiar modern borrowings from one people by another, these terms should indicate some sort of indebtedness. They blend into a slightly larger body of loan-words not always transliterated by Latin authors, used in the realms of cosmetics and coquetry.[7] They suggest broad fashions of behavior. Around them lay a still larger matrix of terms for items of luxury: textiles, garments, dainties to eat. These Grae-

cisms testify to a way of life imported as a package, and on occasion repudi-
ated as such.[8] They designate articles only to be sought from the east or practices (or practitioners) with which Romans at home were not at ease and which
they therefore wished to refer to within a notional setting that did more naturally accept them. Therefore their Roman users left them untranslated. For the
same reason, a generation ago, people aware of prejudices against drinking
would offer a *wee drap*, archly; or, being uncomfortable about some extra-
marital relationship, they referred to it as an *affaire*, *amour*, or *liaison*. The
Scotch, as every Englishman knew, must be forgiven whisky—it was their
national vice; the French, their adulteries; the Greeks—many things, all forbidden.

Second, during the period of the Republic the mentions of male homosexual
connections that involve Romans also involve Greek-speaking regions in a
significant proportion. Scandal touches Romans freshly returned from the
east. Young Caesar in the court of the king of Bithynia comes to mind, the
depraved youth corrupted by, or forcing his attentions on, his Oriental host.[9]
A few years later in Rome, in a conversation that Cicero imagines (*de natura
deorum* 79), C. Aurelius Cotta is put on the defensive, though very gently and
among his own acquaintances, in recalling to them his recent visit to Athens
and his survey there of the ephebes at their exercises. "But hardly a singly
finely formed one could be found," he says. "I see why you smile, but still,
that was the case. And to us who, with the concurrence of the philosophers of
old"—meaning, perhaps, Plato, Diogenes, and Zeno—"take our delight in
youths, often their very defects are pleasing." He goes on to quote Alcaeus
and then verses by Q. Catulus, who loved a youth *pulchrior . . . deo*. The
points of reference for the scene and subject are all Greek. Later still, Cicero
in his own voice, discrediting a hostile litigant, makes great play with the
man's origins in Pergamon and virtual kidnapping of a handsome young Tem-
nian. "I know his type, his habits, his desires," he says—all sinister and un-
mentionable, of course.[10] When he himself was in Laodicea, and the young
Hortensius turned up, that lad propositioned him, as we would say—offered
him sexual relations, to his absolute astonishment. He could hardly be sure
that the invitation to meet in Athens (where Hortensius was going to visit) "so
that we might go home together," meant what it seemed to mean.[11] Very
shocking.

But we must remember that Romans had been taking Greeks home with
them for centuries by then, as slaves especially, and by the hundreds of
thousands, so that Rome in Cicero's day had turned into the largest Greek city
in the world—at least tied with Alexandria for the honor, if by "Greek" we
may mean "inhabited by people whose parents spoke Greek as their first language" (the definition is not an unreasonable one).[12] Markets there offered the
buyer whatever he might conceivably desire, for purchase openly or dis-
creetly. Many a rich Roman household took advantage of the opportunity to

assemble a very full equipment of articles and agents for whatever might increase the master's pleasures in life.

The same sort of rich owner was likely to spend a good part of the year in another of his houses in the Bay-of-Naples area. The stubbornly Greek character of cities there, above all of Naples itself, was well known, even to the drinking of Aegean wines (Romans of Rome bought Italian or western). When Tiberius in his sixties and seventies retired to the area, hostile rumor surrounded the old man with schools of little boys like minnows ministering to his most exquisite lusts; and it was in the same area, naturally, that Nero later found it easiest to begin his own Graecizing publicly.[13] To return, then, to the time of the Republic, we should hardly expect the unregenerate differentness of the richer Romans' resort area to have been itself very Roman, in that earlier age, or that it should not have continued those lessons in the good life that Romans were also receiving in their capital from their staffs of servants.

In the third place, the Greek origin of "Greek love" among the Romans is suggested by its appearance disproportionately in Greek dress in early Roman literature—meaning Plautus above all, who often refers to it, and does so ordinarily in the dramatic setting of Athens. He could say a great deal about foreign places, in the style of the later *Lettres Persanes* and *Rasselas*, that he could never say of "real life." The audience laughed as much at the outrageousness of what they saw as at its intrinsic comicality.[14] But there are other writers as well in whom homosexuality is prominent; and indeed a controversy is well known and of long standing over the question whether some Republican poets present homosexual preferences which are their own and their friends' or which enter their pages only through imitation of foreign literary models.[15] The very existence of the debate, whichever side one takes in regard to whichever poet, points to the foreignness of homosexuality talked about and actually practiced, or merely talked about, in Rome. Had open love of male by male been as much at home in Rome as in Greece, one would not expect the expression of it to be sought in such derivative terms.

But once more (asking a second time what we only appear to have discussed): What can it mean to say these preferences are Greek? No one really supposes Roman men and boys had to read Greek sex manuals or receive coaching in the approved Spartan or Athenian positions. I think rather that sources mean little more than to point to a different *attitude* toward homosexuality, just as one might say today that public displays of grief are foreign (and we whose native language is English would not have to be *taught* to weep at the graves of our loved ones; only we pride ourselves on suppressing certain feelings).

What that Greek attitude was, is well known, and recently surveyed by Kenneth Dover. For its continuation into the period of my discussion, it is enough to recall Plutarch's account of a conversation in which his father took part, about the same time that Persius was being attacked by his puritanical countryman. Plutarch's scene gives us the full range of strong, even violent feelings for and against male homosexuality;[16] the same can be found again in the Pseudo-Lucianic (?third-century) dialogues on the same subject;[17] and both sources recall and extend the traditions of Plato's *Symposium*. What is evident in them, however, and marks them as belonging to a civilization different from Rome's, is the open, unashamed quality of the debate.

In contrast, our own sources assume that Romans in mid-Republican days would have thought it a disgrace to the community and an outrage on nature for an older man to press himself undesired on a younger man, even a slave.[18] It was almost as bad to solicit intercourse without violence; and offering it freely was beyond the pale, too.[19] In the second century, we have reference to a youth defamed as promiscuous;[20] we have another Roman, evidently acquainted with what the Greeks had to say in defense of Greek love, who still condemned at least its open practice. That was Cato, complicated and interesting man of his times.[21] And from Scipio the Younger we have already heard. In a speech of 124 B.C., Gaius Gracchus prides himself that there had been "no very lovely boys standing about in his quaestor's headquarters" and that "your sons [that is, young Romans of all sorts] were treated with more decorum than in a general's tent. . . . If any prostitute entered my home or anyone else's slave boy was sought on my behalf, consider me the lowest and vilest of mankind."[22] The story does not quite confute Balsdon: "it is hard to believe that there was not a great deal of homosexuality in the army"; but it certainly indicates what values were acceptable.[23]

Arriving now on the edge of the last century of the era, and reviewing the various glimpses we have had of earlier scenes, we seem to see isolated but less and less uncommon instances of men of the officer class and aristocracy being detected in or suspected of homosexual desires; and, while these desires are ordinarily vented on slaves, even so, if they are not to draw criticism, they must be kept private. Which leaves everyone else in this society opposed to homosexual practices of any sort. Had that not been the case, of course, critics would have had no audience to appeal to in their highly colored attacks on homosexuality, using such words as "filthy," "vile," "vice," "incontinence," and so forth.

Across a full thirty years of partisan oratory, Cicero offered his listeners or readers many illustrations of these perceptions: enemies like Piso, that "beast," "filth," "the vilest of men," or Gabinius "who could not fend off the foulness of men from the most sacred parts of his body," or "the public prostitute" Clodius, not to mention Verres, Catiline, and Antony—Antony above all—were bound to be addicts of homosexuality.[24] It would be extraordinary if so seasoned and successful a combatant as Cicero in the courts and senate should have routinely appealed to prejudices that simply did not exist; but, beyond common sense, there is some refutation of that possibility in Suetonius' biography of Caesar (§49), where we are told that "except for [Caesar's] lying with Nicomedes [the king of Bithynia] nothing hurt his repute for chastity—but that was a heavy and lasting reproach and exposed him to insult from everybody.'' It seems safe to conclude that ''the man in the street,'' or at least the man in the forum and law courts who constituted the ordinary audience for political statements, could be assumed to be the foe of male homosexuality.

The last great release, or whipping up, of popular feelings about sexual conduct occurred during young Octavian's rise. Even his friends conceded his many acts of adultery, which offered a handle to attack by Antony in a more or less public and certainly very well publicized letter to him.[25]

But attack turned also to more tender areas. As Cicero says (this time defending a client), lovely lads must just expect some slander; and Octavian was a natural target by age, looks, and range of serious enemies. So for a while he was accused of submitting to his uncle, and of being the passive partner to other males too.[26] Such reports commonly punctuated those most ungentlemanly shouting-matches in which Roman competitors for office or for revenge engaged, partly because so much might be at stake, partly because explicit abuse of every kind was thought to be quite tolerable. That fact should not dull our ears. *Maledicta* that Octavian endured were not mere slights or insults. The word meant ''foul abuse,'' and if you could think of nothing worse to call your enemy, surely it follows that whatever you did include in your *maledicta* were acts correspondingly abhorrent to your audience.

Evidently least so was the sexually active role with a boy slave (slaves as instruments of pleasure being seen almost as non-beings, whether male or female); the same role with a freeborn boy was in the second degree generally disapproved; in the third degree, the same role with a grown male, slave or free; in a passive role, as a youth, to an older freeborn man, fourth; for gain, or to a social inferior, fifth and sixth; and even lower, other homosexual acts besides anal copulation.[27] While there is no dispute about the prevalent condemnation of acts at the bad end of the scale, it has been fairly asked whether anyone objected to homosexual pleasure in itself, at the higher end of the scale. The answer is clearly yes. The man who accepted or requested, even without coercing, submission to his sexual wishes was vulnerable to heavy reproach: Gaius Gracchus, if he had used slave boys; Piso and Clodius with their hired catamites; Catiline's followers, corruptor and corrupted equally abhorrent; Cicero's adversary in court, above; and so to the poor prince Gaius whom the senate was willing to condemn to death for no other crime than his love affairs with youths.[28] In many other scenes, for instance, of Tiberius' orgies (n. 13), someone who is plainly (but perhaps not in so many words) held up for detestation is ministered to by boy slaves.

It is true that the opinion expected of contemporaries, whether witnesses or readers of accounts, is not specified by ancient authors. But why should it be? Authors then or today need not designate murder, incest, or cannibalism as reprehensible. In consequence, many hints or scenes of homosexual activity in our sources are presented to us without being clearly characterized, indeed in deliberately vague language, from which it is possible though in my view quite perverse to argue that the subject was held to be ethically neutral. I would rather infer that the subject was very gingerly addressed because it was a hot one, arousing strong feelings of condemnation, shame, and embarrassment[29]—arousing also fierce storms of scholarly debate that toss about the euphemisms, the intentional obscurities, and double-entendres of the Latin or the Greek.

That it seemed no exaggeration to assign homosexual acts to the company of murder, incest, or cannibalism can be shown not only from Aristotle's doing exactly that (*Nic. Ethics* 7.5.7) but from a further consideration: the middle range or degree of disapproval, just discussed, was taken very seriously indeed. Rather than undergo anal copulation unwillingly, even an ex-slave would die—still more, a free man;[30] or he might properly kill the person attempting force.[31] Where life itself was thus outweighed by fear of disgrace, that disgrace can only have reflected very strong condemnation at the bar of public opinion. It seems reasonable to attribute much strength, a little less or a little more, to the adjacent degrees of disapproval as well.

What of a last consideration? Homoeroticism that excluded physical acts, especially if it arose between social equals,[32] may have been quite all right; disapproval may have been saved for loveless acts. A possibility. But, first, no Roman (as opposed to lots of Greeks) makes the distinction now or later. In the second place, there are no declarations of homosexual love on stone (now or later, as opposed to lots that are heterosexual). Tibullus and Catullus could speak more freely because they could better define their audience. It has been called a "coterie dependent on the intimate acquaintance of individuals and [their poetry is] primarily addressed to them rather than to the world at large."[33] And in the third place, total silence about any pair of lovers in some casual episode, case at law, oration, essay, letter, or history of any period (as opposed to what is easily found in Greek literature) is not easily explained save by assuming that such love was given no chance to emerge before the public eye.

Such were the degrees and focus of disapproval during the Republic. What underlay that disapproval was loyalty to an entire cultural inheritance, explaining the not always rational rejection of Greek clothes as well,[34] which by Varro's day had also supplied a name for Plautus' plays, *palliatae*; the rejection of dancing (above, p. 177); also of caviar (n. 8). Greek gourmandizing was bad, not only in itself—it wasted money, and heavy drinking and vomiting were not pretty—but it also led on naturally to sexual promiscuity. The connection was a cliché, in scenes featuring "men who bathe in hot water, eat prepared delicacies, drink unmixed wine, anoint themselves with myrrh, lie on soft couches and sleep with boys for bedfellows—boys past their prime at that.''[35] There was even some feeling against Romans speaking Greek, or at least against citizens not being at home in Latin;[36] and as late as the mid-first century A.D. thoughtful Romans could reflect on ''ancestral customs radically subverted by imported indulgences,'' dissolving into *gymnasia et otia et turpes amores*. ''Imported'' of course meant ''from Greece,'' and the connection between *gymnasia* and vile love affairs of course pointed to male homosexuality —even at that late date, not truly Roman.[37]

But disapproval singled out homosexuality as alien not only to inherited culture, but to an order above nations: to nature itself. So people would strike out at a man who ''dressed and saw to the folds of his costume with great elegance, great care and art; and because his hands during his speech were too much in motion and waving about, he was tossed upon foul, reproachful and libelous talk.'' They would ridicule the man who stood out by reason of his ''dress, his walk, his woman's jewelry.''[38] A man should instead look and talk like other men! As to the man that ''took a woman's part'' (or the like phrase) in sexual intercourse, he was seen as an even harsher violation of nature— *para physin*, a freak for public display, *monstrosus*.[39] Accordingly, Roman parents wished their boys untouched by the love of older males and took precautions accordingly.[40] They also supported laws that protected boys against seduction and rape; and they protected decent citizens (as they would have called themselves) against finding a known homosexual sitting next to them in public gatherings.[41] This last measure we find in Caesar's model charter. It was meant for the use of Italian townships generally and must have responded to their preferences, thus affording us an almost unique glimpse of values outside of Rome. Its significance is confirmed and extended by the rule of law (*Dig.* 3.1.5) forbidding men who had ''used their bodies in woman's fashion'' to act as advocates in Roman courts, anywhere.

But inside the capital in the same period and on to the early second century, we have the series of Catullus, Tibullus, Persius, Martial, and Juvenal all referring openly to homosexual relations, sometimes relations that involved themselves, sometimes other named persons including the emperor Domitian. We have rife and open homosexuality in the *Satyricon*. Beyond doubt, then, in ways and on a scale familiar to everyone acquainted with Latin literature, the choicest circles of writers and readers shared a perfect tolerance of homoeroticism and themselves seem fully to have enjoyed relations with both sexes.

In court circles we have Sejanus playing favorite to a nobleman, we have Claudius' son-in-law dying while in bed with a boy favorite, Vespasian's right-hand man notorious for unchastity and his own son likewise.[42] But that is just a sampling. And we have an almost unbroken series of emperors bisexual in their preferences, including the egregious Nero who actually went through the full marriage ceremony with his favorite Sporus (surgically tinkered with to fit him for his duties).

But we should recall our proper point of focus: *attitudes* toward homosexuality. Evaluation of them may allow us to gain some feel for Roman society as a whole, in order to explain Nero, rather than the other way around. For it is plain that, just as society could not tolerate on the throne a matricide or an idol of the stage, so it could not bear the spouse of Sporus, and threw him off.[43] Far from representing what could be accepted, he represents what could not be. Similarly with the *Satyricon* and other works of literature: we cannot take them as representative—we cannot know what they represented—until we have gained some sense of their whole setting.

That sense may be gained from a passage in Seneca (*Ep.* 123.7ff.) in which he warns of the dangers of trying to keep up with other people. "Everyone," he grants, has crystal goblets; "everyone" has other luxuries. "Everyone's retinue of slaves is carried along, their faces made up to keep their delicate skins from harm by sun or cold. It is something to be ashamed of if there is a slave in your following of boys whose healthy complexion needs no cosmetics"—else the more stylish folk around you may say in disbelief, " 'Have you no girl-favorite, no boy to rouse her envy?' . . . These are the voices of 'everyone' that you must flee. These are the men who pass vice around and communicate it from one place to another."

We have Epictetus, too. He is accustomed to address an audience of all ages but generally of the aristocracy; and he reminds them that it is up to them whether they aim at popularity and the reputation of a good companion, or whether they respect themselves (4.2.7–10). One can go clear to the extreme, he says, joining the ballet-boys and adulterers and cheering the burlesque-dancers, or instead one can decently enjoy oneself—with both sexes.[44]

Finally, we have Quintilian saying (*Inst.* 1.2.8) that we corrupt our own children ourselves when they see "our girls, our boys," *nostras amicas, nostros concubinos*.

From these three commentators we gain a clear sense of various pressures to conform, and counter-pressures which obliged people to conceal a part of themselves from many of their acquaintance, even from their own children. *Their* children must be brought up in other beliefs. Interesting glimpses: "value dissonance," in scientific parlance. We see quite plainly where the conflicts begin, in an upper class some of whose members made manifest a high degree of tolerance for homosexual relationships with slaves. Leaders in tolerance were men of fantastic wealth. Pedanius (n. 42), for example, had a household of four hundred, and Nero—who knows how many thousands? Among such masters it was *en vogue* to live à la Grecque; and to that civilization entire, some gave themselves with taste and abandonment (like Maecenas), some with abandonment only, some with misgivings that required the ministrations of a Stoic chaplain (Greek perhaps, and a slave—one could buy even one's conscience in Rome). He might, like Epictetus (2.10.17), let slip the opinion that the homosexual lover as well as the beloved was no man; he might (like Juvenal 2.82–126) warn against circles within circles "yet more foul," to which aspirants in debauch might be gradually admitted. There always remained, however, even in these elevated social strata (themselves, we should remember, not amounting to a fiftieth part of the city's whole society), a majority of the "old view," as we may call it: dead set against the passive role for any freeborn male, repelled by the parade of instruments for the active lover, and, at the least, upset by the sight of caresses bestowed by an older man on a younger.[45]

That the changes we see at work within the Roman upper class need not have touched all circles equally is easily believed, if we may trust analogy. For illustration: on May 15, 1776, two men could be seen standing together in a London house, guests toward the end of a dinner party. One "held a candle to show a fine print of a beautiful female figure which hung in the room, and pointed out the elegant contour of the bosom with the finger of an arch connoisseur." It is the notorious profligate John Wilkes instructing the adamant moralist Samuel Johnson, while James Boswell looks on delighted. No more than a scene, proving nothing—but every large city in every decade presents such pairs of men of more or less the same class, means, and pursuits or professions, even sharing many of the same haunts and friends and tastes, who yet live out lives utterly incompatible in certain keenly felt respects. That was what made the London scene so exquisitely piquant to Boswell; that was what enabled old-Roman and new-Greek to rub elbows in the forum and the senate, hardly sensing how different they were until reminded by some accident—by entering a new circle, perhaps, like some of Epictetus' or Juvenal's listeners, or by catching a glimpse of their neighbors' children in the latest finishing school, like Scipio.

There are of course also the grand divisions between rich and poor that affect sexual values. Kenneth Dover rightly notes that "the reader who turns from Plato to comedy is struck . . . by its [homosexuality's] displacement from the centre to the periphery of Athenian sexual life; for comedy is fundamentally heterosexual." The explanation he finds in the way of life natural, indeed inevitable, among the less well-to-do, to whom comedy spoke. Homosexuality was for the rich.[46] Differences in sexual customs according to wealth existed also in the city and period we are considering. "You rich," a not-rich litigant is imagined saying in a Roman court, "don't marry, you only have those toys of yours, those boy slaves that play woman for you."[47] The rest of us, the litigant continues, get married and raise a family. Some of the circumstances that Dover uses to interpret the Athenian scene—a less cloistered day for girls and women and less money and leisure for pursuit of boys, among ordinary folk than could be found among the very wealthy—explain the Roman lawyer's statement just quoted. It would have been still more easily illustrated in the little-Hellenized sections of Italy and the west.

We cannot penetrate further into the customs of the ordinary nine-tenths or more of the population. There is no evidence whatsoever that I am aware of.

I discount all sorts of crowd reactions to the likes of Sporus or Nero since our descriptions do not indicate exactly what is condemned and for what reason. I also discount the graffiti of Pompeii, in which too much has been read. Among them, intercourse of male with male and *cunnilinctus* are mentioned with about equal frequency, *fellatio* as often as heterosexual intercourse.[48] From these statistics I do not conclude that the common man in Pompeii most enjoyed the least attested (and, in other sources, the most sharply rejected) forms of sexual indulgence. Rather, I suppose that the graffiti, like their equivalent today, were inscribed for the pleasure they gave to the inscriber: the pleasure of speaking the unspeakable, of violating all the rules of decent (and irksome) society. I would compare the ivory game pieces found in Pompeii, Rome, and other cities. They have any one of a dozen or so words written on them: *cinaedus*, *ebriose*, *moice*, *inpudes*. The most popular are "bird" (*pernix*), "avaricious" (*arpax*), "idiot" (*fatue*), "drunk" (*ebriose* and *vinose*), "catamite" (*patice*), "greedy" (*gumia* and *gulo*). No one would look among them for a true profile of human types prevailing in the world. It was release and titillation that decided what people *wrote* on both these game pieces and Pompeian walls. About what they *did*, this evidence tells us nothing.

In Hadrian's commemoration of the drowned Antinous by the founding of a new city in the youth's honor, we approach the end of the history of Roman homosexuality.[49] His two successors by their own example turned their faces against it. At the very summit of fashion, fashion thus changed. Still later homosexual or bisexual emperors did little to enhance its repute. The worst in the series, Elagabalus, was the most fantastically addicted, whereas a good emperor would consider legislation against it, or actually ban male prostitution. It continued illegally. Of relevant Latin literature nothing has remained since Hadrian's day save the third-century Nemesianus, chirping in his fourth *Bucolic*, "O cruel boy!" (etc., etc.).

As a sort of epilogue, however, we should glance at "Greek love" among the Greeks of the empire. We can only consider the aristocracy of eastern cities; but in them, youths who had many men hanging about them or who rejected brutal advances were equally honored.[50] Greek love poems like the hundreds by Strato, Hadrian's contemporary, went on being composed by males to males just as they had been in Hellenistic times. Greek novels continued to be written and to include heroes alternately in love with lovely men and lovely women.[51] On the other hand (since as we have seen both extremes of view were openly, violently expressed), the Stoic teaching of Zeno that had once recommended sexual relations with boys on equal terms with the heterosexual was, by Sextus Empiricus (*Pyrr. hyp.* 3.245), dismissed as having nothing to do with real choices in the real world, no more than intercourse with one's mother. In the same decade or so as this author, Tatian, a Christian, declared with venomous humor that "pederasty . . . among the Romans merits special rights of pasturage, and they try to collect herds of boys like grazing horses.'' But he here uses against his preferred target, the Romans, a gibe originally aimed at *Greeks* and applied by his teacher to male prostitution in the empire everywhere.[52] His statement thus fits quite easily with those non-Christian passages known from Seneca or the accounts of Elagabalus, or from another Greek observer, Herodian (1.17.3). Herodian refers to the fashion among rich Roman fops or voluptuaries of having naked little boys idling about the rooms of their houses.

A century later, we gain a last look at the Greek world and its attitudes, afforded by a small handful of writers. Responding to the distress of the leading families in Antioch at the loss of their sons to a monastic life—"To whom, you ask, should you leave your fields, houses, slaves, and gold?"—John Chrysostom dilates on the rewards of that choice. One reward is the removal of the youths from homosexual temptation. It is, he says, "a hideous disease," so rife that "the female sex may even prove superfluous"(!).[53] His contemporary, Gregory of Nyssa, paints and condemns a trite scene of the very rich with their varied attendants, "dancers, . . . boys like girls with long hair, and licentious girls." On the pagan side, Julian cannot resist a swing at the monks for homosexual aggression,[54] but he also uses exactly the same vocabulary as Gregory on another target, the degenerate Antiochenes.[55] Libanius' *Twenty-fifth Oration* rather confirms Julian: in Antioch the older man hanging about his beloved boy and heaping him with presents, to his own humiliation (§26), is a familiar sight; but he is indulged by his friends since most of them, too, have felt the same desires (27). And the *Fifty-third Oration* rather confirms Chrysostom, like Chrysostom speaking of homoeroticism as a disease (10) and remarking on its prevalence "in these days." Only, Libanius has no intention of seeking its cure.

In rich Antiochene society (the rest being hidden from us), from the 360s to the 380s, the range of view and the distinctions drawn regarding the active and passive role display a familiar inconsistency. They differ not a whit from those discoverable three centuries earlier. Time has stood still—or one may say, the Greeks are still Greek. Elaborate all-male banquets go on, fathers worry about their sons at school, there is sharp censure aimed at tasteless, bought indulgence; and yet, and yet—the infatuation of a man for a boy, so embarrassing, is so common a thing and so overwhelming, too, that it must somehow be forgiven. Not by a Christian. *There* was a different attitude. It was to be imposed more sharply on Rome in A.D. 390 through the renewal, after nearly a century and a half, of the ban on male prostitution—this time, more decisively enforced.[56]

Over the course of five hundred years, a perception of homosexual urges and acts that was relatively very tolerant and open had appeared on the edges of Roman consciousness, where it touched the Greek, and that perception gradually penetrated past the edges. The resistance it met tells us that all other parts of the citizen body, notably those who were neither rich nor lived elbow-to-elbow with neighbors of Greek descent, were little affected. Minucius Felix (28.10) offers a useful reminder: he accuses Romans of tolerating all sexual license as *urbanitas*. But of course "elegance" or "sophistication" was something that did not concern most people very much. It did concern those of wealth and leisure who felt themselves beyond the reach of common censure, who were caught up in the effort to be *en vogue*, to be imitated—and who enjoyed it (for no one supposes that the Romans at any time did not number any males among them who felt naturally drawn to other males). The story can then be traced in different social circles, all in the city of Rome. It ends obscurely, in the final rejection of 'Greek love' (meaning, to repeat, an attitude), with what rapidity, at what period, and in what circles, the sources do not allow us to say. The turning point seems to lie in the death of Hadrian.

But surely the most interesting yield of this story is the glimpse it affords of cultural transfer at work on various layers or sets in Roman high society. Perhaps other tests may allow us to gain a better picture of those sets, so as to say that the same people who wrote eclogues (or whatever) were also active in commerce (or whatever). So our knowledge of the Hellenizing process might be gradually refined.

18

PERSONAL POWER IN THE ROMAN EMPIRE

WITHIN THE BOUNDS of the Roman empire, principally its central and eastern parts, I mean to discuss the ordinary inducements to obedience controlled by people who enjoyed "clout." It is not easy to explain that American slang term by any single synonym. "Influence" by itself is too tame. I need to add the specification of physical force that may be perceived by a person's community to lie behind his claims—or *perhaps* to lie behind them. Who could be sure? Force was not something one advertised very widely. Its use, however, especially in out-of-the-way towns and rural areas, was known and had to be reckoned with. What sufficed was to be thought capable of resorting to it if gentler suasions failed. The two forms of inducement, negative and positive, worked as a pair.

My understanding of their use grows out of individual instances. There is almost no generalizing about them by contemporaries. Considering the negative ones to begin with, we have of course a lot of information from the uniquely well-reported province of Egypt, in which weak persons—weak by sex, age, or other handicap—went to the imperial authorities for help against their oppressors.[1] They describe their weakness and others' strength: they have been beaten up, robbed, or frighteningly threatened by persons with a reputation for violence. They fear both for their physical safety and their property. Something similar can be seen in the often-quoted complaint of the farmers on the emperor's own lands in north Africa, at Souk-el-Khmis;[2] yet the types and quantity of sources for such accounts of plain terrorizing, at least as it can be seen through the eyes of the victims, are very unsatisfactory. We know that violence was offered by the strong to the weak. So much we could assume of any period of history, anywhere. Was it, however, a fact of life that a sensible person would consider in his daily doings, or was it rare, more on the order of being struck by lightning?

The search for an answer that can reach beyond scattered anecdotes to something historically significant must turn to slightly higher, or quite exalted, social strata. They will show not the victims but the perpetrators. Suppose the perpetrators were rich enough to own a good handful of slaves: then those latter could be used like an army in assaults on your house, your family, or yourself.[3] We have reports from all over—Italy, Greece, and so on—very much as we would expect, in which the only interesting feature, perhaps, is the great difficulty to be sensed in efforts to bring the criminals to book. The reason for that is the absence of a police force. Law there was, but the state agents to enforce it were not easily called on. They amounted, really, to the honor guard of the provincial governors and posts of regular soldiers sometimes found in rural areas.[4] The owner of a runaway slave could request their help in his search. That gave him a kind of vicarious muscle. But a special decree was needed before he could extend his search onto lands owned by a senator.

From a much earlier time we hear of Roman grandees away from Rome insisting on special privileges, using their servants to beat one if one did not comply.[5] One of these reports concerns special access to a town's public baths. Eventually that was secured by law. Anecdote becomes history. Similarly with the deference due to a grandee on the public roads: lowly folk, if mounted, should get off their donkey or mule; pedestrians should get out of the way, otherwise they could be manhandled with impunity by the great man or his retinue.[6] That explains the wrath of an ex-consul of 79 B.C., Servilius, appearing as a witness at a trial and recognizing the accused: it was the very fellow who, while Servilius was once walking along some road, had passed him without dismounting; whereupon the jury "gave the man no further hearing, but unanimously condemned him."

The consul of A.D. 35, "whenever he dined out in Rome, was conveyed by elephant." Fancy transport and a parade of retinue identified the great in their goings-about.[7] They wore items of clothing that indicated their rank, and expressed it also through gait, bearing, expression, and a general air of *noli me tangere*.[8] The Roman as opposed to the Greek or the Carthaginian or any other grandee bore about these various signs commonly and as a part of his way of life. That much we know from foreigners' comments.[9] But the advertising of high status came to prevail in the provinces as well, so far as we can judge from third- and fourth-century customs. Moreover it had its functional side. Beyond feeding the conceit of those with a great appetite for others' fear and deference, it gave fair warning of the power to hurt and thereby deterred trivial or accidental challenge. The coral snake's bright bands conserve its poison. Roman law forbade a blind man to bring suit "because he is unable to see and show reverence toward the magistrate's insignia" (*Digest* 3.1.5).

Without automatic reverence of that sort, people would be forever testing or abusing each other. Society would revert to the jungle. Nobody wanted that. We can hear a tone of disapproval, even of outrage, in many of our accounts already cited (nn. 3, 5, 6, and 8), where someone with "clout" has to use, or at any rate does use, naked physical force. Force stripped everyone else of all their rights. In its place it should rather be law that intervenes to bring disputes to a peaceful end. However, there was nothing to prevent a quite unprincipled man from attempting and sometimes gaining the purchase of a moment's inattention from the law, while he went about his violent business;[10] or he might request the help of the governor's guardsmen to chase his runaway slaves—if we assume those really were slaves and not simply alleged to be so.[11] Borrowing official strength in this way, Dio Chrysostom was thought to have conspired with the governor of his province to secure the torture and exile of some of his enemies, others of whom were driven to suicide; and his defense against the charges is not very convincing. At least, there do seem to have been wicked goings-on, however plotted by whatever persons—the proconsul included.[12] Since a governor of Africa, Marius Priscus, the consul of 84, was actually convicted of something similar in a trial before the senate and the emperor, we may trust that he really had done what his prosecutors Pliny and Tacitus alleged. The allegations make the actions, or at least people's suspicions, of Dio sound not incredible. Marius had decreed and carried out eight executions for a payment of 300,000 sesterces, one of the victims being an equestrian. For another 700,000 he had had a second equestrian flogged, then condemned to the mines, and at last strangled. For all this he suffered banishment, poor man, but a banishment comfortable and even luxurious: "the exile begins his drinking around noon and so enjoys the very wrath of the gods."[13]

Such tempered justice reflected the convict's status, needless to say. The higher your rank, the less severity to which you might be subjected. Two broad terms in law, *humiliores* and *honestiores*, eventually divided society formally for appropriate treatments by the judge. Each was in turn subdivided. For the finer distinctions, the judge must size up the persons who came before him: among several accusers of a single man, he should allow the best to proceed with the case, the one possessing the advantage of *dignitas* (*Dig.* 48.2.16). Among many witnesses, he should give most credence to the superior *dignitas* (*Dig.* 22.5.3.1). But he should be careful not to exclude from his court persons who might be represented by an advocate without *dignitas* (*Dig.* 1.16.9.4). Evidently the Latin term in these contexts, bearing the usual meaning of worth of rank, pointed to a world outside the law, the values of which could be excluded only with special effort or not at all—for we have just seen the courts used by the lawless to strike and wound their enemies.

But consider other contexts also. To begin with, Cicero (*Sulla* 46) warns a critic of his administration not to wax too critical in his remarks—otherwise "I may have to take some thought for my *dignitas*. For no one ever brought the slightest suspicion on me whom I did not overturn and overwhelm." The sort of *dignitas* he has in mind sounds like rather an active quality, does it not? It is, or can be, demonstrated in annihilating one's enemies. Or again, he is ready to take on the insurrectionaries in the city (*Cat.* 4.20): "If," he declares, "if that gang, roused by someone's rage and wickedness, should some day be able to prevail over your own and the state's *dignitas* so as to bring about my end, I will still not regret my opposition to them," etc. The ultimate power of defense to be ranged even against revolution is that personal and institutional force, *dignitas*. And one more illustration, from Caesar (*B. G.* 8.24): while he despairs of catching his enemy Ambiorix, nevertheless "he considered it vital to his *dignitas* to strip Ambiorix's territory of citizens, buildings, and cattle so completely that'' the Gauls themselves would reject him. What Caesar wants to assert through total war is a certain perception of himself, the same perception that Cicero values. He must be seen as capable of ruthless and effective action. So important to him is such an image that he will lead his country into civil war in its defense.[14] And it must of necessity be at least a part of that other meaning in the key word, worth or rank.

While Cicero is shocked by the lengths to which Caesar presses the matter, it remains well within the bounds of ordinary Roman values. Indeed Cicero himself says, later and in another context, that ''no war can be rightly undertaken *save for vengeance* or defense.''[15] There is the closest of connections between *dignitas* and the power to strike back, just as Cicero had reminded his opponent during his defense of young Sulla; likewise, of young Caelius. In the latter trial (*Cael.* 21) he praises people who ''defend their friends and do what men of courage generally do, that is, they feel resentment if they are injured, and let themselves go, if their wrath is roused, and fight when they are challenged.'' What else were the Gracchi taught by their impeccable parent? ''You say,'' Cornelia tells Gaius, ''it is a lovely thing to be avenged upon your enemies—and to no one does this seem more important or lovelier than to myself.''[16]

We can follow the subject further among the moralists of the empire, both Greek and Roman. It is, they say, the right thing to do, to repay people in kind, both with benefits and injury, and you may count yourself lucky if you are able to do both equally.[17] Never a hint that you should turn the other cheek! At the end we have even a bishop commending a candidate for the episcopal throne as being just ''such a person as could injure his enemies and help his friends.''[18] Along the way to this late Roman view we encounter explicit characterizations of effective, energetic persons who rigorously balance their accounts with others. True, the empire's political rivalries were not quite so rough-and-tumble as those of the later Republic. The times called more for words than deeds—rivalries were more civil, on the surface. Yet the ethic didn't change.[19] For Pliny (*Ep.* 2.9.1), when he senses that ''the respect accorded me, my standing, my *dignitas*, are all in the balance,'' it is over a matter of career advancement and weight with the emperor, and not even his own career at stake but a young protégé's. Nevertheless all that was terribly important to him.

Occasionally the bland and decent Pliny shows that he understands the need for strong action. Still, he acts for another. His young friend Atilius has come to him with certain difficulties, including concern about insulting behavior that had been shown to him in public by a tribune (*Ep.* 6.8.3). Should he suffer this tamely? ''I replied, 'Over my dead body.' '' And, continues Pliny to his correspondent, turning to Atilius' other concerns, ''Why mention this exchange? To let you know that Atilius cannot be wronged so long as I am around. . . . Indeed I would count any loss or insult to him as my own, or not merely that, but something more serious still. But why go on with denunciations and, almost, threats?'' (6.8.9). The point is made, he resumes his usual blander tone.

If you simply accepted insulting behavior, you lost face. That was serious. You became a Nothing—as even an emperor might. Dio Cassius describes a day at the races which he probably witnessed himself in A.D. 217. Macrinus and son were present only by proxy (the latter's birthday was the special occasion). The populace began massed shouts that they needed a leader and Jupiter it should be; whereupon the senators and equestrians from their reserved sections in the Circus took up loyal counter-shouts, praising emperor and prince together and inviting the crowds to join in. But the latter resumed the chant, "*He* (Jupiter) is the Romans' Augustus. If we have him, we have it all." Being vastly louder, they prevailed. "Henceforth they regarded both Macrinus and Diadumenianus as absolutely non-existent and already trampled upon them as if they were dead; and this was one important reason why the soldiers despised him and paid no heed to what he did to win their favor."[20]

We have met the word *contumelia* before (n. 14), where it is opposed to *dignitas*. Caesar, in mention of whom it is referred to by Cicero, speaks of it himself (*B. G.* 7.10). He reasons that he must rigorously confront threats to an ally. Otherwise it might seem "that there was no help to be sought for his friends from him''; and, "where such *contumelia* was suffered, all his adherents would be lost to him.'' The line of reasoning tells us a great deal about power in his world. Dio Cassius, just quoted, describes Rome three generations later. Nothing has changed. Power depends in part on the appearance of it, on perceptions, on symbols and gestures; and particularly persons who are ambitious and attempting to broaden the base of their adherents insist on the conventional signs of allegiance from others

> as necessary to make their *dignitas* complete; and if they are not accorded them, they resent it as if they had been ill spoken of, and are angry at the *contumelia*. Thus people are more careful toward such men than to the emperors themselves, you might say. To the latter it is a virtue to forgive an offense, while, in the former, that would be taken as an indication of weakness; and attacks and vengeance are thought to provide the validation of their great power.[21]

A few generations later still, Pliny agrees: "Regulus is *formidable*; for he has money, faction, and wide backing, and is still more widely feared; and that affords more strength than being liked'' (*Ep.* 1.5.15). Recognition of the rules of life in the Roman world, as we see, extends from Republic to empire. For that matter, it extends throughout society, down to the master and his slave or a man of modest standing among his neighbors.[22] You must insist on respect—else you will be trampled on and abused. Others must see you insisting, and be warned. If you want a great deal of respect, your warnings must be dire, perhaps followed up by dire action. Which must be talked about, to yield best results.

But negative inducements to obedience went in pair with the positive. Through various quoted passages, that fact has already emerged quite plainly: in the pairing of being feared and liked, doing "good or harm," "revenge or rewards," and so forth. For ourselves who live neither in Renaissance Italy nor Mafiosa Sicily, it seems more natural to understand Roman patterns of motivation through advantages or privileges sought rather than through deterrents. And indeed the former, *beneficia*, were in constant circulation, the currency by which the person who had much to give gained adherents and their services in turn.

No one, of course, had more to give than the emperor. His *beneficia* are referred to in many, many contexts. They help to define the term itself, which means not simply nice things done for someone or gifts given but grants out of the giver's position of authority.[23] The emperor's authority, however, was infinite; and in formal terms later, in panegyrical terms earlier, it was acknowledged as such. "Whatever he decides is as good as law." "The emperor is owner of everything."[24] Therefore (it is argued), his actions toward others could not but differ radically from those of even the greatest of his subjects: toward him, the recipient could never feel an obligation, no more than to "The Government" in the abstract—no more than to the weather. Moreover, the favor he showed could not be purely arbitrary. Its special nature can be read in his treatment of promotions within his service. Did they proceed according to rules, principally those of seniority? Or were they rather earned by merit and suitability? In either case he was not free to enjoy his own sweet will. So it is argued.[25]

But discrepant bits of evidence need to be considered from discrepant points of view, near to the throne or remote, and of different periods. By Fronto's time, in his letter to Marcus Aurelius (5.37), you could recommend someone for promotion "in due form, in due turn, and proper time," with a sense of decades of precedents. The patterns of movement into the heights of governmental power, though perhaps they lacked strict rules, had become familiar. The emperor as well as petitioners knew them, and one could see, if not their lines, at least their shadow in records of many an individual career. Dio Cassius (79.22.2, A.D. 217) indicates their operation in describing a person "due to be made aedile." That is, the position was owed him, but he was irregularly balked. It would have been insulting, however, to tell the emperor (what certainly was not true) that he absolutely had to do or decree anything at all. Instead, if only out of tact, recipients tended to emphasize the arbitrary element and offer their assurances of gratitude.

Moreover, the emperor always needed more support, however powerful he might seem to be. He must buy it, then. It was proof of a specially lofty benevolence in Nerva, as Pliny recalls (*Paneg.* 39.3), to have expressed this quality through group legislation rather than through favorable responses to individual requests; for thus "he deprived himself of so many opportunities for *beneficia*, such numerous occasions for laying persons under obligation and getting them into his account books." The latter, in physical form, made up a "Book of Grants," a *liber beneficiorum*, and a small secretariate under a Keeper.[26] Their administration was not, perhaps, very different from that under any great dynast of the Republic, though obviously on a grander scale. Caesar had had a special servant to keep his *beneficia* books, so Cicero mentions (*Ad fam.* 13.36); the servant, it was discovered, was inventing and selling grants of citizenship. In the empire, governors of a province or legates of a legion kept their books too, like mini-emperors, and counted the promotions at their disposal (apparently there might be a fixed number at the outset of their own terms of appointment).[27] Rights to appointments were treated like bearer bonds: so many issued to you when you took over your post, the names of the beneficiaries to be filled in ad lib. You first satisfied the most insistent claims of your own dependents and then gratified your peers by admitting some of theirs, without necessarily knowing the merits or even the names of the recipients; and a recipient might make over the *beneficium* to someone else without asking your permission, thereby creating a welcome obligation to himself. For that, he would thank you.[28] It was all very well for a philosopher to protest that "no one enters his *beneficia* in an account book nor, like some greedy bill-collector, calls them in on the day and hour due."[29] High-minded nonsense! Even the same philosopher also says, "When I have received a *beneficium* and not returned it, I must keep it safe; for so long as it is in my hand it should be secure. Then it must be returned to the man who asks it back."[30] In actual practice, anyone in a position to help others to get what they wanted could do so by a *beneficium* in the expectation of being able to ask for some service, some *officium*, in return. He banked his claim, his *gratia*, wherever he could. That *gratia* among persons indebted to him constituted their potential obedience, and their obedience was his power.

For the system to work required that claims be recognized without the need of physical force. Society conspired to that end in the usual manner, by elevating such recognition to the level of morals. "You have," declares Publilius Syrus (*Sent.* 149 Duff), "said everything possible against a man when you call him an ingrate." Contrariwise, you have praised him most highly when you speak of his loyalty, his *fides*; in illustration, Cicero, again and again in his letters of referral speaking of the recommended person's capacity of gratitude. Or of the person's love toward himself—meaning, demonstrated gratitude. Again in Fronto's letters, or in Pliny's, these same points are stressed.[31] In Latin inscriptions we have a great many advertisements of the debt owed by whatever person commissioned the text, to his benefactors. He acknowledges the condescension, honor, bountiful affection, benevolence, and esteem they have shown him.[32] More simply, he calls them his incomparable, his ever-present, patrons. He sings their praises for their active concern on his behalf ("What an edifice of good fame did he not erect about me, among his friends and before the public, even in the view of the emperor!" exclaims Pliny about one of his patrons, *Ep.* 4.17.7). His show of thanks not only makes known their ability to gain the good things in life for their loyal dependents but demonstrates that loyalty itself, on which depend further grants. And the ethical norms that tie the two parties together and secure the working relation between *gratia* and *fides*, leverage and gratitude, and between *beneficia* and *officia*—those norms may be sensed very clearly in, for example, some of the more sententious passages of Pliny's letters.[33]

Evidence for the relationship that I describe is most often found among the upper classes in Italy, predictably; for they were Roman, and, in its formalities, so was the relationship. Also, of course, they had power and could therefore bestow as well as receive *beneficia*. But the terminology could be applied, perhaps a little peculiarly, to benefactors lower down in the social scale.[34] It became familiar in the provinces settled and shaped by the Romans—that is, the west (seen in inscriptions, e.g., n. 23); and the Greek east learned of it too. To go no further back than Pompey, we have reference to a special grant regarding citizenship which he had accorded to the natives of Pontus province, whether made known to them first in Greek or Latin we cannot say. It appears as a *beneficium* when it is later referred to; in Greek it would be *charis*.[35] The term *beneficium* appears translated as a loan-word into Greek and Hebrew around the turn of the third and fourth centuries. The fact suggests that it designated something that had been at some point seen as characteristically Roman, an odd foreign custom. Its oddity can have lain only in the obligation that accompanied the grant; for obviously all peoples have the custom of doing casual, unreciprocated favors. What distinguished the practice as Pompey or Pliny taught it was the particular insistence implied in the word *fides*.

It is ethical norms that we want for the writing of history, not anecdotes. But anecdotes often contain a hint of the sense of right and wrong in surrounding society, from which we can draw general distinctions between our own world and the past. For one thing, the readiness to avenge insult and do some injury to the person responsible would earn approval among the likes of Cicero or Pliny. Submit to a slight? No, only "over my dead body!" *Dignitas* might sound the same threatening note to be heard in the word "respect," on which some modern mobster-chief insists. But, in the second place, Cicero and Pliny would also give approval to the exact recording of one's non-monetary debts to others. That was taken for granted in a respectable person. It could be counted on. Occasionally it is made explicit as the reason for performing some action, although, among the usual mixture of motives, we would not expect to be told very often that a *beneficium* was intended solely or chiefly as a sort of investment in someone else's future compliance or service.[36] Between these two forms of inducement, however, it is plain that the persons of local or empire-wide authority, equally, built up their power and controlled the world around them.

19

HOW TO REVOLT IN THE ROMAN EMPIRE

IF ANY of the emperor's subjects ever compiled a handbook on insurrection, explaining in detail how it must be undertaken, his work of practical instruction has not survived. Perhaps, like too-readily-understandable books about atom bombs, it was seized by the sinister *agentes in rebus* or their equivalent of earlier reigns. In any case, the matter remains for us quite unexpectedly mysterious: no vignettes of the plotters at dinner, no inside stories of how they hoped they could recruit support, no day-to-day account of how the project developed.

Nevertheless revolts as distinct from palace assassinations occasionally were attempted, and we might expect to hear a lot about them. They generally originated among the best-known people, aristocrats distinguished by their tremendous names: L. Arruntius Camillus Scribonianus (cos. 32), C. Calpurnius Piso Crassus Frugi Licinianus (cos. 87), even a Cornelius (Priscianus, legate in Nearer Spain in 145);[1] perhaps the mysteriously annihilated M'. Laberius Maximus (cos. 89) or T. Atilius Rufus Titianus (cos. 217). Dio Cassius (72[73].5.1f.) describes what he evidently sees as a convincing sort of insurrectionary—who, however, chose not to make his move: a man "enjoying very great repute, command of a great army, and the soldiers' loyalty." It was P. Salvius Julianus (cos. 175). At the death of Marcus Aurelius he had his chance; but he eschewed it, we have no way of knowing exactly why.[2] A century and more earlier, L. Verginius Rufus had likewise turned down the offer of the throne from his troops. Tacitus (*Hist.* 1.52.4) says it was on account of his "equestrian origin, his father an unknown"—in short, the name not long enough.

Speculation similarly focused on another man at another shaken moment of the empire's history, after the assassination of Domitian. The candidate, to us with no name at all,[3] was "at that time in control of very great armies in the east, borne on strong though ambiguous rumors." Perhaps it was more the moment than the man that fed the rumors. A weak emperor or a new one not yet settled into the throne provoked contempt from his soldiers and ambition in their higher officers.[4] The latter might half glimpse their opportunity. While their resolution was forming, the gods could be consulted. A favorable answer, if it were spread around, could provide validation of projects otherwise dubious. Any resort to seers or oracles was therefore liable to the severest punishment by the sitting emperor; but Lucian makes it sound as if consultation nevertheless went on all the time, "hazardous and over-venturesome—

you know what questions the rich and powerful are likely to ask."[5] Similarly, distribution of money to soldiers except in the emperor's name called for instant punishment. However, the risk might have to be taken.[6]

So far, the project remains within the bounds of the familiar. A good deal of additional detail and illustration could be easily added; easy also to follow out somewhat more advanced stages of action. Plain common sense, but, again, familiar accounts as well, would indicate the need to attract a core of well-placed persons from one's entourage or province, to join in the revolt for the pay-off held out to them. They would win rapid, even instant, promotion. The prosopographers must deal with the resulting evidence—all, however, circumstantial. Direct, express testimony to the moment of suasion—"Join me and I will make you a governor"—is difficult to come by, even when the outlines of the participants' later careers are well attested.[7] From an original inner membership, invitation then moves out tentatively to wider circles. Aspirant to the throne, the praetorian prefect Nymphidius Sabinus seeks candid advice from a well-informed friend, who "did not think there was a single tenement house ready to call Nymphidius 'Caesar.' "[8] So the prefect made no move. A wider canvass by letter was possible though dangerous. "You are out of your wits" was the reaction of one correspondent when approached by Avidius Cassius. But Avidius was not deterred.[9] We would give a good deal to know more about the delicate business of taking soundings preliminary to armed uprisings. One could hardly ask people outright, "Just how disloyal are you?"

Nymphidius, just referred to, was confident of his hold over the praetorian guard but not so sure the capital's civilian population would accept him. Their importance, unarmed though they were, should not be under-estimated. We have seen them challenge Macrinus and weaken his reputation. On two other occasions they demonstrated their power. Sejanus, in good control of the Guard and seeing the imperial succession about to settle on young prince Gaius, nevertheless deferred his coup upon discovering the masses "strongly pleased by the things said about Gaius, on account of their memory of his father Germanicus" (Dio 58.8.2). And, like Sejanus, the Roman senate two centuries later determined it simply could not continue with its proposed candidates for the throne, Pupienus and Balbinus, in the face of the determined opposition of huge crowds of people in the streets. They had stones and cudgels and were noisy and threatening. So, "at someone's suggestion" (how nameless are the great shifts of history!), a child of the well-liked Gordiani was sent for.[10] So great was the power of the "mob"—and it may have been better organized than the term implies (below, p. 202).

On the other hand, the sounding of Herodes Atticus needs no particular explaining. Besides being in effect the king of Athens and tied in to a network of important people, he was quite gigantically rich. A revolt originating in any eastern province, like Avidius Cassius', would need money and would naturally turn to him for support, if it could be had. Money had to be collected to be given to the soldiers. That was standard, as a reward for deserting or a confirmation of their zeal; and, unless you were willing to lose civilian support by simply seizing all your supplies and transport, moving soldiers about was an expensive business.[11] Tacitus (*Hist.* 1.57) describes how the leading men, the *principes*, of every type of settlement in northern Gaul in 69 joined in providing Vitellius' cause with "volunteers, mounts, weapons, cash"; and Dio (75[76].5.1f.) records the bizarre story of a school teacher taking off from Rome to Gaul where, in 196, he presented himself as a senator on mission from Septimius Severus to assemble an army; did so; and used that army, among other ventures, to seize or somehow acquire 70 million sesterces for the cause.

We have only the two specific details to tell us what objects of preliminary testing would be of the first importance to an insurrectionary movement: provincial millionaires (Herodes Atticus) and broad popular support (the *plebs* in Rome). We are, however, well served by these two. Although popularity with soldiers was crucial, not only among the candidate's immediate command but among his former troops as well,[12] if his movement were to spread, nevertheless the military element in success was only a part of the whole. It may easily receive more attention than it deserves. In fact, as other evidence indicates, success required a broad base because claiming the throne was a complicated matter, no tip-and-run raid on power. Effort had therefore to be given to financing, propaganda, the entire civilian aspect of the thing.

The Augustan History (*Maximini* 15.6f.) presents "a specimen of the letters that the senate sent out" in 238 against the emperor. Granted, the document is invented and the purported author an institution, not some individual pretender himself. Still, it was meant to be a plausible example of propaganda, and succeeds. Just as we would expect, it is addressed to a comprehensive list of Roman magistrates and officials, as well as every sort of urban settlement large or small. Naturally it indulges in a good bit of name-calling and exhortation. At the end it denies the emperor's very legitimacy: he is declared an enemy of the state. The document as a whole, in its general tenor, may be compared with Gordian's early letters requesting support (Herodian 7.6.3f.), reported in a condensed form, and with speeches at the outset of their movements by Vindex, for example, or Galba; also, with the coinage of certain pretenders.[13] From the slogans or rhetoric of these various media, nothing of special interest emerges except their banality. Pretenders supposed they would best gain support through the advertising of familiar virtues and objectives, not through innovation. Indirectly they affirm the socioeconomic stability of the empire during the Principate.

After all, they were addressing a conservative audience: big property holders. Gain these, and the rest—local rural population and individual cities— would follow. Certain figures would be known for their ability to swing entire provinces with their weight: in Crete, where Claudius Timarchus "was accustomed to declare it within his gift whether thanks should be expressed to the governor who got Crete" (Tac., *Ann.* 2.72.2); "in Histria, . . . where the Crassi had long possessed their network of dependents, their lands, and good will toward their name" (Tac., *Hist.* 2.72.2); and elsewhere in the literary and epigraphic record, men identified perhaps through the award of the title "Number One in the province," or sometimes instead through the accumulation of offices, honors, and testimonials to their benevolence.[14] The provinces, quite aside from their Councils and high priests, quite aside from governors, procurators, legionary legates, and other imperial officials, obeyed the authority of an entirely unofficial hierarchy. Its members and order would be familiar to everyone. Similarly, cities: possessing both magistrates and "leaders," however one referred to them.

Into this existing structure of authority pretenders must fit their claims. It was not to be done alone, or so much, by the promise of better rule, still less by the promise or threat of radical change. Claims less grand but more persuasive—of kinship, familiarity, and clientage—are what our sources talk about. It would naturally be assumed that your relatives could be counted on for aid and cooperation.[15] The assumption did not always work out. It would be supposed also that anyone contemplating revolt would base himself in the region where he was born.[16] Native sons started out with a special advantage. For that reason governors and legionary legates were not routinely sent out to the regions they knew best, their own home provinces; rather the reverse, as was affirmed by law in the wake of Avidius Cassius' revolt.[17] Given the almost universal practice of using one's authority to create dependents, supporters, and indebtedness to oneself, in the normal course of a law-abiding life, there was really no way to prevent individuals emerging with the potential to revolt, in the form of political and other obligations owing them in scattered regions of the empire.

Insurrection meant division, as we have seen (n. 15): in Campania, responding to energetic but conflicting propaganda on behalf of two pretenders, "the Puteolans were especially zealous for Vespasian while on the other hand Capua was loyal to Vitellius; and the two were engaged in war through small-town rivalry" (Tac., *Hist.* 3.57.1). In much the same way Lyons favored Nero, Vienne helped Vindex. The one city had been penalized by Galba while the other was honored. Come the Vitellian troops, the advantage was once more reversed and the inhabitants of Lyons urged retaliation upon their neighbor.[18] An eastern rivalry inclined Nicaea to choose one side because its neighbor Nicomedia was vigorously supporting the other with promises of arms, supplies, and so forth;[19] and in the moment of choice, if Antioch came out for Pescennius Niger, Laodicea necessarily inclined to Septimius Severus. After the fighting was over, the victor repaid all the help he had gotten not only by assigning the revenues of the hostile city to his ally (apparently), but bestow-

ing on the latter direct gifts of dole money, tax exemption, and civic promotion.[20] From the chance mentions of food, equipment, transport, lodging, and,
above all, cash that were afforded to the armies favored by a city, it seems
safe to infer that the post-war settling of accounts we sometimes hear about
concerned a good deal more than hurt feelings.

As between cities that were neighbors and rivals, so within cities too, the
news of a revolt and the need to choose up sides no doubt caused sharp division. Perhaps the recollection of one such is to be read in a dedication to
"Septimius Haddudân, illustrious senator, son of Septimius Ogeilu Maqqai
who lent aid to [the troops of Au]relian Caesar [our Lord]" in A.D. 272 in
Palmyra. Among the four tribes that together constituted the urban population,
that of the dedicatees effectively owned the temple of Bel, and appears to have
been the only one to help Aurelian. It was quite rich enough to make a difference.[21]

Reference was made to the survey of opinion conducted in Rome by the
praetorian prefect (above, p. 199). The results were given him in terms of the
different big housing units (synoikiai). Cities of which we have any real
knowledge seem always to have been divided into more or less self-conscious
sub-units of population, sufficiently organized for joint, directed action. That
may be recorded for us in votes of thanks to some important person; sometimes in support at elections. What underlay organization was normally the
dominant trade practiced in a neighborhood, itself formed into an association,
collegium or however called.[22] In trying to understand just how, in detail,
opinion in a city could be brought to a focus in favor of some political decision, we have before us the materials for an easy reconstruction: urban leaders
would come to an agreement with the groups of which they were the designated patrons or semi-honorary officers. The groups themselves, known to us
very familiarly across a variety of data, were likely to include not only a good
share of the entire male population, but in unforced, natural associations as
well, through which people's views could be easily sensed and communicated. In actual fact, the potential of such associations for political action was
amply demonstrated in the capital during the later decades of the Republic,
and remained a reality centuries later. A letter of Trajan to Pliny (Ep.10.34)
speaks of them with distrust, as generally a cause of political unrest in the
cities. It is no rash conjecture, then, to ascribe the partisan acts of whole cities
for or against a pretender in terms of civic leaders bringing together neighborhood, trade, and cult groups (where all three were not identical). In turn, the
leaders negotiated with the pretender.

Individuals like cities were paid off according to opportunity, impulse, and
their past actions. A rash of armed risings were attempted in 218 among the
eastern legions. Their leaders were all executed. They had never had a chance,
and a contemporary (Dio 80.7.2) judged "they were out of their minds," like
Avidius Cassius in the judgment of Herodes Atticus. But their fate should be

balanced against the lack of evidence for widespread campaigns of retaliation aimed at the office-holders on the losing side;[23] against the ample evidence for successful careers riding right through revolts and violent changes of power;[24] and against indirect but also ample evidence for the rewarding of the winners.[25] Joining a revolt need not have appeared a horrible gamble because, I suppose, careers and ambitions were tied into an immensely resilient fabric of mutual obligations and multiple dependencies. These discouraged both upheavals and reprisal. The fact, combined with the fundamental weakness of the imperial government, allowed for the empire's survival through reigns like Gaius Caligula's, Commodus', and Elagabalus'—with which only penny-dreadful historiography need be much concerned.

JUDICIAL SAVAGERY IN THE ROMAN EMPIRE

ROM THE ENTIRETY of the past, historical clichés and catch phrases isolate images that are specially vivid and striking, if only to the unreflecting mind. In English, for example, we speak of "barbarous cruelty" and "medieval torture." These are features of their times that we notice very much. Per contra, we do not associate them with Rome. Rome is essentially different. And in fact the catch phrases speak truly. Sights and sounds to make one shudder, not issuing from eccentric savagery but from communally approved action, could indeed be seen in A.D. 550 and later but not in 150, in the eastern regions of the Mediterranean as well as in the western. Can the change, thus highlighted, be traced and accounted for?

First, a peculiarity in penal action. Among Romans, everything depended on status. Several large distinctions received recognition in the courts: between those who were citizens, and aliens (most often called provincials, in the period of empire), or between those who were free, and slaves. Additionally, judges recognized the status of senators, town councillors (decurions or *curiales*), their kin and descendants, and looser categories both social and moral. Of the social, we have many signs, perhaps the clearest being the first question directed by a judge to anyone, witness or accused, who appears before him: "What is your condition, your rank (*condicio, fortuna, tyche*)?" For this, we have a number of trial transcripts to rely on. As to the moral categories, the signs may be read in the opinion of a jurist of around the turn of the second century. He speaks of notorious bandits whose very notoriety earns special penalties. "Our ancestors in every sort of sentence dealt more harshly with slaves than with freeborn and with men of ill repute than with those of good repute."[1]

The standing of the accused having been determined, and the nature of his act, the two could be put together into a suitable penalty. It bore harder on a person low in the scale, lighter on persons higher up. Slaves at the bottom could not be very much worse treated in the later empire than in the later Republic since they were virtually without rights and since the governing classes took for granted their moral worthlessness.

Because a good part of the story has been carefully told by others,[2] I need only review it quickly and selectively. Most of it may be traced in the obvious sources, too: in the *Digest, Codex Justinianus, Pauli Sententiae*, and *Codex Theodosianus*, supplemented here and there by other texts like the *Collatio* of Mosaic and Roman laws. Their chronological coverage is of course uneven.

They permit the fullest and easiest statements for the period around the turn of the third to fourth century, with which other periods may be compared. I concentrate on severe penalties, above the level of hard labor for life in mines, quarries, and mills; for condemnation to such work-places, though it is more often talked about as the records of the Christian persecutions multiply, does not seem to have changed character across the whole history of the empire.[3]

Prior to A.D. 200, capital punishment visited persons found guilty of making slaves eunuchs (*Dig.* 48.8.4) or stealing livestock (*abigei*, sentenced to gladiatorial combat, *Coll.* 11.7.1). Both sentences were defined by Hadrian. In addition, in his day, parricide was a capital crime punished by tying the offender in a sack with snakes and other animals and drowning him (*D.* 48.9.9 praef.). Attacks on the emperor by magic or by physical means were naturally punishable by death; also arson, temple-robbing, or actual or attempted murder of their masters on the part of slaves, for which they could be crucified (Mart., *Spect.* 7.8–10). [An edict (of Augustus?) in Palestine assigns the death penalty to the violation of monuments meant to serve ancestor worship (*FIRA*[2] 1.416), though ordinary violation was not a capital matter (*Pauli Sent.* 1.21.4f.).] Most cattle-rustlers were executed (*Dig.* 47.14.1); likewise, brigands, some by crucifixion (*Jos.*, *B. J.* 2.75, 241, and 253; Philostr., *Vit. soph.* 541; and Petron. 111.5). To these categories we must add Jews and Christians dying for their faith in both the first and second centuries.[4] And the slave who enlisted in the legions (Plin., *Ep.* 10.30) or pretended to be a citizen (Suet., *Claud.* 25.3—presumably slaves, not free persons) or the slave who proved traitor in time of war (Tac., *Hist.* 4.3.4), or who deliberately moved boundary markers (*Dig.* 47.21.3.1, Nerva), or the convict who broke out of jail (*Dig.* 47.18.1, Marcus Aurelius), was to be executed as well. Poisoning leads to condemnation to the beasts; at least it does so in a fictional account (Apul., *Met.* 10.28 and 34). But that is credible enough. The seventeen or so capital crimes in all these oddments and enactments indicate the height of severity, before the great age of the jurisconsults.

There is more to be said, however, before we leave the first two centuries A.D.; and that more is to be found not in legal sources but in literary, often in anecdotes that lie in the realm between what is done by a law, and what is done by a lawfully appointed authority. In Lyons, for example, the governor identified one Christian in particular, Attalus, as a Roman citizen. He set him aside while he sought instruction about his fate from Marcus Aurelius; he received the command to behead the citizens and crucify the rest; but instead he sentenced the non-citizens and Attalus, too, "as an indulgence to the crowd," to death among the beasts of the amphitheater. In short, he did exactly as he pleased.[5] So likewise did a mid-first-century governor in Spain who sent a poisoner to the cross and, despite the criminal's asserting his citizenship, went right ahead with the crucifixion as decreed, illegally (Suet., *Galba* 9.1); similarly a governor of Asia under Augustus who, "when he had leveled with the executioner's axe three hundred in one day, went about among the corpses with an expression of pride, as if surveying some grand accomplishment." The affair is reported by Seneca in an *Essay on Anger* (2.5.5), as an instance of something almost irrational. And we have a general evaluation of a governor's conduct as "going beyond all bounds in punishing crime."[6] Contemporaries could identify tolerable or praiseworthy exercise of authority and distinguish it from the intolerable. The bounds were not fixed by law, at least not in the minds of ordinary observers; rather, by moral considerations. Governors had a right to freedom of action, they did a great deal more than mechanically apply some rule-book.[7] Really, it was they who determined the level of judicial savagery quite as much as the central government.

It was they, but also that government. Naturally what emperors decided in their judicial as in their legislative capacity weighed heavily on the routines of provincial life, even granted the effective independence of their representatives. For every autocrat in Vienne, violating the rights of Roman citizens, no doubt there were as many or more Younger Plinys, scrupulously referring their uncertainties to their sovereign. The particular preferences of the occupant of the throne at any given moment would be known, as we may judge from the many anecdotes that have come down to us: Augustus and Hadrian kind even to slaves, Tiberius and Caligula inventively savage, Claudius and Domitian more conservatively so.[8] Extremes of imperial vengeance were on display from time to time, for maximum publicity: best known, no doubt, the Christians in the wake of Rome's fire in A.D. 64, fixed to crosses and burned like torches in the evening, as Tacitus tells us (*Ann.* 15.44), while others were wrapped in the hides of beasts of the hunt, set before dogs, and so torn apart. Vespasian had one leader of the Jewish revolt led about the Forum while he was beaten, then to be despatched in the adjoining jail, and another such leader, or brigand, was first tortured and afterward (necessarily in a public place) burnt alive.[9] Under Domitian the character in a play, Laureolus, who is crucified on stage, was acted in the amphitheater by a convict actually despatched on the spot.[10] Similar dressing-up of criminals who were to be executed, and the setting of them into some drama so as to present their death as part of an entertainment, is recorded in Carthage and elsewhere.[11]

Tolerance, even the demand, for severe punishments is often attested. Cruelty served the moral ends of society, so it was argued; and that explains and justifies publicity, too: for how else could convicted criminals serve an exemplary purpose?[12] So authority makes an exhibit of them, even in a theater, amphitheather, or the Roman Circus Maximus. They were, moreover, people who deserved all they got: defeated enemies, foreign or domestic; dangerous, cunning, wicked folk for whom hanging was literally too good.[13] Or the crowds simply didn't bother their heads over moral questions and shouted for more, more, without discriminating between the pleasures of violence and vengeance. With those shouts Christians were familiar in Vienne in 177, in

Carthage according to Tertullian's and Perpetua's reports, and elsewhere, too.[14] At least some large parts of the population of a great many cities, at some moments, more than merely accepted a high level of brutality in the name of their civilization. Particularly for suffering inflicted in the course of public shows, they obviously had a strong appetite. It is worth noting, however, that that appetite as expressed in gladiatorial combat began to diminish slowly around the time of these dates, the later second and early third century,[15] while in judicial contexts its increase steadily continued.

Away from the crowds, at the opposite end of the spectrum of opinion, we find the moralist as his role was conceived of at the time: the philosopher clad in his cloak, or someone taught by such a person. One of them protests, "the executioner and noose are long out of date. Laws have been laid down to determine punishment without any harshness called for from the judges or scandal against the times."[16] But another bids his listeners, "Think now of the jail, the cross, the rack, the hook, and the man pierced right through so that the stake comes out his mouth." He presents these images to arouse dread, not abhorrence.[17] Of course scenes of that description *were* dreadful; yet, in a society where gladiatorial combat was a fixture, they were not likely to be judged literally intolerable. Indeed, they were destined to become more common in the empire's cities as time went on.

Just how common, it is very hard to determine for any period. If we keep our focus fixed on the empire of the first two centuries A.D., we can hardly say whether a criminal's corpse suspended on a gibbet was a sight quite beyond ordinary experience, or not (as in the Middle Ages). "Thoughts of crucifixion seem to have caused nightmares even for those who ran no risk of such punishment."[18] In the wake of some specially great disturbance, the bodies on crosses along the road must produce an overwhelming impression.[19] What mention is made of them may reflect shock rather than their frequency. On the other hand, reinforcing our impression of prevalent and accepted judicial violence in that world, Epictetus warns us of the very real possibility that we may be tortured if we embark on litigation of any sort, and Cyprian points to court hearings as likely to involve brutal interrogation.[20] Common or not, depending on time and place, pictures of brutal routines of law in action were no doubt stored away in the memory of every citizen.

Pain, while a sentence in itself for slaves convicted of certain crimes, was also normally inflicted on them as a way of getting true testimony. Sometimes it was very effective. An example appears much later in a hearing before the governor of Africa in 315: just tying up the witness preparatory to further measures makes him change his story instantly and most damagingly.[21] Freeborn persons, however, if they were also Roman citizens, were at first exempt from force used in interrogation. They were exempt whether as witnesses or accused; and that was St. Paul's point (Acts 16.37 and 22.25): "They have beaten us publicly, uncondemned, men that are Romans. . . . Is it lawful for you to scourge a man that is a Roman, uncondemned?'' By what stages this security was lost does not appear clearly in the record.[22] Augustus affirmed the exemptions but his successor already disregarded it in cases involving treason; and peasants possessing citizenship were beaten by a local imperial official in Commodus' reign, apparently just to coerce and terrify them. Granted, they were lowly folk living in a remote area. From the general indifference displayed toward the qualification of citizenship throughout the *Digest*, from the lack of interest in its universal gift displayed by everyone in and after A.D. 212, and from the clear interest that is by contrast displayed in social status as a determinant of penalties, we can judge where the weight of reality lay. It lay in one's local prominence, wealth, and office—in everything that peasants and the bulk of the population lacked. Indeed, by the date of their complaint to Commodus, the ruling had issued from so scrupulous an emperor as Marcus Aurelius that town councillors and higher ranks (*honestiores*) were not to be flogged either during interrogation or as a penalty; whereas, by implication, those exemptions did not belong by automatic right to persons of lower rank (*humiliores*), and were already coming under attack or question for *honestiores*. Hints of how that attack developed, more against defendants than witnesses and more often in the context of serious charges, can be found in various texts of Severan times.

The long period just surveyed is thus one of steady degradation in the legal right of the individual to decent treatment, only a little modified by touches of *humanitas*. That latter has received a great deal of study and emphasis. It constitutes an element in the history of Roman law that draws admiring comment. The vast majority of citizens, however, were they asked what era they would wish to live in, Cicero's or Marcus Aurelius', for the enjoyment of physical safety in the empire's courts, would no doubt have preferred the former. The statement, to be sure, applies only to Romans. It is clear that treatment of "aliens" in some very broad sense of that term was quite a different matter, and seen to be so; and members of the ruling class when they found themselves abroad were prone to behave as if among a lower species of some sort that had no claim on their humanity—in short, behaved as they would have toward their own slaves at home. In time, habits of law-giving abroad exerted an influence over law-giving even to one's full fellows. So I would explain the development manifestly to be traced in our sources from milder to more severe penal routines. In illustration: during Gaius Verres' provincial governorship in the 70s B.C., "no distinction whatsoever was made" in respect to flogging "between Roman citizens and other people. And the result of this practice was that before long his lictors were in the habit of actually laying hands upon the persons of Roman citizens without so much as waiting for his orders."[23] Cicero and his audience are shocked by such lawless savagery. Time passes, these developments that I have traced increasingly prevail in the empire's courts, and the great jurisconsults of the early third century report on the results.

In describing them now it will be clearest if I do so as I described the state of affairs prior to A.D. 200, that is, beginning with capital offenses. Some fifteen crimes so punished continue on the books[24]—unless two of them no longer count as capital (which is most unlikely): the two that concern slaves who join the legions, and who betray the state to an enemy. For some crimes formerly capital, the penalty has been raised from decapitation by blow of sword, to crucifixion, burning, or wild beasts. Far more striking, however, is the number of additional crimes counted now as capital. Some are against the state: civilian desertion to the enemy (*Dig.* 48.19.38.1 and 49.16.3.10) and sedition (*Dig.* 48.19.38.2), both punished by *bestiae* or *furca*, or flight from the place of one's exile (49.19.28.13). Others violate religion: divination (P. Coll. Youtie I 30, a. 198/199), the killing of sacred animals in Egypt (Min. Fel. 28.8), circumcision of non-Jews (*bestiae* being the penalty for slaves, *Dig.* 48.8.11), or the disturbing of burials to rob them (*Dig.* 47.12.11, the death penalty aimed only at *humiliores* unless arms are employed, 47.12.3.7). Still others concern abuse of litigation: by the slave who brings suit against his master (SHA *Pertinax* 9.10; *CJ* 4.55.4.1, a. 224) or by any person whose false testimony results in the execution of another (*Dig.* 48.8.1.1; Herodian 1.9.5). Finally, there is homicide: of his master by a slave, now punished by burning at the stake (*crematio*, *Dig.* 48.19.28.11); by any robber or poisoner (*Dig.* 48.8.3.5), to be sentenced *ad bestias* if a *humilior*; or accidental homicide through a potion (*Dig.* 48.19.28.5). The total of charges for which one could expect to lose one's life has almost doubled, compared with that of Antonine times.

At a third point in time, around A.D. 300, the anonymous *Pauli Sententiae* allows us to take some further measure of the progress of cruelty.[25] The work survives only in fragments, in which it is nevertheless possible to find nearly the full list of the older crimes.[26] A few of them now receive a milder form of the death penalty, but most receive a harsher one. Moreover, eleven new crimes have been added to the capital list: insurrection (*PS* 5.29.1, "formerly exile"); human sacrifice connected with divination (*PS* 5.23.16, *bestiae* for *humiliores*); the invention of new and unsettling cults by *humiliores* (*PS* 5.21.2); hexing (*PS* 5.23.15, *crux* or *bestiae*) and magic and nocturnal rites in temples (*PS* 5.21.2f. and 5.23.15 and 17, decapitation, or *crematio* for the performer, *crux* or *bestiae* for his customers); the assuming by *humiliores* of the insignia of higher officialdom in order to practice extortion (*PS* 5.25.12); the sale of inside knowledge by court employees (*PS* 5.25.13); counterfeiting by slaves and *humiliores* (*PS* 5.12.12 and 5.25.1, *crux*); kidnapping, if by a *humilior* (*PS* 5.30B.1, *crux*, "formerly a fine"); sexual assault on either a boy or a girl (*PS* 5.4.14); and altering or falsifying a will (*PS* 5.25.1, *crux* for *humiliores*, beheading for freedmen of the will). In the specification of penalties, incidentally, I have indicated the more severe, where some choice was left to judges; and, where there is no specification of rank, I have assumed that all ranks were intended. Some erosion of the difference between *humiliores* and *honestiores* can be seen here in progress, destined to develop further in the century that follows.[27]

The rising level of penal severity that appears in the *Pauli Sententiae* appears also in other sources a little earlier or a little later. I need not depend only on the one witness. Indeed, where I aim to speak generally of moral and judicial values among sixty or so millions, I cannot have enough variety of witnesses. A papyrus of A.D. 278 contains a circular addressed by a high official to district and town magistrates, announcing the rules for the year's dike corvées and threatening infractions with death.[28] No such threat can be found, I think, in prior records of Roman Egypt; but the novelty may be compared to the death penalty directed at extortion in other branches of the government, as they are found in the *Pauli Sententiae*. With that work, another bit of evidence also is entirely consonant: I mean the description of a scene of daily life used by the author of an early fourth-century (?) language-instruction booklet. It shows us the forum of some provincial city in the morning:[29]

> The governor arrives to take his place on the platform between the guards. The platform is prepared. The judge mounts the platform and announces through the herald's voice, "All parties stand." The accused man stands, a brigand. He is interrogated as his doings deserve. He is tortured. The interrogator hammers him, his breast is torn. He is hung up . . . , he is beaten with rods, he is flogged, he passes through the series of tortures and still denies [his guilt]. He is to be punished, undergoes sentencing, is led off to be beheaded.

It is a vignette thought to be useful to the traveler from one province to another, as today we are taught by phrase books to know our way around foreign airports. What a very chilling world it must have been for the tourist then! In those years in particular the persecutions were under way at their worst. What we are told about them fits very naturally into that snapshot of some western Roman forum just offered us. With the persecutions, however, we find ourselves generally in eastern cities, especially of Palestine where Eusebius was resident, took notes, and preserved the memory of his co-religionists' various exquisite sufferings. One novelty especially he records: mutilation. A martyr's leg is broken, the Achilles tendon cut, an eye put out, or a nose or ear cut off.[30] Everyone watches, tourists or residents alike. The scene is quite public: the local amphitheater or, ordinarily, the market-place or public portico where the governor presides from his tribunal. What everyone sees, becomes matter-of-fact; at least it accustoms the eye. Moral and judicial expectations are simultaneously expressed and shaped.

The impact of the frequent witnessing of judicial violence can be measured in a peculiarly useful type of source: handbooks for the interpretation of dreams and horoscopes. These served a clientele of small towns as well as cities, and of the not-very-rich as well as the prosperous. Several of them cluster in the last quarter of the second century, against which we may compare Firmicus Maternus' work that reflects the first third of the fourth century. In both the earlier group and this later one the vicissitudes predicted had to be fairly representative of their times if the diviners were to make sense to their customers and stay in business. Their witness therefore has some historical value. But in the earlier ones, while beatings for slaves, jail terms, fines, even decapitation are mentioned, and while crucifixion arouses a special horror, nevertheless the over-all picture is nowhere nearly so grim as in the fourth century. Then, the courts and their consequences threaten everyone; and their measures are more violent.[31] The "ultimate sentence," *summum supplicium*, is seen as terminating one out of every five or six lives—a statistic of course not literally accurate but all the more revealing of people's fears.

And the severest penalties were applied with diminishing respect for rank. A Duke might burn, so the stars predicted; and they did so more truly than the laws, whose prescriptions did not control practice. A town councillor might be strung up for torture and only when he had broken would he be asked the routine question, "What is your status?" (above, n. 18).

Firmicus Maternus saw in his lifetime a perceptible acceleration of change in the history I am tracing; for Constantine's reign produced several dozen laws for which the sanction was death; and the great majority of these broke new ground.[32] Necessarily these latter were aimed rather particularly at problems of the moment, since the broader categories of serious crime had long since been defined and dealt with. The emperor on a grand scale is thus using the ultimate threat very much as did that regional supervisor in Egypt a generation earlier, in an ad hoc administrative fashion. He expresses special fury against his own government servants, assigning to the greedier ones the punishment of amputation of their hands or the fate of being tortured to death (*CT* 1.16.7 and 1.22.1). He initiates also the form of execution through pouring molten lead down the throat (*CT* 9.24.1.1); and at the thought of those accountants in his government who persist in their venality, he explodes with threats of *tormenta et eculei atque lacerationes* (*CT* 8.1.4).

Was Constantine deranged, a madman? If that were the case, how could he serve us in any attempt to trace and understand the growth of barbarism in the empire? At most, he might have made that element familiar, but not more tolerable. In fact, his admirers characterized him as unusually merciful and mild.[33] He was merely of his times. His savage measures, looked at from a distance, fit very well into the curve of penal development discovered thus far.

There was much worse to come. Valentinian, as any reader of Ammianus Marcellinus knows from an abundance of vivid incidents, was really a man to watch out for lest, in his proximity, you gave offense, and heard the order for your tongue to be cut out or your hand to be lopped off on the spot.[34] More serious matters he dealt with more deliberately, by burning men at the stake.[35] Of Valentinian's brother ruling in the east, Ammianus has quite horrible tales to tell, especially those centering in a case of divination;[36] and his son Gratian, when provoked, could annihilate wrongdoers "with immense tortures,"[37] quite in the family style. As to Valentinian's general Theodosius (again our source is Ammianus), he maintained military discipline by burning men alive or more often cutting off their hands.[38]

In the violence of these great men, resort to mutilation attracts special attention. It is characteristic of their period; for, as a judicial penalty, it makes no appearance before the start of the fourth century.[39] It continues in use thereafter into the fifth and sixth centuries, in just the manner we have seen, rarely as a statutory sanction, more often as an expression of rage or infliction of insult[40]—for example, threatened against a bishop by Constantius and, in the earlier fifth century, applied to great courtiers, enemies of the state, and similar celebrities.[41] One element shared between mutilation and other drastic pains employed by Constantine and perhaps by third-century emperors, too, is dramatic appropriateness: the person who gives wicked advice is to be choked with molten lead, the seller of false promises, "smoke," is asphyxiated over a slow fire; and similarly amputation, whether loss of a foot for a deserter, of a hand for the destroyer of public buildings, or of sexual organs for the pederast (under Justinian), proclaims symbolically the particular evil being punished.[42]

Proclamation is of the times, too. There had never been a moment when Roman Justice, aroused and representing the cause of right, had hidden her acts of vengeance behind a screen;[43] but as the crimes multiplied that earned dramatic retribution—not a mere fine, not even exile, but some more violent assault upon the body of the person convicted—then, more and more, justice is acted out before the people assembled. The stage chosen in Rome is the Septemzodium, where the prefect has an insolent rabble-rouser summarily seized, tied, hung up, and his sides torn.[44] Or, in a small provincial city, Ptolemais, the stage is "the Royal Stoa, for long a court of justice, now displayed as a torture chamber" by the governor.[45] Clearest of all, it is Antioch, thanks to descriptions by Libanius. Behold the councillor Kyriakos after receiving 250 lashes and more. He is a mass of blood and water (since a water jar was smashed by the torturer in the midst of his exertions). We see how successive governors, in the name of questioning, "draw forth streams of blood in their courtrooms by floggings, but beat upon bodies bereft of their souls, abusing mere dumb clay."[46] The crowds look on, with what emotions we can only imagine. In the very streets they are pursued by the sights of savagery; for beaten men are paraded about the city to exhibit their torn backs.[47]

In sadistic men, no doubt prevailing standards of permissible severity brought out the worst. Contemporaries knew and recognized the likes of Urbanus, Andronicus, Eutropius, Festus, Maximus, and others less famous.[48]

But, by those same standards, conduct that we shudder at was acquitted or vigorously defended.[49] Protest might be raised sometimes against violent steps that emperors have in mind or have just taken in individual cases: Ambrose rebukes Theodosius over the massacre in Thessalonica, Augustine tries to soften Honorius' agent in Carthage (*Ep.* 139.1f.), Themistius dissuades Valens from excessive application of the death penalty (Soc., *H. E.* 4.32), John Chrysostom and Libanius independently urge mercy toward those involved in the rioting of 387 in Antioch, and Libanius alone often addresses Theodosius to moderate the punishment of the city's councillors. Spokesmen of eminence were expected to represent both their own communities and the cause of mercy in the abstract. But the right of the emperors to legislate as harshly as they thought necessary is never challenged, and legislation continues to develop along the lines I have been following, that is, toward ever-higher levels of violence.

Now to finish the count of capital crimes, which had risen above sixty-odd at the end of Constantine's reign, including a great many to be punished by something more awful than mere decapitation: heretics continue to be executed in the course of the next three generations, as before, and counterfeiters, rapists, informers, and slaves bringing charges against their masters. New laws reiterate the old on all these and other matters, too, where it is not thought sufficient simply to maintain the legislation of Constantine or his predecessors on the books.[50] But many, many acts hitherto not specified as illegal at all, or not judged serious enough to deserve capital punishment, now qualify for the death penalty. Pagan rites qualify (*CT* 16.10.4 and 6), but also any failure to enforce anti-pagan measures on the part of a governor's staff-members (*CT* 16.10.13.1). That last has about it the ad hoc quality which begins to appear in the later third century. So likewise does the ban on proposal of marriage to a nun (the suitor is to be burned alive, *CT* 9.25.2), or on officials' falsely claiming to be on a search for deserters (*CT* 7.18.17). It is death, again by fire, to divert the waters of the Nile flood from their natural course (*CT* 9.32.1; cf. *Dig.* 47.11.10); death, for a supervisor of an imperial post-station to be absent without leave for more than a month (*CT* 8.5.36); and death to clerks in Rome who put citizens on the dole illegally (*CT* 14.7.6). Anyone reading instead of destroying libelous writings is to be beheaded (*CT* 9.34.7). As for government servants who sell or suspend or bend their authority, of course for a price, they are the target of a particular bombardment of horrific threats, very much in the spirit of Constantine's earlier.[51]

Arriving at some date around the sack of Rome, we find ourselves here confronting a system of penal repression announced, open, unapologetic, and in full accord with the brutal impulses recorded of individual emperors. We cannot dismiss any one of them, no matter how bloodthirsty they may appear, as an unrepresentative departure from moral values and standards in the surrounding society. Men and laws are of a piece.

But the development in turn leading up to that system of repression can be followed out at the level of day-to-day judicial activitiy in the provincial courts. There also the tendency to severity is manifest. Its early targets had been people of no weight or standing in their communities, *humiliores*, whose gradual subjection to torture as defendants and even as innocent witnesses has been outlined (see pp. 208ff.). Much of that process of degradation of *humiliores* is inferred from a similar process working upon their superiors, town councillors and higher, the *honestiores*; and the loss of rights by these latter is likewise a gradual thing. Protest by Lactantius early in the fourth century illustrates what is happening (*De mort. persecut.* 21.2f.): a Roman emperor is modeling his conduct on that of an Oriental despot, who treats all men as if they were slaves; and "not only are town councillors tortured by him but the very foremost in cities, men of rank 'Distinguished' and 'Most Excellent,' and even in trivial and purely civil matters." It is outrageous, and Lactantius supposes his readers will be shocked, that traditional rights are being so violated. Only a few years later, however, Constantine (*CT* 9.19.1, a.316) takes up the matter of forged wills and provides for the torture of the accused, town councillor or not. Then in 319 (*CT* 9.21.1) he recognizes the special status of decurions as opposed to mere plebeians, in regard to permissible penalties for counterfeiting. For magic, however—a serious charge—"although the bodies of persons of rank are exempt from torture," yet even such a one "shall be handed over to the rack, and have his sides consigned to the tearing claws" (or "hooks," *CT* 9.16.6, a. 358).

Back and forth, without consistent practices, the tendency of the laws and judges alike vacillates; yet generally in an Oriental direction, as Lactantius would say. At last we arrive at Antioch of Libanius' day and at those horrific beatings of decurions which he details.[52] More than one of their victims died under the lash. The harshest times begin in the late 370s or 380s, and conclude the process by which more and more of the population is reduced to the judicial vulnerability of slaves. To this end, governors in provincial settings have contributed quite as much as emperors and legists in the capital.

To recount the history of judicial savagery in the empire, to follow it from its least to its most pronounced form over a span of four centuries and more, to quantify its effects in terms of capital punishment especially, and to indicate how pervasive it was and how naturally it seems to conduct the civilization of the ancient world into the medieval and Byzantine—all this is one thing. Explanation is another.

Some preliminary statements: first, it is safe to say there is no explanation for which any real demonstration has been offered. Second, it is not likely that so broad a development will have a single cause. And third, the devices of cruelty, crucifixion in particular, and the willingness to use them, did not have to be invented for the uses of the empire. They could be drawn from neighbors or absorbed in the course of conquest.[53] In the end, however, they had to be applied internally. It hardly counted that they might have been turned against the enemy in defeat, like the Astures whose hands were cut off (Dio 53.29.2, in 24 B.C.) or the Jews who were crucified in 70 (Jos., *B. J.* 5.450); against the mercenaries who had deserted to the enemy and were later caught and thrown to the beasts in 147 B.C. (Val. Max. 2.7.13), or the full citizens who defected from the empire and could be burned alive as if enemies (*Dig.* 48.19.8.2). Special brutality may be reserved for the outsider by any code of law without implying a match in the measures it employs on members of its own community.

It is worth recalling at this point the protection accorded to citizens in the Republic. They were neither tortured nor executed. At worst they might be deported, like Milo; or like Verres they might seek voluntary exile as their best choice. Only in two settings in Roman society was this protection absent: where masters confronted their slaves, or officers, their men. In both settings, so long as there was provocation, extremest severity was looked on as entirely proper. And, for members of the ruling class, both settings formed a part of their normal life experience, thus providing a particular, variant, but acceptable standard in the use of force by superiors against inferiors. In various ways and arguments, the importance of the slave and soldier model has been recognized.[54]

The psychological explanation has been recognized, too, by which standards of humanity that governed other relationships could be dispensed with: for rank and distance set apart the men who ordered and the men who suffered violence. Tocqueville has been quoted to good effect: "à mesure . . . que les peuples deviennent plus semblables les uns aux autres, ils se montrent réciproquement plus compatissants pour leurs misères, et le droit s'adoucit."[55] Contrariwise, in the Roman empire, as men were distanced from each other, they might try to bend others to their will with ever greater ferocity; for they could not imagine themselves ever having to suffer what they inflicted on their inferiors. The ultimate restraint was thus lost: the restraint of inner pain and horror felt vicariously. Penal law merely rationalizes this.

It is easy to identify distance and antipathy sufficient to explain how Augustus, Tiberius, or Claudius could mistreat conspirators against themselves. As the monarchy became more established, moreover, so the gulf continued to widen between the emperor and everybody else. To so high a person as himself, it might seem right to treat even the most eminent citizens as if they were delinquent aliens, slaves, or private soldiers. It is easy, too, to understand the loss of traditional guarantees against corporal punishment in the face of the emperor or his immediate delegates presiding over appellate courts in the capital, say, in Pliny's day. The impact on penal law of the monarchy itself has often been discussed.[56] We are not even surprised that harsh treatment might be employed against provincials by someone like Pliny, thoroughly decent according to the values and standards of his own society. Like so many men of his class at some point in their careers, he found himself fifteen hundred miles from home, High Commissioner or Gouverneur-Général over colonial folk totally different from himself and totally subject to his authority. Some who alleged Roman citizenship knew no Latin to speak of, or speak with. How could they say, then, that they were entitled to the same consideration that this decent man would show to his neighbors around Como? Distance, again. Being compounded of social and cultural memberhip as much as the bare law, citizenship was vulnerable to extra-legal attack, and gradually yielded its associated guarantees against *tormenta et eculei atque lacerationes*. It yielded to considerations of wealth, accent, education, dress, and demeanor. These were what established your claims to be considered "one of our kind" by your judges.

Evidence? We have only one courtroom speech from all the period of the empire: Apuleius' *Apologia*. In it he is at pains to establish the alignment of his own with the judge's general culture, which is, of course, Greek and Latin rhetoric plus the supporting parts, or tags, of ancient literature, history, and philosophy. The value set on such knowledge, to the point of defining a person's whole merit and admission into the governing cadre, is easily discovered at any point in the second century.[57] One might compare the weight, equivalent to all that could be won in mathematics and science, assigned by the British Civil Service examinations to a knowledge of exactly those things that defined Pliny and Apuleius. Over these examinations, cultural leaders were still asserting their personal supervision well into our own century.[58] Extraordinary!

Definition of citizenship in terms of culture rather than according to the letter of the law seems to me the best explanation, over most of the Principate, for the denying of rights to a person having technical title to them; for the central phenomenon we must explain is (to repeat) not new cruelty, but cruelty applied to new categories of person. The perception of the targets then must have undergone some gradual change, expressed among the more powerful members of society by a bearing and tone of address that we call "autocratic." Gradually, too, but after a lapse of time, change found more formal expression in law—at which point (but as a symptom, not a cause) we can describe the judicial consequences found in such terms as *humilior*, *inferior*, and so forth. But it is important not to confuse cause and effect.

Another cause has been suggested, too: jurisdictional changes. Perhaps by the Severan period they were beginning to make a difference. Much civil litigation—eventually all—passed from jury trials to the criminal courts before a judge. The latter tended more naturally toward severity.[59] However that may be, from Severan times onward the life of the emperor more often involved him directly in warfare, he spent more time in camp, he more often rose to the throne from the camp, and the cumulative effect of the circumstances may explain an increasing disregard for civilian niceties in sentencing. Finally, in the fourth century of "férocité maximale,"[60] the ambitions of the imperial government overtopped its ordinary powers of enforcement; it imposed too many, too complicated, and too painful obligations on its citizens, who would not do as they were told; and it resorted increasingly to extraordinary punitive pressure. Judicial cruelty was the "signe parmi tant d'autres d'un pouvoir qui se voudrait obéi et se sait impuissant."[61]

So a succession of causes and changes carry my subject to the edges of another era. But I should not leave the last word to the angry oratory of imperial legislation. After all, it is men who make laws, not vice versa. Their ideas of right derive from their whole experience; they are taught by the whole of their society and by all the roles they may have played. At the end, there is less of the reader of Paul's *Sententiae* or the *Gregorian Code*, and more of the army commandant and master of slaves, in the character of that great power at court and future emperor, Constantius. Surely he appears before us, around the time of the sack of Rome, a more medieval or Byzantine man than Roman.

> Constantius as he circulated kept his eyes down and his expression lowering. He had large eyes, also a thick neck, a flat head always held low over the neck of the horse that bore him. Thus he seemed to everyone, as the saying has it, "most truly autocratic."[62]

By the plotting of this ugly and sinister man and no doubt in the presence of Honorius (for executions of high officials ordinarily did take place before the throne), the ex-Master of Offices "was killed through being beaten with clubs at Constantius' orders, after having his ears cut off."[63]

21

SOCIAL HISTORY IN ASTROLOGY

N AN ARTICLE now long forgotten,[1] Lynn Thorndike set himself the question, What social history can be mined from astrology? The possibilities of the question are still inviting. From the period of the Roman Empire alone, the surviving astrological corpus matches in bulk the entire historical corpus; and though examined in detail by students of ancient religion, language, and science, it has been quite neglected by the social historian.

How much of the corpus can be used? Astrologers defined the positions of the stars at a given time and place, and then indicated the sort of person and event that should result. Astronomical calculations, as well as the theory justifying connections to some future outcome, constitute the greater part of our texts. Much else is blurred and general: this or that astral conjuncture "will lead to ill health, domestic tribulations, pain in the joints, sudden reverses, and death by misadventure," *vel sim.* There remains, however, that fiftieth part (let us say) offering more specific illustration. Here the ancient reader looked for facts that answered to his sense of everyday possibilities. He was, to be sure, not interested in the humdrum. Thus spectacular turns of fate received undue emphasis in what was served up to him. Further, the tradition of the science carried down, from generation to generation of practitioners, out of date terms and examples. But when both dramatic and tralatician elements are pruned away, something remains from which to form a true picture of the past.

That formed the foundation of astrology: fact as tested by inquiry. Astrologers—some of them, at least—kept records of the horoscopes they calculated and the fate of their clients as it actually developed. We can sometimes connect their casebooks with our history books. We are told, for instance, of a man twice consul, subsequently exiled, father of a son who was himself exiled on charges of adultery, later restored to favor, placed in charge of Campania, next of Achaea, then of Asia, and last of the prefecture of Rome. "Whose *genitura* this is, noble Lollianus," says the astrologer to his dedicatee, "you know best"—because it is Lollianus' own ancestors who are described.[2] Again, we are told of a man fleeing from a battle, who fell wounded from his horse. The enemy overran the field but left him for dead. He survived to take over command of the army. His horoscope dates these events to 163–64, and history provides a likely setting: the Parthian campaigns of those years.[3] Finally, we are presented with the governor of a province, whose position and

popularity aroused envy. His tenure of office was cut short by riots and disturbances, and he subsequently died of a painful disease. Dating suggests that he
may be Valerius Eudaemon, prefect of Egypt in 142.[4]

We may now turn to the last quarter of the second century, and to three
writers of the time, Vettius Valens, Claudius Ptolemy, and Artemidorus of
Daldis. In all we find much derivative material,[5] much timelessly vague terminology to describe various careers and vicissitudes, much repetition. They
apologize for their prolixity without being able to amend it, "for many and
innumerable are the things that befall men."[6]

If you are well schooled and eloquent, they say, then you may become rich
and prominent through a distinguished acquaintance, or through the opportunities that await the learned, as teachers, professors, surveyors, astronomers,
poets, political speakers, "of a good disposition, moderate, well disposed."[7]
"Such a one will enjoy good fortune from letters and learning—beloved and
eminent, deemed worthy of offices, honors, gifts, and fame."[8] Another line
of probability leads out from education to business, to control of great men's
affairs.[9] But intellectual gifts may be abused. They may produce the type who
takes his neighbor before the judge on a false charge, who forecloses on debts,
who forges documents, perjures himself, and sets traps for others.[10] The picture of the educated person is a thoroughly mixed one, then. Marked by fame
and fortune, it may also include, in a strange company, "merchants, interpreters, surveyors, lawyers, philosophers, but all mischievous, keen, clever
liars."[11]

A man of this sort turns to the law courts as his natural hunting ground. "He
will trump up lawsuits and charges and not only divorce his wife but also
convict her of adultery."[12] Anxieties about contracts, bequests, property (especially land), or civic status appear throughout our three authors.[13] Artemidorus records an unusual trial for crimes while in municipal office, as a result
of which the defendant lost all his estate and suffered banishment.[14] Something still more serious must account for the seizing of a man's property by
the fiscus, after his death abroad or in exile.[15] But fugitives from the consequences of incest, forgery, "rash remarks" (i.e., treasonous?), and weight of
debts are all attested, too,[16] along with the clear reason for their flight: dread
of punishment. Beatings for slaves, long jail terms, beheading, and fines are
sometimes mentioned; crucifixion brings perfect nightmares.[17] If it is easy to
understand why retributive violence should figure thus in the responses of
dream- and horoscope-analysts, it seems clear also that their clients were prepared from their life's experience to accept predictions of drastic justice.

Political prominence comes from friendship with rulers, education meaning
eloquence, knowledge of law, but most often sheer wealth.[18] Army commands
and imperial posts as governor or procurator seem to lie outside normal expectation, though they do receive occasional attention.[19] Much more within the

reach of ambition—it is, after all, the Greek provinces that our authors dwell among, with only an occasional glance at Italy—are civic eminence and offices. These bring salaries, honorific statues and decrees;[20] they indicate one's good standing with the populace—purchased, it must be added, by lavish expenditure on public needs. That explains the connection between wealth and office.[21] But popularity could quickly turn into its opposite. For all their glory, city magistrates, even a governor, could be conceived of in the darkest terms, involved in violence, base arts, and wickedness,[22] and one group, the market-dues collectors "always stationed at exits" and in the center of "continual disputes about tolls," is the target of particular contempt.[23] Artemidorus, speaking of the invidium and criticism that a citizen may encounter, adds that "one cannot be a market-supervisor without these."[24] In this author as in others we hear of frequent riots, "disturbances and opposition,"[25] though only once in any detail: the theater claque supporting a popular dancer raised a storm, and he escaped punishment for it at the hands of the governor only through the intercession of influential friends and the entreaties of the populace.[26]

Another characteristic source of trouble was the brigand and pirate[27]—who in turn imply travel. Indeed, the clients who wish their horoscopes or dreams to be interpreted seem to have trips often on their mind, or even long absences abroad. Their concern is timeless, responses to them usually vague.[28] A single point emerges: though the life of the uprooted or exile was a wretched one, sea voyages liable to shipwreck, and foreign trade a chancy business, affairs at home might go still worse.[29] Sufficiently hard-pressed, a farmer might turn shipper, while a shipper, "gaining much money, repaid his creditors who held a mortgage on his ship."[30]

Wealth occasionally came from high office, as we have seen, and from export and import; from money-lending, too, and tax-farming.[31] Toll collectors and peddlers enjoyed little respect.[32] Wealth might be inherited, regularly in the form of land,[33] about which the references carry us into different kinds of land use: for livestock, vineyards, oleiculture, and cereal production. It is, however, surprising to find nothing on large-scale proprietors in one writer, Artemidorus, and silence about the small farmer in Vettius Valens and Ptolemy.[34] Tradesmen and artisans, per contra, make up a long list in the last named—as smiths, masons, builders, perfume- or dye- or drug-sellers, jewelers, weavers, carpenters—without being of much interest to Vettius Valens or Artemidorus.[35] It is idle to speculate on the reason for these differences, concerning in any event the occupations so often passed over in other genres of ancient literature.

As to the ways of losing wealth, some have already been touched on. Litigation must involve a loser to each suit; the presence of the money-lender implies borrowers; hence the fear of "judgments and debts, disturbances arising from documents and money matters''—all ''notorious scandals.''[36] The unfortunate scraped a living in noxious jobs such as tanner or grave-digger, as miserable drawers of water or bailers on a treadmill;[37] faced unemployment and poverty;[38] and shuddered at the thought of being reduced to servitude by condemnation or capture.[39] From that, flight alone offered hope, and we must suppose, from many passages, that the runaway slave was no uncommon figure.[40]

A very few hints indicate resentment felt by the ''have-nots'' for the well-to-do. A person's slaves might be his enemies—small wonder—and ''a rich man must . . . encounter plots and envy'';[41] but there is nothing to match the passion of a fragmentary third-century prophesy: ''. . . tumult and war . . . and it will go badly for the rich. Their arrogance will be cast down and their goods confiscated and delivered over to others. . . . And the poor will be exalted and the rich humbled.''[42] The source and period of this latter document recall another, of which M. Rostovtzeff with his unerring eye saw the significance: a list of questions submitted to an oracle in Egypt, including the desperate inquiries, ''Am I to become a beggar?'' ''Shall I take to flight?'' ''Shall my flight come to an end?''[43]

Though nameless, impossible to date to a year or even a decade, and addressed to persons whose condition can only be guessed at, all evidence of this sort nevertheless has a peculiar value. It trades in everyday assumptions— which is to say, *generalizations by contemporaries*. Whether a prophesy or oracular response, whether the interpretation of a dream or a birthday, its very unselfconsciousness insures its veracity. Its prime quality is, in the word that scholars choose to describe it, ''empirical.''[44]

That term especially applies to Firmicus Maternus.[45] Writing toward the year 337 with a style and vocabulary quite of his time, the more closely tied to the contemporary scene by his relatively shallow immersion in the technical aspects of astrology, his work contains far more specific illustrations and terminology than can be found in any of his predecessors.[46] If we arrange the material in his *Mathesis* in the same order that we followed in discussing the second-century writers, it will serve to bring out the changes wrought over the intervening 150 years.

The educated man is found at the center of a group who ''gain the greatest of fortunes from their trained facility in speaking, from legal advocacy, from business, or from priestly incomes,'' ''the associate of rulers for their literary training and teaching.''[47] In many such overlapping lists, three types of career may be discerned. One, with an academic quality, includes ''long-haired philosophers,'' rhetors, teachers, professors, physicians, priests, astronomers, and surveyors, men upright and detached, ''learned and famous.'' Little new here, save the prospects of profit in such occupations and the mention of public chairs for professors.[48] Another group of skills less honored has to do with numbers, with accounting, with business records and secretarial positions to men of importance, *magni viri*;[49] and we should just note the presence of money-changers, money-lenders, custodians of warehouses and deposits, and public notaries.[50] As to the legal profession, though Firmicus had entered it himself, he had quit it with disgust at its mercenary eristics[51]—a disgust highly characteristic of his century, as often to be found in private individuals' writings as in the law codes.[52] "Fear of law suits seemed terrible to the unfortunate," Firmicus recalls from his experience.[53] At the same time, the "accusations, incarcerations, and frequent convictions," the exiles and fines, seem not only a more recurrent motif in the *Mathesis* than in earlier astrologers, but involve a new danger: outlawry.[54] Criminal cases now in the fourth century overshadow the civil.

The third type of career open to educated men may be defined as the governmental. While Firmicus knows of city magistrates, occasionally specified as owing their positions to *litterae*,[55] and while the urban scene of the second century survives at least in outline, with its offices won through public benefactions, its rich leaders shouldering their community's burdens, its popular enthusiasms for this or that nobleman, and its recurrent riots,[56] yet on the other hand a number of Firmicus' terms appear fixed to his own day: "top-ten men," the higher municipal aristocracy that increasingly in the later Empire bore the responsiblity for local government;[57] the city "defenders," an invention of Constantine's reign;[58] and the curators of cities, representing at the same period "the summit of a curial career."[59] More generally, we can see the cities now quite bereft of their autonomy. Not only are defenders and curators appointees of the emperors, but entire cities are described as subject to "men great, powerful, formidable, vigorous, who master the largest cities by virtue of some authority," *qui maximas civitates potestatis alicuius licentia subiugent.*[60] *Civitates* are lumped together with regions, peoples, and provinces, as being "under" some one official,[61] in contexts and phrases quite alien to writers of the earlier Empire. The central authority is evidently treating municipal magistracies as so many extensions of itself.

The men who enjoy power and influence may exert it over more than one city; they have their own secretarial staff, their slaves, rural estates, great mansions like palaces; they are patrons to fine craftsmen; they trail a retinue of hangers-on and dependents.[62] Their hostility is a thing to dread, their favor the key to wealth, fame, promotion.[63] They live among secrets and intrigues, liable to sudden fall from office through the abuse of it—"the highest judges, magnates, holding power over life and death, but rapacious thieves who seize the property of others with the clutching instinct of greed; though still, for these same men, after the widest pillage, the widest thefts and vast robberies, [their *genitura*] yields banishment or a violent death."[64]

No distinction can be made between *potentes* or *magni* or *maximi viri* and imperial officials. In the *Mathesis* they blend into each other, as equivalents, at least as equals, connected in the author's thoughts and, he tells us, by their very *genitura*. "It produces commanders and tribunes of soldiers, but terrifying and raised up on tyrannous powers, or defenders or chiefs of cities, but those who never remain within the bounds of those powers, and who in various ways always offend."[65] Every city cowers under their scowl.[66] A striking glimpse, this, of the baneful weight of government pressing on the emperor's subjects, baneful because of its rapacity and omnipresence in an age of bureaucratic despotism. It weighs upon Firmicus' mind. He devotes an extraordinary number of passages (that is, assigns a quantity of horoscopes) to careers in the imperial service, military, gubernatorial, judicial, or financial.[67] Some lie in the secretariats—*notarii*, for example[68]—but the majority concern taxation and money matters.[69] A good portion of the funds collected as tribute clearly reverted to the pockets of the bureaucrats, to whom office promised *bonorum incrementa non modica*.[70] Further, the emperor had it in his power to reward his servants with direct gifts, too, or to admit them to the luxurious life of the court, as his intimates and agents.[71] Nothing similar to Firmicus' emphasis on the style, size, and ubiquity of the central government can be found among earlier writers in the astrological tradition; where in the second century the city occupies the center of the stage, and abuse or admiration is fixed on municipal officials, these have later been replaced by larger figures, living in a larger, harsher, more predatory world.

The ways to wealth, other than wealth gained through public positions, were strewn with difficulties. Trade meant long absences abroad,[72] while business, except for its links with usury, remains a very fuzzy concept in Firmicus' mind.[73] A wife might bring a fortune with her, but the most common fortune of all, by far, is acquired through inheritance.[74] The less lucky must work. Dozens of crafts and jobs are mentioned, among them a special number given over to luxury.[75] Agriculture appears rarely, and then mostly livestock farming.

To our surprise, considering the hardness of the times, the lowest classes arouse active charity, and draw from Firmicus descriptive passages filled with pity for "laborers bound to eternal toil, who are forever hiring out their bodies to some task."[76] He knows "the straits of poverty, supported in wretched beggary," "the wretched burden of beggary," "the begging poor covered with rags and sunk in wretched calamity," "pressed down in the wretched filth of want, vagrant and never at home."[77] These are not the only sufferers. Many children are exposed at birth, many orphaned; free persons are made captive, and sold into servitude;[78] and there are scores of references to loss of property, *amissio patrimonii*, for the most part unexplained, sometimes attributed to spendthrift generosity or to conviction and subsequent confiscation.[79]

The rise and fall of fortune, touching so many occupations, only matches the migration of people from one place to another. There is much wandering about, preyed on by highwaymen and pirates, patiently endured by outlaws, rewarding to traders ''carried hither and yon on various enterprises.''[80] A final reminder, here, of the profit to be found in the ''empiricism'' of astrological treatises, against the distortion of our other sources. From literary writers, we learn only of an upper-class world that never heard of beggary; from the legislators in the law codes, we learn of a static world, fixing every man in an inherited home and condition.[81] But clients resorted to Firmicus Maternus for a truer picture of the fourth-century empire.

22

THE LEGION AS A SOCIETY

HISTORIANS usually and rightly look at the outside of legions and at their impact in battle. Armies have historical importance only because they win or lose. Of course it is recognized that certain of their internal features have a bearing on their success or failure, notably their training and supply. As a guide to the archeologist or as the yield of excavation, studies exist on military living conditions and leisure facilities. But an attempt to understand anything so romantic as the soul of the soldier has, I think, yet to be made. Modern military leaders are well aware that that subject is of crucial interest to their own profession. If they appear to trust to their own folk wisdom over anything scientific, they nevertheless have fostered a small library of useful analysis drawing on experiences in and after the Second World War.[1] In similar fashion, ancient military leaders also paid a great deal of attention to the state of mind of their troops. Yards and yards of speeches exist in ancient authors, supposed to have been delivered just before some combat commenced; military handbooks emphasized the need of such hortatory eloquence. Evidently maintaining morale has been a real concern in real settings ancient and modern. It ought then to be investigated within the better reported period of about two centuries from the Gallic Wars on.

The evidence naturally does not permit a psychological, to say nothing of a properly scientific, approach. Approach can only be sociological. We should begin by noting the peculiar nature of military life and those who lived it. When short-term enrollments of earlier times gave way to terms of years or even decades, civilian values and character were bound to be distorted by the longer influence. "Les soldats appartenaient à un monde à part," as Paul Veyne says. "Etre soldat n'est pas un métier comme les autres."[2] New entrants were not prepared for the inveterate venality, for example, that they discovered in camp life, and they had to explain it to civilians in tones of surprise.[3] They found their men's accent strange also, to the degree that the men had been serving at a distance from Italy (below, n. 54). By the close of the Antonine period, an observer in Rome would exclaim at the sight of men brought down from the frontier, "most savage to look at, frightening to listen to, and boorish to talk with."[4]

Cicero does not damn the military entire, but he does turn a very jaundiced eye on those in Antony's cause, "grasping adventurers eager for senators' Campanian villas, and country yokels into the bargain"—*agrestes*, "if such creatures really are men and not animals."[5] More generally, though later (A.D.

23), Tacitus explains that "it is for the most part people without property or home who take up military service,"[6] while those of better means resorted to bribery to avoid conscription.[7] Some went into hiding.[8] There is evidence for various kinds of criminals, too, ending up in the army.[9] The picture is mixed, suggesting that the scourings of conscription produced more down-and-out recruits in Italy than in the provinces. There were many volunteers, too. But there was little inducement to enter the legions for a young man with any prospects at all in civilian life, whether he belonged to the longer established citizen ranks or came from more remote territories. Moreover, while the Roman Republican army from the turn of the first century B.C. was thus changing in character and losing its "sturdy peasant" qualities, leadership levels also were beginning to wonder aloud whether national service in arms was so very wonderful a calling after all. Their doubts appear in poetry—Lucretius, Horace, Ovid, Tibullus, and others—more self-revealing a genre than prose.[10]

The army appears to our view as a society rather sealed off from the ordinary, that is, from the civilian. It contained a disproportionate number of men who had failed in that other life or wanted deliberately to turn their backs on it. Analogies with the French Foreign Legion come to mind. The Roman legion was not like some urban union of bag- and rag-dealers, *centonarii*, or the ferry-boatmen down the Tiber; it was by no means just another métier.

Leaving it, then, after one's term of service, one felt a bit lost and clung to one's fellows. The government did not oppose that. Tacitus recalls from much earlier times how "legions as wholes were settled in colonies with their tribunes and centurions and men each in his own rank, so as to create a republic through their harmony and mutual affection."[11] There is an ample epigraphic record of legions forming blocks in the population of *coloniae*. Sometimes they had to be split up among several adjoining towns, as in Mauretania; only rarely were they mixed together.[12]

The characterizing of veteran behavior in order thereby to characterize the sense of place and fraternity that bound soldiers together while on active service might involve some circular reasoning. However, inscriptions again afford a little help. They record moments when units acted as such both during service and afterward. Or the active and the veteran might combine in a single action.[13] Internal relations during and after service seem equally close. They are suggested in the phrasing *commilitones . . . Iovi optimo maximo votum solverunt*, "the comrades paid their vows together," or "Sacred to Hercules Saxsanus, Celsus centurion of Headquarters' infantry (*singulares*) and the Headquarters comrades of the legate . . . paid their vows."[14] Similarly, as veterans: "To Jupiter Best and Greatest . . . , the veterans of the Seventh Legion paid their vows."[15] Veterans acted as voting precincts in Lambaesis[16] or corporately affirmed their New Year's loyalty to the emperor, with or without (but at any rate distinct from) civilian blocks.[17] They corporately demanded their promised benefits from the government by means of envoys corporately chosen to represent them[18] and united in local associations with their own presidents and treasuries in provincial towns.[19] Such *collegia* did no more than perpetuate after retirement the social forms familiar within the camps, where all but the lowest ranks are found from the earlier second century clustered in clubs for mutual aid, particularly for funeral benefits. The members called each other *fratres*, as if they were one big family;[20] they remembered their fellows in honorific memorials and served as custodians and guardians of their place of burial. From their first promotion to their discharge, and from the lowest to the highest ranks in their retirement, the men, many or most of them, joined hands in a fraternity that was not dissolved even after death.

During active service they called each other by the friendly term "tent-mate," as in a letter one of them receives from a distant comrade (but the text is fragmentary): "greet . . . and Elpis, Ju . . . all the *contubernales*."[21] They dined as *contubernales* off common plates, they marched off to their posts as a group, and as such they prepared for battle and fought.[22] Expanded, the term *contubernales* comes to mean not only the normal eight men of a barracks block but whatever group a person was assigned to for service.[23]

Better known, the term *commilito*, "fellow soldier," was favored by great commanders who had earned the right through their own active campaigning and who wished to flatter their armies by an egalitarian and affectionate address.[24] *Commilitones* appear, too, in the same sort of contexts as do *contubernales* in inscriptions and elsewhere.[25]

There was hardly room in the army to stand apart. Barracks blocks were terribly crowded in the standing camps. They provided about nine square meters of living space, or more truly of sleeping space, for mere rankers, and less than that in marching camps.[26] (Officers enjoyed greater comfort—see below.) Crowding did not prevent their quarters from being "beloved like true homes by the soldiers, through long service and familiarity," as Tacitus puts it (*Hist.*, 2.80). Moreover, the bare necessities inside the wall were supplemented by a large non-combatant population outside. Many—in successful campaigns with lots of captives, most—men had one or more slaves attached to them. Freeborn signed on as personal servants, *calones*. Both are familiar figures in warfare from Republican times on to the end of the empire.[27] Vegetius supplies a definition that helps to explain their duties: he speaks of *lixae* "that go by the name 'helm-men,' *galiarii*" (i.e., porters).[28] The term *lixae*, however, is used by Sallust, Tacitus, and other writers to mean camp-followers of all sorts and services, including actors and actresses, seers and holy men, the thousands of prostitutes in the Roman camp at Numantia back in the second century B.C., and, above all, peddlers supplying every sort of necessity in shacks and booths outside the camp[29] or even inside; for we read that all these people in times of danger might have to be cleared out so it could be better defended. Evidently some of them stayed at their masters' side in times of peace. If the legions quit their quarters on a sortie, *calones* and *lixae* took their place to guard the wall, occasionally to make a sally of their own. They thus constituted a useful population even in a strictly military sense; but on the other hand, they also served by their initiative as collectors of food for sale to their hosts in uniform. Their latter role was necessarily very important, perhaps also pretty profitable. No ordinary inducement could account for the dozens of tiny stalls and shops set up in the most inhospitable semi-desert around the besieging force at Masada.[30] They contribute a tangible detail to the picture we have of legionaries surrounded and often equaled in number by a mass of civilians. The two groups were symbiotic, mutually useful; also, peripatetic, very slowly. Our picture recalls many an eighteenth-century army in the field, inching across the Netherlands or through the wilderness of Colonial America.

Within the whole mass of a Roman army, the core and reason for its being was the legion. That had its subdivisions capable of drawing members into a community more intimate and less imposing. One form was the *collegia* already mentioned (they could be found in auxiliary units also). Another form was derived from the birthplace of recruits. Auxiliary *alae* and cohorts, as is well known, were initially organized out of tribes and even from single districts, with all the loyalties to be inferred from that quality.[31] In the course of time, however, fresh drafts to depleted auxilia were collected more randomly; the ethnic community was dissolved, at least diluted. The same process gave character to the legions in Republican times. It is likely that they preserved within them some of the sense of community that had originally brought and kept together all the recruits from this or that district in Italy. At any rate, Caesar describes how, in the uncertain choices of civil war, men raised for Pompey around Corfinium withdrew into their own assembly, so to speak, and there reconsidered their allegiance; but, of their number, the Marsic tribesmen broke away for a while; and even after many months of campaigning, the Marsi as such still acted together, the Paeligni likewise, and the Marrucini (who were explicitly brigaded together).[32] Like the auxilia, however, the legions lost their ethnic traits, and did so much earlier—we cannot say just when.

That left more properly military subdivisions within the legion. Most meaningful was the century, no doubt because it was the very smallest of all. It served as one's mailbox, as can be seen on letters addressed to soldiers; it identified individuals on duty rosters; and in universal reverence throughout the army the guardian Genius of each century was worshipped—not of cohorts or maniples, "obviously because the soldiers attached to their *centuriae* the strongest feeling of identity and belonging."[33] Cohorts, however, did have great tactical importance, requiring advertisement on each man's shield, so Vegetius tells us, "lest the soldiers at any time in the confusion of battle lose their *contubernales*." Advertisement was by symbols called *digmata*,[34] to which might be added the individual's name and century (by the centurion's name) and, in the civil wars, the name of the leader of their cause: Pompey,

Caesar, Cleopatra.[35] Normally, of course, under the Principate, the leader was advertised by his carved or painted portraits—the emperor's.[36] These, being housed in the chapel when the legion was at rest, no doubt took on some totemistic or supernatural aura and thereby served as more than a rallying point in time of battle.

While the decoration on surviving shields or on those shown in works of art display various symbols, and while these must be the *digmata* that Vegetius refers to,[37] they have yet to be decoded. We know also that men identified themselves by other items of equipment besides their shields; but just how, does not emerge from the descriptions.[38] Lastly, some of the symbols on equipment indicated awards won, like those displayed by the champions of two opposed armies who advanced to a duel in full regalia, "the inlay on their shields flashing forth their honorific decorations."[39]

The obscurity of particular insignia does not obscure what is doubtless their chief significance: they expressed a soldier's claim on the society he lived in for that society's esteem. If you took away the very high value he set on his fellows' opinion, the *hasta pura* and other such symbols, being no more than symbols, would have lost all significance. The same truth can be expressed in a slightly different way: awards for valor and identification of one's unit combined to produce one effect; and that effect—namely, resolute conduct—was what determined the legion's failure or success in battle.

I reach beyond Roman history for a little further discussion of this point. Since accounts of conduct in battle are peculiarly subject to self-serving, dramatic, or ideological distortion, it is specially desirable to bring to bear whatever wisdom and clarity modern studies may afford; and the unanimity to be discovered among them suggests that they may be used to shed light on quite other times and circumstances.

I begin with the results of post-combat interviews with some four hundred infantry companies of Allied forces in the Pacific and European theaters of the Second World War, interviews conducted by Brigadier General S.L.A. Marshall.[40] He sums up his principle finding on the collapse of units under pressure, in the course of his discussion of stragglers:

> Individual stragglers had almost no combat value when inducted into a strange organization. The majority of them were unwilling to join any such solid unit which was still facing the enemy. The minority, after being given food and little rest, took their place in the line. But the moment the new unit came under enemy pressure, these individuals quit their ground. . . . On the other hand, that was not true of gun crews, squad groups, or platoons which had . . . managed in some way to hold together during the fall-back. Upon being inducted into a strange company, they tended to fight as vigorously as any element in the command which they had newly joined. . . . There was scarcely a commander who fought on that ground [the Ardennes] and who had experience with both these categories but

commented to me on the absolute contrast between them. . . . [It] derives from
. . . the inherent unwillingness of the soldier to risk danger on behalf of men with
whom he has no social identity. When a soldier is unknown to the men who are
around him he has relatively little reason to fear losing the one thing that he is
likely to value more highly than life—his reputation as a man among other
men. . . . It is the man whose identity is well known to his fellows who has the
main chance as a battle effective.

Next, a psychologist's study of some hundreds of veterans of the Lincoln
Brigade who had seen combat in Spain:[41]

Men take a kind of hard pride in belonging to a famous outfit even when doing so
exposes them to exceptional danger. This is an essential element in the psychology
of shock troops. Pride in outfit is rooted in self. It is one of the most reliable
antagonists of fear. Practically every informant emphasized that being a member
of a distinguished outfit had made him a better soldier. . . . The wish not to let
friends down is also a strong motive. Ninety-four per cent of the men stated that
they were better soldiers because of the fear that if they showed weakness they
would endanger the lives of their friends. Here shame at endangering friends is
pitted against fear of the dangers of battle.

And finally, two social scientists, E. A. Shils and M. Janowitz,[42] in their
attempt to explain "the extraordinary tenacity of the German army" in the
latter part of the Second World War, a tenacity which

had frequently been attributed to the strong National Socialist political convictions
of the German soldiers. It is the main hypothesis of this paper, however, that the
unity of the German army was in fact sustained only to a very slight extent by the
National Socialist political convictions of its members, and that more important
in the motivation of the determined resistance of the German soldier was the
steady satisfaction of certain *primary* personality demands afforded by the social
organization of the army. . . . It appears that a soldier's ability to resist is a function of the capacity of his immediate primary group (his squad or section) to avoid
social disintegration. When . . . [it] offered him affection and esteem from both
officers and comrades . . . , the element of self-concern in battle . . . was mini-
mized. . . . In the Wehrmacht, desertions and surrenders were most frequent in
groups of heterogeneous ethnic composition in which Austrians, Czechs, and
Poles were randomly intermixed. . . . The factors which affect group solidarity
in general were on the whole carefully manipulated by the German general staff
. . . the army was to a great extent carefully protected from disintegrating influences of heterogeneity of ethnic and national origin. . . . German combat soldiers
almost always stressed the high level of camaraderie in their units. They frequently referred to their units as "one big family."

These passages both illustrate and give more force to what has been said about the social organization of the legion: its coherence, manifested in various ways unconnected with combat, served the needs of combat in essential ways. Training of ancient and modern soldiers alike was also essential. So were logistics. The quality of leadership could make an enormous difference. But when the claims of all these other factors have been fully met, there remains in the minds of the best modern observers a special importance attaching to human relationships in small networks, not of thousands but of hundreds or even of dozens of comrades. These latter are what determine whether men fight or run.

To return now to the point of departure: awards for valor in the Roman army were displayed with every sign of pride, even polished up and worn into battle. If men must die, they wanted to do so with all the proofs of their courage about them—proofs recognized by their fellows and received from the hands of their commanders. In that respect, war really was just as the romantic portrayals of it, ancient or modern, would have us believe. Ceremonies of the most careful staging, advertisement before the most complete assembly, really did help an army to win; and they are correctly emphasized in accounts of the most successful leaders, Scipio Africanus or Caesar.[43] The commander must stand on a platform, he must know his men by name, he must address them one by one, he must add some speech of praise, and the awards must be seen as fairly earned. Consider a scene of rebuke to the cowardly—officers at that. They had originally gained promotion "by favor not bravery." They are dismissed as of the moment (all this being said in the presence of the whole army) and, lest they require too much needed transport, each of them may take only a single slave with him. Their disgrace would pursue them into civilian life and disqualify them there for civilian honors.[44] Stripping them of their household added weight to the disgrace, just as the cash prizes, sometimes enormous sums handed out at post-battle meetings, served as testimonies to the honor in which a man was held.[45] They were of course also wonderful inducements: 50,000 denarii, for example, at a time when one denarius was a good day's pay. In our terms, that would be a million dollars.[46] Officers might be promoted or demoted, too, with implications not only for their pay but (more substantial) for their percentage of the wealth won in war.

Of course the donkey obeys both the stick and the carrot. To have one's booty stripped away or lose one's share in future victories served as a reminder of what conduct was expected. And penalties like rewards received maximum publicity—for example, "the man that is the first to quit the line in flight shall suffer capital punishment as an example to all, *while the soldiers watch.*"[47] Our handbooks are full of details on decimation and so forth—rightly, for bonuses and punishments could do much to shape conduct. But they contributed only a part of soldiers' motivation, the less important to the extent that the non-material were enhanced and publicized—which returns us to the relationships formed inside the legion.

Simple rivalry to earn esteem appears in the heightened efforts made because one's comrades were watching.[48] Pride could be challenged if the choice of an ignominious alternative would be clear to all[49] or if public accusation of cowardice must be repelled. Suetonius' father used to tell a remarkable tale to illustrate the fact.[50] A sense of being chosen for a dangerous assignment, that is, of being elevated above one's fellows to an honorific peril, roused men to an extra effort, just as the Lincoln Brigade reported; but the experience is universal.[51] A good commander could remind his men of many decades of regimental history in the confidence that they would understand what he was talking about and rise to the memory.[52] The spur of being a member in a unit whose whole repute was challenged, and therefore one's own repute bound up with it—*that* too was a feeling universally reported in military histories.[53] So intense might this inter-unit rivalry grow, and so narrow the focus of loyalty on one's own little society of fellow soldiers, that all sense of the purpose of war was forgotten. Shils and Janowitz' findings prepare us for such a paradox. Grand political objectives had to give place to petty struggles among the Pannonian troops early in the Principate ("they were deterred [from joint action] by rivalry, for each wished the honor for his own legion") or later in the Dominate ("dissensions arose between [two of] them, as they competed over honor and place").[54] In these moments, however, we see only the misdirecting of the same feelings that could be used to good effect against a proper enemy by a leader like Caesar.

Caesar reports that his men fought the better under his own eye through consciousness that they were being watched and through their zeal to win his praise.[55] The report should not be suspect simply because it is to his own credit. He says the same of troops under the eye of their lower officers, as Livy does also of troops under Scipio.[56] In a healthy state of mind, legionaries took over an officer as their own. He became one of their fraternity, though a special member. By a cliché of panegyric, he laid aside his own richer way of life to share all their hardships, even down to the rigor of their training.[57] They would recall him later and still feel the tie to him, as he too might remind them of it.[58] The fact no doubt underlies a lot of civil war history not otherwise explained to us, in the latter decades of the Republic as in certain junctures of the Principate, notably A.D. 69–70 and 193–197.

The leaders and the led, however, faced each other across great differences in wealth and class. The differences could be easily quantified. At the time of the division of spoils, tribunes could expect a hundred times what rankers received (the figures varied, of course, but I choose a representative one that reflects also the probabilities of pay differences during the Principate).[59] Inside the camps, dining couches for officers in the second century B.C. as in the first century A.D. were gigantic, compared to those for rankers; living quarters for officers were vastly more spacious, even if we discount the palaces reserved at the center for the legate with his slaves and other servants and personal entourage; while, after retirement, the veterans settled into their assigned *coloniae* in allocations just as crudely unequal, each according to his rank. There was nothing a "democrat" like Caesar could or probably would have done to diminish the differences.[60] Nevertheless, they constituted a gulf not easily bridged by understanding. Therein lay a cause of difficulties, or worse.

The relationship may be illustrated through two passages, the first written by one of Caesar's officers (*Bell. Afr.* 85). He describes a moment directly after the battle of Thapsus. The victors had turned their wrath against a mass of the defeated, though the latter offer surrender. Caesar himself with his officers tried to prevent the slaughter; but his troops, "mad with rage and bitter resentment . . . , wounded or killed some of his own army, men of cultivation and distinction, *inlustris urbanos*, who they said were to blame." The term used, *auctores*, suggests two worlds, high and low, that were required to form a single community. For the moment, one turns upon the other as the reason for all the previous horrors of civil strife, and the gentlemen must not intervene now with their own rules of good sportsmanship, to jeopardize an end to that strife, once and for all. The description then continues, with the flight from the scene of "a number of Roman knights and senators, thoroughly terrified, lest . . . they also, themselves, should be killed."

The second passage is from Sallust.[61] It preserves the words of a tribune of the people speaking before an informal assembly, a *contio*, at Rome in 73 B.C. He declares that "peasants," meaning soldiers of that extraction, "are butchered in the feuds of the mighty, they are handed over as presents to magistrates [for service] in the provinces." His thought is the same found in the 40s B.C. among Caesar's men gathered at Placentia, mutinously grumbling at the prospect of yet more fighting abroad: they "cried out against their leaders for prolonging the campaigns and not getting them the money that Caesar had promised them."[62] And it is the same thought that stirs the men at Thapsus: it is not *their* war that they fight but the gentlemen's. Gentlemen of course never understood such a mulish point of view. "Brutus' party," says Dio, "held up before their men liberty, democracy, and no tyrants and masters, and the virtues of equality and how monstrous monarchy was"[63]—all ideals utterly remote from the views and values of their audience, indeed, fit only to fool an audience "of distinction and cultivation." Dio continues, "the other side, to their army, extolled vengeance upon the assassins [of Caesar], acquisition of their property, and the ambition to rule over all their fellow citizens; and (what most reinforced their resolve) they promised each of them 5,000 denarii." *There* were appeals a little more comprehensible. For poor men without other means of improving their lot would indeed sign on, if they were adequately paid, in the defense of whatever nonsense their betters might proclaim.

Again in Tiberius' reign the men grumbled. "Simple-minded fellows," they wanted more money; and Germanicus rose to their demands with a noble speech—on such subjects as veneration and loyalty.[64] "The veterans only raised a most hideous clamor" at all this, and reasserted their grievances. Germanicus then threatened suicide. They proffered—"you will hardly believe it," Tacitus declares—a sharper blade to do the job. In the scene and in our reporter, it is easy for us to judge who were really the "simple-minded." But their misreading of the men they commanded is after all not hard to understand, given the differences in way of life between them.

It is in such settings as the one just described, in some camp at a moment of dissent or decision, that we best see army class relations at work. Speeches by officers and commanders were preserved in antiquity, if not preserved to the present day; and in their style we have many invented examples by Livy, Tacitus, and the like.[65] Some were delivered in council meetings at which only commanders, tribunes, and top centurions consulted together; but the lower ranks could and did hang about to listen;[66] for they regarded their superiors as being in a certain sense responsible to them, even elected by them (above, n. 44).

Splits did develop. In Gaul, while Caesar was away, two commanders of equal authority disagreed about the best strategy. One yielded to the other and to the preponderance of the tribunes and top centurions. In Pannonia in A.D. 14 the legionaries were divided, too, "the better elements" (as Tacitus calls them) against the worse. The latter's ringleaders were evidently mere rankers. At a similar juncture in 43 B.C. the commander bade his tribunes identify "the seditious soldiers (for record is always kept of character, man by man, in Roman armies)."[67]

In the chaos of A.D. 69–70, the men sometimes appear at odds with their own officers. They suspect them of acting as a block to betray them to the enemy. Tribunes and centurions are evidently seen as a unit, and perhaps linked with the senate. The same sort of split is reported among the Dalmation legions in A.D. 42.[68] But what seems never to be reported is a vertical division whereby the two sides both have a fair share of the legion's whole population, high and low alike. Very much as we might expect, considering the sharp differences in wealth that distinguished them, the upper ranks and lower are ranged against each other as blocks. It is reasonable to assume that such loyalties also animated the conflicts not known to us in any detail, down through the whole long crowded list of mutinies or insubordinate outbursts in Roman military history.[69] But they have no ideological tendency—rather, a limited focus on personalities, recent outrages, or conflicts over pillage and discipline. Whatever their outcome, they leave civilian institutions around them quite unchanged.

A sort of secession from the field army of Scipio in Spain (206 B.C.) is reported in unusual detail. A part of the force resented the inadequate reward they had received for their efforts, withdrew to a camp of their own, chose commanders and centurions, administered the usual oath of service to themselves, and got generally organized.[70] The whole process recalls much earlier parallels of the Republic beginning in 494 (or better, perhaps, in 342 B.C., Livy 7.39); but, rather than borrowing from these remote memories, it belongs to an unbroken and rich tradition of self-government peculiar to the Roman army. Its instruments are of the simplest: word of mouth passed up to the commander through tribunes and centurions[71] or, for more formal deliberation, an open space, generally the drill ground, and a little mound or elevation of sods or stones to serve as speaker's platform. From this, anyone of any sort of authority could address the throng.[72] He must be prepared, and no doubt wished, for back talk from his audience in the form of spontaneous reactions, whether murmurs, cheers, or shouted interruptions.[73] While daily routine certainly went on without need for any active participation by rankers in the affairs of the legion, in more eventful moments the means of making their wishes known were ready to hand and applied quite matter-of-factly. That is (to judge from our more detailed accounts), the men generally expected to be advised of what the leadership intended, and to shape or even veto what seemed a bad idea. Among them, the more forceful individuals naturally stood out and enjoyed special weight in decision-making, irrespective of their rank or lack of it.[74]

Throughout its history, the society of the legion continued to function reasonably well—that is to say, it served its members in combat by holding them in their assigned places and constraining them to help each other. The closeness of their community enabled them to fulfill their individual potential as soldiers. It served them well also in situations where much was at stake, though less than life and death. Through its traditions they were able to meet together, arrive at consensus, and despatch their elected representatives to treat for them before the senate or with the Republican dynasts, before a provincial governor, or even in the emperor's court.[75] During the 40s B.C. they had pursued their interests in a businesslike fashion, so far as the chaos of the period permitted (they were hardly to blame for the *inimicitiae* that raged above their heads); and during the Principate they were able gradually to assert their own drill ground and speaker's hillock as the empire's political center. Here the most ancient and quintessentially Roman dilution of democracy produced for the Roman world each succeeding emperor in the 70s, and again in the 190s, and more and more frequently in the third century. Occasionally by its rules a predecessor was tried and found wanting, too.[76] If legitimacy is the quality investing a claim that is generally accepted, even above some written law, then we must acknowledge the army's decisions to be the rightful as well as the necessary determinant of the imperial succession. By contrast, the senate in that role was explicitly rejected in the third quarter of the third century.[77] Only in the fourth century were still other means tried, after the effective abolition of the legion itself.

23

LATE ROMAN SLAVERY

CHANGES IN the legal condition of the labor force and in the relations between worker and employer are generally credited with a large role in the transition from antiquity to the Middle Ages. Both medievalists and ancient historians are interested; and, having often described those changes, they seem in consequence to be settling into some sort of consensus. Before it prevails, some effort should be made to check its chief findings against a generous sampling of the surviving evidence, paying attention to two points especially: *how numerous* were slaves and *what work* did they do?

It is convenient to see the Roman empire as if it were a clock-face, and to begin a survey at the top, in Noricum. There, servitude as an institution was native, and most of its population in Roman times were native, too, as can be judged from their names. They are found in many different sorts of work including employment away from cities; but the rural slaves are, from their titles, or they may be where undefined, overseers and personal servants, not field hands. Slaves and freedmen together total only two hundred or so in the surviving inscriptions. Of these, the bulk predate the Marcomannic wars; and the falling off in numbers by no means corresponds with the curve of numbers in the epigraphic material as a whole.[1] It appears that the institution suffered from there being less money to spare in the later second and third centuries and that farming, which was of course the basis of the economy, at all periods rested on the backs of the freeborn.

A similar picture emerges in the adjoining provinces of Pannonia. There, too, slavery predated the Roman conquest and continued to recruit from Boii and other tribes. There, too, the evidence is almost entirely epigraphic, it presents almost no large individual work force at all, and there is a preponderance of representation in domestic service and lower administrative positions: a *servus saltuarius*, for example, or various *ancillae* and *vernaculae*; but the majority work for governors and procurators. In the upper province, that majority becomes prescriptive in the third century. We would suppose slavery then to have otherwise disappeared, on the Norican pattern.[2] However, in Lower Pannonia the evidence of the first and second centuries, very sparse, becomes less so after Marcus Aurelius' wars, thereby better fitting the frequency curve of Latin inscriptions over-all (the pattern of the western empire attains a high in A.D. 200 or a little after and then drops off precipitously). Slaves appear almost only in cities and camps, where soldiers often owned them.[3] In the wake of wars of the 350s, we read that "the region of Pannonia was a land rich in slaves."[4]

In Dalmatia, the officers and men of two legions are discovered owning a slave or occasionally a pair, but these servants appear less often after the first century (for all centuries, only 38 texts out of the roughly 444 that record the province's slaves and freedmen, both together). Most texts (223) present the civilian-owned in one city, Salona. They are almost a third as numerous as the freeborn in the epigraphy of Salona. Prior to about A.D. 150, 95 percent of the 444 inscriptions regard freedmen only. The delight in epigraphy among persons of that status is extraordinary here as elsewhere, and helps to account for the bizarre ratio, roughly a third, of slave-plus-freed to freeborn.[5] That ratio itself moderates after the mid-second century, as does also the ratio of combined freed-and-slave to freeborn, except in Salona. There alone it rises for a time.[6] At all periods, slave and freed are found in households as personal servants, or as their masters' agents; or they work as craftsmen. They are rarely employed in rural settings save around the coastal citizen colonies.[7] Their minute numbers in the countryside suggest that they played no significant role in agriculture, and any picture of chained field hands is hard to credit—certainly quite unattested. Objection, of course, may also be raised against any detailed conclusions at all based on so small a corpus of texts. Our conclusions, at the most rigorous, might be reduced to the plain fact that slaves are present in the epigraphy of the cities, especially Salona, and in domestic employment above all other types.[8] They nevertheless continued to be some part of the population, as we would assume, since Jerome's very wealthy correspondent in Dalmatia in A.D. 406 "lost all [his] lands and slaves" to the barbarians at that time (*Ep.* 118.2 and 5).

Elsewhere in the Balkan peninsula Dio Chrysostom in the later first century takes slaves for granted as personal servants in Athens and Greece generally.[9] Otherwise, there is little information save for two sets of manumission inscriptions, at Delphi and in Thessaly. In Thessaly, their numbers in quarter-century intervals diminish from 97 in 50–25 B.C. to 9 in A.D. 50–74, thereafter rising slightly in the next half-century, and so up to 89 in A.D. 125–149. Only 16 survive from any date subsequent.[10] At Delphi, the series of texts appears to show a similar "decline of slavery as such" after A.D. 100. Such is the interpretation drawn from their diminished numbers.[11] Yet only ten miles away, slaves in the time of Pausanias (10.32.9) were on sale at the annual fair of Tithorea, and an imperial edict of 124/125 assumes that slaves and freedmen will be employed in oil production in Attica.[12] A law of 327 indicates slaves attached to rural estates in Macedonia; others around Corinth (?) were perhaps employed on the land; and an excavated villa in Thrace may, or may not, have had space set aside for its slaves.[13] Such various kinds of evidence, each presenting its own difficulties and uncertainties, at least serve to show how important it is to check one sort of testimony against some other. In the upshot, perhaps all we can assert is the very sparse presence of slaves and the apparent connection between their numbers and the general level of prosperity in the Balkan region.

In Asia Minor and the Aegean islands prior to the fourth century, epigraphy yields very little that is useful to my inquiry. I know of only three mentions of slave shepherds.[14] Among testimonies to slaves in households, it is interesting to note a certain Roman-ness, as if certain relationships had been imported;[15] interesting also to note that Cibyra under Claudius possessed over a hundred public slaves.[16] Galen's assertion that in his day slaves in Pergamon accounted for a quarter (some 40,000) of the population can represent only a more or less casual guess by some member of his class, or by himself. He might know the total of citizens with reasonable accuracy, and extrapolate the numbers in servitude from his impressions of the households he knew. I am not inclined to dismiss the figure, since it fits not too badly with other evidence that will soon appear;[17] but its proportions are credible only for rich cities, not ordinary smaller ones, and certainly not for the rural population, which vastly preponderated in antiquity.

After A.D. 300, our sources become a little less grudging. Early in the century, census records of Tralles, Lesbos, Chios, Thera, and Magnesia show generally underpopulated lands in which only a small minority of farms had any slaves at all; a few, 2 or 3 slaves; and two farms, 21 and 22 slaves respectively, the rest of the labor force being free.[18] Included in these records are several very large estates of hundreds or thousands of acres, with senatorial owners and decurions, skillfully diversified farming and, no doubt, slaves in the position of bailiffs. Later in the century, a law addressed to the eastern provinces expects to find slaves with *coloni* on the land, and St. Basil refers to slaves employed in agriculture as farmers, shepherds, and so forth, around Caesarea in the 370s.[19] In addition, there are occasional undifferentiated references to servitude of the period.[20] What is most common, however, is the slave around the house, weaving, fetching water, cleaning the stables, or performing various personal or menial tasks.[21] From the specific details but also from silence, we may suppose that servitude within urban settings involved only, or almost only, domestic service, not manufacturing or commerce.[22]

It is true, however, that slaves and freedmen are sometimes encountered on the land, not in the towns. They appear there almost wholly as overseers of one sort or another: in Bithynia, in Pisidia, in Galatia of the second and third centuries, representing landowners including the emperors. They are great folk locally, serving with village officials to date public documents.[23] We find their like in Syria, in A.D. 344.[24]

In the Levant of the Principate, while commerce in slaves is amply attested along with large households of them in Palestine,[25] there is otherwise nothing known; but for the period after 350 and especially in and around Antioch, the sources are exceptionally rich and the picture exceptionally clear: slaves were abundant in the city, very rare in the countryside. Libanius speaks of them casually as one might mention horses or children, simply to illustrate some point he is making.[26] They may occasionally be found in manufacture or at a corn mill but not in agriculture.[27] In domestic service they are so much taken for granted among the circles in which he moves, and to which he speaks, that the possession of few or no slaves defines "poverty." A person who has no more than two or three, and of course rents (not owns) his lodgings, is an object of pity.[28] John Chrysostom sees it the same way: no one really needs more than two or three, though in his congregation "you may think it disgraceful if you don't lead whole herds of them around with you" (disgraceful—therefore a priest too should have a servant "so that he need not bring shame on himself").[29] Like Libanius, Chrysostom addresses an audience that take slaves as a fixture in their lives and houses, often in great numbers.[30] In a passage familiar in scholarly discussion, he rebukes the really wealthy Antiochenes: "You!—consider how many acres and acres of land you possess, and ten or twenty dwellings or more, and as many baths buildings, a thousand slaves, or twice that number, and silver-decorated chariots."[31] The specific figures are set in a context of exaggeration and discredit themselves by their own offhand doubling. But in a grand urban mansion and in an additional dozen country houses, a single millionaire might well count some hundreds on his staff. There is, incidentally, no reason to imagine Chrysostom's thousands at work in the fields.[32] Such employment is not attested in the province, where by contrast peasant labor and tenancies are very well known.[33] It is the peasants whose villages come under the bailiffs already encountered in this as in every other province.

Egypt would be almost too richly documented to be treated in a summary paragraph or two, were it not that the numbers and employment of the servile element in the population have been so carefully evaluated already. It is thus possible to say that, over the course of the first and second centuries and far into the third, slaves made up less than a tenth of the total population, except in Alexandria where, at a guess, the proportion was an eighth or more. In the rest of the province, their contribution in crafts and industry was minute; and, while they might be donkey-drovers or forest-guards or messengers in rural areas, they "played no significant role in agriculture."[34] Because of corvée, census, and tax lists, the reliability of such statements about many moments and places in Egypt is infinitely greater than anything possible through epigraphic evidence, in other provinces. The level of detail is far greater, too, enabling us to show slaves to be 6 out of 466, or slaves and freedmen combined to be 4 out of 214 names in A.D. 192 and 128/129 respectively; alternatively, we hear of an enormous establishment of over a hundred slaves in A.D. 111, the owner being an Alexandrian millionaire and his staff being assigned to book-keeping, accounts, and oversight in scattered country residences. That whole list shows "the dimensions of domestic servitude."[35]

In the third century and later, slaves are perceptibly fewer in Egypt[36] and cost a great deal more, at the least in tandem with a general inflation. Sales and purchases continue to appear in papyri, but rarely; in the fourth century appear also the first records of people pledging themselves or their children into servitude.[37] As in earlier centuries, slaves are employed as domestic servants but are little or never attested in manufacture or agriculture.[38] When we find large estates in the early or late fourth century with their own bakers or potters, those resident workers are freeborn.[39] Synesius in the adjoining province of Cyrenaica around the turn of the fifth century notes how common Gothic house slaves are, so that every family has one or two to wait on table, help in the kitchen, and fetch and carry;[40] but their abundance is a passing thing.

Across the rest of the north coast of Africa, to judge from any evidence we possess, the servile part of the population seem to have counted for only 5 to 10 percent of the whole.[41] The estimates derive from inscriptions modified by a few mentions in legal and literary sources, in a fashion by no means scientific. Of slaves employed in commerce and industry there is scarcely a trace. The *Apologia* of Apuleius in the second century by itself supplies some of the most useful information, including the remark (17.2), "Why should you think three slaves a sign of poverty?" His estimate recalls others encountered in Antioch and Augustine's similar remarks, that even a poor man would have several slaves (*Sermo* 356.6), and that they could be found in virtually every home (*Enarr. in ps.* 124.7). Besides the really rich Pudentilla whom Apuleius marries, capable of presenting her son with 400 slaves without stripping the work force on her own scattered properties, we know of only one similar sign of anything like such large numbers,[42] prior to the absolutely remarkable wealth of Melania the Younger in the early fifth century.[43] Some of it lay in Africa. As discussion will show (below, p. 245), we may guess that some part of her very large numbers of slaves were employed in the fields. Despite the *custodes*, *vilici*, *actores*, *tabellarii*, *dispensatores*, and *saltuarii* of servile status encountered in inscriptions, and despite the need for domestic work in the rural residences of the well-to-do, the really large private work forces—at least, Pudentilla's—must have included not only overseers and servants but some proportion of field hands. It is physical labor and productivity with which a certain fourth-century law is concerned, too, when it speaks of both urban and rustic slaves in Numidia.[44] And a second passage from Apuleius' *Apologia* (17.1) adds confirmation for an earlier time, when he wonders in passing "whether you have slaves to cultivate your fields or yourself exchange labor mutually with your neighbors," as if both alternatives were familiar.

It remains true and accepted that field labor was very largely in the hands of peasants. Stéphane Gsell considers whether in fact rural slaves were really very numerous and supposes that they worked on neither the large nor small estates—rather, "sur des propriétés moyennes."[45] His attempt to find a place for the occasional testimonies we have to great numbers of workers is not very successful. It must remain a matter of local variation.

A second question is likewise difficult to answer: whether any changes in the history of servitude in the African provinces appear across time. For Pudentilla in the 150s in Tripolitania, was there a match in the fourth century? When desert tribes ravaged that region in A.D. 364, they slaughtered the peasants outside the cities, although we would expect mention also of slaves if there had been any;[46] and Augustine, who takes the presence of slaves for granted, thinks of them in domestic service, while in the fields he sees peasants.[47] In part of his recently discovered correspondence, "the presupposition of the letter is that in North Africa there is a large population of poor but free labourers, vulnerable to being made captive and sold into slavery in overseas markets. Only a small minority of the labour force in Africa consists of slaves."[48]

Continuing our circuit into the western European provinces, we come first to Spain. There, information about slavery is most unsatisfactory. At the turn of the Christian era, the few mentions in literary sources do not allow a clear view of the two matters of special interest here: numbers (or percent) of persons in servitude, and their form of employment. Still, it is agreed that they were the principal element in the extraction of precious metals.[49] The heavy use of servile labor on the land is assumed, perhaps by analogy with Italy, but not proved.[50] When inscriptions grow too few to be of any use, as the third century moves on, occasional mentions crop up in other sources, only sufficient, however, to show that slaves continued in existence.[51] Two noblemen in the north of the peninsula led their tenants and slaves in resistance to the barbarian invaders of the early fifth century.[52] The wording of the story rather suggests the slaves were house servants while the tenants came off the land.

In Gaul, the evidence is almost exclusively epigraphic. In the southern towns the relevant texts indicate considerable activity in trade and crafts matching that in low-level government jobs, and some activity in industry, matching that in gladiatorial shows (the total in economically productive roles is obviously limited). Numbers of all inscriptions that record slaves or freedmen come to a peak generations earlier than in the north and center, where the evidence is overwhelmingly from Lyon. North and south combined yield only a small proportion, under a tenth, from rural areas, and no texts indicating any role in agriculture.[53] That is not surprising. Pre-Roman Gaul made use of a more or less tied-down peasantry, not slaves, in agriculture, and the supply of such freeborn labor continued abundant throughout the Roman period. The typical center for the exploitation of the land was the isolated farmstead drawing on the native populace, and such remained the case, by the most likely supposition. The alternative, some real restructuring of agriculture by the Gallic rich along Italian lines, would have required a great supply of slaves for which there was neither the need nor the money, and of which there is no adequate trace; nor is there any likelihood that immigrant Romans would have bought the estates but rejected local patterns of labor when they moved in— all of which is quite unrelated to the question of their own living quarters and personal servants. Expensive rural dwellings on Italian lines were built by the native rich quite like the immigrants. Around them were their dependent villages.[54]

In at least the larger of such villas, can any sign be seen that a large servile labor force was lodged, so as to bring to bear the archeological record on the historical question? The southwest Gallic villa of Montmaurin, exceptionally well known and studied, is obliged to carry the burden of the argument. In its rambling layout, the centralization of quarters is noted for a "specialized work force . . . , either agricultural or in their work rooms," prior to the devastating flood that struck the villa at the end of the second century; and thereafter in its rebuilt form it was a sort of pleasure mansion, all the subsidiary buildings having been dispersed over the estate.[55] As to the occupants of those clustered earlier buildings, we have no knowledge. *Coloni* are mentioned in inscriptions of the province but not specifically at Montmaurin; and a large landowner in the eastern regions had a number of free artisans—his clients, including iron-workers and stone-masons—employed by him under his slave as overseer.[56] For what the example may be worth, the one large industry in Gaul that we know of, producing fine pottery on the Italian model, made almost no use of slaves.[57] The scanty evidence at our disposal thus does not point to slave labor as the natural recourse for the well-to-do in Gaul.

Yet they certainly owned slaves, no doubt in large numbers, for the upkeep and luxury required in their rural and urban dwellings.[58] In the later empire, high levels of domestic service among the upper classes were taken for granted.[59] You were pitied, or a saint, if you had about you a staff of only two or three. In your fields worked your peasants.

They rose against the rich when they got the chance, in the disturbed conditions of the later third century and again in the first half of the fifth century, especially in Brittany. Their name in revolt was "Bagaudae." It was attached to their like in various times and parts of Gaul and northern Spain. They are described as rustic laborers and country folk,[60] also as "brigands" and "revolutionaries"—hardly popular with any local landowner, whose slaves joined them whenever opportunity offered. When in A.D. 417 a strong hand reduced a recent outbreak in Brittany, the rich no longer felt in servitude to their own staff.[61] But not long afterward, "in the remoter parts of Gaul," a new leader arose and "almost all of Gallic slavery joined in the Bagaudic movement."[62] With this last reference to slaves, we may leave them to the medievalists, who discover their continued existence and in all likelihood their prevalence for centuries to come.[63]

Germany resembles Gaul, but even less revealed. We have a glimpse in a bas relief showing a sheep. The picture decorates the tomb of a freedman at

Mainz (a shepherd, then, or overseer of shepherds?);[64] elsewhere, a swineherd and a bailiff; but otherwise a total of only 260-odd inscriptions almost wholly from cities, while the individuals in them are almost wholly engaged in urban service and oversight positions. Their numbers follow the "Mrozek curve" (above, n. 3), diminishing abruptly in the third century.[65] Still, the commerce in slaves is known to have continued into the late empire and beyond, and they are predictably found in the late imperial palace at Trier.[66]

My circling survey of the provinces is now completed, leaving only the center to be discussed. That center is *sui generis*. Into the Italian peninsula, Roman adventures of the last two centuries of the Republic brought many war captives, along with money to buy up whatever else was available in the slave markets (principally in the east). The demographic shift resulting was on a scale unprecedented in all of prior history. Defensible estimates suppose a free population of Italy during that period to have remained more or less stable, amounting at the time of Augustus to four or four and a half millions—but side by side, now, with another three millions of slaves.[67] The absorption of such a human capital into the economy taught a way of life so distinct in quantifiable terms as to be distinct and new in quality as well.

Because of their prominence in scenes of ancient literature, we may first notice the slaves so abundantly employed to wait on their masters and mistresses and to do whatever was needed around the house, in the days of Horace or Suetonius. Over that period it is a reasonable guess that senatorial families in the capital and as a skeleton staff in their nearby villas employed some average around sixty slaves in domestic service, while equestrian families might own, let us say, forty, and another well-to-do fifty thousand families, ten each: a total of a million house slaves for the richest 5 percent of Italy's population. Still in the later fourth century the high and mighty are seen parading about Rome at the head of troops of slaves or assigning them at home to hairdressing, weaving, cooking, and other such tasks; or they are similarly attested in the wealthy households of Verona and Milan.[68] Nothing appears to have changed, nothing appears much different from what we have seen in Antioch, save perhaps in the greater wealth of the peninsula. Where, then, is the uniqueness of Italy?

We must look beyond domestic service. In the capital itself, the number and variety of other jobs performed by servile labor was prodigious. Gummerus and Ciccotti in particular have drawn attention to the epigraphic record. When Latin inscriptions in general diminish after the turn of the second to third century, we cannot determine whether there was any coincidental diminution in the use of slaves as craftsmen and producers of goods, but there is little reason to think so.[69] The only industry that we know Italy lost was the ceramic for export, and that had begun its decline as early as Augustus' reign. The Arretine potteries, a hundred miles or so from Rome, had, however, in their heyday employed nothing but slaves. The uniqueness of Italy begins to appear in the fact that potteries in Cisalpine and Transalpine Gaul relied on freeborn workers (above, n. 57). Moreover, if the servile part of the population of central and southern coastal cities (Capua, Puteoli, Brundisium) is compared with that of six inland and northern cities, within the epigraphic record, it is half again as large.[70] In the six themselves, however, the servile part is still appreciably larger than can be found in the epigraphic record of another nine Gallic and Spanish cities.[71] The further away from Rome, the smaller appears the impact of slave labor in manufacture and the less inventive and pervasive its deployment.

Perhaps the same is true of servile labor in the agriculture of Italy, in both the administrative aspects and the physical. How dominant were slaves? Completely—so it is often said. Let us test the facts. To begin with negatives: we may at the outset discount house slaves occasionally used in farm tasks.[72] From a total of slaves amounting to three millions we must similarly set apart the million we have hypothesized in domestic labor. The remaining two millions or less could constitute only something under a half of the total work force. Beyond such general figures, an alert scholar has examined the fortune of a certain millionaire freedman, Isidore, of the early empire, who owned more than four thousand slaves plus 3,600 pairs of oxen and 257,000 other livestock. When these statistics are interpreted in the light of the agronomists, "only a small proportion of Isidore's lands under the plough could have been cultivated by his own slaves . . . and most of it was leased to tenants or (less probably) worked by free *operarii*."[73] Our one and only set of specific numbers concerning the whole of an individual's holdings thus reveals how a very big quantity of privately owned slaves might still have to be matched by a vastly greater force of free laborers.

As still another point of reference through which to test our impressions about the role of slave labor in Italian agriculture, we have the handbook on farming by Columella. It reflects farming wisdom at a date around A.D. 60—but wisdom of a particular sort. While he does mention lands exploited through tenants, his readers would assume servile labor to be pretty nearly universal.[74] But he is speaking of lands close to Rome which produce wine and oil; also, of lands in a certain size of property. His testimony thus allows of no universal application. When the sizes of properties are examined in sources other than farmers' handbooks, they are found—in the well-known field surveys of south Etruria as in two or three inscribed land registers—to vary enormously, just as anyone would predict; and even in the *Digest*, with its bias toward the concerns of the same sort of Rome-centered rich people that Columella addresses, there are many glimpses of even large farms worked only by the freeborn.[75] A last kind of evidence, hoped for through the close archeological inspection of individual villas, has so far not yielded very much of value, in part because the total of sites is still small.[76]

It follows from my survey that the two questions of special interest here, regarding numbers of slaves and their type of employment, must be answered in a very impressionistic fashion. We can say only that those of Italy in Columella's day constituted an extremely large minority in the total population, of whom in turn a majority were assigned to the fields. Any attempt to translate that "majority" into some exact figure could only generate idle argument.

Yet even the little that can be said suffices to show the uniqueness of Italy. That quality is still apparent toward the turn of the fourth to fifth century and subsequently, in occasional glimpses. Well known is one rich estate near Rome with four hundred field hands in sixty farmhouses owned by Melania and her brother. She freed eight thousand out of many more slaves near or at Rome, and possessed estates all over the peninsula and the provinces.[77] While she later retained, even in her ascetic days, a staff of dozens of slaves and freedwomen around her, the earlier accounts seem clearly to indicate a large agricultural element among her total holdings of slaves scattered among Italian land-holdings. About agricultural slavery there as in Sardinia and Sicily, in fact we hear quite frequent mention.[78] But close to the date at which Melania owned such vast numbers of slaves on her estates, in the neighborhood of the capital, it could be taken for granted that richer men there would rely on free labor to work their villas, while senators in Italy as a group saw their interests sharply threatened by army recruitment touching their estates. Since only free men were ordinarily liable to service, the senators' reaction is revealing.[79] Finally, the last of the Latin agronomists, Palladius, writing in this same period, discusses rational farming in much detail without mentioning slaves, it is true, but nevertheless assuming the employer's control over a range of specialist laborers in quite the relationship of a master.[80] It is not easy to point to a passage in his work which could not possibly describe an estate worked by slaves. The ambiguity of his description, whether deliberate or not, suits the realities of his region and period, in which both free and servile labor, both on a large scale, were taken for granted.

In the light of the foregoing survey, however rapid it must be, I may now attempt an answer to my two opening questions.

First, how numerous were slaves? In the countryside, villages, and smaller, poorer towns of the provinces, I would suppose they amounted to only a few percent at any point in the first four and a half centuries of the era, while in the middle-sized or larger cities the picture we have seems to accord with a figure approaching 25 percent. I have no illusions, incidentally, about the reliability of these estimates; but it would be difficult to halve or double them without thereby also making some other good piece of data difficult to accommodate. I attach special weight to indications (above, at nn. 28f., 41–42, 53, and 59) of perceived prosperity and poverty in terms of size of domestic staff. To pass for upper class among educated, influential people, one needed several servants at the least (and I assume that our ancient authors, when they speak of "everyone" or "every home," mean only persons more or less like themselves). If they in turn constituted a few percent in the urban population, that few may be multiplied by their individual slave establishments, to suggest a slave total. We must beware, however, of an over-estimate arising from freedmen's use of the epigraphic record as a mode of social climbing, which thus produces, here and there, their quite unbelievable prominence among surviving inscriptions (above, at nn. 5, 50, and 53). On the other hand, we must beware of an under-estimate owing to the ancient authors' ignoring of the lowlier sort of people, and the latter's inability to assert themselves in any sort of written record.

Then, too, our impression may be distorted by Italy's thrusting itself forward as if to speak for the whole empire. The sources through which we most naturally describe the empire as a whole, or any aspect of it, are dominated by Italy. The laws were largely issued from, and their interpretation shaped in, Rome itself. So the *Digest* essentially tells us about Italy. Half of the surviving inscriptions come from Italy and reliance on them must therefore compensate for that fact.[81] Literary sources so far as they concern the west concentrate very heavily on Italy, most particularly the handbooks on agriculture by Cato, Varro, Columella, and Palladius. In consequence, the chain gangs of the great landowning senators around the capital or to the south, or on Sardinia and Sicily, tend to invade the modern picture of the provinces as well—only the most careful scholars can keep them at bay![82]

Since the uniqueness of slave numbers and deployment in Italy resulted from special events and processes (call them rapine, in sum), it is often supposed, too, that they were necessary to sustain those results, and that, as times changed, slavery on the Italian scale would pass away: no wars, or fewer wars—then, fewer slaves. To the extent that slaves were an expensive luxury, their numbers might well diminish in periods of less prosperity, too. That can be suspected in Noricum, the Balkan provinces, and Egypt in the third and fourth centuries. Why not in Italy as well? Must not some of its accumulated wealth, and the power to attract still more, gradually ebb away into the provinces? Whatever the logic of the matter, however, I can think of no piece of relevant evidence from the early empire which, removed to the later, need produce any sort of contradiction or appear out of place. The number of slaves may then have remained very nearly on a level, from Augustus to Alaric.

That is by no means the scholarly consensus. Instead, it is agreed that slave numbers throughout the empire went down in the second century. I cite some representative authorities in a note.[83] The ungainly bulk of these names is meant not only to show how widespread is the belief in a decline of the whole institution. It is meant also to draw attention to the lack of substantiation for this view. In fact, the frequency of mentions in inscriptions seems to be the most important kind of data on which scholars have depended. The epigraphic curve, however, invalidates this line of reasoning. In sum, the second-century decline in slavery, whether or not it may be ultimately demonstrable, has yet to be argued in a serious fashion.

It is thought to continue and to become more decisive after the third century, due to revolts in the west and the displacement, there and everywhere, of servile labor by tied free labor (the "colonate"). As to the first of these causes, it seems to have originated in a misreading of the evidence, many times repeated.[84] The errors have congealed into a whole history of slave masses in revolt in the western provinces, preparing the way for serfdom as a more satisfactory means of working large landed estates.

As to the second cause for the decline in slavery, we may agree that tenant laborers, viewed from above and as taxable entities, came to resemble slaves engaged in farming. The change was gradual, spread over centuries.[85] The reluctance of the free rural population to leave their tenancy or village was matched by the desire of the landowner to keep them in place; and indebted peasants might, within familiar terms of law and custom, be forcibly prevented from moving. The distance separating the rural free from the servile population was thus not very great at any time, in regard to mobility. It lessened over the course of the third and fourth centuries. As we might expect, then, the vocabulary to describe the two groups, as it is used by high persons, confuses them or lumps them together.[86]

But we should not on that account simply add all *coloni* to the body of slaves. In fact, no one who reads the late law codes can suppose that servile status had no dire significance. It is, for example, explicit in the famous proclamation of A.D. 332, that *coloni* who flee from one estate to another "must be bound with chains and reduced to a servile condition, so that by virtue of their condemnation to slavery they shall be compelled to fulfill the duties that befit a free man" (*CT* 5.17.1). And on occasion even a rhetor who is obliged to speak of the matter with more than passing attention will protest if "the workers on the land are treated as slaves," *oiketai*; he will contrast "rich and poor, *oiketai* and free, *eleutheroi*"; and he can hardly confuse the peasants with slaves when the former on his own estates are able to defend their independence of action and be upheld by the courts![87]

If the two, the *coloni* and slaves, are seen only as field workers, then it is logical to suppose that the former might displace the latter. Hence a great change in the course of the centuries of the colonate: "The entire economic life of the fourth century was dominated by that notable development, the decline of slavery" in agricultural production.[88] But the premise itself must be examined. To what extent *were* slaves engaged on the land rather than in other work? We come thus to our second major concern, the nature of their labor.

Everywhere but in Italy and Sicily in the later empire as in the earlier, a decided majority of slaves did nothing productive at all. A great many served as batmen to soldiers,[89] who could get them cheap, being near a principal source of supply: namely captives through war. Occasional windfall quantities of them thus came on the market.[90] Slaves are routinely busy for their masters and mistresses around the house, to dress their hair or prepare their horse, to write their letters or deliver them, to satisfy their sexual needs or their need simply for display. Status in itself was a great thing, a good in itself, and eagerly sought through parade of luxury. "Tell me, who draws people to her in the forum—the woman with a large retinue or a small? . . . or the woman elegantly dressed or simply? . . . and what is shameful, *aischron*—to be looked at or to be ignored?"[91] The question would be a rhetorical one in Rome as in Antioch. And, as we have seen, to be bereft of one's personal slaves was, for the secular or ecclesiastical upper class, to suffer real deprivation.[92] Granted, slaves of the big houses did weaving for the household[93] and represented their masters in running the household and organizing the work force, in the later empire as in the earlier. In their administrative role we generally find them on rural estates.[94] There is some economic implication to these activities; but what there is, set against the ordinary patterns, amounts to very little. We hear nothing of small shops and industrial skills in the hands of servile labor, as had been common in first-century Rome. Perhaps the lack of inscriptions is to blame.

Like private individuals, the imperial family had a house staff to serve them, of course a very impressive one. Eunuchs were the most prominent members. The less menial duties were assumed by the freeborn, to a degree unknown in the early empire.[95] Imperial estate overseers continue to meet us in the law codes; imperial factories were worked in some minor degree by slave and convict labor, though mostly free.[96]

For the part of the population bound in servitude, all this amounts to a good deal of visibility not matched, however, by a significant economic role. No matter. It is agreed on all hands that what counted in the economy was agriculture. We have then to recall information for the later empire scattered across our survey, looking for the presence of servile labor in farming. Some was discovered in central Asia Minor, some also in Numidia and Macedonia. Our sources for the latter two were the law codes, which also mention rustic slaves as well as urban in the provinces at large, when they are discussing private property and tax liability.[97] It is sometimes made plain that these mentions concern laborers, not overseers. Of course, their weight in the economy is not directly indicated—not in any terms that could be quantified. It would be natural to suppose it was no different than it had been in the earlier empire (that is, quite inconsiderable, everywhere except in Italy), unless there had been new developments in the supply of slaves. Other than moments of glut in the market, however (above, n. 90), the only identifiable change seems to be an increase in the sale of persons into slavery through debt and poverty, an increase suggested in the third century by the marked rise in discussion of the subject by lawyers of the period A.D. 225–325 and by the sustained interest in the subject thereafter.[98] Whether this phenomenon betokens a rise in the proportions of the servile population or a fall in levels of prosperity that would then normally produce a fall in the numbers of slaves, we cannot be sure.

In view of the whole picture sketched, then, how can anyone speak of the entire Roman world as a "slave-owning society"?[99] How is it possible to assert that slaves in general "dominated large-scale production in the countryside"?[100] In part, the answer lies in assigning the evidence of the Latin farming books to all of Italy, whether consciously and explicitly or not, and then using it still further to describe the whole Mediterranean world;[101] in part, it lies in the plain disregard of the known, or knowable, evidence. By way of illustration: one recent writer demands, all in italics: if serfdom was no real factor in the empire, *"How then, if not by slave labour, was the agricultural work done for the propertied class? How, otherwise, did that class . . . derive its surplus?"*[102] An answer to these pressing demands is easily found: first, in the form of labor preferred by the state on its own crown lands, where only peasants are encountered in Egypt, Asia Minor, or Africa,[103] and beyond that, in the farm and village population empire-wide, which, indirectly through taxes or directly through rents, provided the vast bulk of surplus wealth—as everyone agrees. We cannot say with this author, Ste. Croix, that the particular portion of profit derived from slave labor in agriculture constituted the defining surplus of "the propertied classes," somehow distinguishable from all the rest of their income.[104] Against any such logic a proper protest was lodged by Keith Hopkins twenty years ago: "It is meaningless to think of slavery as somehow a basic, or as the basic, moulding institution of classical civilization. . . . In no sense did . . . society rest upon the productivity of slaves any more than upon the productivity of other workers."[105] In short, we should not disregard the plain teachings of quantification (the numbers of slaves) in our attention to their function (what work they did).

A word of summary: granted the remarkable transformation that took place within the Italian labor force as a result of Roman expansion over the course of the later centuries of the Republic, the changes in the empire thereafter seem to have been rather inconsequential even so late as the fifth century. The dynamic that has been detected in the history of Roman slavery, especially in the second to fifth centuries, seems to have been much exaggerated; therefore the causative role of slavery in the late empire has also been exaggerated. Its general proportions at the time of the sack of the old capital are likely to have been roughly what they had been three hundred years earlier. The period of transition to the medieval world is therefore not best explained in terms of slave, especially rural slave, labor.

24

THE HISTORICAL ROLE OF THE MASSES IN LATE

ANTIQUITY

THE LAST CENTURY and a half of the Roman empire—Diocletian's imperial reign through Augustine's episcopal, let us say—is one of more obvious and important changes than the age of the Antonines or, indeed, the whole Principate. Whatever the changes, no description of them can be very satisfactory which does not take account of the participation of the mass of the population. Accordingly, that participation has been often discussed in modern accounts, and attention called to different categories of person, in the search for that particular category which did most to shape the outcome. In the ancient accounts, by contrast, history moves forward according to the logic of largely horizontal connections: a bishop confronts an emperor and faces him down, an emperor confronts a bishop and sends him into exile, a tribal leader (Firmus or Tribigild) or a great court figure (Eutropius) or senator (Petronius Probus) says or does something to which some similar figure on about the same plane of power reacts. So the narrative proceeds. But such figures responded also to the logic of vertical connections. They were joined to other planes, where they enjoyed such support and following as could make leaders of them. A bishop needed his flock; a senator, his peasants and his minor cousins; chieftains, their people. No one was heard unless his was a voice listened to by many.

Links to the masses that made a following determined in large part why things happened as they did or, equally, why things didn't happen otherwise: no Knights' Rebellion in the Roman empire (though there were *equites*), no Framebreakers (though many *fabricenses*), no barricades in the streets of Carthage or Alexandria. Yet people's ties to or on planes other than the highest, where the drama lay, receive hardly a mention in our surviving sources. Ancient and, for that matter, medieval and early modern historiography never wasted much time on such matters, with which every reader was familiar; so what was obvious was not reported, and was lost, and can now be recovered only in the most broken outline. That is the task for modern historiography: to trace out those interconnections, at least in their larger patterns, as an aid to understanding the flow of events.

What are those larger patterns? They may be recognized by their including large numbers of people and therefore by their helpfulness in explaining the shape of large events. The best possibilities to be considered are those defined according to *culture, law, class*, and *power*. The four, in terms of which this essay is organized, must be looked at one by one.

Culture in the anthropological sense divided the population of the Mediterranean world long before the Romans assembled it all into a single political entity. If the descendants of any of these separate traditions were then picked out for obloquy or government action, we hear none of it. An exception: still at the end, the Jews, most distinctly themselves, retained a way of life centered in a common religion, and were on that account seen as set apart and unassimilable, at least by Christians. Hostile stereotypes long familiar appear in passing mention by Rutilius Namatianus or more pointedly and theologically in the sermons of Ambrose, Chromatius, or Chrysostom;[1] sometimes in events, at Tiberias where the apostate Count Joseph was used by Constantine on a mission of conversion,[2] or again at Callinicum, when monks destroyed by fire a synagogue and a meeting-place of heretics. Ambrose in defense of what was done faced down the emperor at Milan (A.D. 388), in the first famous measuring of the two thrones, episcopal and imperial, against each other. Despite these scattered testimonies, however, it cannot be said that the century over-all was much influenced by Jewish-Gentile relations.

Nor were the barbarians within the empire in the cultural sense a larger factor, however enormous a role they came to play in the military. Rather, because of that role they could not be easily fenced off as internal aliens. The wish to do so can be sensed for example in Ambrose's horror at seeing a Roman in barbarian costume or in the law against the wearing of trousers by the Roman nobility. Earlier, Eusebius had turned a more admiring eye on such dress, if only for their natural wearers, in the antechambers of Constantine's palace.[3] They had supplied a touch of the exotic and proof, too, of the reach of Rome's supremacy to even the most remote of peoples. As the consequences of Hadrianople slowly sunk in, however, post-378, Goths and the like were bound to be seen in a different light. The change can be traced in the eastern court orations of Themistius in the early 380s, through Pacatus' at the end of the decade, and so to Synesius in 399, urgent for the expulsion of the northern intruders and a return to a purely Roman army.[4] Yet it was that same Synesius, a decade later still, who could not lavish enough praise on the Hunnic troops sent him for the rescue of his own province's defenses. By then, and despite a brief surge of antibarbarian sentiment in both capitals, against Gainas in 399 and 400 and Stilicho in 408, the presence of many scores of thousands of barbarians inside the frontiers had become a fact of life, essential to imperial defense.

As such, they had been for centuries allowed or invited to join the army through direct enlistment of their young men or indirectly through resettlement of large, even hundred-thousand, blocs. As refugee families, these latter were assigned to vacant lands under some sort of loose oversight in northern Italy, Moesia, Pannonia, Gaul. Thereafter they would contribute taxes and very likely also a draft quota to the auxiliary forces. Naturally they brought with them their own way of life. Its trace is readily discoverable in the archeological record, though there is none in the written. Immigrants seem to have been successfully absorbed into the host civilization, at least until the fourth century. From that point forward they begin to appear more and more prominently both as high military officers and as small, distinct fighting units, ordinarily under their own chiefs as commanders.[5] While their military role is of no concern here, it might be expected to have had a match in the civilian sphere and to have produced moments of friction, at the least. When the orders went out from Count Julius, late in 378, for the simultaneous slaughter of the Gothic enclaves in all the cities of Asia Minor, that at least suggests how widespread they were. Had they not had any noticeable contact with the civilians around them? Did not the news of this horrible act agitate the garrisoned barbarians in cities of other regions? To the contrary: all we have by way of an answer to these questions is the record of frequent intermarriage at the very highest levels, including the royal house, from Constantius on, between Frankish and other German commanders and the Roman aristocracy, and the steadily growing predominance of barbarian contingents in active campaigns throughout the second half of the century. A distinct element in the population that should have had a whole history was thus confined within an almost purely military-political role.

The possibility of something of further significance remains: it may have been easier for the various northern peoples of the major invasions after 406 to be absorbed, as they were, with surprisingly little disruption, because of a perceptible barbarization of material culture throughout the empire's northern provinces over the course of the previous several generations. With the importation of material culture had come modes of burial, visible in the so-called "armed graves" of Lower Germany and elsewhere, as well as other customs that have left no mark. The same period saw the processes of Romanization actually reversed in several broad regions of the empire, most clearly in respect to language. Testimonies to the continued use of Celtic and Libyan, Syriac, and Coptic are more often encountered, and in the latter two a literature can be seen developing after centuries of silence. Styles that are characteristically native are used in the decoration of jewelry, pottery, headstones, or the statues of the gods; practices of religion assert themselves against Jupiter and Zeus in purely native fashion; and unexpected revivals across every aspect of life, every craft, touch not only Britain, Germany, and Gaul, but Pannonia and Moesia, Egypt, and north Africa.[6] It was very far from a single Greco-Roman civilization that was handed on to Byzantium and the barbarian kingdoms of the west.

Of far greater consequence than the differentness of Jews and barbarian immigrants was that which defined the rustic population and set it apart from the urban. It was among the rustic that non-classical languages and independent traditions of relief decoration survived—all of those traits and arts just mentioned. The fact is easily illustrated by mosaic depictions of poor farmers' and goatherds' huts in Numidia or Augustine's descriptions of the olive-harvesters in his home territory; by Norican farm-women portrayed in their characteristic jewelry, turbans, and smocks on their funerary stelae, or Jewish villagers working Libanius' land in Syria. In contrast to the remarkable degree of homogeneity attained among the cities of the empire in their over-all plan, in their chief buildings, local administration, favorite public amusements, and so forth, country life remained far more heterogeneous.

Yet city people cared nothing for that. Those who lived in the smaller centers had eyes only for the larger; those in the metropoleis looked over their shoulders at each other, imitatively and competitively. The rural world they quite ignored, except to find it alien: themselves, *urbani* to be contrasted with *rustici,* that is, *docti,* "civilized" or "cultivated," as opposed to *indocti.* They themselves were also the "few" as compared to the "many."[7] Indeed, they made up a very small minority (how small, must depend on the definition of "city"). It follows that the part of all the world here under inspection about which we are most seriously ill-informed constituted that great rural majority.

Country-dwellers were not only most numerous but also the dominant force in the economy. They served it by their labor as independent farmers and casual or migrant workers; in large numbers as tenants on someone else's land; and, rather rarely except in Italy, as slaves. In the latter two capacities they provided the platform on which others stood above them: small-town civic leaders, towering magnates of the Roman senate, and all intermediate representatives of landed property. Complex relations between rustics and urban dwellers, involving managers, storage of produce for deferred sale, local and regional markets, transport, and a cash economy, must be inferred as much as they can be demonstrated; but they lay at the center of the empire's productive capacities.[8]

The rural population well understood the facts of their dependence, direct or indirect, on persons above them on the economic scale. They were reminded, for example, by the custom of providing free gifts to their patrons out of their produce or their hunting or fishing. If one of them wished to call on a rich man, "he does not barge in on him abruptly, but comes, stands outside his gateway, and tells his servant, 'So-and-So is standing at the gate of your court. Perhaps you will permit him to enter' "; or again, if they were called on by the owner for special help, they must respond, whether in some building project that required many hands or for rough stuff of whatever sort, self-defense or police work.[9] It was by the threat or reality of physical force mustered by the big landowners against the little that the latter were, we are often told, robbed of access to water, encroached on, or obliged to sell out against their will and at a ruinous price. By such means, dependent relations were regularly reinforced.

In the course of time, as Christianity gained great numbers of adherents among the urban population, the differentness of the rural became more accentuated, giving a new meaning to the old word *paganus* and giving, too, a special color to the history of Europe over many centuries to come. It cannot be easily shown, however, that country dwellers, despite their great preponderance numerically, did much to shape the political narrative of the later empire. Only two rural blocs have been distinguished, the members of which may have considered themselves, or can in retrospect be called, a single force with a common purpose and some sort of organization; and both, Circumcellions and Bacaudae, are best taken to be about what they appear at first sight: the wilder enthusiasts within the Donatist church in north Africa, on the one hand, and the wilder victims of civil war, invasion, and economic dislocation in Gaul, on the other hand.[10] What is in question is not their powerful effect on certain decades and certain provinces, but rather the connection between their violence and their differentness in culture and economic status. Were their attacks on property, property-holders, and officialdom really acts in a broad revolution? Did they intend to get Rome off their backs entirely? To suppose so raises needless complications; for the phenomenon of divisive passions in the Christian communities of every province is most amply attested, as will appear. Nothing further is required to explain the rage of the extremists in Numidia in the 340s and again in the period of Augustine's episcopacy. Similarly of the Bacaudae: given the disturbed conditions in western Gaul of the 280s and 290s and again after 406, great numbers of the dispossessed and desperate might naturally be looked for, as their lawless behavior might be expected, too; for those same conditions produced brigandage and various degrees of separation in northwestern Spain in the last third of the century, as in Mauretania and above all in Isauria.[11] It was surely an accident of language alone that the Isaurians from the third century on were not called Bacaudae by their neighbors (whatever the real meaning of the term in Celtic). A further argument, that vertical rather than horizontal dependencies were in any case the prevalent and obvious in antiquity, and so would be inevitably used to express discontents, can be left for later discussion. But in sum: Circumcellions and Bacaudae cannot be used to diagnose some general disease in the huge mass of the work force.

That force was subjected to strict constraints, possibly first under Diocletian but more probably under Constantine. We turn now to the second category of analysis, law, by which society may have been significantly defined and divided: in A.D. 332 an imperial constitution forbade *coloni*, "farming people," to quit the land they worked, on pain of being manacled like slaves.[12] Their vulnerability to such an order seems to be taken for granted, not some harsh innovation; so it predates the law. In the same reign, other smaller blocs of labor essential to the state, in transport and manufacture, were also tied to their occupations. The law of 332 has been used to support the view that the empire's peasantry had been reduced to an almost servile status and, by subsequent restrictive legislation and change, passed insensibly into serfdom. Were all this true, it would constitute by far the most important development known in the history of late Roman social relations. The truth, however, appears to be more complicated. While a large landowner might indeed refer in a lordly and proprietary way to "my farming people," as the emperor himself did, meaning tenants long resident on his estates, and while such persons henceforward could not legally move about, nevertheless they still did so. Quite openly and in writing, those of an estate in Numidia threatened the owner to pack up and leave if the local bishop, an extortionate scoundrel, were ever allowed by Augustine to return to his see (it was characteristic of such a situation that most of the *coloni* spoke neither Greek nor Latin, and that the proprietor resided far away in Rome). From the preceding ninety years since the promulgation of Constantine's law, numerous other mentions or clear indications survive of its being ignored, and none to show it enforced or so much as thought about. The power structure simply did not bring top and bottom into contact with each other very often, except through intermediaries; and the latter very often preferred to ignore the top, the emperor, and to deal with their problems in their own way. So the legislator's intention, which seems to the modern student so invitingly express and authoritative, turned into reality only to the extent that some quite independent-minded official or provincial magnate might wish it. The same was true, as many mentions in non-legal sources demonstrate, for all the emperors' restrictions placed on all the various labor blocs.

Besides, not all farming people were resident tenants. They might be nonresident, only visiting the fields they leased to get the work done or hiring a third party to do it for them; some were landowners themselves, others, landless laborers. A minority of the resident were slaves. On each of these categories, under different terms, as *originales*, *originarii*, *adscripti*, *adscripticii*, *censiti*, or *tributarii*, different obligations were imposed. These varied from province to province. Generally they were not so restrictive as for resident tenants. The government's purpose was not, in the end, the creation of a caste or civic condition; rather, the assuring of tribute from every single citizen whether directly or, if he were poor, through more financially responsible persons—which tribute and assurance, both, required the backing of real property. The *colonus* need not lose his right to sue the landowner if the terms of the tenancy were violated. He could lease land, hold, inherit, and bequeath property, become a priest or monk. If he was forbidden to leave the place where he was registered to pay his tax, so also was it forbidden to a town senator to withdraw himself from the town's list. Such close binding of all his subjects to their point of obligation, their *origo*, followed from Diocletian's new tax system, though it was his successor who fulfilled its logic.

Even then, logic could tolerate other forms of taxable unit than big estates

with their *coloni*. Alternatively, cities might be the unit, responsible for raising tribute from independent farmers in their territories; or villages as corporations might do so. At the end of the fourth century, measured against these
alternatives, it is safe to say that *coloni* made up only a minority of the agricultural work force, though whether that minority was large or small, evidence
does not suffice to show.[13] It receives altogether disproportionate attention in
the law codes because it lay at the center of common contentions. The way the
tax system operated, the obligation of a unit was not lightened if its membership diminished; those individuals remaining simply had to pay more. Hence
their howls for help against any loss of members. At the same time, fugitives
who could secure a tenancy from some other landowner, undetected or uncor-
rected by the tax-authorities, stood to gain along with their new patron. That
fact explains the situation disclosed in a complaint of the same year as Constantine's law: a village protests against a certain big man of the locality who
is taking in its runaway farming people and defying its headmen behind his
barred gates and armed servants.[14] He needed and welcomed more laborers
and dependents, they for their part needed his protection against the tax-collectors. Whether pure muscle and arrogance won the encounter, we are not
told; but legists like Julian and Gaius in the heyday of the Principate acknowledged that indeed it might do so, especially in the empire's rural parts;[15] and
late antiquity was certainly not a more governed period or more law-abiding
than the reign of Hadrian. What always counted, besides the emperors' will,
were the walls around one and enough people to serve one in case of need: in
short, local power, personal power.

Coloni on close inspection thus shrink in apparent numbers, shrink in importance, and lose definition as a group. The various restrictions by which they
were defined can be seen to be only a part of a far larger tangle encumbering
the lives of such other groups as shipowners and decurions—restrictions from
which these likewise could and did escape by appeal to more effectual realities
than law.

Contemporaries make it abundantly clear that social stratification existed in
a very marked form and that one must always bear it in mind. They knew, as
their court records show, that one could expect to be asked exactly what one's
place was in the world, if one were ever unlucky enough to stand before a
judge. The right answer would give weight to one's testimony, the wrong
would have a very prejudicial effect both in the course of litigation and in
sentencing if found guilty. Fines quantified the sense of rank, for example,
those to be paid by heretics (*C. Th.* 16.5.52, of A. D. 412): fifty pounds of
gold, a gigantic sum, if *illustres*; forty, if *spectabiles*; less in descending order
of amounts by senators, *clarissimi*, *sacerdotales*, *prinicipales*, decurions, *negotiatores*, *plebeii*, and Circumcellions. Fine distinctions are characteristically drawn near the top, among persons of the absolutely highest government
rank (praetorian prefects, notably) down through titular and actual senators,

provincial priests of the imperial cult, members of the governing board of municipal councils, and the councillors themselves (*principales* and *decuriones*). But all of these ranks together, as "the More Honorable," can have constituted only some two-tenths of one percent of the population.

In contrast, the same law of 412 lumps together all merchants, rich or poor, and leaves no room at all for service occupations, manufacture, or trades. All sorts of people working and living on the land are called *coloni* as a single bloc. The members of these latter several enormous groups naturally did not agree in such dismissive categorizing of themselves and, as they looked around at each other, detected as many subdivisions as their betters discovered at the top.[16] They or their families wished all the world to know that they had not lived their lives as indiscriminate *plebeii* but as innkeepers, clothiers, tinkers, oil-sellers, bakers, gardners, construction workers, locksmiths, sausage-sellers, litter-bearers, and so forth; for in such terms they were memorialized in both western and eastern cities.

Minute particularizing of place and occupation, high or low, serves to emphasize how stretched out, or stretched up, the social pyramid really was. Speaking more comprehensively, however, contemporaries saw it in simpler terms, made up of rich and poor. Wealth, the third category of definition proposed at the outset of this survey, was what came first to their minds—and they generally carried their social analysis no further. "How much you'll have is how much you'll be," so ran a proverb that Augustine quotes; division according to wealth, as he says also, was determined "by the law of mankind as by the emperors."[17] In sermons of east and west, our fullest witnesses on such matters, references to the distance separating the rich and poor abound. They dwell on the extreme forms of each; they contrast Lazarus and the rich man in dramatic scenes. But if the world consisted only of rich and poor with nothing in between, exactly what did that signify? Did money define high and low in absolute terms and so determine everybody's value absolutely?—meaning, that wealth was the sole, or at least the principle, *bonum*?

In fact, snobbish attacks on nouveaux riches show one competing claim for value according to plain seniority. Familiar in every period, it is asserted often, for instance, by Libanius. Another claim that he favors is lavish giving, including personal service in administration, to one's native city; still a third is *logoi*, oratorical capacity, both in that same service and for itself. People should be honored for their cultivation. In recommending Themistius for enrollment in the senate, Constantius II comprehensively praises his "famous forbears, abundant wealth, civic labors, and formidable command of words."[18] The four terms of eulogy are thoroughly at home in classical antiquity. The three which are not wealth itself require wealth.

But most important was power. That last term of definition by which to understand the workings of late Roman society rises naturally out of a discussion of wealth, in an analysis of unique length and insight, often quoted. It is found in Salvian's essay on divine governance. He was writing in Marseilles in the 440s; but, as will be seen, he sums up conditions prevalent in the preceding century. Central to his view is the opposition of rich and poor, to which he often recurs (4.4, 4.6, 5.7, and elsewhere). The rich are also the really powerful, *praepotentes* and *sublimes*, able to gobble up the lands of the weak and so to get richer (4.6). Though they themselves are few (5.4), yet, with their households, they bulk as the largest element in cities (8.3), and are joined in their predatory behavior by their agents and followers (5.4, *obsequentes*). The equivalences running through these pages are even expressly strung together as a trio: "extremely powerful," "extremely prominent," "extremely rich" (8.3). Such are the municipal authorities, decurions; more, they have gained higher office, reaching the rank of ex-governors (4.4, *praefectura*; 5.4, *potens et honoratus*; 5.8, *defensores*). Their means of doing so is purchase. Salvian treats it with outrage and contempt, hammering home the words "bought," "price," "trade" (5.7), and "profit" (5.4). What is worst of all, however, is the offer of protection, *patrocinium*, to the weak—an offer in itself to be praised, except that this too can only be had through purchase (5.8). Upon anyone who has not paid for his security, the *potentes* then practice extortion in the name of tax collection, and so recoup their expenses.

Several points in this portrait need to be highlighted. First, perhaps, should be Salvian's shock at the mercenary behavior of average, representative officialdom as he encounters it in his own part of the world. He expresses the reaction of an older man, reared in different values. Once there had been a different inducement to defend the weak: they constituted the chief element in one's community standing. Reward enough. But now noblesse oblige was not the only teaching in town (however much it, too, may have been essentially selfish). Now it was accepted that access to any position of public authority could and should be turned into a source of illicit, or grudgingly tolerated, gain.

A half-century and more before this date, in his forty-seventh oration, Libanius was already to be heard protesting that his patronage over the folk of a village he owned had been usurped by a local army commander. The commander now received a regular rake-off from the villagers while they, under his protection, could refuse to pay their due rents and taxes. Like Salvian, Libanius was outraged. His moral sense had been assaulted. But the man who had replaced him as patron in turn had his own debts to pay off, incurred in the process of gaining his present high position. Salvian (4.4) well understands that fact: *reddunt miseri dignitatum pretia*, the unhappy victims of an official must repay him for the costs of his appointment. Libanius makes clear in other contexts that he too understood the system; Augustine understood and approved.[19]

Also to be noted in Salvian's analysis is the cooperation of several layers of greed and officialdom in the process of extortion. A contemporary and re-

markable description of the process at work in the west can be found in a
Novella (1.3.2) of Valentinian.

> When such a [certain form of tax-] investigator comes to some frightened prov-
> ince, accompanied by agents of false accusations and borne aloft on costly ser-
> vices, he is all arrogance. He demands the assistance of the governor's staff; he
> also joins to his services the scholarians, and with his men and offices thus mul-
> tiplied, terror extorts what greed pleases. To introduce himself, the visitor pub-
> lishes and reiterates fearful commands concerning many and various tax catego-
> ries. He unrolls clouds of minute computations jumbled in unintelligible
> obscurity, which are the more effective as they are the less understood by persons
> ignorant of deceit. They require tax receipts consumed by length of years and age
> which the simplicity and trust of owing nothing have not the wit to preserve. . . .
> The palatine official as his colleague in thefts encourages him, the apparitors tur-
> bulently join the attack, the soldiers ruthless press for action.

What is here offered as a living picture from the western provinces is more
easily found in our sources for the eastern; and with the evidence of Salvian,
it begins to explain one of the two new figures dominant on the late Roman
stage: office-holders (church leaders being the other of the pair, to be set in
place a little later). Of these, quite predictably, there are many descriptions
because such people had a hand in so much business and attracted so much
notice. To the art of the astrologer in Constantine's day, they were known as
"governors, military commanders, masters over life and death, tribunes fearful to provinces and cities," "military commanders, leading an army, great
men, imperious, who are in every way fearful and hold provinces and cities in
the grip of their power, naturally wealthy, rich, and monied, able by the simplest means to get whatever they want and triumphant in every struggle,"
"military commanders, military tribunes, but fearful and borne up on tyrannous powers, and *defensores* or chief men in cities, who change about in the
enjoyment of those powers." To the same effect, Chrysostom describes "the
man in power who gives everyone orders, the cynosure of everyone for his
high rank. He has a splendid herald, a belt of office, and great retinue of
courtiers." And more fully still, Basil speaks of

> the man famous for his overflowing wealth, for the throngs of flatterers about him,
> for the guard of those pretending to be his friends and so to gain his favor; for the
> throngs of kinsmen, real or alleged, a swarm of followers, and a thousand who
> attend him to be fed or to gain other necessities, whom he trails about with him,
> coming and going, and on this account is the envy of passers-by. Add to his
> wealth, his power in the city or as an imperial official, a governor of provinces,
> commander of armies. His herald with great shouts goes before him, his lictors
> strike fear in everyone they meet by reminding them of floggings, confiscations,

sentences of exile, prison—all of which inspire among those subject to him an intolerable terror.[20]

The type here presented shares much with the great men of Nero's or Marcus Aurelius' day, certainly: conspicuous consumption, parade of self and position, swarms of dependents. But essential now are the elements of terrification characteristic of this fourth- and fifth-century elite, and, beyond that, an imperial office which is the instrument of terror. The two are combined to assure wealth; also, to assure a firm seat or promotion in the emperor's service, which to a notorious degree required purchase from others around one—so much so, that one really could not succeed at all without it. As a contemporary says of two particular successes, Stilicho and Rufinus, ''both engaged in indiscriminate plundering, in the conviction that riches were power.'' The same would not have been said a century earlier; nor had the bulk of rich villas, where their owners can be identified, nor the bulk of rich works of art, for example in Spain, always belonged to office-holders in the imperial government.[21] But times had changed. One major development could even be measured, at least approximately: government had increased over Constantine's lifetime not by a mere doubling or trebling but ten- or twentyfold, and continued to grow in numbers throughout the period here surveyed. Its members, however elevated and rewarded in its service, inevitably provoked the scorn of an older elite. That mattered little. They could send their sons to the right schools (Libanius', for one) and marry into the best families. Both ex officio and of their own ample funds, too, they could easily outspend all but the grandest noblemen on their native city itself, forever the focus of aristocratic pride; for primacy in ''evergetism,'' civic munificence, passed into their hands as well as every other aspect of power. They thus represented no departure from the traditional ethic of local leadership—only from the traditional means of getting there. And, in fact, a great number of the new provincial governors, counts, and prefects came from long-established families: Petronius Probus, to name the best known, four times a praetorian prefect in the west, famous for his extortionate tenure.

At the top, new patterns of power in the fourth century accommodated themselves to the greater importance of the center, resulting from the quite unchallenged authority of the emperor to command and the vastly increased number and presence of his agents throughout the cities of the empire; but the degree of independence, to a great extent venal, which was claimed by those agents produced unpredictable, shifting court parties, conspiracies, and ''arrangements.'' Thanks to Ammianus they are detectable in Carthage where Count Romanus had his headquarters, as in Cologne, where Silvanus commanded; thanks to the Collectio Casinensis, we can look into the very minds of intriguers and count the monies to be distributed to the persons they judged key in Constantinople: wives, chamberlains, aides, and assistants to great of-

THE MASSES IN LATE ANTIQUITY **261**

ficials but not the latter themselves (who perhaps cost too much?).[22] The inclusion of women should not surprise—or rather, of "ladies," *matronae*, of the aristocracy. They appear in many mentions as enjoying the influence naturally accorded to wealth and wide kinship. Theodoret reports how the supporters of one of the candidates for bishop of Rome, when the throne was in dispute, hesitated to present evidence in his favor even though they were "persons in office and high rank," knowing the hostility of the emperor (who was visiting the city at the time); but a delegation of their wives approached him and talked him around. Thus Liberius was recalled.

Measured against each other, the *potentes* of the later empire, like those earlier, accepted the consequences of their continual rivalries and expected to encounter adversaries. All the more reason to cultivate good sources of support and information, which even quite lowly dependents could provide. "For who on this earth lives without enemies?" asks Augustine rhetorically; and he goes on to describe attacks on one's dwelling, one's servants, one's lands. It was all very well to praise the meek, as scripture does, but "how can a spirit be meek and gentle amid wealth, amid anxieties and secular concerns, from which flow endless business dealings, lawsuits, charges, feuds, animosities?"—so, the bishop Chromatius of Aquileia. And Basil, true to an ethic long at home in the ancient world, takes for granted the need to make oneself known as a dangerous man to cross. A brother bishop Musonius he praises as "a steadfast helper for his friends, *a most formidable foe to his enemies.*"[23]

He recalls, too, the memory of Musonius among his fellow citizens: "those enjoying office called him their governor; the mass of the people, their defender; those in need of the barest necessities, their sustainer." Being a true leader among people of many ranks on whose compliance he could count, he could therefore count also on the respect of his peers or near-peers. The structure of the world he exemplifies remained still as it had been for centuries, arranged in alliances narrow at the top, as broad as possible at the bottom. Organization was vertical, not along lines of common socioeconomic status. Still as in the past, it was a structure of domination and dependency, in which wealth was the chief contributory part, now joined by authority exercised through imperial appointment. What defined one's place in the end was the ability to bring force to bear in self-defense or aggression, to be "a formidable foe"; and contemporaries certainly saw it this way. In their ordinary terms of social analysis, even more often than synonyms for "rich," they used those for "the powerful"—"bosses" as we would say. Beneath them, in Jerome's words, were "*clientes* and the poor and farmers," subject not only to unofficial authority but also to "those in office and on the bench, who oppress others through their power, or steal, so that they may supply to the poor a little, taken from the many, and so glory in their crimes."[24] Thus he excoriates their "charity."

Ordinarily, the system functioned very well. That is, dependence expressed itself in requests for a loan or a bit of advice; for a word to be spoken to an encroaching neighbor, to the other party in some business deal, or to the public authorities concerning the petitioner's tax dues or liturgies. More on a level, one might apply to someone important for a handful of "letters of recommendation to a friend, as if one were his closest familiar" (Amm. 15.5.3), so as to hand these out like calling cards to other important people. In return, the man of influence expected that his interests would be considered by everyone on whom he had a claim, even without his having to make his wishes express. The system can be seen at work in many scores of letters surviving as literature or as papyri; likewise, in descriptive texts already quoted from Libanius or Salvian.

The building of power one favor, one person, at a time was a slow, laborious process. Surely it could be bettered by reaching out to whole blocs of people: a village, for example, all of it owned by some single rural magnate (and the countryside was of course where the bulk of wealth and population resided). Yet dependent relations in rural settings were too diffuse to be easily brought to bear. When applications of personal influence are sought that can in any sense be called historical, they are found to involve large groups in cities. Ammianus lifts the curtain on such evidence in Antioch when the Caesar Gallus was living there; Libanius speaks of a corps of several hundred claqueurs who sold their shouts not only to actors to get the theater crowds started in cheering a performance, but also to individuals ad hoc, who wished to create a noise about this or that matter of public interest; and there are informative glimpses of coherent groups in action in Rome, which happens also to be relatively well reported.[25] In both cities, the clustering of some craft or commerce in a particular precinct had occurred naturally, and so produced some more or less cohesive scores, or hundreds, or one or two thousands of people. They appear, indeed, formally organized everywhere in the empire: not as trade unions but as friendly, cooperative associations. Even members of trades with no locus of congregation, such as construction workers or bakers, commonly joined together. To assure urban food supplies and certain necessary manufactures, the government of the Principate had first recognized, then privileged, then defined, and eventually in the fourth century controlled and dictated to many of these groups, in an increasing number of cities other than the two capitals. Thereby their action as units was assured—not always in ways the government desired. It was for their own purposes that they sought out patrons. In the later empire they did so normally not among local magnates but rather among imperial officials whose particular charge brought them into contact with workers of some sort: for example, a prefect of the grain supply approached as patron by shippers. From that invitation would derive an instant increase in his standing. He would be looked to for even more than an official role in moments when the city faced a threat of shortage. But direct evidence for this is very rare. Instead, associations' own officials might be appealed to, at least in Rome, along with the city's "precinct chiefs," whatever those persons may have been; or undefined clusters among the populace, enough to make a mob, find some momentary leader, a Valvomeres in Rome or nameless others elsewhere. In short, blocs existed; the openly organized ones constituted elements in the train and sometimes in the control, of *potentes*; but they are not seen to be very effectively manipulated by these latter (exception made of religious struggles, to be discussed below).

The mass of the people instead were never heard from save when a part, perhaps no representative one at all, disturbed the peace. It happened all the time, evidently.[26] So contemporary sources indicate in casual comments. The means of gaining their ends, the people found most often at their entertainments, occasioning such a statement as that of the urban prefect after being driven from Rome by threats against his life and lodging: "Our recall, the votes of the citizens demanded at the theater performances." To modern eyes, a ludicrous humiliation!—but routine. Governors with equal deference, even with apprehension, gave ear to the shouts of the masses for an evaluation of their term of office, since the results, being noted for content and force and so reported to the emperor, could advance or terminate a man's career. Here, too, a claque might help: *clientelae*, as Constantine calls them. Other occasions for demonstrations arose out of rival fan-clubs, most often for chariot races. Thessalonica produced such a riot, a famous one; Constantinople, numberless others. There are many episodes, too, of mob violence (but not much was needed) to rescue persons from the hands of the authorities, the latter being everywhere, even in Rome itself, supported by only exiguous numbers of men at arms. A praetorian guard no longer existed. It had been dissolved by Constantine and no ordinary substitute put in its place; but sometimes garrison troops within a city or on loan from a neighbor could be brought to bear. The surprising weakness of both municipal and imperial government, whose members could only imagine themselves in the role of patron—lofty, benevolent, never tyrannous or oppressive—inevitably invited the urban populace to express their wishes in emphatic form. They expected their lordly leaders to attend their assemblies at the circus or theater to hear whatever they had to say, if some need should find expression in unison shouts: petitions for the lavish provision of entertainment and public amenities, as a matter of course; more pressing demands brought out by too much to drink or too little to eat, or the prevalence of indebtedness. Remarks about "the vinous rage of the mob," or similar phrases, can be heard from Chrysostom or Ambrose. A Roman prefect had the taverns closed except within restricted hours (but not *very* restricted). Then, too, rumor or reality of a food shortage would inevitably provoke demonstrations; sometimes, a lynching or arson. And (for the third condition that contemporaries specified as general) we have Jerome commenting on a reference in Isaiah (56.6) to "savage notes of hand," "in which," he says, "are contained the charges of the usurers, so the poor are oppressed by debt; and this is the chief cause of rioting in every city.''

It appears, then, from this very brief review, that the urban masses did from time to time exert their strength sufficiently to shape the conduct of their masters. It is an obvious question, whether they did this out of their weakness, their poverty and hunger, in a way to make an institution out of the response. If hunger and poverty were always at the door, and the rich and powerful would not support some counter-force to keep the commons quiet, then did they never find other, more constructive ways of meeting the problems? Of course, they did: at least in Rome, by a dole (no Roman invention) from the period of the Republic onward. In the later third century A.D. it began to be imitated in other cities; next, in Constantinople in the fourth. A long history, a large subject. The point to be made here is only that systems for subsidized food supply remained a great rarity. No attack on the basic causes of urban unrest was attempted; yet they were not exploited, either; and the reason lay in the broad and hardly changing sense of role among both rich and poor. On both levels, individuals thought of themselves as such. It was as individuals that they reached up or down, in patterns of dominance and dependence.[27]

Libanius in an interesting passage describes a custom of recent memory that brought together crowds of countryfolk around the more prominent men of the villages, in charge of local temples. They presided over festival banquets; and ''those persons provided help to poverty through their own endeavors for old men and women and orphaned children, most of whom were crippled in some serious way.'' Similar relief is known in various eastern shrines of the Principate, though it was apparently rare. It may have been this sort of thing that was in Basil's mind as he reproached his own congregation: ''Let us feel shame,'' he says, '' at the tales of loving-kindness among non-Christians. Among some of them, there is a law of the sort enjoining a single table and food in common.''[28] Concern about the obligations of the rich toward the poor was of course ordinarily looked for among Christians, not pagans, in this period. Extended treatment of the subject, or hortatory passages, can be found in almost all the dozen or so homiletic collections that survive from the 350s up to Augustine. Within that period, indeed from as early as St. Anthony and so to the younger Melania, there are a number of specific cases of Christians reported to have given away all or most of their estates to the poor; and bishops set an example, in the routine managing of their funds (below). To the extent that the Church established norms of conduct, then, the two broad categories in which society was divided, or at least thought of—rich and poor—should have grown closer together; relations should have been less troubled. However, no evidence actually points in that direction. Instead, people could be seen winning admiration for generous gifts to the poor while gaining an even wider reputation for the savage greed with which they extracted the wherewithal from the weak beneath them. Setting the tone, Christian emperors continued to speak of the "slavish offscourings" and "vulgar vileness" that made up the lower classes; and Ambrose insisted that "priests should have nothing of the masses about them, nothing of the people, nothing in common with the pursuits and manners of the barbarous multitude." Beggars, cripples, old crones by the church doorstep, faceless desperation, all these, preaching held up as an urgent invitation to Christian charity; but they were acknowledged rather for their part in the salvation of the rich than as individual men and women in distress.[29]

The key to this fact is the obvious change accomplished in the character of the Church's leadership as a consequence of Constantine's conversion and of subsequent imperial favor extended to Christianity by his sons and their successors. The position enjoyed by bishops immediately became attractive to a better class than before. In the period of interest here, they were drawn from that upper fraction of one percent defined as curial (above, p. 257). It was this local elite, then, which was called on to lead and to determine the teachings of the Church; and to their role they naturally brought the views they had been reared in. It was inevitable that an aristocrat like Ambrose would speak as he is heard to do, in the preceding paragraph. He or Nectarius or Chrysanthos, the latter two in the eastern capital, had been great men in the empire, major figures of their time before ever they climbed into a bishop's throne.[30] How else but as themselves could they be expected to think and act? It was likewise inevitable that they should have been chosen bishops as and for themselves, meaning (among candidates equally good Christians, or even beyond such) for their distinguished families and their wealth; and of course they expressed and increased their influence as people of their sort normally sought to do in secular affairs through the same two claims, *genos* and *ploutos*, or on occasion by their intimidating harshness (so, Epiphanius reports of a Palestinian bishop). Like secular magnates, they "had to be borne about on splendid spirited horses" and "to parade around and be hailed on all sides," not simply from personal pride but because such display served to increase respect and, therefore, power. So Gregory Nazianzenus characterizes their ways, disapprovingly. Jerome acknowledges the root cause in his remark, "When Christ's church came into the hands of Christian princes, its power and wealth increased but its virtues were diminished." Such were the realities of the world post-Constantine; and they had to be recognized.

Epiphanius (in further illustration) adds to his mention of that unworthy bishop in Palestine, that his power derived not only from his capacity to deal out rewards or injuries, but "from his acquaintance and liberty to speak with Constantius." In this respect, too, bishops behaved like their peers who enjoyed secular office and prominence. To the dismay of some of their number, they besieged the palace for a precious interview, hung about the edges of the court, or boasted of their easy access to its very center—in short, sought control over their affairs at its source, very much as if they had been senators, provincial presidents, or delegates from the curia of some major city. The need to do so most often lay in their inability to agree among themselves, not in any wish to magnify the emperor's authority; but, especially in the east, they had no choice; so, from almost the beginning of the period under review here, they are seen resorting to the emperor for support. At the crudest, they borrowed his soldiers. That happened frequently, as an indication of the emperors' command over the high points and high moments of eccelesiastical history, to say nothing of details. It had been Constantine, for example, who was expected to settle the rights of episcopal election between Majorinus and Caecilian in 312; it was Arcadius's eunuch who brought John Chrysostom from Antioch to be bishop of the eastern capital, and the empress Eudoxia's eunuch who called him back from his first exile in 403; and in between these dates, and on into the latter century, the summoning of ecumenical councils and the setting of their venue, or the choice of what candidate with what doctrine was to enjoy what degree of authority in what see, lay with the crown when its occupant wished to say so.[31] The extent of Caesaropapism need only be mentioned here.

But even against soldiers bishops might prevail; and in the absence of such armed force they had often to confront each other. The means they then made use of was the mass of people in their cities who rallied to them and their cause. The response they offered at the summons of the bishops took on the forms long familiar in the empire and natural to the participants high and low; for the latter expected to be drawn into the rivalries of the former and, as their dependents, to afford the support properly owing: applause and loyal speech and physical presence when called upon. In the fourth century even before Constantine's conversion, and more clearly still in the fifth century, such support played an important part in the making of history; for there is no denying that history during all that long period consisted more in religious disputes than in anything else.

In proof, a test: imagine the largest hundred cities each informed by a weekly gazette, and imagine its headlines and leading stories over the years. They would include a half dozen pretenders, all of whom, however, left the world very much as they found it (Procopius, Attalus, Magnentius, even Julian). They would include occasional wars; minor and, eventually, major invasions; the course of life will be increasingly agitated by barbarian masses within and without the borders of the empire. But by far the most frequent item of news, and the steadiest influence on the course of historical development, must certainly be the cities' excitement, angry divisions, even bloodshed, and broad involvement in disputes about due worship.

Consider Rome. Except for a single visit from the emperor and fears (not the reality) of food shortages, nothing in secular affairs disturbed the ancient capital for almost a hundred years after the battle of the Milvian Bridge. What rather aroused the liveliest attention were legations and controversies brought to the bishop there, and the question, just who *was* the bishop, beginning in

309 and attaching at a later point to the bodies of 137 (or 160) partisans who had died for it. Nor did the deathroll in Rome end with the victory of Damasus. As to Alexandria, its boldest headlines would have announced the casualties to violence associated with the struggle for control of the see in every decade from the 330s to 370s; and there were more to come when Christians turned against pagans and Jews in the later fourth and earlier fifth century. At Antioch, the see was the object of a dispute among rival claimants, as many as four at a time, over the ninety years ending in 414, the occasion of many fatalities; and Carthage's headlines over the same stretch of time would have been likewise monopolized by the division within the Church and the lists of its victims. Constantinople's deaths came only in the 340s and later; but they numbered 3,150 on one occasion, "so it is said," and in 403/404 "filled the church."[32]

From this conspectus of life in the empire's major centers, no one should conclude that they alone suffered such sanguinary disturbances; rather, that their doings were more often reported, and the report more likely to survive; for, by chance, we also hear of violent deaths in smaller cities—of Christians attacked by pagans, most rarely, or of pagans at the hands of Christians (also unusual), or, by far the most frequently, of Christians at the hands of each other. Our sources supply the names of more than a dozen lesser localities thus disturbed in the east, such as Gaza or Caesarea of Cappadocia; others, nameless; a dozen in north Africa; and still others among the western provinces.[33] To count up those centers, large and small, where religious strife led to the loss of life certainly makes for a very odd inventory, but the purpose of the count is surely evident. In the shortest way possible, it dramatizes a new, widespread historical phenomenon; and, further, it suggests the dimensions of that phenomenon by leading the imagination from persons actually killed to some vastly greater number of scenes where only lighter wounds were inflicted, only general brawling occupied the streets and plazas, houses but not their occupants were destroyed by fire, kidnapped persons were safely ransomed, those under threat of death found a safe exile, and floggings and torture fell short of lethal savagery—as unquestionably happened and could unquestionably be cast into a kind of gigantic index to the newspapers imagined over the hundred years or so in question. Among the cities of the ancient world, which, one may almost say, *were* the ancient world, nothing similar had ever been known; not even the much longer tale of the Persecutions had, in the end, spilt anywhere near so much blood. The period thereafter, post-313, is therefore properly to be characterized, as it certainly underwent its chief changes, through the prevalence and the high level of violence over religious differences.

How to explain the passions that moved this violence, and where it tended, may be left to a later page. For the moment, all that needs discussion is the new power structure created by its leaders—ordinarily bishops—to achieve their aims when force of argument alone could not prevail.

First, the character of episcopal rule: in administrative action it was highly independent, making little kings of those who were entrusted with it (hence the term applied to it, "monarchical"). Next, the values to which its occupants adhered through their background and class traditions: they would wish to enhance their influence and their standing in the community as a whole; they would wish to acquit themselves honorably, not only of their duty to God, but of the responsibilities of their rank. To do so in the normal manner, local leaders had always involved themselves in contentious affairs, sometimes to help one side or the other, sometimes impartially at the request of both for adjudication, sometimes as envoys to a third party such as a governor or emperor. Bishops' correspondence post-Constantine is filled with appeals or other forms of pressure they bring to bear on the recipient at the request of some petitioner; their jurisdiction was formally acknowledged since 318 by the secular authorities as independent—in some ways more than the equal— of the civil courts; and their service on embassies is dramatically attested, for example, in Eusebius' visit to Constantine in 324, Ambrose's to Magnus Maximus in 387, or Chrysostom's to Gainas in 400. Basil's description of bishop Musonius' place in his community, on whom everyone for miles around depended and to whom they all looked for advice and assistance (above, p. 261), is matched by the picture of Augustine, who "often spent all the morning and sometimes the whole day hearing causes."[34] We thus have in the empire's urban centers, rapidly emerging, a new authority. Toward the end of the period under review here, it is in fact recognized as chief in the ordering of the series: bishops, clerics, *honorati* (of the rank of governor, retired), *possessores* (independent landowners), and *curia*, who are collectively to see to the election of the cities' *defensores*.[35] How had the world changed!

Augustine's letters illustrate the play of forces universal in late antiquity, pitting the powerful against the weak and manipulating imperial authority for predatory purposes. Here, the Church could and must intervene. The emperors were requested to appoint more *defensores ecclesiae*, lay officials intended to protect ecclesiastical interests and especially the interests of the dependent classes "from the wickedness of mighty folk, who oppress them in any way," "against the powers of the wealthy."[36] The bishop's hand thus gained more reach and strength; but there were still other agents more directly his to command: in Rome, many hundreds of salaried *fossores* (they happen to be mentioned in African cities as well), through whom a burial plot could be bought; in Antioch, the funeral staff used in the organizing of demonstrations in 449; and in Alexandria, *parabalani* who were sufficiently distracted from their proper tending of the sick to inspire general terror in the city, by 416, and whose numbers could not be controlled within the permitted five hundred, thanks to the pressure from applicants to buy their way in (enrollment being evidently a good investment).[37] In addition, a law office served the see, not only in Rome; a secretariat, too; and financial officals, some of them clerics. It is rare to find mention of such staff, high or low, but by Ambrose's time the salaried totals must have topped a thousand at the largest—something less in little towns, yet still sufficient to match and more than match the service under any but the greatest local magnate. At the same time, bishops could compete in disposable wealth with governors and the less affluent senators. Best known, the see of Rome already under Constantine possessed estates on three continents and an income from them of 26,000 solidi, in addition to certain rents in kind, at a time when a single solidus would support a man in all he needed for several months. Oversight of properties must involve the bishop in travels and draw him into worldly affairs, unless he delegated them to "an agent in business, estate manager, and accountant for rents," as the job is described.[38] The bulk of rents went to salaries, but what remained, combined with special gifts from time to time, permitted the routine feeding and clothing of the local poor as well as major building projects, both ecclesiastical and secular. Bishops were thus brought into a relationship of monied dominance over slaves, at the bottom of the heap, and casual labor employed on agricultural properties, peasants and tenant farmers, bailiffs, construction workers, and other labor ad hoc, as well as retailers and subordinate partners in business and some of the urban indigent—all, outside of the Church itself in addition to the see's salary lists. How important such various connections were bound to appear to their communities in strictly economic terms can be sensed in the phrase, "clients of his patronage," to whom a bishop left bequests at his death, or again, in the near-riots that disturbed congregations competing to bestow clerical status on an extremely wealthy candidate.[39]

Though all in the service of the Church, the power of bishops could hardly develop except along lines natural to the secular economy and society, within which, however, its growth was spectacular. Those who controlled it labored to enhance it; what each achieved passed on with little risk of diminution to his successor; and in the peace that followed persecution they could speak out openly with the authority uniquely theirs, as interpreters of divine omnipotence. The larger sees inevitably became objects of ambition and rivalry. Once possessed, they might subserve still further rivalries, in which the whole of that network of dependent connections, just outlined, could be employed. Such was the dynamic of their history.

In their elevation, an active role was traditionally reserved to the people. Their unison shouting and acclamations were considered entirely proper to overcome a candidate's reluctance, and are reported at the election of St. Martin or Ambrose or Augustine—also, in less well known settings, or with "disordered yelling and cries," as Augustine describes it.[40] Expressions of popular preferences maintained their importance in western sees. In the eastern, they lost some of their weight toward the turn of the fourth century; yet there is no better proof of the power of the people to be found throughout our period than in Constantinople at the time when John Chrysostom's supporters were tumultuously resisting the emperor's efforts to get rid of him.

On a number of occasions it was the masses who were successful against all force in determining who was to sit on the see's throne: more than once, in Alexandria, where support for Athanasius was fervent; in Rome under Valentinian through action both of the *multitudo* and its leaders, *proceres*;[41] earlier, under Constantine in Constantinople, when the two largest parts of the Christian community faced off against each other in defense of their opposing candidates. The Master of Cavalry Hermogenes was killed trying to enforce the will of one of the two. It was just such junctures that demonstrated the decisive importance of the whole of a bishop's power structure, beyond merely the upper parts: beyond the circle of his peers in the region, his clerics, and senators. The latter groups sufficed to settle matters subject to no more than ordinary dispute; but what could avail except brute strength when disputants refused to accept the lawfulness of any opposition at all? Witness Honorius' difficulties in 405, rousing his praetorian prefect against certain Arian bishops who, instead of submitting to exile, "hang about and look for popular demonstrations, assemble disturbers of the peace, constitute themselves instigators of mass unrest, declare themselves still guiltless after judgment, gather the people and are addressed as bishops, petition the sacred imperial court and obtain responses and furtive rescripts" (evidently issued by the proper authorities but against the emperor's will)—very much as Urbanus of Parma had once done so insolently, for years, back in the 370s, being abetted by the inaction or sympathy of the *vicarius* deputed to evict him. Urbanus in turn was no different from certain disobedient clerics in Egypt, accused of disregarding imperial commands of the 390s, as *they* exactly resembled that string of other delinquents of the 380s, including Eunomians, Arians, Macedonians, Pneumatomachi, Manichaeans, Encratites, Apotactites, Saccophori, and Hydroparastatae who "shall not assemble in groups, shall not collect any multitude, shall not attract any people to themselves, and shall not dress up private houses to look like churches," anywhere in the eastern provinces.[42] It was of course of the essence for all these religious activities and movements, as for Novatianists, Priscillianists, Pelagians, and others, that they should consist of more than their uncompromising leaders. Every bishop must have followers. Followers alone could make a leader. And, properly led, they could then be dispersed only by force: on an Alexandrian scale, force superior to the six hundred armed men serving one bishop as his private guard toward the end of the period here studied (A.D. 412), or more than five thousand in aid of another, toward the beginning.[43] For smaller settings with less at stake, smaller forces would do. Even unarmed crowds were intimidating, and their sheer numbers, if not confronted by soldiers, could reduce the highest officials, even the emperor himself, to subterfuge or retreat.[44]

In bringing to bear a mass of support, bishops could count on *parabalani*, *fossores*, *lecticarii*, and similar groups already mentioned; then, too, they had a rank of men of acknowledged repute and influence within their congregations, *proceres* and *domini*; next, reaching out a little further, they had their *clientes* bound to them by their past services and favors; and a special resource was ready to hand in the workers' associations whose prominent participation in religious battles is indicated in our better-reported scenes and cities: Constantinople and Rome, but also Cyzicus, Hadrianople, and Antioch. In Antioch, they were under the official oversight of decurions; elsewhere, under their chosen patrons, through whom they could be commanded. In Milan, Ambrose solidified good relations with the large wholesaler and transport associations, capable of providing quite crucial support against official force in aid of doctrines under ban.[45]

He provides a few details that show how negotiations with his foes at a time of armed confrontation were shared with his flock, or much of it (the *populus*), from whom also he did not hide his bitter weeping and his prayers and to whom he addressed some very inflammatory language.[46] It was rather expected that they would respond in the same animated way that they were used to in another setting, the theater, with applause and murmurs or cheers of approbation. In Constantinople, John Chrysostom indeed reproaches them for too much of that; but the eloquence which won him his name was of course enormously valued by all churches, and to exploit its powers better he himself stepped forward from the altar area where his predecessors had spoken, to the pulpit mid-nave. From there he tells his listeners, "if you should hear anyone speaking of God irreverently in the street or town square, go right up to him, rebuke him, and if he needs to be beaten up, don't hold back, but strike him in the face, give him a bash in the mouth." And Augustine can later be heard stirring up a crowd with what amounted to battle cries, at one point in his struggles with his religious opposition, much as the bishop of Sirmium in 366 had addressed *his* excitable listeners. They then demanded his opponent's death. The scene is vivid and revealing.[47] Without any such summons to engage the emotions of large audiences, their actions can hardly be explained.

But at the same time, leaders had causes which might not lend themselves to easy encapsulation (as was certainly true of the homoousion/homoiousion difference and, again, of Nestorianism); nor did they very much want to involve the masses in an understanding of what was in dispute. Rather the reverse: the description of everybody in the bazaars of the eastern capital so eager to offer his theological views, which Gibbon was the first to make familiar, was intended by its ancient author in criticism of such presumptuous folly; and passages from Ambrose and other writers show that it was thought best either to keep doctrine apart from the ordinary worshipper or to present it to him in the most condensed form, ex cathedra. Two rare reported moments, allowing some estimate of common people's actual insight and interest in religious questions, show their focus to be clearly on the leaders involved, not on the subject of disagreement: once in a small town in Africa when an argument between two antagonists was attended by a large crowd, among whom, however, "only a very few persons appeared anxious to explore the issues in any useful cleansing manner, while the rest had assembled more like theatergoers to see our altercation as a show," and the second time in a small Spanish town where everyone was agog over the news of a challenger in doctrine confronting their local hero; but, when one of the two bishops suffered a stroke at the opening of the contest, the audience knew instantly where the merits of the case lay: "See you not God's miraculous demonstration of the accursed falsehood?"[48]

How then to mobilize broad support? Not through the routine of sermons: for preachers generally saw before them the local elite and their slave servants. Not at the occasional great, indiscriminate gatherings on a martyr's feast-day or at baptisms; for the audience would not understand contentious matters. What served rather was the compression of the issues at stake into labels and slogans to be set to music.[49] There was an ample supply of popular tunes which might carry new words. They were pressed into service, for example, among the dockside population of Alexandria or in the forums of north African towns early in the period here reviewed; in Edessa and Nisibis against all wrong doctrine by the tireless Ephraim, composer of some 300,000 didactic verses to which his congregation were to respond antiphonally; later, in triumphant moments of massed chants rising to the skies above Antioch in Julian's reign, above Hippo of Augustine's day—at the birth of Latin accentual verse, indeed—or in Constantinople (as in other eastern cities also) between competing sects in the 380s and in 431. Responsive singing, laity answering clergy, was instituted sucessfully by Ambrose, who boasted, "they [the Arians] say the people are ensnared by my songs—and I certainly do not deny it." Later (A.D. 401) in Constantinople a musical war is recorded between those friendly and those hostile toward the city's principal bishop, one side gathering in the public arcades twice a week to sing out their own beliefs and their challenging phrases, such as, "Where are the people who say the Three are One Power?"—these, throughout most of the night—and, in conclusion, at sun-up, parading across the city; while, in reply to them, the other side, illuminated by candles that the empress supplied and directed by one of her chief eunuchs, responded antiphonally in the words he had composed and taught to them. That mode of religious singing had a long life thereafter. At the time, however, it only led into a confrontation, and a fight, and partisans slain on both sides.

Through such a scene we approach the psychology of violence; and how can it be understood without psychology? Singing together in close-packed crowds, feeling at the same time embattled, perhaps under a night sky and with the edgy sense of the unusual, since prominent persons were present and participant, the crowds may be very easily imagined in a state of high excitement. Indeed, they are so described by observers of the moment. We may compare the impressive torchlight procession accompanying the relics of the holy martyr Phocas across the city of Constantinople, its dark streets successively invaded and left again in darkness as "a river of fire" (in Chrysostom's words) swept past. The very emperor made one of a vast throng, signalizing its importance. And again, another parade of the city's Christians: this time with the empress attending the casket of other martyrs' relics to their new home in a martyrium nine miles beyond the walls, Eudoxia in her imperial jewels walking every step of the way. Relics of John himself were later brought to the capital by torchlight assembly, first of small craft in the Bosphorus across which they were conveyed, then of crowds on foot at the harbor, where they were received by the prayers of the emperor Theodosius and so conducted to their designated resting place.[50] While such scenes as these were entirely peaceful, they united the participants in a solemn purpose, having a powerful effect on them and making out of them a single group.

A fourth scene: at Antioch in 363, Christians expressed their defiance of the apostate Julian while still obeying him, by not merely removing the bones of the holy bishop Babylas from a non-Christian shrine outside of the city but making a great event of it, in great crowds singing psalms along the road and, at each pause before the next, chanting "Shame be on all who kneel to graven images." In times of unchallenged Christianity, it was the emperors themselves who initiated the recovery of relics and their transport to more splendid or more accessible shrines, as was done by Valens and by Theodosius, to the accompaniment of miracles.[51]

The union of religious rivalry and the veneration of martyrs belongs to the times, and to the question, also, how the masses could be engaged in such rivalry. But the answer is plain to anyone who can in imagination enter into such episodes of urban history: they were moving and important to their participants. They brought men in touch physically, or almost physically, with the divine. Nor were they only eastern. In the west, best known is Ambrose's recovery, in 386, of the remains of Gervasius and Protasius, whose resting place was revealed to him in a dream. Transferred from a minor to a major church, the "Ambrosian" basilica in Milan, they came under the care of a sexton whose sight they had restored (the miracle had been witnessed by a huge crowd at the time), and they continued thereafter to expel demons from the possessed and heal diseases. To Florence, Ambrose subsequently brought the relics of Vitalis and Nabor from Bologna. Their whereabouts had likewise been revealed in a dream, and they too demonstrated the power to exorcize demons. To yet another Milanese church he brought relics of the apostles and, a little later, of the martyr Nazarius, miraculously revealed and rescued from obscurity in the suburbs. Elsewhere, we see the bishop presiding over a martyr's miracles as, one might say, an impresario. Reception of St. Nazarius rose to a special point of drama in the midst of Ambrose's sermon of welcome: he was interrupted by the outburst of a demon possessing one of the audience, whom, however, he prostrated by his firm rebuke.[52]

Such leaders as he commanded enormous authority beyond their wealth, social class, and secular connections. God acted through them, giving them special powers—also special protection, as those who opposed them would learn to their cost. Retribution for heretical views, despite the warnings of a good bishop, Basil or some other, would be exacted even from the mighty of this world, in the tradition of the stories told about the persecutors' deaths, Galerius and others—retribution whereby a prince dies in Antioch, an empress is brought to death's door, two *cubicularii* are killed in Milan, diseases afflict hostile bishops and hostile laymen of Constantinople in their fevered bodies, itching skin, swollen feet, suppurating and palsied hands, putrefying bellies, and nightmare-ridden nights.[53] Yet these stories were more than matched by others in which good bishops with or without the aid of martyrs' relics healed the blind or restored the health of petitioners suffering from other intractable illnesses—even raised the dead—at Trier, Paris, Tours, Milan, Aquae Tibilitanae in north Africa, Jerusalem, Antioch, Caesarea, and Constantinople.[54] Accounts come to us from everywhere. Bishops were thought capable of miraculously breaking a famine, draining lakes, disciplining rivers, moving mountains; of floating a grounded monster of a ship or killing a monster of a dragon, merely by spitting at it; of immobilizing their enemies in a state of frozen powerlessness; and of all sorts of supernatural divining, telecommunication, speech with the dead, and the like, especially exorcism.[55] It is often specified that the wonders performed by them were witnessed by great numbers of people, much discussed at the time, held long in memory afterward, and, if the details were sometimes confused, specially recalled in memorial sermons or biographies, before at last they found a place in the more standard ecclesiastical histories. Even there, they did not lose all of their drama. In Theodoret (2.34), for example, no reader can mistake the conclusion to be drawn by contemporaries from the train of events reported: on the very night of the day bishop John is deposed from his throne, an earthquake shakes the capital, and Eudoxia in terror sends for his return. God had been watching over him. He was not as other men. Testimony to his special character had thus been made geophysically manifest, the talk of the town.

Not every bishop commanded divine attention to this degree; but the rank itself created among the masses a presumption, a readiness to accept episcopal authority. Let him then only believe in his own credo with sufficient strength, expressing himself with sufficient passion, and he would find a following to set all of the city ablaze. Constantinople's churches, at least those of them judged heretical by the new occupant of the see in April 428, accordingly went up in smoke, as many before them had been consumed in the cause of correct doctrine. They were no more than a match in bricks and mortar for the flesh and blood that was destroyed in the same cause.[56]

For all that violence in the empire's cities, of which a survey was made some pages earlier (pp. 266–67), the explanation so far offered is therefore quite uncomplicated: it was inspired at the level of the urban elite, among whom the local ecclesiastical leadership from time to time was rent apart by rivalries, unable within itself to bring such rivalries to an end, and tempted to seek a deciding power through appeal to the masses. So, trained in rhetoric and accepted as interpreters of divine intent, ecclesiastical leaders did most persuasively appeal; and the audience they addressed could hardly disobey them, representing as they did a class familiar in the role of command and capable, beyond that, of extracting howls of supplication from the very demons in the bodies of the possessed.

It remains still to be explained why questions of right worship were so often brought to the point of bloodshed by church leaders; for it was the articulate, the educated and privileged, normally the higher clergy, that were responsible for such divisions. Just what right worship was, of course they could not agree. John Chrysostom draws attention to the fact (beyond the pagans Julian and Ammianus, who note the fractious violence of Christians as a whole): a candidate for conversion can, he says, only scratch his head over which sect to approach as the true; "for there is much fighting and division among you [Christians], and much uproar. What doctrine, then, shall I choose? How can I make my selection? For each person says, '*I* speak the truth.' "[57] Differences in doctrine notoriously divided the Church—at which point, entered the conviction that divine vengeance would fall on the incorrect, as blessings would reward the correct. This, unknown in the non-Christian world, was of all ideas the most likely to increase the heat of disagreements. But it could only express itself in action and publicity when Christianity itself could do so. First blood was accordingly not spilt until 309, in the old capital, the persecutions being then finished in the west and the emperor of that time and place being well disposed to the Church. Thereafter, taught by their leaders, congregations can be seen insisting on having the right leader at their head—better none at all, as they protested at Alexandria or Cottiaeum, than the wrong one. The sense of the great seriousness of right belief was joined to a second idea, also essential within the Church, that the community of worshippers was one whole, and must be kept so, uniform in its teaching, not split into independent fractions; and *that* explains not only the continual advocacy of disputed views within the Christian world through rival broadsides put into circulation, and continual meetings in small or large synods, but the intervention of the emperor as well. It was most important to the success of his reign, as Constantine could see within only months of his conversion, that Caecilianists and Donatists should be reconciled; and his successors held to the same underlying conviction, with more or less aggressive enforcement, at other junctures and in other regions of the empire. They can be seen regularly in alliance with one side or another of a doctrinal dispute, lending it their prestige, their edicts, and their armed forces. In reply, the opposition can only depend on the masses. It was they who, seeming to embody public opinion, could give the emperors pause; for the emperors were, after all, no Oriental despots.

Beyond the two beliefs that correct doctrine was of almighty importance, and that the incorrect must be suppressed, the secular norms of the elite by themselves rather favored intransigence. Theirs was a combative class. A good quantity of circumstantial evidence suggests that bishops continued on their thrones to express these norms to a degree giving a special character to late antiquity; and occasionally they indicate in so many words what pressures they came under. Jerome, for example, takes issue with a priest who thinks he must, absolutely must, take up sides in the religious controversies of his milieu, and who, at the same time "fears that someone so eloquent in Syriac and Greek [as I, Jerome] will make the circuit of the churches [in Syria], draw over the people, and produce a schism." Plain neutrality was unimaginable. In a different mood, much later, Jerome wrote to Theophilus of Alexandria to congratulate him on taking the offensive in a doctrinal controversy of the day, after too long delay: "Hurrah for your courage, hurrah for the fervor of your faith! You have shown that your silence was of set purpose, not agreement. And may I speak freely to Your Reverence: I was distressed by your excessive long-suffering. . . . But I see now, you suspended your raised hand and the blow that you might only strike the harder."[58] And the sense of a church historian of the time confirms in more general terms what Jerome's letters indicate, when Sozomen explains why it was so very nearly impossible to end a dispute over doctrine once and for all: "In my opinion, the truth is that most people concurred in this same doctrine that accepted the Son as of the same substance with the Father. However, some continued the battle in contentious fashion against the term 'homoousios'; for, by my interpretation, some had opposed it at the outset and, as happens with *most people, considered it a disgrace to appear to be defeated.*"[59] It was the fear of losing face and of thereby losing power that pricked them on to disagree, to renew debate, carry it beyond the walls of the first encounter, publish angry tracts, hurl insults and accusations, canvass fellow bishops, intrigue for help from the court, and, failing there, draw in the physical weight of their congregations in the largest sense possible. Much of the history of the times, both secular and ecclesiastical—how the episcopacy developed, how doctrine itself took shape—can only be explained in such sequences. They gave as nothing else gave a speaking, singing, shouting part to the usually voiceless masses.

NOTES

Abbreviations used in the notes are all standard, or fuller than standard. Complete citations can be found in the list of abbreviations of such works of reference as Liddell and Scott's *A Greek-English Lexicon*, or l'Année philologique.

1. INTRODUCTION

1. Suet., *Divus Iulius* 82.2; Dio 44.19.5; Apul., *Apol.* 82; and L. Robert, "Bulletin épigraphique, 257: Afrique du Nord," *REG* 66 (1953) 201, on Greek in Africa, emphatically placing Tripolitania within "the Roman or Romanized world" (the more surprising, the Apuleius text). The closest approach to a synthesis was P. Boyancé, "La connaissance du Grec à Rome," *REL* 34 (1956) 111ff., until the appearance of J. Kaimio's work, *The Romans and the Greek Language* (1979)—the latter, probing and comprehensive (though by chance ignoring most of the items above).

2. By A. Alföldi, in the *Römische Abteilung des Deutschen Archäologischen Instituts* of 1934, later reprinted as the first half of his *Die monarchische repräsentation im römischen Kaiserreiche* (1970).

3. On A.-E. Plique and Lezoux pottery, see J. Déchelette, *Les vases céramiques ornés de la Gaule romaine (Narbonnaise, Aquitaine et Lyonnaise)* (1904) 1.139, 142f., and 147; on the continuation of the terra sigillata story, see, e.g., M. Rostovtzeff, *The Social and Economic History of the Roman Empire*[2] (1957) 617 n. 30; and, on developments subsequent to this author and, in turn, his sources, see H. W. Pleket, "Afschied van Rostovtzeff," *Lampas* 8 (1975) 267ff., and K. Greene, *The Archaeology of the Roman Economy* (1986) 156ff.

4. Besides the introduction of wine and olive production into Spain, Gaul, and even Britain, notice the improvement in wool through the replacement of the Iron Age sheep (the Soay strain relegated to St. Kilda's in the Outer Hebrides) by the so-called "Roman" sheep. For specialization, see the cooks, peddlers, bakers, and merchants of straw, linen clothing, beans, etc., recording themselves on the tombstones of a little African cemetery, in H.-G. Pflaum, "Remarques sur l'onomastique de Castellum Celtianum," in *Carnuntina*, ed. E. Swoboda (1956) 134f., and even more minute definition of one's speciality in an eastern cemetery, below, chapter 24, n. 16.

5. On lightened punishment of one's slaves in legal thought, see E. Ciccotti, *Il tramonto della schiavitù nel mondo antico* (1899), in the 1977 reprint, 282ff., looking for explanation in economics where his predecessors had looked to Christianity; or, for a recent view, A. Watson, *Roman Slave Law* (1987) chap. 8, looking to strictly juridical technical explanation; on views of marital norms, P. Veyne, "La famille et l'amour sous le Haut-Empire romain," *Annales: ESC* 33 (1978) 35, 37, and 39; and for further notes on both slavery and on gladiatorial combat, below, chapter 13, pp. 147f., and 149.

6. H. Halfmann, *Die Senatoren aus dem östlichen Teil des Imperium Romanum bis zum Ende des 2. Jahrhunderts n. Chr.* (1979), passim, with the Cappadocian (pp. 78 and 198) and Thracian senators (p. 206) noted, and exclusion made of Italian colonists,

veterans, emigrant traders, and their descendants (pp. 78–81). The thoroughness of tabulation shows in comparison with the totals in M. Hammond, "Composition of the senate, A.D. 68–235," *JRS* 47 (1967) 77, where he finds only two (not twenty-three) and ten (not fifty-nine) names. C. R. Whittaker unfortunately bases his discussion on the older figures, in "Trade and the aristocracy in the Roman empire," *Opus* 4 (1985) 65. Still earlier than Hammond, careful work was being done by P. Lambrechts in the 1930s: see his citations, p. 74.

7. A. Deman, "Matériaux et réflexions pour servir à une étude du développement et du sous-développement dans les provinces de l'empire romain," *ANRW* II, 3 (1975) 67f.

8. J. H. Hexter, "Fernand Braudel and the *monde Braudelien*," *Jnl. of Mod. Hist.* 44 (1972) 485–91. The whole essay provides an excellent view of the school.

9. The mode was, to my knowledge, first used by W. R. Macdonell, "On the expectation of life in ancient Rome, and in the provinces of Hispania and Lusitania, and in Africa," *Biometrika* 9 (1913–1914) 370 and 373, to show life expectancy in the regions indicated in his title, compared with data from England; next, by Bernhard Laum, to plot the rise in numbers of *Stiftungen in der griechischen und römischen Antike* I ([1914] 8); next, by Gunnar Mickwitz, to express precious metal content in late imperial coinage (*Geld und Wirtschaft im römischen Reich* [1932] 114); then by F. A. Hooper, "Data from Kom Abou Billou on the length of life in Graeco-Roman Egypt," *Chron. d'Egypte* 31 (1956) 339f.; next, after my own paper mentioned, that of K. Hopkins, "The age of Roman girls at marriage," *Population Studies* 18 (1965) 324, who has made extensive use of graphs in subsequent publications, here studying a body of just under four hundred inscriptions from Rome; thereafter, in virtuoso fashion, by A. Mocsy, using inscriptions to indicate the profile of "Die Unkenntnis des Lebensalters im römischen Reich," *Acta antiqua academiae scientiarum Hungaricae* 14 (1966) 393ff., and in his subsequent publications devoted to the same subject; in 1974, in my *Roman Social Relations* (p. 96), indicating wealth distribution through inscriptions, better handled in the graphs drawn by R. Duncan-Jones, "Some configurations of landholding in the Roman empire," in *Studies in Roman Property*, ed. M. I. Finley (1976) figs. 1ff.; and so on through many later uses of the medium. A better bibliographer than I could no doubt improve on this little survey.

10. B. Frier, "Roman life expectancy: Ulpian's evidence," *HSCP* 86 (1982) chart 1 at p. 218; studies with tabular presentation earlier, by A. G. Harkness, "Age at marriage and death in the Roman Empire," *TAPA* 27 (1896) 35ff., referring to still earlier studies; W. F. Willcox, "Length of life in the early Roman empire," *International Congress for Studies in Population* II (1937) 14ff., R. Etienne, "Démographie et épigraphie," *Atti del terzo Congresso Internazionale di Epigrafia greca e latine . . . 1957* (1959) 415ff., J. D. Durand, "Mortality estimates from Roman tombstone inscriptions," *Am. Jnl. of Sociology* 65 (1959–1960) 365ff., J. Szilagyi, "Zur Frage der durchschnittlichen Lebensdauer in der römischen Kaiserzeit," in *Sozialökonomische Verhältnisse im alten Orient und im klassischen Altertum*, ed. R. Günther and G. Schrot (1961) 285ff., A. Degrassi, "L'indicazione dell'età nelle iscrizioni sepolcrali latine," *Akte des IV internationales Kongresses für gr. und lat. Epigraphik . . . 1962* (1964) 72ff., and H. Nordberg, *Biometrical Notes* (1963)—to carry the story no further.

11. Hooper, *Chron. d'Egypte* 31 (1956) 332ff.; B. Boyaval, "Remarques sur les indications d'age de l'épigraphie funéraire grecque d'Egypte," *ZPE* 21 (1976) graphiques I–II.

12. R. Bagnall, "Religious conversion and onomastics," *ZPE* 69 (1987) 246f., redating a document crucial to his "Religious conversion and onomastic change in early Byzantine Egypt," *BASP* 19 (1982) 105ff., with graph, p. 124; but it is the target he chooses, and the application of a method from another field of history, that are interesting; on graphed economic activity, see J. M. Blazquez Martinez, *La economia de la Hispania Romana* (in *Historia de España Menendez Pidal* II, 1, 1982) 440.

13. M. Flory, "Family in *familia*: kinship and community in slavery," *Am. Jnl. of Anc. Hist.* 3 (1978) 82f., on "social ties" and "close bonds," having to be inferred from very exiguous evidence; B. D. Shaw, "Latin funerary epigraphy and family life in the later Roman empire," *Historia* 33 (1984) 489 and passim, discovering a sense of family generally confined within the nuclear unit, through a study of much larger samples: (for example) some 3,500 Christian funerary inscriptions.

14. Veyne, *Annales: ESC* 33 (1978) 35, the main contention of the essay being subsequently challenged from this side of the ocean; A. Rousselle, "Observations féminine et idéologie masculine," *Annales: ESC* 35 (1980) 1104f.; and the table used to present findings from among medical writers, in K. Hopkins, "Contraception in the Roman empire," *Comparative Studies in Society and History* 8 (1965) 133f., regarding various methods of birth control.

15. Constantius, *Vita S. Germani* 7.36; A. C. Dionisotti, "From Ausonius' schooldays?" *JRS* 72 (1982) 104f.; and below, chapter 20, at n. 47.

16. A. Rousselle, *Porneia: On Desire and the Body* (1988; in French, 1983) 5f., drawing of course not only on Soranus et al.; on the execution scene for adultery at Vercellae, Hier., *Ep.* 1.3–7, cf. Ambros., *Ep.* 26.3 (*PL* 16.1042C), showing the seriousness attached to sexual conduct, and especially the whole of his *Ep.* 5, on extended litigation regarding a Veronese woman's virginity, appealed to Milan.

17. R. Browning, *The Emperor Julian* (1975) 165. The evaluation quoted could be matched from many other scholars.

18. Dodds' work of 1965 has received a most admiring reception, of which P. Brown's is representative: "I have learned from Professor Dodds more than from any other living scholar that men are not so simple," and so forth, in his *The Making of Late Antiquity* (1978) 5, or J. G. Gager saying, "few small books have had as much impact as this one" (*Pagan and Christian Anxiety: A Response to E. R. Dodds* [1984] 1). For the quoted terminology of psychoanalysis in Dodds' work, see pp. 20, 42, 27f., and ("a period . . .") 135, adducing Seneca, Epictetus, Porphyry, and others, as (p. 41) he adduces St. Paul up to Synesius in laying out the Geist of "our period" (pp. 202–22), "this time" in Seneca and Jerome (pp. 28f.), and evidence in Marcus Aurelius and Celsus and so on to Proclus (d. 485).

19. Dodds, *Pagan and Christian* 57, adducing P. Oxy. 1477, often used by others before and after him; but see G. M. Browne, *The Papyri of the Sortes Astrampsychi* (1974) 17 and passim. The text is not what it seems to be, as was shown back in 1939, and doesn't prove what it has been thought to prove; and for Braudel caught in similarly unlucky moments, see Hexter op. cit. (n. 8) 513f.

20. R. P. Saller and B. D. Shaw, "Tombstones and Roman family relations in the Principate: Civilians, soldiers and slaves," *JRS* 74 (1984) 135.

21. Below, chapter 17, pp. 185f., on groups with different ideas about sexual behavior within a single society, the city of Rome; my *Corruption* 153f. and chap. 3 passim, on adjacent groups with different views regarding extortion.

2. ROMAN ELITE MOTIVATION

1. Polyb. 31.23–24.

2. For this version of Junius Pullus's death, see Cic., *Div.* 2.71; Cic., *Nat. deor.* 2.7; Val. Max. 1.4.3; on Cato's aide, see Plut., *Cato maior* 10.5; on Junius Silanus and Aemilius Scaurus, see Val. Max. 5.8.3–4; Livy, *Per.* 54, in the year of the city's founding 613–615; Frontinus, *Strat.*, 4.1.13; cf. Naevius, in Festus, 461.14–15: "and they would rather die on the spot than return to their fellows in disgrace."

3. Val. Max. 2.9.9.

4. Aul. Gell. 4.20.

5. Polyb. 6.37.4 and 13.

6. Cicero, *De rep.* 5.4; cf., for example, Naevius, in Festus 461.16–17: "But if they desert those bravest of men, it would bring great shame to the people among all nations."

7. Polybius, in Athen. 14 p. 615, in 167 B.C.

8. Plin., *N.H.* 35.22–23, in 145 B.C.

9. App., *Pun.* 9.66; for others who employed poster politics, including Scipio, see Plin., *N.H.* 35.22–23.

10. The quotation is condensed from Plin., *N.H.* 7.28.104–5, in 197 B.C.; very similar is the speech of Spurius Ligustinus, in Livy 42.34, in 171 B.C., rehearsing numbers of campaigns, promotions, and awards for bravery. [For Sergius' fame advertised on coins, see J.-L. Voisin, "Les romains chasseurs de tetes," *Du chatiment dans la cité* (1984) 235f.]

11. Livy 45.39.17, in 167 B.C.

12. Plut., *Cato maior* 19.5.

13. *ORF*³ 1.20–97, esp. 20–21, 28, 53.

14. Ibid., 101.

15. *ILS* 23.

16. Cic., *Pro Arch.* 2.5 and 9.22; Cic., *Tusc.* 1.3; Aul. Gell. 18.9.3; Val. Max. 8.14.3

17. Cic., *Pro Plancio* 59.

18. Val. Max. 2.1.10.

19. Polyb. 6.55.4; Cic., *Pro Archia* 14; on the ballads, see A. Momigliano, "Perizonius, Niebuhr and the character of early Roman tradition," *JRS* 47 (1957), esp. p. 111. They exalt *virorum laudes atque virtutes*, the praises and deeds of men; cf. Cic., *Tusc.* 4.2.3, and Cic., *Brut.* 19.75.

20. T. B. Macaulay, *Lays of Ancient Rome* (1842), "Horatius at the Bridge," stanzas 27, 65–66. For the date of the statue and the truth about the hero, see M. Delcourt, "Horatius Coclès et Mucius Scaevola," in *Hommages à Waldemar Déonna* (1957) 172ff.

21. The three quoted passages are from Polyb. 6.56.3; Plin., *N.H.* 7.43.141; Cato, *De agr.* 14.3 and 5.

22. Polyb. 31.26.8–9 and 27.11.

23. Livy, 42.47.1 and 4.

24. Polyb. 36.9.9–10.

25. Ibid., 1.39.7, *oi d'en tei Romei*, trans. as "Roman government" in *Polybius, The Histories*, ed. W. R. Paton, 6 vols. (1922–1927) 1.109, and as "les autorités" in *Polybe, Histoire*, ed. D. Roussel (1970) 44. For another instance, note the senate on the edge of declaring war on Rhodes in 167 B.C. for having the impudence to offer its services to both sides (Macedonia and Rome) as peacemaker. Cato (ed. Malcovati, 1.66) barely dissuaded the senators: "Should we be angry at someone for being even more arrogant (*superbi*) than ourselves?" Cf. a reason Caesar offers for going to war on the Germans: their arrogance cannot (that is, should not) be borne: Caes., *B.G.* 1.33.5; cf. ibid. 46.4. But it is rare to have a contemporary's open discussion of the leadership's motivation, with their very words, in this period.

26. K. Hopkins, *Conquerors and Slaves: Sociological Studies in Roman History* 1 (1978) 31–32, 35. I choose for my criticism a work of notably interesting scholarship.

27. For the second and early first centuries B.C. the draft pool can best be conjectured by use of P. A. Brunt's fine *Italian Manpower* (1971). He is frank to declare what reviewers must also note, the extreme recalcitrance of the evidence. At various points, "one guess [is] as probable as the other" (so K. Hopkins, in *JRS* 62 [1972] 192); "no solution seems certain" (so P. Salmon, in *Latomus* 31 [1972] 920); "the results issue rather out of his [Brunt's] personal estimates than from true demonstration" (so J. LeGall, in *REL* 50 [1972] 375).

28. A good phrase from H. Lüthy, *From Calvin to Rousseau* (1970) 9. For a thesis similar to Weber's, compare "the contrast of national characters" between France and England sketched by Taine and developed by Halévy from 1906 on, with its concentration on "that singularly influential class," the bourgeoisie: B. Semmel, in his edition of E. Halévy, *Birth of Methodism in England* (1971) 16 and 8.

29. M. Weber, *The Protestant Ethic and the Spirit of Capitalism*, trans. T. Parsons (1958) 17, 19, 178, and passim, indicates the universality of the Protestant differentia, in some degree.

30. R. Duncan-Jones, *The Economy of the Roman Empire: Quantitative Studies* (1974) 152–53.

31. *P[assuum]* not *p[edum]* in ibid., 158, no. 463, produces costs of HS 11.42 or 7.71 (not 22.32) depending on an entrance fee of HS 2,000 or 3,000 (or up to 10,000; see p. 152). In no. 467 (p. 159), the possible cost ranges from HS 8.05, 3 × 2,000 ÷ 248 *p[assus]*, up to HS 36.2, 3 × 3,000 ÷ 248 *p[edes]*. For *p[assus]* on road-paving, contrast ibid., 124 n. 5, or 159, no. 467h. Ibid. 159, no. 467f shows that some Augustales paid half or less of the "familiar charge" (the donors are plural, however many, but together give what a single donor gives in nos. 467d–e).

32. Dio Chrysos., *Or.*, 46.2–3. On the meaning of *euphemein*, see E. Peterson, *RhM* n.s. 78 (1929) 223; on the meaning of *philotimia*, see R. MacMullen, *Roman Social Relations* (1974) 168.

33. Plut., *Moral.* 830E; cf. ibid. 57D, with hypocrites "calling civic generosity a

thankless pursuit of empty glory,'' the passage throwing doubt on the genuineness of despair in 830E.

34. Joh. Chrysos., *De inani gloria* 4–6.

35. P. Veyne, *Le pain et le crique* (1976) 406: "a satisfaction, call it irrational or in any case basic (*irréductible*), which was not power but prestige: public giving (*évergetisme*) would remain incomprehensible if it were not granted that, among the possible elements in social differentiation, prestige belongs of a right quite as basic as power or class interest.'' Cf. Weber, op. cit. (n. 29) 71, explaining the ultimate motivation of the capitalist character in terms of the irrational: "He has nothing from his wealth for his own person—save the irrational feeling of duty well done (*guter Berufwerfüllung*)''; cf. also his attacks on the view "that valid scientific cognition is possible only in quantitative terms'': J. Freund, *The Sociology of Max Weber*, trans. M. Ilford (1968) 42. Most recently H. Putnam writes, in his *Meaning and the Moral Sciences* (1978) 74–77, "what we 'know' by empathy needs to be checked, and so is not *knowledge . . .* but *even this checking is ultimately intuitive . . .* Without a standard of objectivity provided by the imitation of physics, what are we to do? . . . The social sciences might become, in part, more 'literary'—some books might even be written well!'' (emphasis in original). It is comforting to find someone sensing the same impasse that I do, while arriving at it from so different a direction (see the whole of Putnam's lecture—with my thanks to H. Frankfort for the reference).

4. PROVINCIAL LANGUAGES IN THE ROMAN EMPIRE

1. K. Holl, *Hermes* 43 (1908) 240–54; a wider survey with bibliography in J. Sofer, *Wiener Studien* 65 (1952) 140–52.

2. Dig. 32. 11 pr. More usual is his *Regulae* 25.9, in P. F. Girard, *Textes*[6] (1937) 486, "A *fideicommissum* written in Greek is binding, but a bequest written in Greek is not binding''; or *Dig*. 46.4.8.4, *acceptilationes*, as they come under *ius gentium*, can be given in Greek if the Greek words closely fit the Latin formulae.

3. Assyrian means what we now call Syriac, as *Assyrii* means "Syrians'' (Jerome, *In Is*. 5.19.23; Hippolytus, *Philosophoumena*, ed. F. Legge, 1.123, n. 6, at 5.7; Lucian, *Octogenarians* 4) and Assyria often means Syria (idem, *Goddess of Syria* 1 [Loeb] n. ad loc.; Lucan, *B.C*. 7.636; Tatian, *Or.*, col. 888).

4. The Roman Citizenship (1939) 278 n. 7, on *Dig*. 32.11 pr.

5. On the necessity of using Latin and on limited exemptions to types of cases, to individuals, or to privileged groups, see R. Taubenschlag, *Opera minora* (1959) 1.219, 221; L. Mitteis, *Röm. Privatrecht* (1908) 1.282; H. Zilliacus, *Zum Kampf der Weltsprachen* (1935) 80–92; S. Riccobono, *Il Gnomon dell' Idios Logos* (1950) 120, with bibliography, p. 120, n. 2.

6. On the interpreters, Taubenschlag, op. cit. 2.167–70, collects the papyrological references; literary sources and inscriptions are covered without special attention to law in W. Snellman, *De interpretibus Romanorum* (1919).

7. On loan-words into Greek, see R. Cavenaile, *Aegyptus* 32 (1952) 193f.; S. Daris, ibid. 40 (1960) 177f.; and A. Cameron, *AJP* 52 (1931) 237f. The vocabulary of law and of administration, hard to separate, makes up about a third of the total of loan-words. On the use of Latin into the very late Empire (fourth and fifth centuries) in the

Greek east, see L. Hahn, *Zum Sprachenkampf in röm. Reich* (*Philologus*, Suppl. Bd. 10 [1907]) 695f., 708; C. Wessely, *Wiener Stud.* 24 (1902) 99f., esp. 122f.

8. The Book of the Laws is discussed by S. Mazzarino in *Rapports du XIe Congr. int. des sciences historiques* (1960) 2.37f.; Eng. trans. in vol. 8 of *Ante-Nicene Fathers*, 730f. The date is in dispute and may fall later in the century. On his bilingualism and his son in Athens, see A. Baumstark, *Gesch. der syrischen Lit.* (1922) 12, 14. On the mixture of local elements, Hellenism, and Palestinian Christianity, ibid. 24, 50f.

9. Jerome, *Vita Malchi* 2 (near Antioch, a Syriac-speaking monk born at Nisibis); *Vita Hilar.* 22 (monk in Gaza, whose followers at Elusa, ibid. 25, also spoke Syriac); *Ep.* 17.2 (implying a parity between Greek and Syriac in Syria generally); Chrysostom, *On the Statues, Homil.* 17.3; 19.1 (farmers around Antioch speak Syriac); Theodoret (himself reared in Syriac), *Hist. relig.* 5 (monks at Zeugma in the fourth century sing hymns, some in Greek, some "in the native tongue"; cf. ibid. 14 and 17, monks knowing only Syriac); idem, *Hist. eccl.* 4.9–10 (two groups of heretics, Audiani and Messaliani, the former from the name of its founder, the latter from Syriac "praying people," speaking Syriac, especially in monasteries near Melitene and Antioch, later in Pamphylia); Marc. Diac., *Vita Porphyr.* 66–68, mother and child in Gaza know only Syriac; *Patrologia graeca* 20.1459 (Procopius born in Jerusalem, reared in Syriac, employed as church interpreter in Scythopolis); *S. Silviae peregrinatio* 47 (*C.S.E.L.* 39, p. xiii), villagers in 385 near Jerusalem speak only Syriac or a little Greek, but the bishop, knowing Syriac, still insists on Greek for the services and is translated aloud by his Elders; for Antioch and vicinity, P. Peeters, *Tréfonds orientale de l'hagiographie* (1950) 14–17; V. Chapot, *Hellénisation du monde antique* (1914) 341, emphasizing the importance of the late revival of place-names like Hierapolis-Bambyce as a proof of a resurgence of language; R. A. Pack, *Studies in Libanius* (1935) 26 n. 3.; G. Haddad, *Aspects of Social Life in Antioch* (1949) 89, 101–3, 106–7, 115, describing the intimate mixture of languages in the middle Empire, Syriac prevailing among rustics and resurgent in the fifth century.

10. A. Vööbus, *Studies in the History of the Gospel Text in Syriac* (*Corp. script. christianorum orient.*, Subsidia 3, 1951) believes that the *Diatesseron* was originally written in Syriac (p. 12) and only slowly replaced by the "Vetus Syra" in the earlier fourth century and by the "Peshitta" (pp. 48f.) in the later fourth. Details of his views are still disputed.

11. The more important references in ancient sources to Syriac authors are generally highly admiring: Theodoret, *Hist. eccl.* 4.26; Soz., *Hist. eccl.* 3.16; Euseb. *Hist. eccl.* 4.30; Callinicus, *Vita S. Hypat.* pr. 2 (ed. Teubner, p. 4). On Syriac authors, modern authorities are Baumstark, op. cit. (n. 8) 1–100 passim (the basic treatment); Haddad op. cit. (n. 9) 114–15; A. Schall, *Studien über gr. Fremdwörter im Syrischen* (1960) 28–29; J.-B. Chabot, *Litt. syriaque* (1934) 9–41; E. M. Buytaert, *Héritage littéraire d'Eusèbe d'Émèse* (1949) 95 and 105; and C. Brockelmann, in *Handbuch der Orientalistik*, ed. B. Spuler, 3 (1954) 146–74 passim.

12. C.R.C. Allberry, *JTS* 39 (1938) 343; on early Manichaeism and its texts, ibid. 338–49; T. Säve-Soderbergh, *Studies in the Coptic Manichaean Psalm Book* (1949) 156–65, who mentions also the Mandaean elements in the work.

13. P. Ryl. 469; Allberry, op. cit. (n. 12) 348; W. Seston, in *Mél. R. Dussaud*

(1939) 1.230–34, supposing that they were incited as fifth columnists by Persia against Rome.

14. G. Steindorff, *Lehrbuch der koptischen Grammatik* (1951) 2; idem, in *Coptic Studies in Hon. of W. E. Crum* (1950) 192; M. Chaine, *Éléments de grammaire dialectale copte* (1933) xvif., xxiv; W. C. Till, *Bull. John Rylands Lib.* 40 (1957) 230f.; and H. P. Houghton, *Aegyptus* 42 (1962) 3–5. Old Coptic texts run into the fourth century, and are all pagan except for a few very late ones. On the distribution of the dialects, see J. Vergote, *Chron. d'Égypte* 36 (1961) 237f., esp. the map on p. 242. I owe the reference to Dr. D. W. Young, whom, with Dr. Cyrus Gordon, I must thank for their kindness in reading and correcting the sections on Syriac and Coptic.

15. *Monumenta Eucharistica et liturgica vetustissima* 57 (a. 325); E. R. Hardy, *Christian Egypt* (1952) 34–35 and 217 n. 28, fourth century interpreters in provincial Egypt; yet services in Egyptian, not Greek, became more common.

16. Baumstark, op. cit. (n. 8) 84f.; *Patrologia orientalis* 3.433.

17. See above, n. 9.

18. On the isolated Greek-speaking minority of a Pachomian monastery, see Hardy, op. cit. (n. 15) 73; cf. a Syrian monastery split between Greek and Syriac, in G. Bardy, *La question des langues* (1948) 20; on Anthony speaking Coptic, see Athanasius, *Vita S. Anton.* 16 and Jerome, *Vita S. Paul.* 4. E. Amélineau, *Les actes des martyrs de l'église copte* (1890) 215, 226, describes the writers and traditions of martyr stories. E.A.W. Budge, *The Paradise of the Holy Fathers* (1909) 1.xvii and 99, tells of a visitor to a community of monks in the 290s who met a number with names like Busiris = Pa-Asar. For such visitors who knew no Coptic, the monasteries had to supply interpreters (Rufin., *Hist. Monach.* 7).

19. For Bambyce, see above, n. 9; for the revival of ancient place-names in Egypt, see W. L. Westermann in *Coptic Papers Read at a Symposium . . . Brooklyn Museum 1941* (1944) 16. He does not date the changes, but I presume they appear first at a late date.

20. V. Martin, *Recherches papyrologiques* 2 (1962) 62; idem, *Mitt. aus der Papyrussammlung der Oesterr. Nationalbibliothek*[2] 5 (1956) 85–89; R. Calderini, *Aegyptus* 22 (1942) 5–31; C. E. Holm, *Gr-äg. Namenstudien* (1936), esp. 46f., 168.

21. Calderini, op. cit. (n. 20) 21; P. Oslo. 3 p. 100. "Ta-" is the feminine equivalent of "Pa-," which is also more often attested in later nomenclature.

22. S. G. Kapsomenos, *Mus. Helveticum* 10 (1953) 250–58; C. H. Roberts, ibid. 273; C. Préaux, *Mitt. aus der Papyrussammlung der Oesterr. Nationalbibliothek*[2] 5 (1956) 109f., noting a "slow deterioration of the Greek language" among ostraca going down to A.D. 258.

23. This emerges from my count of the names in G. Heuser, *Prosopographie von Aegypten 4: Die Kopten* (1938)—he covers only "A" to "E"—and in H. Munier, *Recueil des listes épiscopales de l'église copte* (1943) 3–15. The proportions do not change significantly over this period (though they do in the fifth and sixth centuries), and show Greek, Egyptian, Latin, and Hebrew in about the ratios 5:1:1:1. An exception is the group of Meletian bishops at Nicaea, 2:1:0:1 (Munier, pp. 2–3).

24. This argument and the various friendships involved appear in Peeters, op. cit. (n. 9) 28–31 and Hardy, op. cit. (n. 15) 73–74; on Shenoute and Siut, see P. du Bourguet, *Bull. de l'Inst. Fr. d'arch. orientale* 57 (1958) 119, 121, and Rémondon, ibid.

51 (1952) 68; Houghton, *Aegyptus* 42 (1962) 6; and F. Zucker, *Sitzb. der deutschen Akad. Kl. für Sprachen* (1950) 1. 17.

25. Hardy, op. cit. 53.

26. This view, often defended in recent years, is now attacked by E. Tengström, *Donatisten u. Katholiken* (1964). There is neither space nor necessity to take sides on the question here.

27. On "Berber" inscriptions being really neo-Punic, see the very convincing treatment of G. Levi Della Vida, *Oriens antiquus* 2 (1963) 65–94. R. G. Goodchild, assuming that the language is Berber, nevertheless detects much Punic in it (*Antiquaries Jnl.* 30 [1950] 141); W. Vicychl, *Jnl. Near Eastern Studies* 11 (1952) 198, 200f., and O. Rössler, in *Sybaris, Festschr. H. Krahe* (1958) 120, both go further. For Latin elements in third-century Berber (?) inscriptions, see Goodchild and Ward-Perkins, *JRS* 39 (1949) 94; on names in one district revealing Romanization among Berber-speaking people, see H.-G. Pflaum, *Carnuntina: Vorträge beim internationalen Kongresses der Altertumsforscher* (1956) 126ff., esp. 145.

28. Aur. Vict., *Epit.* 20.7, of a man reared in Lepcis before 200; Augustine, *Sermo* 288.3, of his own time.

29. Almost the only source on the question for the period after 200 is Augustine. Key passages showing Punic prevalent among Donatists, in rural areas as well as urban, lie in *In Ep. Ioan.* 2.3 (*PL* 35.1991) and *Ep.* 66.2; 108.4; 209.2–3. Some of these are well discussed by E. F. Gautier, *Le passé de l'Afrique du Nord* (1952) 135–36; more fully in the excellent article of M. Simon, *Annuaire de l'Inst. de philol. et d'hist. orientales* 13 (1953) 614–29, with careful weighing of the contrary views of Frend, Courtois, and Green. *Pace* Frend, I cannot believe that Augustine means Berber when he writes "Punic" (see *Sermo* 113.2; *Contr. litt. Petil.* 2.239).

30. A curious illustration is offered by about one hundred texts in Neo-Phrygian, all that are known, mostly curses called down on the head of whatever man violates the inscribed tomb. Some have been recently translated (A. Heubeck, *Indogerm. Forschungen* 64 [1958] 25). All these texts seem to date to the third century. It is argued either that the people who commissioned these inscriptions feared the loss of efficacy of the magic, if translated into Greek, though they themselves no longer spoke Phrygian easily (O. Haas, *Die Sprache* 6 [1960] 13 n.); or that the texts represent an artificial revival, to reach and confirm in their paganism the rural population, tending toward Christianity (W. M. Calder, *JRS* 2 [1912] 249; *JHS* 31 [1911] 163f.; *JHS* 46 [1926] 22; and on the Tekmoreian Association aimed against the Church, W. M. Ramsay, *JHS* 32 [1912] 151f.).

31. Philostorgius, epit. by Photius, *Hist. eccl.* 2.2—just as Augustine (*Retract.* 1.20; *Ep.* 54.34) "to reach the attention of the humblest masses and of the ignorant and obscure, and to fasten to their memory as much as we can," wrote anti-Donatist hymns in Latin on the model of Donatist hymns.

32. For material on Celtic gathered summarily see chapter 5, pp. 45f.; on place-names, E. Meyer, *Zeitschrift für Schweizerische Gesch.* 22 (1942) 416; C. Jullian, *CRAI* 24 (1896) 295.

33. *RhM*² 84 (1935) 301–56, esp. the map on p. 322.

34. I omit the earlier scattered Narbonnese texts in Greek letters. On those in Latin letters, see G. Dottin, *La langue Gauloise* (1920) 146–213, though his no. 52 is not

Celtic (see R. Egger, *Ogam*, 14 [1962] 431f.). For magical spells, see Dottin 43, 214, and G. Must, *Language* 36 (1960) 193–97.

35. J. Whatmough, *Keltika* (n.d. [1947]) 30.

36. Italians in the senate first drop below half (sharply, from 55 to 42 percent) under the early Severi (M. Hammond, *JRS* 47 [1957] 77, and Fig. 1 above in chapter 1; the enrollment of the senate in the first to the third centuries is discussed compendiously, ibid. 74–81). The jurists' origins are studied by W. Kunkel, *Herkunft u. soziale Stellung der röm. Juristen* (1952) 157f., where he discusses, for the period from the mid-second to early third centuries, the possibilities, great or small, of an African origin for jurists numbered in his lists 36, 41, 53, 56, 70 (cf. p. 310) and the eastern origins of nos. 55, 63, 68, 69 (cf. p. 312).

5. THE CELTIC RENAISSANCE

1. H. Koethe, "Die keltischen Rund- und Vielecktempel der Kaiserzeit," *BRGK* 23 (1933) 11f., esp. 32f. The earliest examples belong to Flavian times, and to the areas most penetrated by the Greeks, i.e., the south of France, but they represent a characteristically Celtic divergence from the more ordinary rectangular Greek and Roman temples. A similar translation of a native preference into a new medium is the niche with pilasters favored in Gallic mausolea, found from the late second century on, in all regions subject to Celtic influences: Cisalpina, Noricum, Pannonia, Germany, and the Pyrenees. See J.-J. Hatt, *La tombe gallo-romaine* (1951) 236–37.

2. L. Lengyel, *L'art gaulois dans les médailles* (1954), the photographs superb, the text to be read with extreme caution. P. Le Gentilhomme, "Le trésor de Coesmes," *Gallia* 5 (1947) 336 and 344–46, points to some more specific features of traditional Celtic art appearing in Gallic coins of the third century A.D.

3. In addition to many of the works cited below, see, on Gallic art, F. Le Roux, "Contribution à une définition de l'art celtique," *Ogam* 7 (1955) 200f.; M. Pobé and J. Roubier, *Kelten-Römer* (1958); P. Jacobsthal, "Einige Werke keltischer Kunst," *Die Antike* 10 (1934) 17–45; idem, *Early Celtic Art* (1944); and F. Hubert, *Les Celtes depuis l'époque de la Tène* (1932). The first of these, Le Roux, emphasizes the looseness and heterogeneity of the Celtic people, and of their arts, and consequently of the very word "Celtic." In an essay like the present one, it would be impossible to observe the precautions and qualifications that he recommends.

4. R. Lantier, "Masques celtiques en métal," *Monuments Piot* 37 (1940) 115; idem, "Recherches archéologiques en Gaule en 1939," *Gallia* 1 (1943) 206–7; G. Fouet, "Céramiques estampées du IVe siècle dans la Villa de Montmaurin," *Ogam* 13 (1961) 278; Hatt, op. cit. (n. 1) 183 and 243; E. Meyer, "Römisches und Keltisches in der römischen Schweiz," *Zeitschrift für Schweizerische Geschichte* 22 (1942) 406f.

5. Terra nigra, flourishing in northern Gaul for a period in the mid-first century: Hatt, "Aperçus sur l'évolution de la céramique commune gallo-romaine," *REA* 51 (1949) 110–14.

6. On Celtic techniques applied to terra sigillata, see H. Schoppa, *Die Kunst der Römerzeit in Gallien, Germanien und Britannien* (1957) 35; W. Deonna, "La persistance des caractères indigènes dans l'art de la Suisse romaine," *Genava* 12 (1934) 146f. and 154f.; Lantier, "Le vase de Gundestrup et les potiers gallo-romains," *CRAI*

1932, 303, describing the introduction into Gallic Arretine of "the stiff yet tortured forms whose popularity was due to the Celts," in, e.g., scenes of the chase.

7. Hatt, *REA* 51 (1949) 110.

8. G. Faider-Feytmans, "L'occupation de sol à l'époque romaine dans le bassin supérieure de la Haine," *Latomus* 5 (1946) 48f.; Lantier, *Gallia* 1 (1943) 207; and W. Unverzagt, "Studien zur Terra sigillata mit Rädchenverzierung," *Prähistorische Zeitschrift* 16 (1925) 124 and 156.

9. Unverzagt's was the first study (op. cit. [n. 8], esp. 124–29, 139, and 150–58), and mentions signs even of a return to polychromy, along with the more assimilable delight in plant and animal forms, in fourth-century Argonne ware. The closeness of the fourth-century to the first-century ware shows best in a comparison of his pls. 1 and 21. G. Chenet takes up the subject more recently and fully in his *Céramique gallo-romaine d'Argonne du IVe siècle* (1941), esp. 90f.

10. R. von Uslar, "Zur spätkaiserzeitlichen Drehscheibenkeramik in West- und Mitteldeutschland," *Germania* 19 (1935) 255.

11. See H. Zeiss, "Spätrömische stempelverzierte Keramik aus Portugal und Spanien," *Homenagem a Martins Sarmento* (1933) 468f., on the prevailing La Tène character of the fourth-century pottery, shown in a fondness for rosettes, concentric circles, etc., and general "geometrizing," in Spain; Deonna, *Genava* 12 (1934) 161f., on late Swiss pottery, in which, for example, incised decoration replaces relief, in the third century; A. Stroh, "Römischer Töpferofen mit einheimischer Keramik von Hailfingen," *Germania* 18 (1934) 99f., coarse ware copying La Tène styles being produced to the east of Strasbourg from the later second century; and a number of authorities who have noted in Gallic pottery a return to La Tène, beginning in the later second century and becoming more pronounced after 300: Hatt, *REA* 51 (1949) 118; Lantier, *Gallia* 14 (1956) 140; idem, *CRAI* 1932, 304; Chenet, op. cit. (n. 9) 6; and Fouet, *Ogam* 13 (1961) 276, on the period after 300.

12. On the degree of continuity in pottery from the early to the late Empire, see Lantier, *Gallia* 1 (1943) 206; Chenet, op. cit. (n. 9) 163; Deonna, *Genava* 12 (1934) 117; and Fouet, *Ogam* 13 (1961) 278.

13. Hatt, op. cit. (n. 1) 31; Lantier, "Tête d'un jeune chef Aquitain," *Monuments Piot* 37 (1940) 27; cf. Aquitanian pottery, Fouet, *Ogam* 13 (1961) 278. Pottery and sculpture trace a parallel course in another instance: the brief flourishing of Celtic styles in southern Gaul about the time of Claudius. See Hatt, *REA* 51 (1949) 110 and Schoppa, "Keltische Einflüsse in der provinzial-römischen Plastik," *Bonn. Jbb.* 158 (1958) 270. Celtic influences appear early in other less Romanized areas, e.g., around Nimwegen. See F. Winter, "Stilzusammenhänge in der römischen Skulptur Galliens und des Rheinlandes," *Bonn. Jbb.* 131 (1926) 9.

14. Schoppa, *Bonn Jbb.* 158 (1958) 272; Lantier, *Monuments Piot* 37 (1940) 27 and 37; Deonna, *Genava* 12 (1934) 122f.; Lantier, *CRAI* 1932, 307f. Similar "geometrizing" shows in the eyebrows, through an almost penciled treatment, or in the use of symmetrical whorls in beards.

15. Examples from Switzerland, Deonna, *Genava* 12 (1934) 132, sometimes transformed into abstract designs, ibid. 107; from Austria, the facing animals added to a Hellenistic motif, the pelta to produce a zoomorphic, Celtic interpretation (J. Zingerle, "Kyknos-Relief in Wien," *JOAI* 21–22 [1922–1924] 242–48); or from such fourth-

century works as the Notitia Dignitatum and the Arch of Constantine, showing the very common adaptation of the motif as the identifying device of Roman army units (A. Alföldi, "Ein spätrömisches Schildzeichen keltischer oder germanischer Herkunft," *Germania* 19 [1935] 325–27).

16. Hatt, op. cit. (n. 1) 209f.; idem, "Observations sur quelques statuettes gallo-romaines en bronze du Musée de Strasbourg," *Rev. arch. de l'Est* 12 (1961) 318; idem, "Esquisse d'une histoire de la sculpture régionale de Gaule romaine," *REA* 59 (1957) 95f. and 102f.; Schoppa, *Bonn. Jbb.* 158 (1958) 270f. and 287; L. Hahl, *Zur Stilentwicklung der provinzial-römischen Plastik in Germanien und Gallien* (1937) passim; Zingerle, *JOAI* 21–22 (1922–1924) 248.

17. What the strips were attached to is disputed. See my "Inscriptions on Roman armor," *AJA* 64 (1960) 25 n. 20; E. Meyer, "Zur Zeitlichen und kulturellen Stellung des Dolchortbandes von Gundorf," *Arbeits- und Forschungsberichte zur sächsischen Bodendenkmalpflege* 8 (1960) 7f.; and W. Coblenz, "Ein reiches kaiserzeitliches Grab aus Zauschwitz," ibid, 29f. The technique of fretwork letters goes further in some late second-century ones wholly detached, to be sewn on a baldric, from the Rhone region (P. Wuilleumier, *Gallia* 8 [1950] 146f.).

18. L. Armand-Calliat, "Deux disques en bronze de style celtique flamboyant découverts à Autun," *Gallia* 13 (1955) 86f., dating them to the third century.

19. See a study of examples from Austria by R. Noll, *Kunst der Römerzeit in Oesterreich* (1949) 28, with emphasis on the more flourishing period of Kerbschnitt technique in the fourth century (pp. 29f.), due to the barbarizing of the army and the stimulus of Germanic culture. Kerbschnitt typifies Argonne pottery, and appears also in late Roman stelae of Spain (G. Weise, "Die geistigen und formalen Grundlagen der Kunst des Mittelalters," *Die Welt als Geschichte* 1 [1935] 157).

20. For a discussion of various aspects of revived Celtic practices in jewelry (fibulae, bracelets, etc.), see A. Grenier in the *Economic Survey of Ancient Rome*, ed. T. Frank, 3 (1937) 589; K. Raddatz, "Germanische und römanische Schnallen der Kaiserzeit," *Saalburg Jb.* 15 (1956) 97, acorn terminals on buckles derived from the "Celtic renaissance" of the middle Empire, along with certain shapes of buckles; Deonna, *Genava* 12 (1934) 131–36, on bracelets with animal shapes and lozenge-and-circle decoration, in Switzerland, characteristically Celtic, with some especially striking comparisons between La Tène and fifth-century A.D. objects (p. 168, fig. 34; an equally good comparison between the metal-work of the two periods in Unverzagt, op. cit. [n. 8] 158).

21. Deonna, "Phalères celtiques et gallo-romains avec décor de têtes humaines," *Rev. arch.*[6] 35 (1950) 35f., and 147f.; the quotation from p. 176.

22. Unverzagt, op. cit. (n. 8) 158; J. Gricourt, "La terre sigillée argonnaise du IVe siècle décorée à la molette, à Bavai," *Gallia* 8 (1950) 71–72. To the older symbols, new ones of eastern origin were added from the third century on.

23. A. Schober, "Zur Entstehung und Bedeutung der provinzial-römischen Kunst," *JOAI* 26 (1930) 24f., the "Noric maiden" depicted with hair and costume worn in the old Celtic fashion; the same for Asclepius (Deonna, *Genava* 12 [1934] 118f.) who is also, with other gods, sculpted in a style of frontality and stiffness (ibid, 120–22; W. Schleiermacher, "Studien an Göttertypen der römischen Rheinprovinzen," *BRGK* 23 [1933] 138). On the continuation of Celtic iconography into the later

periods of more obvious Celtic revival, see e.g. Lantier, *CRAI* 1932, 307f.; idem, "Art celtique et art romain," *Mélanges . . . Martroye* (1941) 210; and Schoppa, *Bonn. Jbb.* 158 (1958) 274.

24. Lantier, *Gallia* 14 (1956) 145; Schleiermacher, *BRGK* 23 (1933) 109–38 passim; J. J. Jully, "Une statuette de bronze inédite de Jupiter Apollon," *Ogam* 10 (1958) 199f.; F. Drexel, "Die Götterverehrung im römischen Germanien," *BRGK* 14 (1922) 8f.; D. van Berchem, "Aspects de la domination romaine en Suisse," *Schweizerische Zeitschrift für Geschichte* 25 (1955) 158; and Zingerle, *JOAI* 21–22 (1922–1924) 232f. Schleiermacher and Drexel offer systematic studies to which the other references add confirming details. [Contra, see E. M. Wightman, *Gallia Belgica* (1985) 179 and 185, interpreting un-Romanized religion in sculpture and funerary rites as only the consequence of lower social strata being able or inclined to memorialize their traditional ways.]

25. The change in their position is not decisive, but detectable. See E. Bachelier's cautious treatment, "Les Druides en Gaule romaine," *Ogam* 11 (1959) 295 and 304.

26. The best historical treatment of the subject is C. Jullian's, in his *Histoire de la Gaule* 6 (1920) 110–23. To this, later writers can add little or nothing. Two recent returns to the question are those of P.-F. Fournier, "La persistance du gaulois au VIe siècle," *Recueil des travaux offert à M. Clovis Brunel* (1955) 1.448f., with bibliog., and J. Sofer, "Der Untergang der gallischen Landessprache und seine Nachwirkungen," *Zeitschrift für keltische Philologie* 22 (1941) 93–126. For specifically linguistic studies, see J. Whatmough, "The dialects of ancient Gaul" (microfilm-typescript 1949–1950) 55f. and passim, and J. H. Hubschmied, "Sprachliche Zeugen für das späte Aussterben des Gallischen," *Vox Romanica* 3 (1938) 48f., often cited and doubtless intelligible to linguists.

27. Koethe, "Zur gestempelten belgischen Keramik aus Trier," *Festschrift für August Oxé* (1938) 106f.

28. Hatt, op. cit. (n. 1) 31; idem, *REL* 26 (1948) 66; Meyer, *Zeitschrift für Schweizerische Geshichte* 22 (1942) 412–16. J. Sautel's interesting article on the transition of names from Celtic to Roman does not attempt to establish chronological patterns ("L'onomastique des Voconces," *Mélanges J. Sauner* [1944] 175–80).

29. Meyer, *Zeitschrift für Schweizerische Geschichte* 22 (1942) 416; Jullian, "S'il-y-a des influences celtiques dans l'empire des Gaules au IIIe siècle," *CRAI* 1896, 295; and K. F. Stroheker, *Der senatorische Adel im spätantiken Gallien* (1948) 21.

30. Schober, *JOAI* 26 (1930) 12f., passim; discussed sometimes critically by Schoppa, *Bonn. Jbb.* 158 (1958) 268f. and 280, and by Hahl, op. cit. (n. 16) 56–61 and passim. Both Schoppa and Hahl take account (as Schober often does not) of the fact that a flat, frontal, linear style may be the result not of some native tradition but of simple clumsiness on the part of the artist.

31. On the barbarian invasions as the impetus to the revival of Celtic art, see Chenet, op. cit. (n. 9) 92 and 163; Lantier, *CRAI* 1932, 304; Deonna, *Genava* 12 (1934) 116–17. On Kerbschnitt work diffused all along the northern frontiers—Rhine and Danube—see

W. Grünhagen, *Der Schatzfund von Gross Bodungen* (1954) 73 and n. 4, and Noll, op. cit. (n. 19) 29. Some isolated areas attesting Germanic penetration are discussed by Lantier, "Un cimetière du IVe siècle au Mont Augé," *Antiquité classique* 17 (1948)

393–401; M. Labrousse, "Un cimetière romain du IIIe siècle près de Brive," *Gallia* 6 (1948) 363–64; von Uslar, "Die germanische Keramik in den Kastellen Zugmantel und Saalburg," *Saalburg Jb.* 8 (1934) 63 and 83–86.

32. A. Alföldi, "Rhein und Donau in der Römerzeit," *Jahresbericht Pro Vindonissa* 1948–1949, 15–16.

33. Strasbourg was hit, and Arras, and there is scattered destruction elsewhere in the period, confirmed by a significant increase in coin hoards. A careful collection of the evidence might yield interesting results, but, to begin with, one can refer to Hatt, *Histoire de la Gaule* (1959) 185; idem, *REA* 51 (1949) 106; and Lantier and others in *Gallia* 1 (1943) 195–98; 2 (1943) 42, brigandage; 5 (1947) 225; and 12 (1954) 136.

34. Lantier offers a useful collection of references on scattered industrial sites, in *Gallia* 12 (1954) 552. Rostovtzeff handles villa autarky in his *Social and Economic History of the Roman Empire*² (1957) 616 and 634, to which examples should be added from Lantier, *Gallia* 5 (1947) 219 and 8 (1950) 225.

35. E. A. Thompson, "Peasant revolts in late Roman Gaul and Spain," *Past and Present* 2 (1952) 18, speaking of the movement in the 280s and later.

36. Le Gentilhomme, *Gallia* 5 (1947) 336–42; Hatt, op. cit. (n. 1) 211; H. Mattingly and E. A. Sydenham, *Roman Imperial Coinage* 5² (1933) 331; and A. D. Nock, "The emperor's divine comes," *JRS* 37 (1947) 105.

37. EXPECTATE VENI. One wonders how many of his subjects in Britain recognized the quotation. Yet Tetricus in Gaul addressed Aurelian, "Eripe me his, invicte, malis" (SHA, *Trig. Tyr.* 24.3, if the story has any value), and on the very roulette-relief ware characteristic of the fourth-century revival we see scenes from Vergil (Faider-Feytmans and J. Hubaux, "Moulages du IVe siècle à décors virgiliens retrouvées à Trèves," *Mélanges Grégoire* 2 [1950] 253f.).

38. *RE* Suppl. 6 (1935) col. 409 s.v. "miliarium." The leuga as a unit of distance is first encountered (rarely) under Trajan and Hadrian, and is generally adopted by Septimius Severus and later emperors. See also P. Lebel, "Bornes, centuriations, et cantonnements le long de la voie de Lyon au Rhin," *Rev. arch. de l'Est* 1 (1950) 155–56. The use of the leuga is one of the few facts to which scholars can point who believe in a resurgent nationalism in late Roman Gaul.

39. The best short summary of the scanty evidence is that of A. N. Sherwin-White, *The Roman Citizenship* (1939) 277f. Jullian's article, *CRAI* 1896, is incisive but too emphatic.

6. BARBARIAN ENCLAVES IN THE NORTHERN ROMAN EMPIRE

1. *CIL* 3.3653; 8.18224; R. Laur-Belart, *Vindonissa* (1935) 75; cf. R. Egger, *Anz. der oesterr. Akad. der Wissen.* 88 (1951) 223, for other military *macella*.

2. W. Schleiermacher, *Germania* 32 (1954) 326f. on *nundinenses* at an army camp; on border controls, L. Leschi, *Études d'épigraphie, d'arch. et d'hist. Africaines* (1957) 145f.; E. A. Thompson, *Hermes* 84 (1956) 376f.; Dio 72.11.13; 72.15; 72.19.2; *CIL* 8.6357.

3. A.E.R. Boak, *Manpower Shortage* (1955), despite contrary views expressed before and after the appearance of his book, seems to me utterly conclusive: the empire did suffer an absolute decline in population in the centuries after Marcus Aurelius, [at least at some identifiable points in the northwest quadrant most touched by barbarian

immigration—see archeological evidence referred to in my *Corruption and the Decline of Rome* (1988) 15, 19, and 22f.]. J. F. Gilliam, *AJP* 82 (1961) 225f., shows, however, that the plague under Marcus Aurelius, supposed to be the first major cause of the decline, was neither unique nor as grave as usually described; that plagues of varying severity were many and almost endemic throughout the Empire. There is some confirmation of this, and some qualification against Boak's chronological emphasis, in the unbroken series of measures to stimulate large families, especially on the countryside, from the days of the Gracchi into the fifth century A.D.

4. Strabo 7.303, on which see A. Alföldi, *JRS* 29 (1939) 28f., and in *Arch. Ertesitö* 51 (1939) 265f.

5. ILS 986, on which see Alföldi, loc. cit. (n. 4), and E. Condurachi, *Epigraphica* 19 (1957) 49f.

6. "Zumpt and Huschke offered forty-four references to forced settlements of barbarians in the Empire," according to the count of R. Clausing, *The Roman Colonate* (1925) 77, with reff. For treatments of these passages, see Clausing, 77–91; O. Seeck, *Gesch. des Untergangs* vol. 1 Anhang (1910) 590–93; and Boak, op. cit. (n. 3) 28f. and 137f. Questions of citizenship, the status of *dedititii*, and especially the relevant laws in the *Theodosian Code* are handled by E. Léotard, *Essai sur la condition des barbares* (1873).

7. The term is known only in Britain, in this connection: the *Regio Bremetennacensium* given over to Sarmatians under a *praepositus numeri et regionis*; see I. A. Richmond, *JRS* 35 (1945) 19f. The area was assigned from crown lands (H. F. Pelham, *Essays* [1911] 287 n. 5 and 293–96); from the land of *civitates* (Zos. 2.22 on Sarmatians, Constantine *dianeimas toutous tais polesin*; C. Jullian, *Hist. de la Gaule* 8 [1926] 83 n. 5, using the identifying names of barbarian troops units in the *Notitia Dignitatum*); or from the *territorium* of forts and camps, as we may presume.

8. Jullian and Richmond, locc. citt. (n. 7); R. Cagnat, *L'armée romaine d'Afrique*[2] (1913) 263f.

9. See, e.g., Orosius, *Hist. adv. paganos* 7.25.12, Sarmatians dispersed *per Romanorum finium praesidia*, confirmed by the archeological evidence.

10. A. Alföldi on the Lyons medallion, *Schweizer Münzblätter* 8 (1958) 64f. He sees in the event the settling of Germans near Mainz by Constantius Chlorus and Maximian in 296.

11. H. Vetters, *Dacia Ripensis* (1950) 5, speaking of the effect of the Gothic invasions on Dacia. He goes on to illustrate his point from the evidence of nomenclature and language, pp. 16–18. Zosimus' description of the settlement of the Bastarnae, in about the same time, on which Léotard lays stress (op. cit. [n. 6] 62, on Zos. 1.71), *tois Romaion nomois*, is mere nostalgia.

7. NOTES ON ROMANIZATION

1. Luke 2:3; Tabula Heracleensis lines 142ff. (*FIRA*[2] 1.151).

2. J. F. Gilliam, *BASP* 2 (1965) 66.

3. My own views in *JRS* 54 (1964) 50–53 and *Roman Government* (1976) 203f. and passim, on the limited powers of the central government, are in harmony with those offered to readers of F. Millar's *The Emperor in the Roman World* (1977). Defenders of traditional views, however, resist. See e.g. N. Lewis in *BASP* 13 (1976) 162 and

R. S. Bagnall in *CJ* 75 (1980) 182, where the arguments for *local* initiative, so long as it is not centrally directed, are really not relevant. Also, J. Bleicken, *Sitzungsber. Wiss. Gesellschaft J.-W. Goethe Univ.* (Frankfort) 18 (1982) 184–215, effectively answered by J. Crook, *CR* 33 (1983) 275f.

4. The army's role in individual regions is described in a hundred accounts. I attempt an overview in *Soldier and Civilian* (1963) passim, e.g. the building of aqueducts, pp. 32f., adding K. Majewski in *Latomus* 22 (1963) 504f. for Bulgaria and J. Olami and J. Ringel in *Israel Expl. Jnl.* 25 (1975) 148f. for Palestine; for ceramic production by troops, see my *Soldier and Civilian* 25 and n. 24, adding E. B. Thomas, *Römische Villen in Pannonien* (1964) 132, 181, 207, 226, 232, 257, 304, and nn. 90f.; also V. Culina in *Pontica* 3 (1970) 375f. on the *fig(lina) kas(tri)* in Bulgaria and G. Alföldy in *Epigraphische Studien* 4 (1967) 44–51.

5. As G. Barruol expressed it in a valuable essay in *Assimilation et résistance à la culture gréco-romaine . . . Travaux du VIe Congrès int. d'études classiques . . . 1974* (1976) 399.

6. A. Garcia y Bellido in *Hommages à Leon Herrmann* (1960) 374–82; cf. A. S. Anderson in *Britannia* 10 (1979) 112–14 on other legionary potteries in Britain and the Continent; on the army role in introducing Roman pottery, see MacMullen in *Phoenix* 22 (1968) 340.

7. Strabo 3.3.8. On the translation of *politikous*, see A. Garcia y Bellido in *ANRW* I/1 (1972) 483 n. 45.

8. On crops, see MacMullen in *Phoenix* 22 (1968) 339–41, adding A. Mocsy in *Acta arch. acad. sci. Hung.* 29 (1977) 385 on the Roman introduction of wine into Pannonia. On the *prata legionis* in general, see my *Soldier and Civilian*, 9–14 and, on those of Santander, Garcia y Bellido in *AEA* 29 (1956) 184–94, discussing fourteen *termini*.

9. My article, *Phoenix* 22 (1968) esp. 339, anticipates and supplies some data in support of the rich theoretical discussion by K. Hopkins in *JRS* 70 (1980) 101–4. I question only his surmise (101) that frontier armies must have "consumed" taxes beyond those raised locally, and must thus have brought about the importing of goods equal in value to the difference. But the difference may have been covered by goods produced locally. So far as acculturation is concerned, what counts is only that those goods should be of Roman style.

10. On *mercatores* in Gaul, see Caes., *B. G.* 6.37 and passim; on the quantity of money in troop neighborhoods, MacMullen and Hopkins, locc. citt. (n. 9), and my *Roman Government* (1976) 106f. with notes. We should remember also the money put into circulation prior to conquest, by subsidies, e.g. Caes., *B. G.* 1.31 (Gaul); Dio 67.7.4 and 68.6.1 with Plin., *Paneg.* 12 (Dacia); and Dio 62.2.1 (Britain, where the subsidies helped to pay for the recipient's sumptuous and purely Roman villa; see B. W. Cunliffe, *Fishbourne* [1971] 166f. on this extraordinary example of acculturation).

11. X. Yacono, *La colonisation des plaines du Chélif* (1955) 2.72f., the mid-nineteenth century, noting also the immense stimulation rendered to local agriculture. On markets near Roman camps, among many discussions, see R. von Uslar, *Saalburg Jb.* 8 (1934) 63, 83–88, and 96; idem, *Klio* 28 (1935) 295f.; and F. Diechle, *Historia* 11 (1962) 175.

12. L. Musset, *The Germanic Invasions* (1975) 14, instancing *kaufen*, *pferd*, and other words.

13. *CIL* 6.32567 (Thracian *midne* = *vicus*); C. Jullian, *Histoire de la Gaule* 4 (1914) 337, *vergobret* in Gaul; *portae* in African cities, T. Kotula in *Klio* 54 (1972) 230; and organization by regional *centuriae* in northwestern Spain, M. L. Albertos Firmat, *Organizaciones suprafamiliares en la Hispania antigua* (1975) 32f.

14. In Gaul, cf. J. F. Drinkwater, *Latomus* 37 (1978) 818; in Spain, Garcia y Bellido, *ANRW* I/1 (1972) 488, small denominations by Gades with legends in mixed Neopunic and Latin.

15. On the Tabula Heracleensis, see above, n. 1; on the practical importance of citizenship, see J. Crook, *Law and Life of Rome* (1967) 255f.; and on the ambitions of the leading classes, see below, p. 64 at nn. 31ff.

16. Despite the emphasis laid on the Constitutio Antoniniana in modern accounts, the *argumentum e silentio* certainly suggests that it was of no great importance or interest. People did indeed now call themselves Aurelii; but the Egyptian authorities distinguished among these not only through traditional grades of privilege (see P. Garnsey, *Social Status and Legal Privilege in the Roman Empire* [1970]) but also through other, new grades as well. See D. Hagedorn's discovery of first- and second-class citizenship post-212, in *BASP* 16 (1979) 54.

17. For example, inscriptions on ceramic material in Spain, in R. Etienne et al., in *Assimilation* (op. cit. [n. 5]) 98, similar to the Celtic inscriptions on south Gallic terra sigillata, or specifically at Enserune; cf. M. Clavel, *Béziers* (1970) 578f.

18. Clavel, *Béziers* 581; or Plin., *N. H.* 3.28, noting barbaric names in a corner of Spain.

19. M. Bénabou, *La résistance africaine à la romanisation* (1976) 502, where 815 of 1,945 Fortunati are African (a trait of nomenclature recalling the African fondness for -*ianus* endings).

20. L. A. Curchin, in his excellent University of Ottawa dissertation, "The Creation of a Romanized Elite in Spain" (1981), catalogues 1,236 names of *duumviri*, *sacerdotes*, and the like. Of these, 66 seem to me demonstrably or possibly indigenes (7 are doubtful; 29 date to the reign of Augustus or earlier): nos. 85, 187, 261, 278, 309–11, 315–16, 329, 339, 392, 399, 410, 411, 417, 418, 444, 445, 457, 479, 503–6, 521, 549, 550, 557, 569, 571, 580, 583, 584, 587, 588, 600–602, 726–31, 735, 843, 855, 858, 867, 900–902, 991–93, 1113, 1114, 1118, 1162, 1183, 1190, 1202, 1209, 1211. I have made use of I. Kajanto, *The Latin Cognomina* (1965) and *CIL* vol. 6 to check possibilities like Allius, Reburrus, and Pila (nos. 459, 589, and 1201).

21. In *CIL* 13 (excluding Germany and Narbonensis; thus Aquitania and Lugdunensis only) I have identified 119 elite, in Curchin's sense of the word, out of a total of 3,252 inscriptions. Excluding 25 texts (1642–1714) from the Gallic sanctuary at Lugdunum, only 22 remain that seem clearly indigenous: *CIL* 13.5, 17, 966, 1036, 1042–45, 1048, 1390, 1541, 1571, 1577, 1606, 1911, 1922, 1985, 2449, 2453, 2669, 2839, and 2949. I have used A. T. Holder, *Alt-celtischer Sprachschatz* (1896–1913) to identify certain doubtful cases.

22. I draw on J. G. Liebenow, *Liberia* (1969) esp. 24–27 and 134–37; I. K. Sundiata, *Black Scandal* (1980) 7–9; and T. W. Schick, *Behold the Promised Land* (1977) esp. 100, and the quotations from 107 and 142.

23. For the named estates, and others like Traius, Curius, Paternus, or Rabulius, see F. Didierjean in *Mél. de la Casa Velazquéz* 14 (1978) 22.

24. Garcia y Bellido and J. Gonzalez Echegaray in *AEA* 22 (1949) 245, the inscription often noted since, e.g. by M. Vigil, *Boletín de la Real Acad. Hist.* 152 (1963) 225f. Note misspelling (*possuit*), Celtic filiation (*Cesti f.*) and locative usage (gen. plu. *Aunigainum*). Among numberless illustrations of the weak Romanization of rural cults, see for instance M. Le Glay, *Saturne africain: Histoire* (1966) 268 and passim, or Aisus (misspelled, Esus) invoked in a fifth-century A.D. Celtic spell, in G. Must, *Language* 36 (1960) 197. For illustration of how pottery is used as a clue to Romanization, see e.g. Didierjean, op. cit. (n. 23) 30 (terra sigillata only in urban and rich rural settings), and G. Fouet in *Ogam* 13 (1961) 278 or R. Etienne, *Ruscino . . .* I (1980) 367 (indigenous styles survive only in cheap coarse ware). For illustration of Latinity being used as an index, see e.g. G. Dottin, *La langue gauloise* (1920) 70, who notes Gallic inscriptions still in the third century on spindle weights used by common folk; also examples in MacMullen, *AJP* 87 (1966) 5, 9, and 14, to which other items could be added: Y. Yadin in *Israel Expl. Jnl.* 12 (1962) 235, for instance, who publishes an archive showing the owner simultaneously using Nabataean, Aramaic, and Greek.

25. Eugippius, *Vita S. Severini* 14.3, "the woman . . . did the work in the fields with her own hands in the fashion of the country"; J. Fitz in *Arch. Ert.* 84 (1957) 152f. on fibulae etc. and non-Roman nomenclature; G. Piccottini, *Die Dienerinnen- u. Dienerreliefs des Stadtgebietes von Virunum* (1977) 6 and 22 with Taf. 5 no. 190, on costume and the Norican cult of the dead; for the style of sculpture, see A. Schober in *JOAI* 26 (1930) 24f., W. Deonna in *Genava* 12 (1934) 122f., D. Protase in *Studii clasice* 3 (1961) 133f., and esp. R. Laur-Belart in *La rayonnement des civilisations grecque et romaine . . . Huitième Congrès int. d'arch. classique 1963* (1965) 174 in combination with J. C. Balty in *Eikones . . . Hans Jucker . . . gewidmet* (1980) 57, 60 and 62. The last two scholars point up the essential Celtic-ness of a gold portrait bust (wrongly identified as Marcus Aurelius) and identify it convincingly as Julian.

26. Garcia y Bellido in *ANRW* I/1 (1972) 490 on the *lingua barbarica* (the date of the text contested); on Coptism established as the most dynamic element in Egypt by the mid-fifth century, see my sketch in *Aegyptus* 44 (1964) 197; on other languages, above, nn. 14, 17 and 24.

27. To my survey in *Enemies of the Roman Order* (1966) 228–34 with notes, much could be added, e.g. D. Gabler on post-250 revivals in ceramic styles, in *Arch. Ert.* 103 (1976) 52.

28. Irenaeus, *Contra haer.* 1 praef.; more generally on attitudes toward the hinterlands, see my *Roman Social Relations* (1974) 30–32 and 45–47.

29. Bénabou, op. cit. (n. 19) 496, speaking of burials among "les couches d'Africains qui sont à la périphérie de la romanisation"—the very strata in which indigenism is represented.

30. Above, n. 25; J. Garbsch, *Die norisch-pannonische Frauentracht* (1965) 3, notes that female costume retains Celtic character "in opposition to male costume," e.g. fig. 3 and p. 146; the same relief in Piccottini, op. cit. (n. 25) 22 and Taf. 5 no. 190, with the inscription *C. Tertinio Statuto aedilicio Catronia Severra*, etc. (note Romanized husband, office-holder; misspelling of her own name; and on her name's

derivation, Holder, op. cit. [n. 21], s.v.). Compare also J. Klemenc in *Omagiu lui Constantin Daicoviciu* (1960) 307, the wife of Q. Ennius Liberatus (good Roman name) in "typical Celtic costume" (p. 305, date early Antonine); E. Neuffer in *Germania* 16 (1932) 24f. on a three-part relief showing a woman in native costume with her husband *togatus* (first century A.D.); also J. Marion in *Bull. d'arch. marocaine* 4 (1960) 175, Libyan cognomina easier to find among women than men (but I do not accept Marion's unsubstantiated guess that men = fathers chose such names), and retention of Semitic names by Syrian women generations after the males were given Greco-Roman, as noted by J.-P. Rey-Coquais in *Actes du VII Congres int. d'épigraphie grecque et latine . . . 1977* (1979) 177. On the other hand, as exceptional, H. J. Leon, *The Jews of Ancient Rome* (1960) 109 and 121, notes that Jewish female children pass under alien customs—ordinary Latin names, or Greek or Latin names rhyming with Jewish—more rapidly than males.

31. Even in so richly informed a work as that of M. Bénabou (op. cit., n. 19), there are only two or three lines (p. 499) devoted to the motives for cultural change; and I recall nothing more than that in all my reading.

32. E.g. Strabo 3.3.5–8 and 3.4.5; Velleius 2.106.2, 117.3, and 118.1 (Germans); Tac., *Agr.* 21.1 (British tribes *in bella faciles*); and A. Van Doorselaer in *Helinium* 5 (1965) 119f. and 127, on Gallic burials with arms run on from pre-Roman days to become more common in the second century, a "survival of pre-Roman traditions which now reappeared thanks to economic improvement among the Romanized ruling classes."

33. Caes., *B. G.* 1.1, 2.15, and 4.2.

34. Cic., *Pison.* 53 and *Font.* 33; Suet., *Iul.* 80.2; in contrast, *togati* with full overtones of "acceptable" in, e.g., Strabo 3.2.15 and 3.4.20.

35. Dio Chrys., *Or.* 36.17, of a scene in Borysthenes; cf. Philostr., *Ep. Apollonii* 70, "no [Athenian] ever grew a full beard. . . . The flatterer stands at their [the Romans'] door, the sycophant before their gates" at Sais in Egypt (second century?).

36. For the complete rejection of Romans by natives, notice how the richer cities of Asia and the whole province of Cyprus in Cicero's day (*Ad. Att.* 5.21.7) paid huge sums not to have troops wintering in their homes; and for the same situation later, see my *Soldier and Civilian* 77f.

8. ROMAN BUREAUCRATESE

1. The two passages are from *Cod. Theod.* 1.12.1 and 1.16.7. Repetition in the latter may be less hysterical than rhetorical. Cf. 6.4.15, where Constantius speaks to the senate about a certain precedent which "ought, it ought, to have reminded others also" of the duties of their rank.

2. For example, palatine troops are exempt from all public burdens whatsoever, in *Cod. Theod.* 6.35.1 (A.D. 314), which is repeated in 6.35.2–6 and 8–11, over the years 314 to 381; and governors are told eight times not to initiate any new building till they have completed older projects, in 15.1.3 (A.D. 326), 15, 16, 17, 19, 21, 29, and 37 (A.D. 398). Tacitus is right: *in pessima republica plurimae leges*.

3. *Or.* 47.37–8; P. Petit, *Libanios et la vie municipale à Antioche . . .* (1954) 68 n. 1.

4. J. A. McGeachy, *Quintus Aurelius Symmachus* (1942) 85 on *Relatio* 31. Other

particularly glaring examples of the impotence of the emperor are discussed in C. H. Coster, *The Iudicium Quinquevirale* (1935) 6, and B. H. Warmington on Count Romanus, in *BZ* 49 (1956) 55ff.

5. On these guilds the best account is A.H.M. Jones', in *JRS* 39 (1949) 41ff.; but there is valuable material also in W. G. Sinnigen, *The Officium of the Urban Prefecture* (1957) 11ff., 64ff. They refer to the earlier works of E. Stein, J. P. Waltzing, and T. Mommsen. Two quite neglected authorities are worth mentioning: A. Marchi, in *Archivio giuridico* 76 (1906) 291ff., whose treatment of the sale of *militiae* is essential; and (if only as a curiosity) P. Louis-Lucas, *Étude sur la vénalité des charges et fonctions publiques* (1883), especially vol. I. Louis-Lucas is incredibly prolix (in I.241–94 there are sixty lines of text and over three thousand of notes!), but on some questions uniquely thorough. G. Kolias, *Ämter- und Würdenkauf* (1939), concerns himself mostly with a later period, but see pp. 20ff. On the corruption prevalent in the late Roman period, there is an embarrassment of material. In more modern works, see A. Alföldi, *A Conflict of Ideas* (1952) chap. 3, esp. pp. 35–36; S. Le R. Wallace, *Taxation in Egypt* (1938) 323; E. Stein, *Histoire du bas empire* I (1959) 50; R. Grosse, *Römische Militärgeschichte* (1920) 247ff., and J. Karayannopulos, *Das Finanzwesen* (1958) 13ff. The phrase quoted in the text, *cum suis commodis*, ''with its perquisites'' (*Dig.* 31.1.49, Paul; cf. 32.102.2, Scaevola), suggests that posts in the bureaucracy were yielding a fair profit, and fetching a fair price on the market, as early as Severan times.

6. J. P. Waltzing, *Corporations professionnelles* (1895–1900) I 54, speaking of the *decuriae apparitorum* and *scribarum* in Rome, with a history reaching back to the Republic, sometimes even calling themselves *collegia*. Whether the incorporated *officia* of the fourth century developed from these (largely Roman) guilds, or, with the militarization of the civil service, from the guilds of army officers permitted from Septimius Severus' time, is not clear.

7. *Cod. Theod.* 8.9.2 (382) on the dividend and Lydus, *De mag.* 3.25, on the amounts due to the chiefs of staff. Army staffs were obliged to pay their chiefs a certain sum (derived historically from their superiors' embezzlements) countenanced by law, or at least by custom: Mommsen in *EE* 5 (1884) 642ff.; L. Casson, in *Aegyptus* 32 (1952) 58ff.; *Publications of the Princeton Archaeological Expeditions to Syria* III A 2 (1910) 29ff., esp. 35. Corporate organization in troop units is shown in the provision that the whole company of his *commilitones* should divide the unconsumed rations of a deceased comrade. See, e.g., *Cod. Theod.* 14.17.8 (380).

8. *Cod. Theod.* 11.30.8 (319) is an especially clear instance of a normal arrangement. If a *iudex* delays action on an appeal, the entire staff (*universum officium*) shall pay a fine. ''For the office staff must urge Our decrees upon the *iudex*, and if he should ignore their recommendations, they must oppose him; and as though by forcible seizure they must lead him into court, deliver him to the office of the fiscal accounts, and obligate him with the bonds of the former statute, if they should perceive that he is violating Our sanctions.'' They must ''admonish'' him (11.30.34 [364]), and pay a fine for connivance. See 11.30.29, 11.30.58, and 12.1.85.

9. Lactantius, *De mort. persecut.* 22; *Cod. Theod.* 14.1.1 (357/360), that no one shall rise in the *decuriae* who is not ''so polished that words proceed from him without the offense of imperfections.''

10. SHA *Ant. Pius* 11.1, *Sev. Alex.* 36.2–3, 67.2.

11. O. J. Zimmermann, *The Late Latin Vocabulary of the Variae of Cassiodorus* (1944) 107; on the custom of soliciting *suffragia*, G.E.M. de Ste. Croix, *Brit. Jnl. Sociol.* 5 (1954) 33ff. (passim) and H.-G. Pflaum, *Les procurateurs équestres* (1950) 195ff.; and on *introitus* similarly narrowed to mean "entrance fee," Marchi, *Arch. giurid.* 76 (1906) 318ff.

12. For *stillatura*, see *Cod. Theod.* 7.4.28.1 (406), "an emolument under the title of *stillatura*" on which the recipients are trying to get a further "rake-off" by juggling the commutation rates of supplies in kind and in cash. For *salgamum*, ibid. 7.9.3 (393), demands made *salgami nomine*. For *sportulae*, a common word with a long history, see e.g. PSI 1026 (150); G. Behrens, in *Mainz. Zeitschr.* 35 (1940) 82; and *Cod. Theod.* 6.24.3 (364/365)—examples from papyri, inscriptions and laws, covering four centuries of the Empire. For *munusculum*, *Cod. Theod.* 11.11.1 (368/370/373), the affectionate diminutive, from *munus*, like *lucellum* from *lucrum*, 1.31.2 (368/370). For Gr. *xenia*, 11.11.1 and *Dig.* 1.16.6.3. The word, like "bakshish," "lagniappe," "douceur," and "largesse" in English, was adopted into Latin (*xenia*) probably because its foreign extraction served better to muffle its meaning. J.N.L. Myres, *JRS* 50 (1960) 25f., shows how, in the second half of the fourth century, *gratia* shifted from "favor" to "favoritism," *gratiosus* from "gracious" to "corrupt," and *potentia* and *potentes* from "powerful" to "wickedly powerful, oppressive."

13. Anon. *De rebus bell.* 4.1 (ed. E. A. Thompson, *A Roman Reformer* . . . [1952]); *sollemnia lucra*, developing into payments under the name *ton kaloumenon solemnion*, in Justinian's day (Karayannopulos, op. cit. [n. 5] 16)—another example of the usefulness of a foreign word (see preceding note).

14. Amm. 22.6.5 and Lydus, *De mag.* 3.27.

15. *IGR* 3.1119 (third century); *Cod. Theod.* 8.5.21 (364), a *novum rapinarum aut fraudium genus*; and 7.4.12 (364?). Tacitus mentions taxes "bearing names invented by the collectors" (*Ann.* 13.51) but there is of course more evidence for a later period. See the petitioners complaining that "we do not know into what account [our payments] have gone" (P. Cair. Isidor. 73, A.D. 314) or against the collectors *onomata heautois exeurontes*, "making up titles for themselves" of P. Oxy. 58 (288).

16. *Cod. Theod.* 14.1.1 and 6.26.1. On the extraordinary prestige enjoyed by rhetoricians and *literati*, see Coster, op. cit. (n. 4) 11 and Alföldi, op. cit. (n. 5) 106ff., who both turn to China for a parallel "veneration for culture, and especially for literature." Alföldi's full and excellent treatment is marred only by an unwillingness to see earlier precedents for the condition. In the second century, or in the first, for that matter, while literature alone might not carry a man to the top, it was still often a vital companion to a career. See some examples in H. Bardon, *La littérature inconnue* II (1956) 179ff., 208, and 214; A. Calderini, *I Severi* (1949) 6ff.; *CAH* 10.610 (M. P. Charlesworth) and 828 (G. H. Stevenson); Frontinus, the Plinies, Silius Italicus, Appian, Tacitus, and some of the men whom the last mentions (*Hist.* 1.8), and A. Claudius Charax (C. Habicht, in *Istanbuler Mitt.* 9–10 [1959–1960] 110f.). Three decisive passages show advancement specifically on the basis of scholarly pretentions: Dio 72.22.2, 72.35.2, and SHA *Hadr.* 3.11.

17. Alföldi, loc. cit., gathers much evidence. A very incomplete list of such figures would draw on Eusebius, *H. E.* 7.32.2–3; Amm. 17.5.15, 22.1.2, 27.9.6, 28.1.45;

Zos. 4.41.3; Eunapius, *Vit. soph.* 465, 490; Auson., *Praefatiunculae* 35ff., *Domestica* 41ff., *Parentalia* 14.9ff., *Ep.* 12, *Comm. profess.* 1.9ff., 15.18, 17.12ff.; *Grat. act.* 4, 7, and 9; Bardon, op. cit. (n. 16) 290, 299; McGeachy, op. cit. (n. 4) 159ff.; H. Bloch, *HThR* 38 (1945) 206; L. Robert, *Hellenica* 4 (1948) 24ff.; A. Steinwenter, *ZSS* 65 (1947) 114ff.; and A. Fitzgerald, *The Letters of Synesius* (1926) 258 n. 2. The men whose works survive include Ausonius, Zosimus, Tiberianus, Macrobius, Symmachus, and Latinius (author of the last of the Latin panegyrics).

18. Amm. 30.4.14.

19. Amm. 30.4.11–13; H. Hagendahl, *Studia Ammianea* (1921) 100ff.; and A. Müller, in *Philologus* 64 (1905) 574ff.

20. A.H.M. Jones, *JRS* 47 (1957) 88, instancing *Cod. Theod.* 11.1.15, which substitutes *sortes* for *iugatio*; A. J. Fridh, *Terminologie et formules dans les Variae de Cassiodore* (1956) 73ff. (finding in the Codes eighteen names for the letter of authorization issued by the emperor [*beneficium, oraculum, ordinatio*, etc.]), 112ff. (similar variants for other types of document [complaints and petitions] sent in to the emperor); and F. Zucker, *BZ* 30 (1930) 152ff., on the multiplication of synonyms, e.g. (*Studien zur Palaeographie und Papyruskunde* 20 [1921] 121), *omologo ekousiai gnomei kai authairetoi kai ametanoetoi kai adoloi proairesei*, in papyri of a legal or official type—in this truly wild example, a bill of sale. Cassiodorus offers some late parallels, in his letters of appointment (*Variae* 7, passim); but that this practice was not of his invention can be seen in Ausonius, *Grat. act.* 9 (lines 291f. Peiper), where Gratian says *te consulem designavi et declaravi et priorem nuncupavi* (A.D. 379).

21. G. Orwell, *Shooting an Elephant and Other Essays* (1950) 88.

22. *Nov. Just.* 13.4; Zimmermann, op. cit. (n. 11), 136, 140; *Cod. Theod.* 11.1.20, 11.24.1, 11.24.6; D. van Berchem, *BSAF* 10 (1937) 130.

23. Trans. E. R. Graser, in *Economic Survey of the Roman Empire*, T. Frank, 5 (1940) 314.

24. *IGLS* 1998 (Domitian) is a good instance of the explanatory preface, though it is a relatively modest and succinct one. Further development can be illustrated by a comparison of the laws relating to the lease of imperial land in Africa, an edict to Trajan beginning abruptly, *qui eorum intra fundo . . .* , and that of Hadrian beginning, *quia Caesar noster pro infatigabili cura per quam adsidue pro humanis utilitatibus excubat, omnes partes agrorum . . .* (Bruns, *Fontes iuris Romani antiqui* 1 [7th ed. 1909] nos. 114, 115). For the role of Hadrian in the history of chancery Latin, see below. A further step is clear in various Severan edicts: *OGIS* 515 (209/211) lines 47–52, just cited in the text; the *Constitutio Antoniniana*; and P. Fay. 20 (Severus Alexander; see W. Schubart, in *Archiv für Papyrusforschung* 14 [1941] 57). Philostratus, *Vit. soph.* 2.24, speaks of a rhetorician called Antipater, who "weakened the force of his ideas by the rhythmical effects of his style," but who, when the emperor supplied the ideas, "proved brilliantly successful," partly through "the pleasing effect secured by the use of asyndeton." He was *ab epistulis* to Septimius Severus. For the mature, or already over-ripe, specimens of such diction, the better-known texts are the *Edictum de pretiis* (301; trans. Graser in *Economic Survey* 5.314); P. Cair. Isidor. 1 (297)— "Our most provident Emperors . . . to root out this most evil and ruinous practice . . ."; and the Brigetio Table (see E. Paulovics, in *Arch. Hungarica* 20 [1936] 49) beginning, "since in all things we are desirous always of taking notice of the comforts

and needs of our soldiers, as befits their devotion and labors, so in this instance, by the foresight of our provisions, we believe.'' See more generally Fridh, op. cit. (n. 20) 40ff. (early instances even under Augustus), 49ff. (the fully developed explanatory preface appearing under Diocletian), and passim; and E. Vernay, in *Études d'histoire juridique offertes à P. F. Girard* II (1913) 263–74, giving Diocletian's as the reign that sets the mode, though with first-century precedents.

25. For the reversion to a clear, terse language in the sixth century, see E. Grupe, *Zeitschr. für Rechtsgesch.* 14 (1893) 225ff., 15 (1894) 341ff.; and F. Schulz, *History of Roman Legal Science* (1946) 328.

26. For these stages and participants in the history of chancery, Schulz, op. cit. (n. 25) 96ff., 258ff., 328; E. Volterra, *Mél. H. Lévy-Bruhl* (Publications de l'Institut de droit romain de l'Université 17, 1959) 327ff.; Steinwenter, op. cit. (n. 17) 93ff., 108ff., 118; Vernay, op. cit. (n. 24) 268–74; and H. P. Jolowicz, *Historical Introduction to Roman Law*[2] (1952) 481; on the union of rhetorical and legal training in the persons of the upper administration, above nn. 16, 17.

27. Jolowicz, loc. cit. (n. 26): ''This rhetorical style . . . frequently makes the legislator's intention very difficult to discover''; and Schulz, op. cit. (n. 25) 328: ''it is a labor to extract the sense from the flowery verbiage.'' To this opinion the chief witness is the large number of ''interpretations'' added to the constitutions of the Theodosian Code.

28. *Cod. Theod.* 9.38.6 (381); cf. 8.15.5, to ''those who under the name of prison registrars guard the prisons that are loathed by unhappy men.''

29. Julian, *Ep.* 56, the basis of *Cod. Theod.* 9.17.5 (W. D. Wright, in the Loeb edition of Julian, III 190 n. 2). Yet the letter is no more involved than the labyrinthine one of Constantine to the Antiochans (Eusebius, *Vita Const.* 3.60). To A.H.M. Jones, *Constantine and the Conversion of Europe* (1948) xiii, a very proof of the genuineness of such documents in Eusebius is the fact that ''they are written in a uniformly turgid and long-winded style.''

30. The sophist Heliodorus instructed a friend, ''as though he were an advocate at the bar, what to put at the beginning of his speech . . . or with which figures of rhetoric he ought to aim at brilliant passages'' (Amm. 29.2.8), while Symmachus could remind Patricius, *magister memoriae, tuum sacris tibiis carmen incinere*, ''it is your task to sound the song upon the imperial pipes'' (*Ep.* 7.60.2)—a regular invitation to versify.

31. *Edoxen autou tei megalioteti*, W.H.C. Frend, *JRS* 46 (1956) 47, part of a third-century decision rendered ''in language at once servile and ornate'' (ibid. 52); *tes ses andreias*, P. Cair. Isidor. 66 (299); *dignationis suae respectu*, in *CIL* 10.520 (end of the fourth century); and B. H. Warmington, *PBSR* 22 (1954) 46, commenting on the change in the fashion of address to a patron, from the relative simplicity of the first two centuries to ''the extravagant terms then [in the third century] becoming popular.''

32. M. J. Higgins, in *Traditio* 3 (1945) 74ff.

33. Zucker, *BZ* 30 (1930) 148–49; and P. Collinet, *REL* 5 (1927) 254ff., finding the use of rhythmic *clausulae* so common in later laws that they can be used even to detect interpolations. Rare before Diocletian, usual in the fourth, such *clausulae* become mandatory in the second quarter of the fifth century.

34. H. Zilliacus, *Eranos* 54 (1956) 161ff.

300 NOTES TO CHAPTER 8

35. Zucker, *BZ* 30 (1930) 151; Zilliacus, *Eranos* 54 (1956) 162ff.; G. Böhlig, *Untersuchungen zum rhetorischen Sprachgebrauch* (1956) 232.

36. Zilliacus, *Eranos* 54 (1956) 165; C. L. Hrdlicka, *A Study of the Late Latin Vocabulary . . . in . . . St. Augustine* (1931) 2; A. Ernout, *Aspects du vocabulaire latin* (1954) 180ff.; and R. G. Kent, *TAPA* 50 (1919) 98.

37. Higgins op. cit. (n. 32) 3.91ff.; Steinwenter op. cit. (n. 17) 92ff.; P. Lond. 1927.

38. E. Löfstedt, *Late Latin* (1959) 151; Fridh, op. cit. (n. 20) 159ff.; Paulovics, *Arch. Hung.* 20 (1936) 47 n. 33; *Cod. Theod.* 6.24.6, 6.26.13, 15.1.38; above, n. 31.

39. *Dig.* 1.4.1

40. In *Cod. Theod.* 12.12.14, Theodosius II invites recommendations from his praetorian prefect; 8.9.1 (335) declares that *ordines decuriarum . . . oblatis precibus meruerunt*; Fridh, op. cit. (n. 20) 116 writes on *desideria*, which generally expressed the wishes of a city or whole province; and see, on *suggestiones*, Fridh 122ff.; S. Dill, *Roman Society in the Last Century of the Western Empire* (1899) 230; and especially W. Ensslin, in *Studi in onore di A. Calderini e R. Paribeni* I (1956) 315ff. Evidence for these petitions seems more abundant in the second half of the fourth century.

41. On Synesius, see Coster, *Byzantion* 15 (1940–1941) 16ff., 26ff.; Fitzgerald, op. cit. (n. 17) 25; and L. Harmand, *Libanius, Discours sur les patronages* (1955) 98. On Libanius, ibid. 99ff., esp. 104; P. Petit in *Historia* 5 (1956) 479ff. (passim), esp. 495f., 500f.; R. A. Pack, *Studies in Libanius* (1935) 45, 49, 108. On Symmachus, McGeachy, op. cit. (n. 4) 13, 47ff.

42. That rulers should make every effort to encourage communications from their subjects was agreed among ancient philosophers. Late examples include Themistius, *Or.* 1.19; Synesius, *De regno* 17 (reinforcing the point with a quotation from the *Iliad*); and Julian, *Panegyric in Honor of Constantius* 17, where, in direct address to the emperor, he says, "[you] granted to your friends . . . the privilege of addressing you as an equal and full freedom of speech." See also his *Heroic Deeds of Constantius* 97, making the same point, which Julian knew (none better) was a pure lie.

43. These false praises include Julian's speeches to Constantius, Symmachus' to Valentinian (Alföldi, op. cit. [n. 5] 84), and that of the envoy recorded in Amm. 30.5.8–9.

44. Suppression of the name of the emperor's enemies had a long history, best visible in erasures of inscriptions. An early instance in literature is Augustus' detour around the name of Lepidus (*Res gestae* 10.2). Later instances are Eusebius, *Vita C.* 1.49; *Incerti panegyricus Constantio dictus* 6.1 and 12.1 (ed. E. Galletier, *Panégyriques latins* 1 [1949] 86, 91); and Themistius, *Or.* 1.13.

45. On the council sessions, see C. Zakrzewski, *Eos* 31 (1928) 405ff., esp. 413, and A. Christophilopulu, *BZ* 44 (1951) 80ff. Utter silence was possible, to be sure, only before imperial announcements, especially those summing up the decisions of the council sitting in a judicial capacity. But there is no doubt that debate was extremely stiff and limited. Jones, op. cit. (n. 29) 164–65, mentions, at Nicaea, the "paralyzing . . . effect [Constantine's] imperial presence had on free discussion." It was significant, too, that in about this period (the first use of the word in Lactantius) the room for writing or sealing of documents began to be called the *secretarium*, though *secretarius*

(hence our "secretary") dates to the mid-fifth century (A. Kraus, *Römische Quartalschr.* 56 [1960] 45ff.).

46. *Praef.* 3 and 10 (trans. Thompson, op. cit. [n. 13]).

47. *Pan. vet.* 6(7).7.1 and 2, 6(7).14.1, 10(4).5.1 (ed. Galletier, *Panégyriques latins* 2 [1952] 21, 28, 170). Charlesworth's interesting article, *JRS* 37 (1947) 34–38, gathers the texts on imperial deportment, but add *Pan. vet.* 7(6).4.4 (3.57 Galletier), on Constantine's *adspectus: eadem in fronte gravitas, eadem in oculis et in ore tranquillitas.*

48. R. Marichal, "L'écriture latine de la chancellerie impériale romaine," *Aegyptus* 32 (1952) 336–50, analyzes the writing of the period around 300, giving examples, papyrological and epigraphical, where the recipient of a chancery document simply could not read what had been sent to him. The close wedding of "the rhetorical bombast of speech" and the chancery hand of the fourth century is stressed by Schubart, *Griechische Palaeographie* (1925) 86–87.

49. L. Lafoscade, *De epistulis aliisque titulis imperatorum magistratuumque Romanorum* (1902) 75, 93, 99.

50. There are two ways of attacking the question: the literary, which tends to be an outcry not an analysis, and the sociological. Of the first, "Vigilans," *Chamber of Horrors*, introd. E. Partridge (1952) 9–10, supplies a good bibliography (note esp. various works of A. P. Herbert, and add chap. 5 of D. Macdonald, *The Ford Foundation* [1956] on "foundationese," and R. C. Doty, *New York Times Magazine*, October 18, 1959, on "military agglomerese"). With the help of colleagues, particularly Dr. James Price, I have made a fairly thorough search for a sociological study of bureaucratese, in vain. Sociologists, notoriously bad writers of English, are apparently not sensitive to the problem. At any rate, *Current Sociology* 7, no. 2 (1958) lists nothing—though it does say of one item (no. 93): "Answers to all questions posed are integral aspects of the requirements for a systematic appraisal of the ideological goals and institutional framework of the societies in question"!

51. Above, p. 69; add F. M. Marx, *Review of Politics* 3 (1941) 100: "the unprecedented growth of bureaucracy is one of the striking features of totalitarianism."

52. Karayannopulos, op. cit. (n. 5) 13, says something on the sluggish pace of government; see also above n. 1; but the sources are full of postponed trials, forgotten appeals, and delays of action. As to forms, they were a necessary part of legal documents and naturally dominated bureaucratese. New ones were invented as need arose (e.g. L. Mitteis, *Hermes* 30 [1895] 567ff., on a form new in the third century) and became more cumbersome (above, n. 20).

53. Jones, *JRS* 39 (1949) 50.

9. SOME PICTURES IN AMMIANUS MARCELLINUS

1. On the ceremonies of the later Empire, generally studied with reference only to the emperor himself, the literature is now very abundant. The name most often cited is A. Alföldi, whose kindness in criticizing this paper deserves special thanks. His own two classic articles, "Die Ausgestaltung des monarchischen Zeremoniells am römischen Kaiserhofe," *Mitt. Deut. arch. Inst., römische Abteilung* 49 (1934) (hereafter "Ausgestaltung") and "Insignien und Tracht der römischen Kaiser," ibid. 50 (1935) (hereafter "Isignien"), are the main foundation for the subject, which has since been

divided and pursued by narrower specialists: R. Delbrück, for instance, on costume, in his *Die Consulardiptychen* (1929); "Der spätantike Kaiserornat," *Die Antike* 8 (1932); and "Zu spätrömischen Elfenbeinen des Westreichs," *BJbb* 152 (1952); on ceremonial architecture, A. Boethius, "The reception halls of the Roman emperors," *Annual of the British School at Athens* 46 (1951), among others; on the *adventus*, H. P. L'Orange, "The adventus ceremony," in *Late Classical Studies in Honor of A. M. Friend* (1955); F. Cumont, "L'adoration des mages et l'art triomphal de Rome," *Atti della Pontificia Accademia romana di archeologia, Memorie* 3 (1932–1933); and esp. E. Kantorowicz, "The 'King's Advent' and the enigmatic panels in the doors of Santa Sabina," *Art Bull.* 26 (1944). A convenient general résumé is W. Ensslin, "Der Kaiser in der Spätantike," *HZ* 177 (1954) 177ff.

2. On the tendencies of late Roman private architecture toward more grandiose effects, see R. Stillwell, "Houses of Antioch," *Dumbarton Oaks Papers* 15 (1961) 55ff.; I. Lavin, "The House of the Lord," *Art Bull.* 44 (1962) 1ff.; R. Meiggs, *Roman Ostia* (1960) 260ff.; and L. Crema, *L'architettura romana (Enciclopedia classica, Sezione* III: *Archeologia e storia dell'arte classica*, XII: *Archeologia*, I, 1959) 604ff., esp. 608.

3. Translation of L. J. Swift and J. H. Oliver, "Constantine II on Flavius Philippus," *AJP* 83 (1962) 248ff. It is astonishing when one thinks of it, that all this and a great deal more in the same vein was carefully written on stone.

4. Translation of H. I. Bell, *Jews and Christians in Egypt* (1924) 83. For further discussion of the style of late Latin and Greek, and of the influence of the capitals like Constantinople on the language of the man in the street, see above, chapter 8.

5. U. Monneret de Villard, "The temple of the imperial cult at Luxor," *Archaeologia* 95 (1953) 85ff., 105; D. Levi, *Antioch Mosaic Pavements* (1947) 329–32 (hereafter *Mosaic Pavements*). On clothing, see further below, the section on symbolism in uniforms.

6. The influence of the *scaenae frons* on other edifices can be traced through J.-P. Cèbe, "Une fontaine monumentale," *Mél. Rome* 69 (1957) 190ff.; P. Grimal and J. Guey, "A propos des 'Bains de Livie,' " ibid. 54 (1937) 153; H. Stern, "Nouvelles recherches sur les images des conciles dans l'Eglise de Nativité à Bethléen," *Cahiers arch.* 3 (1948) 83ff.; F. Wirth, *Römische Wandmalerei vom Untergang Pompejis bis ans Ende des dritten Jahrhunderts* (1934) 33ff., 226; and G.-C. Picard, "Le Septizonium de Cincari," *Monuments Piot* 52 (1962) 77–92.

7. Curtains in architecture: C. Daremberg and E. Saglio, *Dictionnaire des antiquités*, s.v. Velum; on their use to close stage doors, see E. Bethe, "Die antike Terenz-Illustrationen," *Jb. des Deut. arch. Inst.* 18 (1903) 107 and figs. 5–7; E. R. Fiechter, *Die baugeschichtliche Entwicklung des antiken Theaters* (1914) 120. Curtains on later doorways can be seen in Stern, *Cahiers arch.*, 3 (1948) 94ff.; G.-C. Picard, "Une schola de collège," *Karthago* 3 (1951–1952) 177ff. and fig. 5; J. Strzygowski, *Die Calenderbilder des Chronographen vom Jahre 354* (1888) pl. 35 and pp. 90ff.; W. F. Volbach, *Frühchristliche Kunst* (1958) fig. 152; idem, in *Altchristliche Mosaiken* (1947) 14 and fig. 12.

8. *Or*. 1.4C; cf. 2C, the orator's art "does not forbid flattery, nor is it generally counted a disgrace to the speaker to praise falsely those who do not deserve praise." Augustine recollects with more shame the occasion in Milan "when I was preparing to

recite a panegyric on the emperor, wherein I was to deliver many a lie and, lying, was to be applauded by those who knew I lied" (*Conf.* 6.6). Add some more references to similar occasions listed in chapter 8, n. 43.

9. H. I. Marrou, *MOYCIKOC ANHP* (1938) 8, 138ff., and passim.

10. Alföldi, "Ausgestaltung" 79ff.; further, F. Staehelin, "Felicior Augusto, melior Traiano," *Mus. Helv.* 1 (1944) 179ff., and H. U. Instinsky, "Kaiser und Ewigkeit," *Hermes* 77 (1942) 350, pointing to the reflections of acclamation style in the dedications of the later Empire, e.g., in *ILS* 597. In the Byzantine amphitheater, the claques also waved colored handkerchiefs.

11. Alföldi, "Ausgestaltung," 83–86.

12. P. Oxy. 41, late third–early fourth centuries.

13. Lactantius, *De mort. persecut.* 46.6 and 11, the moment being Licinius' joining of battle with Maximin in 313.

14. SHA *Sev. Alex.* 57.5; *Firmus* 9.1; *Gordiani* 8.4. The SHA are particularly rich in the texts of acclamations, or alleged ones, a few running to several pages, but they occur in other authors too, e.g., *Cod. Theod.* 7.20.2; Herodian 1.4.8; 2.2.4.

15. The common words are *feliciter* or *vivas* in the early Empire, *gaudeas* or *floreas* later (H. Stern, *Le Calendrier de 354* [1953] 119). But variants are many: *utere felix, zeses, ave, bibe*, etc.

16. Amm. 16.8.9, *exclamasse ex usu "vincamus," verbum sollemne*; similar *Glückwünsche* to protect the house, written over its doors, *in his praediis NN . . . et filii . . . vivant, senescant, et meliora perficiant, CIL* 8.22774, or *spes in deo* (8.21533). The practice goes back at least to the *Salve* of a Pompeian mosaic, and the greetings of slaves to the same period. Cf. Trimalchio's first and second "shifts," *illi quidem exclamavere, Vale Gai, hi autem, Ave Gai* (Petr., *Sat.* 74).

17. R. Zahn, "Zur Sammlung Friedrich L. von Gans," *Amtlicher Bericht aus den Königlichen Kunstsammlungen* 38 (1916) 42–46, the inscription on a decorative disk attached to a necklace; cf. "Good luck to the Tungri," on a gold torque, A. Roes, "Some gold torques found in Holland," *Acta arch.* 18 (1947) 179; "Long life to Julian," on a gold fibula, *CIL* 3.1639; and similar phrases on largesse-dishes of glass or silver, coins or medallions, or items of military equipment. On the last with *utere felix* or *optime conserva*, see P. Wuilleumier, "Information de la XVe circonscription, Rhône," *Gallia* 8 (1950) 146ff., and A. Ruhlmann, "Communication à propos d'une plaquette de caractère militaire," *CRAI* 1935, 69ff.

18. M. P. Charlesworth, "Imperial deportment," *JRS* 37 (1947) 36. Yet wigs may rather have served the purpose of giving a very full head of hair, which was thought to express a plenitude of power. See H. P. L'Orange, *Apotheosis in Ancient Portraiture* (1947) 33ff., 68ff., 94. Themistius had proclaimed that the good ruler should indeed resemble an *agalma, eikon*, or *indalma*. The references and earlier sources for this extraordinary view are collected by L. Delatte, *Les traités de la royauté d'Ecphante* (1942) 157 and 216. Some aspects go back to Plato. Compare his *Rep.* 420C and *Politicus* 277A with Synesius, *De Regno* 5.1068.

19. P. Castelfranco, "L'arte nella moneta nel tardo impero," *Critica d'arte* 2 (1937) 13ff., and C. C. Vermeule, "Roman numismatic art, A.D. 200–400," *Num. Circular* 65 (1957) 2–6, on the coins; L'Orange, op. cit. (n. 18) fig. 66, p. 91, and p.

118, on both coins and portrait busts. This feature of art begins suddenly at the turn from the third to the fourth centuries, and though there are some later developments, the ideal image remains remarkably stable throughout the next 250 years.

20. *Pan. vet.* 7[6].4.4, referring to Constantine. *Serenitas* is a frequent title, e.g., *Cod. Theod.* 1.12.5; 5.29.3; cf. L'Orange, op. cit. (n. 18) 95, on the *prosopou galenen entheos*, the calm that bespoke divine power resident in the philosopher or ruler, recalled in Synesius' address on kingship (*PG* 66.1069). *Tranquillitas* is more often ascribed to the empire than to the emperor, but coins of the second and third centuries carry the legend *Tranquillitas Augusti* or *Augustorum*, and *Beata tranquillitas* is familiar in the fourth century. *Gravitas* harks back to Republican ideals of *weighty* calm, but it too is ascribed to the emperor (*Pan. vet.*10[4].9.5).

21. Meaning "oven," which gives the wearer's point of view. On these troops see my article, "Inscriptions on Roman armor," *AJA* 64 (1960) 30ff.; ibid., passim, for many references on elaborate armor, adding H. Klumbach, "Ein römischer Legionarshelm aus Mainz," *Jb. Röm.-Ger. Zentral Mus.* 8 (1961) 96ff., on helmets mostly of the early Empire.

22. The precise origin is disputed, but it is generally eastern. See H. Seyrig, "A helmet from Emesa," *Archaeology* 5 (1952) 69, and B. Rugin, "Die Entstehung der Kataphraktenreiterei," *Historia* 4 (1955) 264–83. Another piece of equipment with an eastern home was the ring-pommel used on the hilts of longer swords, introduced into the Roman army from Severan times on. See H.-J. Hundt, "Ein tauschiertes römisches Ringknaufschwert aus Straubing," in *Festschrift des Römisch-Germanischen Zentralmuseums Mainz* 3 (1953) 109–18, and on the overall Orientalization of the later army, R. Grosse, "Bewaffnung und Artillerie des spätrömischen Heeres," *Arch. Anz.* 1–2 (1917) 43.

23. On the commander's extravagant costume, see *Pan. vet.* 10[4].29.5; Claudian, *De Cons. Stil.* 2.88ff.; Amm. 23.3.6. The quotation on the guards is from Amm. 31.10.14. The SHA often mention gifts by the throne to favored officers, upon advancement, and stress the elegant results of this generosity: "fine bright uniforms," "nobly armed" (*Sev. Alex.* 33.3ff.; 50.3), belts with gold and gems (*Gallieni* 20.3) or gilded (*Claudius* 14.5), etc. I am inclined to believe that they are accurate statements of conditions in the period when they were written, though of little value for the period which they pretend to describe. They are confirmed by the soldiers' uniforms, some with *segmenta*, shown in frescoes and mosaics; by the gold and silver-chased helmets of *Cod. Theod.* 10.22, 1; and by the evidence referred to in nn. 21 above and 28 below.

24. Gold torques went back to the Republic, borrowed from Germanic and Gallic usages (Alföldi, "Insignien" 54; A. Büttner, "Untersuchungen über Ursprung und Entwicklung von Auszeichnungen im römischen Heer," *BJbb* 157 [1957] 133ff., 152ff.) but are far more frequently noticed in the late Empire, becoming by the mid-fourth century a standard instrument of coronation ceremonies (Amm. 20.4.18; 29.5.20). Several authors speak of gifts by emperors of torques, rings, fibulae, and armillae to troops (MacMullen, "The Emperor's Largesses," *Latomus* 21 [1962] 159ff.). One branch of the Roman army got its name from its ornaments, Bracchiati (Alföldi, "Cornuti: A Teutonic Contingent in the Service of Constantine the Great," *Dumbarton Oaks Papers* 13 [1959] 174ff.), and Roman civilians put on jewelry that

bore Germanic motifs in decoration (idem, "Eine spätrömische Helmform," *Acta arch.* 5 [1934–1935] 114; J. Heurgon, *Le trésor de Ténès* [1958] 40ff.).

25. D. P. Dimitrov, "Le système décoratif et la date des peintures murales du tombeau antique de Silistra," *Cah. arch.* 12 (1962) 38ff.

26. The so-called *Zwiebelknopffibel*, in, for example, R. Laur-Belart, "Spätrömische und frühmittelalterliche Gräber," *Ur-Schweiz* 21 (1957) 7ff. and fig. 6; Heurgon, op. cit. (n. 24) 23ff.

27. The views of Plotinus are discussed by A. Grabar, "Plotin et les origines de l'esthéthique médiévale," *Cah. arch.* 1 (1945) 18ff.

28. Amm. 18.2.17; 21.13.15; 27.2.6; 27.5.3; 28.5.3; 29.5.15; 31.10.9. The enemy *pavore torpescent, territi stetere*, etc., because of the Romans' flashing eyes, splendid equipment, shining standards, etc. Ammianus is not saying that splendor terrifies by implying military efficiency, but that it terrifies by itself alone.

29. Vegetius 2.14, cited by Alföldi, *Acta arch.* 5 (1934–1935) 117.

30. Dio Cassius 67.10.1. In M. Rostovtzeff et al., *Dura Preliminary Reports* 6 (1936) 466, we have the written mark of a maker or owner; stamped or punched on *tabulae ansatae* or *umbones* in E. Hübner, "Römische Schildbuckel," *Arch.-epigr. Mitt. aus Oesterreich* 11 (1878) 105ff.; and a late example (fifth century) in J. Werner, "Kriegergräber aus der ersten Hälfte des 5.Jahrhunderts," *BJbb* 158 (1958) 406ff.; on the general practice, consult Grosse, *Arch. Anz.* 1–2 (1917) 42. Against Dio, probability favors the use of shield inscriptions simply to protect the articles against loss.

31. The quotation is from Vegetius 2.18. A neglected text is clearer (Amm. 16.12, 6): *Alamanni enim scutorum insignia contuentes, norant eos milites . . . quorum metu aliquotiens . . . abiere dispersis*. Cf. corps identification implied earlier in Tac., *Hist.* 3.23. As to shield insignia, the earliest examples that I find are in Trajan's column, and then on the Antonine Column. All the others are abstract. Later pictures can be seen in G. V. Gentili, *La Villa Erculia de Piazza Armerina. I mosaici figurati* (1959) pls. 24, 30, 31; B. Pace, *I mosaici di Piazza Armerina* (1955) pl. 17; Volbach, op. cit. (n. 7) pl. 2; Levi, *Mosaic Pavements* 73; P. Muratoff, *La peinture byzantine* (1935) pl. 7; H. Stern, "Les peintures du mausolée 'de l'Exode' à El-Bagaouat," *Cah. arch.* 11 (1960) 112ff.; and W. F. Volbach, *Early Christian Art* (1961) pl. 89.

32. I presume that the shield devices on the Trajanic and Antonine columns represent painted ones, but the earliest surviving example in color that I know is on the mural in the Temple of Gaddé at Dura, a scale design on a gold and reddish-brown shield, dated in the second half of the first century (*Dura Preliminary Reports* 7–8 [1939] 232, 269ff.). The Monza diptych of Stilicho (fig. 3) has a similar scale pattern.

33. Homeric scenes on shields painted in the year 256, ibid., 326ff., 349ff., and pls. 41–45; vivid colors and borders, Gentili, op. cit. (n. 31) pls. 24, 30, and 52; Pace, op. cit. (n. 31) pl. 17; Volbach, op. cit. (n. 7) pl. 2. There is one mention, SHA *Alex.Sev.* 50.5, of special corps with silver and gold shields.

34. Claudian, *De Bello Gildonico* 1.423.

35. Domaszewski, "Die Tierbilder der Signa," *Abhandlungen zur römischen Religion* (1909) 3, and again in E. Petersen et al., *Die Marcus-Säule* (1896) 112ff.

36. Domaszewski, op. cit. (n. 35) 12ff.

37. On these, on the Cornuti, and on their connection with animal cults and horned helmets of later centuries, see Alföldi, *Dumbarton Oaks Papers* 13 (1959) 172ff., add-

ing the shield shown in E. Schaffran, "Eine Völkerwanderungszeitliche Bronzestatuette," *Riv. arch. cristiana* 32 (1956) 245ff. It dates ca. 600. For lions on various objects in metal such as fourth-century belt buckles, see J. Lafaurie, *Le Trésor de Chécy* (suppl. to *Gallia* 12, 1958) 301ff.; for a dolphin and horse motif on a fourth-century buckle, see J.M.C. Toynbee, *Art in Roman Britain* (1962) 178. On the general subject of the revival of animal forms in western provincial art of this time I have gathered some references in chapter 5, p. 43.

38. "Beasts" or the like as a term of vituperation: SHA *Maximini* 17.1; Zos. 2.47.5; Pacatus in *Pan. vet.* 12[2].24.6; Julian, *Or.* 1.38C; 2.62C, the monster of Lerna; *Pan. vet.* 2[10].4.3, *monstra biformia* like the ones Hercules faced; Euseb., *Mart. Pal.* 2.16; idem, *Vita Const.* 1.49; 2.1; 3.66; Athanas., *Hist. Arian.* 3, 20, and 25; idem, *Vita S. Antonii* 9; Amm. 16.5.17; 28.1.12; 28.3.4; 28.6.4; 31.15.12. Examples of Homeric metaphors are Amm. 19.3.3 and 29.4.7, *leo magnitudine corporis et torvitate terribilis*; Julian, *Or.* 1.48C, *hosper tina lukon*; 2.84D, cf. *Iliad* 17.20; 2.87A; 2.98C, cf. *Iliad* 22.262; Synesius, *De Regno* 6.1069, comparison with the Hydra. Earlier authors exercised a tyranny over the imaginations of their successors in Latin and Greek, and readers tire of this borrowed and mechanical savagery as of other stock types of metaphor, nautical (pilots, storms, rudders, favoring winds), medical (doctors, wounds, diseases), military (bastions, walls, towers, armor, weapons), and miscellaneous old favorites such as shepherds, watch-dogs, seasons of the year, rivers, sun, stars, etc., etc., to all of which men or events are likened. The animal and other metaphors in Ammianus to which I draw attention are, however, much further elaborated than in Tacitus, Cicero, or other writers. Such is my own impression, confirmed *per litteris* by Prof. Geo. Kennedy, whose kind response I must acknowledge.

39. P. Fargues (*Claudien* [1933] 322ff.) gathers the references and distinguishes between the old (lions, horses, bees, etc.) and the new animals. The latter he derives without discussion from images in vulgar speech. M. P. Brown, *Authentic Writings of Ignatius* (1963) 112, even fixes on a fondness for extended and exotic animal metaphors as among the differentia of the mid-fourth century Pseudo-Ignatius, as opposed to the more limited range of metaphor in the genuine Ignatian corpus.

40. Amm. 14.4.1; 14.9.9; 15.3.5; 28.4.10; 28.6.13.

41. It is a safe assumption that these existed, given the use of placards in triumphs and in the light of other public paintings described below (see the ample material from the Republic and Empire assembled by L. Friedländer, *Darstellungen aus der Sittengeschichte Roms*[9] [1920] 3.50ff.); but there are three direct references. Herodian (1.15, 4) speaks of animals collected for Commodus' games which "we then saw that we had [earlier] wondered at in pictures." SHA (*Carus* 19.1) mentions games "which we can see painted in the Portico of the Stables, on the Palatine," and *Gordiani* (3.6), a picture set up in the House of Beaks showing 200 stags, 30 wild horses, 100 wild sheep, 300 red ostriches, etc. The number of animals was probably written on a representative of each species, as is done in a surviving mosaic (L. Poinssot and P. Quoniam, "Bêtes d'amphithéatre sur trois mosaiques du Bardo," *Karthago* 3 [1951–1952] 140), and on gladiators' figures on cups and mosaics to show the total of their victories (J. Gricourt, "Les 'Marques chiffrées intra-décoratives' de la Graufesenque," *Hommages à Albert Grenier* [1962] 2.763–70).

42. Poinssot and Quoniam, *Karthago* 3 (1951–1952) 144ff. (later fourth century).

43. Amm. 14.5.6; 14.7.13; 15.2.4; 15.7.4; 18.4.4; 28.1.7; 28.1.33.

44. It is first seen on Trajan's column, borne by eastern auxiliaries only, but in Vegetius' day it is found also among the legions. It was known among Germans, Dacians, and Sarmations (J. Dobias, "Roman Imperial Coins as a Source for Germanic Antiquities," *Trans. Int. Num. Congr. 1936* [1938] 170ff.) but its more obvious origins were recognized: *Persici dracones* (SHA *Aurelianus* 28.5); [cf. the long description in Lucian, *How to Write History* 29]. On its history, see R. Grosse, *Römische Militärgeschichte* (1920) 231. There is only one picture of it, dating to the fourth century. See Stern, *Cah. arch.* 11 (1960) 112ff.

45. Athanas., *Vita S. Antonii* 6; idem, *Hist. Arian.* 80; Theodoret., *H. E.* 1.14, a political enemy is "that dragon"; Claudian (an Egyptian), *De III Cons. Honorii* 138ff., idem, *In Rufin.* 2.177ff., 346ff., *Epithalamium* 193, *De IV Cons. Honorii* 545, *De VI Cons. Honorii* 566ff.; Euseb., *Vita Const.* 2.1; and add the two eastern provincials just cited, Ammianus and Themistius [with Greg. Naz., *Or. adv. Julianum* 1.66] (but also Prudentius *Peristeph.* 1.35, *Contra Orat. Symm.* 2.713, *Cathemerinon* 5.56). The earliest reference to *dracones* that I know is in the African poet Nemesianus (*Cynegetica* 85), of the later third century.

46. *Vita Const.* 3.3; cf. Licinius again a *drakon*, ibid., 2.46; [and Diocletian in his edict against the Manichees, trans. J. Stevenson in *A New Eusebius* (1957) 283, comparing Manichaeism to "the poison of a malignant serpent"]. The scriptural allusions are to Revelations 20:2 and Isaiah 27:1 (cf. Lk 10:19 and Ps. 91:113ff.), which Constantine's allegory closely follows. The Eusebius passage is discussed by G. Rodenwaldt, "Eine spätantike Kunstströmung in Rom," *Mitt. Deut. arch. Inst., römische Abteilung* 36–37 (1921–1922) 85ff., and by Alföldi, *The Conversion of Constantine and Pagan Rome* (1948) 84ff. The picture is repeated in Constantine's coinage for wider circulation and again (ibid., p. 134 n. 28) in Firm. Matern., *De err. profan. relig.* 21.2.

47. J. Strzygowski, *Hellenistische und koptische Kunst* (1902) 27 fig. 16; 35 fig. 19; and 37.

48. G. Schlumberger, "Amulettes byzantins anciens destinés à combattre les maléfices et maladies," *REG* 5 (1892) 73ff., esp. 91; N. Thierry, "Notes sur l'un des bas-reliefs d'Alahan Manastiri," *Cah. arch.* 13 (1962) 43.

49. G. Downey, "The Pilgrim's Progress of the Byzantine Emperor," *Ch. Hist.* 9 (1940) 207–17; ibid. 10 (1941) 367–76. He finds vices presented as animals, and their conquest as a *venatio*, in a second-century moral tract, and in later art.

50. In Prudentius, *Peristeph.* 5.176 and 381ff., 14.112; Firm. Matern., *De Err. profan. relig.* 5.1; Gregory Thaumaturgus, *Sermon on all the Saints, PG* 10.1201; and in Perpetua's vision (*Passio SS. Perpetuae et Felicitatis* 4), in which her first step upward to salvation is trod upon the head of a dragon: *calcavi illi caput, et ascendi.*

51. Strzygowski, op. cit. (n. 47) 35 and fig. 19, the Aachen reliefs with the standing warrior type crushing a monster beneath his foot; Levi, *Mosaic Pavements* 243, 341 (citing Downey's articles).

52. For their presence in parades welcoming Athanasius in Alexandria, see E. R. Hardy, *Christian Egypt: Church and People* (1952) 61; for their banners, see Friedländer, op. cit. (n. 41) 1.167; M. Rostovtzeff, "Vexillum and Victory," *JRS* 32 (1942) 105; and G. Lugli, *Roma antica* (1946) 614ff. The scene recalls Gallienus' triumph in

Rome (SHA *Gallieni* 8.6–7) featuring "50 gilded spears borne on both sides of him, 100 *vexilla* besides those of the guilds, *dracones*, and *signa* of all the temples and legions . . . as well as men dressed to represent foreign nations, like Goths, Sarmatians, Franks, or Persians," and in the early Middle Ages (Gregory, *Hist. Francorum* 8.1) celebrating the king's entry into Orleans with standards, banners, acclamations, and the rest—the whole rigmarole of the *adventus* perpetuated in the west.

53. *Paneg. vet.* 8[5].8.4; cf. Herodian 4.8.8, Alexandrians receiving Caracalla with "instruments of every style, stationed everywhere." As this second passage is the earliest that I find, perhaps the use of instruments in *adventus* may be ascribed to eastern initiative.

54. Amm. 28.2.13; further evidence in MacMullen, "Imperial Bureaucrats in the Roman Provinces," *HSCP* 68 (1964) 308.

55. MacMullen, *Soldier and Civilian in the Later Roman Empire* (1963) 83.

56. Claudian, *De Cons. Manlii Theod.* 313–19; Basil, *Homil. in Gord.* 19 (*PG* 31.500), flutes and organs in the theater in the early fourth century; horns of various kinds, and organs, in mosaics also, e.g., of Zliten and Antioch; and tax exemption for the winners of trumpet contests in third century Egypt, in P. Oxy. 2338.

57. Amm. 14.7.21; 15.2.1; 16.8.11; 20.5.2; 26.4.5; 28.1.14; 29.1.14; 31.13.1; Oros., *Hist. libri septem* 7.39, "the trumpets of salvation," has different origins.

58. *Dura Preliminary Reports* 7–8, pp. 232, 269ff.

59. Ibid. 326, 330–37, 363ff. Some of the costumes are thought to follow Roman models.

60. Patroclus depicted with square *segmentum* on left shoulder, in Levi, *Mosaic Pavements* 46ff. and pl. 8a.

61. Gentili, op. cit. (n. 31) 69 and pl. 52.

62. MacMullen, *HSCP* 68 (1964) 309, on uniforms of green, of fur, silver-decorated, etc.

63. *Cod. Theod.* 14.10.2 restricts the use of trousers in Rome. They were called *braccae* (whence our "breeches") in Gaul, and their popularity had spread into the army even before the second century (Alföldi, "Insignien" 61ff.). They are attested in Palmyra long before the Romans came (M. Morehart, "Early Sculpture at Palmyra," *Berytus* 12 [1956–1957] 76) along with the long-sleeved tunic, to which cavalry added the skirted riding coat—*scaramangion*—known to the Romans from the third century and prominent as an item of Byzantine military and ceremonial costume (F. Cumont, "L'uniforme de la cavalerie orientale et le costume byzantin," *Byzantion* 2 (1925) 181ff., with Kondakov's article, "Les costumes orientaux à la cour byzantine," ibid. 1 (1924) 7–49.

64. Gentili, op. cit. (n. 31) 70, on the hats ("of a clearly eastern origin," says Pace, op. cit. [n. 31] 66) which we can see also on the famous statue of the Tetrarchs in Venice, "costume ufficiale dell'età tetrarchica"; Alföldi, "Insignien" 47ff., on the Dalmatic; and Herodian 4.7.3, on the kind of cloak worn by the Germans and adopted by Caracalla.

65. Hier., *Ep.* 60.9, on the emperor's bodyguard in white; white shirt not of wool but of silk, a piece of real finery, in SHA *Claudius* 17.6; white for officers, or reserved for troops only on festal occasions, in E. Sander, "Die Kleidung des römischen Soldaten," *Historia* 12 (1963) 153ff., and white with mystic meaning in E. R. Good-

enough, *Jewish Symbols in the Greco-Roman Period* 9 (1964) 165ff. I must thank Prof. Goodenough for letting me see his volume in galleys. For embroidery on uniforms, SHA *Aurelianus* 46.5–6 and Monneret de Villard, *Archaeologia* 95 (1953) pl. 31c, supply more details.

66. Themist., *Or.* 10.135A–B, in the year 367; Amm. 21.6.8; Zos. 5.41.6.

67. *RE* s.v. *Dies imperii* col. 478; on the general importance of purple, W. T. Avery, "The adoratio purpurae and the importance of the imperial purple," *MAAR* 17 (1940) 66–80.

68. Sander, *Historia* 12 (1963) 153; MacMullen, op. cit. (n. 55) 170ff. and the appendix.

69. MacMullen, ibid.; idem, *HSCP* 68 (1964) 309; and below, n. 86.

70. Euseb., *Or. to Constantine* 5.613; cf. Jos., *A. J* 19.8.2, "Agrippa put on a garment made wholly of silver and of a wonderful contexture . . . [that] glittered in a surprising way and was so resplendent as to inspire fear and trembling in those that looked intently upon him."

71. *Cod. Theod.* 6.8.1, *praepositi sacri cubiculi*, at the ceremonious Adoration of the Purple, "shall of course wear the conventional garb." Cf. 14.10.1 (382), stipulating that senators must wear togas in public hearings, applied more widely to anyone appearing in the courts, whence the reminder in P. Oxy. 123 (third to fourth centuries) that a *notarius* (apparently) must remember to attend sessions *meta tes aisthetos*, "with the [proper] dress." [Cf. Julian, *Letter to a Priest* 3–3B.]

72. P. DeJonge, *Philological and Historical Commentary on Ammianus Marcellinus* 4 (1953) 12; on *palliati*, Amm. 15.8.1 and Alföldi, "Insignien" 150ff. and 156.

73. Soz., *H. E.* 3.4, 111. Initiates of Isis received special robes embroidered with beasts, dragons, and griffins, and other pagan and later Christian rites employed symbolism in dress. See Goodenough, op. cit. (n. 65) 9.144.

74. Livy 1.20, 4, quoted by P. Perdrizet, "La tunique liturgique historiée de Saqqara," *Mon. Piot* 34 (1934) 116; Levi, *Mosaic Pavements* 48, ascribing the origins of the practice to "a very early age," for various priesthoods, one example coming from the Egyptian hieratic garment from Saqqara described at length by Perdrizet. It dates to the second century.

75. R. Forrer, *Die Gräber- und Textilfunde von Achmim* (1891) 19.

76. E. Vogt, "Frühmittelalterliche Stoffe aus der Abtei St-Maurice," *Zeitschr. für Schweiz. Arch. und Kunstgesch.* 18 (1958) 122ff., on the fourth- or fifth-century cloth from St. Maurice abbey; H. Seyrig and L. Robert, "Sur un tissu récemment publié," *Cah. arch.* 8 (1956) 27ff., on a fragment of a figured curtain from Egypt woven in Syria or Bithynia; R. Forrer, *Römische und byzantinische Seiden-Textilien aus dem Gräberfelde von Achmim* (1891) 15; S. Donadoni, "Stoffe decorate da Antinoe," *Scritti dedicati alla memoria de Ippolito Rosellini 1943* (1945) 114ff. and pls. 20 and 23, showing Egyptian pieces of the third/fourth and fourth/fifth centuries.

77. Forrer, op. cit. (n. 76) 15–18 and pls. 3.3–4 and 5.1; A. F. Kendrick, *Catalogue of Textiles from Burying Grounds in Egypt I: Graeco-Roman Period* (1920) 64ff.; [and Asterius Amasenus discussed by H. Koch, *Die altchristliche Bilderfrage* (1917) 65–68].

78. Stern, op. cit. (n. 15) 167, detects astrological meaning in certain signs and symbols, but not all of them seem to answer his interpretation; on the fish, alpha and

omega, and cross embroidered on garments, see Forrer, loc. cit. (n. 77); idem, op. cit. (n. 75) 22; M. Chéhab, "Mosaiques du Liban," *Bulletin du Musée de Beyrouth* 14–15 (1958–1959) 64 and pl. 30.2. The letters on garments H, I, X, Z, etc. are more obscure (G. Wilpert, *Le pitture delle catacombe romane* [1903] 1.89). A late parallel is interesting: personified Philosophy with pi and theta on her robe, for Practice and Theory (Boethius, *De Consolatione philosophiae* 1.1 pr. 18ff.).

79. L. W. Jones, "The archetypes of the Terence miniatures," *Art Bull.* 10 (1927) 117; below, n. 86.

80. Ms. Vat. Barb. lat. 2154. Stern, op. cit. (n. 15) 153, accepts it, though from a Carolingian manuscript, as a faithful copy of the fourth-century original.

81. Heurgon, op. cit. (n. 24) 41, from Rome; cf. a similar belt-end in gold fretwork with four tiny medallion scenes surrounding a relief, all with classicizing figures in them, in O. von Falke, "Spätantike Goldschmuck aus Alexandria," *Pantheon* 14 (1934) 370ff. (cited by Heurgon).

82. Theodoret., *Or.* 4.541; Auson., *Grat. actio ad Grat.* 11.51ff.

83. SHA *Trig. tyr.* 14.4; on the propaganda value of Alexander in the struggle of late paganism against Christianity, see A. Alföldi, *Die Kontorniaten: Ein verkanntes Propagandamittel der stadtrömischen heidnischen Aristokratie* (1942–1943) 57ff.; but on the merely formular nature and unreliability of the word *hodie*, see W. Hartke, *Römische Kinderkaiser* (1951) 21–23.

84. Levi, *Mosaic Pavements* 336 n. 81, on early *clavi* going back to the later second century (pls. 11, 20, and 48); Goodenough, op. cit. (n. 65) 9.134–153, traces the use of *clavi* on religious dress back through Pompeian frescoes into Etruria, south Italian Greek, and ultimately eastern Hellenistic uses. J. Leroy ("Mosaiques funéraires d'Edesse," *Syria* 34 [1957] 316ff.) describes second- or third-century cloak *segmenta* from Edessa, derived (p. 335) from Persia in the second century, the garments so decorated being called *oculatae* according to O. Marucchi, "L'ipogeo sepolerale de Trebio Giusto," *Bull. arch. cristiana* 17 (1911) 214; and Gentili, op. cit. (n. 31) 69, deriving the hemmed tunic from Egypt of the third century.

85. Goodenough, op. cit. (n. 65) 9.134ff.

86. In addition to the early fourth century Sicilian mosaics, there are third- and fourth-century paintings and mosaics from Rome, France, Switzerland, Germany, and Africa showing such details. See Wilpert, op. cit. (n. 78) 1.88ff. and pls. 142, 146, 192, 237; Volbach, op. cit. (n. 31) pls. 7–10 and 130; [H. Schlunk, in E. Boehringer, ed., *Neue Deutsche Ausgrabungen* (1959) Abb. 1–6, of date ca. 325;] J. Moreau, *Das Trierer Kornmarktmosaik* (1960) pls. 1, 2; V. von Gonzenbach, *Die römischen Mosaiken der Schweiz* (1961) pls. 49, 52; H. Stern, *Recueil générale des mosaïques de la Gaule*, suppl. to *Gallia* 10 (1957) 53; idem, op. cit. (n. 15) pls. 3.2; 42.2, 3; and 45.5. In Wilpert's very large collection of the catacomb paintings, the only figures clearly lacking *clavi* belong to servants, shepherds, and laborers (pls. 51, 95, 107, 112, 132), which rather supports Goodenough's belief (op. cit. [n. 65] 9. 164) that *clavi* indicated rank. Yet Goodenough specifies rank in the sense of degree of saintliness, so that the figure of Christ, apostles, and Joseph will differ in richness of dress. In this narrow interpretation he seems to be mistaken.

87. Especially the tunic, with *segmenta* and *clavi*. The examples are scattered in P. Gauckler, *Inventaire des mosaïques de la Gaule et de l'Afrique*, vol. 2 of plates

(1911) no. 967; Moreau, op. cit. (n. 86) 11; Stern, op. cit. (n. 86) 53; R. P. Hinks, *Catalogue of the Greek Etruscan and Roman Paintings in the British Museum* (1933) 129 and 143; and Monneret de Villard, *Archaeologia* 95 (1953) pl. 33, a Tripolitanian figure.

88. Levi, *Mosaic Pavements* 336 n. 81.

89. Cypr., *Ep.* 1.7, *veste pretiosa*; Tert., *De spect.* 23; and Plut., *Moral.* 554B.

90. Wirth, op. cit. (n. 6) 126ff. and pls. 29–39; Lugli, op. cit. (n. 52) 614ff.

91. L. Leschi, "Une mosaïque achilléenne de Tipasa," *Mél. Rome* 141 (1937) 25–41. He identifies some of the figures (Achilles, centaur) but not the probable scene.

92. All this has been discussed at length by Alföldi, "Insignien" 59; idem, "Das Problem des verweichlichten Kaisers Gallienus," *Zeitschr. für Numismatik* 38 (1928) 172ff.

93. E. A. Thompson, *Historical Work of Ammianus Marcellinus* (1947) 83, seems to misinterpret Amm. 22.4.1, but has picked out the perfect passage in Socrates' *Historia ecclesiastica* 3.1.50 (= 172): "To give up the overwhelming impression wrought upon the masses [*tois pollois kataplexis*] by the emperor's wealth would bring the monarchy into contempt."

94. *Or. to Constantine* 5.613. There is a like tone in Symm., *Rel.* 4.1–2: "such ostentation is inconsistent with a self-respecting office."

95. Amm. 28.6.20; 30.5.19; SHA *Sev. Alex.* 28.4; 36.2; cf. the cruel joke played on a criminal as a punishment, *Gallieni* 12.5, and Claudian *In Rufin.* 2.436ff.

96. Oros., *Hist. libri sept.* 7.33; cf. Euseb., *Vita Const.* 1.59, "And still the stroke of God was laid cruelly on him, so that his eyes protruded and fell from their sockets, leaving him blind; and thus he suffered, by a most just sentence, the very same punishment which he had been the first to devise for the martyrs of God."

97. Euseb., *H. E.* 9.10.365; *Vita Const.* 1.57; Hier., *Vita S. Hilarionis* 34; Amm. 14.11.24; and Lact., *De mort. persecut.*, passim. See J. Moreau's edition of the last work (1954) 1.60ff., tracing the vigorous tradition of fitting deaths back to Herodotus.

98. *Clementia*, in *Cod. Theod.* 11.7.15; 11.8.7; etc.; Gentleness (*mansuetudo* or *hemerotes*) in Symm., *Rel.*13.2; 29.2; 34.2; *CSEL* 35, p. 52; Athanas., *Apol. ad Const.* 621B; Julian, *Ep.* 110 (Bidez).

99. SHA *Maximini* 17.1; *Gordiani* 13.3; *Sev. Alex.*17.2; on Julian, *iratus et frendens*, Amm. 24.5.6; on Valentinian, *ira vehementi perculsus, et inter exordia respondendi tumidior, increpabat verborum obiurgatorio sonu*, 30.6.3; on Theodosius, Zos. 4.51.4.

100. Alföldi, "Ausgestaltung" 37ff.; *Cod. Theod.* 1.16.7; [cf. Themist., *Or.* 7.110 Dindorf (ɪ p. 137 Schenkl), later, and Euseb., *H. E.* 6.43.7, earlier (ca. 250)].

101. Besides those on military standards and on the labarum, see Lact., *De mort. persecut.* 42, *imagines ubicumque*; SHA *Gordiani* 13.6; Herodian 4.2.7; Euseb., *H. E.* 7.18.265, "the likeness of the Apostles Paul and Peter, and of Christ himself, are preserved in paintings, the ancients being accustomed, as is likely . . . to pay this kind of honor indiscriminately to those regarded by them as deliverers." Cf. the portraits on *segmenta* and robes, above, n. 82, and Claudian, *De Cons. Stil.* 2.350ff.

102. SHA *Maximini* 12.10, placed in front of the senate house; Herodian 7.3.8, "large paintings" displayed in the same place; idem, 3.9.12, displayed "publicly" in Rome.

103. *Ho ton palaismaton agonothetes Christos*, the martyrs *hoi athletai*, in fourth-century paintings of the eastern provinces. See the phrase in both Greg. Nyss., *Or. de S. Theod.* (*PG* 46.737) and Basil, *Homil.* 17 (*PG* 31.489), and a fuller and extremely vivid description of such a painting in Asterius, *Homil.* 12 (*PG* 40.335ff.). Originally the symbolism of the athlete fitted martyrs who died in the arena. It was, however, applied indiscriminately later. Moreau in his edition of Lactantius, p. 295, traces earlier examples of the athlete metaphor, among pagan as well as Christian authors.

104. Rodenwaldt, op. cit. (n. 46) 79–97 and passim; R. Bianchi Bandinelli, "Continuità ellenistica nella pittura de età medio- e tardo-romano," *Rivista dell'Istituto Nazionale d'Archeologia e Storia dell'Arte* 2 (1953) 122–45; M. Bonicatti, "Industria artistica classica e tradizioni popolari nella cultura del basso impero," *Scritti di storia dell'arte in onore de M. Salmi* (1961) 1.61.

10. CONSTANTINE AND THE MIRACULOUS

1. Soc., *H. E.* 2.28 (Gallus, with parallels afforded by Philostorgius, *H. E.* 3.26 (ed. Bidez, *GCS* 1913), involving Constantius, and by Soz., *H. E.* 2.3, where Constantine's physician, his conversion not yet complete, is won over to Christianity by a vision of the cross and a voice explaining its significance as the guarantor of salvation; cf. ibid. 4.5, a cross fifteen stadia high seen by multitudes in Jerusalem, who rush to the churches to be shriven or converted.

2. Theodoret., *H. E.* 2.26.

3. Exod. 8.16f; Ps. 105.31f; cf. Theodoret., *Graec. affect. cur.* 10.58 (ed. P. Canivet, *Sources chrét.* 57.2 [1958] 378 n. 2), on pests of mice, bats, snakes and scorpions; the last, with various stinging insects, appear often on magical amulets (S. Einrem, *Symb. Oslo.* 7 [1928] 70–73; cf. Cypr., *Ep.* 69.5). In Arnobius' day (*Adv. Nat.* 1.3) plagues of locusts and mice were still blamed on Christians.

4. Soc., *H. E.* 5.25, "so powerful was the emperor's prayer."

5. Dio 72.8.4; cf. Euseb., *H. E.* 5.5.1–3, adding the detail of lightning-bolts, and E. R. Dodds, *JRS* 37 (1947) 56; full treatment in J. Guey, *Rev. Phil* 22 (1948) 17f.

6. M. R. James, *The Apocryphal New Testament* (1924) 339; date (ibid. 228) revised upward by P. M. Peterson, *Andrew, Brother of Simon Peter* (1958) 26.

7. Dio 55.1.3f., 79[78].25.5; cf. 73.13.3, and Plin., *Ep.* 7.27, and Soz., *H. E.* 7.23.

8. A catalogue of pagan epiphanies—of Asclepius alone—would be endless. For a selection of those sent to Christians, see Constantine's being led on the founding circuit of Constantinople by some divine being, in Philostorg., *H. E.* 2.9; Theodosius' vision of "the blessed Meletius," in Theodoret., *H. E.* 5.6; and of St. John and St. Philip on the eve of battle, promising him success, ibid. 5.24 (confirmed by a second witness); Constantius' beholding of his own guardian angel or genius, in Amm. 21.14.2; Arnobius' conversion by visions, in Hier., *Chron.* A.D. 326/327; and the angel sent to Licinius in a dream, in Lact., *Mort. Pers.* 46. For Christ appearing to Constantine, see Soz., *H. E.* 1.3.

9. Paneg. vet. (ed. Baehrens[2],1911) 10[4].2.6, 12.1, 13.5, 16.2, 17.1, 28.1.

10. Amm. Marc. 29.5.40, 16.12.13; cf. frequent references to the emperor's *numen* or *divinitas* in the *Paneg. vet.* 3 and 4 (e.g. 4.15.6, 4.17.1); and Constantine's conversion *aphrastoi tini dynamei*, in Soz., *H. E.* 1.18. Even such loosely conceived Powers

might still be thought of as actually operating on history. We see events taking place *hypo tinos daimoniou tyches*, in Herodian 1.9.4; *ex epipnoias tinos theias*, in Dio 79[78].8.2; cf. 76[75].4.5; or *hosper hypo pneumatos deinou tinos*, in Euseb. *H. E.* 4.2.2.

11. Interesting passages: SHA *Avid. Cassius* 2.2; 8.2f., 11.8, quoting Hor., *Od.* 1.17.13. I cannot recall any earlier pagan texts hinting at the existence of a divine plan for history, though it is easy to find the belief that the accession and demise of an emperor were divinely intended. See J. Béranger, *Recherches sur l'aspect idéologique du principat* (1953) 155f., 164f. In the fourth century, no doubt in a spirit of anti-Christian polemic, Eunapius (*Vit. soph.* 476) describes Julian's "conquering all [the barbarians] because he worshipped the gods"—a more explicit statement of cause and effect than fits in the earlier Empire. Cf. infra n. 17.

12. Firm. Mat., *Err. prof. rel.* 16.4, 20.7, 29.3; bishop Dionysius in Euseb. *H. E.* 7.11.8; cf. Tert., *Apol.* 33; Orig., *C. Cels.* 8.68 and 70; and, of course, Eusebius throughout the *Vita Const.*, e.g. 1.38.

13. The basic text was Deut. 32.8f (and Dan. 10.13), with later adherence clearest in Orig., *C. Cels.* 1.24, 3.2, 4.8, 5.25, 5.30; see H. B. Kuhn, *Jnl. Bibl. Lit.* 67 (1948) 218–31; E. Peterson, *Theol. Zeitschr.* 7 (1951) 81–90; and C. M. Morrison, *The Powers That Be* (1960) 18–23 and passim.

14. Euseb., *Vita Const.* 1.38.

15. Some slight help from A. D. Nock, *JRS* 37 (1947) 112–14.

16. Julian, *Adv. Gal.* 115D; Orig., *C. Cels.* 8.35; Ael. Arist., *Or.* 43.18, cited from H. Chadwick, *Origen: Contra Celsum* (1965) xix; Iambl., *Myst.* 5.25; Morrison, op. cit. (n. 13) 84f.; on the related idea of a supreme god with angel-agents, like the Persian king surrounded by his satraps, which was fitted into both Origen's and Neoplatonic thought, see P. Cumont, *Rev. hist. rel.* 72 (1915) 163–74.

17. Note the references, of a new explicitness, by the Egyptian prefect Aemilianus, to "the gods that preserve their [scil., of Valerian and Gallienus] monarchy," or by Maximin, to the city that is "by many proofs revealed to flourish through the presence of the heavenly gods," etc., or his assertion that "by the gods the government of the state and all individuals in it have their being" (Euseb., *H. E.* 7.11, 9.7.5, 9.7.7f., 9.9A.6). Pagan supporters attributed Julian's spectacular success against Constantius to Julian's divine protectors (Eunap., *Vit. soph.* 476; Greg. Naz., *Or.* 4, *Adv. Julianum* 1.47). For even approximate parallels to such views, one would have to go back three centuries and more to Vergil's age (R. Syme, *The Roman Revolution* [1939] 448f.).

18. On Maxentius' desperate measures, see *Paneg. vet.* 9[12].16.5; Euseb. *Vita Const.* 1.36; *H. E.* 8.14.5, 9.9.2; Lact., *Mort. pers.* 44; Zos. 2.15.4; for these clichés of the tyrant's last days, compare SHA *Julianus* 7.9f.; Soz., *H. E.* 1.7; Dio 74.16.5, 80[79].11; Euseb., *Vita Const.* 2.4f., *H. E.* 8.14.8; and Zon. 13.1.2; for the prognostic sacrifices, also Amm. Marc. 29.2.17.

19. A. Alföldi, *Conversion of Constantine* (1948) 17f., argues for the *chrisma*, but points out (126 n. 7) the magical properties which it as well as the cross might be supposed to possess.

20. On the power given to Constantine by use of the cross, see Soc., *H. E.* 1.2; Soz., *H. E.* 1.4, the cross venerated by soldiers and the *labarum* work miracles; ibid. 1.8, cross marked on weapons; Theodoret., *H. E.* 1.17, and Soc., *H. E.* 1.17, Helena

sends her son nails and wood from the true cross, which he uses on his equipment and bears into battle "in order to avert the missiles of his enemies."

21. Firm. Mat., *Err. prof. rel.* 20.7, the *labarum* called the *vexillum fidei*; and, on its warlike properties, Alföldi, op. cit. (n. 19) 84 and n. 3, coins of Constantine showing "the imperial standard with the emblem of Christ piercing with its point the snake of paganism."

22. Thunderbolts on shields in W. F. Volbach, *Altchristliche Mosaiken* (1947) pl. II; E. Petersen et al., *Die Marcus-Säule* (1896) pls. 5.1, 10.1f., 11.1, 15.1, etc.; *RE* s.v. Scutum (1921) col. 919, on Trajan's Column; for identification of units by their shields, see Tac., *Hist.* 3.23; Dio 64.14.2; Amm. Marc. 16.12.6; for Vespasian's name on his *vexilla*, Suet., *Vesp.* 6; for apotropaic animal symbols on shields, see above chapter 9, p. 90f.

23. A. Ruhlmann, *CRAI* 1935, 67f.; P. Wuilleumier, *Gallia* 8 (1950) 146f.; J.M.C. Toynbee, *Art in Roman Britain* (1962) 168 and pl. 107.

24. For example, Cypr., *Ad Demetrianum* 15; *Acta Andreae* 9; Theoph., *Ad Autol.* 2.8 (*PG* 6.1061f.); Marc. Diac., *Vita Porph.* 61; *Consultat. Zacchaei et Apollonii* (ed. G. Morin, 1935) 1.5; Greg. Nyss., *Vita Greg. Thaum* (*PG* 46.916A and 949D–952D); Soz., *H. E.* 4.16 and 5.2; Theodoret., *H. E.* 3.1, 5.21; Athanas., *Or. incarn. verbi* 48 (*PG* 25.181); idem, *Vita Anton.* 13.23, 35, 40, 53, 63f., and 80; Lact., *Mort. pers.* 10.2f.; Euseb., *C. Hierocl.* 4; Julian, *Ep.* 79 (ed. Bidez); and *Acta Xanthippae et Polyxenae* (ed. James) 17f.

25. To the references in MacMullen, *Enemies of the Roman Order* (1966) 319, on apotropaic statues, add Suet., *Nero* 56, Philostr., *Vita Apollon.* 4.10, and Dio 37.9.2; cf. effective apotropaic rites against the enemies of the state, SHA *Aurelian* 18.5, 20.5–7, 21.4, described with considerable emphasis to match, in pagan history, the miracles wrought by Christians. On Constantine's statue, see Soc., *H. E.* 1.17.

26. J. Stevenson, trans., *A New Eusebius* (1957) 312, Council of Ancyra; *Concilium Laodicenum* (ed. Jonkers) 36; cf. Basil on medical magic resorted to by his congregation, *PG* 29.417. Further, on superstition prevalent among Christians, cf. Stevenson 308 (Council of Elvira, A.D. 305), infra n. 44, and esp. compare Plut., *Mor.* 356E with Aug., *Conf.* 8.12.29.

27. Euseb., *H. E.* 7.18.1–3; Soc.. *H. E.* 1.17; R. Arbesmann, *Traditio* 10 (1954) 3f. Note that, as Christ was lowered to a healer of bodies, pagan propaganda sought to raise Asclepius to a healer of souls—Julian, *Adv. Gal.* 200B. At the same time the ability of the gods, notably Asclepius, really to heal their worshippers was persistently depreciated, e.g. in Cypr., *Idol. vanit.* 6f.; Tat., *Ad Graec.* 16; Tert., *Apol.* 22; Ps.-Clem., *Hom.* 9.15f.; and Athanas., *Vita Anton.* 33. F. Dölger, *Antike u. Christentum* 6 (1950) 242–54, discusses some of these and other passages.

28. Cypr., *Ad Demetr.* 2f.; Arnob., *Adv. nat.* 1.1 and 3; Porphyry in Theodoret., *Graec. affect. cur.* 12.96f. For a pagan and a Christian in competition to avert plague from Rome, only the Christian successful, see Dodds, op. cit. (n. 5) 57.

29. Medical details meet us in Plut., *Sulla* 36, but earlier examples that he draws from Greek literature could be easily multiplied. See the full history of *theomachoi* in W. Nestle, *Griechische Studien* (1948) 568f. Other roots of the genre reach into Judaism, continued by Christian writers against pagans, persecutors, and heretics, and usurped for use against Christians by pagans. See 2 Chron. 21.15 and 18; 1 Macc. 6.8;

2 Macc. 9.8f.; Acts 1.18, 12.23; Herod smitten, in Joseph, *A. J.* 17.168–70, *B. J.* 1.656–60, both texts familiar to Eusebius (*H. E.* 1.8.5f.); Arius smitten in answer to bishop Alexander's prayer, in Soc. *H. E.* 1.38 and Theodoret., *H. E.* 1.13; Galerius smitten, in Lact., *Mort. pers.* 33 and Euseb. *H. E.* 8.16.3–5; Julian, uncle to the Apostate, smitten in Soz., *H. E.* 5.8, in Theodoret., *H. E.* 3.9, and in Philostorg., *H. E.* 7.10 (ed. Bidez), adding the names of other victims of *phtheiriasis*; and used against Christians by Julian, *Ep.* 55 and 90 (ed. Bidez).

30. Euseb., *H. E.* 9.7.10; cf. Marc. Diac., *Vita Porph.* 56; Iambl., *Myst.* 5.6 and *Vita Pythag.* 135; and supra n. 5. Though this evidence deals only with storms, much more could be gathered on other types of natural disaster.

31. The poisoned source for the incident is Eunap., *Vit. soph.* 462f.

32. Marc. Diac., *Vita Porph.* 19; Cypr., *Ep.* 75.10.1f (ed. Bayard, 1961).

33. Zos. 2.7; Z. Petre, *Studii clasice* 7 (1965) 263f., noting (264 n. 4) "the obviously magical nature of these games."

34. K. Svoboda, *La démonologie de Michel Psellos* (1927) 11–14, 31, 34f.; F. Cumont, *Lux perpetua* (1949) 81–95; idem, *Rev. hist. rel.* 72 (1915) 159–74; T. Hopfner, *Griechisch-ägyptischer Offenbarungszauber* 1 (1921) 6, 8, 21f., 43f.; and the sources, from the less important forerunners like Plutarch (e.g. *Moral.* 361Af.), Albinus (e.g. *Epit.* 15.1), and Artemidorus (e.g. *Oneir.* 2.34) to the chief Neoplatonists, Plotinus (*Enn.* 3.5.6), Porphyry (*Ep. ad Anebo*, passim; Aug., *De civ. Dei* 10.9.26; Procl., *In Tim.* 142C), Iamblichus (*Myst.* 1.3–9, 12, 20; 2.3; 3.16; etc.), and Proclus (*In Crat.* 122).

35. Demons caused pests, etc. in Porph., *Abst.* 2.40 and Iambl., *Myst.* 2.6 and 56; they cure the sick, ibid. 3.3; bring oracles, ibid. 3.2 and 16, and Plut., *Moral.* 362; respond to *defixiones*, in Iambl., *Myst.* 2.7, and Cumont, *Rev. hist. rel.* 72 (1915) 175; they attack men at the command of magic, Marc. Diac., *Vita Porph.* 10; Liban., *Or.* 1.43, 36.1–3 (cf. Zon. 13.8.17f., and Amm. 26.3.2)—though the pure were immune, Plot., *Enn.* 4.4,43; and MacMullen, op. cit. (n. 25) 317.

36. Svoboda, op. cit. (n. 34) 24f., 29–31; Iambl., *Myst.* 2.9f.

37. Euseb., *Praep. ev.* 4.23 (Porphyry); C. Bonner, *Studies in Magical Amulets* (1950) 15f.; Dodds, op. cit. (n. 5) 64f.; *Corp. Herm.* (ed. Nock, II, 1945); *Asclepius* 37; Macrob., *Sat.* 1.23.13; Porph., *Vita Plotin.* 10; Hopfner, op. cit. (n. 34) 1.14.

38. Fronto, *Ep.* 3.9.1–2; Celsus in Orig., *C. Cels.* 5.25; Iambl., *Myst.* 1.20, 5.25; Julian, *Adv. Gal.* 143A–B; Hopfner, *Ueber die Geheimlehren von Jamblichus* (1922) 243, adding Procl., *In Tim.* 142C; and supra n. 16.

39. Iambl., *Myst.* 3.3; Dio 65.25.5, 79[78].7.4, 80[79].18.1; supra n. 7. "The term [*daimon*] ordinarily indicates, in Dio Cassius, a divinity of the second rank often foreign, entrusted with functions among mortals"—J. Beaujeu, *La religion romaine à l'apogée de l'empire* (1955) 344 n. 4

40. Constantine attributed *stasis* in the Church to the operation of "the envious *daemon*" (Soz., *H. E.* 1.19). For similar views on the deceitful activity of demons who control events through the control of men's minds, see Athenag., *Pro Christ.* 27; Cypr., *Idol. vanit.* 6f.; Theoph., *Ad Autol.* 2.8 and 28; Arnob., *Adv. nat.* 1.56; Greg. Naz., *Or.* 1.47, 39.7; Theodoret., *H. E.* 1.1C; Euseb., *H. E.* 2.14.1, 3.8.9, 4.7.1, 9, and 10; 5.14.1, 7.17.1; Justin., *Apol.* 1.5 and 26, 2.13; Orig., *C. Cels.* 3.32, 4.32, 4.92, 5.5; Tert., *Apol.* 27; and Lact., *Mort. pers.* 3.

41. See the discussion and sources in MacMullen op. cit. (n. 25) chaps. 3–4.

42. Demons were seen as intermediary beings (Arnob., *Adv. nat.* 2.35; Euseb., *Praep. ev.* 4.5), formerly angels until their fall (Tat., *Ad Graec.* 12; Tert., *Apol.* 22; Laect., *Div. Inst.* 2.15; Euseb., *Praep. ev.* 7.16; Athenag., *Pro Christ.* 24; *Consult. Zacchaei* [ed. Morin] 1.30f.; Phot., *Bibl.* 234f. = Methodius; Svoboda, op. cit. [n. 34] 6f.). What pagans called gods were either formerly mortals (Euhemerism: Arnob., *Adv. nat.* 1.37; Firm. Mat., *Err. prof. rel.* 2.3, 7.6; Cypr., *Idol. vanit.* 1; Athenag., *Pro Christ.* 28) or simply demons (Tat., *Ad Graec.* 22; Justin, *Apol.* 1.5; Clem. Alex., *Cohort.* 1.2.63 and 69; Tert., *Apol.* 22; Euseb., *C. Hierocl.* 25 and *Praep. ev.* 4.5 and 23; *Consult. Zacchaei* 1.5; Soc., *H. E.* 3.23; Soz., *H. E.* 2.5; Theodoret., *H. E.* 1.1C, 3.3). They lodged in cult statues (Ps. 96.5; Ps.-Clem., *Hom.* 9.15; Cypr., *Idol. vanit.* 7; Rufin., *PG* 12.789B; Basil, *PG* 30.532C; Firm. Mat., *Err. prof. rel.* 13.4; Athenag., *Pro Christ.* 26f.), delighting in the smoke and blood of sacrifices (Orig., *C. Cels.* 7.5; Tert., *Apol.* 22; Firm. Mat., *Err. prof. rel.* 13.4; Basil, *PG* 30.165C and 532C), issuing deceitful oracles to pagans (Cypr., *Idol. vanit.* 6; *Consult. Zacchaei* 1.27; Svoboda, op. cit. 34); they sought sexual license through possession (Ps.-Clem., *Hom.* 9.9f.; [Clem. Rom.], *Recog.* 4.16; *Consult. Zacchaei* 1.30; Svoboda, op. cit. 31). Especially by controlling men's minds and impulses they intervened to shape historical events (Justin, *Apol.* 1.44.12; Cypr., *Idol. vanit.* 7; Euseb., *Vita Const.* 1.45, 1.49, 3.12, 3.26, *H. E.* 3.8.5, 4.7.2, 4.11.9, 9.10.2; Greg. Naz., *PG* 36.341B; Soc., *H. E.* 4.19; Theodoret., *H. E.* 1.1C). They could be called or banished by spells (Arnob., *Adv. nat.* 1.43–45), but could not hurt the pure (Lact., *Div. Inst.* 2.16). Nations and peoples were assigned to the oversight of angels (supra n. 13; Clem. Alex., *Cohort.* 2; J. Daniélou, *Origène* [1948] 236f.; idem, *Recherches de science religieuse* 38 [1951] 132–34).

43. Theodoret., *H. E.* 2.7.

44. Ibid. 1.28; Soc., *H. E.* 1.27; Soz., *H. E.* 2.25, 4.10—all recounting accusations against Athanasius; also against Eusebius of Emesa (Soc. 2.9; Soz. 3.6), Cyprian (Prudent., *Perist.* 13.21f.), Constantius (Amm. 21.1.6), and various heresiarchs (Iren., *Adv. haer.* 1.13.3, and Euseb., *H. E.* 4.2 and 4.11.4, quoting Irenaeus and Justin; Tert., *De praescr. haer.* 43; idem, *Adv. Marc.* 1.18). One set of charges against a certain Syrian bishop in 444 is interestingly analyzed by E. Peterson in *Miscellanea Pio Paschini* 1 (1948) 95–99. The usual term of abuse was *goes* and *goeteia* (*cf.* Joseph., *A. J.* 20.5.1, 20.8.5f., 20.8.10).

45. On *Christus magus* see Lact., *Div. Inst.* 5.2, refuting Hierocles' comparison of Apollonius and Christ; ibid. 5.3; Athanas., *Or. incarn. verbi* (*PG* 25.181); and Arnob., *Adv. nat.* 1.53; cf. Athanas., *PG* 25.129 and 149, and *Consult. Zacchaei* 1.13, on *magica carmina*.

46. See nn. 35, 37 and 42, and esp. Porph., *Vita Plotini* 10, with Theodoret., *Graec. affect. cur.* 12.96f.; Arnob., *Adv. nat.* 2.2; Tert., *Apol.* 46; Orig., *C. Cels.* 1.60, 3.29; Euseb., *H. E.* 7.10.4, 9.3; Soc., *H. E.* 3.18; Soz., *H. E.* 5.2, 5.19; and Hopfner, op. cit. (n. 34) 1.14 (a Neoplatonist view).

47. Euseb., *Vita Const.* 2.50; *H. E.* 7.10.4, cf. 7.17 and 9.3; Soc. 3.18, 4.24.

48. Eunap., *Vit. soph.* 481; cf. the attack repulsed by Plotinus, in MacMullen, *op. cit.* (n. 25) 100f.

49. Euseb., *H. E.* 8.14.5; supra n. 18.

11. DISTRUST OF THE MIND IN THE FOURTH CENTURY

1. Sufficient, concerning all these persons, to refer to the article in *RE* s.vv.; L.Friedländer, *Roman Life and Manners* (1907) 4.48. Add such lesser names as Annius Tiberianus (s.v., *RE* col. 766f.) and Optatianus Porphyrius, prefect of Rome (G. Chmiel, *Untersuchungen zu Publ. Opt. Porfyrios* [1930]); also, those other writers whose works are known to us only indirectly, and who likewise attained high office—for example, Protadius and Minervius (J. Vesserau, *Cl. Rutilius Namatianus* [1904] 224f.) and Nicomachus Flavianus (B. H. Warmington, *North African Provinces* [1954] 104).

2. Firm. Matern., *Math.* 3.5.37; see further illustration in Paneg. vet. 5[9].5.4; 7[6].23.1f.; Amm. 27.9.6; Auson., *Profess.* 1; among modern works, especially H.-I. Marrou, *History of Education* (1956) 311f.; T. Haarhoff, *Schools of Gaul* (1920) 135–74; and P. Petit, *Etudiants de Libanius* (1956) 154–88.

3. Like the circles of Aulus Gellius and of Plutarch, later groups clustered around Macrobius, Ausonius, or Symmachus, overlapping and sharing their members and correspondence. For literature as an inheritance, we may instance Protadius (Vesserau 224) or the Flavii Postumii Titiani (A. Chastagnol, *Fastes de la préfecture de Rome* [1962] 41f.).

4. Clearest through his correspondence; but on his appointment of orators and *literati* to office, see e.g. Liban., *Or.* 18.158f.; Amm. 21.10.6; 22.1.2; 27.9.8; *Cod. Theod.* 13.3.5; Paneg. vet. 11[3].1.4 and 23.4; Himerius, *Or.* 7.1.

5. Constantine, *civilibus artibus et liberalibus studiis deditus* (Eutrop., *Brev.* 10.7) showed favor to Sopater as to the less well known Nicagoras—see P. Graindor, *Byzantion* 3 (1926) 209f., and O. Schissel, *Klio* 21 (1927) 369.

6. Aurel. Vict., *Caes.* 42.23, cf. 42.4 and Amm. 21.16.4.

7. On Valens, see *Epit. de Caes.* 45.6, balanced by the remarks attributed to him in Amm. 27.6.9, in which he recognizes the value of liberal studies; on Theodosius, Auson., *Praefat.* 3 (ed. Peiper, p. 3), and Themistius, *Or.* 34.7.

8. Especially in the Augustan Histories and Aurelius Victor, but also in other writers—*Epit. de Caes.* 41.8; 44.4; 45.6; 47.4; Eutrop., *Brev.* 10.7; 10.10; Amm. 14.6.1 and E. A. Thompson, *Historical Work of Ammianus Marcellinus* (1947) 14 n. 1; in general, the excellent pages of A. Alföldi, *A Conflict of Ideas in the Later Roman Empire* (1952) 102–4, with further material.

9. H. I. Marrou, *MOUSIKOS ANHR* (1937) 215 n. 37; on the cultural difference, Petit, *Libanius et la vie municipale* (1955) 180; SHA *Alex. Sev.* 16.3; Paneg. vet. 11[3].20.1.

10. Liban., *Or.* 18.288 (quoted in the text) and 158; cf. Lact., *De mort. persecut.* 22, judges being *humanitatis litterarum rudes*; *Cod. Theod.* 14.1.1 (357; 360), forbidding promotion to the scribe who is not so trained that *citra offensam vitii ex eodem verba procedant.*

11. *Cod. Just.* 10.31.6 (Diocl.).

12. Sulpicius Lupercus Servasius, *De cupiditate* 29f., charges that lawyers "lack Latin, and mangle ridiculous words, to the horrible sound of their turbid speech" (fourth or fifth century); cf. Paneg. vet. 11[3].20.1, "the science of civil law . . . was declared a skill for ex-slaves," under Constantine. On official language, see above, chapter 8, pp. 67ff.

13. Aurel. Vict., *Caes.* 39.26; [and, on the prestige enjoyed by immigrants, see my *Corruption and the Decline of Rome* (1988) 199–202].

14. *Epit. de Caes.* 37.1; 40.10; 40.15; 40.18; 41.9; Firm. Matern., *De errore profan. relig.* 16.1; Amm. 21.10.8; 30.4.2; 31.14.5; Paneg. vet. 11[3].21.2.

15. H.-I. Marrou, *St. Augustin* (1958) 170 and 273; F. Kühnert, *Allgemeinbildung und Fachbildung in der Antike* (1961) passim, esp. 18 and 20.

16. Amm. 22.16.17 (cf. 26.1.8); also Julian, *Adv. Galil.* 131C, on the west in general; in medicine, Amm. 16.8.1, Joh. Chrysos., *In Ep. ad Coloss.* III *homil.* 8.5 (*PG* 62.357f.), and, more broadly, F. Jürss, *Klio* 43–45 (1965) 382f.

17. Lact., *Div. Inst.* 3.5.4; Basil, *Homil. in Ps.* 45.2 (*PG* 29.417); and compare the statement of Marcellus Empiricus, in the early fifth century, that he had "learned chance, simple remedies from peasants and lowly folk," *De medicamentis* (ed. Niedermann) pr. 2; for medicinal magic practiced by the educated, cf. Concilium Laodicenum (ed. Jonkers) 36; Firm. Matern., *Math.* 3.5.32; Liban., *Or.* 1.201; Amm. 16.8.2; *Cod. Theod.* 9.16.3 (321); Veget., *Mulomedicina* 3.12; and Eunap., *Vit. soph.* 499, on the use in the medical schools of Alexandria of *theiasmos . . . hosos ex iatrikes es anthropous hekei ton kamnonton es prognosin*; for amulets, S. Eitrem, *Symb. Oslo.* 19 (1939) 59, and C. Bonner, *Studies in Magical Amulets* (1950) 13.

18. Himerius, *Ecl.* 3 pr.; 4.12.

19. Typical is Themistius, *Or.* 18.267, re-using phrases from *Or.* 1.1 and 34.460, and Ammianus' thirty-five synonyms for "at dawn"; cf. H. Hagendahl, *Studia Ammianea* (1921) 101f.

20. P.-M. Camus, *Ammien Marcellin* (1967) 41 and 88–99.

21. *Math.* 3.7.13; 3.9.10; cf. 3.10.14.

22. *Cod. Theod.* 14.9.1 (370); on the size of the bureaucracy, see my article in *HSCP* 68 (1964) 306f., confirmed by A.H.M. Jones' much fuller calculations, *The Later Roman Empire* (1964) chap. 16. Notice also that, from Diocletian into the sixth century, the chief law school (at Beirut) was restricted to an enrollment of twenty-five; cf. Marrou, op. cit. (n. 2) 302.

23. Liban., *Or.* 1.214 (cf. 234); Petit, op. cit. (n. 9) 347f., 365f.

24. Arnob., *Adv. nat.* 1.58; Lact., *Div. Inst.* 5.1.10f.; cf. 5.1.15 and 17 (comparing Aug., *Ep.* 44.1); and 1.1.8.

25. Paneg. vet. 11[3].1.20, *oratoriam dicendi facultatem ut multi laboris et minimi usus negotium nostri proceres respuebant*.

26. *Epit. de Caes.* 41.8—not a new charge, of course; see e.g. Philostratus, *Vit. soph.* 499.

27. Aurel. Vict., *Caes.* 39.26; Lact., *De mort. persecut.* 22.4.

28. Zos. 4.14f.: *hapantas tous epi philosophia tenikauta diaboetous e allos logois entethrammenous*.

29. *Philosophi* in Amm. 29.1.36, 37, and 42; 29.2.25; cf.19.12.12; Eunap., *Vit. soph.* 478–81; Liban., *Or.* 18.287.

30. Amm. 29.1.41; 29.2.3; cf. the chilling incident in Joh. Chrysos., *In Acta Apost. homil.* 38 (*PG* 9.273f.), where two youths find and pick up by chance a suspect volume thrown away, just as a soldier comes into sight. Death if they're caught with it!

31. Eunap., *Vit. soph.* 478.

32. Paneg. vet. 11[3].23.4.

33. Ibid. 32.4–6; cf. Aug., *De civ. dei* 5.2, where Poseidonius is *hoc philosophus astrologus*; Hier., *In Dan.* 2, astrologers are *philosophi Chaldaeorum*; and notice the connections of profession implied in Julian, *Or.* 6.197, or in Firm. Matern., *Math.* 3.2.18 and 3.2.6, *philosophi, mathematici, magi philosophi et caelestia saepe tractantes* being all strung together. For the background, see my *Enemies of the Roman Order* (1966) 320f. and 325.

34. Clem. Alex., *Strom.* 4.80; later, and of course quite against the temper of his times, Julian, *Or.* 6.197D.

35. A. D. Nock, *JEA* 15 (1929) 222, points out that magical papyri mostly survive from fourth-century editions, and there is a similar profile of evidence for *defixiones*, etc. Cf. MacMullen, *Paganism in the Roman Empire* (1981) 179 n. 35. The quantity of heretical writings hardly needs comment, whether they be Ophitic, Manichaean, or Arian. I am struck also by the popularity of such a tale as the duel between St. Peter and Simon Magus in Rome, familiar in its details to Arnobius (*Adv. nat.* 2.12) and Cyril (*Cat.* 6.14f.) and re-copied in P. Oxy. 849 (early fourth century). For the burning of books, see Paul, *Sent.* 5.23.18 (cf. 5.21.4), magical treatises; *Mos. et Rom. legum coll.* 15.6 (A.D. 297); and, for the burning of Christian writings, from a hundred testimonies, Lact., *De mort. persecut.* 12.2.

36. On medicine, above, n. 17; on the *ars mathematica damnabilis, Cod. Just.* 9.18.2; on the meaning of *mathematicus*, MacMullen, op. cit. (n. 33) 320f.; on *sophia* and *sophistes* as "magic" and "magician," see Julian, *Or.* 6.197D, Greg. Naz., *Or.* 1.55 *Contra Iulianum*, and Eunap., *Vit. soph.* passim; but also Philostratus, *Vit. Apollon.* 7.39 and passim, and Porph., *Vit. Plotin.* 10, of the third century.

37. On rioting, consider the reception of Eusebius of Emesa, after his years of studying *ta philosopha* at Alexandria: *diastasianton ton Emisenon . . . eloidoreito gar, hos mathematiken askoumenos* (Soc., *H. E.* 2.9). On similar charges against Constantius et al., to references gathered above in chapter 10, p. 316 n.44, add Amm. 15.7.8; Liban., *Or.* 1.194; and Sulp. Sev., *Chron.* 1.46, quoted in the text.

38. Alex. of Lycopolis, *Manichaei opin. disp.* (ed. Brinkmann) 1 p. 3; Arnob., *Adv. nat.* 2.10; cf. the closely similar passage of the mid-third century, *Asclepius* 1.12b (Scott): *multi etenim incomprehensibilem philosophiam efficiunt, et eam multifaria ratione confundunt . . . in varias disciplinas nec conprehensibiles eam callida commentatione miscentes*; and for still further fourth-century texts saying just the same thing, see my *Paganism* (n. 35) 179 n. 137. It is likely that the popularity of Sextus Empiricus (Greg. Naz., *Or.* 10.21.12) was due to his feeding of prejudices, through distortion or simplification of his doctrines.

39. Lucian (in the Loeb ed.), *Hermotimus* 56; *Zeus Rants* 42; *Philosophies for Sale* 21f.; Tert., *De praescr.* 7; and Hippolytus (if it be he) quoted in Euseb., *H. E.* 5.28.14f.—all expressing a like point of view. Origen, *Homil. in Ps.* 36.5.1 (*PG* 12.1359), in vain protests against "hating and opposing those who pursue the study of wisdom"; later, only Julian (*Ep.* 28.410C) protests against the common perception. I cannot take proper account, here, of specifically Christian views, which approached the problem of secular knowledge from their own bases; but the views expressed in the so-called *Little Labyrinth* (Euseb., *H. E.* 5.28.13ff.) are illustrative.

40. Lact., *Div. Inst.* 3.2.8f.: *cum vero tot temporibus, tot ingeniis in eius* [scil., *sapientiae*] *inquisitione contritis non sit comprehensa, apparet nullam ibi* [scil., in

philosophy] *esse sapientiam*, etc. Cf. 1.1.18 and 3.1.1, and notice further how a pseudo-philosophy like the Hermetic commands his respect, in many passages, esp. *Div. Inst.* 4.9.3 and *De ira dei* 11.12f. The same source of wisdom is cited side by side with Plato and Pythagoras in Arnob., *Adv. nat.* 2.13.

41. Euseb., *Praep. ev.* 15.62.16, cf. 15.62.1; Philastrius of Brescia, *De haeresibus* 102 (*PL* 12.1216A), of the 380s, quoting the Septuagint, and Philostorg., *H. E.* 12.10 p. 147 (Bidez-Winkelmann), emphatically of the same opinion (which later, by half a millennium and more, Photius found heretical). Earlier, "Lactantius explicitly rages against science, *Naturforschung*" proposing answers to questions out of Scripture, or a cessation from any at all, which might be impious prying. Cf. J. Geffcken, *Zwei griechischen Apologeten* (1907) 293f.

42. Origen, *Homil. in Ps.* 36.5.1 (*PG* 12.1359); Euseb., *H. E.* 5.28.15; cf. Palladius, *Hist. Laus.* pr. 4, and passages in John Chrysostom discussed by G.J.M. Bartelink, *Rev. d'ascétique et de mystique* 36 (1960) 482 and 490.

43. Ibid. 487; Soz., *H. E.* 1.17; *Mart. S. Apollonii* 33 (Knopf-Krüger, *Ausgewählte Martyrerakten* [1929] 54).

44. *LSJ* s.v. (Galen, vol. 5 p. 9, ed. Kühn), contradicted, however, by the same author making a distinction between Christian believers and philosophers, "those who philosophize," in R. Walzer, *Galen on Christians and Jews* (1949) 57. In Clement of Alexandria, Eusebius, and others after these, *philosophein* means the "practice of Christianity," "living . . . rationally and virtuously, and esp., in accordance with Christian morality" (Justin, Clement, etc.), "implying esp. poverty" (Clem., Joh. Chrysos., etc.), "live as an ascetic," the *vita austera* without luxury or expense, in Euseb., Greg. Nyss., Chrysos., Soz. 8.12, and Theodoret, all in Stephanus s.vv. and G.W.H. Lampe's *Patristic Greek Lexicon* (1961) s.v. *philosopheo, philosophia*, and *philosophos*; add passages from Joh. Chrysos such as *In 2 Thess.*, *PG* 62.434f. and *In Ep. ad Coloss.* 1 *homil.* 1.6 (*PG* 62.207). For the background, see G. Bardy, " 'Philosophie' et 'philosophe' dans le vocabulaire chrétien des premiers siècles," *Rev. d'ascétique et de mystique* 25 (1949) 97f. and 107, from whom I draw the Eusebius text that I quote: *Praep. ev.* 12.29.1 (*GCS* 8, 2, 119), on the prophets' devotion to contemplation, *pros mono to Theo ten dianoian echontes*; but notice how the same author (*H. E.* 6.4.13) can use both meanings of the *philosophos/ia*, "disciplined ratiocination" and "asceticism," in the same sentence, seemingly unaware of what he is doing. In Latin, the shift in meaning may be exemplified by Paulinus in his biography of Ambrose (§7, *PL* 14.29B) recording how the saint *philosophiam profiteri voluit, futurus sed verus philosophus Christi, qui contemptis saecularibus pompis*, etc.

45. Philostrat., *Vit. Apollon.* 8.6 and 879, before Domitian, allegedly (the work of literature being of the first half of the third century).

46. Athanas., *Vita S. Antonii* 34 and 60 (*PG* 26.893B and 931f.).

47. Rutil. Namat., *De reditu* 517–26. Cf. the characterization offered by a sophist (also, of course, a pagan), Eunapius, in his *Vit. soph.* 472: "The so-called monks, who live a pig's life and flaunt their shamelessness in public."

48. Athanas., *Vita. S. Antonii* 73; cf. 72 and 74, with similar stories in which the saint, *anchinous* and *synetos* despite lack of culture, routs "the Greeks" or "those who were thought wise among the Greeks."

49. Rufin., *Hist. mon.* 28 (*PL* 21.452); cf. F. Nau, *Rev. de l'Orient chrétien* 14

(1909) 369 = *PL* 73.891, for the Greek and Latin versions of a similar confrontation between "the Greeks" and a simple ascetic.

50. *Apophthegmata patrum*, *PG* 65.88f.

51. I. Hausherr, *Orientalia christiana periodica* 2 (1936) 352; cf. ibid. 351–62, on the meaning of the saying.

52. Rejecting as silly the religious ideas of *rustici* and *anoetoi*, see the interestingly nuanced discussion in Plin., *N. H.* 28.4.22ff.; Plin., *Ep.* 8.5ff., with a sense of the ludicrousness of rustic religion; Lucian likewise, in his *Alex.* 9 and 17; Apul., *Apol.* 3.6, 27.1, and passim; and MacMullen, op. cit. (n. 35) 70f. with notes. In the later empire, distinction may be made in terminology ("as the vulgar call it," *vel sim.*) without there being any distinction in the substance of opinion; cf. *Cod. Theod.* 9.16.4 (357) and 6 (358), Amm. 29.2.6 (who, however, elsewhere sets himself apart from the excesses of the book-burning variety of superstition), and Hier., *In Is.* 47.12 (*PL* 24.457), "*vulgo appellantur . . . mathematici*" etc. Only Julian distinguishes know-nothing anti-intellectualism as the *doxa ton pollon*, *Or.* 6.197B–D.

53. Euseb., *Mart. Pal.* 4.15; above, n. 41, on Philastrius and Philostorgius; and below, chapter 24, p. 274.

54. *Les moines d'Orient* 1 [1961] 21.

55. Momigliano, "Popular religious beliefs and the late Roman historians," in *Popular Belief and Practice*, ed. G. J. Cuming and D. Baker (1972) 9 and 17, going on to say, "Anyone who reads in Socrates and Sozomenus the story of the two banishments of John Chrysostom is left in no doubt about the weight of mob theology."

56. Brown, *The Cult of the Saints* (1981) 19, quoting Momigliano, op. cit. (n. 55) 18 on the non-existence of "popular beliefs" as opposed to those of "the elite." The former are, in the quoted words, "never treated . . . as characteristic of the masses and consequently discredited." For the surrounding discussion by Brown, see his *Cult* 12–22 and 28–33, his article "The rise and function of the holy man in late antiquity," *JRS* (1971), republished in his *Society and the Holy in Late Antiquity* (1982), esp. 107ff.; ibid. 8–13 and passim (a study belonging to 1977); and *The Making of Late Antiquity* (1978) 7–11, on "lower class . . . elements" and " 'a failure of nerve,' or a 'decline of rationalism' "—all, terminology which is to be rejected.

57. For the exploitation/influence explanation, see esp. Brown's *Cult* 32f. and *Making of Late Antiquity* 57 and 59, and 63f.; for the poet's apostrophe to Dullness, meeting Professor Brown's quotation in *JRS* 58 [1968] 87 = *Religion and Society* (1972) 284 and *Cult* 18, see Pope's *Dunciad* 1.169f. (not that dullness is by any means Professor Brown's style).

58. Momigliano, op. cit. (n. 55) 12.

59. Callistus bishop of Rome 217–222, a freedman (Hippol., *Philos.* 9.7); and bishops unable to sign their names, in E. Schwartz, *Acta conciliorum oecumenicorum* (1927–1930) 1, 1, p. 63 no. 190, the bishop of Gadara unable to sign his own name; similarly, others, 1, 7 p. 101–104 nos. 17, 19, 24, 26, etc., 112 no. 8, 114 no. 94, 116 no. 163, and 117 no. 184; and western examples in Africa, *PL* 11.1302 col. 2 line 9, and R. Kaster, "Professio litterarum," in *Guardians of Language: The Grammarian and Society in Late Antiquity* (1988) 37 n. 16, the ref. thanks to E. A. Meyer.

60. Euseb., *Vita Const.* 2.68–69 and 71, writing on Arianism. For similar views in

one of Constantine's intellectual advisers, Lactantius, regarding philosophers, see Geffcken, op. cit. (n. 41) 294 n. 1.

61. *Or. ad sanctos*, on which see my *Paganism* (n. 35) 179f. n. 38.

62. *Cod. Theod.* 1.4.1 (trans. Pharr) and *Cod. Just.* 6.9.9; cf. above, n. 26.

12. TWO TYPES OF CONVERSION TO EARLY CHRISTIANITY

1. See *Acta Pionii* 19.11 p. 162 of the edition of H. Musurillo, *Acts of the Martyrs* (1972), by which I cite most of the martyr acts from here on; also see my *Paganism in the Roman Empire* (1981) 83 (hereafter *Paganism*), adding from later times Aug., *Ep.* 16.1: a pagan's doubts about Olympus, while believing in *salutaria* numina (but also in "the one god all-high, without beginning or offspring, a grand and magnificent father").

2. See my *Paganism* 76 and P. A. Brunt in *Studies in Latin Literature*, ed. C. De-roux (1979) 512, on pagan skeptics; on the Christians' involvement, see *Acta Acacii* 2.7 p. 58 of the edition of R. Knopf, *Ausgewählte Märtyrerakten*, ed. 3 by G. Krüger (1929).

3. P. Oxy. 1382 (mid/late second century), in an aretalogy; on a third-century gem, A. Dimitrova-Milceva in *Vorträge des 10. int. Limeskongresses* (1977) 285; more examples in my *Paganism* 186; and the interesting scene in the *Acta Petri* 26 p. 73 of the edition of R. A. Lipsius, *Acta apostolorum apocrypha* 1 (1891), where the crowd in Rome shouts *unus deus, unus deus, unus deus Petri*.

4. Plin., *N. H.* 2.5.22, *Fortuna, toto mundo et omnibus locis . . . Fortuna sola invocatur . . . et cum conviciis colitur*. For demons causing plague etc., cf. Philostr., *Vita Apoll.* 4.10, the same view being Origen's at *C. Cels.* 1.31 and 8.31, and in Just., *2 Apol.* 5, or Tert., *Apol.* 22.4.

5. See sources cited in my *Paganism* 185.

6. *Test. animae* 1; cf. A. D. Nock, *Conversion* (1933) 192.

7. Orig., *C. Cels.* 1.8; P. Bodmer 20 cols. IV–V; cf. Just., *2 Apol.* 3.

8. Caution dictates the use of only as few. See W. Schneemelcher in E. Hennecke, *Neutestamentliche Apokryphen*[3], Eng. trans. (1965) 2.275, dating the *Acta Petri* to the 180s and (pp. 261ff.) showing its use by the *Didascalia* and in Origen; ibid. 351, the *Acta Pauli (et Theclae)* dated to ca. 185–195; and texts in Lipsius, op. cit. (n. 3).

9. Lucian, *Peregrinus* 11–13; Galen, in R. Walzer, *Galen on Jews and Christians* (1949) 15; Minucius Felix, *Octavius* 9.6, given maximum proportions by P. Frassi-netti, *Giornale ital. di filol.* 2 (1949) 238–54; and Just, *2 Apol.* 3.1.

10. Acts 10.25 (Peter) and 14.11–12 (Barnabas and Paul) and 28.6, cf. Musurillo 348 and *Acta Petri* 28 p. 78 Lipsius (Peter worshipped). For a wholly pagan parallel, see Philostr., *Vita Apoll.* 4.44 and 7.32, Apollonius saluted as a god.

11. Acts 8.11.

12. Lk 9.33.

13. Acts 8.19 and 16.16.

14. *Hypsistos* in Acts 16.17.

15. Acts 14.12.

16. E.g. Musurillo 148 and 158 (*Acta Pionii* 9.9 and 16.4); cf. Celsus supposing Jesus would be an angel, in a Jew's eyes, or anyone else's, *C. Cels.* 2.9.1 and 2.44, and pointing out the flaw in Christian monotheism, 8.12. Further, pagans could only

have understood *theou pais* as "God's slave," at Musurillo 42, cf. Acts 3.26 and elsewhere.

17. E.g. Musurillo 162, Zeus *basileus* compared with Christ *basileus*, ibid. 8 and 188, or Paul to the Areopagus, Acts 17.24, Christ *kyrios*.

18. *Apol.* 24.3ff., cf. Min. Fel., *Octavius* 20.1, and Athenagoras, *Leg.* 6, attributing a widespread belief in One God to pagans generally, or to "the philosophers" (as does Clement, *Protrepticus* 5, PG 8.164ff., and meaning especially Plato, *Protr.* 6, PG 8.172ff.). Further, see my *Paganism* 86ff. and above, n. 1.

19. As H. Chadwick says in his translation of the *Contra Celsum* (1965) p. xvii: for subscribers to a sort of Platonism, "monotheism and polytheism are not mutually exclusive." But my own interpretation includes not only philosophers.

20. Eusebius (*H. E.* 2.3.2) says the disciples induced people to reject *daimonike polytheia*, but I find no other uses of the term in Christian sources before A.D. 337 (nor the word *monotheia*).

21. *Acta Acacii* 1.9ff. p. 58 (Knopf-Krüger).

22. E.g. Acts 17.29 and 19.26 and Musurillo 24, 94, and 296; often in the Apologists, e.g. Theophilus, *Ad Autolycum* 1.1 and 2.2, and Athenag., *Leg.* 15.

23. *Daimones* = pagan "gods" in Tert., *Apol.* 23.11, Just., 1 *Apol.* 56, 58 and 62–64, *Acta Claudii* et al. 1.4 and 8 p. 107 (Knopf-Krüger), or Musurillo 22 (or in Jewish sources like Jos. *A. J.* 8.2.5), more often *daimonia* (regularly in NT, also Musurillo 306 and *Acta Claudii* et al. 5.2 p. 108 Knopf-Krüger); demons, not gods, in idols do miracles; cf. Athenag., *Leg.* 23 and 26; Orig., *C. Cels.* 8.62; Tert., *Apol.* 22.8ff.; and pagan predecessors in these views, in my *Paganism* 82. For *daimonia* as a derogatory term, see Acts 17.18 and Jn 10.21.

24. 1 Cor. 8.5: *eiper eisin legomenoi theoi . . . hosper eisin theoi polloi kai kyrioi polloi, all' hemin heis theos*, cf. Gal. 4.8, and perhaps some reflection of the point of dispute in Celsus' calling Hecate along with other powers "*daimones*," *C. Cels.* 1.9, or angels, "gods," 5.4.

25. *Apol.* 23.2.

26. *Acta Petri* 23 p. 71 (Lipsius).

27. Mt 10.8.

28. *Apol.* 23.4, trans. T. R. Glover (Loeb ed.), where *dominus* = "god" like Gr. *Kyrios*.

29. See passages quoted in my *Paganism* 168 n. 4, and conversions wrought upon seeing exorcism, in Euseb., *H. E.* 5.7.4 = Iren., *C. haer.* 2.32.4 (Gaul in the 180s). They continued to exert their power later, e.g. in Augustine's world, *Civ. dei* 22.8 (*CSEL* 40, 2, pp. 602ff.).

30. *Acta Pauli (et Theclae)* 17 p. 246 (Lipsius), Paul addressing the throng at Iconium.

31. Tert., *Apol.* 17.6; Orig., *C. Cels.* 8.45; and more evidence in my *Paganism* 32. For Christian stories of divine punishment, cf. for example Acts 4.5–10 and 13.10–11 (compare 1 Tim. 1.20); Tert., *Ad Scap.* 4.3; *Acta Petri* 15 p. 62 (Lipsius) (the wicked are stricken dumb); *Acta Andreae* narr. 36 (Ep. Gr. 15) (the wicked a suicide); Euseb., *H. E.* 6.9.5, comparing Acts 12.23 and more famous victims among the persecutors, e.g. in Lactantius. For God as spyer-out of wickedness, see Min. Fel., *Octavius* 10.5:

Christians "would have Him a hostile figure, restless, shameless and inquisitive," etc., repeated at 23.9.

32. Lk 3.9 and 17; 10.12 and 12.5; 1 Thess. 1.10, and, as general impression, A. von Harnack, *The Mission and Expansion of Christianity* (1961) 90.

33. Above, n. 30, and Mt 10.7 and 15 (cf. Lk 3.7–9; 10.12; 12.5; 19.27; and elsewhere); at Thessalonica, warning of God's wrath, *Acta Andreae* 12; but not at Lystra, Acts 14.15ff., and barely at Athens, 17.31.

34. *C. Cels.* 8.48, trans. Chadwick; cf. Just., 1 *Apol.* 8 and 68, offering the parallel of Rhadamanthus and Minos (as do Theoph., *Ad Autol.* 37, and less clearly Min. Fel., *Octavius* 35) which he expects to be told is incredible. On divine retribution threatened in martyr scenes, see Musurillo 10, 22 and 32 (bare mentions only, by Polycarp, Carpus, and Pamphilus) and the *Acta Acacii* 1.8 p. 107 (Knopf-Krüger).

35. Musurillo 126; cf. the preaching to the populace on the night before, pp. 124, and 14–44 (Pionius, at length and explicitly), and implied at lines 8ff. of the *Passion of Phileas*, ibid. p. 332.

36. Musurillo 332, similar to the pagan's challenge, *ipso corpore*? etc., in Min. Fel., *Octavius* 11.7; cf. also Acts 17.32, the Athenians hearing of the raising of the dead "jeered"; and among the Apologists conscious of the difficulty of the doctrine, notice Theoph., *Ad Autol.* 1.8; Tat., *Ad Graecos* 6; Origen meeting Celsus' protests, *C. Cels.* 4.56ff., 5.14, 5.18 (Celsus' ridicule), and 8.49; and special treatises on the resurrection by Athenagoras, Justin, Tertullian, and others.

37. *Peregrinus* 13; and, for the rarity of beliefs in immortality, my *Paganism* 53–57. C. B. Welles in *Excavations at Dura-Europus, Prelimin. Report* 9 (1944) 179, reports the Durene epitaph containing the wish, "may the *psychai theai* receive him," but can find no parallel to this thought. I am also struck by the evidence in W. Peek, *Griechische Vers-Inschriften* 1 (1955), where, among many hundreds of epitaphs of the Roman period, only a handful (among nos. 1755–77, passim) offer the distinction, "the earth holds the body but the Aether [or Heaven, the Gods, the Muses, etc.] hold the soul." All the rest are silent about eternity, or they urge the reader to "drink up, you see what you will come to" (e.g. no. 378), or they refer to the soul in its earthly existence (no. 540).

38. Origen, *C. Cels.* 2.5 and 6.11, knowledge less stated than hinted at by Celsus; knowledge declared, by Justin to his tormentors, Musurillo 52; and indicated, by imagined pagans, ibid. 206 (the *Passio SS Mariani et Iacobi* 8.7) and Min. Fel., *Octavius* 11.5; preached to the unconverted only by Apollonius martyr (not a source to be pressed), Musurillo 100.

39. *Acta Pauli (et Theclae)* 11 p. 243 (Lipsius).

40. Ibid. 17 p. 246 (Lipsius); Acts 17.30–31; and taught by Peter in Judea, *Acta Petri* 17 p. 64 (Lipsius).

41. *C. Cels.* 3.59 and 8.48–49, cf. 4.10; above, n. 31. As to punishment after death, I find almost nothing. F. Cumont in *Afterlife in Roman Paganism* (1923) cites outright denials of it (p. 83), discounts the unusable (pp. 84f.), and is left with only the Syrian novel, Heliod., *Aeth.* 8.9, and the *Apocalypse of Peter*. The pictures they present claim no generality and their origin is unknown. S.G.F. Brandon, *The Judgement of the Dead* (1967), chap. 4, adds nothing from the centuries A.D. except (p. 93) Lucian's *Menippus*, which is surely a *jeu d'esprit* and nothing more (like the *Cata-*

basis, e.g. §§3 and 13). In Plutarch's *De sera num. vind.* a company of the widely learned, including a high Roman, discuss divine punishment of the wicked after death; they enjoy the idea as a novelty (566f.); but it seems to me decisive (cf. esp. 555D) that they know no such living faith anywhere.

42. *C. Cels.* 8.11, trans. Chadwick.

43. Tert., *Apol.* 2.18, trans. Glover—cf. "our fight is not against human foes but against Cosmic Powers, against the authorities and princes of the dark world," etc. (Ephes. 6.12).

44. Musurillo 102.

45. On the overwhelming respectability (to say no more) of worshipping in the way of one's fathers, see my *Paganism* 3ff.; on Christians' consciousness of their innovating predicament, see e.g. Clem. Alex., *Protrepticus* 10, or Just., 1 *Apol.* 12.

46. Though without any thorough search, I find only one possible active evangelist attested in post-Biblical times, outside of Asia: a certain Alexander in Gaul, Euseb., *H. E.* 5.1.49. I discount another possibility, see my *Paganism* 98 and J. Reynolds et al., *JRS* 71 (1981) 136; I also discount teachers one-to-one, inside private homes, such as Origen's (Euseb., *H. E.* 6.3.1 and 5) or such as Celsus describes, *C. Cels.* 3.55, and teachers against heresies in public but only a Christian public, in Euseb., *H. E.* 5.16.4, 6.37, and 7.24.7; and I discount Justin in a public setting at Ephesus, *Dial.* 122.4, since the interested bystanders are apparently Jews or *sebomenoi*, and in Rome as well, where Eusebius (*H. E.* 4.16.1: Justin "in debates with listeners present often refuted him," i.e. Crescens) seems only to draw out the implications of Just., 2 *Apol.* 3, *demosiai*, and 5, *prothenta me kai erotesanta auton eroteseis tinas*. But the mob in Smyrna does know Polycarp as "the teacher of Asia . . . teaching many not to offer sacrifice nor venerate the gods," Musurillo p. 10; and see further below, p. 140.

47. It was not cynical in Julian the Apostate to stress the importance of the eleemosynary factor: notice the consternation in the Roman Christian community when its chief patron withdrew support, *Acta Petri* 8 p. 55 (Lipsius).

48. For example, Just., *Dial.* 8 (but so elaborate in setting—a dialogue within a dialogue—and so indebted to Plato, e.g. *Symp.* 201ff., that I cannot take it as truly autobiographical); Tat., *Ad Graecos* 29 (quoted); Theoph., *Ad Autol.* 1.14 (brief mention of prophecies); Tert., *De paenit.* 1.1 (conversion unexplained); Greg. Thaumat., *Paneg. to Origen* (hints hidden in the verbiage, esp. chaps. 5, 13, and 15). From the fourth century I can add, besides Augustine, only two cases: of Victorinus briefly described by him, *Conf.* 8.2.3f., cf. C. Monceaux, *Hist. littéraire de l'Afrique chrétienne* 3 (1905) 377f., and Synesius, cf. J. Bregman, *Synesius of Cyrene* (1982), chap. 1 and passim—both coming to Christianity through Neoplatonism, and doing so as philosophers.

49. *Vita Pachomii* 2 p. 4 (Athanassakis), cf. Just., 2 *Apol.* 12, observation of martyrs discredits slanders about their vices (but here there is no connection with conversion).

50. Musurillo 116 and 124 (*Passio S. Perpetuae* 9.1 and 16.4), recalling the terrified jailer's conversion through the miracle at Philippi, Acts 16.25–34, and a disciple's deepening of belief in his teacher's divinity, Philostr., *Vita Apoll.* 7.38.

51. *Vita Pachomii* 5 p. 6 (Athanassakis).

52. Soc., *H. E.* 7.30 (they promptly won the battle, destroying three times their weight in enemies).

53. Musurillo 38 (*Passio SS Ptolemaei et Lucii* 2), cf. the *Acta S Dasii* 4.2 p. 93 (Knopf-Krüger).

54. Acts 22.3–21, esp. 6–13; and in letters, Gal. 1.16, 1 Cor. 9.1 and 15.8, and Phil. 3.12.

55. *Acta Petri* 20 p. 67 (Lipsius).

56. Schneemelcher in Hennecke, op. cit. (n. 8) 2.389.

57. *Ad Scap.* 4.6.

58. Notice *phasi*, PG 46.916B, *legetai* at 917B, etc., and caution at 957D.

59. Ibid. 917Aff. (of the *neokoros*), 920Cff. (of the Neocaesarian crowds), 924D (the same, plus countryfolk), and 957B (relief of plague). Compare above, n. 29; and the last pre-Constantinian scene I find, of Agapetus (s.v., in Suidas) making conversions "through miracles," e.g. raising the dead and moving mountains, and so, ca. A.D. 300, "won over many pagans to enroll themselves in Christianity" (Philostorgius, *H. E.* pp. 19f. Bidez).

60. Above, nn. 3 and 58, and Marc. Diac., *Vita Porphyrii* 21 and 31, the pagans exclaim at the miracle, *Ho Christos monos theos*, and *megas ho theos ton christianon*.

61. *Acta Petri* 10 p. 57 (Lipsius); 12 p. 60 (the call, *alium signum nobis ostende ut credamus*); 13 p. 61 (*secuti sunt plurimi hoc viso et crediderunt in domino*); 17 p. 63 (*propter hoc enim factum credent*).

62. Tert., *Apol.* 21 and 31, paganism wins devotees: *quibusdam signis et miraculis et oraculis fidem divinitatis operatur.* Also material in my *Paganism* 95ff.

63. I know of no collection of the evidence. As a beginning, notice Soz., *H. E.* 5.15 (in Gaza ca. A.D. 350, instantly upon seeing a devil exorcized); Soc., *H. E.* 1.20 (PG 67.129ff. = Theodoret, *H. E.* 1.23, *PG* 82.971ff. = *H. E.* 1.24 in *GCS*², 1954), in the reign of Constantine; ibid. 5.21.7 (*PG* 82.1244), in A.D. 388, pagans burst into hymns to God at a miraculous temple-destruction; Hier., *Vita Hilarionis* 25 (*PL* 23.41), of the A.D. 380s near Gaza; Rufinus, *H. E.* 2.4 (*PL* 21.512Cff.) of A.D. 373 or a little later, near Nitria in Egypt (cf. Soc., *H. E.* 4.24); and, of date ca. A.D. 400, Marc. Diac., *Vita Porphyrii*, locc. citt. and elsewhere. For the nature of that work, likely to be least distorted in its descriptions of miracle scenes, see the introduction in H. Grégoire and M. A. Kugener's edition (1930). Miracles often change the minds of persons already Christian, of course, e.g. Soz., *H. E.* 6.27 (*PG* 67.1369B) and 8.1(1509B).

64. On the simple folk, see *C. Cels.* 3.44 and 55, and *Acta Petri* 1 p. 44 (Lipsius); on the highly educated, see Min. Fel., *Octavius* 40.1.

65. *C. Cels.* 1.46, "even if Celsus, or the Jew that he introduces, ridicule what I am about to say . . ." (trans. Chadwick); cf. also 8.47, and compare Augustine's views: the foundations of Christian faith were laid through miracles, for we find in Scripture *quae facta sunt, et propter quod credendum facta sunt*, etc. (*Civ. dei* 22.8, *CSEL* 40, 2, p. 596).

66. *C. Cels.* 1.9 and 18; 5.15, 19, and 29; and elsewhere; also among Apologists, e.g. Min. Fel., *Octavius* 19.15, or *J Th St* 17 (1966) 111, and cf. Clem. Alex., *Stromat.* 1.12, *PG* 8.753, care taken to avoid guffaws of the masses, like the warning by

Menander Rhetor, p. 14 (Russell-Wilson), not to "look unconvincing and ridiculous to the masses" through subtlety of theological argument.

13. WHAT DIFFERENCE DID CHRISTIANITY MAKE?

1. I cite the question in my *Christianizing the Roman Empire* (1984) 154 n. 25 (hereafter, cited as *Christianizing*).

2. For example, wine, 2.20.3; dancing, 2.40f.; theater, 3.76.3; loose jokes, 3.77.1f.; cosmetics, 3.5.1 and 3 and 3.10.3; luxurious, fancy clothes, 2.105.2, 2.107.5 and 3.55.3; jewelry, 3.60.1—all, sex-connected. Special emphasis on male homosexuality and depilation, etc., in its service, the whole being *to para physin*, 3.20.2 (on depilation, Clement confesses *thermainomai hypo tou logou*, 3.19.3, and goes on to dilate on the improprieties of male hair dress and adornment, 3.3 passim, 3.57f., etc.). The same connections were drawn later, e.g. by Basil, *Homil. in Hexaemeron* 4.1f. (*PG* 29.77Af.), calling musical performances schools of licentiousness.

3. For slave-owning, notice, e.g., 2.23.2, 2.60.1, 3.47.3, and 3.39.1. The high social class addressed by Clement is recognized by L. M. White, "Scholars and patrons," in *Christian Teaching: Studies in Honor of L. G. Lewis* (1981) 328f. Similarly in the fourth century, the preacher's audience was the wealthy and powerful, cf. Basil, *Homil. in Ps.* 45 (*PG* 29.417B), *Homil. in Hexaemeron* 5.2 (*PG* 29.97Df.), and J. Bernardi, *La prédication des pères cappadociens* (1968) 71 and 77; on Greg. Naz., ibid. 106 (*Or.* 14.15); and on Greg. Nyss., ibid. 266. Only in martyr veneration did congregations draw from society at large (ibid. 31 and 306). To indicate the order of magnitude of slave-owners I deem likely in the urban population, let me point to Rome, where the slave percentage was atypically high. I sketch some proportions: suppose a population of half a million, in which the senators to the number of 600 owned an average of 100 slaves each, while each of 5,000 equites owned 25 slaves and non-equestrian rich persons each owned 5 slaves—then ca. 4 percent of the city population would own 175,000 slaves, and the remaining 300,000 persons would be free (including free men). A similar curve of distribution I believe would be found in other, less slave-heavy urban and small-town populations.

4. The derivative elements are abundantly noted by H. I. Marrou in the edition *Sources chrétiennes* vol. 70 (1960), e.g. I 49–52, 67, 71, 85f., and 90; II 45 and 65 and notes to those pages; further, H. Chadwick, *Early Christian Thought and the Classical Tradition* (1966) 36, 41, and esp. 104: "Celsus complains that Christians have nothing new to say in their ethical teaching. . . . Origen . . . simply accepts the proposition without demur."

5. Forty years ago, Fritz Schulz thought Romanists liable to overestimate the contribution of Christianity and to underestimate that of "ancient *humanitas*" in law. See his *History of Roman Legal Science* (1946) 298 with notes; more recently, G. R. Stanton, "Marcus Aurelius, emperor and philosopher," *Historia* 18 (1969) 570–87. B. Biondi, *Il diritto romano cristiano* I (1952) 103 and II (1952) 139, persists in the older view.

6. W.H.C. Frend, *The Rise of Christianity* (1984) 133. He quotes Ignatius of Antioch, the *Didache*, and other commonly adduced texts. See recently G.E.M. de Ste. Croix, "Early christian attitudes to property and slavery," in *Church Society and Politics*, ed. D. Baker (1975) 20f., quoting these and others, or similarly, H. Gülzow,

Christentum und Sklaverei (1969) 105 n. 3. Like Frend, Ste. Croix (p. 23) finds no rejection of slavery, nor do G. Boulvert and M. Morabito, "Le droit de l'esclavage dans le Haut-Empire," *ANRW* ii, 14 (1982) 160, nor again E. J. Jonkers, "De l'influence du christianisme sur la législation relative à l'esclavage," *Mnem.*[3] 1 (1934) 247— not even Biondi: "la chiese non a ragione di combattere la schiavitù." See his *Diritto* ii 376, or 379, quoting the acceptance of slavery by Leo XIII.

7. Constantine prepared for approximation to slavery of a large new category of the population, the *coloni*, through *CT* 5.17.1 (332); and, as Boulvert and Morabito point out (op. cit. [n. 6] 162), his new laws for the freeing of slaves "seem far more a complex of pro-Christian or anti-Jewish or anti-pagan measures, than pro-slave." Even his law (*CT* 2.25.1, a. 325/334) banning the splitting up of slave families upon sale applied, so far as we know, only to those on his crown estates in Sardinia; and, after all, they were still sold, not freed. For some pagan precedents, cf. *Pauli Sent.* 3.6.38 and *Dig.* 33.7.12. Slave rights he actually pruned back in *CT* 4.8.6 (323—Interpretation), 9.12.1 (319), and 4.8.7 (331) with 4.8.9 (393); and he provided revocation of freedom for ingratitude, *CJ* 6.7.2 (320). Prohibition of prostitution forced on a slave woman against her will (and only then) came not till A.D. 428 (*CT* 15.8.2), and built on pagan law that forbade prostituting a slave sold on condition that she be spared that. Constantine barred senators' sexual relations with slaves (*CT* 12.1.6, a. 318/319), but the object clearly was to force them to marry, have children, and so continue the line of their service to their communities (the slave women in such a relation were condemned to hard labor for life). Use of slaves in direct service to the emperor was banned not because servitude was immoral but because it was unseemly that such lowly creatures should be seen in the imperial palace. See W. W. Buckland, *The Roman Law of Slavery* (1908) 599. For many other matters in the same balance, see Jonkers, and Boulvert and Morabito, artt. citt. (n. 6) passim.

8. *CT* 9.12.1f. On these, I am not persuaded by the arguments of A. Watson, "Roman slave law and Roman ideology," *Phoenix* 37 (1983) 61–63; nor does he give a fair interpretation (p. 60) of *Inst. Just.* 1.8.1.2, where Antoninus Pius' own references to an *asperitas* that might be *intolerabilis*, and constitute *intolerabilis iniuria*, surely show that some cruelty to slaves could not be borne. Further, see *CT* 9.5.1.1 (320/323), whereby the slave *delator* against his master is to die on the stake (or cross: *patibulum*); to be burned to death, if accomplice in the rape of a free woman (*CT* 9.24.1.5, a. 320/326); or to be thrown to the wild beasts, if guilty of kidnapping (*CT* 9.18.1, a. 315).

9. Back in the second century, slave-ownership is nothing that Christians need to conceal (above, n. 6); and Athenag., *Legat.* 35 (*PG* 6.968f.), almost boasts that "some of us have many slaves." Compare also *Acta Pauli* (*et Theclae*) 1.266 (Lipsius), later, where Thecla is followed about by a large retinue of slaves (Gülzow, op. cit. [n. 6] 103 n. 4) and later still, many reff. showing the church, bishops, or *clerici* as owners. See F. Fabbrini, *La manumissione in ecclesia* (1965) 232, 233 n. 65, and 236f. n. 76, and *CJ* 1.13.2 (321). Note Melania's thousands and thousands of slaves in the west, in Pallad., *Hist. Laus.* 119 (*PG* 34.1228, 1230) and *Vita S. Melaniae* 10.1 and 18 (24,000 in her Sicilian holdings alone!); in Antioch, Joh. Chrysos., *Adv. oppugnatores vitae monasticae* 3.7 and 16 (*PG* 47.360 and 377); in Constantinople, idem, *In ep. ad Coloss.* 2 (*PG* 62.363); and bishop Synesius, *De regno* 15 (*PG* 66.1093B) tells us in the

Pentapolis "every household in the least prosperous has its Scythian slaves," cf. Aug., *Enarr. in Ps.* 124.7, in Africa of his acquaintance *prope omnes domus habent huiusmodi potestatem*, speaking of the work force (both texts are not to be taken literally, of course, simply meaning that "we" of "our class" own slaves—we who are rich). Add Hier., *Ep.* 118.2, on his friend Julian's slave-holdings (in Dalmatia: §5).

10. Joh. Chrysos., *In ep. I ad Cor. homil. XL* 5 (*PG* 61.355), "you have herds upon herds of slaves" and "you deem it a disgrace if you do not lead whole flocks of them around with you." Compare the picture of Antioch here with similar north Italian ostentation of slave-hordes, rebuked by Ambrose, Zeno of Verona, Gaudentius of Brescia, and Maximus of Turin. See L. Cracco Ruggini, "Vicende rurali dell'Italia antiqua," *Riv. storica italiana* 76 (1964) 267. Specially revealing is Greg. Naz., *Or.* 40.27 (*PG* 36.369D), urging his congregation, "Do not scorn to be baptized together with a poor man, if you are rich, or with some lowly person, if you are high-born, or with someone who has been up to now your slave, if you are his master."

11. See the rich and interesting note by N. Adkin, "Some notes on the dream of Saint Jerome," *Philologus* 128 (1984) 119 n. 1, instancing Cypr., *Zel.* 2 and *Hab. virg.* ii and various fourth-century writers: Joh. Chrysos., *De lib. educ.* 35, Ambros., *Hel.* 15.54, Gaudent. Brix., *Sermo* 8.17, and of course Jerome himself at several points.

12. Aelian, *Variae hist.* 2.38; cf. Clem. Alex., *Paedag.* 2.30f.: wine heats the young and leads to sex.

13. Reff. below, chapter 15, n. 4.

14. *Dig.* 47.10.15.15, 19–21 (seductive language is abduction, though not *per vim*), and 23 (good *mores*).

15. Menander Rhet. 364, p. 66 (Russell-Wilson).

16. So I take the locale to be in the anon. *Epp. ad virgines* 2.4f. It is worth quoting: "If we [itinerant ministers] happen on some place where we find only one believing woman and no other Christian person there but only herself, we do not stop there or pray there nor read the Scripture there, but we flee as from before the face of a serpent and as from before the face of sin. Not that we disdain the believing woman—far be it from us to be so minded toward our brethren in Christ!—but because she is alone, we are afraid lest anyone should make insinuations against us in words of falsehood" (trans. M. B. Riddle in *Ante-Nicene Fathers* VIII [1899]).

17. Method., *Sympos.* pr. 6: *panta gar akallopistos en kai nothon epheren ouden—*date, later third century?

18. Hippolyt., *Refutat.* 9.11.10 (*GCS* 3 p. 247), *ousa philotheos pallake Komodou.*

19. P.R.L. Brown, "Aspects of the Christianization of the Roman aristocracy," *JRS* 51 (1961) 7 n. 50, drawing attention to the texts in conflict. The Ps.-Aug., *Quaestiones CXV* 12 (*CSEL* p. 322) is scandalized by the idea of a woman remarrying, though *coeperunt enim cottidie licenter viros suos demittere*, i.e. times are changing. On the Christian rules themselves, see e.g. P. Nautin, "Divorce et remariage dans la tradition de l'église latine," *Recherches de science religieuse* 62 (1974) 24, 37, 39, 44f., and H. Crouzel, "A propos du Concile d'Arles," *Bull. de litt. ecclésiastique* 75 (1974) 25f. and 189f. On the emperor Valentinianus, the Benedictines (note to Malal. p. 341, *PG* 97.508Bf.) say simply, *duas simul uxores habuit*; further, on the first wife "apparently still at court in 367," see *PLRE* s.v. Marina, *re* Aur. Vict., *Epit.* 45.4; also Amm.

28.1.57, in the late 370s; and the later explanations, unlikely-sounding in Malal. loc. cit. and John of Nikiu, *Chron.* 82.10–13 p. 83 (Charles). For Jerome's case, see *Ep.* 77.2 (*CSEL* 55.38f.), concerned only with "Fabiola, the praise of Christians," who (77.3) has "aroused a storm of her critics [who] oppose me because she left one husband and chose a second." He confronts Mt 19.9 with 1 Cor 7.9, "better to marry . . . than burn." *Adolescentula erat.*

20. Cic., *Pro Plancio* 30f., rape of "a little chorus girl," *mimula*, "as, it is said, is done by the young men of Atina according to an old right [*vetere iure*] against actors, and certainly very crude"—but permissible, *quod licuerit.* Cf. *Pro Caelio* 28.

21. And not only in Roman society. Notice Dio Chrysostom, *Or.* 7.133f., repelled and indignant about the prostitution of slaves and insistent (138) that "all humanity has been held in honor, and in equal honor, by God, who begat it, having the same marks and tokens to show that it deserves honor" (trans. J. W. Cohoon); but (139) "this dishonored fornication, so very shameless and unchecked," must be ended, not only because it is bad in itself but because it may turn next to "honorable women." Further, *Or.* 15.5., "do not many Athenians have intercourse with their slave women, some hiding it, some openly?" Also, Plut., *Moral.* 752C: enjoyment of sex is for prostitutes (in *matruleia*, brothels) but "it is improper for decent women, of course, either to receive or offer sexual love"; and again, 753B, "a woman declaring sexual love, a man would flee from, disgusted."

22. Cf. *CJ* 5.27.1 (336): not respectable would be a *scaenica, tabernaria, humiles vel abiecta*, their daughters, or a *lenonis aut harenarii filia.* Their issue (i.e. sexual union) has no legitimacy.

23. I have described these in "Roman attitudes to Greek love" (chapter 17), emphasizing differences in Italy between Rome and elsewhere (p. 184), with exception made of Hellenized Bay-of-Naples towns (p. 180, adding G. Rohlfs' art. on their Greek character in *CJ* 62 [1967] 167); also, differences between high and lower classes in both Rome and the Hellenized eastern empire (pp. 181 and 186). Of course the chief distinction lies between the west and the east.

24. Isolated condemnation of homosexuality in the interval, in the *Digest*, in Marcus Aurelius, and Dio Chrysostom prove nothing, perhaps, but the silence on the other side, i.e. approval of homosexuality, is suggestive (below nn. 31 and 49).

25. With extreme caution and indirectness, he approaches his real subject only at *Or.* 33.38, veers away, returns at 48, defines his target as men talking like women in violation of their nature (51f.), and finally lets out the key word at 54: *kinaidos.* C. P. Jones dates the speech to around A.D. 100, in *The Roman World of Dio Chrysostom* (1978) 136, but, like other commentators, quite misinterprets its object (73f.—the mysterious *rhenkein* is, I suppose, some sort of nasal drawl). For the characterization of homosexuality as against nature, see further 60, *meden hos pephyke*, and 63, *he tes physeos techne*; again, *Or.* 7.149; and passages in Max. Tyr., Epict., and various Latin authors of the time, below n. 39.

26. Dio Chrysos., *Or.* 32.4, quoted; further, at such spectacles, irreverence, idle contention, silly lamenting over the teams that lose, abusive language (32.5 and 74), fights and coarse laughter (32.30), silly, brainless tastes in music (32.65). Tert., *De spect.* 99, is closely similar.

27. Greg. Naz., *Poemata* 2.4 (*Ad Nicobulum*) lines 150–57 (*PG* 37.1515f.); Basil,

Homil. in illud Lucae, destruam 3 (*PG* 31.267Df.). Compare Joh. Chrysos., *In ep. ad Coloss.* 2 (*PG* 62.362), "Nowadays [in Constantinople] your children prefer Satan's songs and dances like cooks and bakers in choruses."

28. Symm., *Rel.* 6.3—and there are plenty of other testimonies to spectacles: horse-racing in mosaics, and races notorious in the hippodrome of the eastern capital; theatrical spectacles provided for in, e.g. *CT* 15.5.1 (372)—5 (425), and the revealing concession of 15.6.1; in general, 15.7–10.

29. I draw for all this on G. Ville, *La gladiature en Occident des origines à la mort de Domitien* (1981) 320f. and passim, and idem, "Les jeux de gladiature dans l'empire chrétien," *Mél. Rome* 72 (1960) 278, 291 (adding Euseb., *Vita Const.* 4.25 to the law of 325), and 313 (the institution disappears in the west). But notice *CT* 9.18.1 (315), where Constantine still condemns criminals to death *in ludum gladiatorium*.

30. Ville, *Mél. Rome* 72 (1960) 294, 296f. (on *CIL* 11.5265, Hispellum in A.D. 333/337), 299 (in Rome in 393), 316, 318f., and 331. On Constantius' legislation, see *CT* 15.12.2f. (357–397).

31. Ville, *Gladiature* 406 n. 117 (Dio 72.29.3, to be balanced by *CIL* 2.6278).

32. E.g., Athenag., *Legat.* 35 (PG 6.96A), including *venationes* in the condemnation; Theophilus, *Ad Autol.* 3.15 (*PG* 6.1141A); Iren., *Contra haer.* 1.6.3 (*PG* 7.508).

33. On the pagan side, such is the apparent reaction of Dio Chrysos., *Or.* 31.131f. (human bloodshed near places of worship), and Philostr., *Vita Apollonii* 4.22; on the Christian side, see Tert., *De spect.* 92, 93, 96, 97 (to watch is idolatry, for *amphitheatrum . . . omnium daemonum templum est*). Notice words like *inquinamentum* and *contaminamur* (94); similarly, Novat., *De spect.* 4 (*PL* 4.814).

34. Watching, a man becomes *skaios*, see Lucian, *Anacharsis* 37; he becomes cruel and inhuman, Sen., *Ad Lucil.* 7.3f; Lucian, *Demonax* 57; Tert., *De spect.* 100f. (with words like *crudelitas, saevitia, immisericordia*). We watchers are accessories to murder, Sen., loc cit. (*mera homicidia*), and Tert., *De spect.* 100v. For further ancient texts and comment, see MacMullen, *Enemies of the Roman Order* (1966) 350.

35. *CT* 15.12.1, *cruenta spectacula in otio civili et domestica quieta non placet.* "Le prince, à la rigueur, pourrait tolérer la gladiature en temps de guerre," comments Ville, *Mél. Rome* 72 (1960) 305.

36. Aug., *Conf.* 6.13, Alypius reporting his feelings, evidently in vivid detail, to his friend. Both at the time (A.D. 383/384) adhered to Manichaeism, to which, however, Augustine (probably not Alypius) had been converted from Christianity.

37. Quoted by Ville, *Mél. Rome* 72 (1960) 293n., where the authors cited hold in scorn men who fight merely to earn their bellyful of food.

38. Ibid. p. 331, where Ville attributes the end of gladiatorial combat to some lost law or policy of Theodosius II, which would explain also the choice of laws on the subject for inclusion in the *Code* of 438. The underlying reason in turn he attributes in the east as in the west to a combination of economic causes and loss of the taste for gladiatorial combat simply through its discontinuity as entertainment (p. 334). The hypothesis is unsupported and I prefer my own (also unsupported). P. Veyne inserts his own explanation in Ville's book (pp. 465–72): Christianity gave special support to the more humane elements in society. This seems to me untenable in the light of the inhumanity I point to, below; and surely Veyne cannot use Aug., *Conf.* 6.13—a passage which (p. 470) "rend un son nouveau"—as the key to saying that Christianity

tout court was the explanation. See above, n. 36. The penalty *ad bestias* continued to be invoked—only once in the *Theodosian Code*, to my knowledge (*CT* 9.18.1 a. 315), but cf. Liban., *Or.* 19.37, where Theodosius' Master of Offices and Master of Soldiers throw rioters to the wild beasts in A.D. 387. The practice and necessary animals existed, then—the reference to them in the *Code* perhaps deleted?

39. I discuss the phenomenon more fully in chapter 20.

40. *CT* 10.10.2 (312). There is debate whether the law prescribes literal strangling and mutilation. T. Spagnuolo Vigorita, *Exsecranda Pernicies* (1984) 96f., thinks no (and I agree). But the literal interpretation was assumed by, and seemed quite in order to, the legists of the *Code* later.

41. *CT* 9.5.1.1—*ad patibulum*. J.-P. Callu, "Le jardin des supplices aus Bas-Empire," in *Du châtiment dans la cité: Supplices corporels et peine de mort dans le monde antique. Table ronde . . . 1982* (1984) 339 n. 110, takes the date to be 320/323 and the meaning to be "hanging"; Spagnuolo Vigorita, op. cit. (n. 40) p. 69 n. 68, hesitates, supposes it need not mean crucifixion, and surveys other scholarly opinions. T. D. Barnes, "Three imperial edicts," *ZPE* 21 (1976) 275, accepts crucifixion as the meaning but wants to attribute the law to the pagan Licinius, through "a small and easy emendation." It involves rewriting the emperor's name and the office of the addressee (in consequence also displacing a known occupant of the time—pp. 276f.).

42. *CT* 9.7.3 (342), against a male homosexual marrying—not a homosexual marriage (!) as J. Boswell imagines, *Christianity, Social Tolerance, and Homosexuality* (1980) 123f., cf. D. Grodzynski, "Tortures mortelles et catégories sociales," in *Du chatiment* (op. cit., n. 41) p. 378 n. 50; *CT* 9.7.6 (390), against catamites; *CJ* 4.42.1 (Constantine), on castrating a slave; *CT* 9.24.1.5 (320/326) and 9.24.2 (349), on abetting rape; 9.25.2 (364), on soliciting sex from a nun; 16.1.1 (364/365), 16.10.4 (346/356), and 16.10.6 (356), all aimed at paganism; 16.8.6 (339), 16.9.2 (339), and 16.8.1 (315/339), all aimed at Jews; and the largest category, that aimed against Christians pronounced heretical: 16.1.4, 16.2.3, 16.4.1, 16.5.9, 16.5.34, 16.5.36, 16.5.51, and 16.5.56. The laws run from Jovian's reign in 363/4 up to 412 (where I simply end my period of study, a hundred years after Constantine's conversion). But the series properly begins in 333 with the edict against the Arians, in H. Opitz, *Athanasius Werke* 3, no. 1 (1935) 68.

43. E.g. Soc., *H. E.* 4.32 (*PG* 67.552B), Valens punishes homoousians with the death penalty; the burning alive of an executioner for stripping a female convict on her way to be beheaded, Amm. 28.1.28; *matronae* executed for fornication, Hier., *Ep.* 147.4 (*PL* 22.199); and the death of a young man accused of adultery, after hideous tortures, while his partner in the accusation escapes only because her decapitation is miraculously botched (*Ep.* 1.3–15).

44. Libanius, for example, often discusses judicial savagery, e.g. *Or.* 4.37 or 28.13; so also Ammianus, e.g. 28.1.7f; on the Christian side, Basil, for example, *Homil. in Ps.* 7 (*PG* 29.214A), taking torture for granted in judicial interrogation; or Synes., *Ep.* 57 (*PG* 66.1389C) or Theodoret, *H. E.* 1.11 (*PG* 82.1025). Ambrose in one incident appears less quick to torture accused persons than most officials who presided over courts (Paulin., *Vita Ambros.* 7, *PL* 14.29Af.): "contrary to his custom, he ordered torture to be applied to people" (simply to dissuade the throngs of witnesses from urging his episcopacy—but rather hard on the individuals tortured). Augustine

was not opposed to torture or execution in themselves, but urged moderation in their use. See Biondi, *Diritto* 3.515f., and esp. A. Houlou, "Le droit pénal chez St. Augustin," *RHD* 52 (1974) 14f., 18, and passim. Notice esp. *Ep.* 104.17, 133.1 and 139.1–2. But, as H. Chadwick points out, "New letters of Augustine," *JTS* 34 (1983) 431, "flogging is a frequent penalty for delinquents brought before the episcopal court"; and Synesius at one point recommends (*Ep.* 44, *PG* 66.1372D–73A) that a judge should "run through all your means of torture and hunt out the truth" in a certain case (it involves a recalcitrant witness). "You have the man. Get to work on his body. . . . He ought to be bound and hung up and his sides torn open. Torturers are wonderful at research. They have invented certain nails, for instance, that have the force of analytical syllogisms."

45. J. Le Goff, *La naissance du Purgatoire* (1981), draws principally on the *Apocalypse of Peter* and the *Apocalypse of Paul*, the first dating to the early second century, the second, to the mid-third (pp. 54 and 56); see W. Schneemelcher, *New Testament Apocrypha* 2 (1965) 664; tortures described in *Apoc. Petri* 7 (ibid. 672f., including mutilation, 716f.), compared with *Or. Sibyll.* 2.255–307.

46. *FIRA*² 2 p. 581 (*Mos. et Rom. legum collatio* 15.315–16).

47. MacMullen, *Christianizing* 100. Abbot Shenute offered exactly the same argument, later (ibid., 163).

48. Ambros., *De off.* 2.150f. (*PL* 15.152B), where a woman entrusts property, no doubt silver plate and the like, to a church for safe keeping, and the owner (as legal process determines) claims it—in vain.

49. Greg. Naz., *Or.* 43 (*In laud. Basil.*) 57 (*PG* 37.569A). Cf. priests of the church in Nola hiding a fugitive from conscription for a month, in Paulin., *Poema* 19.445f.

50. Biondi, *Diritto* 3 p. 457; and he goes on to note (p. 459) that "postclassical and Justinianic penal law has been judged to be barbarous and inhuman; but heavy legislative repression" reflects that imposed by the Church itself. Indeed, "benignità e clemenza spirano da ogni parte del Corpus Iuris" (2 p. 138; cf. 128 and 150). This opinion seems to me entirely mistaken. It is founded in small part on undeniable but, on balance, not very significant manifestations of lenity in e.g. the administration of prisons; in much larger part, on statements of the 530s and later in the Justinianic *Code*. The mid-sixth century is not the fourth. For recent discussion, seeming to me very judicious and giving access to much bibliography, see R. A. Bauman, "The 'leges iudiciorum publicorum,' " *ANRW* II, 13 (1980) 189–92 (esp. 192) and 212–14.

51. Biondi, *Diritto* 3 p. 415.

52. MacMullen, *Christianizing*, chap. 9.

53. The material obvious in the Theodosian *Code* has been looked at more than once, for example, by G. R. Monks, "The administration of the privy purse," *Speculum* 32 (1957) 748–79; A.H.M. Jones, *The Later Roman Empire* (1964) index s.v. fees; and W. Schuller, "Prinzipien des spätantiken Beamtentums," with other essays also, in *Korruption im Altertum: Konstanzer Symposium . . . 1979* (1982) 201–8.

54. P. Abinnaeus 35, of the 340s. The editors elsewhere in the collection capitalize the deity's name; but, faced with the circumstances of this context, they demote Him to a nameless lower-case heathenism; similarly in P. Abinnaeus 59 (345), which I go on to quote.

55. *Histoire de Saint Pacôme* 33f., the text in J. Bousquet and F. Nau, *Patrologia Orientalis* 4 (1908).

56. Greg. Naz., *Or.* 21.21, the speech written more than twenty years after the event, and in a hostile spirit; yet the condemnation of bribery is interesting. See below, at n. 59.

57. Basil, *Ep.* 190.2 (*PG* 32.700B). On the good cause in question, see T. A. Kopecek, "Curial displacements and flight in later fourth century Cappadocia," *Historia* 23 (1974) 327. The Migne-editors refer to *CT* 6.22 to show Basil's and Amphilochius' plan illegal—more accurately, 6.22.1 (321/324), which condemns the purchase of assignments to liturgy-exempt positions. But such purchases were routine throughout the century, e.g. in *CT* 12.1.5 (317), earlier, or 13.5.19 (390), later.

58. J. F. Matthews, *Western Aristocracies and Imperial Court* (1975) 196, the reference to Probus' patronage pointing to Paulin., *Vita Ambros.* 5: Probus "chose Ambrose as an adviser . . . and later welcomed his election as bishop."

59. *Conf.* 6.11.18—the interpretation suggested by C. Lepelley, *Les cités de l'Afrique romaine au Bas-Empire* 1 (1979) 272f. Compare the borrowing from wives to buy bishoprics, below, n. 65, and "the promise of eighty Numidian stallions, fattened on the estates of the church, as douceurs for" certain influential persons in a church dispute—the promise offered by the bishop of Thagaste. See P. Brown, *Augustine of Hippo* (1967) 362, quoting *Op. imp.* i.10.

60. *Sermo* 13.7, *iudex esse vis* (*non potes meritis*), *vel pecunia. Fortasse enim prodesse cupis rebus humanis, et emis ut prosis.*

61. *Ep.* 153.23.

62. Some examples in my *Christianizing* 165f. or Aug., *Ep.* 66.1.

63. Synes., *Ep.* 67 (*PG* 66.1428B); Max. Taurinensis, *Sermo* 26.4; Basil, *Ep.* 53.1 (*PG* 32.397A), adducing in rebuke Acts 8.20 against Simon.

64. Palladius, *Dial. de vita S. Joh. Chrysos.* 53 p. 94 (Coleman-Norton), cf. 24 p. 41, priests "in Cple arranging the purchase of promotions in the Egyptian province from the appointed governors, *archontes.*"

65. Ibid. 51 p. 90 (quoted), in a long and instructive story (48 p. 84 to 51 p. 91). Date, around A.D. 400.

66. Aug., *Sermo* 302.15; Max. Taurinensis, *Sermo* 26.3; Ambros., *In Luc.* 2.77 (*CSEL* 32.83); cf. Synes., *Ep.* 129 (*PG* 66.1521B), against extortion by soldiers.

67. *Conf.* 6.10.

68. Paulin., *Vita Ambros.* 41 (*PL* 14.44A).

69. Zos. 4.28.5; Procop., *Anecdota* 21.9f.

70. I have, throughout this paper, avoided pointless correction of views that seem to me inappropriately defensive, in various authorities I cite. That such a tone may be found, the reader can easily discover in a work like Biondi's, or at n. 54, above.

71. There was undoubtedly more *talk* about commiseration with the poor, charity, and (not quite the same thing) *caritas* among Christians in the fourth century than among pagans then or earlier. I assemble information in my *Enemies of the Roman Order* (1966) 345f.—though cf. Sen., *Ep.* 95.51–53, *praecipiemus ut . . . cum esuriente panem suum dividat? . . . Homo sum, humani nil a me alienum puto*; also Dio Chrysos., *Or.* 7.103, 32.9, 43.7, and 50.3; Lucian, *Dialogues of the Dead*, passim, and *Saturnalia*. On the other hand, actuality was complicated, as I try to show in *Chris-*

tianizing 53f. with notes. The main point is that poverty-relief institutions like burial clubs and festival banquets rapidly disappeared as open cult-acts became risky. On the grander aspiration of loving even one's enemies, see J. Whittaker, "Christianity and morality in the Roman empire," *Vig. Christ.* 33 (1979) 209–25. He considers the position of Feindesliebe in the ancient world, and, against the views of W. C. van Unnik, he finds this virtue traditional in non-Christian moral writings and ideals (pp. 214, 218, 222, etc.). I owe the reference to the kindness of W. A. Meeks. But far more conclusive on the matter than the discussion of Feindesliebe in hortatory forms is the history of Christians' behavior toward their chief foes, namely, persons of differing religious preference. Witness the bishops cutting each other up with swords at the Council of Serdica, *Ep. synod. Sardicensis ad univ. ecclesias* 3 (*CSEL* 65.11) or at the election of a pope, *Avellana coll.* 1.5–7, comparing the bloody conflicts in Palestine, too (ibid. 2.109) [or in Alexandria in the early 370s (Greg. Nyss., *Or.* 25.12)]. I point out further evidence in *Christianizing* 160–62.

72. Above, pp. 148f., and Grodzynski (op. cit., n. 42) 375–77.

73. For example, in Trier (Aug., *Conf.* 8.6.15) or north Africa (Aug., *De haeresibus* 87 [*PL* 42.47]) the Abelonii.

74. G. Blond, "L' 'hérésie' encratite vers la fin du quatrième siècle," *Recherches de science religieuse* 32 (1944) 170–73, 182, 198, and 206f., describing eunuch-priests and bishops forswearing sex along with their congregations.

75. Besides Origen's castration, notice the long and emphatic discussion in the third book of Clement's *Stromateis*, e.g. 3.91 (*GCS* 15 p. 238) on Julius Cassianus' *peri enkrateias e peri eunouchias*; further, J.E.L. Oulton and H. Chadwick, *Alexandrian Christianity* (1954) 34f.

14. ORDINARY CHRISTIANS IN THE LATER PERSECUTIONS

1. *Or.* 4.74 (*PG* 35.599A).

2. A round number, as in my *Christianizing the Roman Empire* (1984) 135f., with reff.

3. H. Grégoire et al., *Les persécutions dans l'empire romain*[2] (1964) 166, with closer discussion in appendix II, 181f., and the differences of an opponent, E. de Moreau, "Le nombre des martyrs de persécutions romaines," *Bull. Acad. roy. de Belgique* 38 (1952) 63–68, answered by Grégoire, "Nouvelles observations sur le nombre des martyrs," ibid. 37–60. For a more recent specialist's view, see W.H.C. Frend, *Martyrdom and Persecution in the Early Church* (1965) 413, on the 250s (comparing Grégoire, loc. cit., "a few hundreds" pre-Diocletian), and 537, on the early 300s, where he would raise Grégoire's estimate to 3,000–3,500.

4. Euseb., *H. E.* 8.3.3f. and *Mart. Pal.* 1.4.

5. J. R. Knipfing, "The *libelli* of the Decian persecution," *HThR* 16 (1923) 351f., followed by G. W. Clarke in his excellent edition of *The Letters of St. Cyprian* (1984–1986) 1.30 (hereafter *Letters*), collects a number of details, e.g. *primores* and *magistratus* in Cypr., *Ep.* 43.3.1 (Carthage), cf. the *archontes* in Greg. Nyss., *Vita S. Greg.*, *PG* 46.944C, or in Euseb., *Mart. Pal.* 4.8, long recension, *GCS* 2.[2] 914; *logistai*, *strategoi*, and *taboularioi*, ibid. 9.2; *tabularii* again, with *duoviri* and *scribae*, *Acta purgationis Felicis*, in Optatus appendix II, p. 197 (Ziwsa); a *flamen perpetuus* and *curator*, ibid. 186 (in Cirta); a *procurator ducenarius* (Cypr., *Ep.* 56.1.1, Spain); a

neokoros (*Acta Pionii* 3.1, Smyrna); in the Egyptian *libelli*, a *prytanis* and *grammateus* or simply *hoi epi ton thysion heirmemenoi* (Knipfing 363f.); and town criers (*Acta S. Cononis* 1.2; Euseb., *Mart. Pal.* 4.8).

6. G.E.M. de Ste. Croix, "Aspects of the 'Great' persecution," *HThR* 47(1954) 97 and 102.

7. See Gregory Nyssenus' biography of Gregory Thaumaturgus, *PG* 46.945A, where confiscations are spurred on by delators and their hope of reward, some of them being Christian apostates, 944B; Euseb., *H. E.* 4.16.9 and 4.17.8; Clem. Alex. quoted ibid., 4.26.4, "informers and greedy for what belonged to other people"; and 6.41.21 (under Decius). For the Great persecution, see ibid. 8.12.3, informers acting from *phthonos* of a rich lady, and idem, *Mart. Pal.* 3.4; Can. 9 of the Council of Ancyra, in K. J. Hefele, *Histoire des conciles* 1 (1907) 308f., and Can. 3 p. 305, *hypo oikeion paradothentas*, the betrayed having perhaps been hiding in their own or kinsmen's residences or estates; and Theodoret., *H. E.* 1.19 (*PG* 82.961) = 1.20 (*GCS* p. 66).

8. Cypr., *Ep.* 20.2.2, cf. idem, *De lapsis* 7f., and, for Rome, *Ep.* 21.2; *Acta Pionii* 4.1, a local Smyrniote official bids Christians *peitharxesai katha kai pantes*, everyone else has subscribed to the sacrifices, cf. 20.3, "many others have sacrificed"; and more generally, Cypr., *Ep.* 30.5.4, *totum orbem paene vastatum*. Among descriptions of widespread surrender that convey no sense of numbers, see, for example, Hefele, op. cit. (n. 7) 1.306, Can. 4 of Ancyra, Euseb., *H. E.* 6.41.11, and the inference of C. Schmidt, *Fragmente einer Schrift Märtyrerbischofs Petrus von Alexandrien* (1907) 16, from the pressing nature of the *lapsi*-question, that the number of them must have been *ungeheuer*.

9. *Passio S. Crispinae* 1.7, *omnis Africa sacrificia fecit, nec tibi dubium est*, which the martyr does not contest; Euseb., *Mart. Pal.* 2.1; and Optatus 3.8 p. 90 (Ziwsa) and 1.13f. p. 15f., on *traditores*, among whom he names various bishops.

10. Cypr., *Ep.* 57.3.1, cf. earlier, Plin., *Ep.* 10.96.5.

11. In Decian times, Cypr., *Ep.* 55.14.1; in 306, Peter, *Ep. can.* 5–7, 10, and 12 (*PG* 18.473f.), of A.D. 306, cf. J. Quasten, *Patrology* (1950) 3.115.

12. The *Martyrology of Saint Coluthus* in E.A.E. Reymond and J.W.B. Barns, *Four Martyrdoms from the Pierpont Morgan Coptic Codices* (1973) 147, with a similar picture offered there of another bishop, of Lycopolis, nowadays (in 304) "not at all ashamed [of having sacrificed], and everyone honors him"; in Rome, "the case against Marcellinus would appear to be a strong one," Frend, op. cit. (n. 3) 504; and in north Africa, Optatus 2.25 p. 65 (Ziwsa). Cf. in Decian times Eusebius, *H. E.* 8.2.1f., on evidently prevalent surrender of some sort by Egyptian bishops, and "the head of your community, Euctemon," who sacrificed in Smyrna, *Acta Pionii* 15.2; Cypr., *Ep.* 67.6, Spanish bishops who sacrificed; and 54.10, a number of Numidian bishops likewise, one of whom was followed in surrender by his congregation.

13. Passages often cited: Clem. Alex., *Stromat.* 4.4.17f. (*PG* 8.1229Bf.), Frend, op. cit. 357 adding 7.11.66; Cypr., *Ep.* 81.1.4, Clarke, *Letters* 1.318f. n. 11 adding other texts; and comparison with Lucian, *Peregrinus* 1f. But there were different messages, e.g. Origen's *Exhortation to Martyrdom*.

14. *H. E.* 6.42.1 and 9.1.7; *Mart. Pal.* 1.3.

15. Cypr., *Ep.* 58.4.2, cf. the *grammaticus* Victor of Cirta fleeing *in montem Bellonae*, in the *Acta purgationis Felicis*, Optatus appendix II p. 186 (Ziwsa) (*fugivimus*,

perhaps with a cluster of fellow refugees); in the caves neighboring on the Dead Sea, cf. the *Vita S. Charitonis* 2 and 13, in G. Garitte, "La vie prémétaphrastique de S. Chariton," *Bull. de l'Inst. belge de Rome* 21 (1941) 12 and 17; in Egypt, Hier., *Vita Pauli* 5 (fictional?), and Euseb., *H. E.* 6.42.2f.; and in the east of unspecified regions, Euseb., *H. E.* 10.8.18, "once again, flight on the part of the pious, once again the rural areas and deserts, glens and mountains." Compare the support network of local Christians coming to the aid of the brethren, in Cypr., *Ep.* 55.13.2, or of a woman exiled for her religion to the Oasis in Egypt, in M. Naldini, *Il Cristianesimo in Egitto* (1968) 132f.

16. Pontius, *Vita S. Cypr.* 14.3; cf. Euseb., *H. E.* 6.41.13, a Pontus bishop flees into Palestine; 8.12.3, an Antioch Christian leaves the province, *allodapes* (surely not beyond the empire); Athanas., *Hist. Arian. ad monach.* 64, cited by Ste. Croix, op. cit. (n. 6) 100 to show fugitive Christians in Egypt sheltered by compassionate pagans; and Bishop Peter of Alexandria given asylum in Oxyrhynchus by the clergy there, cf. Schmidt, op. cit. (n. 8) 7.

17. Cypr., *Ep.* 75.10 (*CSEL* 3, 2, 816f.), "large numbers fled from the province" of Cappadocia, to which, earlier, Clement of Alexander had fled with his disciple, choosing never to return home; cf. Quasten, op. cit. (n. 11) 2. 5f.

18. Clarke, *Letters* 1.34 adduces Cypr., *Ep.* 30.8.1, people from overseas take shelter in Rome; 21.2.2 and 4.1, specifically from Carthage, in Rome; and 8.2.2, Romans shelter in Carthage, or (Clarke 1.69, on Cypr., *Ep.* 8.3.1) Africans in Carthage; cf. hiding in Alexandria, Euseb., *H. E.* 7.11.24. In the Great Persecution, we have a fugitive from the little town Apthunga hiding in Cirta, cf. *Acta purgationis Felicis*, Optatus appendix II p. 201 (Ziwsa).

19. Euseb., *H. E.* 6.3.1, "everybody having fled from the threat of persecution," including the clergy; Firmilian, in Cypr., *Ep.* 75.10; Dionysius, in Euseb., *H. E.* 6.41.6, "the brethren" without distinction slipped away; *Vita Greg. Thaumaturg.*, *PG* 46.945B and 948D, *panton pros phygen tetrammenon*; Cypr., *Ep.* 58.4.1, with Clarke's *Letters* n. 3 p. 230; and add, for whatever historical value it may have, *Acta S. Cononis* 1, an entire Pamphylian hamlet emptied of its inhabitants at the onset of persecution. For the Great Persecution, I can quote only Eusebius, *H. E.* 10.8.18.

20. Confiscation is a penalty in the early 200s, in Euseb., *H. E.* 6.2.13, and in the 250s, ibid. 7.11.18 and Cypr., *Ep.* 19.2.3, 24.1.1, 66.4.1, and 80.1.2, and in the Great Persecution, as seen in Can. 3 and 6 of Ancyra, Hefele, op. cit. (n. 7) 1.305 and 308f.

21. Clarke (*Letters* 1.34) notices the greater vulnerability of *insignes personae* (Cypr., *Ep.* 8.1.1—the other letters 5, 13, and 14 which he cites seem not to be relevant). Cf. Euseb., *H. E.* 7.11.24, where bishop Dionysius of Alexandria reports that some Christians have found a hiding place in the city itself, but two others, "the better known in the world, are wandering around Egypt."

22. Euseb., *H. E.* 9.6.1. Similar cases could be easily adduced.

23. *PG* 46.9945D; Euseb., *H. E.* 6.41.13.

24. Grégoire, op. cit. (n. 3) 51, and Frend, op. cit. (n. 3) 413.

25. Above, n. 9; Cyprian of his own clerics, *Ep.* 29.1.1, *nostros plurimos absentes esse, paucos vero qui illic* [in Carthage] *sunt*; and Euseb., *H. E.* 6.3.1, on Alexandria in Severan times.

15. WOMEN IN PUBLIC IN THE ROMAN EMPIRE

1. The complaint in *Roman Social Relations* (1974) 179 n. 86 is made also by E. A. Judge, *JAC* 14 (1971) 28, noting the gap in NT studies. I exclude studies that do exist of figures like Boudicca and Zenobia, who tell us no more about their sex than Mithridates or Maximinus Thrax can tell us about men; and I exclude studies of women in *CIL* VI, who for obvious reasons have received some attention.

2. P. Paris, *Quatenus feminae res publicas in Asia Minore, Romanis imperantibus, attigerint* (1891) (hereafter *Quatenus*).

3. Münzer in *RE* s.v. Sulpicius cols. 809f., the consul of 166 who died shortly before 149. The lapse of time may explain Plutarch's confusion (*Moral.* 267C): the wife was divorced because she *was* veiled. See also Isid., *Orig.* 104.5, referring to a custom of the remote past, *apud antiquos*, that if you burst into someone else's house unexpected, you must never see the *mater familiae* or *virgines*, though a less likely interpretation is offered in P. G. Maxwell-Stuart, *Greece and Rome* 24 (1977) 1.

4. Plut., *Moral.* 267A, supporting the text often used, Dio Chrysos., *Or.* 33.48, and an obscure one brought to notice by L. Robert, *Hellenica* 5 (1968) 66, who also points to Palmyrene reliefs, ibid. 68 n. 3 (he adduces *FHG* II p. 259, but it is too early to apply). Add, fourthly, Euseb., *Mart. Pal.* 4.15 (long recension, G. Bardy, *Sources chrétiennes* no. 55 p. 136), referring to citizens of Caesarea in 306 flocking to a public spectacle, "even the women who are (generally) hidden and in the quarters and others still unmarried." Lastly, Tertullian, *De virgin. veland.* 2.1 (*PL* 2 Col. 890) speaks of young women veiled "throughout Greece" and among Christians in some African cities, though (3.1, col. 891) not in most. "Veiling" meant the head (3.7f.), only in Arabia the face as well (3.17, col. 912). For the majority custom, see the confirmation in funerary reliefs, e.g. in N. Firatli, *Les stèles funéraires de Byzance gréco-romaine* (1964).

5. *CIL* 10.810, cf. the Temple of the Genius of Augustus on the forum, built by Mamia, also *sacerdos publica* (*CIL* 10.816). On Eumachia's family, see P. Castrén, *Ordo populusque Pompeianus* (1975) 95; ibid. 71f., 94, 97, 133, 188 and 225 (on Arellia Tertulla), on other priestesses. Also M. D'Avino, *Women of Pompeii* (1967) 103 and 106.

6. Ibid. 26, 30 and 38 (not altogether reliable, I think); A. Scalera *Rend. Lincei*[5] 28 (1919) 388–400.

7. *CIL* 4.913; 171; 1083; 3291; 3403; 3527; etc. The phenomenon in inscriptions of Rome is interpreted by M. B. Flory, "Family and Familia . . ." (Ph.D. diss., Yale University, 1975) 61–68 and 82–84.

8. J. Andreau, *Les affaires de Monsieur Jucundus* (1974) 119f., with *CIL* 4.8203f.

9. Ibid. 105 (Umbricia Antiochis), 114, 139f. (fourteen women in Jucundus' books), 290 (Babinia Secunda), 296f. (freedwomen of Umbricius Scaurus), and 319 (one sale of HS 8,562).

10. For the degree of freedom women enjoyed in conducting their business, see J. Crook, *Law and Life of Rome* (1967) 114f., using the Herculanean tablets, for example: Calatoria goes bail for Petronia, the necessary spokesman being a freedman of her deceased husband. Hardly a tyrannous *tutela*. On women in the Codes, see L. Huchthausen, *Klio* 56 (1974) 226, listing them by categories.

11. *CJ* 5.14.2; 5.16.3; 5.23.1; 6.38; 4.21.1—all of A.D. 213; also 5.16.8 (233); 2.4.3 (233, ref. to a woman's *negotia*); 8.44.5 (212, *praedia mercata*).

12. Huchhausen, *Klio* 56 (1974) 199f., 203f.— more than half from the provinces (p. 205), and all classes save the highest (209f., 212).

13. *IG* 14.760, a.71: *t[ou hierou?] ton gynaikon oikou*, cf. the unexplained *collegium mulierum* of *CIL* 6.10423, a cult- or burial-society for women of one house?

14. *CIL* 14.2635 (burial to Pluria, *sodalis, l. d. d. d.*); 2631; 9.4696, memorial by *sexvir Augustalis, magister invenum;* 5.5907, memorial largesses by members of deceased's urban precinct (*vicus*); cf. also 9.1153, Aeclanum, late first century, a priestess-flamen of Julia Pia Augusta, as well as of several goddesses, and many women presiding with priest-husbands over the imperial cult in Spain, J. Deininger, *Die Provinziallandtage . . .* (1965) 129 and 131 n. 5.

15. Above, n. 13; and the *curia mulierum* in Lanuvium (*CIL* 14.2120), mysterious despite A. Donati, *Riv. storica dell'antichità* 1 (1971) 236, and J. Straub, *Bonner Historia-Augusta-Colloquium 1964/1965* (1966) 229.

16. L. Cracco Ruggini, *Akten des VI. int. Kongresses für griechische und lateinische Epigraphik* (1972) 297f., Mothers of centonarii, fullones, fabri, *CIL* 9.2687, 5459 (the *mater* married to a freedman); 11.1355 and 5748; 3.1207; or Mothers of cult groups, 5.4411; 14.69; 13.8244; 3.7505 and 7532; 3.870, A.D. 235, *Asiani* at Napoca in Dacia, a Bacchic group of men and women, J. P. Waltzing, *Etude historique sur les corporations professionelles chez les Romains* 3 (1899) 81. For *patronae*, see *CIL* 5.5295 and 5869; 9.4894 (*ob merita*); 11.2702 and 5749 (wives of local magnates; *patronissa, IG* 14.1671 (Rome). Without special title, patronesses in *CIL* 5.5272 (for a bequest given); 14.3677; in Narbonensis, 12.2824, *ob merita.*

17. G. Clemente, *Studi classici* 21 (1972) 160–213 passim, provides 261 identifiably male patrons, 19 female, but the lists are not complete.

18. Whatever evidence held economic data was gathered by R. Duncan-Jones, *The Economy of the Roman Empire* (1974) 143 and passim. I can add only *AE* 1971, 85. Texts without economic data no doubt exist in considerable numbers, e.g. *CIL* 11.3303 and 7803.

19. *CIL* 9.4697; *ILS* 6468, 6271 and 5196—the last including *mulieribus honor(atorum?*—or *atis?*), according to different completions of the abbreviation by Duncan-Jones, op. cit. (n. 18) 195 and S. Mrozek, *Epigraphica* 34 (1972) 49. Other texts including women are *CIL* 9.977 and 981 (men and women at the same rate); 9.5376; 10.109 and 415; 11.4663 and 5716; *ILS* 2666, 6530, 6643, and 6583 (a woman of a very prominent family, cf. *CIL* 11.3801, 3805, 3807 and 6489–93, with Mommsen's comments).

20. Duncan-Jones, op. cit. 264f., 266 and 267, 268f., 270 and 274, and 271, takes as excluding women the words or phrases *omnes cives, plebs urbana, municipes, universus populus* or plain *populus*, in Siagu (Africa) and various Italian cities. I concur.

21. Many of the women appear in references in K. W. Harl, "Political Attitudes . . . in the Third Century A.D." (Ph.D. diss., Yale University, 1978) 210, 222, 225 and 654.

22. *CIG* 2782, and discussion by A. D. Macro, *AJP* 100 (1979) 94f.

23. Paris, *Quatenus* 86f. and passim.

24. *AJP* 100 (1979) Macro, 95; Deininger, op. cit. (n. 14) 41, 75 and 154; D. Magie, *Roman Rule in Asia Minor* (1950) 1608.

25. *CIG* 3415 (Phocaea, *PIR*² F 285); J. Keil, *Anatolian Studies . . . Buckler* (1939) 120f., Ephesus; J. T. Bent, *JHS* 8 (1887) 425, Thasos; or further, *IGR* 4.1571 = L. Robert, *Etudes anatoliennes* (1937) 25, a provincial high-priestess is simultaneously priestess of the city's guardian god Dionysus, at Teos; ibid. 258, a woman also queen, married to the King Archon of Heraclea in Bithynia (cf. *IGR* 3.81 for that local office).

26. Paris, *Quatenus* 132–36 (*IGR* 3.800–802). For the pecking order, cf. also *IGR* 4.46, or J. Hatzfeld, *BCH* 51 (1927) 92, at Panamara, distributions by a woman to "the citizens and women."

27. Deininger, op. cit. (n. 14) 76 and n. 1; R. Cagnat in note to *IGR* 3.583, cf. man and wife as Pontarchs, *IGR* 3.97.

28. *TAM* 3, 1.57 and 178f.

29. *AE* 1956, 178; O. Walter, *Arch. Anz.* 57 (1942) 178, 183 and 176 (the Macedoniarchissa).

30. Paris, *Quatenus* 58–76, mentioning an epimeletes as aide to a woman, 65f., cf. also L. Robert, *REA* 62 (1960) 295f., *IG* 12, 2.258 and 12, 5.39, *IGR* 4.100 (a hypogymnasiarch subserves a woman of the imperial house) and 3.504 (a woman herself is an Assistant Warden, hypophylax).

31. Examples of high honors to priestesses in F. Dunand, *Le culte d'Isis . . .* 3 (1973) 114f.; W. M. Ramsay, *Cities and Bishoprics of Phrygia* 2 (1897) 760; R. Harder, ed., *Die Inschriften* (in T. Wiegand, *Didyma* 2, 1958) nos. 307f.; *IG* 7.1869; 10, 2².176, 189 and 191; *Sardis* 7, 1 (1932) 60 and 67–69; *Forschungen in Ephesos* 3 (1923) 144; L. Robert, *Hell.* 9 (1950) 21.

32. B. Pace, in *Anatolian Studies . . . Ramsay* (1923) 306; L. Robert, *Hellenica* 7 (1949) 42, crowning, as in *CIG* add. 23471; and *OGIS* 513, Pergamon, *a.* 215.

33. Priestesses were often wives or daughters of priests, e.g. *RE* s.v. Panamara col. 452; Ramsay, op. cit. (n. 31) 1.293; Dunand, op. cit. (n. 31) 3.164; *IG* 10, 2².176, 189, 191 and 194. For double colleges of men and women serving deities, see e.g. P. Roussel, *BCH* 51 (1927) 124, and Paus. 7.20.1.

34. To F. Poland, *Gesch. des griechischen Vereinswesens* (1909) 345f., add, for Cybele at Cumae, *Inschriften von Kyme*, ed. H. Engelmann (1976) 90, a *doumos* = *oikia . . . ton gynaikon*; P. Herrmann and K. Z. Polatkan, *Das Testament des Epikrates . . .* (1969) 55f., for Men in Lydia; C. Edson, *HThR* 41 (1948) 167f., for Dionysus in Salonica; G. Deschamps and G. Cousin, *BCH* 15 (1891) 204 *politeuma ton gynaikon* for Hera in Panamara.

35. Paris, *Quatenus* 43–45, on the gymnasiarchs, to which many additions could be made; ibid. 108f., on gerousiarchs, again allowing additions, e.g. *IG* 10, 2².177.

36. Paris, *Quatenus* 19f., on spokesmen; for female virtues, note honors awarded by a public vote *sophrosynes te kai philandrias heneken*, Ramsay, op. cit. (n. 31) 1.333.

37. *Acts of the Pagan Martyrs*, ed. H. A. Musurillo (1954) 19, *parouson de kai ton matronon*. For discussion of another text that adds credibility and parallels, see Straub (art. cit., n. 15) 225f.

38. D. I. Pallas et al., *BCH* 83 (1959) 498f. I draw the reference from A. J. Marshall, *Anc. Soc.* 6 (1975) 123, who well sees and describes the role of the woman.

39. G. E. Bean and T. B. Mitford, *Journeys in Rough Cilicia 1964–1968* (1970) 27, and 22–29 passim.

40. Cursorily among sculptures and more carefully in mosaics of Syria, Lebanon, and Palestine, I have looked in vain for any representation of a veiled woman, not to be found even in Antioch street scenes. But contrast the elaborate hairdos in terracotta statuary from Smyrna of the first and second centuries, in A. Delhaye-Cahen, *Bull. des Musées royaux d'art et d'histoire* 40–42 (1968–1970) 27–38 and passim.

16. WOMEN'S POWER IN THE PRINCIPATE

1. The women indicated begin with Livia (Dio 57.12; Suet., *Tib.* 50.2f.—an interesting tug-of-war); then Messalina, in Dio 60.16.2, 60.17.5, and 60.18.2 (compare Gessius Florus made procurator of Judaea in 64 thanks to his wife, "through her being a friend of Poppaea, Nero's wife, and through her wickedness no less than his he gained the position," Jos., *A. J.* 20.252); further, P. Galerius Trachalus, orator and cos. 68, saved from execution by his kinswoman Galeria, Vitellius' wife, Tac., *Hist.* 2.60.2; then Nero's freedwoman, in Suet., *Otho* 2.2; then Caenis in Dio 65(66).14.3, cf. Antoninus Pius' mistress like Vespasian's selling government positions, in SHA *Ant. Pius* 8.9 (but Caenis sold the emperor's decision also); then Titus' daughter Julia, naming a consul for A.D. 84, in Dio 67.4.2; and last, Julia Domna, in Herodian 5.7.1, handling Elagabalus' official correspondence, Dio 77(78).18.2 and 78(79).4.2f., while generally she enjoys "great power," 78(79).24.2. Or one could instance Hadrian's wife's power in making appointments, SHA *Had.* 4.1 and 4, or Severus Alexander's mother in Herodian 5.7.3; also Aggrippina in Tac., *Ann.* 12.27.1, 12.59.1, and elsewhere, and in Dio 60(61).32.1, where she rules "by fear or by favor."

2. *ILS* 4928f. (and O. Hirschfeld, *Die kaiserlichen Verwaltungsbeamten²* [1904] 304).

3. Tac., *Hist.* 1.73: *totius postea* (after Macer) *civitatis gratiam obtinuit . . . , potens pecunia et orbitate, quae bonis malisque temporibus iuxta valent*; further, Dio 62.12.3f. On her first husband's and her bricks and amphorae widely marketed, see *PIR²* C 363.

4. Tac., *Ann.* 3.33.3f.; *repetundae* and *ambitio aut avaritia*, cf. 1.69.1f. and 2.55.5; so stay-at-homes were more praised, Sen., *Cons. ad Helv.* 19.6. M. T. Rapsaet-Charlier, in *Historia* 31 (1982) 64–69, catalogues eighty-nine senatorial women sojourning in the provinces in the first two centuries; Pflaum, cit. ibid., 59, added thirty-three wives of procurators; and, on wives' extortion in general, see Juv. 8.128f. and Tac., *Ann.* 4.19.4; particular cases in Tac., *Ann.* 6.29, Plin., *Ep.* 3, 9, 20, 29, and 34, and Mart. 2.56 (Gallus' wife)—the texts all cited by Rapsaet-Charlier.

5. Tac., *Ann.* 3.15 and 17, on her trial; 2.43, on her *nobilitas ac opes*; and 3.15 again, on her *maior gratia*, Livia's *preces*, and Tiberius' predicament. On her career, see *PIR²* M 737 (she committed suicide in A.D. 33).

6. *ILS* 1136, at Venafrum, cf. *PIR²* M 22; for the second woman, *ILS* 5628 and R. Syme, in *Historia* 17 (1968) 73–76; for the third, Vitrasia daughter of cos. II A.D. 176, killed in 183, cf. *ILS* 1115, Dio 73.5.1, and SHA *Commod.* 4.10.

7. *ILS* 6972 (such public funerals are more commonly attested in Asia); in Tarraco, see G. Alföldy, *Flamines Provinciae Hispaniae Citerioris* (1973) 49–53 and 94–97.

8. In the enlightening and interesting essay of R. Van Bremen, in *Images of Women*

in Antiquity (1983), see 231–33 on the background in Hellenistic law, with scattered texts from Cicero to Gaius the jurist; further, using papyrological information, the remarks of R. Taubenschlag, in *ZSS* 49 (1929) 126, though they are not very broadly founded. On the *matrona stolata* and the meaning of the phrase in Roman Egypt, see J. J. Rea, in *Collectanea papyrologica . . . in Honor of H. D. Youtie* (1976) 461; on the legal rights and position of women in Asia Minor, A. Balland, *Fouilles de Xanthos*, 7 (1980) 254f.; on the freedom of Roman women in legal business, see *Historia* 29 (1980) 210 n. 10 or such parts of the *Corpus Iuris* as *CJ* 4.28. I am not aware of any full discussion that compares the two legal traditions, in the period of the empire. Perhaps, as Van Bremen suggests, the little evidence we have is enough for our purposes.

9. Examples in *ILS* 8825; *Inschr. v. Ephesos* no. 1618; *IGR* 3.958–59; also 800, a little misunderstood by Van Bremen, op. cit. (n. 8) 223, since the main gift is from Menodora's son, through his last will, and he is not likely to be still a "boy" while serving as *demiourgos*.

10. T. Reinach, in *REG* 19 (1906) 94, the phrase *ton proton* or *genous proton* being common in praise; and C. Picard, *Ephèse et Claros* (1922) 241, the woman here being also *kosmeteira* of Artemis at Ephesus. Compare the wife of a Lyciarch honored as descendant *ton nauarchon kai strategon, syngenida tou proteuontos en Lykia genous*, in Balland, op. cit. (n. 8) 235f., and *IGR* 3.464, a woman high-born, *taxeon ton proteuonton tes poleos*. I instance other women of the same order and prominence in eastern provinces, *Historia* 29 (1980) 213f., and, p. 215, consider the evidence for their personal active involvement in the duties of their office. On that matter see also S. Jameson, in *ANRW* ii 7, 2 (1980) 847f., instancing certain female gymnasiarchs (compare *IGR* 3.373, for example, *SEG* 31 [1981] 958, from Ephesus, or my art. cit., p. 215 n. 35).

11. *TAM* 2.188 ii lines 13f.; compare M. M. Alves, in *Madr. Mitt.* 19 (1978) 270f.

12. *Patronissa* is simply the feminine of the borrowed *patron*, itself not an everyday word—but see for example *MAMA* 6 no. 258 (Acmonia), a city patron of the first half of the first century b.c.; *Inschr. v. Ephesos* no. 3006, of 3 b.c.; *IGR* 4.1462 (Smyrna). For "patronesses," see the inscription in a village I know well, Cyprian Palaepaphos, published by the regretted T. B. Mitford, *Inscriptions of Kourion* (1971) 183; *TAM* 3, 1, no. 117 (in Termessus), the wife of a priest; *Inschr. v. Ephesos* no. 998, *he patris etimese ten patronissan*; *IG* 10, 2, 1, no. 187 (in Thessalonica, the daughter of a local and provincial magnate and Helladarch, honored in the 190s *kata ta doxanta tei kratistei boulei kai toi ierotatoi demoi*); *IG* 14.1671 (Rome); and *TAM* 3.58 (in Termessus, a highly prominent office-holder honored with a statue by her freedman, the text cited by Van Bremen, op. cit. [n. 8] 228f.).

13. *TAM* 3 no. 62, in Pergamon, *hoi techneitai* to a *euergetin auton*. Compare the *matres* or *patronae collegiorum fabrum* (and *centonariorum*, or other groups) so titled by the guild, in J.-P. Waltzing, *Etude historique sur les corporations professionnelles chez les Romains* 1 (1895) 430 and 4 (1900) 369f. and 373.

14. *ILS* 1105 and *AE* 1935 no. 26; compare the gift of a town banquet and cash to everyone, too, by a woman to whom the town has voted a statue, at Anagnia (*ILS* 406—she had renovated the town baths), and lordly gestures of the same sort as Fal-

conilla's by Sittia Calpurnia of Cirta, *ILAlg*. 693, and other citizens, 6486 and 6495, or *CIL* 2.1956, 3240.

15. *Dig*. 18.1.69 (the ancient Lake Anguillara).

16. Fronto, *Ad amicos* 2.8 (Naber p. 199). The fragments terminate, *id populo quoque*, indicating the public nature of the project.

17. Plin., *Ep*. 10.58–60 and 81.2. A. N. Sherwin-White, *The Letters of Pliny* (1966) 642, supposes the dispute was over a will, perhaps over suborned testimony.

18. On the very interesting evidence of the Justinian Code, see L. Huchthausen, in *Klio* 56 (1974) 199f. and 203–12. She points out elsewhere, in *Klio* 58 (1976) 56, that female litigants of the 290s include many from the northern provinces. For my own figures, confirming hers but focused differently, I have checked the cases recorded for the first half of the third century, and find 242 of 1048 (23 percent) women; but a good number of the men are soldiers. Were they excluded, women would bulk larger. There is no good way of determining what percent of them reside in the east or west. I have not counted women incidentally mentioned by litigants, as defendants (e.g. *CJ* 1.9.1) or plaintiffs (1.3.5).

19. At Pompeii, *Historia* 29 (1980) 210f.; at Ostia, H. E. Herzig, *Historia* 32 (1983) 79–81.

20. T. Helen, *Organization of the Roman Brick Industry* (1975) 23: out of 150 *domini* 43 are women (most often as landowners, however, p. 110), with 20 of the *officinatores* also women. P. Setälä, *Private Domini in Roman Brickstamps* (1977) 223, describing yards largely around Rome, notices that two-thirds of the *dominae* are daughters of senators. The whole industry was dominated by the big *gentes*. But at least one smaller yard in Ostia was owned by a local woman (Herzig, *Historia* 32 [1983] 81).

21. Tac., *Hist*. 1.81.1; *celebre convivium primoribus feminis virisque*; for the adjective, see Suet., *Domit*. 8.3: *primores viri ac feminae*; Tac., *Ann*. 2.29.1; or earlier, Cic. 2 *Verr*. 1.153.

22. Dio 72.31.2, *hai dynamei proekousai*, A.D. 176, cf. 78(79).18.2, A.D. 217, the senators rage against the accomplices of the dead Caracalla, including "many of the most prominent women, believed to have drawn up secret reports and to have lodged false suits in court in his reign."

23. Epict., *Diss*. 3.7.13.

24. *IGR* 3.500, the main source. In drawing the stemma, Figure 2, I have relied on many additional sources. Among the modern are R. Heberdey and E. Kalinka, *Bericht über zwei Reisen in südwestlichen Kleinasien* (Denkschrift d. oesterr. Akad. d. Wiss. 45, 1, 1877) 41–46 with fold-out; H. Halfmann, *Die Senatoren aus den östlichen Teil des Imperium Romanum* (1979), stemmata on pp. 150, 166 and 185; S. Jameson, *Anatolian Studies* 16 (1966) 125–36 with fold-out, supplemented and (regarding certain individuals and connections) corrected by Balland, op. cit. (n. 8) (consult his index nominum); further, the fold-out stemmata at *PIR*[2] C 776 (facing p. 164) and 947; L 947; and M 222. On particular individuals, see *PIR*[2] C 947 and M 229; *ILAlg* 652; *TAM* 2 no. 915 (emending the text to add Lyciarchies to Opramoas' sons); *OGIS* 490 (Sossia Polla); and E. Groag, *Die römischen Reichsbeamten von Achaia* (1939) 107f., on Vilius Titianus Quadratus. Near the center of Figure 2 is Aelia Platonis, whose

father, unknown, may be Apollonius or Hermaios; but I think the authorities I depend on have removed other plain uncertainties from the stemma.

25. In addition to the 600,000 HS counted up by T.R.S. Broughton, in T. Frank, *An Economic Survey of Ancient Rome* 4 (1938) 780, and gifts such as the temples of Fortune and of Nemesis to his native city of Rhodiapolis itself (pp. 783f.), there are other items amounting to another 4.5 million. See A. Balland, in *Actes du colloque sur la Lycie antique* (1980) 93 n. 8. Hence, no doubt, enough for six senatorial census. And perhaps we should add to the family the only author to enter the Teubner canon entirely epigraphically. See C. W. Chilton, ed., *Diogenis Oinoandensis Fragmenta* (1967) xivf.

17. ROMAN ATTITUDES TO GREEK LOVE

1. Macrob. 3.14.7. (And here at the outset I thank G. Williams for helpful comments.)

2. Aul. Gell. 6.12.2 = *ORF*[3] 1.127, of 142 B.C.

3. Persius 4.33ff., of A.D. 62? Cf. [Quint.], *Decl.* 298 p. 176 Ritter, similar views attributed to the stereotypical *rusticus: quid turpius, quam luxuria?*—cf. p. 177, perfumes on a man are *perditae vitae signa*.

4. Hence I disagree with various *obiter dicta* (the subject has been barely touched by classical scholars): M.-H.-E. Meier and L.-R. de Pogey-Castries, *Histoire de l'amour grec* (1930) 178, using only Polyb. 32.11 to show that "la débauche pédérastique était devenue ordinaire à Rome"; P. Veyne, e.g. using Horace, in *Annales* 1978, 51; Festugière, below, n. 51; also J. P. Sullivan, *The Satyricon of Petronius* (1968) 235, believing he can find one over-all "fairly standard ancient view"; and most of all with J. Boswell, *Christianity, Social Tolerance, and Homosexuality* (1980), e.g. p. 22 n. 42, "Romans were quite open about homosexual feelings and gay relationships were . . . generally accepted"; p. 49, "homosexual desire, which everyone apparently considered . . . entirely ordinary"; p. 58, "few classicists have doubted that homosexuality occupied a prominent and respected position in most Greek and Roman cities at all levels of society and among a substantial portion of the population"; p. 62 n. 4, "Roman sexuality was virtually untrammeled . . . The attitude . . . probably typical of Roman males . . . : 'Can it matter where or in whom you put it?' "; p. 72, "Nowhere is there any indication that such [homoerotic] passions or acts might be illegal or disapproved, until the time of Juvenal"; and p. 78 n. 84, "Homosexuality per se was not a subject of controversy"(!).

5. Polyb. 31.25.3: *euchereia* and *akrasia*. He goes on to show that he means only very rich circles. See also W. Kroll, *RE* s.v. "Knabenliebe" (1921) col. 905, "to the Romans pederasty appeared a Greek custom"; and he cites Cic., *Tusc. Disp.* 5.58, the clearest passage, describing a young man surrounded by lovers *more Graeciae*; J.P.V.D. Balsdon, *Romans and Aliens* (1979) 225, citing the same work, 4.70, *mihi quidem in Graecorum gymnasiis nata consuetudo videtur*, where Ennius is cited, *flagitii principium est nudare inter civis copora*; and less explicit, Sall., *Cat.* 11.55ff. with 13.1. Besides, would Plato have written, *Symp.* 182B, that pederasty was generally held in dishonor in "barbarian" lands, if the opposite had been true in Italy of the time? For later years, see below, n. 37.

6. Others, too, e.g. *inberbi androgyni, barbati moechocinaedi*, Lucilius 30.1058

(Marx); *concubitus . . . clinopalem vocabat* (Domitian), *Domit.* 22; *embasicoetas*, Petron. 24.1; *tunc primum ignota antea vocabula reperta sunt sellariorum et spintriarum*, Tac., *Ann.* 6.1, cf. Suet., *Tib.* 43; and *laecasim*, Petron. 42.5, cf. H. Jocelyn, *Proc. Cam. Philol. Assoc.* 206 (1980) 17.

7. For words regarding coiffure and cosmetics, see O. Wiese, *Die griechischen Wörter im Latein* (1882) 187–92, and J. Griffin, *JRS* 66 (1976) 93 n. 94; also Hor., *Sat.* 1.2.94 (*depygis*); Lucr. 4.1160–69 (a string of euphemisms and arch periphrases); Lucilius 17.2 (540–46 Marx), Greek untransliterated as also at 8.1 (303–4 Marx), where the obscenity is thus veiled; Plaut., *Asinaria* 627 (3.3.37), *calamistratus*; Mart. 1.87.5, *diapasma*; Augustus calling Maecenas *malagma moecharum*, Macrob. 2.4.12; and a standard good summary in L. R. Palmer, *The Latin Language* (1954) 82.

8. In Cato's pages even the word *elegans* indicates censure, and he explodes almost as violently against Pontiac caviar as against catamites. Cf. Aul. Gell. 11.2.1 and Polyb. 31.25.5. Note also Scipio's revulsion from dancing, cf. n. 24 below.

9. Suet., *Iulius* 2, the story elsewhere also; or Plut., *Cimon* 1.2ff. of the 70s B.C.

10. *Pro Flacco* 21.51 and 29.70 (Pergamon).

11. *Att.* 6.3.9, the whole behavior *flagitiose et turpiter*, cf. 10.4.6, the lad is corrupted by nature.

12. As Glasgow was at one time the largest Irish city and at another time New York was the largest Jewish city, so Rome was Greek. My (quite unprovable) estimate draws on L. R. Taylor, *AJP* 82 (1961) 113, 118, and 125; P. M. Fraser, *Ptolemaic Alexandria* (1972) 1.91 and 2.172 n. 358; and P. A. Brunt, *Italian Manpower* (1971) 383. Dio 79.20.2 (A.D. 217) reports the Roman masses as still bilingual in the third century, with some confirmation in I. Kajanto, *Onomastic Studies . . .* (1963) 57ff.: names on dated Roman epitaphs even after 313 (to A.D. 410) are ca. 30 percent Greek (earlier, ca. 45 percent, tables 13–14); [and notice H. J. Leon, *The Jews of Ancient Rome* (1960) chap. 4, esp. p. 76 (cross-transliteration of Latin in Greek letters and vice-versa): the Jewish communities were essentially Greek-speaking but bilingual, without evident change till ca. 300].

13. Livy 35.16.3; Tac., *Ann.* 15.33, and Griffin, *JRS* 66 (1976) 92ff., excellent pages. On the wine-drinking, see C. Panella, *Dial. di arch.* 7 (1963) 344; and note the ratio of freed or slave to freeborn, in categories of Puteolan inscriptions: 16, 10, or 7 to 1, in J. P. D'Arms, *JRS* 64 (1974) 112 n. 7. [On the Bay area and the entire south of Italy, also G. Rohlfs, *CJ* 62 (1967) 167.] On Tiberius in the Bay area, see Tac., *Ann.* 6.1, Suet., *Tib.*, 43ff., Dio 58.22.1, and Balsdon, op. cit. (n. 5) 227 (like other scholars, rightly dismissing the picture as fiction); on Nero, speaking Greek and applauded in the Greek manner, see Suet., *Nero* 20.2.

14. E. Segal, *Roman Laughter* (1968) 37–41.

15. Plautine passages such as *Asinaria* 703, with others in Kroll, "Knabenliebe" cit. above at n. 5; Q. Lutatius Catulus in Aul. Gell. 19.9.14, see G. Williams, *JRS* 52 (1962) 40; the three *veteres poetae*, i.e. of the second century B.C., in Aul. Gell. 19.9.10–14; and the controversy recently renewed by Griffin, *JRS* 66 (1976) 87ff.

16. Plut., *Moral. (Amatorius)* 751C, *para physin* contrasted with *eros te physei*; 751D, anal copulation is *nomo tetrapodos, para physin*, and ungraceful; it merely "pretends friendship" (752A, Loeb trans.); or contrariwise, it is pronounced rather the best form of love (750C–E); Pisias' rejoinder, 752B.

17. *Amores* 21, the debate ending at §52.

18. Livy 8.28 (326 B.C.), Val. Max. 6.1.9 adding that the senate defended Romans' *pudicitia* with a law and a jail sentence; similar and early, Dion. Hal. 16.4 (292/290 B.C.), an attempted seduction, then force attempted by an officer on a young *contubernalis*. The *akosmia* is seen as *koinon adikema tes poleos* and the *hybris* offered *para physin* is punished with death.

19. Val. Max. 6.1.7 (later third century B.C.), *quod filium suum de stupro appellasset*; also in Plut., *Marcellus* 2.3ff. Kroll (loc. cit., n. 5) defends the historicity of the tale. Its usefulness for my purposes is not tied to the true date or purport of the Lex. The same solicitation earlier (312 or 292/290 B.C.?) is described in the same words and meets equally sharp condemnation: *universae plebis sententia crimine impudicitiae damnatus*, Val. Max. 6.1.11; [and notice Dion. Hal. 20.13.3, in an early third-century context, contrasting Athens with the Romans, among whom one finds "no wantonness and corrupting of youthful comrades"].

20. *Famosa*, in a woman's role, in ca. 170 B.C.; see Cic., *De orat.* 2.277.

21. His saying that "the soul of the man who loves dwells in the soul of the man beloved" is a thought I cannot suppose arose in Cato's mind spontaneously (Plut., *Moral.* 759C; slightly different in *Cato Maior* 9.5). It is pure Greek, cf. e.g. Plato, *Symp.* 183E. He is also recorded protesting against buying boy slaves, Polyb. 31.25.5—only on account of the extravagance? So A. E. Astin, *Cato the Censor* (1978) 173 n. 46, Veyne, *Annales*, 1978, 50, and Boswell, op. cit. (n. 4) 72. But why then should his lieutenant *commit suicide* when discovered buying (on the battlefield, surely for pennies) three boy captives, *paidaria* (Plut., *Cato Maior* 10.5)? And why should Cato often reprobate L. Cornelius Scipio for (the mere possession of) a hired catamite, Livy 39.42.9? The same boy induced from his lover an act of barbarous cruelty (ibid. and Plut., *Flamininus* 18.3ff.), which many persons besides Cato reprobated.

22. Aul. Gell. 15.12.2ff. = *ORF*³ 1.181; see also Plut., *C. Gracchus* 4.4, in which he pours contempt on a man *diabeblemenos* for *malakia*, explained as intercourse with men; and capital punishment awaiting the young soldier who prostituted himself, Polyb. 6.37.9. [Livy (21.3.4, trans. de Selincourt) later projects his own views and, presumably, those of his readers into the past, in the comment, "Heaven forbid that under the veil of a military training we should subject our young men to the lusts of our generals."]

23. Balsdon, op. cit. (n. 5) 226, citing also Plut., *Marius* 14.3ff., the story of the young Marius also in Val. Max. 6.1.12 and Cic., *Pro Milone* 4.9. Notice also Cic., *Phil.* 3.31, and Tac., *Hist.* 3.33, pillaging troops carry off both girls and boys; and [Caes.], *Bell. Hisp.* 33, an officer with *concubinus* on campaign.

24. *In Pisonem* 1.1, *belua*; 6.13, *caenum*; and 29.72, *homo turpissimus*, etc., consort of *illa saltatrix tonsa*, Gabinius, 8.18, cf. 36.89, *tuis teneris saltatoribus*, consorting with certain *formosi fratres; Post reditum in sen.* 5.11 (quoted, on Gabinius); *De domo sua* 19.49 and *Pro Milone* 55, on Clodius; Plut., *Cic.* 7.5, on Verres' son; Cic., *Cat.* 1.4.7, 2.2.4, 2.4.8, and 4.6.12; and, on Antony's homosexuality, many passages, e.g. *Phil.* 2.77 and 2.18.44ff. Even the wretched Rullus is pictured *cum suis formosis finitoribus* or succumbing to an *adulescens bene capillatus*, *Leg. agr.* 2.53 and 59. Lost verses by Gallus evidently presented Cicero himself as the lover of Tiro

(Plin., *Ep*. 7.4.3 and 6)—possible, but see A. N. Sherwin-White in his edition of Pliny (1966) ad loc.; [and Clodius himself orchestrated abuse against Pompey as being "a man that seeks other men" and scratches his head with one finger, on which gesture, see n. ad loc., Plut., *Pomp*. 48.12, in the Budé ed.].

25. His adulteries *ne amici quidem negant*, Suet., *Aug*. 69, with the text of Antony's letters, *an refert ubi et in qua arrigas?*—"designed for publicity," says R. Syme, *The Roman Revolution* (1939) 276. Boswell, p. 62 n. 4 (see above, n. 4) quite distorts the text.

26. Cic., *Pro Caelio* 3.6, *maledicta pervulgata in omnes* (scil. *adulescentes*), cf. Suet., *Aug*. 68, *stuprum* and *cinaedus*, and 71.1, *crimina* and *maledicta* aimed at (among other things) *infamia impudicitiae* —"the old themes," as Syme says, loc. cit. (n. 25), or "die stereotypen Vorwürfe," as W. Kroll says, *Die Kultur der ciceronischen Zeit* (1933) 2.55, cf. 164 n. 63 for many examples, likewise in I. Opelt, *Die lateinischen Schimpfwörter* (1965) 155ff.

27. I offer here a mechanically schematized ranking drawn from a good deal of modern discussion, perhaps most clearly worked out by K. Dover, *Greek Homosexuality* (1978) chap. 2. The ultimate in shame was *irrumatio*, that is, compelled *fellatio*, cf. e.g. Suet., *Nero* 35.4, or Catullus 16, and discussion, e.g. by A. Richlin, *CP* 76 (1981) 42, or by Jocelyn, *Proc. Cam. Philol. Assoc*. 206 (1980) 19ff.; but to be a *fellator* was very low also, clearly in an aggrieved soldier's gibe at Scipio, Lucilius 398ff. (Marx), or in Cicero's description of Gabinius, above at n. 24, and later in Mart. 3.82.33 and Dio 62.13.4 and 64.5.2.

28. See above, nn. 22, 24, and 11; Cic., *Cat*. 2.7 and 22f.; and Tac., *Ann*. 5.3ff., *amores iuvenum*.

29. Passages at nn. 1 and 2 and elsewhere, above, or Aul. Gell. 9.10.1, *res operienda*; Athen. 11.506C, "what [Plato] said about Alcibiades in the *Symposium* ought not to be brought up in any discussion"; Quint. 1.3.17, *pudet dicere* the *probra* he is discussing; and the result, perplexity among the learned today, in certain of whose pages the authors are reduced to "silliness," as Jocelyn has the courage to say, *AJP* 101 (1980) 424.

30. Examples from the Empire: Dio 64.10.1 (Sporus), Quint. 4.2.69, and Tac., *Ann*. 13.17 (the death of Britannicus, *stupro pollutus*, was "none too soon, nor cruel"); earlier, above, n. 23, and most generally in *Dig*. 4.2.8.2 (Paulus), sexual defilement, *ne stuprum patiatur*, "good men must fear more than death."

31. Above, n. 23; *Dig*. 48.8.1.4 (Hadrian).

32. Worse, if it demeans the well-born, see e.g. Cic., *Att*. 1.16.5 and *Pro Rab. Post*. 10.26; Dio 58.22.1; and Tac., *Ann*. 13.25.

33. G. Williams, *Figures of Thought in Roman Poetry* (1980) 216.

34. Cicero on cloaks and sandals, *Pro Rab. Post*. 10.26 and *Phil*. 2.76. Vergil deriding tunics, Aul. Gell. 6.26.6 on *Aen*. 9.616ff.; Augustus rebuking men who wear *lacernae*, Suet., *Aug*. 40.5; Tac., *Ann*. 14.21, and Suet., *Nero* 25.1, an emperor in the capital wearing a chlamys, horrors!—and again, *Domit*. 4.4.

35. Dio 62.6.4 (Loeb trans.), the more interesting because it is a description of Romans put into the mouth of a British queen. Compare a fuller scene in Philo, *De vita contemplativa* 50–53, or Mart. 3.82.8ff., and other passages in L. Malten, *Hermes* 53 (1918) 165ff., esp. Cic., *De fin*. 2.83.

36. Dio 57.15.2, the word *emblema* outlawed; 60.17.4, Claudius and citizenship.

37. Tac., *Ann.* 14.20, cf. Tert., *Ad nat.* 1.16.15, *Graeco utere* = pederasty.

38. Aul. Gell. 1.5.3, ridicule in a court scene in 62 B.C.; Tac., *Hist.* 1.30, ridicule aimed at Otho, implying he had risen in the world by serving as a catamite, cf. also *Ann.* 4.1 (Sejanus); and Musonius Rufus, *Discourses* 21 p. 128 (Lutz), men *gynaikodeis* in various respects. Kroll, op. cit. (n. 25) 58, cites other evidence that "it was thought, too that *cinaedi* betrayed themselves by their feminine walk" (not to mention many reff. to excessive jewelry, perfume, etc.). Boswell, pp. 24, 67, and 339–41, still insists that "homosexuality was not associated with 'effeminacy.' "

39. The phrase *para physin* in Plut. and Dion Hal., above, nn. 16 and 18; but see also Muson. Ruf., *Discourses* 12 p. 86 (Lutz); Plut., *Moral.* 990D and F and 991A; Dio Chrysos, *Or.* 7.135 (heterosexual union is *kata physin*—cf. Max. Tyr., n. 51 below) and 7.149; Epict. 3.1.25, the man who wants to be a woman is to be advertised to the public for a show; Suet., *Caligula* 16.1 (*spintriae monstrosarum libidinum*); Mart. 9.7(8).6, boy prostitutes are *monstra*; Juv. 2.121ff., a priest is needed to exorcize homosexual "nuptials," *monstra*, which may be compared to "a woman giving birth to a calf, or an ox to a lamb"; and female homoeroticism in Ov., *Met.* 9.727 and 736, *prodigiosa* and *monstra*. Veyne, *Annales* (1978) 52 and 62 n. 6, denies the whole notion of "l'amour contre-nature" in antiquity; still more emphatically, Boswell, pp. 11–16, 21 n. 50 (having to translate *atopos* "unseemly," though it is applied to things like cannibalism!), 109–13 and elsewhere denying any perception of homosexuality as unnatural. He does not mention the probative words in the very lines he has cited for other purposes, e.g. pp. 58 (Plut.), 63 (Dion. Hal.), 66 and 82 (Juv.), 67 (Mart.), 77 (Epict.), and 152 (Ovid).

40. Nepos, *Praef.* 4ff., is typical (compare various passages above) in contrasting Roman and Greek views on the desirability of a boy having *amatores* (which are among things *infamia, humilia,* and *ab honestate remota*); cf. Hor., *Sat.* 1.6.81ff., guarded against both *obprobrium* and *turpe* at school; Quint. 1.2.2 and 4 and 1.3.17; and Plin., *Ep.* 3.3.4.

41. The purport of the Lex Scantinia is not clear in Cic., *Ad fam.* 8.12.3; Juv. 2.43ff.; and Suet., *Domit.* 8. For penalties inflicted on *stupratores* through private suits, see Quint. 4.2.69 and 7.4.41ff.; *Dig.* 47.10.9.4 (Ulpian); 47.11.1.2 (Paul), 48.5.6pr. (Papinian); 48.6.3.4 (Marcian); *Pauli Sent.* 2.27.12, against rape, and §13, heavy fines for voluntary participation; compare *Tab. Heracl.* lines 122–23, *quei corpore quaestum fecit fecerit*, with 134 and 138ff., forbidding such men (evidently not slaves) even to sit in public side by side with town leaders; further, Kroll, op. cit. (n. 25) 57; and entirely obscure reff. to a *nomos* (or an act *paranomos*) in Muson. loc. cit. and Sext. Emp., *Pyrr. Hyp.* 1.152. Mart. 9.5(6) and 9.7(8) show Domitian issuing decrees against prostituting boys below a fixed age, and against castration (which Hadrian legislated against also). Boswell, p. 69, taking Cic., *Pro Plancio* 12.30, to mean homosexuality "is not a crime," mis-translates "is no (mere) reproach, *crimen*, but a *maledictum*"; so the text reveals nothing about legality (though indeed something about current attitudes). For a sound view on the actual effect of such laws, see Griffin, *JRS* 66 (1976) 100.

42. Dio 57.19.5 (Sejanus); Suet., *Claud.* 29.2 (Gn. Pompeius); idem, *Vesp.* 13 (Licinius Mucianus, evidently *pathicus*); *Domit.* 1.1 (D. as a boy promises a nobleman

a night); and other figures like Val. Asiaticus, Tac., *Ann.* 11.2.2, and L. Pedanius Secundus, *praef. urbi* A.D. 61, with a vast household, ibid. 14.42.

43. Dio 63.22.4, for Nero's relationship with Sporus seen as a cause for revolution. The general reception of Nero's acts is evident across the record of his reign; but, as a sampling, notice Tac., *Ann.* 13.25, *foeda domi lascivia*, with men as well as women; 15.37.8ff., he marries *unus ex illo contaminatorum grege*; and Suet., *Nero* 29.1, "after defiling almost every part of his body, he went so far in violating his own chastity as to devise a new game," a second homosexual "marriage"; Boswell's views (pp. 69 and 82ff.) on this and similar unions seem to me very strange.

44. I count in Epictetus eighteen passages suiting an entirely heterosexual society (1.6.8; 1.11.1–3; 1.11.17; 1.16.9–14; 2.8.15; 2.20.27; 2.20.37; 2.22.11; 2.22.32; 2.23.38; 3.2.8; 3.5.19; 3.12.12; 3.25.6; 4.1.22; 4.9.3; 4.9.5; and 4.9.6); nine passages fitting a bisexual society (2.1.28; 2.10.17; 2.16.29; 2.18.15; 2.2.12ff.; 3.3.14; 3.7.21; 4.1.15; and 4.1.35–36). He sees the boy participants as slaves (that is morally neutral, evidently) or *kinaidoi* (who pay a heavy price, themselves—2.10.17). Even a freed boy slave who "earns a living by his body suffers terrible things," 4.1.35.

45. Censure of the *pathicus* is clear in, e.g. Tac., *Ann.* 11.2.2, and Suet., *Vitellius* 3.2–4.1; and censure of flaunted expense on boy slaves, in Sen., loc. cit.; of caresses in public, *Acta Alexandrinorum* p. 25 (Musurillo), where a speech apparently in a court at Rome under Trajan blackens the accused (that is, takes for granted that the court will more readily find against the accused) for fondling an adolescent at semi-public banquets. See, for the setting, H. A. Musurillo, *The Acts of the Pagan Martyrs* (1954) 152ff. Boswell, p. 30, quite misreads the text, partly through mistaking the nature of the document, which he knows only as P. Oxy. 471.

46. Dover, op. cit. (n. 27) 148, with further discussion, pp. 61 and 149ff. Boswell, p. 49, misreads one of the more significant texts, Ar., *Clouds* 1075–82, through supposing that it is the playwright that speaks rather than "the immoralist Wrong" (Dover's phrase), and through not noticing the change in the subject of the speech, from "pleasures" (including boys) to *anangkai*, "harsh necessities" (not "needs" in the sense of "desires").

47. Ps. Quint., *Decl.* 337 p. 329 (Ritter): *illa ministeria, illi imitati feminas pueri. Der Kleine Pauly* s.v. Quintilian hesitantly suggests a date in the time of Quintilian himself.

48. See the index to *CIL* 4 s.v. *pedico* (4.2210, etc.) in seventeen inscriptions, (*cunni*)*lingit* in fourteen, *fello (fellare)* in forty, *futuo* in forty (and seven times showing sex of partner, female, hence always heterosexual, one may assume); [compare also graffiti in Ostia, in G. Calza, *Monumenti antichi, Accad. dei Lincei* 26 (1920) 370f.]. Without going into details, Boswell, p. 57, sees in the graffiti proof of homosexuality being very common. For suggestive parallels, see the *tesserae lusoriae* in C. Huelsen, *RM* 11 (1918) 227–37, esp. the lists, pp. 233ff.

49. Dio 69.11 and SHA *Had.* 14.5ff. are almost the only sources. Both hesitate about any homosexual connection between Hadrian and Antinous; but the modern consensus assumes it, no doubt rightly. [A sign of a turning point may be supposed late in Hadrian's reign when a Roman aristocrat contemplates suicide on account of his son's effeminacy, *malakia* (Dio 69.23.4), cf. above, n. 22.] For the next two emperors, see M. Aurel., *Medit.* 1.16.3 (Ant. Pius, see also Pius' *pudicitia* praised by Fronto, *Fer.*

Als. 3.5, Loeb ed. 2 p. 8), 1.17.2, and 3.16; [on Verus, in a late source, condemnation contained in the report that he was *iuvenum amoribus infamatus est*, SHA *Verus* 4.4;] on Commodus, Dio 74.5.4 and SHA *Commod.* 10.1 and 8ff. and 19.2 (*impurior Nerone*); similar discredit, *diabole* for Plautianus' various abhorred practices of bed and board, Dio 76.15.7; on male prostitution banned in the 240s (but not heterosexual), see A. Chastagnol, *Bonner Historia-Augusta-Colloquium 1964/1965* (1966) 55f., 76f.

50. In speaking of "Epictetus' world," Veyne, *Annales* (1978) 50, includes the evidence of PTeb. 104; but the text dates to 92 B.C., not A.D. Moreover, in specifying that the husband shall not introduce *mede pallaken mede paidikon*, the marriage contract may reflect special customs of the parties, both "Persians of the Succession" (the term mysterious to the editors of other documents; see Fraser, op. cit. [n. 12] 58ff.); and further, one should not assume prevailing bisexuality from the clause, any more than *tri*sexuality in the cult regulations against intercourse with women, dogs, or donkeys, seen in F. Sokolowsky, *Lois sacrées . . . Supplément* (1962) 160. On such a taboo in a new cult, see the prohibition against pederasty as *asebes* in Lucian, *Alex.* 41. As to seeing in Plut., *Moral.* 990Dff., proof that all classes shared the same practices (Boswell, p. 58), Plutarch actually contrasts the "no-accounts" only with figures of myth, the scene not being on the human level at all. For youths being sought after, see Dio Chrysos., *Or.* 36.8; defending their sexual honor or choice, Philostr., *Vita Apollon.* 7.42; hostility to prostitution of boys or to seduction or pursuit of them if they are "honorable," Lucian, *Alex.* 5 and 41, and Dio Chrysos., *Or.* 7.135, 139, and 149–51; respect for boys' repute and protecting them against *diabole*, Menander Rhetor p. 132 (Russell-Wilson).

51. A. J. Festugière, *Antioche paienne et chrétienne* (1959) 197–98, cites Xen. Ephes. and Achilles Tatius (and in addition only the *Amores* and Hor., *Serm.* 2.3.325) to support the view that "in the literature of the empire the two species of love are seen exactly on a level, one taken to be fully as normal as the other." Among Greek writers of the second century, no doubt more could be found, e.g. Ael. Arist., *Or.* 45 p. 146 (Dindorf), pederasty casually mentioned on a par with heterosexuality, but cf. 33.20 p. 232 (Keil) (paired with various tasteless indulgences); and Max. Tyr., *Diss.* 24(8).2, 25(9).4ff., and 26(10).9, says very roundly, no physical contact between males, "change your pleasures to nature's," *epi ten physin.*

52. Tat., *Ad Graecos* 28ff., *paiderastia . . . pronomias . . . exiotai*, drawing on Just., 1 *Apol.* 27 (*PG* 6.369B); and behind *this* lies Aristides in his *Apol.* 13 p. 109 (Harris-Robinson), specifying "Greeks." Justin addresses alternately the emperor, e.g. here and at §12; inhabitants of Rome (26); and people of the Hellenic tradition (21–22). Boswell, p. 68, seems not to know where the gibe originated and to mis-read the Greek, thinking it shows "pederasty was held in preeminent esteem by the Romans." He also asserts, ibid., of another Christian source, "Minucius Felix says that homosexual relations were 'the Roman religion' (*Octavius* 28)," but I find no such statement in that author, nor does Minucius make mention of "ceremonial fellatio" (Boswell, p. 131). He does reject as lies the accusation against Christians of phallic worship according to priests (28.9) and accuses pagans of *fellatio* —which of course he sees (28.10) as thoroughly repulsive.

53. Joh. Chrysos., *Adv. oppugnatores vitae monasticae* 3.16 (*PG* 47.377). See elsewhere, e.g. 3.7 (47.360), on the wealth of the class in question; 3.9 (47.360) on

the extreme delicacy and shamefulness of the subject, *nosema chalepon*, etc.; notice at 3.8 (47.361) that it is the active role that is being discussed (exclusively?—*arrenes en arsesin ten aschemosynen katergazontai*), and "in the very midst of your cities" (cities, plu.); and, making use of the text on its prevalence, at 3.8 (47.361), Boswell (p. 55) paraphrases without reserve, "Chrysostom suggests very strongly that in fourth century Antioch heterosexual persons were in a small minority"(!). One further Antiochene, Ammianus (31.9.5), shows harsh prejudice against homosexuality. For condemnation of luxurious, licentious households, see Greg. Nyss., *PG* 46.468B, and, in the 370s A.D., Basil, *Ep.* 188 can. 7, and 217 can. 62–63, condemning copulation with males or animals. Homosexuality was also cause for *diabole* against a teacher in Constantinople, Eunap., *Vit. soph.* 495, [and, in Antioch, material for blackmail, while prostitution was punished by loss of citizenship, cf. Liban., *Or.* 18.38 and 15.57].

54. *Or.* 7.224A, taking *"tois xulois" sensu obscaeno*, cf. Stephanus s.v., citing Euripides.

55. *Misopog.* 346A and 350D.

56. *Mos. et Rom. leg. coll.* 5.3 (*FIRA*² 2.557), posted in A.D. 390, on which see O. Seeck, *Gesch. des Untergangs der antiken Welt* 5 (1913) 531ff.

18. PERSONAL POWER IN THE ROMAN EMPIRE

1. I assemble reff. in *Roman Social Relations* (1974) 8–12 and notes.

2. *CIL* 8.10570 and 14464: tortures, beatings, confinement in fetters by land administrators, even for Roman citizens.

3. Cic., 2 *Verr.* 1.66f., Sicily in the 70s B.C.; *Pro Flacco* 73, an incident at Pergamon in the 60s B.C. (?); M. Dubois, "Lettre de l'empereur Auguste aux Cnidiens," *BCH* 7 (1883) 64, at Cnidus under Augustus; Tac., *Ann.* 15.69, slaves used in defense of the house in the A.D. 60s; similarly in *Dig.* 8.5.18, mid-second century (?); Philostr., *Vit. soph.* 588, a decade or two later in Greece; and so up to the fourth century in Egypt, P. Oxy. 1903.

4. On the grudging use of soldiers in police work, notice Plin., *Ep.* 10.78—though soldiers do a lot of the dirty work against Christians, esp. in the Great Persecution. For use at the call of slave-owners, see *Dig.* 11.4.1.2 (Ulpian) and 11.4.2 (Marcus Aurelius, use of *stationarii*).

5. From Gaius Gracchus' speeches, anecdotes in Aul. Gell. 10.3.5 and 10.3.3—the latter regarding public baths at Teanum Sidicinum; compare the often quoted Scaptopara inscription, *CIL* 3.12336 (A.D. 238) = *IGR* 1.674 = *Syll.*³ 888, later frozen in law: *CT* 7.11.1f. (A.D. 406 and 417).

6. Dio 45.16.2, Servilius Isauricus, cf. Livy 24.44.10 (213 B.C.), the consul's lictor announces to anyone approaching "that he must get down from his horse"; and Suet. *Nero* 5.1, Domitius Ahenobarbus, consul A.D. 32, who deliberately runs down a boy in a village street.

7. Dio 49.7.6, a man "so extremely proud . . ." On retinues see L. Friedlaender, *Roman Life and Manners*⁷ (1908) 1.207 and 209; MacMullen, op. cit. (n. 1) 107 and nn. 56f.

8. Notice the incident Pliny describes (*Ep.* 3.14.7): an equestrian will knock you down for the insult of being touched by your slave. Compare Lucian, *Nigrinus* 21: the rich Roman is seen "addressing others on the street by a spokesman, thinking they will

be pleased just by the glance bestowed on them, and the more reverend men expect you to kneel to them''—just as Amm. 28.4.10 indicates later, where the rich ''offer their flatterers their knees to kiss or their hands.'' So Tac., *Hist.* 4.14, speaks of Roman governors' ''arrogant retinue,'' cf. *Ann.* 3.40, ''the arrogance of governors.''

9. MacMullen, op. cit. (n. 1) 195f.

10. Jos., *B. J.* 2.287f.; Lucian, *Alex.* 57.

11. N. 4 above and *Dig.* 22.3.20; and notice how Lucian can borrow soldiers for his own protection from the governor of Cappadocia, ''a friend of mine'' (*Alex.* 55).

12. *Or.* 43.11 and 45.15.

13. Pliny, *Ep.* 2.11.3, 8, and 19; Juv. 1.49f.

14. Notice *B. G.* 4.17, 6.8, and 8.6, for similar use of *dignitas*; for Caesar's own *dignitas* as the key to 49 B.C., a subject often discussed, see the recent E. Wistrand, *Caesar and Contemporary Roman Society* (1979) 30f., with a good selection of passages from Caesar, Hirtius, and Cicero, e.g., *Pro Ligario* 6.18, ''What other object did your armed forces have except to drive off *contumelia*, insult, from you? And, invincible, what did they accomplish except to defend their rights and your *dignitas*?''

15. *Rep.* 3.35, on which W. V. Harris says, in his *War and Imperialism in Republican Rome* (1979) 165 n. 2., ''revenge was morally quite acceptable to most Romans.''

16. Nepos frag. 58 p. 202 (Malcovati). It is irrelevant for my argument whether the speech represents common values of Gaius' day or Cicero's. Cornelia, however, does go on to urge Gaius against harming the state. In Gaius' father, notice the same struggle between revenge and care for the state, in Livy 38.53.6 (*res publica* weighed against ''private feuds''—again, a view of the second century? of Livy's own?).

17. Epict., *Diss.* 2.14.18, ''you have come to me like a man who stood in need of nothing . . . for when a man has done you either good or harm you know how to pay him back in kind''; Sen., *Ep.* 81.7, ''surely it belongs to justice to pay back everyone in kind, with thanks for a *beneficium* and retaliation for injury, or at least ill-will''; and Plut., *Moral.* 563D–E, where someone is held up as a model, ''no one more just in business . . . , no one more pious toward god, no one more baneful to enemies or stauncher to friends'' (and the same ethic is preached by Plato, *Meno*, 71e).

18. Synes., *Ep.* 67 (*PG* 66.1413C).

19. Tac., *Ann.* 13.21, Agrippina celebrates a personal victory with revenge and rewards; Plin., *Ep.* 1.5.15 (Regulus described) and 5.13.2, a senator may be expected to litigate most relentlessly where his ''influence, *gratia*, reputation, and *dignitas*'' are all at stake; and Dio 77.9.3 (A.D. 205) on a grandee ''able to hold all the world in contempt'' because he can ''bestow favors on his friends and vengeance on his enemies'' (similarly, the emperor Severus, 77.16.1).

20. Dio 79.20.1–3 (Loeb trans.).

21. Dio 58.5.3f. I substitute *dignitas* and *contumelia* for *axioma* and *ubrizomenoi* to bring out the thought (he is discussing Sejanus and his like).

22. Liban., *Or.* 47.22, if a slave seeks help from an outside party, ''the master is scorned through the other person's rendering aid''; and *Passio S. Perpetuae* 5.2, a father disobeyed by a child is consigned ''to scorn among men.''

23. A sampling of texts: *CIL* 12.594; 3.781; and 8.26528b, Antoninus Pius' *beneficia* to Arles, Tyre, and Dougga, in the form of confirming certain monetary advan-

tages to these cities; his gift of procuratorships as *beneficia* at Fronto's request, *Ad Pium* 9 p. 170 (Naber): *CIL* 6.2131, promotion to equestrian status; unspecified "great *beneficia* through the emperor's indulgence," 6.1074; 2.4249, "enrolled in the colonia Caesaraugusta by *beneficium* of Hadrian"; special advancement by *beneficia* of the emperor, "earlier through the years than is usually allowed," 12.3164; F. Miltner, *Jahresheft der oesterreichischen Akad. der Wissenschaften* 45 (1960), Beiblatt p. 42, a *beneficium* of the emperor permits reallocation of municipal income; AETERNVM BE-NEFICIVM LAOD[ICENIS] DATVM on a coin of 213 or 216 commemorating the emperor's gift of grain, in R. Ziegler, *Chiron* 8 (1978) 508; a procuratorship or partial citizenship "by *beneficium* of the emperor," *Dig.* 4.4.11.2 (Ulpian); *FIRA*² 2.266 (Ulpian); *FIRA*² 1.445 (A.D. 205); Plin., *Ep.* 10.11, citizenship by "your *beneficium*" (Trajan's); 10.94f., special exemption granted by the same emperor; Sen., *Benef.* 3.9.2, citizenship or equestrian status as an imperial *beneficium*.

24. *Dig.* 1.4.1, cf. 1.3.31; Sen., *Benef.* 7.5.3, *Caesar omnia habet*, cf. Ovid, *Fasti* 2.138, "whatever exists beneath Jupiter on high, Caesar possesses," and *Tristia* 4.15, "for the emperor *is* the state."

25. For access to discussion of these matters, see R. P. Saller, *JRS* 70 (1980) 44, citing H.-G. Pflaum, F. Millar, and P. A. Brunt; idem, *Personal Patronage under the Early Empire* (1982) 24f., e.g., 33 (adding E. J. Champlin and P. Veyne to the debate); most recently, W. Eck, in *Korruption im Altertum*, ed. W. Schuller (1982) 142–47. Among these points of view, Eck's and Millar's, though briefly expounded, seem to me closest to the truth, Saller's and Veyne's least persuasive.

26. Hyginus, *De limit. const.* p. 203 (Blume-Lachmann-Rudorff), cf. p. 295; *CIL* 6.33770 and reff. there.

27. A *beneficiorum numerus*, Tac., *Hist.* 4.48.5, cause of wrangling between two authorities in the same province. For the normal context of *beneficia*, in career advancement, see e.g. *CIL* 6.2131 = *ILS* 4929, a Vestal confers *beneficia* and her *suffragium* on a dependent.

28. Details quite naked in Plin., *Ep.* 2.13.2 ("You command a very large force, giving you an ample store of *beneficia*," etc.); 7.22.1, Pliny requests a military tribunate; another he has in his gift and (3.8.4) the recipient treats it as transferable to a kinsman (Pliny had gotten it in the first place from his friend, who knows nothing of what is happening); further, 2.9.3 and 4.4.1–3.

29. Sen., *Benef.* 1.2.3, adding "it is a disgusting sort of usury to count a *beneficium* as money out at interest" (suggesting that people usually did); cf. 1.1.9, "we give not lend *beneficia*" and (*Ep.* 81.9) "we do not talk about 'paying' a *beneficium*; no word suits as that belongs to indebtedness."

30. *Benef.* 7.19.3. The unreality in Seneca's other statements is seen by Wistrand, op. cit. (n. 14) 11f., who adduces contrary Latin usages and citations from Cicero and Publilius Syrus, *Sent.* 61 (Duff), "You sell your freedom when you accept a *beneficium*" (date in the 40s/30s B.C.). Notice also Marcus Aurelius, *Medit.* 5.6.1, that some people in bestowing a *charis* create a debtor, as they see it.

31. Cic., *Ad fam.* 9.24.1, "my well-being is awfully important to him," so I will readily help him; 3.1.3, 5.11.1, 13.4.1, 13.21.2, and book 13 passim, stressing a person's capacity for gratitude; 13.15.1, 13.21.1, 13.25.1, and 13.38.1, the recommended person is very fond of Cicero; Fronto, *Ep. ad Ant. Pium* 8 (Loeb ed. 1) 236,

the choice of friends to help in governing a province is dictated first by *fides*, then by *diligentia* and *integritas*; and the remark in Sen., *Benef.* 7.19.2, "to return a *beneficium* is a matter of *fides.*" Like Cicero, Pliny emphasizes to his friends that a recommended person loves him, *Ep.* 2.9.5, 3.2.4, 6.6.5, 6.23.3, 10.26.1, and esp. 2.13.9, "he recognizes those *beneficia* of mine so gratefully that, in accepting the earlier ones, he earns subsequent ones." Compare 7.22.2, "the loyalest of friends" is recommended.

32. E.g. *Année épigraphique* (1917–1918) 73; *ILS* 8977; *CIL* 6.1531 and 1624, 3829, 31776; 8.2393 and 12442; 10.4861; and 11.2106.

33. *Ep.* 7.31.7 (trans. B. Radice): "For, according to the code of friendship, the one who takes the initiative puts the other in his debt and owes no more until he is repaid." Also 1.19, "The length of our friendship warrants that you will be ever mindful of this gift; I will even withhold the admonition (though I should offer it, if I did not know you would observe it unasked), to treat that position, given by me, with all possible discretion; for a rank is the more carefully to be maintained, in which there is a friend's *beneficium* also to be protected."

34. B. Cavagnola, *Atti, Centro studi e documentazione sull'Italia romana* 6 (1974–1975) 83: a public slave, now freed, thanked "for his many *beneficia* and easy access granted by the whole household."

35. *Dig.* 50.1.1.2; for the Greek word chosen as a translation, see Miltner, loc. cit. (n. 23), *charites* = *beneficia* in the bilingual inscription; Marcus Aurelius (n. 30 above); Acts 25.3, an irregular request made of a governor by civic leaders *aitoumenoi charin kat' autou*; *IGR* 4.1402 (A.D. 198/209), tax exemption granted by the emperor is a *charis*; and Ael. Arist., *Or.* 32(12).15, saying that rulers once openly bestowed *charites* instead of ordinary gifts very much as in imperial affairs nowadays. Notice D. Sperber, *A Dictionary of Greek and Latin Legal Terms in Rabbinic Literature* (1984) 72, and *Acts of Phileas* (P. Bodmer 20) xi lines 175f., *benephikion toi adelphoi son charizomai.*

36. Plin., *Ep.* 6.18.1, "I would like to place under obligation, *obstringere*, a most distinguished chartered colony, through acting as its lawyer, and yourself, through a favor most acceptable to you"; Publilius Syrus, *Sent.* 59 (Duff), "You have no right to ask if you don't know how to bestow a *beneficium*"; and Plut., *Moral.* 814C, "The Romans themselves are extremely zealous for their friends in matters of political partisanship, and it is a noble thing to gain a harvest of friendship among the rulers," i.e., the Roman governors set over Plutarch's countrymen, "on behalf of the general happiness."

19. HOW TO REVOLT IN THE ROMAN EMPIRE

1. *PIR*[2], C 1418, *vir consularis.*

2. *PIR*[1], S 104. He was legate in Ger. Inf. (not to be confused with the jurist cos. 148, whose age in A.D. 180 would be too great).

3. Plin., *Ep.* 9.13—no doubt some governor of Syria, from mention of the troop command.

4. Dio 57.4.3, the Pannonian troops in A.D. 14 "in the change-over of rule hoped to gain everything they wanted either by frightening him *or by giving the power to someone else.*" Further, Tac., *Hist.* 2.76.2f., Vitellius; Dio 78[79].20.4, Macrinus;

Herodian 6.8.3, Severus Alexander—whose excessive rigor, however, not weakness, is blamed by Aurelius Victor, Eutropius, and the *Augustan History*. Two emperors, Nero and Elagabalus, provoked attack by their homosexual acts: Dio 63.22.4 and Philostr., *Vit. soph.* 625.

5. Lucian, *Alex.* 32; governors routinely seek oracular approval of their terms of office, SHA *Macrinus*, iii, 1.

6. Tac., *Hist.* 1.23f.; Suet., *Otho* 4.2; Herodian 5.3.2.

7. For example, Tac., *Hist.* 2.82.2; but, on the dearth of information, see J. Nicols, *Vespasian and the Partes Flavianae* (1978) 33, 86, and 147; A. R. Birley, *Septimius Severus* (1972) 158; and T. Spagnuolo Vigorita, *Secta Temporum Meorum* (1978) 91f., on the Gordiani. These three junctures are the best reported in the sources.

8. Plut., *Galba* 13.4.

9. Herodes Atticus to Avidius Cassius, in Philostr., *Vit. soph.* 563; cf. Dio 72[73].7.4 and Amm. 21.16.11, where Marcus burns a bundle of intercepted letters which would incriminate Cassius' accomplices. Similarly Otho before he died destroyed the letters sent him during the organizing of his party (Tac., *Hist.* 2.63.1); and the governor of Ger. Inf., cos. 84 (?), puts down L. Antonius Saturninus' revolt and destroys the rebel's files of letters (Dio 67.11.2). Vespasian's letters and agents circulated all over the west in the summer of 69 (Tac., *Hist* .1.75 and 2.82 and 98), just as Septimius Severus' letters blanketed western magnates and governors (Herodian 2.10.1).

10. Herodian 7.10.5–7, and the confirmation of the people's power in 7.8.7.

11. Cash to deserters, e.g. in Herodian 5.4.2f.; transport costs estimated in *Latomus* 43 (1984) 576f.; and the needs of passing armies munificently supplied by a city's millionaire in A.D. 114/115 at Ancyra, *IGR* 3.173, and again in 124, *IGR* 3.208 = *SEG* 6.57, and in 311, at Stratonicea, in A. Laumonier, *Les cultes indigènes en Carie* (1958) 287f. W. Ameling, *Epigraphica Anatolica* 1 (1983) 64, 68 n. 16, and 70 nn. 36 and 38f., instances a number of other men financing or sheltering an army in transit, past Prusias, Side, Palmyra, and elsewhere, esp. in the 230s and 240s.

12. Tac., *Hist.* 1.70.2f., loyalty to the recollection of Vitellius; Suet., *Vesp.* 6.2f., loyalty to the recollection of Vespasian (at an extraordinary congress of troops to decide whom to support among the existing, or conceivable, candidates). Compare the useful popularity of a secondary figure among a detachment of praetorians in Gaul, on behalf of Vespasian, Tac., *Hist.* 3.43.1.

13. See the issues from Carthage of L. Clodius Macer in the third quarter of A.D. 68, in A. S. Robertson, *Roman Imperial Coins in the Hunter Coin Cabinet* 1 (1962) xci, and from Tarraco and elsewhere of Galba (but not yet named on the coins), in A. Mattingly, *Coins of the Roman Empire in the British Museum* 1 (1923) clxxxix.

14. *IGR* 3.173, already cited, with honors shown to a certain *protos Hellenon* (the phrase again in *IGR* 1.1978); in Lycia, the famous Opramoas was one *ek ton proteuonton en tei eparcheiai*, *IGR* 3.739 cap. 56 (cf. 3.640, someone *ek ton proteuonton en tei ethnei*); Lucian, *Alex.* 45, someone *tou Pontou protos*; Plin., *Ep.* 1.10.8, *provinciae* (Syria) *princeps*; Tac., *Ann.* 11.23.1, *primores Galliae; princeps Delmatorum, Desitiatium*, or *Iapodum*, in D. Rendic-Miocevic, *Parola del Passato* 190 (1980) 24; *protos tes nesou* (Malta), Acts 28:7; and *princeps insulae* (Corsica), Tac., *Hist.* 2.16.

15. The assumption explains Festus' concerns (he was on the wrong side; cf. Tac.,

Hist. 4.49.1). It explains imperial suspicions that Valerius Asiaticus might lead a rising in Gaul: "born in Vienne and supported by a large and powerful kin," Tac., *Ann.* 11.1.2. But notice the Hordeonii, thickly clustered at Capua (in *CIL* 10, twenty-one occurrences), compared with Puteoli (four occurrences among far more numerous texts); yet Capua did not for that reason side with Hordeonius Flaccus. J. H. D'Arms, *Historia* 23 (1974) 499f., points to the facts but reverses them.

16. The assumption underlies the suspicion of someone's planning an insurrection in 218, cf. Dio 80.4.7, and the real strength of an agent of Vespasian's in southern Gaul, around Fréjus, cf. Tac., *Hist.* 3.43.1—perhaps of another agent also, see R. Syme, *Tacitus* (1958) 684. But in any case the latter person in question suffices to swing over "his *colonia*" (not named).

17. Dio 71[72].31.1; but in A. R. Birley, *The Fasti of Roman Britain* (1981) 29, 73, 165f., and 189, one can see, long before Cassius' time, a settled prejudice against appointing troop commanders twice in the same army, or where their fathers had commanded, as also against governors serving where they had earlier been stationed as legionary legates. For enthusiasm shown toward a pretender of 270 by provincials, whom he had once governed, see A. Boninu and A. von Stylow, *Epigraphica* 44 (1982) 41f.

18. Tac., *Hist.* 1.51.9; 1.64.7; and 1.65f.

19. Nicomedia coined for Niger, then switched to Septimius Severus; Nicaea was pro-Niger always—see L. Robert, *HSCP* 81 (1977) 25, and Herodian 3.2.7f. Further, F. Millar, *The Emperor in the Roman World* (1977) 416.

20. R. Ziegler, *Chiron* 8 (1978) 501–5. For the punishing or rewarding of cities after revolts, see Robert, *HSCP* 81 (1977) 25 n. 114, where Macrinus strips Pergamon and Ephesus of their titles; K. W. Harl, *Am. Num. Soc., Mus. Notes* 29 (1984) 72, where Philip promotes a friendly city to *colonia* status, and Trajan Decius angrily demotes it; and L. Foucher, *Hadrumetum* (1964) 318, where Capellianus punishes a city in 238 for its disloyalty.

21. M. Gawlikowski, *Palmyre VI: Le temple palmyrénien* (1973), a certain Septimius being "head of the Roman party" (p. 78); the relation of the temple to the tribe (pp. 36 and 68); the text (p. 77); and a similar moment in 261/262 when Alexandria was split, Euseb., *H. E.* 7.21.1.

22. Jerusalem, for example, had its section accommodating "woolshops, smithies, and cloth-markets" (Jos., *B. J.* 5.331); Rome, its *vicus inter olivarios*, cf. R.E.A. Palmer, *Bull. Comm.* 85 (1976–1977) 151, with other *vici* of the same sort; for other cities' sub-regions, see my *Roman Social Relations* (1974) 132–35; on their joint actions in inscriptions, ibid. 136f. and Robert, *REG* 42 (1929) 32–38; also *IGR* 4.425, a second-century thanks-statue to a consul bought and set up by "the occupants of Paspara Square" in Pergamon through two men, one a dyer (all the group, artisan?); and on their serving as urban voting units in north Africa, see T. Kotula, *Eos* 68 (1980) 136–39. Trade associations are named as payees (i.e. enforcers) of fines for tomb violation, cf. L. Cracco Ruggini, *Assimilation et résistance à la culture gréco-romaine* (1976) 469; they corporately support political candidates in Pompeii, cf. P. Castren, *Ordo populusque pompeianus* (1975) 116, and at Rome in the late Republic, cf. J.-P. Waltzing, *Etude historique sur les corporations professionnelles chez les Romains* 1 (1985) 90–111.

23. Retaliation checked the career, e.g., of C. Iulius Septimius Castinus (*PIR*², I 566). Other figures could be instanced—perhaps not many (and the phenomenon has never been especially studied).

24. For careers that make progress both before and after A.D. 69, see *PIR*², A 49, A 69, C 763, C 1206, D 201, E 84, F 91, F 354, M 242, and M 296; before and after A.D. 193, *PIR*², C 1322 and F 27; before and after A.D. 235/238, *PIR*², D 28, H 112, L 452, M 520, and O 9, and K. Dietz, *Senatus contra Principem* (1980) 292 and 296; and even at the turn of the third to fourth century, *PIR*², C 806 and I 36 and *PLRE* 1.977.

25. Winners: for example, Antonius Primus and Cornelius Fuscus resume their ambitions at the call of Galba and go on to prominent careers. See *PIR*², A 866 and C 1365, and Syme, op. cit. (n. 16) 592. Vespasian's early supporters are rewarded, including Ti. Iulius Celsus (*PIR*², I 260) and A. Iulius Quadratus (*PIR*², I 507), and derelict or junior careers are salvaged—see J. K. Evans, *Historia* 27 (1978) 112 and 120. For Septimius Severus' partisans, see A. R. Birley, *BJbb* 69 (1969) 274–79.

20. JUDICIAL SAVAGERY IN THE ROMAN EMPIRE

1. *Dig.* 48.19.28.16 (Callistratus), to which P. Garnsey draws attention in his *Social Status and Legal Privilege* (1970) 231, with brief comment. Moral character was an element in judging always, as one can sense in both Cicero's forensic oratory and Apuleius', passim, across a span of more than two centuries, and, in the interval, less clearly in [Quint.], *Decl.* As to the question, *cuius condicionis es*, see passim in the *Gesta apud Zenophilum*, e.g. p. 185 line 9 of the edition of Optatus of Milevis by Ziwsa (*CSEL* XXVI, 1893); again in other trials of the period, the early fourth century (ibid. 203 line 21; *Martyrdom of Dasius* 6, in H. Musurillo, *Acts of the Christian Martyrs* [1972] 276, and P. Franchi de' Cavalieri, "Note agiografiche," *Studi e Testi* 65 [1935] 50, the *Passio SS. Dativi et al.* 5).

2. T. Mommsen laid the groundwork in his *Römisches Strafrecht* (1899), though his approach obscured the historical dimensions (see esp. 943f., less than a page on the subject of this paper). Subsequent scholars include U. Brasiello, *Il diritto penale* (1937); more recently, P. Garnsey's valuable article, "Why penal laws became harsher: the Roman case," *Natural Law Forum* 13 (1968); A. Rousselle, "La persécution des chrétiens à Alexandrie," *RHD* 52 (1974); M. Hengel, *Crucifixion* (1977); R. A. Bauman, "The leges iudiciorum publicorum," *ANRW* II, 13 (1980); J.-P. Callu, "Le jardin des supplices au Bas-Empire," in *Du châtiment dans la cité: Supplices corporels et peine de mort dans le monde antique*, ed. D. Baker (1984) (hereafter, "Jardin"); D. Grodzynski, "Tortures mortelles et catégories socials," ibid.; and T. Spagnuolo Vigorita, *Exsecranda Pernicies* (1984).

3. The data are carefully assembled in F. Millar, *PBSR* 52 (1984) 124–47. He indicates condemnation *in pistrinum* in Ephesus of Cicero's time (p. 130); to the treadmill in Tiberius' time (p. 136) and to "the works" (i.e. factories?—p. 137) in A.D. 70; to public projects under Nero (p. 133); and *in metalla* and hard labor under Caligula and Trajan (pp. 136f.) as well as earlier and later. Allowance being made for the uneven supply of evidence, distorted through survival of martyr accounts, I see no increase in the use of these penalties except in moments of persecution—*pace* Millar (p. 145: "a radical innovation," etc.).

4. Jewish martyrs, Jos., *B. J.* 2.152f., and in the second century Akiba and others, in W.H.C. Frend, *Martyrdom and Persecution in the Early Church* (1965) 227; C. G. Montefiore and H. Loewe, *A Rabbinic Anthology* (1963) 255, 264, and 269f.; Christian martyr accounts are conveniently in H. Musurillo, op. cit. (n. 1).

5. Euseb., *H. E.* 5.1.44, 47 (*apotympanismos*), and 50. For the definition of the Greek word, see Rousselle, *RHD* 52 (1974) 231f. The arbitrariness and variety of tests and penalties prescribed by judges to Christians in the first two centuries has been many times discussed. The judge sometimes makes explicit his freedom of action, e.g. *Passio S. Polycarpi* 10 or Tert., *Ad Scap.* 4.1–4.

6. Suet., *Galba* 9.1, *acer et vehemens in coercendis delictis vel immodicus*, à propos esp. the crooked money-changer whose hands Galba ordered cut off and nailed to his change-table; 12.1, Galba's *fama saevitiae* ; cf. Sen., *De ira* 1.18, the vivid tale of a Syrian governor—identification in R. Syme, *Tacitus* (1958) 544 n. 8—who flies into a passion of anger, *furens*, etc., and so has three innocent men, all legionaries, executed. Compare Philo, *In Flacc.* 78f., the governor of Egypt disregards distinctions of status, a sign of his *kakonoia*, in the assigning of corporal punishment, and departs from penal routine in other ways; and a governor of Syria burns and drowns assorted criminals and mutilates deserters, and crucifies undisciplined men, all victims of his *crudelitas potius quam severitas*, SHA *Avidius Cassius* 4.1–5.

7. As Callu, "Jardin" 341 n. 117 points out, quoting Ulpian and Callistratus— though norms were certainly present to mind, and for most cases explicit.

8. For Augustus, see Dio 54.23.3, though cf. Suet., *Aug.* 67.2; Hadrian in *Dig.* 1.6.2; Suet., *Tib.* 62.2f.; for *Caligula*, idem, *Caligula* 27.3f., Dio 59.10.3, and P. Giss. 46 = H. A. Musurillo, *Acts of the Pagan Martyrs* (1954), 14, col. iii line 25; Suet., *Claud.* 14, 15.2, and 34.2; Domitian 8.4f., 10.2, and 11.2, and Callu, "Jardin" 328–31.

9. Jos., *B.J.* 7.154, all done "by Roman law"; ibid. 7.450, cf. similar parading of the victim before execution, in Jerusalem, by imperial order, ibid. 2.246 (Celer). Further, on the almost ritual procedure, Dio 60.13.3 and 60(61).35.4. For executions at Claudius' orders *in campo Esquilino*, cf. Suet., *Claud.* 25.3.

10. Mart., *Spect.* 7; cf. A. Nicoll, *Masks Mimes and Miracles* (1963) 111.

11. Tert., *Apol.* 15.5, "Hercules" burnt alive and "Atys" castrated; *Passio S. Perpetuae* 18.4; Apul., *Met.* 10.28 and 34.

12. Hence, the criminal suffers in the same location where he performed his evil deeds: SHA *Avidius Cassius* 4.2 and 5.2 (soldiers); *D.* 48.19.28.15 (brigands); SHA *Sev. Alex.* 23.8 (extortionate imperial slaves); and [Quint.], *Decl.* 274 p. 124 (Ritter), the crucified are displayed on the busiest road so as to arouse fear among the maximum of passers-by (second century?). The last ref. is brought forward by Hengel (op. cit., n. 2) 50. There is a wealth of material in military settings, e.g. Polyb. 6.37f., Frontin., *Strat.* 4.16, and *Dig.* 49.16.

13. The wicked alone receive cruelty, or deserve it: Mart., *Spect.* 7; Sen., *Ad Lucil.* 18.103.2, of those condemned to gladiatorial combat, *latrocinium fecit aliquis, ille meruit ut hoc pateretur*; Lucian, *Alex.* 2; and Tert., *Spect.* 100v.

14. Euseb., *H. E.* 5.1.38, 43, and 50; Tert., *Spect.* 103v, *in nos quotidiani leones expostulantur*; *Passio S. Perpetuae* 6.1 and 18.9, in Carthage; at Smyrna in the 150s, *Passio S. Polycarpi* 3 and 12, pp. 4 and 10 in Musurillo, op. cit. (n. 1).

15. See my discussion in chapter 13, pp. 147f.

16. Thrasea, in Tac., *Ann.* 14.48.

17. Sen., *Ep. moral.* 14.5; compare Lucian, *Piscator* 2, where the point of the humor lies in the philosophers' recommending crucifixion, mutilation, etc., for their enemy.

18. R. Pack, "Artemidorus and his waking world," *TAPA* 86 (1955) 283 n. 9, speaking of the later second century and referring to the *Oneirocriticon* 152.4; cf. Plut., *Moral.* 554A, "every evildoer goes to his punishment bearing his cross on his back" (as if that were the only form of punishment)—quoted by Hengel, op. cit. (n. 2) 77, along with several other mentions in second-century authors.

19. Tac., *Ann.* 15.44, on the Great Fire in Rome; after Jewish defeats, in Jos., *B. J.* 2.75, 241, and 253; *Vita* 420.

20. Epict., *Diss.* 2.2.1: "you who face litigation" may confront a judge (2.2.5) who "will do things to you that are thought to be frightful," at least by non-philosophers; and you must "endure to be beaten to death" (2.2.13); cf. Cypr., *Ep. I ad Donat.* 10 (*CSEL* 3, 1, p. 11), bidding the reader look at the forum, there to behold "the spear, the sword, the executioner handy, who tears at you with his hook; the stocks that stretch, the fire that burns, more torments for a single body than there are limbs." In Apul., *Met.* 10.10, when accused of homicide, the prisoner is racked, beaten, and burned; compare scenes in the persecutions, Tert., *Apol.* 12.4, *ungulis deraditis*, etc.; *Passio SS. Potam. et Basilid.* 4 (boiling pitch dropped on the body); *Passio S. Polycarpi* 2.4, novel tortures of various sorts applied in Smyrna near the mid-second century; and Euseb., *H. E.* 3.32.6, similar scenes, but earlier (A.D. 106/107) in Palestine.

21. *Acta purgationis Felicis* (Optatus appendix II, p. 202 lines 5f., Ziwsa). He was a *decurio*, not a slave (p. 203 line 21).

22. For what follows, I depend on Garnsey, op. cit. (n. 1) 122, 127, 141–43, 241, and 265, and P. Brunt, "Evidence given under torture in the Principate," *ZSS* 97 (1980) 259–63.

23. Cic., *2 In Verr.* 5.140 (trans. L.H.G. Greenwood). For Verres' threats of beating to death, see *2 Verr.* 3.70 and 4.85; actual instances, 5.164f.; "atrocious cruelty" in beating and use of hot metal plates on citizens, 1.122 and 5.163; and crucifixion not only for slaves (5.12) but Romans as well (1.13 and 5.164f.).

24. Castration remains on the books as capital, *Dig.* 48.8.4.2; livestock theft is punished capitally only among *humiliores* unless by someone who attacks with arms, which merits death by wild beasts (*Dig.* 47.14.1.3); parricide remains (*Dig.* 48.9.9 pr.); *maiestas* remains (*Dig.* 48.4.11), as any attack on either the state or the emperor; arson remains a crime punished by *crematio*, *Dig.* 48.19.28.12 (but *bestiae* for *humiliores*, 47.9.12.1, Ulpian); temple-robbing remains (*Dig.* 48.13.7[6], *pro qualitate personae*, some sentenced to the beasts, some to burning, some to *furca*); plotting against his master by a slave remains (*crematio*, *Dig.* 48.19.28.11); brigandage also (*furca* or *bestiae*, *Dig.* 48.19.28.10 and 15); likewise Christianity; moving of boundary markers by a slave remains on the books as a capital crime (*Dig.* 47.21.3.1), as does breaking out of jail (*Dig.* 47.18.1) and poisoning (*Dig.* 48.19.28.9).

25. For the date, see Callu, "Jardin" 336, and Rousselle, *RHD* 52 (1974) 244. Garnsey, op. cit. (n. 1) 221, sets it near the end of the third century.

26. *PS* 5.24, *bestiae* or *crematio* for parricide *hodie*, not *culleus*; 5.19A, disturbance of burials; 5.18.2, *gladium*, no longer *bestiae*, for the *atrox* (= armed) *abactor*; 5.22.1, *crux* or *bestiae* for sedition; 5.29.1, *bestiae* or *crematio* for *humiliores* guilty of *maiestas*; 5.21A.2 civilian desertion; 5.21.4, *crux* for divination about his master by a slave; 5.3.6 and 5.20.1, arson prepense and for the sake of pillage; 5.23.1, *crux* for the *humilior* guilty of poisoning; 5.19, *bestiae* for sacrilege; 5.22.3f., circumcision of non-Jews; 5.23.13, castration for male prostitution; 5.23.1, *crux* or *bestiae* for homicide by *humiliores* but, 5.23.4, if in a *rixa*, the penalty shall be condemnation to gladiatorial combat or the mines; and 5.23.1, *crux* or *bestiae* for false testimony leading to someone's death.

27. Grodzynski, op. cit. (n. 2) 384f.

28. P. Oxy. 1409, *ou monon peri chrematon alla kai peri autes tes psyches to agona*. I cannot find the latter phrase in its present meaning in E. Kiesling's *Wörterbuch der gr. Papyrusurkunden* 4, 1 (1944) 28 s.v. *agon*, or the supplement of 1969.

29. Text in A. C. Dionisotti, "From Ausonius' schooldays?" *JRS* 72 (1982) 104f.; date (123), "late third or more probably fourth century." At §74, *custodis sessurus* = *phylaxein kathemenos* I suspect to be a dative plural, where the editor suspects a word (*provinciae*?) dropped out. At §75, the *quaestionarius* is the soldier to be expected in attendance on the governor. See my *Soldier and Civilian in the Later Roman Empire* (1963) 67, or D. J. Breeze, "The organization of the career structure of the army," *BJbb* 174 (1974) 275.

30. Euseb., *H. E.* 8.6.2f. (Nicomedia); 8.8.1 (Levantine scenes); 8.9.1f. (Egypt); 8.12.1 (Egypt and Cappadocia); 8.12.2 (Antioch); 8.12.6f. (Pontus); 8.12.8–10, "goodness and humanity" advertised by Maximin Daia for his mutilations in the place of executions, cf. Lact., *Mort. persecut.* 36.7, *effodiebantur oculi, amputabantur manus, pedes detruncabantur, nares vel auriculae desecebantur*; most detailed, Euseb., *Mart. Pal.* passim, e.g. 4.10–11, 11.18, or the characterization of governor Urbanus, 7.4, as highly inventive in cruelty, castrating some martyrs, condemning others to the beasts or unarmed combat or the mines; and to the trial description that I quote compare the description (7.7) of the persecutor "rendering judgment from a lofty tribunal among the mass of his military guards—the ruler over the entire province of Palestine." Callu, "Jardin" 333, surveys and quantifies Eusebius' essay: twenty-three cases of decapitation in it, one crucifixion, eleven burnings, five *ad bestias*, etc. But Eusebius reminds us that the torture scenes involving Christians were no different from those involving non-Christians, as Licinius treated them in Antioch (*H. E.* 9.11.6). Their crime, in this passage, was divination and prophecy.

31. See below chapter 21, pp. 219, 222—the findings confirmed and the statistics carried further by Grodzynski, op. cit. (n. 2) 397–403.

32. Eleven of his constitutions with the death penalty develop previous similar legislation: *CJ* 4.42.1 (Constantine—no date), regarding the castrating of a slave, cf. *Dig.* 48.8.4.2; *CT* 1.16.7 (331), cf. *PS* 5.25.13; *CT* 9.5.1.1 (314/320–323), slaves informing on masters, cf. *CJ* 4.55.4.1; *CT* 9.10.1 (317), raising the penalty for *vis* from exile to beheading, on the grounds that *vis* often leads to homicide (which latter is a capital crime, cf. *PS* 5.23.1 and 4); *CT* 9.15.1 (319), parricide; *CT* 9.16.1(319/320), soothsaying, cf. *PS* 5.21.4; *CT* 9.18.1 (315), cf. *PS* 5.30B.1, kidnapping; *CT* 9.19.2.2 (320/326), forgery, cf. *PS* 5.25.1, altering a will; *CT* 9.21.1 (319/323–325), counter-

feiting, cf. *PS* 5.12.12 and 5.25.1; *CT* 9.24.1.5 (320/326), rape, cf. *PS* 5.4.14; and *CT* 9.40.1 (314/315), adultery, homicide, or magic. As to adultery as a capital crime earlier, cf. Bauman, ANRW II, 13 (1980) 191 n. 191, on *CJ* 9.9.9 (224); SHA *Aurelian* 7.4; and perhaps *CJ* 2.4.18 (293—an interpolation?). But Constantine returns to that crime, again with a capital sentence, in *CJ* 9.9.29(30).4 (326). The remainder of the capital penalties he decrees are novel: *CT* 1.16.7 (331); 1.22.1 (316); 1.32.1 (333); 4.13.1 (321); 4.13.3 (321); 7.4.1 (325); 8.4.2 (315); 9.3.1.1 (320); 9.21.2 (318/321); 10.4.1 (313/326); 11.16.4 (328); 11.30.8 (319); and 13.5.5.1—all thirteen of these dealing with official mis-doings; and another thirteen miscellaneous: *CT* 2.30.1 (315); 7.1.1 (323), 7.12.1 (323), 9.9.1 (326/329), 9.10.2 (317/318), 9.22.1 (317/343), 10.10.1 (313), 10.10.2 (312), 10.10.3 (335), 13.5.5.1 (326/329), 14.4.1 (334), 16.8.1 (315/339), and finally, death by fire for heretics, in Constantine's edict of 333, in H.-G. Opitz, *Athanasius Werke* 3, 1 (1935), 67f.

33. *Paneg. vet.* 10[4].3.3 and 8.1, his *misericordia* and *clementia* (in A.D. 321); Euseb., *Vita Const.* 4.31 (*GCS* I 129). It is true, of course, that we hear next to nothing about him from neutral or hostile sources. Only Eutropius (10.8, *multas leges rogavit, quasdam ex bono et aequo, plerasque superfluas, nunnullas severas*) adds a little chiaroscuro.

34. Amm. 28.6.20 and 30.5.19 (note also the characterization of the man and his rages, 27.7.4 and 29.3.2f., with more domestic savagery, as it may be called).

35. E.g. Amm. 27.7.5, cf. *Chron. Pasch.* 557 Bonn; Eunap. frag. 30, cf. Malal., *Chron.* 13 p. 339; or Amm. 28.1.28.

36. Amm. 29.1f., cf. Soz., *H. E.* 6.8 (*PG* 67.1313C).

37. Amm. 28.1.57—Gratian described by Ambrose, *De obitu Valentiniani* 74, as *pius atque mansuetus, puro corde*. Compare the description of Julian as "a mild and gentle emperor" for merely burning alive one person and beheading two others among the population of a city that had resisted him, Amm. 21.12.20.

38. Amm. 29.5.22, 31, 43, and 49.

39. First by Galba (Suet., *Galba* 9.1), but that was impulse not law; dubiously, a century (?) later, as penalty for striking one's father, [Quint.], *Decl.* 372 p. 409 (Ritter), *manus ei incidantur*; next, only in the Great Persecution (above, n. 30) and thereafter in *CJ* 6.1.3 of disputed date (314? 317/323?), cf. Spagnuolo Vigorita, op. cit. (n. 2) 98 n. 44. Constantine's law of 331, *CT* 1.16.7, has also been referred to.

40. *CIL* 5.8768 of the 390s threatens anyone who disturbs the burial beneath the stone with amputation of his hand or a heavy fine—a threat more than a law, surely. It is adduced by E. Patlagean, "Byzance et la blason pénal du corps," in *Du châtiment dans la cité* (1984) 413 n. 40. In 412 the *notarius* Marcellinus had in mind exact judicial retaliation against members of a mob that put out a man's eye and amputated a finger. Augustine wants to talk him out of it, *Ep.* 133.1; cf. idem, *De gestis cum Emerito* 9 (*PL* 43.704), a bishop's tongue and hands cut off in sectarian strife in A.D. 404.

41. Theodoret, *H. E.* 2.28 (*PG* 82.1083) = 2.32.3 (*GCS* ed. 1954) in the 350s; Oros., *Hist. adv. pagan.* 1.42.4, Honorius mutilates Attalus; Olymp. frag. 8, Stilicho mutilated before execution, as the rebel John is likewise treated under Valentinian III. See Procop., *De bell.* 3.3.9 (A.D. 420) and Philostorg., *H. E.* 12.13 p. 149 (Bidez) (with other mutilations earlier, 12.3 p. 142 Bidez and 12.5 p. 144 Bidez). By 458 (*Nov. Maj.* 4.1.1, against destruction of public buildings) mutilation becomes a set penalty

and remains so thereafter in Byzantium, whence it spreads by the mid-seventh century to the west. See R. S. Lopez, "Byzantine law in the seventh century," *Byzantion* 16 (1942–1943) 450–55, and Patlagean, op. cit. (n. 40) 408 and 412 (under Justinian).

42. I have tried to put this quality of punishment in context, without really explaining it, above in chapter 9, pp. 102f.; see further Patlagean, op. cit. 421f., who draws a parallel to the message implicit in the body of the Christian ascetic. Both teach symbolically. But I would not attribute the appearance of mutilation in the empire's history to the domination of Christianity—except perhaps as carrying forward Jewish ideas. See D. Fiensy, *HThR* 76 (1983) 257f.

43. For the Republican background, see Mommsen, op. cit. (n. 2) 914; for the Principate, above, nn. 8–11, and Jos., *B. J.* 2.246, the arch-criminal to be dragged round the city before beheading.

44. Amm. 15.7.3–5; again in Rome, 28.1.16, many executed *publica morte*; cf. SHA *Sev. Alex.* 36.2, the Forum Transitorium is the place of execution—a tale I take to be indicative of the fourth century, not historical—and *Coll.* 5.3.2 (*FIRA²* 2.557), criminals to be burned alive, *spectante populo* (in Rome). Cf. Hier., *Ep.* 1.7, varied and hideous tortures on a woman in Vercellae, all before the governor and the *populus*.

45. Andronicus in Synes., *Ep.* 57 (*PG* 66.1389C); cf. *Ep.* 58 (*PG* 66.1400B), describing "the unheard-of types of torture tools . . . the finger-breaker, the foot-crusher, the presser, the nose-tweezers, the ear-chewer, the lip-twister," employed by this man.

46. *Or.* 28.13f. and 45.29. Libanius, the man of conscience, takes a chance in these descriptions. He returns to the subject, e.g. *Or.* 27 passim; 54.51; or 4.37, where the wicked Eutropius, governor of Syria in 389, is seen flogging people frightfully, "an outrage to the public image of the city, . . . before the eyes of all." Note the governor's "laughter . . . and his delight."

47. J.H.W. Liebeschuetz, *Antioch* (1972) 52, citing *Or.* 1.228 and 29.11. On the disgrace keenly felt through being so displayed, see the description of Nectarius' family, Aug., *Ep.* 103.4; also, comparatively, J. C. Baroja, "Honour and shame," in *Honour and Shame*, ed. J. G. Peristiany (1965) 103, on the disgrace felt through flogging in seventeenth-century Spain.

48. There is Urbanus, governor of Palestine, n. 30; also the governor of Syria in the 360s, Festus, in Eunap. frag. 39 (*FHG* 4.29), "a man of wicked nature . . . , in the penalties he inflicted exceeding the savagery approved by the palace"; or Maximus, *vicarius* of Rome in A.D. 370–371, in Amm. 28.1.10–40; others above, nn. 44f.

49. Constantine, Julian, Gratian, above, nn. 32 and 37; for the argument that harsh laws teach by terrifying, see above, n. 12, and *Dig.* 48.19.16.10, "the *supplicium* of a few malefactors may be a warning, *exemplo opus sit*, to the many," cited by Callu, "Jardin" 342 n. 118; and, for a later period, he cites *CT* 9.24.2 of A.D. 349 (add 11.16.11 a. 365, 9.27.3 a. 382, and 14.3.17 a. 390, all to the same effect; *CT* 8.5.56 [396] and Eunap. frag. 35 [*FHG* 4.27]; not quite so explicit are *CT* 9.16.1 [389] or 11.4.1 [372]).

50. Capital punishment for heretics, *CT* 16.1.4 (386), 16.5.9 (382) and 56 (410)—as also for hiding heretical writings, 16.5.34.1 (398), or permitting meetings of heretics, 16.5.36.1 (399) and 51 (410). Regarding counterfeiters, see *CT* 9.21.5 (343), 9.21.6 (349), 9.23.1 (348/352–356), and 11.21.1 (371); slave rapists, 9.24.2 (349); informers, 10.10.10 (365), 10.10.12.2 (380), and 10.10.13 (380); and slave litigants,

9.6.1 (376) and 3 (397). More or less reiterative laws threaten deserters and their accomplices (7.18.2, 4, 6, and 8), brigands (even though veterans, 7.20.7), assault (9.10.4), magic (9.16.11), astrology (9.16.8), divination (9.16.4), infanticide (for divination, 9.14.1), inflicting injury on *navicularii* (13.5.16) or taxing them (13.5.17), plotting homicide against senators and high officials (9.14.3), and conversion to Judaism wrought by a Jew (16.8.6 and 16.9.2).

51. *CT* 1.16.5 and 11; 7.4.30; 8.1.13; 8.5.14, 41, and 47; 9.27.5; 9.28.1; 9.40.16; 11.1.22; 11.8.1; 11.11.1; 12.1.179.4; 12.6.5 and 30; 12.11.2; 13.10.8; and 14.15.6. Slightly different is the illegal assigning of confiscated estates (5.15.21), peculation of gold from the imperial stores (10.24.2), or exporting of goods raised as taxes (13.5.33). Besides bureaucratic corruption, broadly defined, the death penalty smites libel (a second time, *CT* 9.34.10), and marriage to a niece (3.12.1), to a barbarian (3.14.1), or to a woman, by a male homosexual (9.7.3; Grodzynski, op. cit. [n. 2] 378 n. 50). Self-mutilation to avoid conscription was a capital crime (7.13.5); torturing decurions (if by a judge, *iudex*: 9.35.2) or hiding them if they are fugitives (12.1.50); hiding the property of the proscribed (9.42.5); harboring brigands (if a *vilicus*, *crematio*: 9.29.2); appointing a Christian as a temple-warden (16.1.1); offering violence to a Christian priest (16.2.31); religious rioting (16.4.1); and catamites (9.7.6 = *Coll.* 5.3.2, above, n. 44).

52. Above, p. 212. On cruel and abusive treatment of decurions, see Liebeschuetz, op. cit. (n. 47) 166 and 173f., n. 7; P. Petit, *Libanius et la vie municipale à Antioche* (1955) 258f.; and B. Schouler, *Libanios. Discours moreaux* (1973) 114 and 117.

53. Drawn from Greece, for example. I am not competent to explore the matter. For Athenian judicial savagery, however, Plato, *Rep.* 361C, is most informative and horrible; and, besides the institution of *apotympanismos*, Romans had many a glimpse of Greek barbarism, e.g. Livy 32.38, 39.35.8, and 45.10.14. As to modes of torture, crucifixion is not so likely to be Greek (Hengel, op. cit. [n. 2] 30) as Carthaginian (ibid. 22 and Callu, "Jardin" 337); and most or all fancy devices to inflict pain appear in eastern provincial (therefore originally Hellenistic?) settings.

54. Grodzynski, op. cit. (n. 2) 393 points to the approximation of the *colonus'* condition to that of slaves, as an aid in explaining the fourth-century penal standards—the century of "férocité maximale. Pire qu'avant, pire qu'après" (396, cf. 372). And all writers on penal law from Mommsen through Garnsey recognize in the sources the prominence of the rules of servitude in defining extreme tolerable force—punishment *servili modo* or the like phrase. Of the soldier model, Callu ("Jardin" 318 and 321f.) found prominent mention in the later biographies of the *Augustan History* and used that source (331f.) to illustrate how the army could be seen as "le modèle disciplinaire de la société toute entière" in the later empire.

55. Garnsey, *Natural Law Forum* 13 (1968) 158.

56. Ibid. 141f. (Montesquieu and others); and Bauman, *ANRW* ii, 13 (1980) 202f. and 208f., discussing how the interpretation of crimes like counterfeiting or sedition as *laesa maiestas* might make them subject to harsher treatment. But the evidence all comes from the late Empire.

57. See Apul., *Apol.* passim, for parade of learning, e.g. §30; more especially 25 lines 30f. in the Oxford edition, inviting the judge "to recall with me" a long passage quoted in Greek from Plato; 36 line 12, praising the judge's *eruditio* and knowledge as

well as admiration (41 line 11) of Aristotle's works; and again, appeal to the judge's familiar reading of Plato (64 lines 12f.). Note also the exclaiming over the exquisite literary style of the previous governor, 94 lines 16f.

58. J. Roach, *Public Examinations in England 1850–1900* (1971) 196, on the scoring; E. Abbot and L. Campbell, *Life and Letters of Benjamin Jowett* (1897) 2.350; eidem, *Letters of Benjamin Jowett* (1899) 153; *Dict. National Biog. 1912–1921*, 513; and J. W. Mackail, *James Leigh Strachan-Davidson* (1925), 87—with thanks to F. Turner's kindness in getting at these matters.

59. Garnsey, *Natural Law Forum* 13 (1968) 150 and 157f., without indicating the basis for saying that judges sentenced more harshly than juries. I am not sure the evidence for a comparison exists. The change in any event does not seem to concern the erosion of citizen *rights* as opposed to non-legal claims to a mild sentence.

60. Above, n. 54 (Grodzynski), or A. Piganiol, *L'empire chrétien* (1972) 454: "La législation criminelle du IVe siècle laisse une impression d'horreur; beaucoup de lois semblent dictées par des furieux."

61. J. Gaudemet, "Aspects politiques de la codification théodosienne," *Istituzioni giuridiche e realtà politiche* (1976) 279; on the ineffectiveness of imperial legislation, often noted, see the Theodosian Code passim, noting the repeated laws that had not been obeyed, redoubled harshness of penalties that had not deterred, and a general tone of frustration. For a few details, see my "Social mobility and the Theodosian Code," *JRS* 54 (1964) 49f.

62. *Eidos axion tyrannidos*, Olymp. frag. 23 (*FHG* 4.62).

63. Idem frag. 8 (*FHG* 4.59), on Olympius' death. Stilicho's party had been killed at Pavia before the emperor and so was Eusebius at Ravenna (also by clubbing, Olymp. frag. 13, *FHG* 4.60).

21. SOCIAL HISTORY IN ASTROLOGY

1. L. Thorndike, "A Roman astrologer as a historical source: Julius Firmicus Maternus," *CP* 8 (1913) 415f., dealing with only two books of the author's *Mathesis*. I had finished research and begun writing on the present subject before tracking down the sole—wrong—reference to Thorndike's article that I have seen.

2. Firmicus Maternus (henceforth F. M.), *Math.* (ed. Kroll-Skutsch, 1897–1913) 2.29.10 and 19f.; cf. A. Chastagnol, *Les fastes de la préfecture de Rome au Bas-Empire* (1962) 66, 68, 114f.

3. Vettius Valens (henceforth V.V.), *Anthologiae* (ed. W. Kroll, 1908), p. 175; O. Neugebauer and H. B. van Hoesen, *Greek Horoscopes* (1959) 119f. (henceforth *Horoscopes*).

4. V.V. p. 270; Neugebauer and van Hoesen, *Horoscopes* 86 n. 5.

5. W. Kroll, *Cat. Cod. Astrol. Graecorum* (henceforth *CCAG*) V, 2 (1906) pp. 143–45; W. Gundel and H. G. Gundel, *Astrologumena* (1966) 202, on the date of Ptolemy, and 206f., on his sources; 216–20, for V.V.; O. Neugebauer, *HThR* 47 (1954) 66f., for the date of V.V.

6. V.V. 226; cf. 95, "lest we write too repetitively about the same things," and Artemidorus (henceforth Art.), *Onirocriticon* (ed. R. A. Pack, 1963) p. 100.

7. Ptol. 3.13.163; 4.4.178; V.V. 39 and 40.

8. V.V. 60, 88; Art. p. 119.

9. Ptol. 4.2.174, 178, and 179 (lawyers, treasurers, magistrates, teachers, and party-leaders, *ochlon proestotas*); V.V. 37, 39, 58, 72f.

10. V.V. 37, 42f., 48, "a scandal among the people," "leading a shameful life," "cunning in other greedy ventures, good-for-nought, wily."

11. V.V. 74.

12. *P. Mich.* 3. 148, an anonymous horoscope of the first century, but typical: see, e.g. Art. p. 41, or V.V. 231 *pseudokategoria*.

13. V.V. 37f., 268, 282; Art. 30, in the form *diken echon* or *pheugon*; on land suits, e.g. Art. 66; on *epitimia*, 112.

14. Art. 13; for exile cf. 306 (to an island).

15. Art. 285; a similar, real case, *Cod. Just.* 8.51.18.

16. Art. 93 (incest), 262 (forgery; cf. V.V. 40), and 317 (rash remarks).

17. V.V. 68 (jail); 283 (condemnation to quarries; cf. Art. 66); Art. 303 (decapitation); manacles or bonds common in Art., e.g. 15 or 209, "poverty, slavery, or bonds"; on crucifixion, R. Pack, *TAPA* 86 (1955) 283 n. 9.

18. V.V. 39, 66; Ptol. 3.13.163; 4.4.178; 4.4.180; Art. 26: "a rich man not yet in office," implying that office is to be expected; cf. ibid. 149.

19. V.V. 39, 42, 45, 59, 73, 78 (tribunes and centurions; cf. Art. 265); Ptol. 4.3.176; Art. 265, a works-supervisor becomes an imperial treasurer, and an imperial procurator (p. 305) imposes a corvée (*angareia*).

20. V.V. 39, 45f.; *P. Mich.* 3. 148.

21. V.V. 46f., "catering to the pleasures of the people"; cf. ibid. 82, benefactions to cities, perhaps including the gladiatorial combats implied in ibid. 75, 79 and in *CCAG* 8, 2, p. 85f., which dates to 113, according to Neugebauer and van Hoesen, *Horoscopes* 109; Art. 252, "a rich man must spend freely"; ibid. 149, "ever ambitious for honor, he will spend *eis to demosion*."

22. V.V. 48, 283.

23. Art. 229 and 270.

24. Art. 152; cf. the Inspectors of Weights and Measures found in bad company, in Artemidorus' list, p. 171.

25. V.V. 60; cf. 42f., 45, 74, 230, 283; Ptol. 3.13.163, *stasiastai, emprestai, theatrokopoi*; *CCAG* 8, 1 (F. Cumont, 1929) p. 168, *ochlon ephodous, kindynous, empresmous*; Art. 26, 59, 102, 139, 148, 252.

26. V.V. 231, dated to 123 by Neugebauer and van Hoesen, *Horoscopes* 121; many similar, real cases, e.g. Philostr., *Vita Appolon.* 1.15; Dio 57.21.3.

27. V.V. 74, 77f., 231 (dated to 113 by Neugebauer and van Hoesen, *Horoscopes* 109), 288 (dated to 154 by Neugebauer and van Hoesen, p. 125); *P. Mich.* 3.148; Art. 170, 175, 109, etc.

28. It would be pointless to assemble references, but note travel beyond the empire (V.V. 165), and the topic in such other sources as *CCAG* 8, 2, p. 240, in Balbillus' lost work, the section entitled "On sojourns abroad," and in Maximus, *Peri katarchon* (ed. A. Ludwich, 1887), of the second century (?), the sections III and IV titled "On sailings and business trips" and "On journeys."

29. Chancy: for example, V.V. 165; wretched life, ibid. 65; foreign trade (*naukleria*), 73; and gains from the like, ibid. 38; Ptol. 4.2.174, and Art. 12.

30. Art. 319 (cf. 305; 141). A similar, real case, Synes., *Ep.* 4 p. 640 (Hercher).

The terms are the expected ones, in our sources: *naukleros, emporos, kybernetes* (for example, in Art. 97).

31. The *trapezites* is often mentioned, the *eranarches* and *daneistes* less common; see e.g. Art. 44 and 230; V.V. 38.

32. Above, n. 23; Art. 30.

33. For example, V.V. 69, 76; Ptol. 4.2.176.

34. No peasants in V.V., unless Kroll's index and I have missed a reference; twice in Ptol. 4.4.170f.; but a dozen times in Art. 79, 109, etc. and addressed in Maximus, lines 456–543. For shepherds and vinegrowers, see Art. 167, 169, and half-a-dozen times elsewhere.

35. Vaguely implied in V.V. 69, "contemptible work"; Art. 242, a carpenter flees his country for debts; 59 (tanner), 136 (potters and tanners), 267 (fuller), 140 (unguent- and perfume-sellers); but a full list in Ptol. 4.4.179; cf. 180f.

36. V.V. 37, 42, 43; cf. references to seizure of property, *lepseis* or *nosphistai* or *epithymetai allotrion* in numerous passages of V.V.

37. *Antletai* in Ptol. 179 and Art. 54.

38. *Cheirotechnais de argian kai scholen* in Art. 102, 128, 140, 142, etc. Cf. mentions of poverty and beggars, ibid. 83, 166, 226.

39. Condemned to slavery, V.V. 68 and Art. 288; captive, and/or sold into slavery, V.V. 58, 68, 71, 77, 84.

40. Maximus p. 4, section VIII, *Peri drapeton* e.g., lines 332–36; H. Stern, *Le Calendrier de 354* (1954) 64; but a single reference in V.V. 283, and none in Artemidorus or Ptolemy.

41. V.V. 181, 222, 269, etc., trouble from slaves; envy of the rich, several times in Artemidorus, e.g. p. 151.

42. P. Oxy. 2554.

43. *Social and Economic History of the Roman World*[2] (1957) 479.

44. Neugebauer and van Hoesen, *Horoscopes* 162, of Vettius Valens; Pack, *TAPA* 86 (1955) 284, of Artemidorus.

45. W. Gundel and H. G. Gundel, *Astrologumena* 210 and 384, emphasize F. M.'s dependence on earlier sources and (p. 227f.), with A. Bouché-Leclercq, *L'astrologie grecque* (1899) 400 n. 1, 402 n. 1, criticize his confused and amateurish methods. But this (against Gundel 234 and with Thorndike, *CP* 8 [1913] 421 and passim) does not prevent F. M. being manifestly up-to-date in many items of terminology, as we shall see. W. Kroll, *CCAG* 5, 2 (1906) 143–48, detects various derivative items in F. M., which should rule out his use as a source for his own period. But two exceptions test the rule. F. M. speaks of kings, a difficulty to Kroll (p. 148). The word, however, may be tralatician without invalidating its contexts; note its certain equivalence with "emperor" in V.V. 21 and 268 (and, we may add, 281), through the dating of Neugebauer and van Hoesen, *Horoscopes* 86 and 121f., to A.D. 74 and 122, and similarly in Artemidorus, where (pp. 192, 265) *basileus* and *basilikos* can only mean *sebastos*. Again, F. M. speaks of heralds—typically Ptolemaic, a *scandalum* to Kroll (p. 148), but a feature equally characteristic of the fourth century (Amm. 28.2.11; the *ius praeconum* for certain officials, *Cod. Theod.* 12.1.74).

46. So rich is his *Mathesis* for our purposes that some sort of statistical analysis may be attempted, not in the exact numbers that Thorndike offers, but by a system of aster-

isks, one or two to indicate whether a given item is quite frequent, or extremely often referred to.

47. F. M. 3.7.11; 4.14.16; 3.5.37 (tralatician? cf. V.V. 72, *philosophoi kai mousikoi kai philologoi kai basilikes philias entos ginomenoi*); Thorndike, *CP* 8 (1913) 425 on various kinds of education.

48. Profit, e.g. F. M. 4.10.9; 5.1.3; chairs, e.g. 3.12.1 and 4.9.8.

49. F. M. 3.7.4; 3.7.7; 3.9.10; 3.10.1; 3.12.1; 4.14.1; 5.2.15; agents, stewards, or secretaries to *potentes** or *magni viri**, 3.3.18; 3.7.21; 3.10.1.

50. *Mensae feneratores**, etc., in F. M. 3.7.3; 3.7.13; 3.10.1, gaining thereby glory and riches (4.15.8); *publici tabelliones*, 4.12.4.

51. F. M. 4 pr. 1, venal lawyers exploit the "conflict in law cases"; cf. 3.7.11, *ex advocatione . . . fortunam sibi maximam comparare* (cf. 4.10.8), in contrast to the ruin of the litigants (5.3.31; 5.3.41).

52. The most telling references are to Synesius, *Ep.* 2 and 101 (ed. R. Hercher, *Epistolographi graeci* pp. 638, 699); Lact., *De mort. persecut.* 22.5; and Anon., *De rebus bell.* 21.1.

53. F. M. 4 pr. 1; cf. Thorndike, *CP* 8 (1913) 428, "Sixty-eight passages predicting accusations, judicial sentences and forms of punishment also give a sinister impression of his age," marked by beheading, torture, incarceration, and so forth (crucifixion rare, e.g. 6.31.73).

54. *Proscriptio** and attendant *mendicitas*, F. M. 3.4.22; 3.6.16; 5.3.31; etc. Compare the material in A. Calderini, *JEA* 40 (1954) 19f.

55. F.M. 4.12.4; 4.21.5 (gymnasiarchs).

56. The rich win high office (4.9.2; 4.11.8; etc.) by gifts (5.2.4) and assumption of *munera* (3.10.9; 5.1.12), gaining favor (3.4.33; 5.12.19, etc.) or risking *seditiones** or *rixae* (3.3.16; 6.11.2; etc.).

57. *Decemprimi**, F. M. 3.3.1, etc.; cf. *Cod. Theod.* 9.35.2 (376).

58. *Defensores civitatum* in F. M. 4.14.8; otherwise, first in 322, according to A.H.M. Jones, *Later Roman Empire* (1964) 1299; but he omits *Cod. Just.* 6.1.5 (319).

59. *Curatores civitatum*: Jones, op. cit. (n. 58) 726; F. M. 5.2.15.

60. F. M. 4.4.4 cf. 3.5.21.

61. In phrases such as *provinciis civitatibus praepositi*** (or *principes*, in F. M. 3.10.7; 3.12.4 etc.; with *regiones*, 4.10.1; 7.22.1; etc.). Cf. the phrase *dioiketai poleon* in Paulus Alexandrinus, *Apotelesmatica* (ed. Ae. Boer, 1958) 65, dating to a little after 378 (p. 136). The same author, though much under the spell of second-century astrological traditions, contains elsewhere some limited material such as we have been using thus far—references to factions, exiles, court convictions (p. 25), profits from education (67, 70), magistracies and priesthoods (65–67, 69f.)—without, however, meriting quotation.

62. F. M. 5.1.8; 3.10.1; 5.3.55; 3.6.19; 5.1.24.

63. Hostility, e.g., 5.3.12 and 3.14.7 (*factiosi*); their *gratia** and *amicitia** prepotent, e.g., 3.5.38; 5.2.13.

64. F. M. 3.5.10; cf. 4.19.27; *secreta* and confidences, 5.1.12 and often; *machinationes et callidae circumscriptiones*, 6.11.9; fall from office, 5.1.27; crimes, 3.7.26; 3.11.16.

65. F. M. 4.14.8; *terribilis*** for army officers in 4.11.8, etc.; *gloriosi*, 4.11.9;

efficaces, 4.14.11, etc.; *terribilis* for governors, 3.13.10; cr. *local* magistrates described as noble, wise, good, etc., in 6.25.5.

66. F. M. 3.4.2 and 3.4.28.

67. Thorndike, *CP* 8 (1913) 421 n. 3 and 422 nn. 3f. indicates the numbers involved.

68. F. M. 3.10.14; cf. Paulus Alex. p. 67, *skriniarious e antigrapheus e notarious.* Other technical terms of the bureaucracy occur scatteredly, e.g. 3.4.8 and 3.5.26. Note *curiosi* (3.11.3) and vocabulary datable to F. M.'s own day, stressed by Thorndike, *CP* 8 (1913) 421.

69. *Administratores*** (3.5.4 etc.), *rationales*** (3.3.8 etc.), and references to the *fiscus*** (3.5.14; 6.3.3; cf. Paulus Alex. p. 65, *phorologoi basileon*).

70. F. M. 3.5.13; cf. 3.13.5; 4.10.8; and 4.14.5.

71. Imperial largesses: F. M. 5.1.10, *habebunt sane vitae substantiam ex publicis vel ex regiis locis quibus vitae illis substantia conferetur*; compare Paulus Alex. p. 63; on imperial friends, see F. M. 3.6.24; court luxury, ibid. 3.6.3 and 19; 5.1.4.

72. *Peregrinationes** for unspecified reasons, 3.13.4, etc.; for trade, 4.10.10; 5.2.21; etc.

73. *Negotiatio*** and *faeneratio**, 3.7.3; 4.14.6; etc.

74. Dowries, 3.12.7 and 18; 5.2.12; *patrimonii heredes***, 3.7.17, etc.—of land and cash, 3.10.2.

75. Thorndike, *CP* 8 (1913) 427; F. M. 3.3.14. (*aurifices** and others), plus perfume-dealers, embroiderers, and the like.

76. Charity, F. M. 5.3.22; laborers, 4.14.2 (cf. 3.3.11).

77. F. M. 4.8.1; 4.10.2; 4.14.3; 4.14.15, with other similar passages; *paupertas*** unadorned, 6.31.2, etc. Thorndike, *CP* 8 (1913) 433 draws attention to the note of genuine sympathy, in F. M.

78. Exponere natos*, F. M. 3.6.13; 7.2.1, etc.; orphans, 4.15.1 and 4 (cf. Paulus Alex. pp. 54, 59, 71); *captivi**, 4.14.4, etc.; for slaves bringing danger or trouble on their masters, 3.7.26; 3.2.26; etc.

79. F. M. 3.4.1; 3.4.22; etc.

80. *Latrones**, 6.31.6, 58, 60, etc.; *piratae*, 3.13.2, etc.; *grassatores* and *abactores*, 3.11.10; 6.31.6; *frequenter mutare domicilia* or the like, 3.9.5; 3.13.4; 4.10.10; 8.6.2; traders on the move, 5.2.21.

81. On "empiricism," above, n. 44; on distortions in the laws, MacMullen, *JRS* 54 (1964) 50f.

22. THE LEGION AS A SOCIETY

1. E. Kiesling at Stanford University and W. Murray, professor at the Mershon Center (Ohio State University), kindly steered me to good materials regarding modern warfare and showed me also how little has been incorporated into modern training. See the titles below, notes 40ff.

2. P. Veyne, *Le Pain et le cirque* (1976) 610.

3. P. Mich. VIII 468; Plin., *Ep.* 7.31.2; PSI 446 (133–137).

4. Dio 75.2.6, A.D. 193.

5. *Phil.* 8.9.

6. *Ann.* 4.4.2, *plerumque inopes ac vagi*, cited by P. A. Brunt. He supposes very

reasonably that conscripts were poor people, in *Scripta classica Israelica* 1 (1974) 94 n. 22.

7. Ibid. 97 on Tac., *Ann.* 14.18, in Cyrene in the 50s A.D.; also Dio 72.4.1, in Egypt in the 170s.

8. Suet., *Tib.* 8.3 (23 B.C.), cf. Ps.-Quint., *Decl.* 377 p. 418 (Ritter), a son is compelled to serve against his will by his father, and many further texts on compulsion in conscription in Brunt, art. cit. (n. 6) 92–108—to be modified a little, I think, by G. Forni in *ANRW* II, 1 (1974) 354ff., and R. MacMullen, *Roman Government's Response to Crisis* (1976) 184.

9. *Dig.* 49.16.4.8, on the guilty who avoid trial by fleeing to armed service. On the likelihood of recruits from the upper classes being largely "black sheep," see Brunt, art. cit. 112; ibid., 94f. on Dio 52.27.4f., showing that the army gave a lawful career to types otherwise inclined toward violent crimes. Sallust, *Bell. Jug.* 86.2 is useful for the late Republic: those who answered Marius' draft call were *capite censi plerique*.

10. K. J. Pratt, *CJ* 51 (1955) 22f.

11. Tac., *Ann.* 14.27.3 (referring to Augustan times?).

12. P. A. Brunt, *Italian Manpower* (1971) 295 n. 5, cites *CIL* 9.1603 = *ILS* 2235 and the epitaphs indicating many men of leg. XIII in Beneventum, as H. Dessau points out ad loc.; further, Brunt, *Manpower* 322f., drawing on Nicolaus for further illustration; N. C. Mackie, *Historia* 32 (1983) 342, on the disposition of veterans of three legions in Mauretania; also P.-A. Février, *Cah. arch.* 14 (1964) 27, on the first-century veteran colony at Setif. Where inscriptions show veterans in blocks from several legions, the most likely explanation is successive *separate* settlements, as in Scupi, for example. Cf. A. Mocsy, *Gesellschaft u. Romanisation in der röm. Provinz Moesia Superior* (1970) 70. The clear pattern can be seen in the name *colonia Iulia Tertiadecimanorum* (Uthina) or in the five similar Caesarian colonies in Narbonensis, *RE* s.v. Coloniae cols. 528f.

13. *AE* 1974 no. 570, a dedication by the *sacerdos*, the officer, the enlisted men, and seven veterans of leg. XI Claudia.

14. *Inscripciones Romanas de Galicia* 4 (1968) 72 no. 66; *AE* 1923 no. 33, with similar material in H. Finke, *BRGK* 17 (1927) 29, 81, and 83 (*commilitones* and *vexillari*); J. Fitz, *Les Syriens à Intercisa* (1972) 101; and dedications by army units as wholes, e.g. *CIL* 3.1773, to Diana, *ILER* 55 and 86, and many other examples in R. MacMullen, *Paganism in the Roman Empire* (1981) 198.

15. *CIL* 2.2556 and 3327; the phrase *veterani et veteres* (meaning?) in 2.3734–37 and 3741; and *AE* 1974 no. 571.

16. T. Kotula, *Les curies municipales en Afrique romaine* (1968) 39, e.g. the *curia Hadriana felix veteranorum leg.* III *Aug.* explained, ibid. 47, *Klio* 54 (1972) 236; cf. J. P. Waltzing, *Etude historique sur les corporations professionnelles chez les Romains* 1 (1895) 209, action taken by the *veterani et peregrini* in Germany; *CIL* 8.885 = *ILS* 6803, honor paid *ex decreto paganorum . . . et veteranorum* of Medeli near Carthage; or honors paid to various town groups including "veteranis corporatis," in *CIL* 10.1881 = *ILS* 6328, cf. 6146 = *CIL* 14.409.

17. *CIL* 3.6166, *veterani et cives Romani*; 6162, without civilians.

18. H. Boterman, *Die Soldaten u. die röm. Politik* (1968) 7 and 15, in the 40s B.C.

19. T. Nagy, *Arch. Ert.* 94 (1967) 67f., on *collegia veteranorum*, one such constituting the local fire brigade.

20. Dio 47.22.1 and other texts in H. Schulz-Falkenthal, *Afrika u. Rom in der Antike* (1968) 157 and 163; Waltzing, op. cit. (n. 16) 1.56, 132, 204, 277, and 342; E. Weber in *Roman Frontier Studies 1979* (1980) 615, a *collegium quaestionariorum*; and M. P. Speidel and A. Dimitrova-Milceva, *ANRW* II, 16 (1978) 1548. The palace guard had such a *collegium Germanorum* which set up a memorial to a deceased member, in *CIL* 6.8807 = *ILS* 1725; cf. *CIL* 5.884, *locus sepulturae gentilium veteranorum*; 8.14608, *huic* [a deceased member] *veterani morantes Simittu de suo fecerunt*; or 11.136 = *ILS* 7311, a burial protected by the veterans' group.

21. A. K. Bowman et al., *Britannia* 5 (1974) 475.

22. I. A. Richmond, *JRS* 52 (1962) 146, eight-men triclinia for contubernia; *Dig.* 13.6.21.1, *contubernalibus vasa utenda* . . . ; *CIL* 14.4509; [Caes.], *Bell. Alex.* 16, "each man as he walked along with his tent-mate, friend, or acquaintance had reminded them of Caesar's exhortation before battle"; and Veget., *De re milit.* 2.18, insignia help to rally *contubernales*.

23. *Contubernia*, see H. von Petrikovits, *Die Innenbauten röm Legionslager* (1975) 36, and Richmond, loc. cit. (n. 22); on the wider meaning of the term, Veget. 2.21.

24. *Commilito* used by Caesar, or dramatically *not* used, in Suet., *Julius* 67.2, *blandiore nomine commilitones appellabat*, and ibid. 70 and Lucan 5.358 (he terms them Quirites); the term *commilito* too familiar and demagogic for Augustus, Suet., *Aug.* 25.1, but used by Galba (Suet., *Galba* 20.1), Trajan (Plin., *Ep.* 10.20, 53, 101, and 103), Pertinax (Dio 74.1.3), and Caracalla (ibid. 78[77].3.1).

25. *Inscripciones Romanas de Galicia* 4 (1968) 72 no. 66; *CIL* 6.1064; 13.595 and 7698f., 7710, 7717f., 7727; 3.12067 and 12069; Finke, *BRGK* 17 (1927) 83; *AE* 1926 no. 146; *Cod. Just.* 9.23.5 (Alex. Severus); and [Quint.], *Decl.* 312 p. 226 (Ritter).

26. Only two square meters in marching camps; cf. Petrikovits, op. cit. (n. 23) 35f.

27. Plut., *Paullus* 22.2 (at Pydna in 168 B.C.); Sall., *Bell. Jug.* 45.2, slaves allowed only to officers; Suet., *Julius* 26.3; Caes., *B. C.* 3.6, slaves too many to fit on the transport vessels; [Caes.], *Bell. Alex.* 73; ibid., 74, a *magna multitudo* of slaves compared to a *paucitas* of soldiers with Caesar in Pontus; *Bell. Afr.* 54, the slaves and pack animals of a single officer suffice to fill a transport vessel; ibid. 85; *Bell. Hisp.* 18; Dio 56.22.2b, Varus' limited numbers of troops compared with large numbers of unarmed followers; [Jos., *B. J.* 3.69, *therapontes* in vast numbers train beside troops;] Tac., *Hist.* 2.87, Vitellius' 60,000 men outnumbered (!) by *calones*, "the sutlers (*lixae*) being most impudent even compared with other slaves"; 3.33, the 40,000 attackers at Cremona are also outnumbered by *calones* and *lixae*; Quint., *Inst.* 8.6.42, the army matched in size by its following is a familiar image; and mentions of such civilians in other sources, epigraphic (*CIL* 3.2045 or Finke, *BRGK* 17 [1927] 67) or legal (*Dig.* 41.1.33 or *Cod. Just.* 5.16.2, 9.23.5, or 12.35[36].10) or technical (Veget. 3.7). I have gathered still further material in my *Soldier and Civilian in the Later Roman Empire* (1963) 106. On *calones*, further, see for example Tac., *Hist.* 4.60, and Caes., *B. C.* 1.52, *calones* sent out to collect food supplies.

28. Veget. 1.10, cf. the *skeuophoroi* in Dio 78[77].26.5f., on campaign in Parthia, making a charge on the enemy of their own initiative, and slaves specified as bearers

in *Bell. Alex.* 74. Petrikovits, op. cit. (n. 23) 58, takes the *galiarii* as helmeted drovers, I think wrongly.

29. Sall. *Bell. Jug.* 45.2; an inscription from Germany in Petrikovits, in *Roman Frontier Studies 1979* (1980) 1027f.; App., *Iber.* 85 and Val. Max. 2.7.1, cf. the women in Dio 56.20.2 and 56.22.2.

30. Richmond, *JRS* 52 (1962) 150f., cf. Livy 34.9.12, indicating how an army in the field would ordinarily be fed, through retailers in turn buying from the natives.

31. For instance, the cohors I Morinorum et Cersiacorum raised from the *pagus Gesoriacus* in Belgium near the Morini. See A. Donati, *Epigraphica* 33 (1971) 70f.; also "the [men of the] Vellavian district (*pagus*) serving in the Second Cohort of Tungrians" setting up a dedication, *RIB* 2107, or another by "the [men of the] Condustrian district," *RIB* 2108, cf. 2100.

32. Caes., *B. C.* 1.20; 2.29; and 2.34; [cf. Plin., *N.H.* 2.147, a *magnus numerus* of Lucanians in Crassus' last army].

33. Speidel and Dimitrova-Milceva, *ANRW* II, 16 (1978) 1546.

34. Veget. 2.18, speaking both of the past and his own day. On the back of the shield, he says the bearer wrote his name, cohort, and century. For unit identification on shields, see 27.47.1, at an early date, and, later, Dio 64.14.21. On other items of armor so identified by the owner's name and century, see R. MacMullen, *AJA* 65 (1960) 23 and 37, with other examples in F. B. Thomas, *Helme. Schilde. Dolche* (1971) 33, 38, and 51.

35. Dio 67.10.1; [Caes.], *Bell. Alex.* 58f. and Dio 50.5.1; compare Vespasian's name on vexilla of troops supporting him, in Suet., *Vesp.* 6.3.

36. See the exception, Sejanus' image among the *signa*, in Tac., *Ann.* 4.2, and Suet., *Tib.* 48.2; more normally, the emperor's image, as in Herodian 2.6.11; Tert., *Apol.* 16.8; SHA *Maximini* 24.2; and Dexippus frag. 24 = *FHG* III 682, where Aurelian reviews his elite troops with their "eagles and imperial images and enumeration of legions in gold letters; and they were all on display affixed to silver staffs."

37. Besides the well-known shields of Dura-Europus and such artists as are described by G.M.A. Hanfmann, in *AJA* 85 (1981) 87f., see the depictions of decorated shields on glass, in F. Fremersdorf, *Festschr. R. Egger* (1952) 68, and in relief, in L. Rossi, *Trajan's Column* (1971) 109–13, the latter showing (p. 114) British auxiliaries' symbols that resemble those on British legionary shields.

38. Caes., *B. G.* 2.21, insignia identifying the unit to be attached (to one's person?), cf. 7.45; *Bell. Afr.* 16, *signa decumanorum*, evidently not standards but worn by the individual; *Bell. Hisp.* 23, insignia stripped from a corpse; Tac., *Hist.* 2.89, soldiers on parade *donis fulgentes*.

39. [Caes.], *Bell. Hisp.* 25; see also Rossi, op. cit. (n. 37) 118, inferring unit awards on shield decoration. The clearest passage is Arrian, *Tact.* 34.2, speaking of cavalry helmets as more or less decorated "according to rank or military skill," *kat axiosin . . . diaprepeis e kath' ippiken diapherontes*.

40. See S.L.A. Marshall, *Men against Fire* (1947) 53f., and my quotation from pp. 151 and 153.

41. J. Dollard, *Fear in Battle* (1944) 1, 62, and the quotation from 46.

42. E. A. Shils and M. Janowitz, *Public Opinion Quarterly* 12 (1948) 281, 285 and n. 7, and 282. What the authors here emphasize—the role of a soldier's group and its

cohesiveness in enabling him to sustain prolonged combat—is also acknowledged by A. J. Glass in the introduction to *The Psychology and Physiology of Stress*, ed. P. G. Bourne (1969) xix, and again by the recent and valuable work by Major General F. M. Richardson, *Fighting Spirit* (1978) 9f. (regimental spirit is a manifestation of the regiment as "The Family") and 12 and 171f. (ties in order of strength are to the soldier's immediate group, to the regiment as a whole, and to The Cause).

43. From abundant materials, I instance the scenes in App., *Hisp.* 23; Caes., *B. G.* 5.52; *B. C.* 3.53; *Bell. Afr.* 86.

44. *Bell. Afr.* 54, Polyb. 6.37.4 and 13, and *FIRA*² 1.149 (Tabula Heracleensis 120f.) Cf. other officers' dismissal *ignominiae causa*, and "the harshest of proclamations against them posted up," with similar ceremonies of disgrace in *B. C.* 3.74. Suet., *Aug.* 24.2, describes other varieties of *ignominiae* used by a commander, while material on election of officers (*ex suffragio legionis*, vel sim.) is discussed by E. Birley, *Carnuntum Jb.* 1963–1964, 22f., and J. Reynolds et al., *JRS* 71 (1981) 132. Add Tac., *Hist.* 1.46.1, where the praetorians "chose their prefects themselves," and election of centurions by special concession from the commander, ibid., 3.49.

45. Dio 48.9.1, where failure to provide victory bonuses is seen as dishonor, *atimia*, as well as loss.

46. Caes., *B. C.* 3.54, for a centurion, joined with promotion from eighth to top centurion; cf. the exhortation to men *magnis praemiis pollicitationibusque*, vel sim., *B. G.* 3.26, 7.27, 7.47, and 8.4; *Bell. Alex.* 17, 48, 52, and 77; *Bell. Hisp.* 26, 3,000d. per man.

47. *Dig.* 49.16.6.4, the whole section 49.16 being, with Frontinus, *Strat.* 4.1, our chief source on military punishments.

48. *In conspectu exercitus*, in Caes., *B. G.* 8.42, cf. 3.14 and *B. C.* 1.67.

49. Caes., *B. G.* 4.25, *ne tantum dedecus admitteretur*; 7.17; and *B. C.* 3.101, *ignominiam non tulerunt*, etc.

50. Suet., *Otho* 10.1, where a soldier, rather than be thought a liar or a fugitive from battle, falls on his sword before his commander's feet. Similar incidents of ecstatic pride and devotion are easily found and well attested in other periods and settings.

51. [Caes.], *Bell. Alex.* 16, "they must not fall short of their own and everyone's estimate of themselves, according to which they had been chosen and were now proceeding to the engagement." Cf. Caesar's manipulation of his men's pride, through appeal to the Tenth, e.g. *B. G.* 1.40, cf. *Bell. Afr.* 16; or Tac., *Hist.* 2.27, where the commander assigns tasks to specific legions "so that the division of labor might distinguish the brave from the cowardly and the men be stimulated by the contest itself over honor."

52. Tac., *Hist.* 3.24.

53. Ibid. 2.27, the auxiliaries boast of coming out ahead of a legion, the Fourteenth, and the boast arouses other legions; 2.66, brawling breaks out and, 2.68, two cohorts are destroyed (!) before it is over.

54. Tac., *Ann.* 1.18 and *Hist.* 2.21, where the soldier of one command sees another in a different command as *peregrinus et externus*, and their two forces (2.37) are *linguis moribus dissoni*, incapable of *consensus*; Amm. 29.6.13; and Veget. 2.21, where

"the legionary cavalry hold the cohorts of their *contubernium*, their unit, in affection, even though cavalry do not naturally get along with infantry."

55. Caes., *B. G.* 2.25 and 3.14, cf. 6.8, "fight as if [Caesar] were present," his officers urge.

56. Ibid. 1.52; Livy 26.44.8, the commander's presence as witness "served above all else to rouse the soldiers' spirits."

57. Livy 26.51.8.

58. Tac., *Hist.* 1.70, the officers are *Othonis ignari, Vitellio obstricti*. See similar ties at 2.74 and 3.44, and their recall by Tiberius, *Ann.* 1.25 and 34; also the request of the troops in the fragmentary text, Dio 67.6.6.

59. See my *Soldier and Civilian* (n. 27) 106, and my *Roman Social Relations* (1974) 94, on pay differences; further, B. Dobson, *Anc. Society* 3 (1972) 198–201, and K. Hopkins, *Conquerors and Slaves* (1978) 40 n. 54, pointing out the widening gulf, as pay and bonus differentials increased over the last two centuries B.C. On space allocation, see my *Soldier and Civilian* 95 and Richmond, *JRS* 52 (1962) 148 and n. 36, at Masada and Numantia; at Timgad, in the veteran colony, see E.W.B. Fentress, *Numidia* (1979) 130.

60. In the Caesarian view, luxurious furnishings while on campaign deserved comment as signs of folly, not as morally wrong: at Pharsalus among the Pompeians, *B. C.* 3.96, or *Bell. Hisp.* 26, Pompeian *equites Romani* "on mounts almost hidden under silver [decorations]."

61. In his *Historiae* 3.48.27 p. 130 (Maurenbrecher) = *Opera* (ed. Ernout, 1964) 298 §27, *agrestes . . . caeduntur inter potentium inimicitias*. Cf. his reminding the plebs, ibid. §11, that in civil wars they struggle only to determine who will be their master. [There are a few parallels in Livy, e.g. 27.21.2 (209 B.C.).]

62. App., *B. C.* 2.47, 49 B.C.

63. Dio 47.42.3f., at Philippi; cf. Cic., *Phil.* 8.9f., declaring *his* party offers *its* soldiers only honorable rewards like liberty, laws, justice, compared with the base inducements held out by Antony.

64. Tac., *Ann.* 1.31, *rudes animi*, and 1.34f.; cf. 1.16, *imperiti animi*.

65. For instance, Cato's oration *ad milites* against Galba, mentioned in Aul. Gell. 1.23.1, or Caesar's speeches (if genuine) to his troops in Spain, in Suet., *Julius* 55.4.

66. Speeches in consilia in Caes., *B. G.* 5.30, and Tac., *Hist.* 3.3.1.

67. Caes., *B. G.* 5.28–30, where the losing commander tries to set the men at odds with the united officer corps. Compare Dio 73[72].11.3, where a governor faces down a commander before his legion in ca. A.D. 163. For other incidents, see Tac., *Ann.* 1.16 and 21, and App., *B. C.* 3.7.43, or Tac., *Hist.* 1.18, where some praetorians support Galba and Piso and their officers, and some do not.

68. Otho's base of support was the men in the ranks, whether praetorians (Tac., *Hist.* 1.18) or legionaries (ibid. 1.36, 38, and 80; 2.18). Notice 1.82, *undique minae* (by Othonians in Rome), *modo in centuriones tribunosque, modo in senatum*. But the officer corps of Vitellius later deserted him en bloc, ibid. 3.31 and 61; in contrast, 1.70, where an officer brings over an *ala* to his cause; and officers of Vespasian are for a moment at odds with their men, 3.19. On Scribonian's revolt, officer-initiated, see Suet., *Otho* 1.2; the same sort of initiation by Niger and Sept. Severus, working first

on officers, in Herodian 2.7.7 and 2.9.7; and, in contrast, the revolt against Macrinus begun in a slaughter of all officers, Dio 79[78].32.3f., A.D. 218.

69. W. S. Messer collects much material in *CP* 15 (1920) 163–73, though essentially limiting himself to the period before A.D. 100.

70. App., *Bell. Hisp.* 34. For a similar scene, see Caes., *B. C.* 1.20.

71. For example, Caes., *B. G.* 1.43 and 7.17; *B. C.* 1.64.

72. The *suggestus* is made in the *campus*, see e.g. [Caes.], *Bell. Afr.* 86; Tac., *Ann.* 1.18; Philostr., *Vit. soph.* 488; and SHA *Probus* 10.4.

73. For example, in Caes., *B. C.* 2.33, and 3.6; *B. G.* 7.17, the legions reply, *petebant*; and Tac., *Ann.* 1.34f. and 1.26, *responsum est a contione . . .*

74. The *honestissimi* of Caes., *B. C.* 1.20, or *hoi ton stratioton exechontes* of Herodian 2.77.

75. Aside from the better known events of A.D. 14, in Tac., *Ann.* 1, Dio 57.4.3f., etc., notice Suet., *Claud.* 24.3, *Galba* 16.2, and *Cod. Theod.* 7.20.2 (320); also the very interesting P. Yale 1528 = *Sammelbuch* V 8247 = C. B. Welles, *JRS* 28 (1938) 41f. and 47; and, earlier, in the years after 44 B.C., see Boterman, op. cit. (n. 18) passim, e.g. pp. 15, 28f., and 152.

76. Victor, *De Caes.* 29, Iotapianus "killed by decision of the soldiers," compare Eutrop., *Brev.* 9.7; other emperors "the choice of their legions," Victor, *Caes.* 25.1; Dio 72[71].23.1, cf. Marcus Aurelius' deferential speech to the legions, conceding their right to choose and dismiss emperors, ibid. 72.23.3f.; SHA *Probus* 10.4; *Gallieni* 1.2; and the concession by the senate of all rights in the selection process, Victor, *Caes.* 36.

77. Reluctantly presented in our sources: SHA *Aurelian* 40.2f. and Victor loc. cit.

23. LATE ROMAN SLAVERY

1. G. Alföldy, *Noricum* (1974) 128–32, 173f., 177, and 190f. Notice that potters of Samian ware were freeborn (p. 190); that the largest attested group or household of slaves numbers only six (p. 131); and that the post-180 decline in slave/freedman numbers is ten times greater (to 4 percent) than in inscriptions over-all (to 44 percent, i.e. from 2,295 to 930, p. 136).

2. A. Mócsy, "Die Entwicklung der Sklavenwirtschaft in Pannonien," *Acta Ant.* 4 (1956) 22–226, 230f., and 244.

3. Ibid. 233f. and 245f. (notice that a slave costs two years' pay for a soldier, pp. 238f., suggesting acquisition and raising of them from childhood). For the "Mrozek curve," see my essay on "The epigraphic habit," *AJP* 103 (1982) 242f.

4. J. Rougé, *Expositio totius mundi et gentium* (1966) 18f.

5. G. Alföldy, "Die Sklaverei in Dalmatien," *Acta Ant.* 9 (1961) 123–126 and 128; on inscription ratios, as high as freedman: freeborn: 16:1, see J. H. D'Arms, "Puteoli in the second century," *JRS* 64 (1974) 112 n. 71, with similar findings in Rome of *CIL* VI: freedmen nearly 80 percent, cf. P. A. Brunt, *Italian Manpower* (1971) 387 n. 1.

6. Alföldy, *Acta Ant.* 9 (1961) 131 and 134.

7. Ibid. 130: three *libertae* and two *liberti*, a *libertus negotiator vinarius*, a *sevir*, and four *vilici* (around Salona). These last, J. J. Wilkes supposes in charge of slave gangs, *Dalmatia* (1969) 234. But he detects no barracks for them (pp. 394–406), cf. Alföldy, op. cit. (n. 1) 131, there too no barracks in villas.

8. K. Kurz, "Gnoseologische Betrachtungen," *Listy filologické* 86 (1963) 218f.

9. *Or.* 15.5, 18f., and passim (only in domestic duties).

10. A. M. Babacos, *Actes d'aliénation en commun . . . de la Thessalie antique* (1966) 232–51, by my count of the data there.

11. U. Kahrstedt, *Das wirtschaftliche Gesicht Griechenlands in der Kaiserzeit* (1954) 27.

12. Ibid. 47 on *IG* II^2 1100.

13. *CT* 11.3.2; Julian, *Or.* 14.45; and D. Nikolov, "Une villa rustica thrace," *Actes de premier Congrès int. des études balkaniques et Sud-Est Européennes . . . 1966* (1969) 2.524, detecting the abundant use of slaves in farming and crafts, on the basis of a big room identified as a barrack (p. 520). The conclusion seems to go beyond the evidence, given the contrary evidence of peasant hamlets and tenant lodgings near the same villa and elsewhere in the province. See further, below, n. 76. At some dramatic date in the second half of the second century, an absentee landowner in the Hellespont region engages in farming, with little profit, through slave labor (Philostr., *Heroicus* 16 p. 664—merely a novelistic scene? and slave labor specified as something unusual?)

14. L. Robert, *Hellenica* 10 (1953) 31, on Thasos and in Anatolia; also *MAMA* 4.297 (Phrygia).

15. *TAM* 5, 1, 71, a *kollegion phamilias* (A.D. 140); *IGR* 4.1076 (Cos), by a slave to his *patron*; 4.573 (Teos), a *berna*; elsewhere, rare reff. to slaves and freedmen generally belonging to the highest classes, Roman by name or citizenship—though cf. the quite Greek *oiketes* and *doulos* of *IGR* 4.1031 (Astypalaea) and Ael. Arist., *Or.* 50.105, a landowner uses violence through his *oiketai kai misthotoi* (Mysia). T.R.S. Broughton, "Roman Asia Minor," in *An Economic Survey of Ancient Rome*, ed. T. Frank (1938) 4.690–92, concludes a useful review, "Agricultural slavery was of little importance."

16. *IGR* 4.914, cf. L. Robert, "Documents d'Asie Mineure," *BCH* 102 (1978) 408.

17. Galen, *De cogn. curand.* 9 vol. 5 p. 49 (Kühn), a statement which excludes freeborn children and resident non-citizens. It is "our only fairly reliable figure," according to G. Alföldy, *The Social History of Rome* (1985) 137; W. L. Westermann, *The Slave System of Greek and Roman Antiquity* (1955) 87, accepts it; G.E.M. de Ste. Croix, *The Class Struggle in the Ancient Greek World* (1981) 242, calls it "surely quite unreliable."

18. A.H.M. Jones, "Census records of the later Roman empire," *JRS* 43 (1953) 54 (Magnesia), 55 (Thera), 56f. (Lesbos and Chios). He adds, in *The Later Roman Empire* (1964) 793 (henceforth, *LRE*), that the slaves may have been *vilici*.

19. *CT* 5.17.3 (386/7); Basil, *Homil. in divites* 2 (*PG* 31.285A), *ton allon oiketon arithmos apeiros pros pasan autois polyteleian exarkon: epitropoi, tamiai, georgoi*, etc. The word *oiketes* is usual for 'slave' in this author as for Greg. Naz., cf. R. Teja, "San Basilio y la esclavitud," *Basil of Caesarea: Christian, Humanist, Ascetic* (1981) 1.394 n. 5.

20. Council of Gangra of 340/341, Can. 3, in C.-J. Hefele, *Histoire des Conciles* (1908) 2.172; Basil, *Homil. in Ps. XIV* (*PG* 29.277B), a debtor sells children into slavery; and *CT* 12.3.1 (386).

21. Asterius of Amasea in Pontus, *Or.* 4 (*PG* 40.212B), date ca. A.D. 400; Basil,

Homil. de ieiunio 7 (*PG* 31.176A); Greg. Naz., *Or.* 14.17 (*PG* 35.877Cf.), in Caesarea.

22. Add, that J. Bernardi, *La prédication des pères cappadociens* (1968) 72, infers this from the mention of only freeborn craftsmen in Basil's *Hexaemeron*.

23. L. Robert, *Hellenica* 10 (1953) 31, and in *Etudes anatoliennes* (1937) 241, the *oikonomos, apeleutheros,* or *pragmateutes* overseeing "une population exclusivement paysanne"; other texts, ibid. 243 = *IGR* 3.17 and p. 263 = *IGR* 3.1434; J.G.C. Anderson, "An imperial estate in Galatia," *JRS* 27 (1937) 19ff.; and the four texts of Ormela, *IGR* 4.888–91, A.D. 200–217/218.

24. *IGLS* 1908, the bailiff and village headman appearing together. Cf. Mt 21.33f., Mk 12.1f., and Lk 20.9f., where the master gets work done by paid labor while his slaves do the overseeing and account-keeping.

25. F. M. Heichelheim, "Roman Syria," in *An Economic Survey* (cit., n. 15) 4.165.

26. Liban., *Or.* 16.36; 18.95 and 133f (*oiketai* cannot hide their *douleia,* their slavishness, though in palace service); 47.8 and 21 (the *oiketes* = *doulos* is property of his *kyrios* or *despotes*), referring not only to Antioch but to cities in general (their councils, *hai boulai*); 48.29; 49.24; 50.20; and still other passages from Libanius in J.H.W.G. Liebeschuetz, *Antioch* (1972) 47. Compare Eunap., *Vit. soph.* 458, a rich man (of Apamea around A.D. 300?) has a staff of slaves around him; at some earlier date, a master honors the memory of his *librarios* and barber (*IGLS* 2859, Baalbek).

27. Liebeschuetz, loc. cit. (n. 26), citing *Or.* 42.21 and 53.19. Notice also *Or.* 25 where the orator speaks of *douleia* as existing in houses and fields, but means slavishness or servitude in a metaphorical sense, in the way that the free farmer is a "slave" to the weather (25.38)—and here the silence about real slaves is striking. Further, *Or.* 45.5, "the workers in the fields are treated like slaves," *isa kai oiketais kechrentai,* which would hardly be said if slaves were actually farmers.

28. Liban., *Or* 31.9ff., compare his uncle in straitened circumstances with only eleven slaves and barely money enough to buy a single farm, *Or.* 47.28.

29. Joh. Chrysos., *In ep. I ad Cor., Homil.* XL 5 (*PG* 61.355), "you have droves upon droves of slaves," solely as body servants, but think anything less *aischron; In ep. ad Philipp. II, Homil.* IX 4 (*PG* 62.251), the cleric needs *ton diakonoumenon* in order not to *aschemonein;* cf. *Homil. in Hebr.* II 28.4 (*PG* 63.197), where he "accepts two slaves as the basic minimum for a lady," Ste. Croix, *Class Struggle* 851, and *In ep. I ad Cor. Homil.* XIX 5 (*PG* 61.158), even poor people own slaves.

30. Joh. Chrysos., *Laus Max.* 1 (*PG* 51.226); *De Anna* II.6 (*PG* 54.651); *In ep. ad Ephes., Homil.* 13.4 (*PG* 62.96) and 15.3 (*PG* 62.109); *In ep. ad Tit., Homil.* 4.3 (*PG* 62.685); *In ep. I ad Thess., Homil.* V 4.4 (*PG* 62.427); *Expos.in ps.* 48.8 (*PG* 55.510f.); *Contra eos qui habent virg. subintroduct.* 9 (*PG* 47.507), ref. to homes containing "a crowd of barbarian girls newly bought," who weave, cook, and wait on table, etc.

31. *Homil. in Mt.* 63.4 (*PG* 58.608), Antioch in 390, "possibly within the range of the maximal possibility," says Westermann, *Slave System* 136; a "statement of a rhetorical character," says Ste. Croix, *Class Struggle* 242; and "highly rhetorical," says Liebeschuetz, op. cit. (n. 26) 47 n. 1.

32. As Liebeschuetz does, op. cit. 64.

33. Liban., *Or.* 47.13 (his own family for many generations) and 17 (similarly, "a great many families"); Joh. Chrysos., *Homil. in Mt.* 6.1.3 (*PG* 58.592), extra peasants hired for the vintage, and the regular tenants ill-treated by landowners; and *Homil. in Acta Apost.* 18.4 (*PG* 60.147), a chapel built on their estates serves *pros eirenen ton georgounton.* Liebeschuetz, op. cit. 64 n. 2 declares "only two slave inscriptions are known from the hill villages" in the region inland from Antioch.

34. M. Hombert and C. Préaux, *Recherches sur le recensement dans l'Egypte romaine* (1952) 170; Westermann, *Slave System* 87, 120f., and 134; N. Lewis, *Life in Egypt under Roman Rule* (1983) 116; I. Biezunska-Malowist, *L'esclavage dans l'Egypte gréco-romaine II: Période romaine* (1977) 74, 91, and 157; and the words I quote from p. 83.

35. Ibid. 96f., cf. 74 and 151, stressing the primacy of Alexandrians, and theirs and the emperors' big estates, as slave-owners; also Lewis, op. cit. (n. 34) 57, indicating that most metropolite households would have "at least a slave or two, and many had more"; and M. Drew-Bear, "Les conseillers municipaux des métropoles," *Chron. d'Egypte* 59 (1984) 326, confirming both the role of Alexandria and the metropoleis.

36. Ibid. 326; Westermann, *Slave System* 133; I. F. Fichman, "Sklaven und Sklavenarbeit im spätrömischen Oxyrhynchus," *Jb. für Wirtschaftsgesch.* 1973, II, 152 and 154; and J. A. Straus, "Le prix des esclaves dans les papyrus," *ZPE* 11 (1973) 293, on the price rise from the late 260s.

37. Biezunska-Malowist, op. cit. (n. 34) 16f.

38. Fichman, *Jb. für Wirtschaftsgesch.* 1973, II, 152f.; Jones, *LRE* 793; and I. Hahn, "Sklaven und Sklavenfrage der Spätantike," *Klio* 58 (1976) 466.

39. I. F. Fikhman, "Quelques données sur la genèse de la grande propriété foncière," in *Le monde grec. Hommage à Claire Préaux* (1975) 788 and 790.

40. Synes., *De regno* 15 (*PG* 66.1093B); cf. *Ep.* 4 (*PG* 66.1341A), a slave girl from Pontus.

41. From the fullest recent study, G. Pereira Menaut supposes the lower of these figures, in *Terres et paysans dépendants dans les sociétés antiques. Colloque internationale . . . 1974* (1979) 419, slaves except in Proconsularis "pratiquement inéxistants" (cf. p. 420). Notice (p. 438) the concurrence of J. Kolendo. Further figures in R. MacMullen, *Roman Social Relations* (1974) 185, suggest rather 10 percent, and calculations from Tripolitania and Proconsularis suggest over 17 percent slaves in a small city near Carthage. Cf. R. Duncan-Jones, "City population in Roman Africa," *JRS* 53 (1963) 88. For Mauretania, see E. Gozalbes Craviato, "Consideraciones sobre la esclavitud en las provincias Romanas de Mauretania," *Cah. de Tunisie* 27 (1979) 60 and 66. The over-all study still most valuable is that of S. Gsell, "Esclaves ruraux dans l'Afrique romaine," *Mélanges Gustave Glotz* (1932) 400–415, who abjures the risks of quantifying the servile element (p. 415). I rely much on this article in what follows.

42. H. Pavis d'Escurac, "Pour une étude sociale de l'Apologie d'Apulée," *Ant. afr.* 8 (1974) 92, on *ILS* 2927, adding that modes of land exploitation must have been "perceptibly different" in Tripolitania from elsewhere in Africa.

43. Gerontius, *Vita S. Melaniae* 10 and 20; lands in Africa, Numidia, and Mauretania.

44. *CT* 10.8.4, mentioning both urban and rustic slaves in Numidia.

45. Gsell, op. cit. (n. 41) 400 and 405. For peasant labor, two striking testimonies are Sen., *Ep.* 114.26, "thousands of *coloni*" at work for a single owner in Africa, and Agennius Urbicus in C. Thulin, *Corp. agrimens. Rom.* (1913) I, i, p. 45 lines 16–22, speaking of single African estates of Flavian times with *non exiguum populum plebeium et in vicos circos villam in modum municipiorum.* On the source (Frontinus), see O.A.W. Dilke, *Roman Land Surveyors* (1971) 130.

46. Loss of only *agrestes*, in Amm. 28.6.4.

47. Aug., *Ep.* 108.18 and 185.15, slaves run away to the Circumcellions; *Civ. dei* 19.16 (and Ps.-Aug., *Sermo* 117.12, *PL* 39.1979), advice on master-slave relationships; H. Chadwick, "New letters of St. Augustine," *JThSt* 34 (1983) 433, on the commerce in and living standards of slaves; but Aug., *Ep.* 247.1 and 4 (*CSEL* 57.586f. and 588), show the landowner's "agents [who] oppress his tenants," *coloni, rusticani homines, miseri.*

48. Chadwick, *JThSt* 34 (1983) 433.

49. J. M. Blazquez, "L'esclavage dans les exploitations de l'Hispania romaine," *Mél. de la Casa Velazquez* 8 (1972) 635f., assembles over a dozen references, of which two appear to have no relevance to slaves; one (Caes., *Bell. Hisp.* 12.1) shows a soldier pretending to be a slave; the rest, referring to slaves of unknown use, belong half in an urban setting or in personal service to a master in the army. So the summary, "toutes ces exploitations employèrent essentiellement de la main-d'oeuvre servile," is not well founded. *CIL* 2.1980 is likewise unspecific (a *vilicus* and *familia* in an act of cult, no mention of their work); but *CIL* 2.5042 does appear to show a *fundus* leased to a slave and equipped with *mancipia*. Blazquez (p. 637) argues for exploitation later by free workers. Of his references, only one (not available to me) appears in *Année philol.*, so I cannot control them.

50. Blazquez, above (n. 49); M. Taradel, "Sobre las invasiones germanicas del siglo III d. J. C. en la Peninsula Iberica," *Estudios clasicos* 3 (1955–1956) 109, speaking of "trabajo a base de esclavos," in mining and farming. In the cities, a count has been made by G. Pereira Menaut, "La esclavitud y el mundo libre," *Papeles del Laboratorio de Arqueologia de Valencia* 10 (1970) 170–88, from the *CIL* only, of slaves and freedman in inscriptions, which, on average and together, come close to a half of the names attested epigraphically in twelve cities; but they cannot be believed. *Liberti* among them constitute absurdly high proportions; never less than 13 percent, averaging almost 30 percent, and up to 43 percent (in Corduba). We confront the fact here as elsewhere (above, n. 5) that freedmen were especially given to recording both themselves and their status on stone.

51. Council of Elvira, *Can.* 5, 41, and 80, on relations between owner and slave (Hefele, op. cit. [n. 20] 1.138, 152, and 167); in A.D. 401, the Council of Toledo, *Can.* 9 (Hefele 2.123, Latin text in Mansi 3 p. 1000), a household slave; *Vita S. Melaniae* 10; *CJ* 6.1.6 (332), fugitive slaves.

52. Oros. 7.40.5f., *servuli e praediis*; Zos. 6.4.3, *plethos oiketon kai georgon.*

53. A. Daubigney and F. Favory, "L'esclavage en Narbonnaise et Lyonnaise," in *Actes du Colloque 1972 sur l'esclavage* (1974) 318f., 327, 338, and 347—with my thanks to E. A. Meyer for referring me to the article. Notice (319 n. 3) the ratio of freed:slave :: 9:1 and the connection (320 and 328) suspected between prosperity and larger slave-numbers. But the failure to test the frequency of slave texts against any

over-all epigraphic sample invalidates their use (323) to show a rise and fall in slavery as an institution.

54. See briefly, Westermann, *Slave System* 94. The regretted E. M. Wightman described all this in two special studies: "The pattern of rural settlement in Roman Gaul," *ANRW* II, 4 (1975) 625, 629, and 650f. (native princes in grand villas), 632 and 637f. (villas surrounded by lands and villages with *coloni* = tenants); and "Peasants and potentates in Roman Gaul," *Am. Jnl. Anc. Hist.* 3 (1978) 97f.: the pre-Roman patterns endure, and "there is singularly little evidence for rustic slavery in Gaul," where most *servi/liberti* in inscriptions come from towns and many serve public bodies or soldiers. See ibid. 106, on the unlikelihood of a change-over to slave labor. J. F. Drinkwater, *Roman Gaul* (1983) 170f., quotes a number of recent scholars, to show "it is generally agreed that the [Gallic] landlords of both periods [Caesar's and late Roman] exploited the labour of a, at least nominally, free population, not that of slaves."

55. G. Fouet, *La villa gallo-romaine de Montmaurin* (1969) 44, whose words I quote. Regarding the re-built villa he says (p. 45) only that "the application of servile and rural workers tended to suffer in both quantity and quality," this being the only hint he offers of how he would characterize the work force, by inference from the clustering of the earlier buildings.

56. Wightman, *ANRW* II, 4 (1975) 638 and 646 n. 174.

57. *RE* s.v. Industrie und Handel (H. Gummerus, 1916) col. 1513; C. Delplace, "Les potiers dans la sociéte de l'Italie et de la Gaule," *Ktema* 3 (1978) 64f. Compare also the free labor in north Italian potteries, in G. Pucci, "La ceramica italica," in *Merci, mercati e scambi nel mediterraneo* (1981) 110.

58. Westermann, *Slave System* 95 n. 58, cites from Jullian seven inscriptions, five from Narbonensis, showing domestic service for slaves (*familia urbana, verna, vernacula*).

59. Service in the army to soldier-masters, see Sulp. Sev., *Vita S. Mart.* 2, noting the saint's self-denial in having only one slave; on urban households, whose slaves conspire against their masters, see Paulinus of Pella, *Eucharist.* 334 (ca. A.D. 415 in Vasates) and 537, the author is so poor his house slave must help him in his garden near Marseille in the 430s. Compare the *Vita Caesarii* 1.5 (in Jones, *LRE* 851), where Caesarius goes to Marseille *cum uno tantum famulo*. The passage from Sulpicius Severus is used to show slaves as ordinarily (!) employed in the fields, by C. Verlinden, *L'esclavage dans l'Europe médiévale* (1955) 1.53. Further, in Paulinus of Nola, *Ep.* 24.3 (*CSEL* 29.204), Sulpicius is commended for living as only a tenant in his own house though still with his *vernulae*; Sulpicius Sev., *Vita S. Mart.* 8, a personal servant, *e familia vernulus*, takes care of a rural magnate on his estate near Tours; and Ausonius 3.1.24, indicating a peasant work force in the fields, cf. Wightman, *Am. Jnl. Anc. Hist.* 3 (1978) 107, correctly interpreting *cultores = coloni*.

60. *Panegyrici lat.* 2.4f. (A.D. 289), *rebelles, agricolae, aratores, pastores, rustici*; Aur. Vict., *Caes.* 39.17, *agrestes ac latrones*; Eutrop. 9.20f., *rusticani* and *agrestes*; Hier., *Chron.* a. 2303, *rustici*; Iordanes, *Romana* a. 296, *rustici*; Oros. 7.25.2, *agrestes* and *rustici*; also *rusticani* in the *Querolus* p. 16 (Peiper), a comedy to whose relevance E. A. Thompson drew attention in "Peasant revolts in late Roman Gaul and Spain," *Past and Present* 2 (1952) 18.

61. Rutilius Namatianus, *De reditu suo* 1.215f., Exuperantius *servos famulis non sinit esse suis*. For the date (A.D. 416 or 417), see J. Vesserau, *Rutilius Namatianus* (Paris 1904) 205, and *PLRE* s.v. Exuperantius.

62. *Chron. min.* 1 p. 600 (*MGH AA* 9.660) of A.D. 435, *omnia paene Galliarum servitia in Bacaudam conspiravere*; cf. Thompson, *Past and Present* 2 (1952) 16. On slaves joining "revolutionaries," see above, n. 47.

63. The studies are many: M. Bloch, "Comment et pourquoi finit l'esclavage," *Annales* 2 (1947) 30f., an essay of limited value due to its lack of documentation; Verlinden, op. cit. (n. 59) 1.638f., 2.34f., and passim; H. Nehlsen, *Sklavenrecht zwischen Antike und Mittelalter* (1972) 53–56, finding servitude reflected in many barbarian law codes, e.g. pp. 101, 144, 262, and 276; and P. Bonnassie, "Survie et extinction du régime esclavagiste dans l'Occident," *Cahiers de civilisation médiévale* 28 (1985) 307–38 passim.

64. M. Rostovtzeff, *Social and Economic History of the Roman Empire*² (1957) 151, on *CIL* 13.7070.

65. L. Lazzaro, "Esclaves et affranchis en Belgique et en Germanie," *Quaderni Camerti di Studi Romanistici* 8 (1978–1979) 241f. and 253 (very few artisans: a butcher, a smith . . .), confirmed by B. Böttger and G. von Bülow in *Die Römer an Rhein und Donau* (1975) 163f. and 253. Add Amm. 29.4.4 of A.D. 372, when the Romans beyond the Rhine stumble upon slave-traders.

66. *CT* 6.35.1 (313/314).

67. P. A. Brunt, *Social Conflicts in the Roman Republic* (1971) 18, basing his estimate on his *Italian Manpower* (1971) 224, though in that latter work he supposes a maximum up to seven and a half millions.

68. A rich man of the third century in Rome has seven hundred slaves, if the source may be trusted: V. Ryssel, "Eine syrische Lebensgesch. des Gregorius Thaumaturgus," *Theol. Zeitschr. aus der Schweiz* 11 (1894) 240f. and 249; for the fourth century, Amm. 14.6.17 and 26.3.5; *CT* 14.17.5–6; Ambros., *Ep.* 2.31 (*PL* 16.887f.); *De Nabuthe* 20 and 28 (*PL* 14.756C and 759B); and Zeno of Verona, *Sermo* 1.6.8. L. Cracco Ruggini, "Vicende rurali dell'Italia antica," *Riv. storica italiana* 76 (1964) 267, offers this same picture, though not all of her evidence seems relevant.

69. E. Ciccotti, *Il tramonto della schiavitù nel mondo antico* (1899; reprint 1977), in his second volume, and Gummerus, op. cit. (n. 57), offer much epigraphic evidence without trying to understand its history within terms of the curve of frequency; similarly, E. M. Staerman and M. K. Trofimova, *La schiavitù nell'Italia imperiale* (1975) 73–75 with notes. Moreover, their account essentially ends ca. A.D. 225. A. Carandini, *L'anatomia della scimmia* (1979) 132, supposes a development of small workshops into large, reasoning from the collapse of the Arezzo potteries and the rise of big ceramic officinae in late Roman Pisa. Potteries in Puteoli and the Po valley declined along with the Arretine, cf. Delplace, *Ktema* 3 (1978) 57f. and 62. But these declines are too far separated in time and place from the Pisan to be related (and in addition the argument is weakened by the Pisan evidence not being published).

70. G. Pereira Menaut, "El numero de esclavos en las provincias romanas del Mediterráneo occidental," *Klio* 63 (1981) 376f., where I count the combined *servi*, *liberti*, and Greek names in the three cities (they average 54.3 percent of the total

attested population) as against 38 percent in Brixia, Verona, Milan, Aquileia, Beneventum, and Aeclanum (total of names in all nine cities: 9,305).

71. Ibid., showing in both the four Spanish cities and the five Gallic ones (with
4,567 names) only 30 percent *servi/liberti*/Greek.

72. Mart. 3.58.29–32; Plin., *Ep.* 9.20.2; and above, n. 59, on Sulpicius Severus.

73. P. A. Brunt, "Two great Roman landowners," *Latomus* 34 (1975) 625f. and
the quotation from 628, on Plin., *N. H.* 33.134f.

74. Columella, *Re rust.* 1.7.6, "on distant estates which the owner finds hard to
visit, every kind of land fares better under free tenants than under slaves and a slave
bailiff, and especially grain lands." Cf. the natural conclusion in, e.g., G. Hentz,
"Terre et paysans de l'Italie," *Ktema* 5 (1980) 156, or M. I. Finley, "Private farm
tenancy in Italy," in *Studies in Roman Property* (1976) 113, that Columella implies
slave labor as standard and predominant.

75. On the bias of this source, see R. J. Buck, *Agriculture and Agricultural Practice
in Roman Law* (1983) 8f. and 23f. ("rural slaves as contrasted with *coloni* seem not
especially common"), and P. W. DeNeeve, *Colonus* (1984) 162 n. 213, on mixed
labor forces.

76. K. D. White, *Roman Farming* (1970) 437, on slave quarters in a villa. Carandini, op. cit. (n. 69) has much to say about "slave-owning villas" in general, at various
times and places in Italy. The argumentation is entirely untrustworthy: e.g. (p. 129)
citing for support a work by Dyson, to appear in a certain journal; but in fact it had
already appeared, in a different journal, and makes no mention of slaves, servile labor,
or modes of production; also cited, works by Frederiksen and Johannowski (read Jo-
hannowsky) that are irrelevant (second century B.C.) and another by Potter which
makes no mention of forms of labor nor so much as uses the word "slaves." For further
criticism, see S. Dyson, "Some reflections on the archaeology of southern Etruria,"
Jnl. of Field Archaeology 8 (1981) 82, deploring Carandini's misreading of the archeological record and forcing of the evidence "onto the Procrustean bed of Marxist
theory."

77. *Habebat enim ipsa possessio sexaginta villas circa se, habentes quadringentos
servos agricultores*, in the *Vita Melaniae* (only the Latin) chap. 18 p. 13 (Rampolla).
The *villae = epoikia* in the Greek must be "Ökonomiegebäude," familiar in archeol-
ogy, and cf. SHA *Pert.* 3.4, *tabernam . . . infinitis aedificiis circumdedit . . . et mer-
catus est per suos servos*, in rural Liguria. Had the author meant each villa with 400,
he would have said *unaquaque* or the like (in spite of which the passage is always taken
to show a total of 24,000 slaves!). The locus of the estate is not specified. L. Cracco
Ruggini, "Sicilia III/IV secolo," *Kokalos* 28–29 (1982–1983) 487 n. 13, and S. Cal-
derone, *Enchiridion fontium ad res romanas saec. IIII inlustrandas* (1970) 110, follow
Rampolla in setting the estates in Sicily, but I follow other scholars and the implications of the text, sec. 18 (set in Sicily, but regretting losses, sec. 19, incurred in Rome).
For Melania's 8,000 manumissions, see Palladius, *Hist. Laus.* 61.5; for her personal
slaves, ibid. 6.6, slave women and eunuchs, comparing the personal and domestic
slaves in Amm. 28.4.8f., a *multitudo servorum* accompany the nobleman, 50 attend
him in the bath, and Symm., *Ep.* 8.2 and 9.140 and *Rel.* 31.3.

78. F. Fabbrini, *La manumissio in ecclesia* (1965) 232, slaves owned by the church

in Sicily; and laws on rural slaves and addressed to Italy in *CT* 7.18.2 (379), 10.8.1 (313), 10.9.2 (395), 11.1.12 (365), and 12.1.6 (318/319); and 2.25.1 (334?, Sardinia).

79. Jones, *LRE* 794f., on Ambros., *De off.* 3.47 (*PL* 16.159Af.), and *CT* 7.13.13–14 (397).

80. Alleging the absence of slavery in Palladius (which postdates 372), see E. Frézouls, "La vie rurale au Bas Empire d'après l'oeuvre de Palladius," *Ktema* 5 (1980) 198 and 201f., and R. Martin, ed., *Palladius: Traité d'Agriculture* (1976) viii and xxxi and xii and xvi (date), with p. 94 (note to Pallad., *Opus agr.* 1.6.2, needlessly uncertain whether *rustici* may not mean [*servi*] *rustici*). Palladius is ambiguous in his wording, however, leading V. I. Kuziscin, "Le caractère de la main-d'oeuvre dans un domaine du IVe siècle," in *Actes du Colloque sur l'esclavage . . . 1975* (1979) 242, 244, 247, and 252 n. 24, to suppose Palladius is indeed assuming a servile labor force. Notice Pallad. 1.6.18 and 14pr.2, assuming slaves (but domestic?) among his readers; also 1.21.1f.; 1.42.1; 2.3.2, and 4.11.1f.—all indicating very elaborate and specialized resources—and *de insitione liber* 2, speaking of *argutia famulorum, domini, servilia ingenia*, and (1.6.18) the villa's oversight by *procuratores*.

81. The degree of possible distortion appears in, e.g., L. Halkin, *Les esclaves publics* (1897), whose individual judgments (e.g. p. 224) and whose entire book rest principally on discussion of 391 inscriptions, 88 percent of which come from Rome (149) and Italy (191).

82. P. Veyne, *Comment on écrit l'histoire* (1979) 102 n. 3, is quite right: "l'esclavagisme de plantation, qui seule concerne les forces et les rapports de production, est une exception propre à l'Italie et à la Sicile"; but the opinion is buried in a footnote. D. Konstan, "Marxism and Roman Slavery," *Arethusa* 8 (1975) 145, would agree, but cites only Westermann, *Slave System* 90 (who refers to the period B.C.), and Toynbee (who says nothing relevant, and within a context of fourth/third-century Sicily); and K. Hopkins hits the truth, too, but without occasion to supply substantiation, in "Economic growth and towns in classical antiquity," in *Towns in Societies* (1978) 64. Contrast below, n. 101.

83. P. Garnsey, "Non-slave labour in the Roman world," in *Non-slave Labour in the Greco-Roman World* (1980) 40, using only Italian data, would cast doubt on the rapidity of "the decline of slavery." Earlier writers have no doubt, e.g. C. A. Yeo, "Economics of Roman and American slavery," *Finanzarchiv*[2] 13 (1951–1952) 470 and 481f., seeing a decline after the Flavian era; Verlinden, op. cit. (n. 59) 27, "un sérieux recul" beginning with the second century (citing Stein and Déclareuil, who say nothing at all about a "recul"; also Halkin, who sets the largest number of slaves at the first and second centuries, referring to legal texts but principally epigraphic, and takes no account of the "Mrozek curve"; and lastly, Lot, *La fin du monde* p. 74, likewise citing no evidence himself and saying nothing about a decline); Westermann, *Slave System* 120 n. 39, depending on Ciccotti's lists of (almost only) Italian inscriptions; Staerman and Trofimova, op. cit. (n. 69) 3f. and 57, a decline beginning in mid-second century in Italy and fifty years later in the provinces (no data adduced); Blazquez, *Mél. de la Casa Velazquez* 8 (1972) 637, a general decline in agricultural slaves empire-wide in Antonine times; Carandini, op. cit. (n. 69) 131, Italy's "struttura economica (quella della forma schiavistica) e politica (quella dell'imperialismo romano) è tramontata per sempre" in Severan times; P. Dockès, "Révoltes bagaudes et ensau-

vagement," in *Sauvages et ensauvagés* (1980) 174, few or no slaves in Gaul left at the end of the second century, citing the words of M. I. Finley, *L'économie antique* (1975) 113, that in southeast Gaul "for example" the abandonment of a "predominantly servile work force" can be dated to the opening third century—all this, on the basis of Montmaurin (!—and misunderstood, cf. above, n. 55); and Ste. Croix, *Class Struggle* 144, that "direct cultivation [of fields, anywhere in the empire] by slaves was steadily giving way to letting to tenants during the first three centuries of the Christian era" (with no substantiation offered).

84. With the data in nn. 60–62 above, compare Thompson, *Past and Present* 2 (1952) 11, asserting the "revolts were due primarily to the agricultural slaves." He cites only one source, *Chron. min.*, for one revolt (of 435), which in fact shows that revolt to have been started by others and joined by slaves (whether agricultural or not, is not indicated). Subsequently, Dockès, op. cit. (n. 83) 176 supposes "a massive reduction" in the third-century Gallic slave force, though it still remained substantial. He cites (188) Liban., *Or.* 47.11, as applying to the Rhine area (!) and, in his *Libération médiévale* (1979) 27, describes the Bagaudae as wholly slaves (again, p. 112, modified). His estimate is accepted by Bonnassie, *Cahiers civilisation médiévale* 28 (1985) 314: the Bagaudae were wholly or largely "des révoltes serviles"; likewise by P. Anderson, *Passages from Antiquity to Feudalism*[2] (1981) 103.

85. Often discussed: see my *Roman Government's Response to Crisis* (1976) 173–81 with notes. For the actual degree of freedom enjoyed by real farmers in known situations of the second to fourth centuries, see ibid. 289f., adding *CIL* 3.12336 (Scaptopara in Thrace) and *OGIS* 488 (Lydia, noticing the plaintiffs in the village being *hoi kataleipomenoi*) and my "Social mobility and the Theodosian Code," *JRS* 54 (1964) 49–53.

86. MacMullen, op. cit. (n. 85) 178f.; also Thompson, *Past and Present* 2 (1952) 11. Victor Vitensis protests against his fellow bishops being made by the Vandals to work like "slaves" or "rustic clods" or "men bound by law to the land"—all, terms to stress the grievous unsuitability of the labor. M. I. Finley, *Ancient Slavery and Modern Ideology* (1980) 124, supposes they were literally synonymous in Victor's mind, and therefore indicate some social reality; but that goes too far. See e.g. Cicero's view of *coloni*, and the upper-class terminology for rustics generally, in my *Roman Social Relations* (1974) 28–31 and 161 n. 4. Finley (p. 127) tries similarly to flow together Libanius' words in *Or.* 47: *georgoi, hoi ergazomenoi, oiketai, somata, douloi*, and *ergatai*. But Libanius is quite clear and specific about those persons who endure a shameful status (47.21, as also 18.133f.) and persons who may be sold (47.8, *therapainas = oiketai, Or.* 50.7). On his and others' usage, see above, nn. 19 and 26f.

87. *Or.* 45.5, 18.95, and 47.13f. and 17. Better, perhaps, 25.1 and passim, devoted to the subject and meaning of "slavery." For consistency in his usage, see the preceding note—in defiance of which Finley, op. cit. (n. 86) 127, finds all of Libanius' terms for slave and work "synonymous, all referring to Syrian peasants."

88. A. Piganiol, *L'empire chrétien*[2] (1972) 304, 309, and 448 is the most emphatic; see also Ciccotti, op. cit. (n. 69) 2.311f.; E. M. Chtaerman, "La chute du régime esclavagiste," *Recherches internationales à la lumière du Marxisme* 2 (1957) 114,

124, 128, and 154; W. D. Phillips, *Slavery from Roman Times to the Early Atlantic Trade* (1985) 36.

89. Above, nn. 3 and 59; Alföldy, *Acta Ant.* 9 (1961) 123f.; and *IGR* 3.1434. In the later empire, see *CT* 6.35.3.4.1; 7.1.3; 7.13.16; 7.22.2; and Jones, *LRE* 647.

90. Amm. 31.6.5; earlier, 22.8 and *CT* 13.4.4, *servi barbari* in Africa; later, Ambros., *De off.* 2.15.70, and Oros. 7.37.16, along with Synesius (above, n. 40).

91. Joh. Chrysos., *In ep. ad Hebr.*, *Homil.* 28.5 (*PG* 63.198); cf. above, n. 29.

92. Notice the phraseology in Pallad., *Dial.* 15 p. 23 Coleman-Norton, bishops en route from Italy are rudely confined *hos mede paida echein*; also above, nn. 28 and 59, and at p. 240 above.

93. Amm. 14.6.17 and above, nn. 21 (Asterius) and 30.

94. *IG* 14.63 (A.D. 410, Sicily—but rural?); Salvian, *Gub. dei* 4.15; routinely, *actores*, or less often *procuratores* in *CT* 2.3.1; 4.22.1.1; 5.7.2; 6.1.16; 7.18.2–7 and 12; 9.29.2; 9.30.2; etc.

95. W. W. Buckland, *Roman Law of Slavery* (1908) 599; above, n. 26.

96. Westermann, *Slave System* 133, citing Gummerus and Waltzing, who both are accurate. They cite the fact that workers were paid (*CT* 10.20.14, 16, and 18), lived with their families (Soz. 5.15, *PG* 67.1256C), and could be fined (*CT* 10.20.6), as indications of their status. For further proofs, see MacMullen, op. cit. (n. 85) 284f. Jones, *LRE* 836, correctly says *fabricenses* were free; he is correct that some other workers were slaves (*CT* 10.20.2, 3, 5, and 9), but incorrect in finding slaves elsewhere in the Code and in Euseb., *Vita Const.* 2.34 (actually half convict labor, in the tradition of e.g. *Dig.* 49.15.6, women in *salinae*). He is followed by Anderson, op. cit. (n. 84) 81 n. 4 and others.

97. *CT* 1.42.7 (369); 2.30.1 (315); 5.17.3 (386); 9.42.7 (369); 10.8.1 (313); 10.9.2 (395); 12.1.6 (318; 319); 12.3.1 (386); *CJ* 11.48(47).7; 11.68(67).3 (365–375) and 4 (Gratian).

98. M. Morabito, *Les réalités de l'esclavage d'après le Digeste* (1981) 78; for the new appearance of self-sale in Egypt post-300, see Westermann, *Slave System* 135— but in fact his two references, Taubenschlag and Meyer, afford little support. Better, Biezunska-Malowist, op. cit. (n. 34) 16–19, declaring self-sale never significant in Egypt; in Milan, Ambros., *De Tobia* 29f. (*PL* 14.769f.) and V. R. Vasey, *The Social Ideas in the Works of St. Ambrose* (1982); Basil, *Homil. in illud Lucae, destruam* 5 (*PG* 31.268C), and *Homil. in ps. XIV* (*PG* 29.277B); Liban., *Or.* 46.23; *CT* 4.8.6.1 (323), 5.9.1(331), 5.10.1 (329), 11.27.2 (322), and *Frg. Vat.* 34 (313), all of Constantine, and later texts in F. Affolter, *Die Persönlichkeit des herrenlosen Sklaven* (1913) 55.

99. Hahn, op. cit. (n. 38) 460; Bonnassie, op. cit. (n. 63) 338, "l'Etat esclavagiste"; or "le régime esclavagiste," Chtaerman, op. cit. (n. 88) 124; Carandini, op. cit. (n. 69) 131; Finley, op. cit. (n. 86) 149, the empire was "no longer a slave society" post-300; Dockès, op. cit. (n. 84) 24, "chain-gang slavery is the principal relationship in the society" in the west; Ste. Croix, *Class Struggle* 53; and a number of Russian writers reported by F. Vittinghoff, "Die Bedeutung der Sklaven für den Übergang von der Antike ins abendländische Mittlealter," *HZ* 192 (1961) 265f.

100. Finley, loc. cit.; A. Chastagnol, *L'évolution . . . du monde romain de Dioclétien à Julien* (1982) 318f., saying that as a result of a decline since the third century

"slavery was no longer the most important labor force in the economy"; Anderson, op. cit. (n. 84) 22, also sketching (79, 80, 82, 93, 95, and 97) the general and economic history of the west or the whole ancient world, or "Roman" undifferentiated, in terms of "the slave mode of production" and (p. 25) finding that "the numerical bulk of slave labour . . . was agrarian labour"; finally, Dockès, op. cit. (n. 83) 174, the slave system "dominant" in the second century, "l'âge *classique* esclavagiste."

101. Anderson, op. cit. 75–82; Dockès, op. cit. (n. 84) 82, supposing Columella's estate model and his own property to have lain in Spain not Italy (but cf. K. Ahrens, *Columella über Landwirtschaft* [1972] 12f., and R. Martin, *Recherches sur les agronomes latines* [1971] 290f.); and Ste. Croix, *Class Struggle* passim, e.g. 144f., 172, and the very uneasy and unsubstantiated aside (p. 234) that in discussing the Greek east "(I need make no apology for referring so often to the Roman agricultural writers, since their advice was largely based upon handbooks either written in Greek or dependent on Greek sources)."

102. Ibid. 172.

103. Ste. Croix himself cites some of the evidence (ibid. 215f.); yet, with more italics, he insists on the predominance of slaves in agriculture quite regardless of the lack of evidence (133 and 171). Elsewhere, in more normal fashion (e.g. 158), he develops his arguments on the absence of evidence as well as on its presence.

104. Ibid. 3f., 51, 112, 173 (with more italics), and passim. The whole line of argument which runs through the center of the book seems very tortured. As to its value strictly in terms of Marxist reasoning, I leave it to B. D. Shaw, "Anatomy of the vampire bat," *Economy and Society* 13 (1984) 214f., 222f., and 230, with notes.

105. "Slavery in classical antiquity," *CIBA Foundation Symposium on Caste and Race* (1967) 172.

24. THE HISTORICAL ROLE OF THE MASSES IN LATE ANTIQUITY

1. Rutilius Namatianus, *De reditu* 1.383ff.; L. Cracco Ruggini, "Intolerance: equal and less equal in the Roman world," *CP* 82 (1987) 203ff., with discussion and access to her other essays on the subject.

2. Epiphanius, *Adv. haer.* 30.4.12.

3. Ambros., *Ep.* 10.9, A.D. 381; *C.Th.* 14.10.2, A.D. 397 or 399; Eusebius, *Vita Const.* 4.7.

4. Pacatus, *Paneg.* 32.3; access to other discussions through Cracco Ruggini, *CP* 82 (1987) 197 n. 25.

5. Amm. 31.16.8.

6. On provincial culture of the third and fourth centuries there is no more recent survey than my *Enemies of the Roman Order* (1966) 227–41 with notes; but there are many more recent items to add, e.g. M. Bénabou, *La résistance africaine à la romanisation* (1976) 374, 587f., and passim.

7. Augustine supplies all three pairs of terms to describe the baptismal congregations he would expect to find in Carthage, *De catechizandis rudibus* 23 (*PL* 40.328); further on the urban-rustic split, the two seen as miles apart, such passages as Greg. Naz., *Or.* 2.29 (*PG* 35.437B).

8. See for example D. Vera, "Forme e funzione della rendita fondiaria nella tarda antichità," *Società romana e impero tardoantico* I (1986) 409–12.

9. On gifts, see e.g. Lactantius, *Div. Inst.* 6.18.10; on the proper manners for a client, D. Sperber, "Patronage in Amoraic Palestine," *Jnl. Econ. and Soc. Hist. of the Orient* 14 (1971) 234, reign of Constantine; Greg. Nyss., *Ep.* 25 (*PG* 46.1097), labor projects done by one's peasants; and Joh. Chrysos., *Ep. ad Olympias* 14.3 (*PG* 52.615), and Oros., 7.40.5 and Soz., *H. E.* 9.11, peasants turned into the landowners' militia.

10. In a work that intensified and shaped subsequent debate, W.H.C. Frend proposed that the Circumcellions "indicate the union of social and religious discontent," in *The Donatist Church* (1952) 176 and passim; but the weight of opinion now inclines on the other side, e.g. in C. Lepelley, "Témoignage et attitude de Saint Augustin devant la vie et la société rurale dans l'Afrique de son temps," in *Congrès de Varsovie . . . 1978* (1983) I 74 and 79f., or A. R. Birley, "Some notes on the Donatist schism," *Libyan Studies* 18 (1987) 32f. On the Bacaudae, it was E. A. Thompson who shaped debate, in "Peasant revolts in late Roman Gaul and Spain," *Past and Present* 2 (1952) 11–23; access to subsequent contributions in L. Okamura, "Social disturbances in late Roman Gaul," in *Forms of Control and Subordination in Antiquity* (1988) 292 and passim, to which add a hitherto unused source in D. De Decker, "L'expression des revendications sociales dans l'antiquité tardive," *Dialogues d'histoire ancienne* 5 (1979) 257.

11. On brigandage in Mauretania, see discussion of new data in J. Rougé, "Escroquerie et brigandage en Afrique romaine," in *Les lettres de Saint Augustin* (1983) 185; in Isauria, idem, "L'Histoire Auguste et l'Isaurie," *REA* 68 (1966) 303–10; and Pamphylia, Zos. 5.15.5, "constant conflicts with the neighboring brigands" (A.D. 399).

12. *CT* 5.17.1, cf. D. Eibach, *Untersuchungen zum spätantiken Colonat* (1977) 47ff. and 214 n. 519. For what follows, see this work, passim, and the more controversial article by J.-M. Carrié, "Un roman des origines: les généalogies du 'colonat du Bas-Empire,' " *Opus* 2 (1983) 206ff. Add, on disregard of the colonate, evidence cited in R. MacMullen, *Roman Government's Response to Crisis* (1976) 305, with Aug., *Ep.* 20*.10.2 (Punic, 20*.21.1). On the broad front of legislation to tie people to their occupations, see D. Liebs, "Privilegien und Ständezwang in den Gesetzen Konstantins," *RIDA* 24 (1977) 301ff.

13. Eibach, op. cit. (n. 12) 79 and 246ff.; Carrié, *Opus* 2 (1983) 229; and Lepelley, op. cit. (n. 10) 77.

14. P. Thead. 17, A.D. 332.

15. R. MacMullen, *Corruption and the Decline of Rome* (1988) 94f.

16. For views of merchants, Joh. Chrysos., *In Mt* 74.5 (*PG* 58.686), *kapelikoteron*, a term of scorn; Julian, *Adv. Galil.* 238E and *Ep.* 36.422B; Themist., *Or.* 4.73; and *CJ* 12.1.6. For subdivisions specified within lower ranks, see A. F. Norman, "Gradations in later municipal society," *JRS* 48 (1958) 80f., and epitaphs of Corinth, Ephesus, Korasion, Tarsus, Corycus, Tyre, etc., in J. H. Kent, *The Inscriptions of 1926– 1950* (1966) nos. 522, 525, 561, etc.; K. P. Mentzou, *Symvolai eis ten meleten tou oikonomikou kai koinonikou viou* (1975) 34f., and J.-P. Rey-Coquais, "Inscriptions grecques et latines trouvées dans les fouilles de Tyre 1963–1974, I: Inscriptions de la nécropole," *Bull. Musée de Beyrouth* 29 (1977) 31 and 98 (fourth-century texts) and 27, 40, and 81, undated, perhaps fourth century, with many similar later ones. Compare the population of Cirta reflected in its cemetery inscriptions, above, p. 277 n.4;

likewise the similar though rare epitaphs in, e.g. Cirta, *ILAlg.* 870 (a bean seller) or 1545 (a kitchen-boy).

17. *En. in Ps.* 51.14 (*PL* 36.609) and *In Ioannem evang.* 6.25 (*PL* 35.1437); cf. similar perceptions in eastern sources, J.H.W.G. Liebeschuetz, *Antioch* (1972) 61; A. Gonzalez Blanco, *Economia y sociedad en el Bajo Imperio segun San Juan Chrisostomo* (1980) 62ff., 123f., and 205; and R. Teja, *Organizacio economica y social de Capadocia* (1974) 67; also sources in MacMullen, *Corruption* 60; and, for the west, L. Padovese, *L'originalità cristiana* (1983) 73.

18. A.H.M. Jones, *The Later Roman Empire* (1964) 1220, his sense of the passage shared in Them., ed. Downey, 123 app. crit.; cf. the same four items of praise in Liban., *Or.* 1.2 and *Ep.* 1393, and Joh. Chrysos., *In Mt* 71.2 (*PG* 58.664).

19. MacMullen, *Corruption* chap. 3.

20. On such figures in the west (Sicily and Italy), see Firm., Matern., *Math.* 3.4.28, 4.11.8, and 4.14.8 ; in the east, Joh. Chrysos., *In Mt* 23/24.10 (*PG* 57.320), and Basil, *In hexaemeron* 5.2 (*PG* 29.97Df.).

21. Eunap. frag. 63 Müller = 62.2 Blockley, cf. MacMullen, *Corruption* 280 n. 78; ibid., 27, 29, 49, and 80f., for reff. on the *patrocinium* and "evergetism" of the new elite, a well-recognized phenomenon, and 144f., on their numbers = size of government. Also, J.-U. Krause, "Das spätantike Städtepatronat," *Chiron* 17 (1987) 1ff.; and, for Spanish illustrations of their mark on the world, J. M. Blazquez, *Estructura economica y social de Hispania* (1964) 110f., and idem, "La economia de la Hispania romana," *Historia de Espana Menendez Pidal* 2, 1 (1982) 544 and 592.

22. Amm. 15.5, 28.6, and elsewhere on these figures; MacMullen, *Corruption* 165f.; and, on the emissaries to Constantius in 356, Theodoret, *H. E.* 2.14 (*PG* 82.1040Bf.), comparing pressure from court women a few years later, Philostorg., *H. E.* 4.8 p. 62 (Bidez).

23. Aug., *Sermo* 56.14 (*PL* 38.383); Chromat., *Sermo* 41.2; cf. Teja, op. cit. (n. 17) 46, and Gonzalez Blanco, op. cit. (n. 17) 62ff. and 205, on rural feuds continually afoot; urban rivalries among city magistrates, Hier., *Vita Hilar.* 20; Basil, *Ep.* 28.1 (*PG* 32.305A), going on (§2, 308C) to describe the deceased bishop of Neocaesarea as patron.

24. Hier., *Comment. in Ezech.* 6.18 (*PL* 25.175C); *clientes* again in idem, *Homil. in Lucam* 16 p. 377 Morin (*CCSL* 78.508), *Paneg. lat.* 12(2).9.3, Auson., *Ecl.* 2.40f., or Valerian, *Homil.* 14.4 (*PL* 52.736D), sketching a scene of the 440s at Cimiez near Nice, cf. Amm. 14.6.13f.

25. Amm. 14.7.5f. and 15.13.2; Julian, *Misop.* 368C; Norman, *JRS* 48 (1958) 80f.; Liebeschuetz, *Antioch* 212–16 (claques) and 219–23. For Rome, see Amm. 15.7.4f., with Kneppe, *Untersuchungen zur städtischen Plebs des 4. Jahrhunderts n. Chr.* (1979) 73, 77, 82f., and 94f., and *Coll. Avell.* 21.2ff. (*CSEL* 35, p. 69), 31.6 (p. 71), and 32.3 (p. 79), on the *primates regionum* and *corporati*; on *collegia*, MacMullen, op. cit. (n. 6) 342–45, with ancient and modern sources, esp. (344 n. 19) Kohns and Martindale.

26. Frequent rioting, in the east, Soc., *H. E.* 2.13.3 and 2.15.7, cited in Kneppe, *Untersuchungen* 82f., and in Antioch, Liban., *Or.* 25.44; in Rome, frequent mob arson, Ambros., *Ep.* 40.13 (*PL* 16.1105Bf.), and demonstrations in the theater, Symm., *Ep.* 6.66 (a. 397); acclamations, Liebeschuetz, *Antioch* 209–12, and *C.Th.* 1.167.6.1

(331), a general law, and 8.5.32 (370), for Rome alone; rescue by mobs, Joh. Chrysos., *De incompr. dei nat.* 3.7 (*PG* 48.726), Soz., *H. E.* 7.13 (*PG* 67.1448B), or Hier., *Ep.* 1.10 and 15 (*PL* 22.330f.); Jerome's comment, quoted from *In Isaiam* 16.58.6 (*PL* 24.565); hunger riots, in G. Alföldy, "Soziale Konflikte in römischen Kaiserreich," *Heidelberger Jahrbücher* 20 (1976) 120, and C. Pietri, *Roma christiana: Recherches sur l'eglise de Rome* (1977) 646f. (with bibliog.); and drunkenness, in Kneppe, *Untersuchungen* 49f., and R. Lavollée, *Essais de littérature et d'histoire* (1891) 49.

27. P. Veyne, *Le pain et le cirque* (1976) 685ff. and chap. 4 passim.

28. Liban., *Or.* 30.19f., cf. 2.30; Basil, *Homil. dicta tempore famis* 8 (*PG* 31.325A), on *philanthropa diegemata*.

29. For the elite's view of the masses, see above, n. 16; also passages gathered in MacMullen, *Corruption* 237f.; Kneppe, *Untersuchungen* 162, 165, and 171; *C.Th.* 16.5.21 (392) and 6.27.18 (416), *servilis faex*; Letoios quoted (a pagan), in Liban., *Ep.* 550ff., with Theodoret., *Hist. relig.* 14 (*PG* 82.1413Af.), comparing Jerome on similar Christians, above, n. 24; Ambros., *Ep.* 28.2, comparing Euseb., *Praep. ev.* 13.14 (692b), or Synes., *Ep.* 105 (*PG* 66.1488A), for similar dismissive hauteur; contemptuous dismissal of the opinions of a mere tanner, Palladius, *Dial. de vita. S. Joannis* 19 (*PG* 47.67), and, for the views underlying preaching on poverty, P. Brown, "Late Antiquity," in *A History of Private Life* I, ed. P. Veyne (1987), 277ff.

30. F. D. Gilliard, "Senatorial bishops in the fourth century," *HThR* 77 (1984) 155, 170f., and passim; on Chrysanthos, *PLRE* I s.v.; on *genos* and *ploutos* defining suitability for the episcopate, see H. Chadwick, "The role of the Christian bishop in ancient society," in *Protocol of the 35th Colloquy, Center for Hermeneutical Studies* (Berkeley 1980) 9, quoting Augustine, and Joh. Chrysos., *De sacerdotio* 3.15 (*PG* 48.652); also Epiphanius, *Panarion* 30.5 (*GCS* 25.340); luxury, Greg. Naz., *Or.* 42.24 (*PG* 488Af.), *Coll. Avell.* 2.121 (*CSEL* 35, p. 43), and Hier., *Vita Malchi* 1, "lignes bien connues," in F. Paschoud, "L'église dans l'empire romain," in *Actes du VIIème Congrès de la FIEC* (1979) 207. For bishops besieging the palace the eastern evidence is better known; but see such texts as Can. 7 of Serdica, specifying Africans as the worst, and Sulp. Sev., *Vita S. Martini* 1.20.3, calling the petitioners "imperial clients."

31. On the beginnings of the African schism, see Frend, op. cit. (n. 10) chap. 1, noting the murder with which it began in Carthage (p. 19 n. 3: Aug., *Ep.* 44.4.8); and, on Chrysostom, Palladius, *Dial. de vita S. Joannis* 5 (*PG* 47.19) and elsewhere, Soc., *H. E.* 6.16 (*PG* 67.713), and other sources.

32. For a sampling of the evidence, see, in ROME, the *caedes* over the episcopal election in A.D. 309, Damasus, *Epigr.* 18.5 and 48.4; Amm. 27.3.12f. and *Coll. Avell.* 1.5–7 (*CSEL* 35, p. 2f.), with the death of Macarius to follow, later, ibid. 2.80f. (*CSEL* 35, p. 29); in ALEXANDRIA, whether soldiers or civilians killing civilians, episodes may be found in Athanas., *Ep. encycl. ad episcopos* 3 (*PG* 25.229A) and *Hist. Arian.* 10 (*PG* 25.705B), of A.D. 339; Soc., *H. E.* 2.8 (*PG* 67.197A), of A.D. 341; Athanas., *Hist. Arian.* 60 and 81 (*PG* 25.765A and 793C), *Apol. ad Const.* 27 (*PG* 25.629C), *Apol. de fuga* 7 (*PG* 25.625C), and Soc., *H. E.* 2.28 (*PG* 67.273A), all of the mid-350s, Soc., *H. E.* 2.38 (*PG* 67.325C) of 359, and Athanas., *Hist. aceph.* 2.10 (*Sources chrétiennes* 317, p. 148), and Soc., *H. E.* 3.2 (*PG* 67.381B), lynchings of

A.D. 361; Greg. Naz., *Or.* 25.12f. (*PG* 25.1213C), and Theodoret., *H. E.* 4.19 (*PG* 82.1169A = 4.22.5 and 29, ed. Parmentier-Scheidweiler), of the 370s; later, Christian-pagan troubles in 391, Rufinus, *H. E.* 2.22 (*PL* 21.528C), Soc., *H. E.* 5.16 (*PG* 67.604Cf.) and elsewhere, and ibid. 7.13f. (*PG* 67.761A and 766Bf.), on the Jewish troubles in 415; in ANTIOCH, ibid. 4.17 (*PG* 67.501), and Liebeschuetz, *Antioch* 234f.; in CARTHAGE, above, n. 31, *Gesta apud Zenoph.* pp. 189 and 191 (Ziwsa); *Sermo de passione Donati* 8 (*PL* 8.678B) and Frend, op. cit. (n. 10) 159f., of A.D. 317/321, and 181 and 188f., of A.D. 340s; and in CONSTANTINOPLE, Theophanes, *Chron.* a. m. 5849 (*PG* 108.145A), and Soc., *H. E.* 2.12 and 16 (*PG* 67.208Af. and 217A), for the bloodshed of A.D. 342–344; ibid. 2.27 (*PG* 67.269C) of A.D. 351 and 2.38 (*PG* 67.326C and 332A), Novatian persecutions followed by lethal riots of A.D. 355; Pallad., *Dial. de vita S. Joannis* 2 (*PG* 47.10f.), for the symbolical violation of the baptismal water by blood shed in strife, and Soc., *H. E.* 6.8 and 17f. (*PG* 67.689C, 716A, and 721B), and Zos. 5.23.4, for violence both before and after Chrysostom's exiling.

33. Soc., *H. E.* 4.16 (*PG* 67.500C), scores burned to death in 370 at Dakibyza (near Nicomedia); Greg. Naz., *Or.* 4.93 (*PG* 35.625B), pagans kill Christians in Caesarea, A.D. 362/363; Athanas., *Hist. Arian.* 18 (*PG* 25.713B), an episode in Hadrianople; Bishop Paul executed in Cucusus in 350, ibid. 7 (*PG* 25.701B); *Coll. Avell.* 2.109 (*CSEL* 35, p. 39), Eleutheropolis in Palestine; Soz., *H. E.* 5.9 (*PG* 67.1237B) and Theodoret., *H. E.* 3.3 (*PG* 82.1092C), Ascalon and Gaza in the 360s; ibid. 5.4 (*PG* 82.1204C), a bishop killed in 380 in Doliche; ibid. 3.3 (*PG* 82.1092D), Heliopolis; ibid. (1093A), Durostorum in Moesia; Theophanes., *Chron.* a. m. 5864 (*PG* 108.180), a general slaughter in 370 in Edessa; Soc., *H. E.* 2.38 (*PG* 67.329Af.), pitched battle between soldiers and locals in Mantineion in ca. 360; large numbers of deaths in 428 at Miletus and Sardis, Soc., *H. E.* 7.29 (*PG* 67.804D); Cyril, *Ep.* 169 (*PG* 83.1474Bf. = E. Schwartz, *Acta conciliorum oecumenicorum* I, 7 [1929] 80, *Coll. Athen.* 69 §5), stoning of clergy in suburbs of Chalcedon in A.D. 431; four bishops killed at Cottiaeum over the decade or so before 443, in Malalas p. 362 (Dindorf); and, in Africa, *CIL* 8.21517, martyrdoms at Quiza (Mauretania) in 329; Optatus 3.4 pp. 82 and 85 (Ziwsa) and *De schism. Donatist.* 3.4 (*PL* 11.1008B), large numbers killed in the 340s at Bagai and *locus Octavensis*, cf. Optatus 3.5–6 p. 86, victims unnamed, and *Passio Marculi*, *PL* 8.763, at Nova Petra, also in the 340s; *Gesta coll. Carthag.* 1.133 (*PL* 11.1310A), at Memblosa in Proconsularis, A.D. 405/408; ibid. 143 (1318C), at Quiza in Mauretania, ibid. 187 (1330B), at Rotaria in Numidia, and Aug., *Ep.* 91.8 and 10 (*PL* 33.316f.), at Calama, bloody incidents all in this same period; Bagai again in 403, Aug., *Ep.* 185.27 and 30; ibid. 50 (*PL* 33.191), A.D. 399 in Sufes; Optatus 2.18 pp. 51f., and Frend, op. cit. (n. 10) 189 and 258, at Lemellefense and Tiaret, A.D. 401; Aug., *Ep.* 133 (*PL* 33.509), at Hippo in 412; at an unnamed location (Limata?), the bishop a homicide, Optatus 1.13 p. 16, and, in 408, other deaths reported in unspecified settings apparently at the hands of certain bishops, in J. D. Mansi, *Sacrorum conciliorum nova et amplissima collectio* III (1759) 810; Hilar., *Frag. hist.* 2.12 (*PL* 10.641B), a bishop killed in Aquileia in 343; a lynching at Milan in the 380s, Paulinus, *Vita S. Ambrosii* 16 (*PL* 14.32D), cf. the violence suffered in the city in the 370s by the future bishop of Brixia, in Gaudentius, *Sermo* 21.6 (*CSEL* 68 p. 186); and Hier., *De viris illustr.* 121, Trier in 385.

34. Possidius, *Vita Aug.* 19, cf. Paulin., *Vita S. Ambros.* 25, petitioners come to Ambrose even from Persia.

35. *CJ* 1.55.8 (409).

36. Quoting from Aug., *Ep.* 22.*2.4 (*CSEL* 88 p. 114), and *Reg. eccl. Carthag. excerpta.* 75 (*CCSL* 149 p. 202), *defensores eis* [= to the poor] *adversus potentias divitum*; cf. W.H.C. Frend, "Fussala: Augustine's crisis of credibility (*Ep.* 20*)," in *Les lettres de St. Augustin découvertes par Johannes Divjak* (Paris 1983) 256.

37. Antioch's *lecticarii* and *copiatae*, in Liebeschuetz, *Antioch* 217 n. 1; on *parabalani*, *CT* 16.2.42–43. Appointees both bought and bequeathed their membership.

38. Jones, op. cit. (n. 18) 905 and 933f.; Pietri, op. cit. (n. 26) 570f.; as to travels by bishops entailed in estate management, see Can. 12 of Serdica, and a sample of much other evidence in B. D. Shaw, "Rural markets," *Antiquités africaines* 17 (1981) 70; for a bishop's man of affairs, Sidon. Apoll., *Ep.* 4.11.5, the scene Vienne toward the mid-fifth century.

39. Sidon. Apoll., *Ep.* 7.2.9, *clientibus patrocinii*; Aug., *Ep.* 125f. (explained perhaps by local hard times?); and 124.2; on distributions to the poor, among much evidence, cf. Possidius, *Vita S. Aug.* 23f. (*PL* 32.53f.), Aug., *Ep.* 122, and Hilary, *Vita S. Honorati* 21.1 (*PL* 50.1261).

40. In Barcelona in 394, *vi multitudinis*, Paulin. Nolanus, *Ep.*1.10 (*PL* 61.158 = *CSEL* 29 p. 8); Aug., *Ep.* 9.*5 and 20.*15.3 (*CSEL* 88 p. 100 and 103), at Fussala, *apertis vocibus atque ululatibus clamant*, with *rixae*. In general, see F. L. Ganshof, "Note sur l'élection des évêques dans l'empire romain au IVème siècle," *RIDA* 4 (1950) 469f.; charges of bribery, ibid. 480, Can. 2 of Serdica, and *Coll. Avell.* 1.5, or Hier., *Ep.* 92.3.

41. In Alexandria, in Soc., *H. E.* 2.9 (*PG* 67.200A), an appointed bishop dares not take up the seat; cf. Soz., *H. E.* 4.9 (*PG* 67.1132A); in Rome, *Coll. Avell.* 1.3 (*CSEL* 35, p. 2), cf. *domini plebis* (= *ecclesiae*) in Aug., *Ep.* 268.1, and other incidents, in Cple, where Hermogenes dies (Soc., *H. E.* 2.13, *PG* 67.208D), and Constantius dare not disregard popular support (ibid. 2.37, *PG* 67.321B), or again, ibid. 2.16 (*PG* 67.216A), where the praetorian prefect fears to provoke the crowds head-on, or in 404 once more, when Theophilus fears to assume the see, Pallad., *Dial. de vita S. Ioannis* 2 and 9 (*PG* 47.10 and 30); similarly in Edessa, the praetorian prefect flinching from the consequences of Valens' orders, Soc., *H. E.* 4.18 (*PG* 67.504Af.); in Antioch, where crowds force an ordination, 5.5 (*PG* 67.569D), or block ordinations (at Cyzicus, Philostorg., *H. E.* 9.13 p. 120 Bidez-Winkelmann); cf. similar motivation at work in Jerusalem, in Soz., *H. E.* 2.20 (*PG* 67.984Cf.); Valens fearful of popular outbursts in Nicomedia and resorting to subterfuge, 6.14 (*PG* 67.1329A), as, later in the same city, Nectarius flinches from confrontation, 8.6 (*PG* 67.1532A).

42. *Sirm.* 2; *Coll. Avell.* 13 (*CSEL* 35, p. 54), with *PLRE* i s.v. Simplicius; *C.Th.* 16.2.35 (405), 16.4.3 (392), to the Augustal prefect, and 16.5.11 (383).

43. *Parabalani*, above, n. 37; Athanas., *Apol. de fuga* 24 (*PG* 25.673D).

44. *Populi metu*, the government kidnaps a Roman bishop, Amm. 15.7.10; *nimio terrore*, the vicar and prefect of Rome will not enter the church, *Coll. Avell.* 32.3 (*CSEL* 35, p. 79); "Valens, fearing disturbances by the Alexandrians, wrote that Athanasius should be returned," for the *demos* had not allowed the *archon* to expel him,

Theophanes, *Chron.* a. m. 5861; and numerous other instances of the same phenomenon, above, n. 41.

45. *C.Th.* 16.4.5 (404); *Coll. Avell.* 32.3 (*CSEL* 35, p. 79); Soz., *H. E.* 5.15 (*PG* 67.1256Cf.); Athanas., *Hist. Arian.* 18 (*PG* 25.713B); Joh. Chrysos., *De incompr. dei nat.* 3.7 (*PG* 48.726); Liebeschuetz, *Antioch* 219 and 221f.; L. Cracco Ruggini, "Ambrogio di fronte alla compagine soziale del suo tempo," *Ambrosius Episcopus* (1976) 258f., and Ambrose, *Ep.* 20.5f. (*PL* 16.995), where evidently the *populus* that captures an opposing priest is really the *mercatores* and *negotiatores* of the town square.

46. Ibid. §§2, 5 and 16, cf. Aug., *Sermo* 24.6.

47. Preaching from ambo, Soz., *H. E.* 8.5 (*PG* 67.1528C); cheering, Joh. Chrysos., *Ad pop. Antioch.* 1.12 (*PG* 49.32); ibid. 2.4 (*PG* 49.58), "the church is not a theater where we listen for the pleasure of it. . . . What need do I have of applause, of these praises and hubbub?" with similar phrases and comment to the audience often elsewhere, e.g. 5.7 (47.79), the phrase *krotoi kai thoryboi* in both *In Ep. ad Rom. homil.* 15 (*PG* 60.548) and *In Matt. homil.* 17 (*PG* 57.264); and, for the Sirmium scene, see the *Altercatio Heracliani*, *PL* Suppl. 1.350. In fact, the theater, common setting for secular agitation, sometimes resounded to religious rivalry as well: see Palladius, *Dial. de vita S. Joannis* 8 (*PG* 47.29), referring to the partisan songs sung in the theater of Cple, and religious cheers in that of Alexandria, Soz., *H. E.* 7.20 (*PG* 67.1481B).

48. Greg. Nyss., *De deitate filii* (*PG* 46.557Af.); Aug., *Ep.* 44.1f., A.D. 398 in Tubursi near Cirta; *Coll. Avell.* 2.34 and 38f., Iliberis in ca. 358.

49. R. MacMullen, "The preacher's audience," *JTS* 40 (1989) 506–9; idem, "Sermo humilis," *JTS* 17 (1966) 109f., adding Soz., *H. E.* 6.25.4 (*PG* 67.1357C = *GCS* 50.270f.), on Apollinarian converts made and confirmed in Antioch and other cities through songs sung at work or at festivals, and P. de Labriolle et al., *Histoire de l'église* IV (1945) 74f., on Augustine's invention; in Alexandria, Soc., *H. E.* 1.9 (*PG* 67.84B), and J. Quasten, *Patrology* (1950) 3.11f., on Arius' expression of his theology in meter to be sung, and Soc., *H. E.* 2.11.6 (*PG* 67.205B), on Athanasius' use of singing as a form of crowd control in Alexandria in A.D. 345; at Antioch, Rufinus, *H. E.* 1.35 (*PL* 21.503B), and Soz., *H. E.* 4.28 (*PG* 67.1201C = *GCS* 50.226), psalms chosen and sung as protestations of individuals' credal preferences, and 5.19 (*PG* 67.1276Bf.); in Constantinople, Soc., *H. E.* 6.8f. (*PG* 67.689Af.), and Soz., *H. E.* 8.8 (*PG* 67.1537A), with later scenes still in Greg. Naz., *Ep.* 101 (*PG* 37.193A), and *Coll. Vaticana* no. 66 (Schwartz, op. cit. [n. 33] I, 2, p. 66); esp. in Milan, cf. Paulinus, *Vita S. Ambros.* 13 (*PL* 14.31C), and Aug., *Conf.* 9.7.15, who date the first uses of antiphonal singing to the struggle over the Milan basilica; H. Hucke, "Die Entwicklung des christlichen Kultgesangs zum Gregorianischen Gesang," *Römische Quartalschrift* 48 (1953) 51 and 53f.; Ambros., *Sermo contra Auxentium* 34 (*PL* 16.1017C), quoted; and, finally, Malalas p. 362 (Dindorf), where, in the small town of Cottiaeum in 443, the clergy and congregation of the church, suspicious of the orthodoxy of their new bishop, in antiphonal challenges require him to expound his creed for them. His reply is amusingly adroit.

50. In A.D. 398/399, Joh. Chrysos., *De S. hieromartyre Phoca* 1 (*PG* 50.699f.), for which I borrow the quoted phrase from *Homil.* II *postquam reliq. mart.* 1f. (*PG* 63.469f.); in about the same period, the bishop brings the relics of Habbakuk to

Eleutheropolis, Soz., *H. E.* 7.29 (*PG* 67.1505C); and, for the ceremony of 438, Theodoret., *H. E.* 5.36 (*PG* 82.1265Df.). Augustine knew of bishops who in his time and district brought martyrs' relics to their cities' churches (*De cic. Dei* 22.8 [*CSEL* 40.604f. and 608]), at Aquae Tibilitanae and Uzalis.

51. Soc., *H. E.* 3.18 (*PG* 67.425C), Soz., *H. E.* 5.20 (*PG* 67.1276B), and Theodoret., *H. E.* 3.6 (*PG* 82.1097B), the chant being reminiscent of Ps. 97.7. For the transfer of the head of John the Baptist from Cilicia to Cple, see Soz. *H. E.* 7.21 (*PG* 67.1481Bf.).

52. Paulinus, *Vita S. Ambrosii* 14, 29, and 33, Aug., *Conf.* 9.16 and *De civ. Dei* 22.8 (*CSEL* 40.596f.), and Ambros., *Ep.* 22.2 (*PL* 16.1019Bf.); for bishops as impresarios, the best example is Augustine in *Serm.* 320f. introducing to his congregation people as living testimonials, to tell their stories in their own words. One of them, in *Serm.* 322, mentions that *sciunt multi quanta miracula per beatissimum martyrem Stephanum in ista civitate fiant* (323)—the *civitas* being Uzalis, where the saint is referred to as *patronus noster* in a catalogue of written testimonials (*De mirac. S. Steph.* 1 praef., *PL* 41.834). Kneppe, *Untersuchungen* 30, notes how such miracles "were excellently suited to strengthening Ambrose's position," just as P. Brown speaks of bishops' "appropriation" and "orchestrating" of belief in the saints "under the patronage of the bishop," as a sort of local municipal power-grab (*The Cult of the Saints* [1981] 33, 42, and chap. 2 passim). For Ambrose's exorcizing of a demon from a young man in his audience who interrupts him (Paulinus §33, cit.), see exact parallels in Philostratus, *Vita Apollonii* 4.20 and Greg. Nyss., *Vita Greg. Thaumaturg.*, *PG* 46.941D.

53. Soc., *H. E.* 4.26 (*PG* 67.533B), Philostorg., *H. E.* 4.7 p. 61 (Bidez-Winkelmann), Soz., *H. E.* 6.16 (*PG* 67.1332B), Theodoret., *H. E.* 4.16 (*PG* 82..1161Af.) = 4.19.8, and Pallad., *Dial. de vita S. Ioannis* 17 and 20 (*PG* 47.58 and 72), punishments ending in death for some of the victims.

54. Restoring sight to the blind, in Aug., *De civ. Dei* 22.8 (*CSEL* 40.604); healing in western cities, Sulp. Sev., *Vita S. Martini* 16 and 18, and Paulinus, *Vita S. Ambrosii* 10 (*PL* 14.30B); raising the dead, ibid. 28 (*PL* 14.36D), and Soz., *H. E.* 3.14 (*PG* 67.1077Bf.), and, in Jerusalem, Soz., *H. E.* 2.1 (*PG* 67.934A); in Antioch, raising the dead, Philostorg., *H. E.* 3.6a p. 36; in Caesarea at a time of plague, by Gregory the Wonder-worker, in Gregory of Nyssa's biography, *PG* 46.924A and 957Cf.; in Cple, healing, Philostorg. 4.7 p. 61 and Soc., *H. E.* 7.4 (*PG* 67.745A).

55. Joh. Chrysos., *Homil.* ix *in illud, Pater meus* 1 (*PG* 63.511f.), only John can avail against the city's food shortage; Greg. Nyss., *Vita S. Greg.*, *PG* 46.926C and 929Df., the saint channels a river, others of his miracles also being still held dear in memory more than a century *post eventum*, 957D; Philostorg., *H. E.* 2.8a p. 19f.; Soc., *H. E.* 7.37 (*PG* 67.824B), a story about the Troas bishop, and Soz., *H. E.* 7.26 (*PG* 67.1498Bf.), the bishop Donatus' of Euroea in Epirus "binding" of his foes (attributed to many holy men, more often ascetics), as also in Paulinus, *Vita S. Ambrosii* 20, by Ambrose, and by a Cypriote bishop, in Soc., *H. E.* 1.12 (*PG* 67.104C); other miracles, by a Syrian bishop, 2.9 (200B) and by Paul of Cple, 7.17 (773A); and special powers of mind, Soz., *H. E.* 1.11 (*PG* 67.888B), 4.10 (1132Bf.), regarding Athanasius, 6.28 (1372Df.); Aug., *De civ. Dei* 22.8 (*CSEL* 40.604); and Paulin., *Vita S. Ambrosii* 16, 20, 43, and 51.

56. Soc., *H. E.* 7.29 (*PG* 67.804C), burning of Arian churches; cf. earlier, 2.13 (208D), 5.13 (600Bf.), and 6.18 (721A), in June 404 by John's followers.

57. Joh. Chrysos., *In acta apost. homil.* 33.4 (*PG* 60.243). Eusebius (*H. E.* 8.1.7f.) makes clear what is of course evident in the historical record, that the most strenuous disputes divided the church before Constantine—indeed, themselves were seen as having induced the chastisement of the Great Persecution. But they could not emerge in the form of *open* violence until about A.D. 304 in the west, later in the east.

58. On the high level of acceptance of aggressive and belligerent behavior among the ruling classes, see MacMullen, *Corruption* 67f., 90, and 92; and for Jerome's views in correspondence, his *Ep.* 17 (*PL* 22.360) and 86 (754).

59. Soz., *H. E.* 3.13 (*PG* 67.1068Af.).

INDEX